Developing Effective Educational Experiences through Learning Analytics

Mark Anderson
Edge Hill University, UK

Collette Gavan
Edge Hill University, UK

A volume in the Advances in Educational Marketing, Administration, and Leadership (AEMAL) Book Series

Information Science REFERENCE
An Imprint of IGI Global

Published in the United States of America by
Information Science Reference (an imprint of IGI Global)
701 E. Chocolate Avenue
Hershey PA, USA 17033
Tel: 717-533-8845
Fax: 717-533-8661
E-mail: cust@igi-global.com
Web site: http://www.igi-global.com

Library of Congress Cataloging-in-Publication Data

Names: Anderson, Mark, 1971 Sept. 3- editor. | Gavan, Collette, 1964- editor.
Title: Developing effective educational experiences through learning analytics / Mark Anderson and Collette Gavan, editors.
Description: Hershey, PA : Information Science Reference, [2016] | Includes bibliographical references and index.
Identifiers: LCCN 2015050777| ISBN 9781466699830 (hardcover) | ISBN 9781466699847 (ebook)
Subjects: LCSH: Education, Higher--Data processing. | Learning--Evaluation. | Data mining.
Classification: LCC LB2395.7 .D48 2016 | DDC 378.0285--dc23 LC record available at http://lccn.loc.gov/2015050777

This book is published in the IGI Global book series Advances in Educational Marketing, Administration, and Leadership (AEMAL) (ISSN: 2326-9022; eISSN: 2326-9030)

British Cataloguing in Publication Data
A Cataloguing in Publication record for this book is available from the British Library.

Advances in Educational Marketing, Administration, and Leadership (AEMAL) Book Series

Siran Mukerji
IGNOU, India
Purnendu Tripathi
IGNOU, India

ISSN: 2326-9022
EISSN: 2326-9030

MISSION

With more educational institutions entering into public, higher, and professional education, the educational environment has grown increasingly competitive. With this increase in competitiveness has come the need for a greater focus on leadership within the institutions, on administrative handling of educational matters, and on the marketing of the services offered.

The **Advances in Educational Marketing, Administration, & Leadership (AEMAL) Book Series** strives to provide publications that address all these areas and present trending, current research to assist professionals, administrators, and others involved in the education sector in making their decisions.

COVERAGE

- Advertising and Promotion of Academic Programs and Institutions
- Students as Consumers
- Educational Management
- Consumer Behavior
- Academic Pricing
- Faculty Administration and Management
- Educational Finance
- Marketing Theories within Education
- Educational Leadership
- Direct marketing of educational programs

IGI Global is currently accepting manuscripts for publication within this series. To submit a proposal for a volume in this series, please contact our Acquisition Editors at Acquisitions@igi-global.com or visit: http://www.igi-global.com/publish/.

The Advances in Educational Marketing, Administration, and Leadership (AEMAL) Book Series (ISSN 2326-9022) is published by IGI Global, 701 E. Chocolate Avenue, Hershey, PA 17033-1240, USA, www.igi-global.com. This series is composed of titles available for purchase individually; each title is edited to be contextually exclusive from any other title within the series. For pricing and ordering information please visit http://www.igi-global.com/book-series/advances-educational-marketing-administration-leadership/73677. Postmaster: Send all address changes to above address.

Titles in this Series

For a list of additional titles in this series, please visit: www.igi-global.com

Campus Support Services, Programs, and Policies for International Students
Krishna Bista (University of Louisiana at Monroe, USA) and Charlotte Foster (Missouri Western State University, USA)
Information Science Reference • copyright 2016 • 354pp • H/C (ISBN: 9781466697522) • US $185.00 (our price)

Facilitating Higher Education Growth through Fundraising and Philanthropy
Henry C. Alphin Jr. (Drexel University, USA) Jennie Lavine (Higher Colleges of Technology, United Arab Emirates) Stormy Stark (Pennsylvania State University, USA) and Adam Hocker (Pennsylvania State University, USA)
Information Science Reference • copyright 2016 • 372pp • H/C (ISBN: 9781466696648) • US $195.00 (our price)

Developing Successful Strategies for Global Policies and Cyber Transparency in E-Learning
Gulsun Eby (Anadolu University (College of Open Education), Turkey) T. Volkan Yuzer (Anadolu University (College of Open Education), Turkey) and Simber Atay (Dokuz Eylul University (College of Art), Turkey)
Information Science Reference • copyright 2016 • 355pp • H/C (ISBN: 9781466688445) • US $195.00 (our price)

Impact of Economic Crisis on Education and the Next-Generation Workforce
Patricia Ordóñez de Pablos (University of Oviedo, Spain) and Robert D. Tennyson (University of Minnesota, USA)
Information Science Reference • copyright 2016 • 432pp • H/C (ISBN: 9781466694552) • US $195.00 (our price)

Censorship and Student Communication in Online and Offline Settings
Joseph O. Oluwole (Montclair State University, USA) and Preston C. Green III (University of Connecticut, USA)
Information Science Reference • copyright 2016 • 622pp • H/C (ISBN: 9781466695191) • US $235.00 (our price)

Open Learning and Formal Credentialing in Higher Education Curriculum Models and Institutional Policies
Shirley Reushle (University of Southern Queensland, Australia) Amy Antonio (University of Southern Queensland, Australia) and Mike Keppell (Swinburne University of Technology, Australia)
Information Science Reference • copyright 2016 • 343pp • H/C (ISBN: 9781466688568) • US $195.00 (our price)

Examining the Impact of Community Colleges on the Global Workforce
Stephanie J. Jones (Texas Tech University, USA) and Dimitra Jackson Smith (Texas Tech University, USA)
Information Science Reference • copyright 2015 • 309pp • H/C (ISBN: 9781466684812) • US $185.00 (our price)

Cases on Leadership in Adult Education
Oitshepile MmaB Modise (University of Botswana, Botswana)
Information Science Reference • copyright 2015 • 326pp • H/C (ISBN: 9781466685895) • US $175.00 (our price)

IGI GLOBAL
DISSEMINATOR OF KNOWLEDGE
www.igi-global.com

701 E. Chocolate Ave., Hershey, PA 17033
Order online at www.igi-global.com or call 717-533-8845 x100
To place a standing order for titles released in this series, contact: cust@igi-global.com
Mon-Fri 8:00 am - 5:00 pm (est) or fax 24 hours a day 717-533-8661

List of Reviewers

Chris Beaumont, *UK National Teaching Fellow*
Claire Moscrop, *Edge Hill University*
Lindsey Martin, *eLearning Strategy and Development Manager, Edge Hill University*
Siraj Shaikh, *The Knowledge Transfer Network*
Katie Woods, *University of Wolverhampton*

Table of Contents

Detailed Table of Contents

Visualizations are quickly becoming an integral part of learning analytics for knowledge discovery, sensemaking, and insight. Empowering educators and learners, visualizations make data graphically accessible through a range of perceptual modes. As the embodiment of learners' data, visualizations give them a thing to reflect upon, potentially arriving at insights they may otherwise not have. Visualizations aid educators in behavioral monitoring, formative feedback provision, and strategic intervention. They support learners' motivation and self-regulation, focusing attention on the behaviors associated with academic success. As a mechanism for joint knowledge work, visualizations are collaboratively used to produce, translate, and facilitate communication around shared learning artifacts. This visualization survey explores disposition, predictive, semantic, discourse, collaborative and social learning analytics tools within a variety of learning spaces. In their entirety, they represent both the historical and the novel, from conceptual designs to empirically validated tools.

Real world data sets often contain disproportionate sample sizes of observed groups making it difficult for predictive analytics algorithms. One of the many ways to combat inherent bias from class imbalance data is to perform re-sampling. In this book chapter we discuss popular re-sampling methods proposed in research literature, such as Synthetic Minority Over-sampling Technique (SMOTE) and Propensity Score Matching (PSM). We provide an insight into recent advances and our own novel algorithms under the umbrella term of Over-sampling Using Propensity Scores (OUPS). Using simulation we conduct experiments that result in statistical improvement in accuracy and sensitivity by using these new algorithmic approaches.

The desire to provide personalized learning support for students has been a strong driver of the development of learning analytics capabilities at the University of Wollongong (UOW), Australia. A case study approach is taken to explore the diverse challenges faced when adopting an institution wide approach to learning analytics. Aspects explored include: establishing a clear strategy and governance, implementing foundation technology, developing and applying analytics and visualizations, managing organizational culture change, understanding student expectations, and addressing ethical challenges associated with learning analytics. This chapter draws upon the results of a UOW student survey conducted in late 2013 that explored first year student expectations regarding privacy in relation to learning analytics, and their preferred approach to interventions. Throughout it is noted that the academic endeavor, rather than technology and data management, drives the UOW adoption of learning analytics.

Research and experimentation is uncovering forms of best practice and possible factors on which to centre the analysis of students in an effective way, however learning analytics has yet to be comprehensively implemented country-wide in the United Kingdom. The chapter explores the current impact of learning analytics in higher education at mome discusses and observes the current vacancies with which a framework enabled to function with data visualisation could be utilised. The deliverable seeks to design an initial framework that has the potential to be utilised in a higher education setting for more effective and insightful decision making with regards to learner retention and engagement. This framework will combine the theory and scientific action of predictive analytics with a comparison of the most suitable data visualisation toolsets that are currently available in open-source software.

Learning analytics has vast potential as a tool to further unlock the effectiveness of education in a digital age. The amount of data that can be gathered from varying access points can provide new insight and knowledge into how learners are interacting with course materials, learning systems and even fellow classmates. Research and experimentation is uncovering forms of best practice and possible factors on which to centre the analysis of students in an effective way, however learning analytics has yet to be comprehensively implemented country-wide in the United Kingdom.

Due to the ubiquity of technology use in today's society, 21st century workers are likely to be knowledge workers who can use computer technologies to perform non-routine tasks. Students in this century are also likely to learn computer skills online. A robust instrument to investigate effective strategies while learning computer skills is needed. Although the Motivated Strategy for Learning Questionnaire (MSLQ) have been used widely in a conceptual learning environment, it has limitation in assessing students' use of learning strategies in computer software courses. In addition, there have been concerns about the latent factor structure of the MSLQ. This chapter presents a revised learning strategies section of the MSLQ for assessing learning strategies used in a hands-on, computer-skill learning environment. The new instrument contains five learning strategy subscales and exhibits validity and reliability. This revised instrument can be used to assess learning computer skills online.

Learning analytics is an emerging but rapidly growing field seen as offering unquestionable benefit to higher education institutions and students alike. Indeed, given its huge potential to transform the student experience, it could be argued that higher education has a duty to use learning analytics. In the flurry of excitement and eagerness to develop ever slicker predictive systems, few pause to consider whether the increasing use of student data also leads to increasing concerns. This chapter argues that the issue is not whether higher education should use student data, but under which conditions, for what purpose, for whose benefit, and in ways in which students may be actively involved. The authors explore issues including the constructs of general data and student data, and the scope for student responsibility in the collection, analysis and use of their data. An example of student engagement in practice reviews the policy created by the Open University in 2014. The chapter concludes with an exploration of general principles for a new deal on student data in learning analytics.

This chapter will describe, evidence and critically evaluate a pedagogical journey which takes the reader from a traditional position of the "academic as a domain expert" to what turns out to be a far more effective position as the "academic as a Learning to Learn expert". The evidence used to confirm the value and effectiveness of this changed approach by the author over a period of 5 years or so is based on Learning Analytics which demonstrate significantly improved academic results and achievements. It also demonstrates that the author's teaching styles have a dramatic impact on the so-called BME Achievement Deficit, compared to many modules at the institution. It has also had a significant impact in terms of improving student satisfaction. The confirmatory evidence derived from the Learning Analytics is now being used to make informed choices by other colleagues to change their own pedagogical choices to also develop excellent achievement in their own modules and programmes

The Eynesbury Institute of Business and Technology (EIBT) is one of a growing number of private providers partnering with universities to establish pre-university pathway programs worldwide. As a second chance for prospective students who do not meet initial Australian Higher Education (HE) entrance requirements, pathway providers attract students early in their tertiary lifecycle to secure their destination. EIBT has an abundance of empirically-rich and 'big' data that may be used to find pedagogically useful indicators, predictors and recommendations for teaching and learning advancement by careful evaluation of the findings. The work of 'researchers' often resides in isolation from that of 'educators', whereby the 'gap' may reflect a poor-cycle of communication and interaction between empirical studies and praxis. This chapter is limited to a select and somewhat brief discussion of specific uses of Learning Analytics (LA) in the context of EIBT and related sense-making and predicting of student performance.

Evaluating workplace training often involves using participant surveys to gather information about effectiveness. Unfortunately, how well these surveys are designed will play a major role in the information quality used to make conclusions. Following a proper survey design method will improve data quality and help trainers better understand what these data truly mean. Additionally, as a first step in a chain of evidence, properly designed post-course surveys will play a key role in connecting training with any on-the-job changes. This chapter will describe in detail a survey design process adapted from Spector (1992) to yield key insights about training's design, trainer and participants' interactions during training, and participants' perceived value of attending.

Data analytics, tools and techniques are no more confined to research organizations. These tools are being adopted by many organizations to generate business intelligence for improving decision making. Higher education institutions (HEIs) are beginning to use data analytics for improving their services and for increasing student grades and retention. Educational learning analytics are used to research and build models in several areas that can influence online learning systems. While use of analytics and data mining in education is increasing, sorting out fact from fiction and identifying research possibilities and practical applications are not easy. This chapter intends to help policymakers and administrators of HEIs understand how learning analytics have been used and can be applied for educational improvements.

Preface

Determining the effectiveness of the learning experience within Higher Education is a critical issue that institutions must address. The changing context of a university education has promoted a requirement to not only ensure that students are progressing through programmes academically, but that they are also developing a much broader range of skills that will enhance their employability following graduation. This is, in no small way, exemplified by the developing environment within the United Kingdom in which changes to government funding and student support in the sector have driven a view of students as "consumers" whereby performance factors are not only analysed by those within institutions, but also by external stakeholders such as funding bodies, employers and potential students. With this in mind, the beneficial outcomes that can be delivered through the adoption of learning analytics within an institution far outweigh the cost implications, both financially and temporally, of implementing strategies that place learning analytics as a focal point of institutional data capture.

Learning analytics have been adopted by educational institutions as a means of determining the effectiveness and quality of the learning experience for students (Brown, 2012; Greller & Drachsler, 2012). Derived from the analytic processes that underpin much commercial activity (Larose, 2005; Han & Kamber, 2006; Cooper, 2012), higher education establishments quickly identified that mining and understanding the data that is collected through the breadth of university systems could facilitate the improvement in delivery of courses, particularly with the pervasive adoption of online systems to support teaching and learning that facilitated non-intrusive data collection (Savage & Burrows, 2007; Long & Siemens, 2011). Implementing learning analytic initiatives is not without its issues (Buerk & Mudigonda, 2014), but the importance of implementing and enhancing such processes cannot be underestimated.

Key to adopting Learning Analytics is the growing use of Technology Enhanced Learning (TEL) within Higher Education. Alongside the often cited benefits of facilitating access to course materials for students, and supporting personalised learning experiences, the use of TEL also allows the learner journey to be captured and understood. Drawing upon experiences gained through e-commerce and the related customer journey to enhance the retail experience, educational establishments can gain a much richer understanding of the patterns of engagement. This leads not only to an understanding of how students are progressing, but can also determine points of intervention when students may stop engaging and be considered a risk in relation to retention.

Associated to the field of Learning Analytics is the related study of Academic Analytics [Long and Siemens, 2011]. A clear distinction can be drawn between the two fields: learning analytics focuses on the study of data to benefits tutors and learners, whereas academic analytics maintains a focus on supporting the administrative bodies related to institutions. Learning analytics is therefore more fine-grained in approach, treating courses and departments as central objects to a study, and is therefore more appropriate to consider in the context of this book. It is equally important that one group of stakeholders in relation to the implementation of learning analytics are the students themselves. It is crucial to recognise that a student-centric approach should be adopted in any implementation strategy for learning analytics; an approach that recognises that students are not just conduits to data capture, but undertake an integral role to the successful adoption and implementation of a strategy. Indeed, should students also realise the benefits from such toolkits being implemented then a truly holistic strategy embodying a community approach can be realised.

However, gathering the data is the first stage of the analytic process. Understanding the data, and subsequently acting upon the findings or predictions, form a key stage in the successful implementation of any learning analytics solution. It is therefore a critical requirement that the lecturing staff who are to interact with a learning analytics environment are both conversant and adaptive to the additional tools and facilities that they have access to. Without attaining the support of academics in establishing appropriate strategies for adopting learning analytics as a solution to deliver improved student learning experience, then the implementation of systems to support such strategies becomes challenging if not impossible. The subject of staff engagement, and the means by which academics can be assisted in proactively utilising learning analytics to enhance both engagement and retention, are areas that this book seeks to address.

Interpreting the large amounts of data that can be collected through a learning analytics strategy also provides opportunity for research and development. Drawing from existing fields, such as data mining and visualisation, the evaluation of data that has been collected and determining predictions based on such data sets. Indeed, predictive analytics is a hugely important area in relation to the educational environment. Implementing such strategies and tools facilitates earlier intervention to enhance both retention and also programme outcomes as emerging patterns in collecting data can indicate impending issues prior to their occurrence.

This book will explore the fields of Learning Analytics and Academic Analytics. Both areas are rapidly emerging as topics of great interest to the Higher Education community, both for programme managers and course tutors. Both topics concentrate of understanding the learning journey for students, and the outcomes that module cohorts attain through study. However, Learning Analytics approaches the analysis process from the learner perspective, often relying on data input by learners through virtual learning environments and online questionnaires to determine the effectiveness of the student experience. Academic Analytics, on the other hand, collates data from management systems related to Higher Education Institutions to understand the student journey.

The role that this book will play will be to inform the academic community of the opportunities that exist when the rich data sets collated through university online systems are mined and visualised to understand the impact of student experience on the outcomes of programmes. Equally, neither field should be considered in isolation. In this respect, the proposed publication shall explore cases where both Learning and Academic Analytics techniques have been employed to understand their impact.

A further area that shall be explored is the relevance of Learning and Academic Analytics to educational practices. There has been little research to understand how different pedagogical approaches affect the impact of Learning Analytics and/or Academic Analytics. This is a significant area that the proposed publication shall explore.

Target Audience

With respect to the applicability of learning analytics within the education sector this book has been designed to engage a wide audience of experts from a multi-disciplinary background. The primary audience for this publication are considered to be researchers who are working within this field. As the book draws upon projects that address concerns from a global perspective it is the intention that this would offer a significant resource for researchers in the field to develop and thereby enhance their contribution towards this emergent subject area.

In adopting learning analytics, institutions must engage key groups of practitioners in order to successfully implement strategies and solutions. These groups consist of those who determine effective strategy for embedding best practice; delivering senior management influence relating to the applicability of tools and techniques within the institutional context. Equally the academics who develop and deliver courses must understand the implications of effective data capture and its impact in determining the delivering successful programmes to students. The rationale being that by delivering the desired outcomes identified through analytics will result in an enhanced student experience leading to improved results and retention. The book aims to provide a useful resource to these key groups operating within the sector to aid understanding of successful design and deployment of analytic toolkits. As such, both the human and technology challenges are presented through case studies with a view to assist policy-makers and academics develop a positive relationship with analytics as a beneficial tool.

As the adoption of learning analytics toolkits gathers momentum, the focus turns towards the development of enhanced tools that are both usable and feature-rich. Usability is a critical concern in the design of the interface as this promotes easier accessibility to processing functions and the presentation of outcomes or predictions based upon the data collected. Also, the toolkits must facilitate easy integration with existing educational support systems such as register, timetable, library systems and most significantly virtual learning environments. The book, therefore, provides a resource for systems developers and integrators to assist in identifying the challenges faced when deploying learning analytics systems with the aim of inspiring the design of solutions that ease installation and enhance functionality.

Book Organization

This book is organized into 12 chapters that deal with the impact and experiences that institutions can encounter through the design, implementation and evaluation of learning analytics strategies. A brief description of each chapter follows.

Chapter 1 considers the impact that Visual Learning Analytic Tools (VLATs) can demonstrate when they are applied to interpretation of learning analytics. The chapter evaluates the growing field of VLAT and discusses the future for the implementation and application of these systems.

Chapter 2 explores the issues surrounding class imbalance when collating large data sets and developing prediction models. Class imbalance is a significant factor in the field of learning analytics as it can lead to groups within a domain set becoming over-represented or under-represented and thereby impacting upon the predictive outcomes as the data set is analysed

Chapter 3 presents a case study with the aim of sharing the experience gained by an Australian institution when introducing a learning analytics strategy. The case study explores the development of a strategy with a holistic viewpoint; encompassing technology, governance and culture change factors.

Chapter 4 focuses on a case study in which learning analytic techniques have been applied to understand the effectiveness of introducing new pedagogical approaches to teach a computing module in a university. The data captured for the evaluation was collated throughout the period of the class and thereby gives an excellent insight into the student experience as was captured and evaluated using an analytic and visualisation approach.

Chapter 5 explores the current impact of learning analytics in higher education and the different strategies that can be adopted for visualising data within a learning analytics context. This chapter also discusses and observes the current opportunities in which a framework enabled to function with data visualisation could be utilised. This framework will combine the theory and scientific action of predictive analytics with a comparison of the most suitable data visualisation toolsets that are currently available in open-source software to initialise the implementation of visualisation solutions for learning analytic systems.

Chapter 6 evaluates the perspective shifts that have taken place in e-learning in the past 25 years. The development of e-learning strategies is explored in the context of data collection, which has risen at an incredible rate, and is aligned with a changing viewpoint of learners towards self-regulated learners. The chapter also presents a study that explores the changing learning strategy subscales.

Chapter 7 focuses on the role of students in the successful implementation of learning analytics. In doing so, this chapter challenges the often adopted viewpoint that the student role is merely as a data source to provide institutions with intelligence in relation to performance and engagement. Rather, the chapter argues, students should be encouraged to have a more pro-active and inclusive role; in other words, the chapter proposes a student-centric approach to learning analytics.

Chapter 8 presents a case study that utilises learning analytics as a means of evaluating a changing pedagogical paradigm; one in which the academic is considered as a learning facilitator rather than a teacher. The analytics not only demonstrated the effectiveness of a changed approach, but also uncovered additional benefits to groups of students. In this context, the impact of adopting learning analytics using a range of approaches is demonstrated.

Chapter 9 explores bridging the gap that exists between the technical and educational domains through the integration and deployment of analytic tools. Whilst big data sets can be built using learning analytic tools, the timeframe between collecting the data and then acting upon the findings needs to be reduced in order to ensure that interventions are timely. The chapter explores the strategies that can be employed to ensure that use of the analytics is proactive rather than reactive.

Chapter 10 considers the challenges that are faced when implementing learning analytics in relation to the training of teaching staff to make use of the analytic findings. Whilst learning analytics can yield large amounts of highly relevant and useful data, without understanding the means by which this can be processed and interpreted then the data collection becomes a largely redundant process. This chapter presents one approach to address this issue and affect the impact on change of a course.

Chapter 11 draws upon experiences that have been reported from the commercial world in relation to data analytics. The aim is to identify areas of good practice that can be transposed onto learning analytics systems. Equally strategies that have been adopted for successful implementation may inform implementation of analytics systems within an educational environment. The purpose of this evaluation is to assist policymakers in determining the strengths that an analytic solution can bring to an educational establishment, and to identify the key strategic points that need to be addressed when implementing a learning analytics solution.

Chapter 12 explores the reported experiences in literature and critically evaluates and develops a holistic view of this emergent field. The chapter considers the range of implementations that have been reported upon and considers the functional applications of learning analytics in relation to the scope of implementation. In doing so, the chapter aims to determine strategies that will deliver high-impact implementations of learning analytics in the context of system requirements.

Book Objectives

The field of Learning Analytics, and the associated field of Academic Analytics, has recently emerged as a key field to assist understanding of the student learning experience within Higher Education. The mission for this publication is to collate the latest research in the field from around the globe and assist researchers to understand, and ultimately resolve, the challenges that exist within the field currently. Equally the book seeks to establish the links that can be made between learning analytics and other related fields, and potential challenges that may lie ahead as the field reaches maturity.

As an emergent area of research and development, Learning Analytics is developing rapidly and is thereby attracting a great deal of interest in both the academic and commercial environments. Suppliers of online education systems are actively pursuing opportunities to integrate their platforms with the tools necessary for supporting learning analytics. Aiding the promotion of learning analytics as a powerful tool for understanding student experience and engagement has been a drive to make effective use of Technology Enhanced Learning (TEL) within the sector. For a number of years, TEL has promised to offer a more flexible delivery pattern and enable students to access course materials in different ways to support their own learning styles. The argument also exists that TEL allows students to access materials "on-demand" and so students can adopt a more pro-active approach to enhancing their own learning. The challenge exists for providers of all online systems used by higher education institutions to consider the impact and challenges of integrating analytics tools to capture meaningful data as students progress through their courses.

Academic institutions are equally driving forwards the development of analytic platforms as the benefits of utilising diagnostic strategies are starting to be realised. As a result, there is an active community of researchers working within the field. One of the objectives of this book, therefore, is to collate research output in the area which encapsulates current thinking in all aspects of learning and academic analytics.

In addressing this objective, the book contains a number of case studies with the aim of presenting the experiences and outcomes that have been achieved at Higher Education establishments around the world. Capturing a global context for the case studies has been an important factor when compiling this book. There are a number of nations who are at a more advanced stage of implementing learning analytics within their education systems, and it is imperative that the experiences and strategies of practitioners in these countries are shared to disseminate best practice. It is therefore an aspiration of this book to explore case studies and explore the outcomes of studies within the context of Higher Education.

It is important to acknowledge that the impact realised by adopting learning analytics tools is not only related to the national context of the locale in which related research has taken place, but also the cultural context within the academic department or subject area that may be the focus of an impact case study. Academics who are technology agnostic may benefit from an environment in which greater care has been taken to engage staff with a strategy that is designed to leverage maximum advantage from learning analytic toolkits. Equally, the selection of the most relevant tools to support a strategy becomes a key decision. In particular, the development of visualisation techniques appropriate to the prism of deployment is a critical factor. The role of visualisation is to aid the interpretation of data collected, and ultimately derive predictions drawn from that data. However an inappropriate visualisation technique could hinder rather than assist in the adoption of the techniques for the benefit of the institution and its students. With this in mind, the book draws together research that encompasses the full lifecycle of implementation for learning analytics systems.

Attracting interest from researchers and practitioners around the world, each chapter in the book identifies different aspects or contexts of learning analytics as a field in its entirety. The book serves as an introduction to those looking to adopt learning analytics into their modules or programmes. For those within management in the higher education sector, the book provides a contextual overview of learning analytic systems and the key issues that may be encountered when implementing strategies to embrace such systems within an institution. Equally the book will also serve as a reference for those undertaking further research in the field; considering both the technical and the human factors. The book thereby offers a platform for future research in the field.

REFERENCES

Brown, M. (2012, July). Learning Analytics: Moving from Concept to Practice. *EDUCAUSE Learning Initiative*.

Buerk, J. P., & Mudigonda, S. P. (2014). A Resource-Constrained Approach to Implementing Analytics in an Institution of Higher Education: An Experience Report. *Journal of Learning Analytics*, *1*(1), 129–139.

Cooper, A. (2012). *A Brief History of Analytics. JISC CETIS Analytics Series, 1(9)*. University of Bolton.

Greller, W., & Drachsler, H. (2012). Translating Learning into Numbers: A Generic Framework for Learning Analytics. *Journal of Educational Technology & Society*, *15*(3), 42–57.

Han, J., & Kamber, M. (2006). *Data mining concepts and techniques*. Burlington, MA: Morgan Kaufmann.

Larose, D. T. (2005). *Discovering knowledge in data: An introduction to data mining*. Hoboken, NJ: John Wiley and Sons, Inc.

Long, P., & Siemens, G. (2011). Penetrating the Fog: Analytics in Learning and Education. *EDUCAUSE Review*, (September/October): 31–40.

Savage, M., & Burrows, R. (2007). The coming crisis of empirical sociology. *The Journal of The British Sociological Association*, *41*(5), 885–899. doi:10.1177/0038038507080443

Chapter 1
A Language and a Space:
Visualizing Learning Online

Halimat I. Alabi
Simon Fraser University, Canada

ABSTRACT

Visualizations are quickly becoming an integral part of learning analytics for knowledge discovery, sensemaking, and insight. Empowering educators and learners, visualizations make data graphically accessible through a range of perceptual modes. As the embodiment of learners' data, visualizations give them a thing to reflect upon, potentially arriving at insights they may otherwise not have. Visualizations aid educators in behavioral monitoring, formative feedback provision, and strategic intervention. They support learners' motivation and self-regulation, focusing attention on the behaviors associated with academic success. As a mechanism for joint knowledge work, visualizations are collaboratively used to produce, translate, and facilitate communication around shared learning artifacts. This visualization survey explores disposition, predictive, semantic, discourse, collaborative and social learning analytics tools within a variety of learning spaces. In their entirety, they represent both the historical and the novel, from conceptual designs to empirically validated tools.

INTRODUCTION

Following the Industrial Revolution, schools adopted a regimented learning model focused on routine and rote memorization to meet the labor needs of factories. Fast forward to today and it is knowledge work, rather than labour, that is a key wealth-generating resource (Savage, 1996). As such, information literacy – an intellectual framework for understanding, finding, evaluating, and using information – is a desired competency gaining a foothold in classrooms (Association of College & Research Libraries, 2013). Learning analytics (LA) tools offer a way of presenting data that builds learners' fluency with information technologies, an important competency in today's workplace. Though the impetus for the presence of visualizations in the classroom is motivated by a cultural shift to knowledge work, the visualizations within this chapter represent a wide variety of constructs at varying levels of sophistication. A

DOI: 10.4018/978-1-4666-9983-0.ch001

subset of learning analytics, visual learning analytics tools (VLATs) have been impacted by the increased numbers of online learners, the shift of non-traditional learners to majority status, and the participatory nature of our social media culture.

The appropriation of learning analytics and the visualizations that support them is motivated from the top down – informing administrations of learners' progress and persistence – and the bottom up, from the individuals directly involved in learning practice. With a focus on informing and empowering educators and learners (Siemens & de Baker, 2012), learning analytics are uniquely poised to inform policy and practice. At the core of empowerment decisions are discussions about who should have access to the learning technologies based on greatest need, benefit, or overall impact. Existing visualizations for educators far outweigh those for learners, likely in part because educators may better leverage their pedagogical expertise, power, and influence in learning spaces. Similarly, most existing interventions address the needs of at risk-learners rather than the general population. As we continue to move away from a Socratic model of education, there is a need to create tools for diverse education models, particularly those that are learner led. Use of the term *learner* here is meant to include individuals learning outside of the academic environment the term student implies. This includes learners in the workplace, Massively Open Online Courses (MOOCs), and Personalized Learning Environments (PLEs).

Visualization is an effective way to support a deep understanding of complex interactions (Medina & Suthers, 2009; Saltz et al., 2004; Hirschi, 2010). Though there is clear value in ability of visual analytics to amplify, extend, and enhance human cognition, the design and evaluation of VLATs has been almost a by-product of the research in learning analytics. Visualizations are often implemented and tested only for the aspects of usability they contribute to learning analytics tools. This collection of VLATs is part of an effort to position them as the next phase of learning analytics' maturation, as an entity that will eventually find a space of its own within this nascent field.

BACKGROUND

With little exception, when it comes to taking in information, vision ultimately trumps our other senses. The tight coupling between visual perception and cognition is even evident in our language, in the relationship between *understanding* and *seeing* (Ware, 2005). *Visualization* is both a mental process and a tool for knowledge discovery, sensemaking, and insight. Visualizations as tools transform perception by amplifying or reducing the data they represent. An art and a science, visualization is informed by the nuances of graphical design. Lines, points, curves, position, and color – these attributes are the words of graphical language. Information visualization uses these words to abstract and represent all kinds of data, from observations in the natural world to the relationships formed in simulated learning spaces. The ability of visualization tools to transform complex, multi-dimensional data is one of the many benefits of the science. Its ability to inspire creativity and curiosity is an allowance of the art.

Visual representations of learning data must strike a delicate balance between often-divergent goals. Given a messy data set visualization lends structure, making connections and patterns easier to recognize. Through simplification or filtering, visualization can be used to improve the efficiency of data search. At other times, aesthetics and abstraction are best used to communicate ideas about data, while perhaps even evoking emotion in the process. When it is most important to stress the instability of a system, a logical, uniform data arrangement would not be appropriate. The success of a visualization design is conditional, depending a great deal on the goals of the user, their prior experience, and knowledge. As such, there is yet no optimal visualization for learning.

Though sometimes used interchangeably, an important distinction between infographics and visualizations is interactivity. Infographics are static images, two-dimensional presentations of information that for memorability, are often arranged in an artful way. By design visualizations are interactive, allowing users to pose and answer relevant learning questions through interacting with the visualization. *Analytical provenance* describes the process of how visualizations are used during knowledge discovery and analysis to arrive at insights relevant to the viewer. This graphical approach to analyses means that learners' activities may then be characterized and analyzed in terms of their shape. Linear, cyclical, or branching patterns, their degree of regularity, congruence, or relative position to or in the graph – all of these patterns could potentially represent important nuances of learning (Winne & Jamieson-Noel, 2002). Unanticipated patterns also begin to take shape within visualizations, representing responses to pedagogical interventions or unforeseen events. Many of the visualizations within this survey are in the early stages of development or assessment. Some are quite simplistic, while others belie the complexity of the relationships in highly dynamic learning networks. Even without the benefit of robust empirical validation, these visual learning analytics tools represent the fruitful design space of the technologies re-visioning education.

At a fundamental level learning takes place through engagement – engagement with peers, educators, and learning resources. These occurrences of engagement are then used to infer how, when, and with whom learning takes place. This underlying trace data comes from a variety of sources, including, Learning Management Systems (LMS), intelligent tutoring systems (ITS), e-portfolio systems, and virtual worlds. Though the trace data is both timely and accurate, this does not necessarily mean that the correct inferences will be made, making it understood in the intended manner. This is why visualization design techniques are equally as important as the underlying foundation created by the data. Interactive visualizations support the discovery of hidden patterns that speak to causality or correlation by presenting a breadth of data from a variety of sources. Enough data is represented to allow the information-seeking individual to draw their own conclusions. The more VLATs embody pedagogical, sociological, and psychological theory, the more influential they become as learning tools and interventions (Wise, 2014).

Largely what we see in online learning spaces are cognitive-behaviorist, social constructivist, and connectivist pedagogies shaping the learning activities, assessment criteria, and the technologies used to mediate them (Anderson & Dron, 2011). Though pedagogy is greatly influential, the medium also defines the message (McLuhan, 1964). One of the explicit effects embedded within learning management systems is the promotion of content-driven course models, which in turn promotes visualizations based on that content. While behaviorist theories focus on learning that can be demonstrated by altered behavior, cognitivist theories attend to changes in knowledge or capacities stored in memory. These models came to prominence at a time when understanding of the brain's computational processes was growing, computer models were being used to describe and test learning, and when there were few technologies that allowed many-to-many communication (Anderson & Dron, 2011). Cognitive-behavioural pedagogies beget visualizations that emphasize tacit knowledge development and transfer, individualized learning contexts and assessments represented by automatically generated models of cognition. Cognitive-behavioural distance learning was defined by the absence of social presence, which became a prevalent driver in subsequent social constructivist, and connectivist pedagogies. Visualizations informed by social-constructivist pedagogy emphasize context, relationships, group knowledge construction models, and prior experience.

MOTIVATION AND REFLECTION

The ability to self-reflect is critical to learning (Dabbagh & Kitsantas, 2004; Winne, 2005; Zimmerman, 1989); visualizations can guide this process. Visualizations are already used in some applied sciences such as engineering, biology, earth and atmospheric science; learners in these fields must learn how to analyze data visualizations for success in their intended careers. The application of VLATs in all disciplines helps to establish a common language for learners to be able to externalize and discuss their mental models of themselves and their learning. Visualizations of learner models and dispositions are externalized representations of learners' internal states and feelings about the learning process that serve as personalized, motivational objects of learning to monitor and reflect upon.

Learner Models

Learner models can be used to give learners a more personalized experience (Fancsali et al., 2013), or to predict motivation, disposition, achievement, and course persistence (Cook & Kay, 1994; Dimitrova, 2003; Mabbott & Bull, 2004; Kay & Lum, 2005; Rueda et al., 2006; Bull et al., 2007; Kerly et al., 2008; García-Solórzano, 2012). These models also inform educators' decisions on interventions and pedagogical changes. The underlying data can be quite varied, but often includes learners' demographic and trace data from online learning spaces. Criticisms in the use of trace data to model learners or describe online learning processes are mainly due to a lack of transparency (Oblinger, 2011). Open learner models expose the underlying factors used to develop the models that are theorized to impact learning to learners and educators. Visualizations of open learner models make it easier to identify and monitor the aspects of learning these models are based on.

Cook and Kay (1994) presented one of the first learner model visualizations using a text-based conceptual tree diagram. Almost a decade later, the STyLE-OLM open learner-modeling tool (Dimitrova, 2003) guides the learner through a reflective activity that interactively builds the concept map (Figure 1). The concept map allows the learner to expand their beliefs by exploring different aspects of the domain. When evaluated, STyLE-OLM was found beneficial for knowledgeable learners to reflect on the learning domain, and less knowledgeable learners to inspect and challenge the robustness of their learner models (Dimitrova, 2003).

Mitrovic & Martin's (2007) visual learner model summarizes six aspects of the learning domain with red-green-white color bars. The colors indicate demonstrated achievement with green for correct understanding, red for incorrect understanding, and white for unattempted learning modules in an intelligent tutor. More recently, García-Solórzano et al. (2012) offer data portraits, based on a novel representation graphical representation of user forum participated based on past interactions, introduced by People-Garden (Xiong & Donath, 1999). In People Garden a garden metaphor is used to represent online forum discussions; individuals' unique interaction contexts are represented by flowers (Figure 2). Similarly in Daisy Maps (Icke & Sklar, 2008), learners' strength and weakness scores in areas such as reading and writing are represented by flowers (Figure 2). Scores range from 1 to 4; the daisy petals are color-coded

Figure 1a. Cook and Kay's student model visualizations (Cook & Kay, 1994)

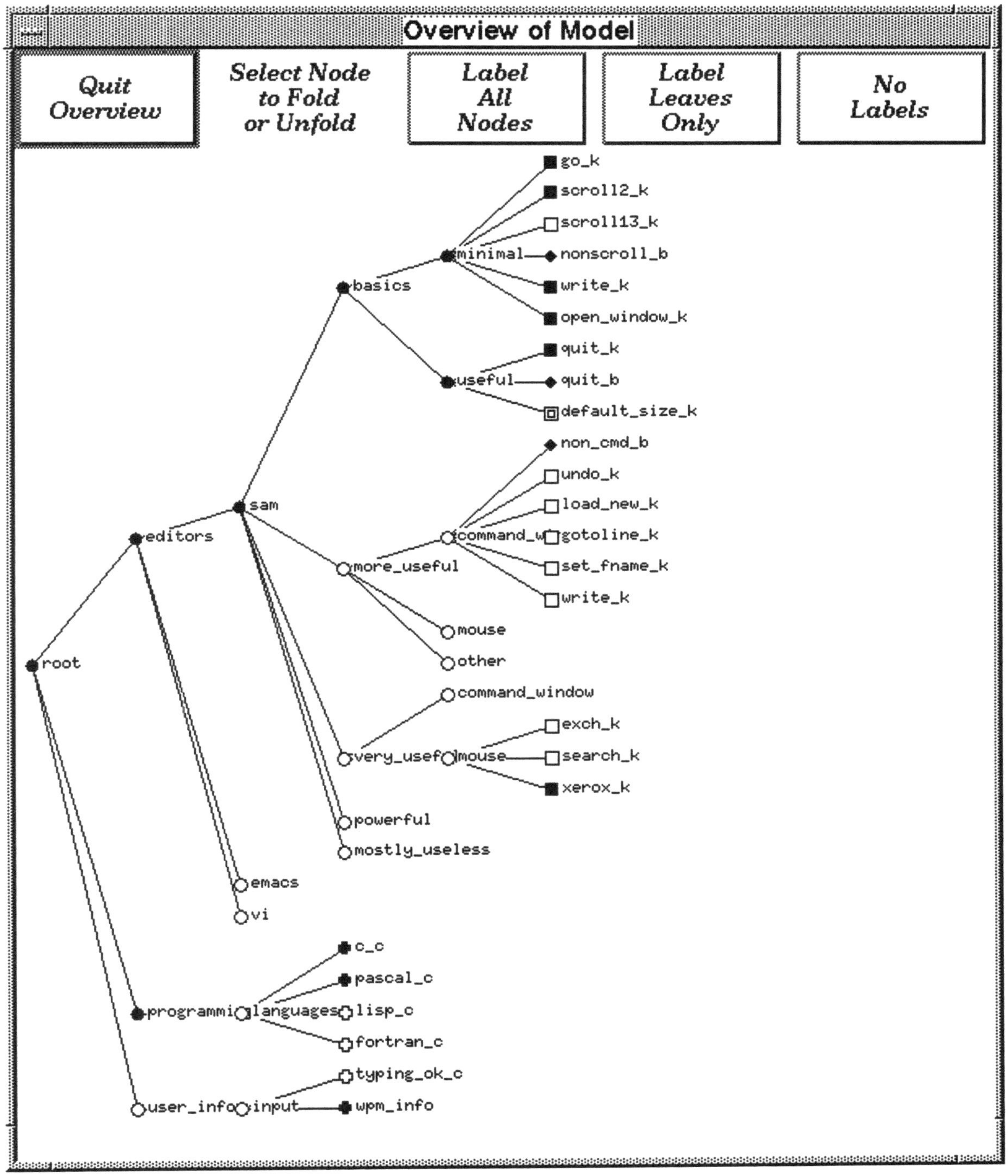

Figure 1b. STyLE-OLM (Dimitrova, 2003)

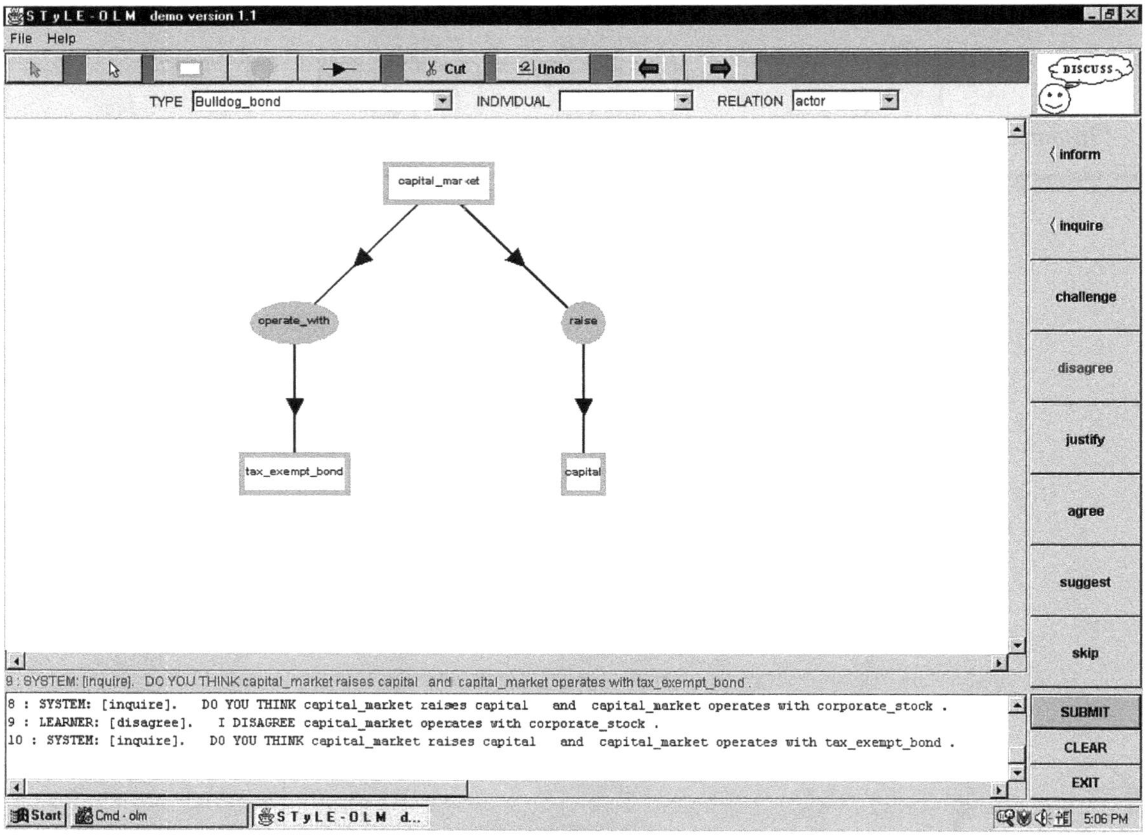

according to these scores. García-Solórzano et al.'s (2012) data portraits are examples of single axis composition (Mackinlay, 1986), when multiple information types are represented on a single axis. From left to right, differences in color opacity indicate the relative numerical values of learners' initial posts, replies, read messages, the messages' average grade, and the number of highlighted messages (Figure 2).

The visualizations of SIV (Kay & Lum, 2005) and DynMap+ (Rueda et al., 2006) enable the exploration of evolving learner models over time. The DynMap+ tool uses concept maps to visualize learner *and* group learning models (Rueda et al., 2006), while SIV uses a word tree (Wattenberg & Viégas,

Figure 2. (left to right) Data portraits of PeopleGarden (Xiong & Donath, 1999), Daisy Map (Icke & Sklar, 2008), and García-Solórzano et al.'s data portraits (2012) of an active learner and an inactive learner who must repeat the course

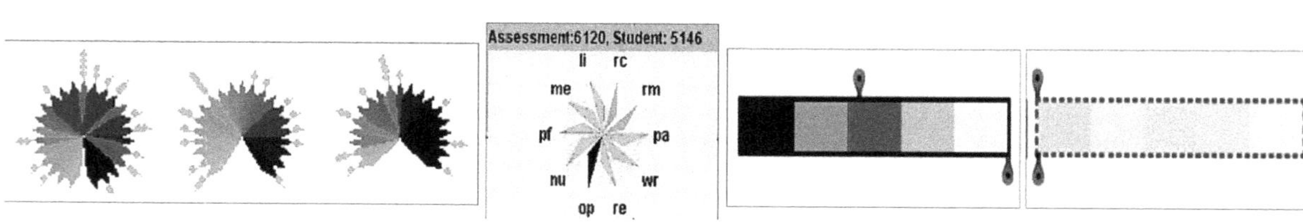

2008). The Flexi-OLM learner modeling tool provides seven views, among them a concept map and a hierarchical structure grouping of related concepts (Mabbott & Bull, 2004). Bull et al. (2007) tested 14 learners' visual attention using an eye-tracker and several visualizations of Flexi-OLM, to see how learners inspect different versions of their learner models. Though the results did not indicate that learners' view preferences impacted their visual attention, the authors argued that the very existence of the learners' preference for particular views warranted offering multiple views.

The CALMsystem represents a negotiated learner model for use in an Intelligent Tutoring System, meant to support the development of metacognitive skills such as self-assessment and reflection (Kerly et al., 2008). Through the use of a conversational agent (Figure 3) the learner is invited to compare their beliefs about their capabilities to those inferred by the system. The belief values are recalculated with each question answered, and learners can choose to negotiate and change their learner model by answering further test questions. When tested with a class of 30 UK primary school children, the CALMsystem was found to increase the accuracy of learners' self-assessments, and to reduce the number of discrepancies between the system and the learners' beliefs (Bull et al., 2008; Kerly et al., 2008; Kerly & Bull, 2008).

Figure 3. The CALMsystem (Kerly & Bull, 2008)

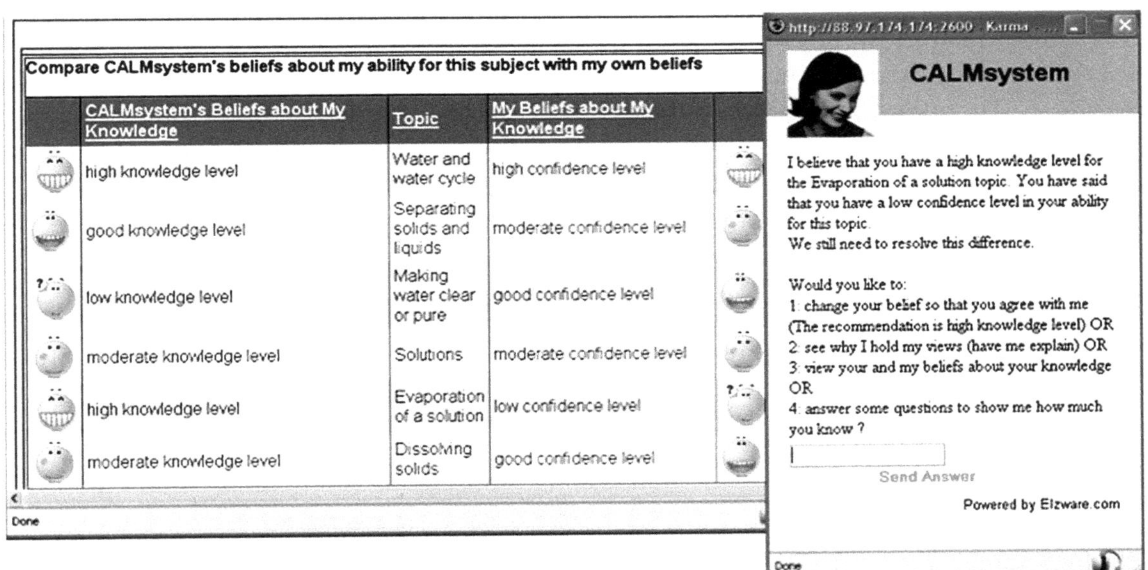

Shaped in part by culture, visual metaphors impact how information is received (Ziemkiewicz, 2008). While the learner models of the Calmsystem are evaluated, the visualizations are not. Deeper exploration of the chatbot's use of a realistic Caucasian female image and smiley face glyphs present an opportunity to better understand how learners receive and trust these kinds of visualizations in context. Are the smiley faces currently used in the classroom to represent a scale that the children already understand? Is the female image a stranger, or is she the children's teacher, someone with whom they already have a relationship? When testing learner's belief systems to ultimately increase their autonomy, acceptance, and negotiation of learning models, it is worthwhle to explore issues of power and identity inherent in the applied visual metaphors.

Disposition Analytics

Learning dispositions, learners' thoughts about learning, are malleable. Linked to identity, agency, motivation, and culture, an individual's disposition enables engaged learning in any context. Disposition analytics visualizations describe the inherent attitudes and feelings an individual brings learning to the experience. The importance of disposition is particularly evident when learners encounter challenging real world problems, as one's disposition represents an inclination for certain behaviors. In recent study, Tempelaar et al. (2014) compared learning dispositions, Blackboard LMS trace data, and data from a computer aided formative assessment tool to investigate their power to predict performance. Using Shum and Crick's (2012) theoretical framework of dispositional learning analytics, their empirical study found that the combination of dispositional and assessment data far outperformed the Blackboard tracking data in predicting learners' performance.

It is thought that sharing dispositional data with learners will aid metacognitive reflection and the development of metacognitive skills necessary for persistence (Kay & Lum, 2006). The Effective Lifelong Learning Inventory (Elli) web survey collected data from learners on the traits that demonstrate *learning power*, a measure composed of 7 learning disposition constructs (Shum & Crick, 2012). A radar graph, also known as a spider diagram, visualized the results for learners, mentors, and educators. Rather than numbers, the axes are labeled with qualitative descriptions.

The visualization graphically summarizes the relative strength of learners' baseline dispositions with their goals. Learners are taught how to perceive the diagram and set future goals in coaching sessions with mentors. The one on one coaching mitigates two problems common to visualization usage – graph

Figure 4. The shaded region of the Elli spider diagram is the learners' initial profile, and the dark line indicates goal targets (Shum & Crick, 2012)

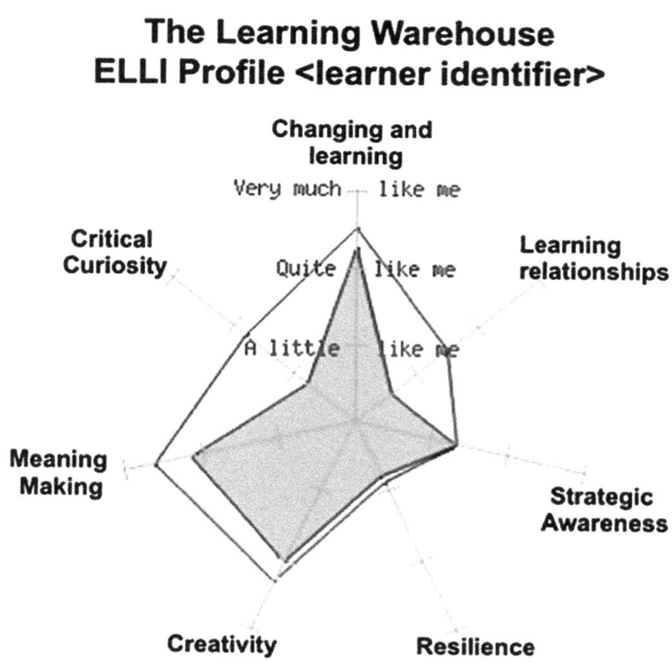

misinterpretation and ignorance of next steps. Educators reported using the radar graph as a curricular planning tool and as a communication tool, fostering conversation about the internal constructs that most impact learning (Shum & Crick, 2012).

Stories, whether told through words or images, are integral to human knowledge and the orientation of oneself in relationship to one's community. Sfard and Prusak state, "identity is the missing link between learning and its sociocultural context" (2005, p. 6). In subsequent studies with the Elli spider diagram, glyphs were added in an effort toward memorability and cultural relevance. Iconic animals were depicted in a study with indigenous youth (Millner et al., 2006), and Simpsons cartoon characters were used in a study with English teens (Deakin et al., 2010). These metaphorical representations of self represented abstract qualities such as strength and courage. For example, in the Millner et al. study (2006), a wedge-tailed eagle was selected by learners to represent strategic awareness due to its representation of confident self-awareness and because it is "the powerful cultural Ka-Wul community totem and the totem of the Wonnarua people" (2006, p. 453). Symbols encoded with meaning are powerful learning tools (Kop & Fournier, 2011). These two case studies represent learning dispositions merged with symbols infused with socio-cultural meaning, resulting in a unique depth of understanding.

Concept Maps

Concept mapping has established methodological value in education (Novak, 2003; Novak & Cañas, 2004). Originally invented in 1972 to explicitly describe children's conceptual understanding (Novak & Cañas, 2006), these visual representations of externalized knowledge make higher-order relations more accessible (Tufte, 1990). Concept maps organize knowledge representations, making meaningful steps or relationships explicit. In online learning spaces they are used in a variety of ways – to visualize group learning models over time (Rueda et al., 2006), track learner progress (Cerezo et al., 2014), assist in self-reflection in diagnostic reasoning (Lajoie et al., 2013), scaffold structured deliberation and argument mapping (De Liddo et al., 2011), and to navigate a complex domain knowledge structure and locate learning objects within it (Wang et al., 2011).

A concept map is particularly useful in *abstracted replay* (Schoenfeld, 1983), a reflective learner activity that focuses on the decisions or actions experts would take in a given situation. Lajoie et al. (2013) employed an expert skeleton map, a concept map of experts' actions, in their study in the virtual world, BioWorld. The expert skeleton maps were used to motivate medical students to reflect on their medical diagnostic reasoning processes, and ultimately improve their accuracy and confidence. The expert skeleton maps acts as the foundation for learners to construct meaning upon, as they compared their problem-solving processes to those of experts. In the study learners who used the expert maps were found to be slightly more accurate than those without the maps, but there was no significant difference in average diagnostic confidence as anticipated (Novak & Cañas, 2004). The authors posited that perhaps self-regulation *during* problem solving is more effective than reflection tasks *afterward*. They also reasoned that learners might have needed more guidance in interpreting the expert visualization maps, perhaps debriefing with a human tutor as seen previously in the Elli study (Shum & Crick, 2012).

Taking the concept map visualization further, Learning Progress Maps (Lesh et al., 1992) borrow from cartography to visualize the conceptual terrain of mathematics learning, with all its inherent complexity. The mountains indicate learners' construction of relevant mathematical models; the growth of a mountain is a physical analogy for increased understanding. The position of these mountains is also important; it indicates the close relationships between ideas, concepts, model, procedures, or representa-

Figure 5. (left) eGraph visualization of differently colored course content, representing the following variables: tasks, task submission, forum view, forum participation, theoretical content, summary, and multimedia content (Cerezo et al., 2014). (right) Richard Lesh's Learning Progress Maps are graphic, n-dimensional displays that trace the evolution of learners' achievements (Lesh et al., 1992)

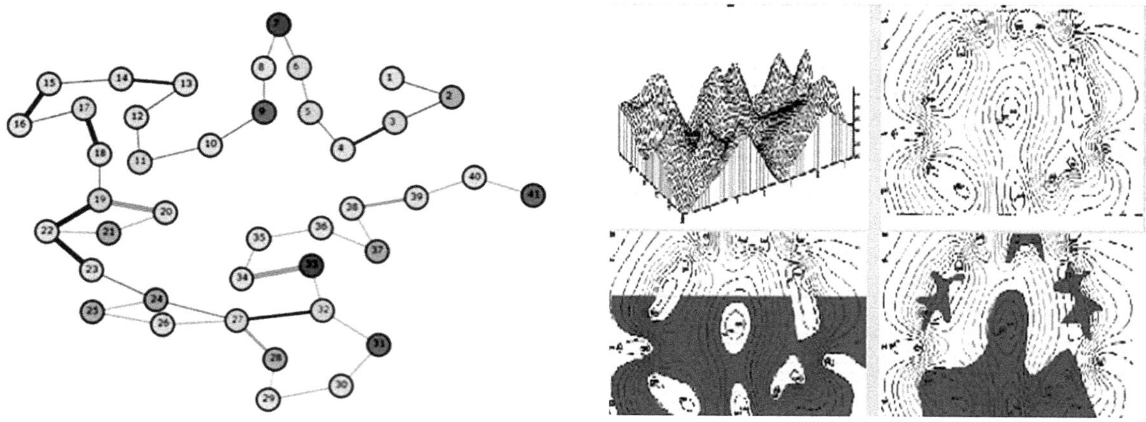

tions. Concepts at the boundaries of the map are simpler than the ones near the middle, where complex models build upon initial concepts. The construction of such a map would require preemptively mapping all of the cognitive analyses learners are expected to perform over the duration of a class, along with all of the activities required for mastery demonstration. Though a tremendous undertaking impractical for most educators, the result is arguable a thing of beauty.

FOCUS AND ATTENTION

As predicted by M. Goldhaber in 1997, we have indeed become an "attention economy" (Goldhaber, 1997). There are so many entities demanding our attention that it is quickly becoming a thing of scarcity. We see this scarcity of attention in online learning spaces too. Learners may have difficulty orienting themselves in online learning spaces, finding collaborators, and assessing their own work. Meanwhile, online educators often have difficulty monitoring learners' activities, finding and assisting those in need of help, providing timely feedback, and updating pedagogy to meet the specific needs of their ongoing courses. Since humans acquire visual information in bursts (Ware, 2012), the initial capture of attention is critically important. To capture and sustain attention, information must be among many things, visually distinct (Duval, 2011) and personally relevant (Sperber & Wilson, 1986). Beyond this, VLATs can offer targeted feedback to educators (Kosba et al., 2005; Kosba et al., 2007; Scheuer & Zinn, 2007) and learners (Arnold & Pistilli, 2012; Raimondo, 2013) to help them make better-informed decisions.

Predictive Analytics

Nudges are subtle interactions that influence people's actions without infringing on their freedom of choice (Carmean & Mizzi, 2010). These sorts of interventions persuade individuals to act, similar to the persuasive technologies prompting behavioural changes like healthy eating or smoking cessation

(Consolvo et al., 2009). Perhaps one of the most successfully adopted nudge analytics tools, the SIGNALS LA tool uses predictive models to incite at-risk learners to action ("Course Signals at Purdue: Using Learning Analytics to Increase Student Success," 2012). Originally designed for educators to give relevant feedback to at-risk students (Arnold & Pistilli, 2012), SIGNALS is based on Tinto's Model (1975) of learner retention. Feedback is visualized for learners using a 3-color stop sign type metaphor (Arnold & Pistilli, 2012); clicking on the signal gives a standard list of resources. The simplicity of the performance indicator visualization (i.e., red for high risk, yellow for moderate risk, and green for low risk of failure) calls into question its usefulness without an educator's input, as so much information is lost in the simplification. Combined with the fact that the indicator only updates when the educator manually updates the SIGNALS system, this lag in feedback could skew learners' perception of their chances of doing well in a course (Smith, 2014). Though large-scale studies indicate higher grades and earlier, more frequent help seeking (Pistilli et al., 2012) from using SIGNALS, the visualization may garner attention unnecessarily, negatively impacting learners' sense of agency (Smith, 2014).

The E2Coach (Raimondo, 2013) is a predictive analytics tool that provides individualized coaching to all University of Michigan physics learners, not just those determined to be at-risk. The model was built from 14 years worth of introductory physics course trace data from the 48,579 learners who took the course. Current learners see their current and predicted grades based on their data and the long-term model. The grey boxes reflect current scores charted against a final grade scale (Figure 6). Learners can estimate and plan for upcoming homework, exams, and participation scores to be able to achieve their desired final grade – all without the need for an educator to interpret the data for them. In reviewing the E2Coach, McKay attributes some of its success to the domain knowledge area, noting that since physics is an observational science, "it's a natural progression into observing data about students and their performance" (Miller, 2011).

Figure 6. E2Coach explaining to learners what grade they are "heading for" (Raimondo, 2013)

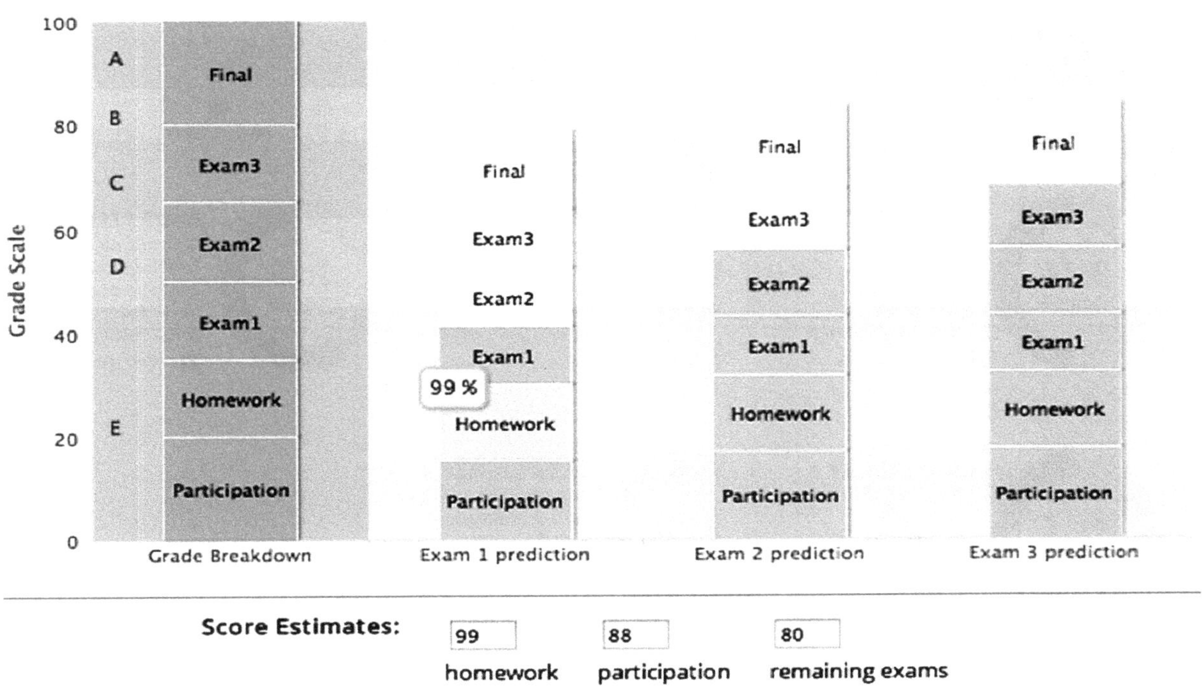

Dashboards

Dashboards have been found to increase persistence across academic programs by guiding learners in informed decision-making (Buerck, 2014; Fritz, 2011; Grann & Bushway, 2014; Verbert et al., 2013; Santos et al., 2011), and providing educators with a way to monitor learners' behaviors (Leony et al., 2012; Pohl et al., 2012; Podgorelec et al., 2011). Arizona State University, one of the largest universities in the United States, uses two data analytics packages to help its 72,000 learners stay on track toward graduation. They use Blackboard LMS with on the ground learners and Pearson Learning Studio for online learners to make ASU seem less monolithic and more personalized (Wishon & Rome, 2012). The university's LMS produce almost three million rows of behavioral data daily. eAdvisor is their learner-facing dashboard, guiding learners in finding a specialization, registering for classes, and monitoring their progress. eAdvisor is credited as an integral part of the strategic goal that has increased the university's one-year persistence rate for first-time, full-time freshman from 77% in 2004 to 84% in 2010 (Wishon & Rome, 2012).

Capella University's competency map dashboard represents the university's alignment with professional practice by visualizing the knowledge, abilities, and professional attributes leaners need to succeed in their given professions (Grann & Bushway, 2014). When initially designed the map contained information on all assignments for all courses, but a focus group of learners found this overwhelming. The initial visualization was a series of slider bars indicating the percentage of criterion passed for each competency, with the bars' color indicating performance level. It was found that learners combined the two metrics erroneously, thinking that the bars indicated progress relative to expected progress (Grann & Bushway, 2014). The final dashboard (Figure 7) is instead defined in terms of small multiples of completed criterion and competencies. When empirically evaluated, the effect of the dashboard on persistence wasn't statistically significant as hypothesized. When all other variables were controlled for however, it did account for 7% of the variance in reregistration behavior (Grann & Bushway, 2014).

Figure 7. Capella University's dashboard (Grann & Bushway, 2014)

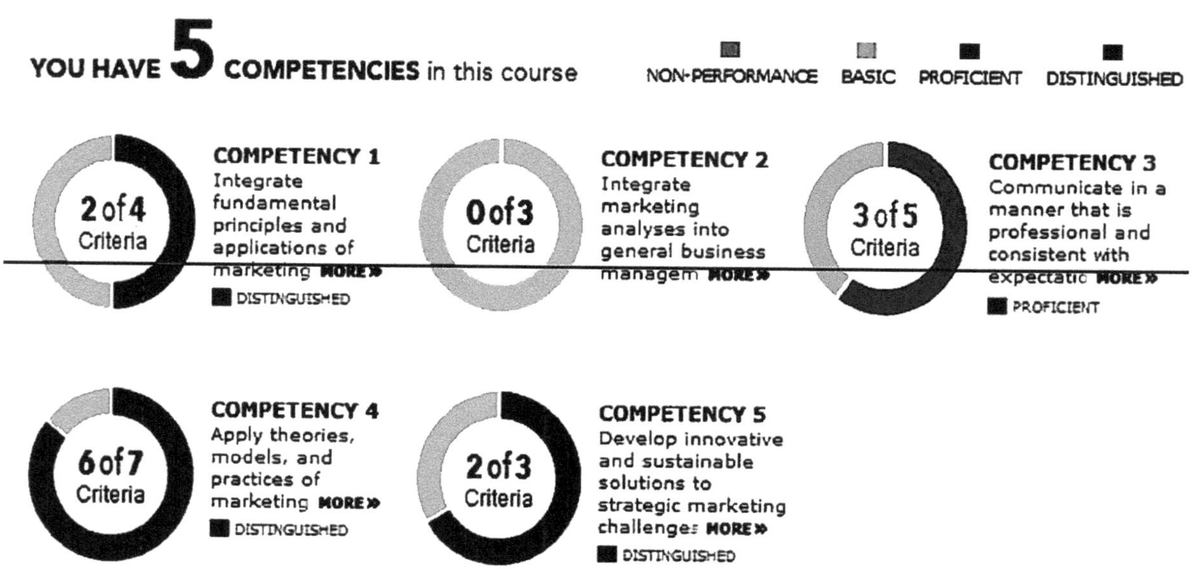

Predictive analytics positively impact learner retention rates in many universities (Schaffhauser, 2013). They're included in this survey not for the novelty of their visualizations, but for their overall impact. Research in this area has precluded and thus influenced much of the research being done in learning and visual learning analytics. These tools trade on the currency of attention – though educators may not know exactly *what* happened with a learner, predictive analytics indicate when an intervention may be necessary. Similarly, the tool may alert learners to a maladaptive behavior or negative result, without necessarily enumerating next steps. Though there is extensive research in this area from educational data mining and user modeling, there is less research on how visualizations indicating poor or average performance are received, or their impact on motivation.

Monitoring

Without the benefit of the interpersonal cues that come from face to face communication, online learner and educators can sometimes struggle. Tools such as Teacher ADVisor (Kosba et al., 2005), Student Inspector (Scheuer & Zinn, 2007), Learnograms (Nachimas & Hershkovitz, 2007), Gismo (Mazza & Botturi, 2007), the Student Activity Meter (Govaerts et al., 2010), and García-Solórzano et al.'s faceted browsing and data portrait tool (García-Solórzano et al., 2012) provide visualizations to aid in monitoring. Increasingly these monitoring tools – many of them dashboards – reflect a systems way of thinking. More specifically, they provide multifaceted data in visualizations that are interconnected, such that the visualizations are more than the "sum of their parts." In an empirical study with educators, Ali et al.'s (2012) results revealed that multiple visualization methods increased educators' perceived value of the feedback offered by their tool, LOCO-Analyst. The significance of their results is evidence that the success of an LA tool can depend strongly on the visual aspects of the system.

Most of the monitoring visualizations for educators are 2-dimenstional rather than 3D (Figures 8, 9, 10), because they are more intuitive (García-Solórzano, 2012). For example, reviewing a row of information in CourseVis indicates how an individual learner has done on all course activities, whereas reviewing a column indicates how the performance of all learners on a single activity (Figure 8). An educator can get a sense of the overall class performance by reviewing the visualization in its entirety. Of these 2D visualizations – often in the form of line, bar, and pie charts – most weren't empirically evaluated in their own right. The evaluations of many VLATs assess usability, ease of use, the clarity or completeness of the data being evaluated rather than the actual visualization (Kosba et al., 2007; Scheuer & Zinn, 2007; Govaerts et al., 2010). When visualization isn't addressed in early design phases with users, the opportunity to test for their visual preferences is missed.

CourseViz (Figure 8) is a monitoring tool for educators developed on WebCT (now Blackboard) to visualize student trace data (Mazza & Dimitrova, 2004). Mazza and Dimitrova (2007) identified the provision of multiple visualizations as a possible extension in their first evaluation of the tool. The evaluation criteria for CourseVis were efficiency, effectiveness, and usefulness, based on a questionnaire answered by 98 educators from 11 different countries (Mazza & Dimitrova, 2004; Mazza & Dimitrova, 2007). A focus group of five educators assessed the usefulness and comprehensibility of the visualizations. The user-driven design model from CourseVis was repeated in the design of GISMO (Mazza & Botturi, 2007), an open source follow-up to CourseViz. GISMO (Figure 9) also visualizes discussions, quizzes, assignments, and course access trace data for educators. While useful for monitoring, it also proved valuable for assessing discussion forum participation and redesigning the course content according to learners' needs (Mazza & Botturi, 2007). In evaluating GISMO's monitoring capabilities with a

Figure 8. (left) CourseVis plot of discussion threads based on post date and the initiator of the thread. The color and size of the balls represent the number of follow-up posts the thread received. (right) Matrix visualization of learners' quiz performance on various domain concepts (Mazza & Dimitrova, 2007)

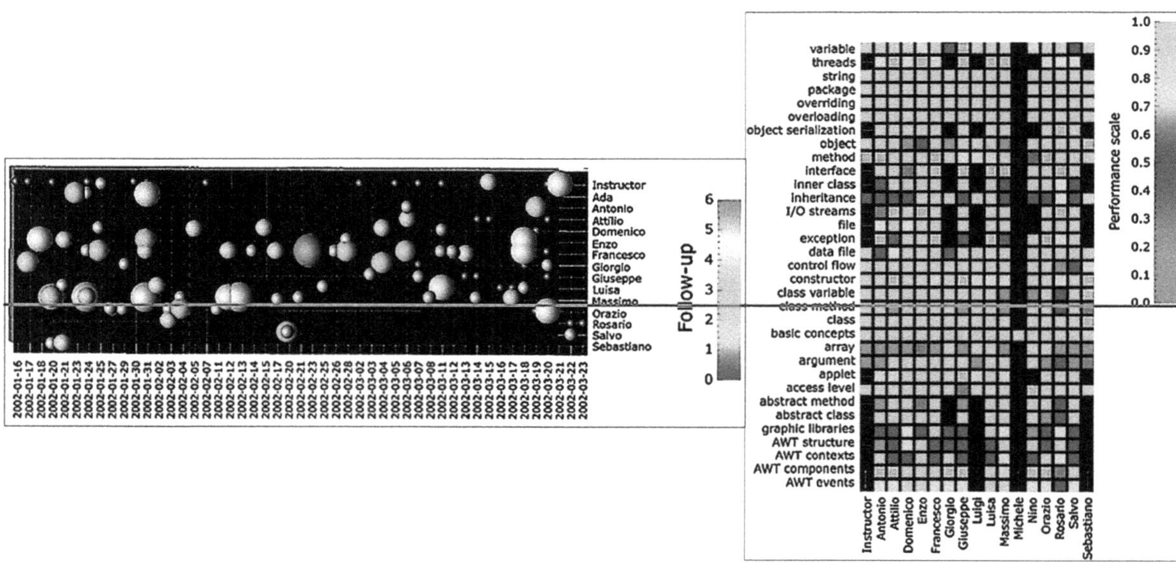

Figure 9a. The Student Activity Meter (SAM), the bar chart and tag cloud visualizations are not shown (Verbert et al., 2014)

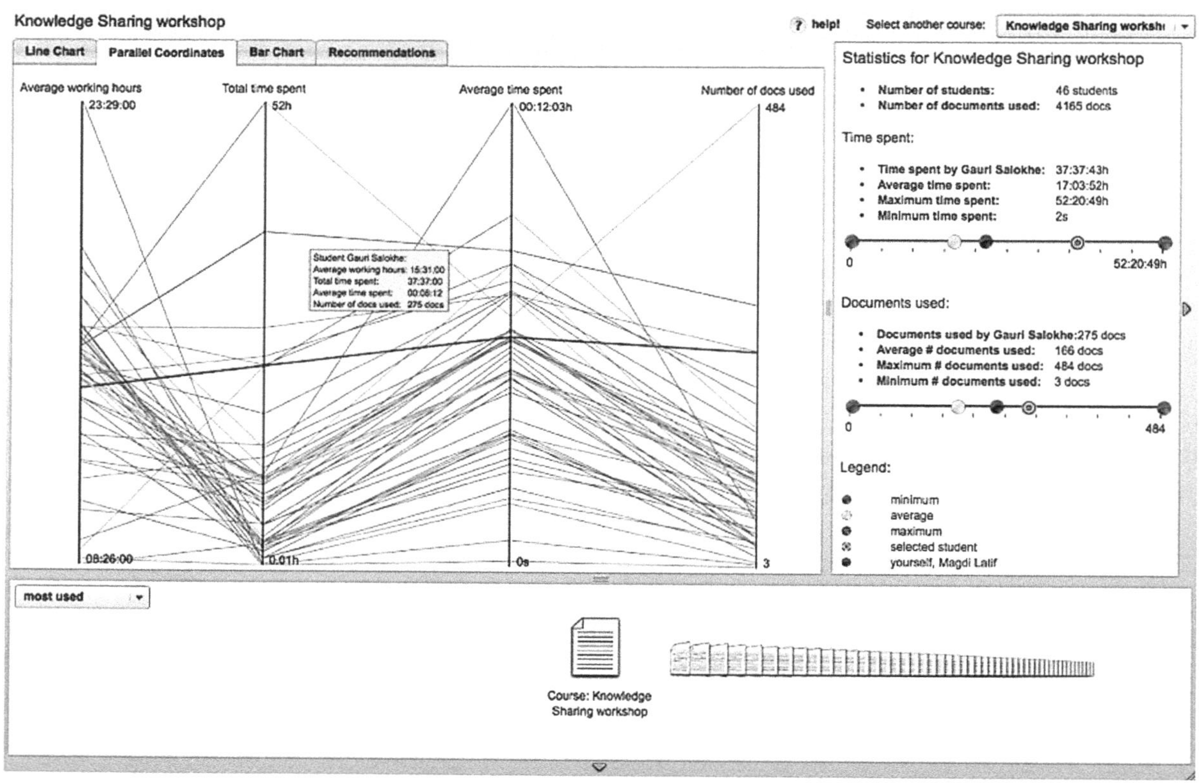

Figure 9b. The Student Activity Meter (SAM), the bar chart and tag cloud visualizations are not shown (Verbert et al., 2014)

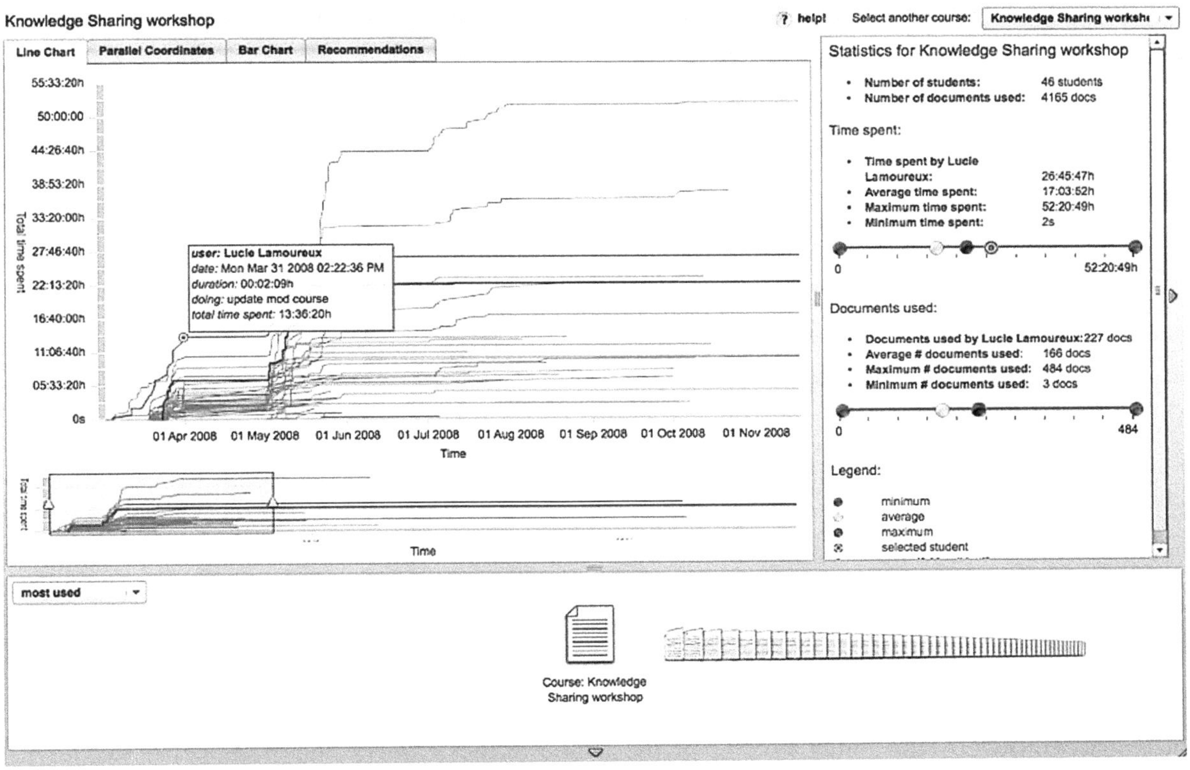

project-based online course, the authors noted something consistent across all visualizations for learning – the same learning behaviors do not equate similar learning amongst learners (Mazza & Botturi, 2007).

The Student Activity Meter (Govaerts et al., 2011) was designed for learners and educators in PLEs. SAM visualizes learners' time on task and accessed resources (Figure 10). Using design-based research methods, its visualizations were iteratively tested first with learners, the primary users in this type of environment, then with educators and learning analytics experts. Over a period of 24 months SAM underwent 4 major iterations. The first iteration was tested with learners using a task based think-aloud protocol, followed by a user satisfaction survey after a month of use. In the CIGAR case study, SAM's visualizations were evaluated by 20 educators; in the Learning and Knowledge Analytics (LAK) course with 12 individuals, 6 of them being educators (Govaerts et al., 2011). Rather than usability surveys, the authors designed their own survey using Likert-like and open-ended questions to use in both case studies. Educators were asked to rate the usefulness of each type of visualization for tasks such as finding isolated learners, giving feedback, and finding the amount of time spent in various activities (Govaerts et al., 2011). The open-ended questions proved valuable, in that the researchers received feedback they otherwise would not have. For example, the educators noted that time on task information helps them manage their own workload, and to see when learners truly began working, rather than relying on self-report. Learning analytics experts from the second case study prioritized new features, from most to least desired: (1) learner-created content, (2) the resource types used, (3) detailed statistics on

Figure 10. Faceted browsing prototype (García-Solórzano et al., 2012)

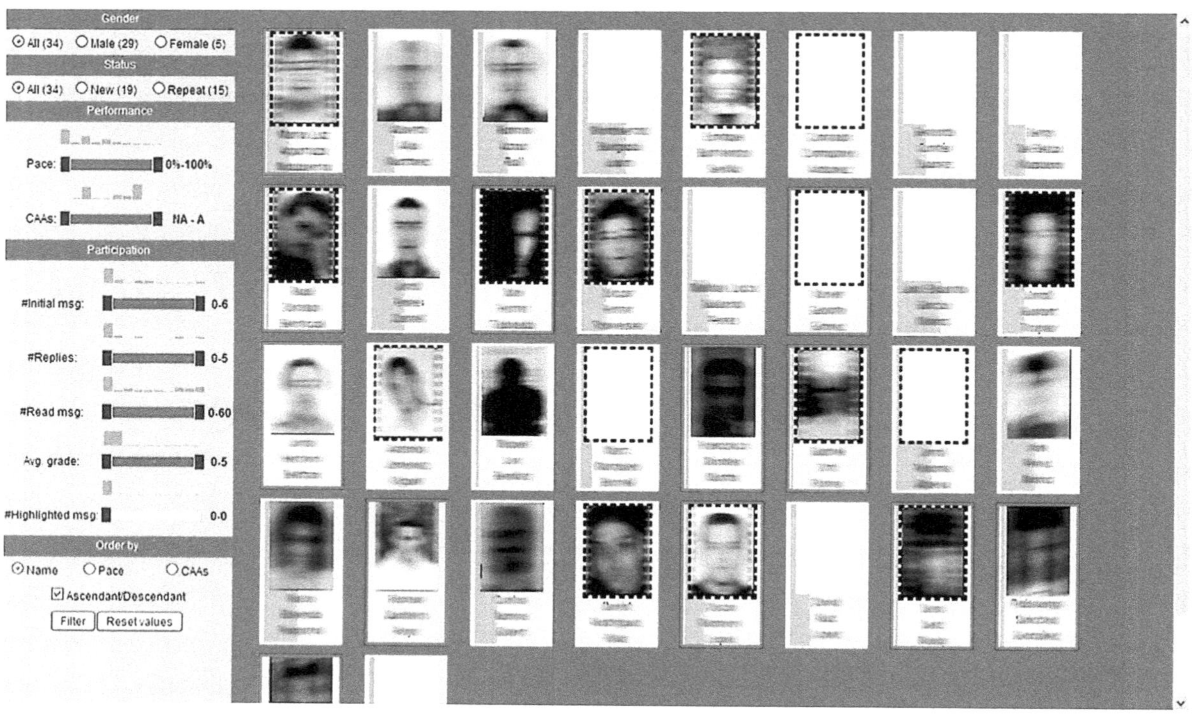

the resources used, (4) the ability to compare the actions of two learners, and (5) more detailed learner information (Govaerts et al., 2011). Filtering, zooming and search functionality were added in the next iteration, which was evaluated again with educators using a survey of 25 open-ended questions and the visualizations of data collected from a semester-long course (Govaerts et al., 2012). Future, larger scale evaluation is planned for SAM.

SEMANTIC AND DISCOURSE ANALYSES

Forums, chats, blogs, and tweets are some of the ways that learners connect to each other and learning content online. Text mining generally refers to the extraction of data from unstructured text. Semantic and discourse analyses extract *meaning* from text, going further to group, classify, and model text-based exchanges to expose previously hidden patterns.

Semantic Analytics

Latent Semantic Analysis (LSA) (Landauer, Foltz, & Laham, 1998) is a statistical technique used to reduce and extract word patterns from documents and discourse. Commercial tools like Turn It In (2015), plagiarism detection software serving 10,000 educational institutions, use the method to discover un-original content from billions of web indexes, learner papers, articles and textbooks. LSA is also used for tutoring (Dessus, 2009), automatic summarization (Whitelock et al., 2014), and formative assessment (Teplovs & Scardamalia, 2007; Villalon & Calvo, 2011).

OpenEssayist (Whitelock et al., 2014) automates the provision of formative feedback, supporting constructivist reflection using reflection prompts and multiple visualizations. Rather than assess accuracy, the tool's summaries focus on essay structure, keywords, and the sentences that represent the essay's cohesiveness (Whitelock et al., 2014). OpenEssayist's visualizations include a scatterplot of keyword dispersion, a word cloud that differentiates high frequency words according to size (Hotho et al., 2005), a tabular keyword word count, and a word limit comparison that augments the learner's original essay with color coded keywords and phrases. When tested with 41 postgraduate learners, the most used features were the highlighted keywords, extracted keywords analysis, and the keyword word cloud (Whitelock et al., 2014).

Created as part of a project developing text-mining algorithms, the Concept Map Miner is another LSA tool designed for use during the process of writing (Villalon & Calvo, 2011). CMM (Figure 11) automatically generates a concept map that reveals the flow of the learner's writing, in terms of the document's structure and lexical coherence (Villalon & Calvo, 2011). After extracting key words, the resultant concept map represents a summary of connected topics and the conceptual relationships they represent. Learners are meant to reflect on the mental models visualized from their work. The provision of automated feedback decreases the amount of time one would normally have to wait for feedback, and allows the learner to repeat the process as many times as desired.

DocuBurst (Collins et al., 2009) is an example of how a radial representation can be used to visualize semantic content. The visualization (Figure 11) reveals patterns in long texts and invites interactive exploration through zooming, filtering, or linked access to source text (Collins et al., 2009). Learners could use it to compare their texts to those of their classmates, or even previous iterations of their own work.

The degree of topic flow between consecutive sentences and paragraphs is consistent with the essay quality, and aids in the assessment and improvement the quality of written works (O'Rourke et al., 2011). In "Visualizing Topic Flow in Students' Essays, " authors O'Rourke et al. (2011) visualize the

Figure 11. (left) A CMM sample essay (Villalon & Calvo, 2011) and (right) DocuBurst visualization of a science text, focused on energy (Collins et al., 2009)

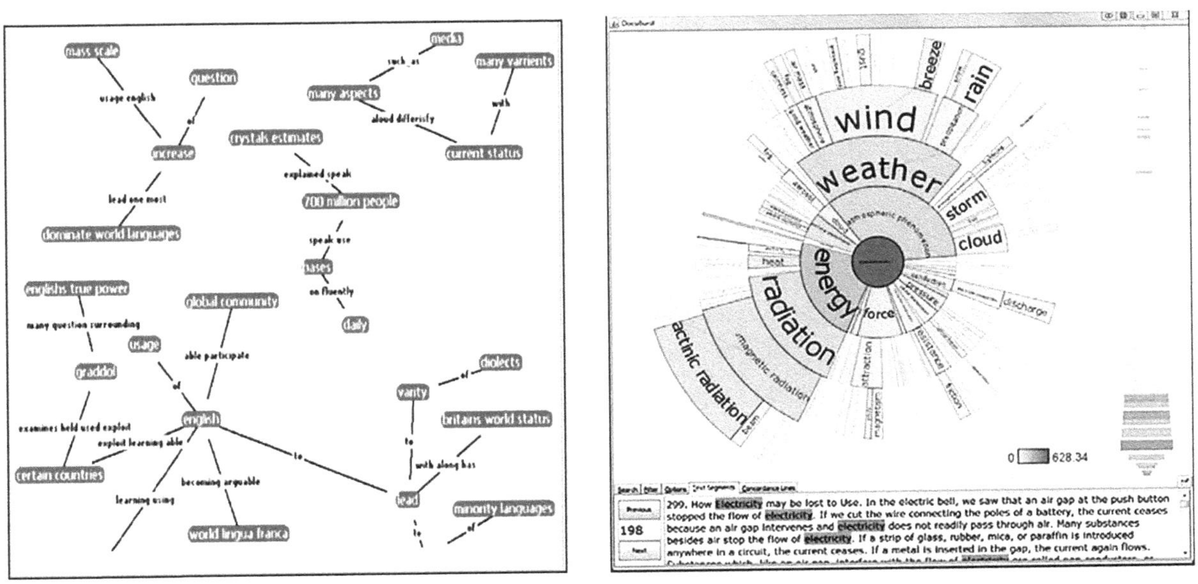

semantic distance between document sections, highlighting the structure and flow of topics between paragraphs (Figure 12). The authors evaluated the tool with 2 tutors with little teaching experience, to see how it impacted the quality and consistency of their assessments as compared to the ratings given by experts (O'Rourke et al., 2011). Presumably this would be an excellent tool for fledgling instructors, tutors, or peer reviewers. Likewise, this sort of tool could also help experienced educators quickly and consistently assess learners' work.

Discourse Analysis

Learning analytics provide insight into textual discourse by looking into the underlying motivations and outwardly expressed consequences of language (Ferguson, 2011). Language, like any other form of self-expression, is mediated by its creators' goals. The strategic use of language can indicate how learners engage with, relate to, express, or explain their own and others' perspectives. Challenging ideas, evaluating evidence and discussions of one's reasoning – these are all social learning strategies.

Education success has been related to the quality of learners' educational dialogue (Mercer, 2004). The discourse-centric visual analyses of message sequences can be used to illuminate the relationships among the processes that contribute to knowledge creation (Van Diggelen et al., 2008). As different kinds of conversation lead to different types of knowledge building (Schrire, 2004), the context, semantics, and knowledge domain are all important to the kinds of models used to visualize the discourse.

Created in 2014, the Knowledge Forum (Chen, 2014) is a prototype for the visualization of discourse by topic, the number learner, of times viewed, and time (Figure 13). Intended for use by learners and educators, Knowledge Forum's multidimensional scaling signifies that it may be particularly useful in large classrooms. The timeseries visualization could be used to track evolution of group discourse. Learners could use it to find semantically connected topics to their own in conversations that they didn't

Figure 12. Paragraph maps of a low scoring (left) and a high scoring (right) essay (O'Rourke et al., 2011)

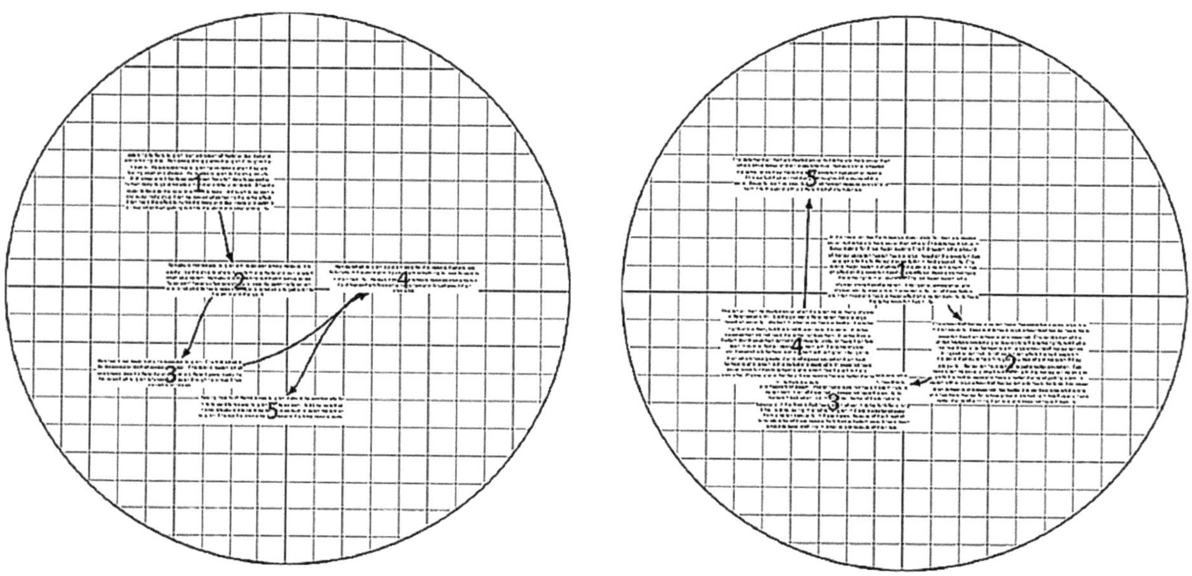

Figure 13. Knowledge Forum notes arranged by topic (color) and views (symbol) and (right) the evolution of the top 5 semantic topics (Chen, 2014)

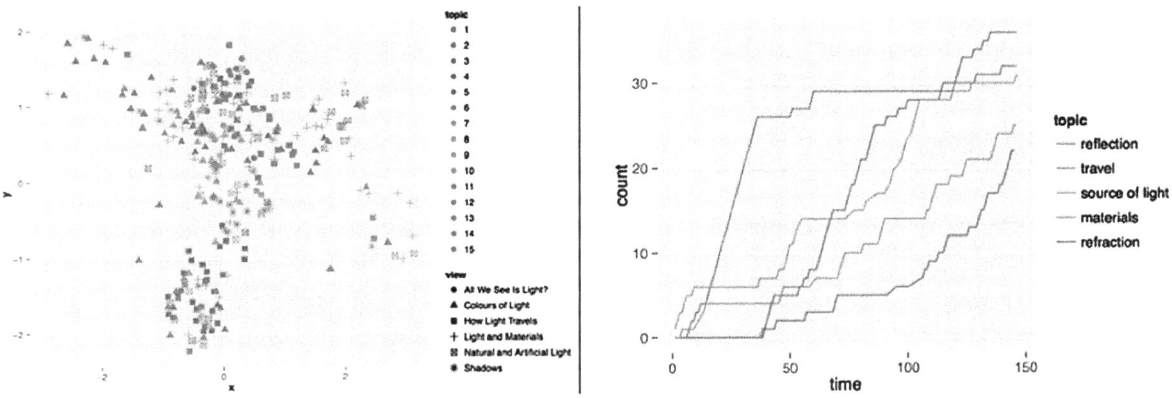

participate in, perhaps finding likeminded peers for collaboration. Similarly, Zhuhadar and Nasraoui offer a recommender system based on learners' interests – culled from their discourse – to provide learners with personalized search capabilities (Zhuhadar & Nasraoui, 2010).

SOCIAL LEARNING ANALYTICS (SLA)

Social stratification – based on wealth, power, labor, or culture – is one of the oldest social constructs, one visualized in everything from city planning to the organizational charts that model the hierarchical structures of the workplace. Created by Dorothy McKenzie, a nursery school supervisor at the University of Toronto's Institute of Child Study, the target sociogram board (Figure 14) is the precursor for modern day digital depictions of social networks with sociograms (Northway, 1952). Like its digital sociogram

Figure 14. (left) Target sociogram board with movable pins connected by elastic bands to facilitate quick prototyping and (right) sociogram of a first grade class (Northway, 1952)

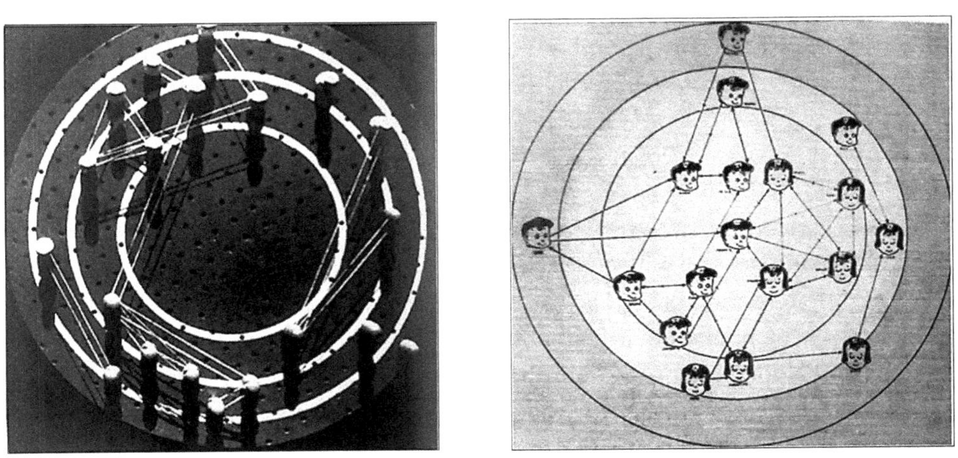

successors, the physical board allows for the quick remapping of relationships based on current behaviors. In PLEs, MOOCs, social constructivist and connectivist (Siemens, 2004) learning environments where the locus of control has shifted more from educators to learners, SLA may be used to promote a sense of social awareness, reinforce the importance of multiple perspectives, and the need for learners to develop self-assessment capacity.

Social Network Analysis

One may observe many kinds of network topologies in natural and digital worlds. The neural network of the brain is responsible for transmitting the synapses that allow us to learn, reason, and commit information to memory. The Internet is perhaps the most complex communication infrastructure ever invented. Networked learning focuses on the socially distributed nature of learning, the diversity of social relationships that people develop, the strategies they use to maintain them, and the value this creates for learning. Social network analysis (SNA) visualizes the relationships between learners, educators, and communities of learning. SNA visualizations can be used to increase social awareness (Lambropoulos et al., 2012), illustrate participatory influence or support (Fritz, 2011), monitor joint knowledge construction (de Laat, 2011), or show how collaborative activities contribute to emerging roles and power distributions (de Laat et al., 2004). These visualizations offer a way of mapping group interactions to answer questions such as *who are the main contributors*, *who is being left out of the discussion, what interactions led to learning*, and *what value do these learning interactions create?*

The metrics use for social network analyses are consistent. Nodes generally represent entities – people or documents – while edges generally represent relationships. Density is a measure of the number of connections between individual nodes. Centrality is a measure of connection, the central positioning of a node relative to the rest of a network. It is also used to describe activity, popularity, and reputation. The more connected a node is, the more central it becomes. Degree centrality counts the total number of connections linked to a node. Concentration measures the clustering of an entire network toward the center. In a directed graph that indicates information flow, in-degrees centrality counts the number of edges pointing into a node. For example, this could represent the number of followers an individual has on their wiki page. Out-degree centrality is exactly that, it counts the number of edges pointing out from a node. An example of this would be the number of people an individual follows. Betweeness centrality measures the brokering capability of a node, as it bridges between two or more additional nodes. It is represented by measuring how often a node lies on the shortest path between two nodes. A node that is frequently on the shortest path between other nodes has a higher betweeness centrality than those not on the path. This measure represents how a node facilitates the transfer of information or content to its neighbors.

The Network Overview for Discovery and Exploration in Excel, NodeXL (Bonsignore et al., 2009; Hansen et al., 2010) has a low barrier to entry (Doran et al., 2011). The open-source plugin integrates a library of common network metrics and SNA visualizations using a Microsoft Excel template (Figure 15). When tested with a diverse set of users NodeXL, was found to be an effective SNA tool *and* a means to teach SNA (Bonsignore et al., 2009). The friendship network and boundary connection visualizations (Figure 16) were created by novices in Bonsignore et al.'s study (2009). NetEvViz (Khurana et al., 2011) extends the codebase of NodeXL with the inclusion of timeseries analyses (Figure 17). Additional features include edge coloring, the ability to specify and edit temporal annotations, and timeline visualization that allows multiple graph metrics plotted over the same timespan.

Figure 15. NodeXL data on left and visualization on the right (Bonsignore et al., 2009)

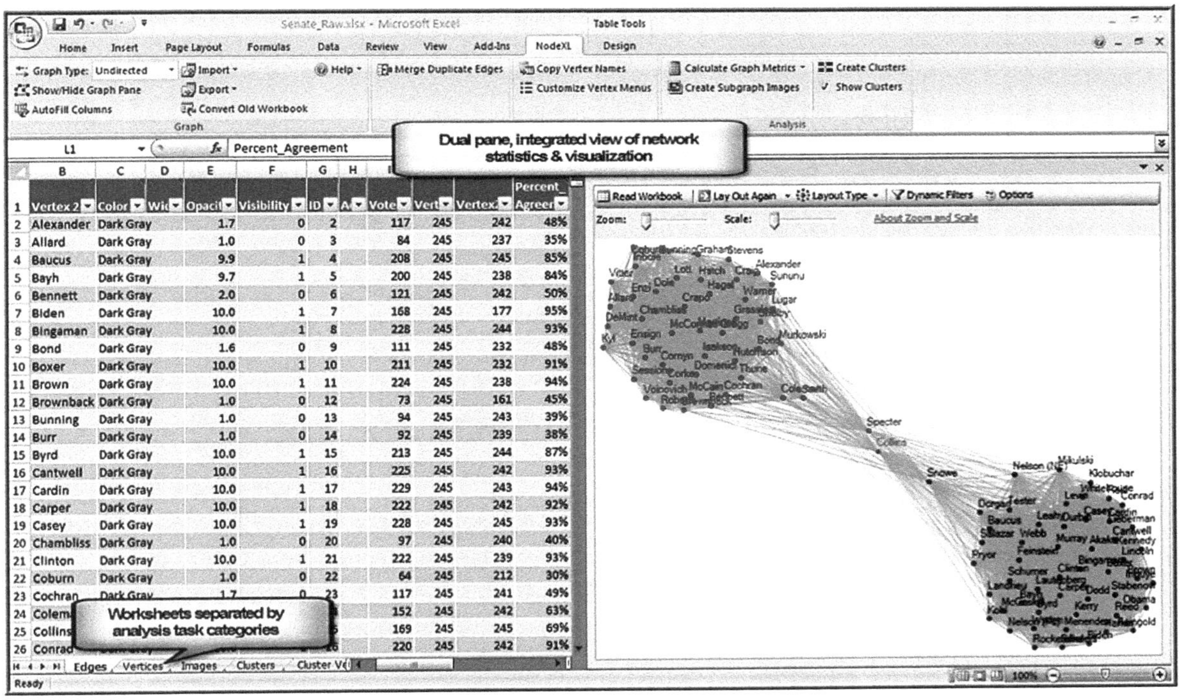

Figure 16. Visualizations created by novices with the NodeXL tool of a friendship network (left) and boundary connections between 3 forums (right) (Bonsignore et al., 2009)

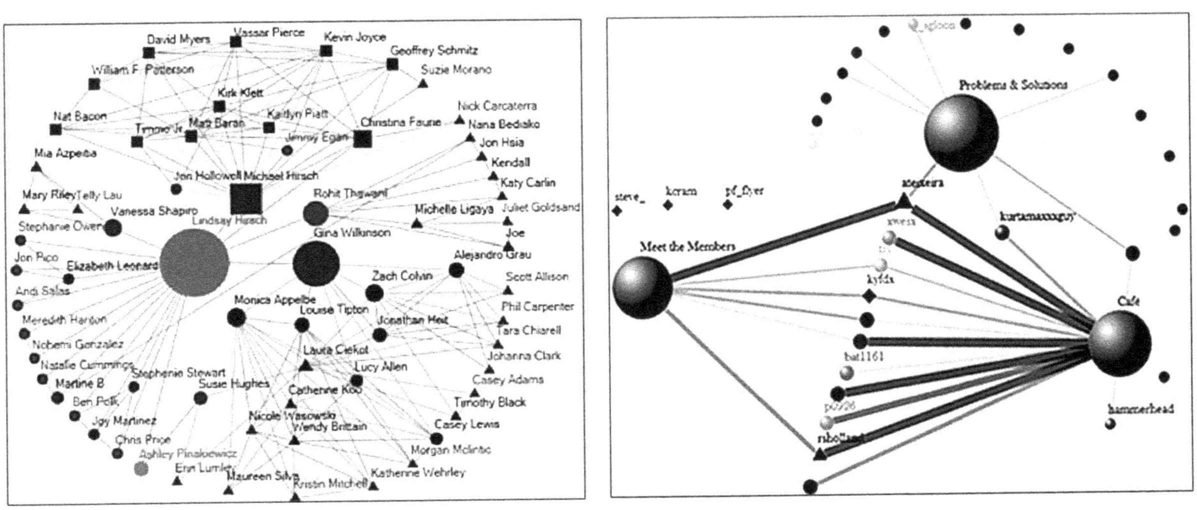

The Social Networks Adapting Pedagogical Practice (SNAPP) bookmarklet (Bakharia & Dawson, 2011) also incorporates time-based visualizations (Figure 17). It is cross-platform and cross-browser compatible, mitigating the hindrance of end-user IT permission issues. SNAPP infers participant relationships from discussion threads, visualizing a chronological message thread tree and a sociogram.

Figure 17. (left) In NetEvViz layout color indicates different days activity occurred (Khurana et al., 2011). (right) SNAPP network visualization showing message flow (Dawson, 2010)

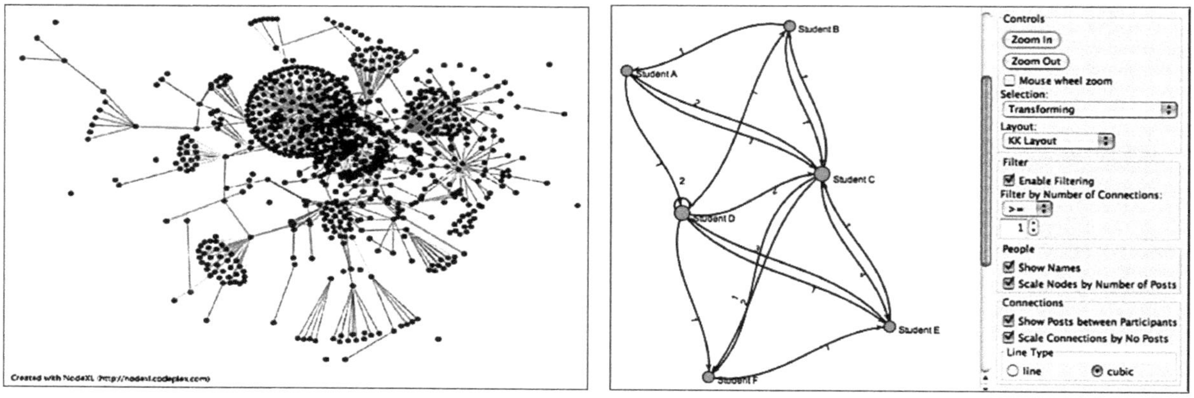

The visualizations may be embedded directly in the discussion forums, helping learners identify how their posts contribute to class discussions. Node size and edge widths can be scaled according to post frequency and relationship strength. Now in its second iteration, SNAPP incorporates all of the features of the previous version, plus the ability to search by date or relationship strength, and to watch animations of network's evolution (Bakharia & Dawson, 2011).

Folksonomy, an amalgamation of *folk* and *taxonomy*, is a means of social classification through tagging that can give insight into the nature of community dynamics. This natural language classification method uses keywords assigned to information or objects to facilitate information retrieval online for social media services like YouTube. Crowd-sourced tags of course content can be used to visually estimate learners' participation or perceived comprehension; differentiations of size, shape, and color aid in the visualization of these tags. Using folksonomy visualizations, educators can quickly identify how learners' tags align with those of the class (Ali et al., 2008; Winne & Hadwin, 2013).

One of few empirically validated VLATs, LOCO-Analyst's (Jovanović et al., 2007; Jovanović, 2008) visualizations include a scatterplot for overall impressions of learning behaviors, an ego network of chat activity (Figure 19), and a folksonomy tag cloud (Figure 18). Statistics about exchanged chat messages quantify the number of one-to-one chats and group discussions involving particular individuals. An ego network reconfigures the ego network based on peer communication patterns. First created in 2006, the 2009 iteration of LOCO-Analyst mainly featured an increase in the number and types of visualizations displayed. Evaluated both quantitatively (Jovanović et al., 2007) and qualitatively (Ali et al., 2012), the feedback garnered from evaluating the second iteration spoke to the immense value visualizations add to LATs. In their validation of the Learning Analytics Acceptance Model based on educators' perceived usage beliefs, authors Ali et al. (2013) found that the use of visualization is an influential factor in the adoption of learning analytics tools.

Collaboration Networks

Engagement with peers or experts in the field greatly expands an individual's network and the possibilities of what can be learned. Moving from VLATs of networked learning to those of the shared cognition

Figure 18. LOCO:Analyst visualizations of (A) learning content hierarchy tree, (B) tag cloud, (C) and ontology (Ali et al., 2008)

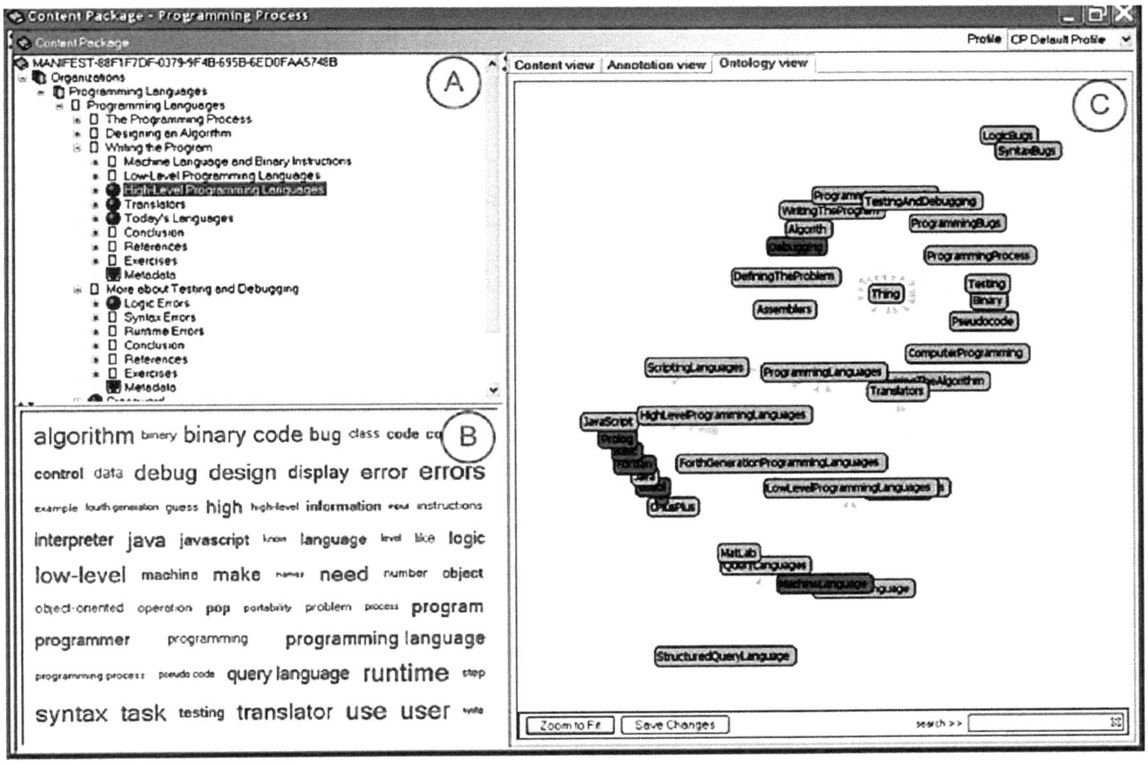

Figure 19. LOCO-Analyst chat visualizations (Jovanović et al., 2007)

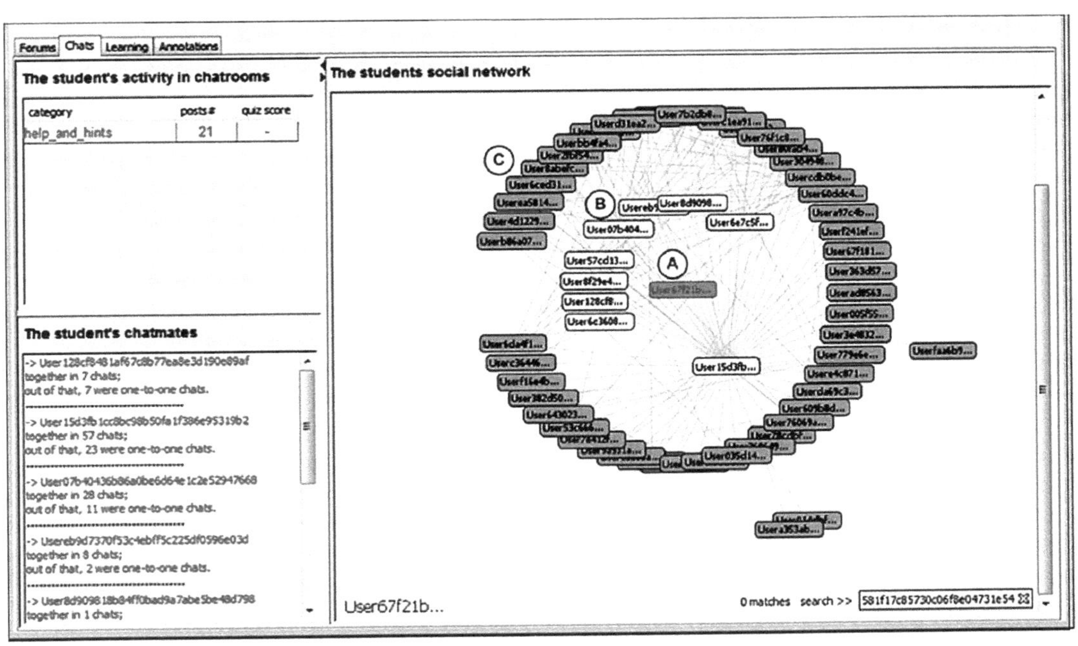

that emerges from highly collaborative learning spaces, these tools visualize peer engagement and support, the formation and dissolution of groups, and the production of learning artifacts. Joint publications (Leung et al., 2011; Ochoa et al., 2014), and even musical scores (Akoumianakis & Alexandraki, 2010) are examples of the outcomes of such collaborations. Some group cognition models link the *objects* of the knowledge work, rather than the individuals who created them (Bereiter, 2002; Scardamalia & Bereiter, 2006). Coauthorship networks like the ones visualized by SocialVis (Leung et al., 2011) illustrate the publication counts of individuals and research teams (Figure 20).

Calvani et al. (2010) used radar graphs to indicate group progress, while Kay et al. (2006) provided them to learners as a means of mutual monitoring. The Forum Plus Moodle radar graph add-on (Figure 21) indicates how groups are doing to the group members, as part of a project that seeks to answer what

Figure 20. SocialVis coauthorship networks (Leung et al., 2011)

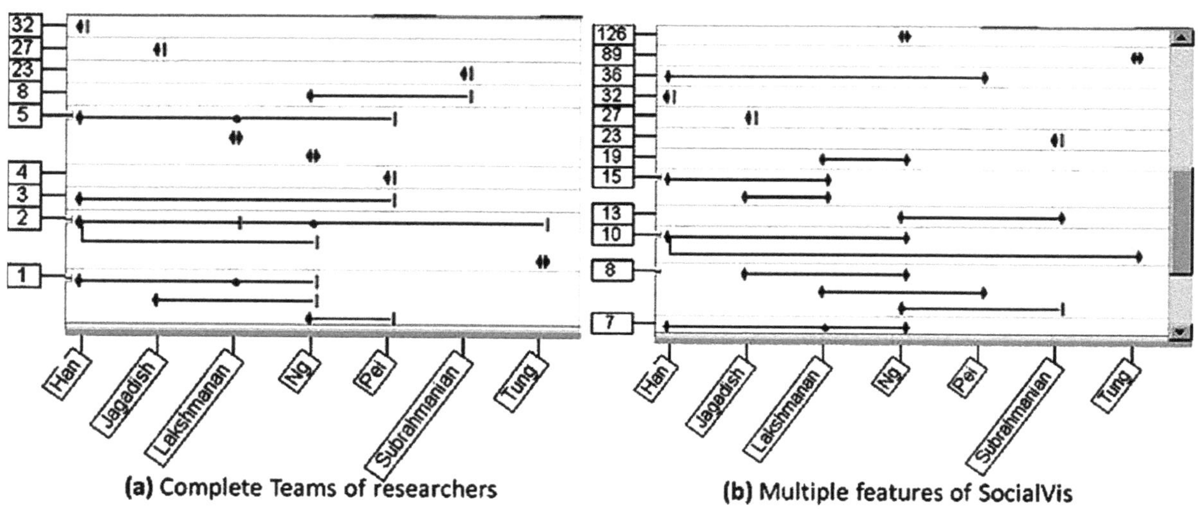

Figure 21. Forum Plus Moodle add-on illustrates effective (left) and ineffective (right) groups (Calvani et al., 2010)

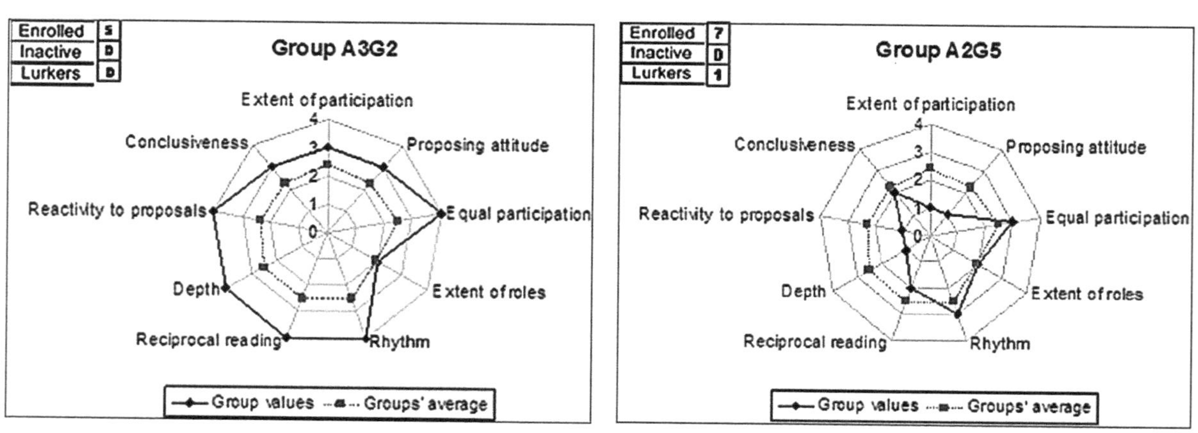

parts of the collaborative process are necessary for group success (Calvani et al., 2010). Kay et al. used a Wattle Tree (Figure 22) to mirror group task accomplishment to programming teams. Along with the radar graphs (Figure 22), the Wattle Tree was evaluated during a semester-long programming course qualitatively with learners and according to the Big 5 theory of teamwork. According to Salas et al. (2005) the five competencies are leadership, a team orientation, mutual performance monitoring, and the work task transparency required to be able to "back each other up," balancing workloads in times of high stress. Rather than provide feedback, which is inherently connected to optimal performance, the visualizations mirror presenting only what transpires.

Collaboratories such as the National Fusion Collaboratory (Schissel et. al, 2004) are large-scale, multidisciplinary, often international science endeavors. Their complex problems require a robust infrastructure that will support large distributed knowledge networks and repeated simulations with the same data. The visualizations in online collaboratory environments are research tools and a means of communication across demographics, disciplines, and even languages. Inspired by collaboratories, Marchese and Brajkovska's (2004) asynchronous collaborative system for molecular visualization is a mash-up of an interactive visualization program and a wiki. The wiki houses comments and visualization annotations, and the included playback function allows learners to step through screen captures of their visualizations.

The Knowledge Space Visualizer (KSV) uses LSA to classify learner text, based on context and coherence (Teplovs & Scardamalia, 2007). It supports individual *and* group knowledge construction, visualizing structural and semantic networks (Figure 23). The nodes are the notes produced by learners (semantic search), or individuals (structural search). Search criteria may include authors' names,

Figure 22. (left) Group activity radar; each dot is an individual and the inner circle represents average participation relative to a group or the course (Kay et al., 2006). (right) A Wattle Tree of a functional group; the density of circles indicates the learners represented on the left-most lines had the highest workload (Kay et al., 2006)

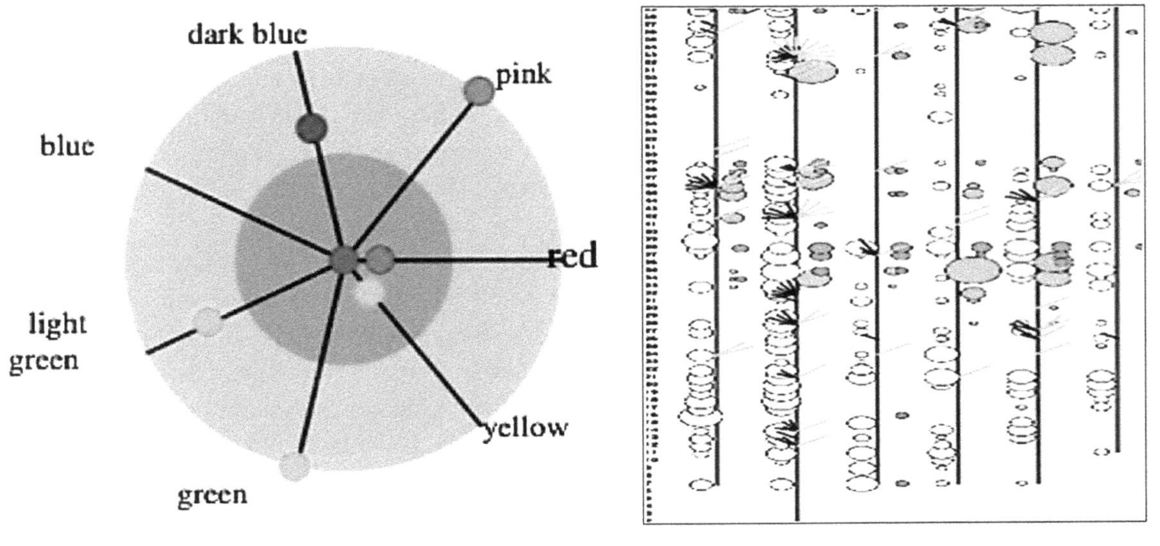

Figure 23. KSV user interface (Teplovs & Scardamalia, 2007)

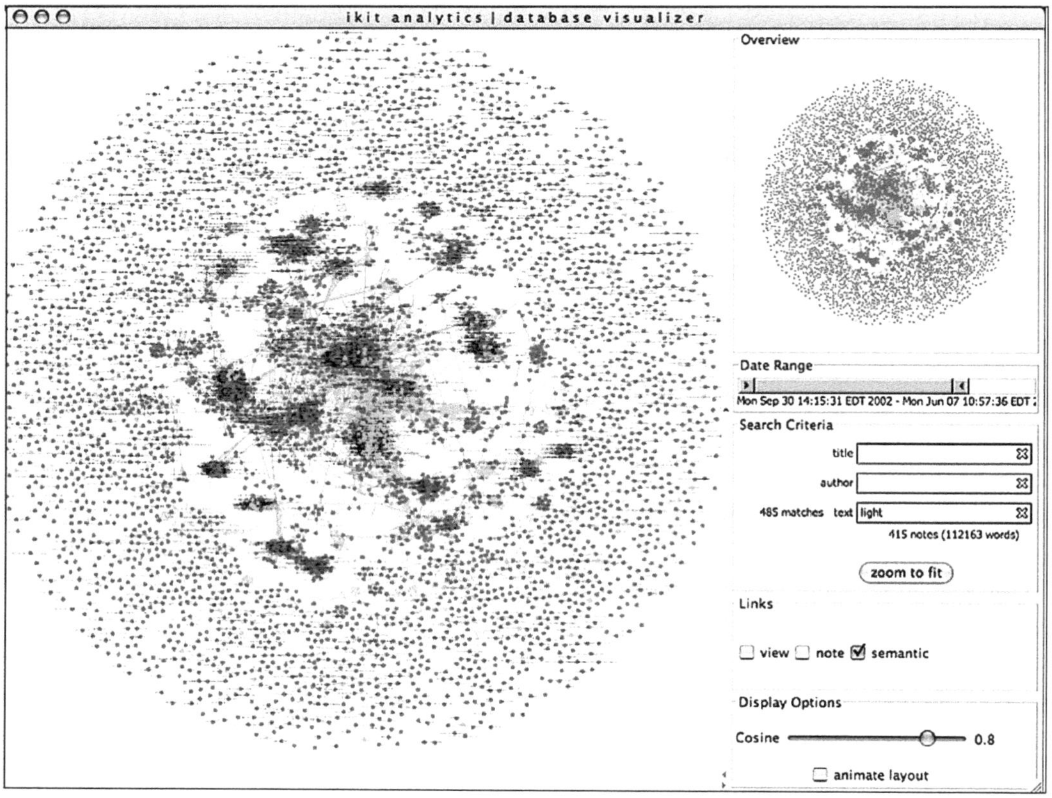

title words, or entire texts. An open source tool, the KSV has been used in multiple contexts to provide formative feedback to learners (Fujita & Teplovs, 2009; Sha et al., 2010). A similar plugin, the Network Awareness Tool, was built to visualize face-to-face workplace social networks. (Schreurs et al., 2013).

When authors Fujita and Teplovs (2009) compared KSV results to a qualitative analysis of discussion transcripts, the idea clusters identified with the KSV were similar to human-created qualitative coding categories. The authors noted that an automated tool like the KSV is useful, but vulnerable to difficult-to-detect themes, or themes needing additional key terms (Fujita & Teplovs, 2009). This is an excellent example of when visualization presents the correct data, in a graphically distinct and aesthetically pleasing way, but is incorrect because of a flaw in the underlying data.

Built on top of KSV, the Knowledge, Interaction and Semantic Student Model Explorer (KISSME) visualizes the collaborative tendencies of individuals based on interactions or the similarities in their work. KISSME combines LSA and SNA, creating interaction visualizations of *content-aware interactions* (Teplovs et al., 2011). KISSME automates content analysis, an arduous, time-staking manual endeavor. The horizontal axis represents time and the vertical scale indicates authorship. Overlaid onto the learner time display, LSA specifies the degree of similarity of the works over time and authorship (Figure 24). The superposition of different link types on the same layout makes this VLAT particularly interesting. *Content-aware interactions* are texts mathematically represented by vectors; the vectors are additive, meaning that a single vector can be made that includes all of an individual's discourse,

Figure 24. Structural links (magenta) and recently opened notes (green) superimposed on KISSME chronological authorship diagram (Teplovs et al., 2011)

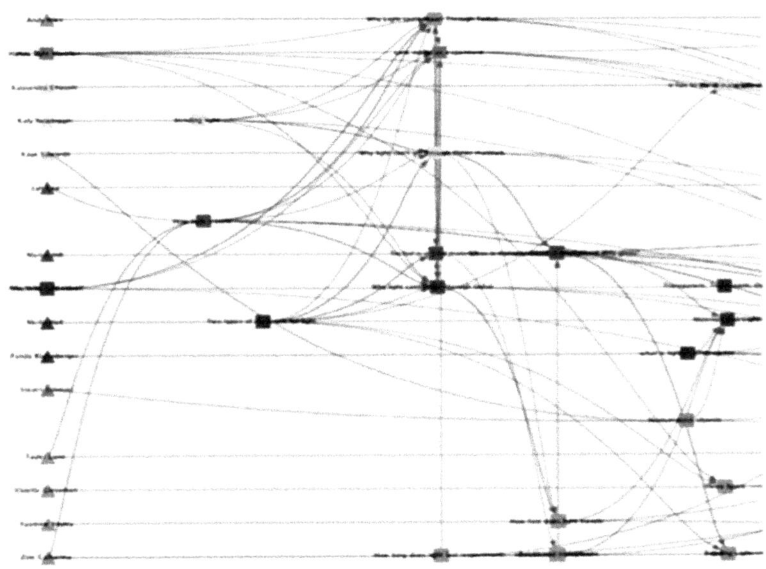

the discourse of a pair, or even a group (Teplovs et al., 2011). KISSME could be used to generate and test predictive models of learner interactions, such as the type and duration of the interactions that will result in learning. Researchers may use it to explore the characteristics of effective collaborative learning of interactions. Teplovs and Fujita hoped the tool could be used to identify the particularly pivotal moments "when individuals whose similarity based on semantic analysis of their writing are given the opportunity to interact" (Teplovs & Fujita, 2013).

SENSEMAKING AND EVALUATION

To detect pedagogically important patterns in visualizations, one must be able to make sense of sometimes-abstract representations. Though VLATs take advantage of the visual system's ability to quickly discern patterns in fractions of a second, sensemaking is perhaps the most challenging aspect of the visualization process. Borrowing from cognitive science, insight is defined as the process when a person suddenly moves to the state of knowing how to solve a problem (Kounios et al., 2006). This cognitive science definition speaks to the necessity of a problem to solve, but learners' insight may be about seeking information about their learning process, or maintaining positive behaviors. Visualizations act as the embodiment of learners' data giving them a thing to reflect *upon*, to potentially arriving at insights they may not have otherwise. To be able to distinguish between the visualizations best suited to attain it, one must be able to measure insight generation. Unfortunately, no clear definition of visual analytics insight exists (Yi et al., 2008). North (2006) categorizes it as (1) complex, (2) deep meaning that builds over time, (3) qualitative, in that it can be uncertain and subjective with multiple levels of evaluation, (4) unexpected and perhaps most importantly, (5) relevant. Rather than attempt to define it, Yi et al. (2008) describe insight generation in terms of its procedural aspects. Yi et al.'s (2008) description is based on four distinctive processes gleaned from information visualization literature and reflected in VLATs – overview, adjustment, pattern detection, and matching to a mental model. Indeed some researchers define the purpose of visualization as *being* insight (Card et al., 1999), even though different kinds of insight exist.

One of the major criticisms of LATs is that they aren't explicit about their theoretical or conceptual underpinnings (Suthers & Verbert, 2013). This is important as LATs are designed with a particular conceptualization of success that defines the data captured and patterns that evidence progress (Shum & Crick, 2012). Without knowledge of these underpinnings it is difficult, if not impossible, to compare the design or evaluation of LATs and their visualizations. Few studies reuse or reevaluate the same data. Though these studies may be ecologically valid, other forms of validity are not yet realized. Still, the perspective evidenced by real-world settings yields greater insight into the actual learning practices of learners, and highlights possible inconsistencies between behaviors and perception (Savage & Burrows, 2007).

While learning strategies, collaboration, and knowledge realization may be inferred by trace data; experience is subjective. What we have seen thus far is a lack of a coherency in evaluating VLATs; many are evaluated for usability rather than perceptual experience. The need to ask and answer questions situated from the perspective of those involved in the learning process points to the need for more phenomenological studies of visualization. The long-term empirical evaluation of VLATs would allow for the examination of the stability of pedagogical constructs over time, the transferability of data visualization literacy skills, and the patterns involved in knowledge discovery, sensemaking, and insight. Information visualization methods could be used to evaluate VLATs, methods such as participatory observation, design as a multistage process, and specifically addressing the long-term nature of insight generation (Lam et al., 2012). The evaluation of insight by measuring its transferability with the application of the new knowledge to a new or different problem may be particularly appropriate for evaluating VLATs (Chang et al., 2010), particularly in domains of applied science that routinely use visualization. The evaluation of insight is not user or domain specific, making it replicable and generalizable, however domain specific information would be lost.

CONCLUSION AND FUTURE WORK

This survey of currently existing VLATs and the challenges they address is a step toward the articulation of what we seek to achieve as a nascent field *within* a nascent field. The successful implementation of VLATs in a variety of learning domains speaks to their significance to online learning. There are however, many challenges still to be addressed. First, there are considerably less visualizations for use by learners, especially those not deemed at-risk. Since learners have the most agency to effect change, there is a particular need for their inclusion. The exposure of the underlying conceptual models VLATs' designs are based on will serve to deepen conversations about the perceptual experiences they provide. Often what is observed and experienced online is a group of people with shared tasks and goals. Fostering a sense of community within online learning spaces is a wicked problem (Rittel & Webber, 1973), one that contributes to learner isolation and dissatisfaction with the overall experience of online learning. Visualizations help to clarify the metrics used to assess performance; now it is important look to how they may be used to truly increase engagement and collaboration between learners.

The amount of available learning data has exploded in the last twenty years, making it possible for VLATs to be used in virtually every aspect of online learning. As more learning spaces adopt similar data standards, the closer the realization of the uniform collection of learning data from kindergarten to college, career and beyond becomes, providing a more complete lifelong learner portfolio than ever before. The amount and granularity of this data increases the number and type of visualization possible. These possibilities are an opportunity for the research community to address difficult questions, such as:

- How do learners operationalize visualizations over time?
- How do learning analytics tools employing visualizations help to establish or reinforce power relationships in learning spaces?
- By moving beyond simplistic glyphs and largely numerical graphical representations, how can the acquisition of knowledge be visualized in novel ways?

As described by Spiro et al. (1991) in the cognitive flexibility theory, to attain advanced knowledge acquisition one must revisit the same information at different times, for different reasons, from a variety of perspectives and contexts. VLATs are tools to reflect on and with, helping to connect learners, educators, learning content, and communities of practice. Visual Learning Analytics Tools have the potential to act as a boundary object between different disciplines, theoretical and methodological traditions, users, and research communities (Suthers & Verbert, 2013). As they evolve VLATs will likely move toward visual storytelling methods, and as time transpires, grow in value as both artistic and cultural digital artifacts.

REFERENCES

Akoumianakis, D., & Alexandraki, C. (2010). Understanding Networked Music Communities through a Practice-Lens: Virtual "Tells" and Cultural Artifacts. *Proceedings of the 2010 2nd International Conference on Intelligent Networking and Collaborative Systems (INCOS)* (pp. 62–69). doi:10.1109/INCOS.2010.65

Ali, L., Asadi, M., Gašević, D., Jovanović, J., & Hatala, M. (2013). Factors influencing beliefs for adoption of a learning analytics tool: An empirical study. *Computers & Education*, *62*, 130–148. doi:10.1016/j.compedu.2012.10.023

Ali, L., Hatala, M., Gašević, D., & Jovanović, J. (2012). A qualitative evaluation of evolution of a learning analytics tool. *Computers & Education*, *58*(1), 470–489. doi:10.1016/j.compedu.2011.08.030

Anderson, E. W. (2012). Evaluating scientific visualization using cognitive measures. *Paper presented at the 2012 BELIV Workshop: Beyond Time and Errors - Novel Evaluation Methods for Visualization BELIV '12*. doi:10.1145/2442576.2442581

Anderson, T., & Dron, J. (2011). Three Generations of Distance Education Pedagogy. *International Review of Research in Open and Distance Learning*, *12*(3), 1–18.

Arnold, K. E., & Pistilli, M. D. (2012). Course signals at Purdue: using learning analytics to increase student success. *Paper presented at the 2nd International Conference on Learning Analytics and Knowledge LAK '12* (pp. 267–270). doi:10.1145/2330601.2330666

Bakharia, A. (2011). SNAPP Presentation. Paper presented at the *Learning Analytics and Knowledge Conference*. Retrieved from http://www.slideshare.net/aneeshabakharia/snapp-learning-analytics-and-knowledge-conference-2011

Bakharia, A., & Dawson, S. (2011). SNAPP: a bird's-eye view of temporal participant interaction. *Paper presented at the 1st International Conference on Learning Analytics and Knowledge LAK '11*, New York, NY. doi:10.1145/2090116.2090144

Bell, F. (2010). Network theories for technology-enabled learning and social change: Connectivism and actor network theory. *Proceedings of the International Conference on Networked Learning*. doi:10.1109/ITHET.2013.6671027

Bonsignore, E. M., Dunne, C., Rotman, D., Smith, M., Capone, T., Hansen, D. L., & Shneiderman, B. (2009). First Steps to Netviz Nirvana: Evaluating Social Network Analysis with NodeXL. *Proceedings of the 2009 IEEE International Conference on Computational Science and Engineering* (Vol. 4, pp. 332–339). doi:10.1109/CSE.2009.120

Bowden, E. M., & Jung-Beeman, M. (2003). Aha! Insight experience correlates with solution activation in the right hemisphere. *Psychonomic Bulletin & Review*, *10*(3), 730–737. doi:10.3758/BF03196539 PMID:14620371

Bry, F., Gehlen-Baum, V., & Pohl, A. (2011). Promoting awareness and participation in large class lectures: The digital backchannel backstage. *Proceedings of the International Conference on Information Systems*.

Buerck, J. P., & Mudigonda, S. P. (2014). A Resource-Constrained Approach to Implementing Analytics in an Institution of Higher Education: An Experience Report. *Journal of Learning Analytics*, *1*(1), 129–139.

Bull, S., Ahmad, N., Johnson, M., Johan, R., Mabbott, A., & Kerly, A. (2008). Adaptive Navigation Support, Learner Control and Open Learner Models. *Proceedings of the 5th international conference on Adaptive Hypermedia and Adaptive Web-Based Systems, LNCS (Vol.* 5149, pp. 275–278). Berlin, Heidelberg: Springer-Verlag. doi:10.1007/978-3-540-70987-9_33

Bull, S., Cooke, N., & Mabbott, A. (2007). Visual Attention in Open Learner Model Presentations: An Eye-Tracking Investigation. *Paper presented at the 11th International Conference on User Modeling UM '07*, Springer-Verlag. doi:10.1007/978-3-540-73078-1_21

Calvani, A., Fini, A., Molino, M., & Ranieri, M. (2010). Visualizing and monitoring effective interactions in online collaborative groups. *British Journal of Educational Technology*, *41*(2), 213–226. doi:10.1111/j.1467-8535.2008.00911.x

Card, S. K., Mackinlay, J. D., & Shneiderman, B. (1999). *Readings in information visualization - using vision to think*. Academic Press.

Carmean, C., & Mizzi, P. (2010). The Case for Nudge Analytics. *EDUCAUSE Quarterly*, *33*(4), 1–8.

Cerezo, R., Suarez, N., Núñez, J. C., & Sánchez-Santillán, M. (2014). eGraph tool. *Paper presented at the Fourth International Conference*, New York, NY (pp. 273–274). doi:10.1145/2567574.2567596

Chang, R., Ziemkiewicz, C., Pyzh, R., Kielman, J., & Ribarsky, W. (2010). Learning-based evaluation of visual analytic systems. *Proceedings of BELIV* (pp. 29–34). doi:10.1145/2110192.2110197

Chatti, M. A., Dyckhoff, A. L., Schroeder, U., & Thüs, H. (2012). A reference model for learning analytics. *International Journal of Technology Enhanced Learning*, *4*(5/6), 318–331. doi:10.1504/IJTEL.2012.051815

Chen, B. (2014). Visualizing semantic space of online discourse: the knowledge forum case. *Paper presented at the Fourth International Conference on Learning Analytics And Knowledge LAK '14*. ACM. doi:10.1145/2567574.2567595

Collins, C., Carpendale, S., & Penn, G. (2009). Docuburst: visualizing document content using language structure. *Computer Graphics Forum*, *28(3)*, 1039–1046. doi:10.1111/j.1467-8659.2009.01439.x

Consolvo, S., Markle, K., Patrick, K., & Chanasyk, K. (2009). Designing for persuasion: mobile services for health behavior change. *Paper presented at the 4th International Conference on Persuasive Technology Persuasive '09*, New York: NY. doi:10.1145/1541948.1541964

Cook, R., & Kay, J. (1994). The Justified User Model: A Viewable, Explained User Model. *Proceedings of the Fourth International Conference on User Modeling* (pp. 145–150).

Dabbagh, N., & Kitsantas, A. (2004). Supporting Self-Regulation in Student-Centered Web-Based Learning Environments. *International Journal on E-Learning*, *3*(1), 40–47.

Dawson, S., Bakharia, A., & Heathcote, E. (2010). SNAPP: Realising the affordances of real-time SNA within networked learning environments. *Proceedings of the International Conference on Networked Learning* (pp. 125–133).

Deakin Crick, R., & Grushka, K. (2010). Signs, Symbols and Metaphor: Linking self with text in inquiry based learning. *Curriculum Journal*, *21*(1).

de Laat, M. (2011). Bridging the Knowledge Gap: Using Social Network Methodology for Detecting, Connecting and Facilitating Informal Networked Learning in Organizations. *Proceedings IEEE International Conference on System Sciences* (pp. 1–8). doi:10.1109/HICSS.2011.88

de Laat, M., Lally, V., & Lipponen, L. (2004). In J. Nall & R. Robson (Eds.), *Proceedings of World Conference on E-Learning in Corporate, Government, Healthcare, and Higher Education* (pp. 1846-1853). Chesapeake, VA: Association for the Advancement of Computing in Education. Retrieved from http://www.editlib.org/p/11592

de Laat, M., Lally, V., Lipponen, L., & Simons, R.-J. (2007). Investigating patterns of interaction in networked learning and computer-supported collaborative learning: A role for Social Network Analysis. *International Journal of Computer-Supported Collaborative Learning*, *2*(1), 87–103. doi:10.1007/s11412-007-9006-4

De Liddo, A., Sándor, Á., & Buckingham Shum, S. (2012). Contested Collective Intelligence: Rationale, Technologies, and a Human-Machine Annotation Study. *Computer Supported Cooperative Work*, *21*(4-5), 417–448. doi:10.1007/s10606-011-9155-x

Dessus, P. (2009). An Overview of LSA-Based Systems for Supporting Learning and Teaching. In *Artificial Intelligence in Education* (pp. 157–164). doi:10.3233/978-1-60750-028-5-157

Dimitrova, V. (2003). STyLE-OLM: Interactive Open Learner Modelling. *International Journal of Artificial Intelligence in Education, 13*(1), 35–78.

Dourish, P., & Bly, S. (1992). Portholes: supporting awareness in a distributed work group *Paper presented at the SIGCHI Conference on Human Factors in Computing SystemsCHI '92* (pp. 541–547). doi:10.1145/142750.142982

Doran, P. R., Doran, C., & Mazur, A. (2011). Social network analysis as a method for analyzing interaction in collaborative online learning environments. *Journal of Systemics. Cybernetics and Informatics, 9*(7), 10–16.

Duval, E. (2011). Attention please!: learning analytics for visualization and recommendation. *Paper presented at the 1st International Conference on Learning Analytics and Knowledge LAK '11* (pp. 9–17). doi:10.1145/2090116.2090118

Dyckhoff, A. L., Zielke, D., Chatti, M. A., & Schroeder, U. (2011). eLAT: An Exploratory Learning Analytics Tool for Reflection and Iterative Improvement of Technology Enhanced Learning. *Educational Data Mining* (pp. 355–356).

Ebbinghaus, H. (1913). *Memory: A contribution to experimental psychology*. Teachers College, Columbia University. doi:10.1037/10011-000

Fancsali, S., Ritter, S., Stamper, J. C., & Nixon, T. (2013). Toward "Hyper-Personalized" Cognitive Tutors: Non-Cognitive Personalization in the Generalized Intelligent Framework for Tutoring. *Proceedings of the International Conference on Artificial Intelligence in Education* (pp. 71-79).

Ferguson, R., & Shum, S. B. (2011). Learning analytics to identify exploratory dialogue within synchronous text chat. *Proceedings of the 1st International Conference on Learning Analytics and Knowledge* (pp. 99–103). doi:10.1145/2090116.2090130

Fritz, J. (2011). Classroom walls that talk: Using online course activity data of successful students to raise self-awareness of underperforming peers. *The Internet and Higher Education, 14*(2), 89–97. doi:10.1016/j.iheduc.2010.07.007

Fujita, N., & Teplovs, C. (2009). Automating the analysis of collaborative discourse: Identifying idea clusters. *Computer-Supported Collaborative Learning*, 2009, 162–164.

García-Solórzano, D., Cobo, G., Santamaria, E., Morán, J. A., Monzo, C., & Melenchón, J. (2012). Educational monitoring tool based on faceted browsing and data portraits. *Paper presented at the 2nd International Conference on Learning Analytics and Knowledge LAK '12*, New York: NY. doi:10.1145/2330601.2330645

Goldhaber, M. H. (1997, April). The Attention Economy and the Net. *First Monday, 2*(4). doi:10.5210/fm.v2i4.519

Govaerts, S., Verbert, K., Duval, E., & Pardo, A. (2012). The student activity meter for awareness and self-reflection. *CHI Extended Abstracts* (pp. 869–884). doi:10.1145/2212776.2212860

Govaerts, S., Verbert, K., Klerkx, J., & Duval, E. (2010). Visualizing Activities for Self-reflection and Awareness. In X. Luo, M. Spaniol, L. Wang, Q. Li, W. Nejdl, & W. Zhang (Eds.), *Advances in Web-Based Learning – The 9th International Conference on Web-based Learning*, Shanghai, China, LCNS (Vol. 6483, pp. 91–100). Berlin, Heidelberg: Springer Berlin Heidelberg. doi:10.1007/978-3-642-17407-0_10

Grann, J., & Bushway, D. (2014). Competency map: visualizing student learning to promote student success. *Paper presented at the Fourth International Conference on Learning Analytics And Knowledge LAK '14* (pp. 168–172). doi:10.1145/2567574.2567622

Gruzd, A., Haythornthwaite, C., Paulin, D., Absar, R., & Huggett, M. (2014). Learning analytics for the social media age. *Presented at the Fourth International Conference*, New York: New York (pp. 254–256). doi:10.1145/2567574.2576773

Hanneman, R. A., & Riddle, M. (2011). Concepts and measures for basic network analysis. In Handbook of Social Network Analysis. doi:10.4135/9781446294413.n24

Hansen, D. Ben Shneiderman, & Smith, M. A. (2010). Analyzing Social Media Networks with NodeXL: Insights from a Connected World. San Francisco, CA: Morgan Kaufmann Publishers Inc.

Haythornthwaite, C. (2011). Learning networks, crowds and communities. *Paper presented at the 1st International Conference on Learning Analytics and Knowledge LAK '11* (pp. 18–22). doi:10.1145/2090116.2090119

Haythornthwaite, C., & De Laat, M. (2010). Social networks and learning networks: Using social network perspectives to understand social learning. *Proceedings of the 7th International Conference on Networked Learning,* Lancaster University, Lancaster, England.

Heer, J., Viégas, F. B., & Wattenberg, M. (2009). Voyagers and voyeurs. *Communications of the ACM*, *52*(1), 87–97. doi:10.1145/1435417.1435439

Hershkovitz, A., & Nachmias, R. (2008). Developing a Log-based Motivation Measuring Tool. In *Educational Data Mining* (pp. 226–233).

Hirschi, C. (2010). Introduction: Applications of Social Network Analysis. *Procedia: Social and Behavioral Sciences*, *4*, 2–3. doi:10.1016/j.sbspro.2010.07.477

Hotho, A., Nürnberger, A., & Paaß, G. (2005). A Brief Survey of Text Mining. *LDV Forum.*

Icke, I., & Sklar, E. (2008). Daisy Map: A Visualization Tool For Student Assessments Data. *Proceedings of the IEEE VisWeek From Theory to Practice Design, Vision and Visualization Workshop.*

Information Literacy Competency Standards for Higher Education. (2000). Association of College & Research Libraries, Chicago.

Johnson, L., Adams Becker, S., Estrada, V., & Freeman, A. (2014). *NMC Horizon Report: 2014 K-12 Edition* (pp. 1–52). Austin, Texas: The New Media Consortium.

Jones, C., Asensio, M., & Goodyear, P. (2000). Networked learning in higher education: Practitioners' perspectives. *HE Association for Learning Technology Journal*, *8*(2), 18–28. doi:10.1080/0968776000080203

Jovanović, J., Gašević, D., Brooks, C. A., Devedžić, V., & Hatala, M. (2007). LOCO-Analyst: A Tool for Raising Teachers' Awareness in Online Learning Environments. In E. Duval, R. Klamma, & M. Wolpers (Eds.), *Proceedings of the Second European conference on Technology Enhanced Learning: creating new learning experiences on a global scale (EC-TEL'07)* (pp. 112-126). Berlin: Springer-Verlag. doi:10.1007/978-3-540-75195-3_9

Jovanović, J., Gašević, D., Brooks, C., Devedžić, V., & Hatala, M. (2007). LOCO-analyst: a tool for raising teachers' awareness in online learning environments. *Proceedings of the Second European conference on Technology Enhanced Learning: creating new learning experiences on a global scale, LNCS* (Vol. 4753, pp. 112–126). Berlin, Heidelberg: Springer-Verlag. doi:10.1007/978-3-540-75195-3_9

Jovanović, J., Gašević, D., Brooks, C., Devedžić, V., Hatala, M., Eap, T., & Richards, G. (2008). LOCO-Analyst: Semantic web technologies in learning content usage analysis. *International Journal of Continuing Engineering Education and Lifelong Learning, 18*(1), 54. doi:10.1504/IJCEELL.2008.016076

Kay, J., & Lum, A. (2005). Exploiting readily available web data for scrutable student models. *Proceedings of the 12th International Conference on Artificial Intelligence in Education* (pp. 338–345). Amsterdam: IOS Press.

Kay, J., & Lum, A. (2006). Exploiting Readily Available Web Data for Reflective Student Models. *Artificial Intelligence in Education.*

Kay, J., Maisonneuve, N., Yacef, K., & Reimann, P. (2006). The Big Five and Visualisations of Team Work Activity. *ITS'06 Proceedings of the 8th international conference on Intelligent Tutoring Systems,* 197–206. doi:10.1007/11774303_20

Kerly, A., & Bull, S. (2008). Children's Interactions with Inspectable and Negotiated Learner Models Paper presented at the ITS '08: *Proceedings of the 9th International Conference on Intelligent Tutoring Systems*, 5091, 132–141. Springer-Verlag, Berlin, Heidelberg. doi:10.1007/978-3-540-69132-7_18

Kerly, A., Ellis, R., & Bull, S. (2008). CALMsystem: A Conversational Agent for Learner Modelling. *Knowledge-Based Systems, 21*(3), 238–246. doi:10.1016/j.knosys.2007.11.015

Khurana, U., Nguyen, V.-A., Cheng, H.-C., Ahn, J.-W., Chen, X., & Shneiderman, B. (2011). Visual Analysis of Temporal Trends in Social Networks Using Edge Color Coding and Metric Timelines. Paper presented at the *Privacy, Security, Risk and Trust (PASSAT) and 2011 IEEE Third International Conference on Social Computing (SocialCom)* (pp. 549–554). doi:10.1109/PASSAT/SocialCom.2011.212

Kop, R., & Fournier, H. (2010). New dimensions to self-directed learning in an open networked learning environment. *International Journal of Self-Directed Learning, 7*(2).

Kosba, E., Dimitrova, V., & Boyle, R. (2007). Adaptive feedback generation to support teachers in web-based distance education. *User Modeling and User-Adapted Interaction, 17*(4), 379–413. doi:10.1007/s11257-007-9031-z

Kosba, E., Dimitrova, V., & Boyle, R. (2005). Using student and group models to support teachers in web-based distance education. *Paper presented at the 10th international conference on User Modeling UM'05.* Springer-Verlag. doi:10.1007/11527886_17

Kounios, J., Frymiare, J. L., Bowden, E. M., Fleck, J. I., Subramaniam, K., Parrish, T. B., & Jung-Beeman, M. (2006). The prepared mind: Neural activity prior to problem presentation predicts subsequent solution by sudden insight. *Psychological Science*, *17*(10), 882–890. doi:10.1111/j.1467-9280.2006.01798.x PMID:17100789

Lajoie, S. P., Naismith, L., Poitras, E., Hong, Y.-J., Cruz-Panesso, I., & Ranellucci, J. (2013). Technology-Rich Tools to Support Self-Regulated Learning and Performance in Medicine. In R. Azevedo & V. Aleven, International Handbook of Metacognition and Learning Technologies, 28, 229–242. New York, NY: Springer New York. doi:10.1007/978-1-4419-5546-3_16

Lam, H., Bertini, E., Isenberg, P., Plaisant, C., & Carpendale, S. (2012). Empirical Studies in Information Visualization: Seven Scenarios. *IEEE Transactions on Visualization and Computer Graphics*, *18*(9), 1520–1536. doi:10.1109/TVCG.2011.279 PMID:22144529

Moere, A. V., & Purchase, H. (2011). On the role of design in information visualization. *Information Visualization*, *10*(4), 356–371. doi:10.1177/1473871611415996

Lambropoulos, N., Faulkner, X., & Culwin, F. (2012). Supporting social awareness in collaborative e-learning. *British Journal of Educational Technology*, *43*(2), 295–306. doi:10.1111/j.1467-8535.2011.01184.x

Landauer, T. K., Foltz, P. W., & Laham, D. (1998). An introduction to latent semantic analysis. *Discourse Processes*, *25*(2-3), 259–284. doi:10.1080/01638539809545028

Leony, D., & Pardo, A., la Fuente Valentín, de, L., de Castro, D. S., & Kloos, C. D. (2012). GLASS: a learning analytics visualization tool. Paper presented at the *Second International Conference on Learning Analytics and Knowledge LAK 2012* (pp. 162–163). doi:10.1145/2330601.2330642

Lesh, R., Lamon, S. J., Gong, B., & Post, T. (1992). Using Learning Progress Maps to Improve Instructional Decision Making. In R. Lesh & S. J. Lamon (Eds.), Assessment of Authentic Performance in School Mathematics (pp. 343–375(. Washington, DC.

Leung, C. K.-S., Carmichael, C. L., & Teh, E. W. (2011). Visual Analytics of Social Networks: Mining and Visualizing Co-authorship Networks. *Human-Computer Interaction*, 2011, 335–345. doi:10.1007/978-3-642-21852-1_40

Mabbott, A., & Bull, S. (2004). Alternative Views on Knowledge: Presentation of Open Learner Models. In J.C. Lester, R.M. Vicari & F. Paraguacu (Eds.), *Proceedings of the 7th International Conference on Intelligent Tutoring Systems* (pp. 689-698). Berlin: Springer-Verlag.

Mackinlay, J. D. (1986). Automating the Design of Graphical Presentations of Relational Information. *ACM Transactions on Graphics*, *5*(2), 110–141. doi:10.1145/22949.22950

Marchese, F. T., & Brajkovska, N. (2004). Dynamically binding image to text for information communication. *Proceedings of the International Conference on Computer Visualization and Graphics* (pp. 707–712). doi:10.1109/IV.2004.1320219

Mazza, R., & Botturi, L. (2007). Monitoring an Online Course with the GISMO Tool: A Case Study. *Journal of Interactive Learning Research*, *18*(2), 251–265.

Mazza, R., & Dimitrova, V. (2004). Visualising student tracking data to support instructors in web-based distance education. *Paper presented at the 13th international World Wide Web conference on Alternate Track WWW Alt. '04*. ACM. doi:10.1145/1013367.1013393

Mazza, R., & Dimitrova, V. (2007). CourseVis: A graphical student monitoring tool for supporting instructors in web-based distance courses. *International Journal of Human-Computer Studies*, *65*(2), 125–139. doi:10.1016/j.ijhcs.2006.08.008

McDonald, B., Noakes, N., & Stuckey, B. (2005). *Breaking down learner isolation: How social network analysis informs design and facilitation for online learning*. Montreal, Canada: AERA.

Medina, R., & Suthers, D. (2009). Using a contingency graph to discover representational practices in an online collaborative environment. *Research and Practice in Technology Enhanced Learning*, *4*(3), 281–305. doi:10.1142/S1793206809000726

Mercer, N. (2004). Sociocultural discourse analysis: Analysing classroom talk as a social mode of thinking. *Journal of Applied Linguistics*, *1*(2), 137–168. doi:10.1558/japl.2004.1.2.137

Miller, K. (2011, May 3). *Gender Matters: Assessing and Addressing the Persistent Gender Gap in Physics Education*. University of Michigan Department of Physics. Retrieved from http://sitemaker.umich.edu/ecoach/press

Millner, N., Small, T., & Deakin Crick, R. (2006). Learning by Accident (Report No. 1). *ViTaL Development and Research Programme*, University of Bristol.

Mitrovic, A., & Martin, B. (2002). Evaluating the Effects of Open Student Models on Learning. In X. Luo, M. Spaniol, L. Wang, Q. Li, W. Nejdl, & W. Zhang (Eds.), Advances in Web-Based Learning ICWL 2010, LNCS (Vol. 2347, pp. 296–305). Berlin: Springer Berlin Heidelberg. doi:10.1007/3-540-47952-X_31

Monroy, C., Rangel, V. S., & Whitaker, R. (2013). STEMscopes: contextualizing learning analytics in a K-12 science curriculum. *Paper presented at the Third International Conference on Learning Analytics and Knowledge LAK '13*, New York: NY. doi:10.1145/2460296.2460339

Morton, K., Balazinska, M., Grossman, D., Kosara, R., & Mackinlay, J. (2014). Public Data and Visualizations: How are Many Eyes and Tableau Public Used for Collaborative Analytics? *SIGMOD Record*, *43*(2), 17–22. doi:10.1145/2694413.2694417

Nachimas, R., & Hershkovitz, A. (2007). A Case Study of Using Visualization for Understanding the Behavior of the Online Learner. *Proceedings of the International Workshop on Applying Data Mining in E-Learning* (pp. 43–52).

North, C. (2006). Toward measuring visualization insight. *IEEE Computer Graphics and Applications*, *26*(3), 6–9. doi:10.1109/MCG.2006.70 PMID:16711210

Northway, M. L. (1952). A primer of sociometry. Toronto, ON: University of Toronto Press.

Novak, J. D. (2003). The promise of new ideas and new technology for improving teaching and learning. *Cell Biology Education*, *2*(2), 122–132. doi:10.1187/cbe.02-11-0059 PMID:12888848

Novak, J. D., & Cañas, A. J. (2004). Building on New Constructivist Ideas and Cmap Tools to Create a New Model for Education. In A. J. Cañas, J. D. Novak, & F. M. González (Eds.), *Concept maps Theory, methodology, technology, proceedings of the 1st international conference on concept mapping,* Pamplona, Spain.

Novak, J. D., & Cañas, A. J. (2006). The origins of the concept mapping tool and the continuing evolution of the tool★. *Information Visualization*, *5*(3), 175–184. doi:10.1057/palgrave.ivs.9500126

Ochoa, X., Suthers, D., Verbert, K., & Duval, E. (2014). Analysis and Reflections on the Third Learning Analytics and Knowledge Conference (LAK 2013). *Journal of Learning Analytics*, *1*(2), 5–22.

O'Rourke, S. T., Calvo, R. A., & McNamara, D. S. (2011). Visualizing Topic Flow in Students' Essays. *Journal of Educational Technology & Society*, *14*(3), 4–15.

Oblinger, D. G. (2011, September 6). Doing Better with Less. *Educause Review Online*. Retrieved from http://www.educause.edu/ero/article/doing-better-less

Pirolli, P., & Card, S. (2005). The Sensemaking Process and Leverage Points for Analyst Technology as Identified Through Cognitive Task Analysis. *Proceedings of International Conference on Intelligence*.

Pistilli, M. D., Arnold, K., & Bethune, M. (2012). *Signals: Using academic analytics to promote student success*. EDUCAUSE Review Online.

Podgorelec, V., & Kuhar, S. (2011). Taking Advantage of Education Data: Advanced Data Analysis and Reporting in Virtual Learning Environments. *Electronics and Electrical Engineering*, *114*(8). doi:10.5755/j01.eee.114.8.708

Pohl, A., Bry, F., Schwarz, J., & Gottstein, M. (2012). Sensing the classroom: Improving awareness and self-awareness of students in Backstage. *Paper presented at the IEEE 15th International Conference on Interactive Collaborative Learning (ICL)*. doi:10.1109/ICL.2012.6402110

Raca, M., & Dillenbourg, P. (2013). System for assessing classroom attention. *Paper presented at the: Proceedings of the Third International Conference on Learning Analytics and KnowledgeLAK '13*, New York, NY. doi:10.1145/2460296.2460351

Raimondo, J. (2013). Analytics' Big Test. *Information Week*. Retrieved from http://twimgs.com/infoweek/green/012813ed/InformationWeek_Education_2013_02.pdf

Rittel, H. W. J., & Webber, M. M. (1973). Dilemmas in a general theory of planning. *Policy Sciences*, *4*(2), 155–169. doi:10.1007/BF01405730

Rojas, I. G., García, R. M. C., & Kloos, C. D. (2011). Orchestration and feedback in lab sessions: improvements in quick feedback provision. *Paper presented at the 6th European conference on Technology enhanced learning: towards ubiquitous learning EC-TEL'11* (pp. 424–429). Springer-Verlag.

Rueda, U., Larrañaga, M., Arruarte, A., & Elorriaga, J. A. (2006). DynMap+: a concept mapping approach to visualize group student models. *Paper presented at the First European conference on Technology Enhanced Learning: Innovative Approaches for Learning and Knowledge Sharing EC-TEL'06* (pp. 383-397). Springer-Verlag. doi:10.1007/11876663_30

Salas, E., Sims, D. E., & Burke, C. S. (2005). Is there a "Big Five" in Teamwork? *Small Group Research, 36*(5), 555–599. doi:10.1177/1046496405277134

Saltz, J. S., Roxanne, S., & Turoff, M. (2004). Student social graphs: Visualizing a student's online social network. *Paper presented at the 2004 ACM Conference on Computer Supported Cooperative Work. Chicago*, IL. doi:10.1145/1031607.1031709

Santos, J. L., Verbert, K., Govaerts, S., & Duval, E. (2011). Visualizing PLE usage. *Proceedings of EFEPLE11 1st Workshop on Exploring the Fitness and Evolvability of Personal Learning Environments* (Vol. 773, pp. 34–38).

Schaffhauser, D. (2013, September 25). The Power of Predictive Analytics. Campus Technology. Retrieved from http://campustechnology.com/Articles/-2013/09/25/The-Power-of-Predictive-Analytics.aspx

Schissel, D. P., Burruss, J. R., Finkelstein, A., Flanagan, S. M., Foster, I. T., Fredian, T. W., & Wallace, G. et al. (2004). Building the US National Fusion Grid: Results from the National Fusion Collaboratory Project. *Fusion Engineering and Design, 71*(1), 245–250. doi:10.1016/j.fusengdes.2004.04.041

Scheuer, O., & Zinn, C. (2007). How did the e-learning session go? The Student Inspector. *Proceedings of the International Conference on Artificial Intelligence in Education* (pp. 487–494(.

Schoenfeld, A. H. (1983). *Mathematical problem solving*. Orlando, FL: Academic.

Schreurs, B., Teplovs, C., Ferguson, R., de Laat, M., & Shum, S. B. (2013). Visualizing social learning ties by type and topic: rationale and concept demonstrator. *Paper presented at the Third International Conference on Learning Analytics and Knowledge LAK '13*, (pp. 33-37). doi:10.1145/2460296.2460305

Sfard, A., & Prusak, A. (2005). Telling identities: In search of an analytic tool for investigating learning as a culturally shaped activity. *Educational Researcher, 34*(4), 414–422. doi:10.3102/0013189X034004014

Sha, L., Teplovs, C., & van Aalst, J. (2010). A visualization of group cognition: semantic network analysis of a CSCL community. *Proceedings of the International Conference of the Learning Sciences* (pp. 929–936).

Shum, S. B., & Crick, R. D. (2012). Learning dispositions and transferable competencies: pedagogy, modelling and learning analytics. *Paper presented at the 2nd International Conference on Learning Analytics and Knowledge LAK '12*, New York, NY. doi:10.1145/2330601.2330629

Siemens, G. (2004, December 12). Connectivism: A learning theory for the digital age. Retrieved from http://www.ingedewaard.net/papers/connectivism/-2005_siemens_ALearningTheoryForTheDigitalAge.pdf

Siemens, G., & Baker, R. S. J. D. (2012). Learning analytics and educational data mining: towards communication and collaboration. *Paper presented at the 2nd International Conference on Learning Analytics and Knowledge LAK '12*, New York, NY. doi:10.1145/2330601.2330661

Smith, D. F. (2014, April 7). Signals Is an Analytical Crystal Ball for Students. *EdTech Magazine*. Retrieved from http:/www.edtechmagazine.com/higher/article/-2014/07/signals-analytical-crystal-ball-students

Song, E., Petrushyna, Z., Cao, Y., & Klamma, R. (2011). Learning Analytics at Large: The Lifelong Learning Network of 160,000 European Teachers. *EC-TEL*, *6964*(31), 398–411. doi:10.1007/978-3-642-23985-4_31

Sperber, D., & Wilson, D. (1986). *Relevance: communication and cognition*. Cambridge, MA: Harvard University Press.

Spiro, R. J., Feltovich, P. J., Jacobson, M. J., & Coulson, R. J. (1991). Cognitive flexibility constructivism and hypertext: Random access instruction for advanced knowledge acquisition in ill-structured domains. *Educational Technology*, *31*(5), 24–33.

Suthers, D., & Verbert, K. (2013). Learning analytics as a "middle space. Paper presented at *the Third International Conference on Learning Analytics and Knowledge LAK '13* (pp. 1-4). doi:10.1145/2460296.2460298

Swenson, J. (2014). Establishing an ethical literacy for learning analytics. *Paper presented at the Fourth International Conference on Learning Analytics and Knowledge LAK '14* (pp. 1-4). doi:10.1145/2567574.2567613

Tempelaar, D. T., Rienties, B., & Giesbers, B. (2014). Computer Assisted, Formative Assessment and Dispositional Learning Analytics in Learning Mathematics and Statistics. In M. Kalz & E. Ras (Eds.), Computer Assisted Assessment. Research into E-Assessment (Vol. 439, pp. 67–78). CHAM: Springer International Publishing. doi:10.1007/978-3-319-08657-6_7

Teplovs, C., & Scardamalia, M. (2007). Visualizations for knowledge building assessment. *Proceedings of the AgileViz Workshop*.

Teplovs, Chris, & Fujita, N. (2013). Socio-Dynamic Latent Semantic Learner Models. In *Productive Multivocality in the Analysis of Group Interactions* (pp. 383–396). Boston, MA: Springer U.S. doi:10.1007/978-1-4614-8960-3_21

Teplovs, C., Fujita, N., & Vatrapu, R. (2011). Generating predictive models of learner community dynamics. *Paper presented at the 1st International Conference on Learning Analytics and Knowledge LAK '11* (pp. 147-152). New York, NY. doi:10.1145/2090116.2090139

Tinto, V. (1975). Dropout from Higher Education: A Theoretical Synthesis of Recent Research. *Review of Educational Research*, *45*(1), 89–125. doi:10.3102/00346543045001089

Torniai, C., Jovanović, J., Bateman, S., Gasevic, D., & Hatala, M. (2008). Leveraging Folksonomies for Ontology Evolution in E-learning Environments. *Proceedings of the IEEE International Conference on Semantic Computing* (pp. 206–213). doi:10.1109/ICSC.2008.15

Tufte, E. R. (1990). *Envisioning information*. Cheshire, CT: Graphics.

Van Diggelen, W., Janssen, J., Overdijk, M., Asterhan, C. S. C., Hever, R., Schwarz, B. B., ... (2008). Analyzing and presenting interaction data: a teacher, student and researcher perspective. *Proceedings of the International Conference of the Learning Sciences* (pp. 375–382).

Verbert, K., Govaerts, S., Duval, E., Santos, J. L., Van Assche, F., Parra, G., & Klerkx, J. (2014). Learning dashboards: An overview and future research opportunities. *Personal and Ubiquitous Computing*, *18*(6), 1499–1514. doi:10.1007/s00779-013-0751-2

Viégas, F. B., Wattenberg, M., & Dave, K. (2004). Studying cooperation and conflict between authors with history flow visualizations. *Paper presented at SIGCHI Conference on Human Factors in Computing Systems CHI '04*, New York, NY (pp. 575–582). doi:10.1145/985692.985765

Villalon, J., & Calvo, R. A. (2011). Concept Maps as Cognitive Visualizations of Writing Assignments. *Journal of Educational Technology & Society*, *14*, 16–27.

Wang, M., Peng, J., Cheng, B., Zhou, H., & Liu, J. (2011). Knowledge Visualization for Self-Regulated Learning. *Journal of Educational Technology & Society*, *14*(3), 28–42.

Ware, C. (2005). Visual Queries: The Foundation of Visual Thinking. In S.-O. Tergan & T. Keller, Knowledge and Information Visualization (Vol. 3426, pp. 27–35). Springer Berlin Heidelberg. doi:10.1007/11510154_2

Ware, C. (2012). *Information Visualization: Perception for Design* (3rd ed., pp. 1–536). Morgan Kaufmann.

Wattenberg, M., & Viégas, F. B. (2008). The Word Tree, an Interactive Visual Concordance. *IEEE Transactions on Visualization and Computer Graphics*, *14*(6), 1221–1228. doi:10.1109/TVCG.2008.172 PMID:18988967

Whitelock, D., Twiner, A., Richardson, J. T. E., Field, D., & Pulman, S. (2014). OpenEssayist: real-life testing of an automated feedback system for draft essay writing. *Paper presented at the #designlearning from blended learning to learning analytics in HE*, Milton Keynes, UK. doi:10.1145/2723576.2723599

Winne, P. H. (2005). Key Issues in Modeling and Applying Research on Self-Regulated Learning. *Applied Psychology*, *54*(2), 232–238. doi:10.1111/j.1464-0597.2005.00206.x

Winne, P. H., & Hadwin, A. F. (2013). nStudy: Tracing and Supporting Self-Regulated Learning in the Internet. In R. Azevedo & V. Aleven, International Handbook of Metacognition and Learning Technologies (Vol. 28, pp. 293–308). New York, NY: Springer New York. doi:10.1007/978-1-4419-5546-3_20

Winne, P. H., & Jamieson-Noel, D. (2002). Exploring students' calibration of self reports about study tactics and achievement. *Contemporary Educational Psychology*, *27*(4), 551–572. doi:10.1016/S0361-476X(02)00006-1

Wise, A. F. (2014). Designing pedagogical interventions to support student use of learning analytics. *Paper presented at the Fourth International Conference on Learning Analytics And Knowledge LAK '14*, New York, NY, 203–211. doi:10.1145/2567574.2567588

Wishon, G. D., & Rome, J. (2012, August 13). Enabling the Data-Driven University. *Educause Review Online*. Retrieved from http://www.educause.edu/ero/article/enabling-data-driven-university

Wong, W.-K., Yin, S.-K., Yang, H.-H., & Cheng, Y.-H. (2011). Using Computer-Assisted Multiple Representations in Learning Geometry Proofs. *Journal of Educational Technology & Society*, *14*(3), 43–54.

Xiong, R., & Donath, J. S. (1999). PeopleGarden: Creating Data Portraits for Users. *Proceedings of the ACM Symposium on User Interface Software and Technology*, 37–44. doi:10.1145/320719.322581

Yi, J. S., Kang, Y.-A., Stasko, J. T., & Jacko, J. A. (2008). Understanding and characterizing insights: how do people gain insights using information visualization? *Paper presented at the 2008 Workshop on BEyond time and errors: novel evaLuation methods for Information Visualization BELIV '08*, New York, NY. doi:10.1145/1377966.1377971

Zhao, W.-Y., Chellappa, R., Phillips, P. J., & Rosenfeld, A. (2003). Face recognition: A literature survey. *ACM Computing Surveys*, *35*(4), 399–458. doi:10.1145/954339.954342

Ziemkiewicz, C., & Kosara, R. (2008). The shaping of information by visual metaphors. *IEEE Transactions on Visualization and Computer Graphics*, *14*(6), 1269–1276. doi:10.1109/TVCG.2008.171 PMID:18988973

Zimmerman, B. J. (1989). A Social Cognitive View of Self-Regulated Academic Learning. *Journal of Educational Psychology*, *81*(3), 329–339. doi:10.1037/0022-0663.81.3.329

Zhuhadar, L., Nasraoui, O., & Wyatt, R. Dual representation of the semantic user profile for personalized web search in an evolving domain. *Proceedings of the AAAI 2009 Spring Symposium on Social Semantic Web* (Vol. 2, pp. 84–89).

Zhuhadar, L., & Yang, R. (2012). Cyberlearners and learning resources. *Paper presented at the 2nd International Conference on Learning Analytics and Knowledge LAK '12*, New York, NY. doi:10.1145/2330601.2330621

Zhuhadar, L., Yang, R., & Nasraoui, O. (2012). Toward the Design of a Recommender System: Visual Clustering and Detecting Community Structure in a Web Usage Network. *Paper presented at the 2012 IEEE/WIC/ACM International Conferences on Web Intelligence and Intelligent Agent Technology (WI-IAT)* (Vol. 1, pp. 354–361). doi:10.1109/WI-IAT.2012.270

KEY TERMS AND DEFINITIONS

Analytical Provenance: Describes the process of how visualizations are used during knowledge discovery and analysis to arrive at insights relevant to the viewer.

Cohesiveness: A measure of semantic similarity that is usually tested on a large corpus of text before its application.

Folksonomy: An amalgamation of *folk* and *taxonomy* coined by information architect Thomas Vanderwall, it is a means of social classification through tagging. It is a system of categorization through keywords assigned to pieces of information. It is used in online services such as YouTube, and Flickr to facilitate information retrieval.

Glyph: Images used of metaphorical representations of sometimes abstract qualities.

Latent Semantic Analysis: Is a statistical technique used to reduce and extract word patterns from documents and discourse.

Learning Disposition: An individuals' thoughts about learning that enable engaged learning in any context; the inherent attitudes and feelings an individual brings learning to the experience.

Visualization: Used here is a subset of learning analytics, a form of analysis, way of graphically depicting information, and a tool for knowledge discovery, sensemaking and insight.

Chapter 2
Advances in Algorithms for Re-Sampling Class-Imbalanced Educational Data Sets

William Rivera
Institute for Simulation and Training, University of Central Florida, USA

Amit Goel
Institute for Simulation and Training, University of Central Florida, USA

J Peter Kincaid
Institute for Simulation and Training, University of Central Florida, USA

ABSTRACT

Real world data sets often contain disproportionate sample sizes of observed groups making it difficult for predictive analytics algorithms. One of the many ways to combat inherent bias from class imbalance data is to perform re-sampling. In this book chapter we discuss popular re-sampling methods proposed in research literature, such as Synthetic Minority Over-sampling Technique (SMOTE) and Propensity Score Matching (PSM). We provide an insight into recent advances and our own novel algorithms under the umbrella term of Over-sampling Using Propensity Scores (OUPS). Using simulation we conduct experiments that result in statistical improvement in accuracy and sensitivity by using these new algorithmic approaches.

INTRODUCTION

With any real world data there is often difficulty in creating prediction models that are highly accurate. In classification of outcomes there is typically a large disparity between the amount of observations collected from equally represented groups or classes. This makes the task of accurately predicting group membership on new data difficult. The problem of disparity between groups is called class imbalance.

Class imbalance is a common property of real world data sets but the issue with class imbalance is that the classifier tends to classify new observations as belonging to the over represented group or

DOI: 10.4018/978-1-4666-9983-0.ch002

majority group because of the inherit bias. The problem is intensified with larger levels of imbalance most commonly found in observational studies. Extreme cases of class imbalance are commonly found in fraud detection, mammography of cancerous cells and post term births. Reported cases of imbalance have been as extreme as 100,000 to (Chawla, 2005; D'Agostino, 1998; Mendes-Moreira & Soares, 2012; Tian, Gu, & Liu, 2010).

Another inherent problem in class imbalance classification is that the classifier will usually contain high prediction accuracy because the underrepresented group is so small thus nullifying the misclassification cost of those observations since the impact is not noticeable. In most cases the target of interest is prediction of the underrepresented group which results in poor predictability.

The first major study to evaluate class imbalance was conducted in 2000. Japkowicz performed experiments on 125 randomly (using uniform distribution) synthesized data sets with varying degrees in complexity, training set size and imbalance in order to search for factors that impact class imbalance data. Using multilayer perceptron networks they identified that domains that contained linearly separable data sets did not suffer misclassification from imbalance. Second, the degree of complexity increases with the level of imbalance and lastly that the error rate is subject to the proportion of imbalance.

Further studies followed suit in highlighting additional reasons why classifiers perform poorly. These include inappropriate metrics for highly class imbalanced data, lack of generalization of classification rules for minority examples and the view minority examples as noise. Data intrinsic properties that perpetuate the class imbalance problem include the degree of class imbalance, complexity of the target concept and the classifier involved (Fernández, García, & Herrera, 2011; X. Guo, Yin, Dong, Yang, & Zhou, 2008; Japkowicz, 2000; López, Fernández, García, Palade, & Herrera, 2013; R. Prati, Batista, & Monard, 2004; R. C. Prati, Batista, & Monard, 2004; Weiss, 2010a, 2010b). The next few sections provide a further overview of these characteristics.

Disjunction

In typical data the minority group will be represented as small disjuncts overwhelmingly surrounded by majority cases. Disjuncts represent clusters spread throughout the data. The size of a disjunct are represented by the amount of observations that it correctly classifies and small disjuncts represent a small region where only a few training examples predict correctly. Small disjuncts have been empirically shown to have higher errors rates compared to large disjuncts which also tend to contribute significantly to the total test error (Weiss, 2010a).

Small disjuncts may appear as noise and most classifiers use induction to represent small disjuncts as a rule. In general there is a lack of information to provide for good generalizations. For instance a classification tree will typically represent each disjunct as a leaf or a given decision at a certain path. The smaller the disjunct the more error prone the classier tends to be (López et al., 2013; Quinlan, 1991; Weiss, 2010a, 2010b). This inherit problem has been of much study and part of what's been considered the data difficulty factor in dealing with imbalanced data sets (Stefanowski, 2014).

Weiss argues that small disjuncts produce higher error rates compared to large disjuncts which is strongly associated with class imbalance (Weiss, 2010a). However the true relationship between them remain uncertain and most research related to disjuncts have typically used decision tree classification algorithms with pruning to provide broader generalization coverage. These algorithms remain highly subject to this problem while other classification algorithms are considered less prone to the issue.

Lack of Data

In general the concept of interest suffers from lack or information since there are so few samples. This usually leads to weaker rules for classification and is often times intensified with highly dimensional data. (Fernández et al., 2011; López et al., 2013; Weiss, 2010b).

The rules induced become too specific which often lead to over-fitting if the learner does not already consider the small sample size as noise. These specific rules do not generalize well on newer instances. Lastly this also may introduce small disjuncts which in itself has issues previously mentioned.

Class Overlap

Regions that contain similar density of observations from both classes are considered overlapped. In 2004, Prait et al. performed experiments on synthetic data sets to measure the degree of class imbalance versus class overlap using 10 artificial domains of 5 attributes consistent of 10,000 instances with varying degrees of class imbalance. They studied degrees of distance of the data between centroids using the C4.5 decision tree leaner and discovered that when the centroid of the minority group lies within 3 standard deviations of the majority set it begins to impact performance while remaining further away has little effect. Although the distance between classes is most relevant, there is notable degradation in performance between highly imbalanced data sets compared to the low imbalanced data set counterparts within the same distance.

In 2010 Denil and Trappenberg followed suit by also creating synthetic data sets to further study the class overlap problem using SVM classifiers. The results also support the claim that the degree of overlap greatly impacts the performance more so than the prior probabilities but not as much as the imbalance ratio provided that the priors lie within the same distance (Denil & Trappenberg, 2010; Fernández et al., 2011; López et al., 2013; R. Prati et al., 2004). Additionally the class imbalance and class overlap are not necessarily independent of one another so there is a need to deal with both simultaneously in order to overcome class imbalance.

Another area of concern closely related to class overlap are observations that lie close to the border of the decision boundary. Borderline examples suffer from the same issues as class overlap particularly because they tend to sit in the overlap region. Another side effect of borderline examples is that the classifier may tend to view them as noise. These borderline or class overlap examples are often termed "unsafe" while those that remain in homogeneous spaces are deemed "safe" because of difficulty in classifying them.

Noisy Data

Noisy data impacts the learner greatly for the minority observations compared to the over represented group. The noise dense areas appear as small disjuncts and will tend to cause the learner to over-fit the data. Noise handling techniques can help manage noise but at the cost of removing both noise and noise free samples resulting in an even lesser representation by the under-represented group.

Noise impacts the leaner in a much greater way then any imbalance although the larger the imbalance the more of an issue it is. Further studies show that under-sampling seem to produce the best results in general and that Bayesian and SVM classifiers tend to outperform rule induced algorithms and instance based learning when dealing with noisy imbalanced data on average (Seiffert, Khoshgoftaar, Hulse, & Folleco, 2014).

Data Set Shift

Data shift can be best described as when the training and test cases follow different distributions as a result of sample selection bias. Most real world data sets have some degree of data shift although many classifiers are not impacted when the degree is small (Fernández et al., 2011; López et al., 2013).

Weiss proposed the following techniques for dealing with class imbalance: obtaining additional training data, using more appropriate inductive bias, Use more appropriate measure of performance, use none greedy search techniques, use human interaction and employ boosting (Weiss, 2010b).

Obtaining more data is often times difficult. However it is still possible that one would have a larger degree of imbalance to contend with so knowing the appropriate amount needed is difficult and would still remain a challenge. Using inductive strategies to eliminate small disjuncts could be accomplished by using significance testing and adjusting for the bias. However, the main concern with these approaches is that they too tend to degrade the overall performance of the classifier.

Non greedy search techniques have attracted a lot of attention including the use of genetic algorithms that have proven to be successful. The major issue with searching or even human involvement becomes when the data sets become extremely large the computation and involvement may become overly complex and too demanding for the user.

The problem with class imbalance is attributed to data intrinsic properties such as the problem with small disjuncts, lack of data, noisy data, class overlap and data set shift which are made further problematic by larger imbalance in the data. To deal with class imbalance the machine learning community has traditionally focused on algorithmic, data processing or ensemble approaches.

Typical evaluation metrics are not relevant in class imbalance data as the misclassification of minority examples usually does not degrade accuracy even though they may all be misclassified. For example let us consider a dataset with and imbalance ratio of 99 to 1. This would imply that if we correctly classified all the majority examples and incorrectly classified negative examples the classifier would result in a 99% accuracy which is not meaningful if the target of interest is the underrepresented group.

Meaningful measures for class imbalance data consist of sensitivity, specificity, precision, F measure, gmean, ROC and AUC. All of which may be derived from a confusion matrix containing true positives, false positives, true negatives and false negative counts from the test set after performing classification.

TECHNIQUES FOR DEALING WITH IMBALANCED DATA

To combat class imbalance the machine learning community has relied upon three broad approaches which consist of algorithmic or embedded approaches, data processing approaches and ensemble learning approaches. (Chawla, 2005; Domingos, 1999; Estabrooks, Jo, & Japkowicz, 2004; S. García & Herrera, 2009; V. García, Sánchez, & Mollineda, 2012; H. Guo & Viktor, 2004; Haro-garcia & Garcia-Perajas, 2011; Hulse & Khoshgoftaar, 2002; Kotsiantis, Kanellopoulos, & Pintelas, 2006; Xu-ying Liu & Zhou, 2006; López et al., 2013; Thanathamathee & Lursinsap, 2013; Zadrozny & Elkan, 2001; Zhang, Zhang, & Wang, 2010).

In this section we outline previous work in dealing with class imbalanced data by briefly discussing algorithmic and ensemble approaches. Because of our interest in processing techniques we provide taxonomy of the more commonly used approaches.

Algorithmic Approaches

Algorithmic approaches represent techniques that are usually implemented within the learner itself or during the learning phase and may be considered internal or embedded approaches. This would include techniques that apply and adjust weights or include a loss function to different samples as well as learners that inherently apply some sub-sampling selection technique. Active learning, kernel based methods and cost assignment approaches fall into this category.

Active Learning

Active learning is a special type of semi supervised learning that allows user querying for label decisions. As part of this approach active learning will take sub-samples of existing data. It typically retains samples closest to the decision boundary thus sub-sampling evenly between groups (Attenberg & Ertekin, 2013). Active learning will greatly reduce the effects of imbalance but that does not mean that it will remove all the bias.

In Active learning the model is involved in selecting samples from a large pool of observations for labeling purposes and both theoretical and empirical results have shown that active learning results in highly accurate models as a result. However, these models still need to be properly tuned in order to handle class imbalanced data. Otherwise they will tend to inherit bias for the majority group simply because there are many more samples to choose from.

Among the most popular approaches for handling class imbalance include density sensitive approaches comprised mostly of heuristic based techniques. Heuristic based approaches use the entire pool of example data and assign a utility score $U(x)$ denoting the improvement gained from training on that instance based on some geometric properties of the data. Popular heuristics include information density on similarity as defined in equation (1.1)

$$U_m(x) = U(x)\frac{1}{|X|}\sum_{i}^{n} sim\left(x, x_i \mid x \neq x_i\right)^{\beta} \qquad (1.1)$$

Where β is the hyper-parameter controlling the tradeoff between the utility score $U(x)$ and the similarity score $sim(x, x_i)$. Other heuristic based approaches include conditional probability of group membership $U_m(x) = (1 - P\{y \mid x\}) \cdot P\{x\}$ or similarly weighted using variations of probabilistic and similarity schemes. A number of improvements to active learning for handling imbalanced data have been researched that typically involve a similarity scoring metric based on covariates distance, cost assignments and even the use of entropy to help combat class imbalance within active learning communities (Attenberg & Ertekin, 2013).

Kernel Based Methods

Support vector machines represent one of the core machine learning techniques that have been widely researched. These robust classifiers seem to be less sensitive to class imbalance compared to other learners when the classes are separable. As a result there has been a large amount of research utilizing SVM modifications to deal with the class imbalance problem. As previously mentioned, they have the interesting property of using kernel functions in order to perform a mapping of input attributes into a dot product space that allows for the use of many kernel types.

Wu and Chang proposed a class boundary alignment algorithm that adjusted the kernel based on the spatial distribution of the support vectors and class skew (Wu & Chang, 2003, 2005) which was soon followed by other adjustment types including kernel target alignment, margin calibration and additional kernel modification methods which typically employ some type of loss function into the algorithm as a way of dealing with the class imbalance (Akbani, Kwek, & Japkowicz, 2004; Batuwita & Palade, 2013; Fan, 2014; Lakshmanan, Priscilla, Ponni, & Sankari, 2011; Ma, Wang, & Shen, 2011; Wu & Chang, 2003, 2005).

Kernel methods are not limited exclusively to SVM algorithms. Kernels are also used in neural networks and other deep learning schemes. Regardless of the case, the kernels themselves usually implement cost based approaches which attempt to account for the importance of certain instances within the learner themselves.

Cost Assignment Approaches

This approach uses a cost or loss function for the model in order to correct class imbalance. Both the over and under-represented group have different costs applied. The goal is to shift the weight of the classifier to the under -represented group thereby removing bias. The optimal prediction is thus defined by (1.2)

$$\sum P\left\{j \mid x\right\} \cdot C(i, j, x) \tag{1.2}$$

where $P\left\{y \mid x\right\}$ is the probability of observation x belonging to class j and $P\left\{y \mid x\right\} \cdot C(i,j,x)$ represents the cost for predicting class i for each example x when the true class is. j The most difficult part is knowing the cost assignment as it may be different for every example even though the calculation formation is straight forward. A cost matrix indicating the overall benefit is usually denoted in Table 1.

The most common approach is to assign the loss function in the problem formulation and then use the new formula on the training set. These approaches have been successfully applied to neural networks, SVMs, Naive Bayes, decision trees and of the like. Studies have empirically shown to increase

Table 1. Cost Matrix

Cost Matrix	Predicted Positive	Predicted Negative
Actual Positive	$C(1,1)$	$C(0,1)$
Actual Negative	$C(1,0)$	$C(0,0)$

prediction accuracy compared to just using the learner alone (Bahnsen & Aouada, 2014; Domingos, 1999; Kretzschmar, Karayiannis, & Eggimann, 2005; Ling & Sheng, 2008; Xu-ying Liu & Zhou, 2006; Zadrozny & Elkan, 2001).

Cost approaches can be divided into two parts direct costs and cost sensitive meta-learning. Direct costs alter the learner while Meta learning approaches manipulate the training set instead. Meta-learning methods can be further subdivided into sampling, threshold and MetaCosts approaches (Ling & Sheng, 2008). MetaCost methods attempt to change the label of the misclassified example to its optimal class as would be using equation (1.2). Sampling techniques are discussed further on and threshold approaches modify the decision threshold to account for the imbalance.

As examples of direct cost approaches, Lakshmanan et al. and Ma et al. proposed Fuzzy support vector machine approaches which apply different fuzzy membership values to account for noise, outliers and class imbalance into the original problem formulation (Lakshmanan et al., 2011; Ma et al., 2011).

Akbani et al. proposed a combination of cost sensitive techniques for constructing an SVM learner with a combination of re-sampling and applied error cost techniques for comparison (Akbani et al., 2004). Kretzschmar et al. proposed costs for each node in a neural network using marginal probabilities of a given label to control both class balance and variance (Kretzschmar et al., 2005). Liu et al. proposed a combination of cost sensitivity and imbalance re-scale ratios (Xu-ying Liu & Zhou, 2006). All these approaches fall under meta-learning.

Boosting is another approach that falls within this category. Boosting is an iterative algorithm that assigns weights to each training sample. For each iteration the weights for incorrectly classified examples are lowered while the weights with the correctly classified example are raised. Boosting is typically a part of ensemble learning which is discussed further on.

One benefit to a cost sensitive approach is the ability to create local and global costs that can be applied in fuzzy systems with different hierarchical fuzzy regions that assign costs to particular partitions where misclassification is higher. One potential downfall is that this approach is algorithm specific and it may not transfer well to other classifiers thus it can become highly specialized and difficult to maintain.

Data Processing Approaches

Data processing approaches are techniques that modify the training set before learning takes place and can also be considered external approaches. These techniques are usually the most simple to implement and empirical studies have resulted in increased accuracy of group prediction. A benefit of data processing is that it allows for the researcher to divide the prediction task into two: the first is dealing with the data intrinsic properties that make class imbalance prediction difficult and the second is the ability of fine tuning the learner. This allows for a divide and conquer approach which makes problems easier to work on (Japkowicz, 2000).

In general active learning and kernel based approaches still have the issue of inherit bias towards the majority group. Cost based approaches are difficult to assess and the cost of misclassification is typically not known beforehand. Data processing approaches, although difficult to tune are both simple to implement and easy understand (Debowski, Areibi, Grewal, & Tempelman, 2012; S. García & Herrera, 2009).

Feature Selection

The goal in feature selection is to select the subset of features $j \subseteq k$ that provide the most optimal classification of a particular target concept while hopefully discarding those features which are not relevant. High dimensional data makes the classification task difficult and reducing the feature size is a way to reduce that complexity.

Feature selection falls into 3 broad categories, wrappers, filter and embedded models (Ghazikhani, 2012; Tan & Liew, 2012). Embedded models implement feature learning and classification simultaneously, wrappers assess feature subsets via building models followed by performance evaluation and filters use mathematical models to evaluate features. A noticeable issue with wrappers and embedded methods are that they have a running complexity of $O(2^n)$ which become intractable in highly dimensional data.

Feature selection is a necessary step in any machine learning process but empirical studies have used feature selection as a way to also combat class imbalance by simply targeting the features that are most relevant for both groups independently and then combining them in a way that generalized well on new data. This suggests that a good feature selection approach provides good separation between groups although this is arguable considering that class imbalance includes additional data intrinsic properties that one must consider (Wasikowski & Chen, 2010).

One reason for pursuing feature selection over re-sampling schemes is that re-sampling may not be the most appropriate approach given the domain. For example in a patient level setting it may not be acceptable to over-sample because it may make many more comparisons to cases that are not actually true and if under-sampling is employed then patients may get omitted.

Re-Sampling

Re-sampling techniques offer simple alternatives to dealing with class imbalance that are easy to implement and understand. Re-sampling consists of both over and under sampling data. In over-sampling, new data is created from the underrepresented group in order to closely match the over represented group size. Under-sampling will reduce samples in order to also match the underrepresented groups. Predictive algorithms can be applied without the need to apply any modifications allowing for simpler models. Re-sampling techniques remain an area for further exploration and refinement.

Over-Sampling

Current research provides four main over-sampling techniques which have inspired the exploration of modified versions. These are focused re-sampling, random over-sampling (ROS), adaptive synthetic (ADASYN) sampling and Synthetic Minority Over-sampling Technique (SMOTE). Focused sampling uses both over and under sampling while SMOTE, ADASYN and random over sampling is a strictly an over sampling scheme.

Random (ROS) and Focused Re-Sampling

Random over-sampling chooses observations at random typically using a uniform distribution to over-sample. The new samples remain exact copies that just become duplicated for the purposes of balancing the data. This can be done with or without replacement.

With replacement makes the chosen sample available to be selected and sampled again. Without replacement does not allow for that sample to be sampled again. A replacement limit can also be an imposed as a small modification. One limitation to using exact copies is that it has the propensity to cause over-fitting which means it does not generalize well on new data.

In focused Re-sampling minority group observations that lie close to the decision boundary are over-sampled while members of the majority group that lie furthest away from the decision boundary are retained. The over-sampled observations are usually duplicated and not synthetically altered in this approach thus there is a high tendency for over-fitting as well.

An extensions to focused re-sampling, selective pre-processing of imbalanced data (SPIDER) provides a two stage approach to re-sampling (Stefanowski & Wilk, 2008). First noise is removed then local characteristics allow for copies of minority examples to be created to balance the data.

As an example let S represent the set of all examples, $l \subseteq S$ represents the subset of examples in the minority group and $m \subseteq S$ represent the subset of examples in the majority group. First each observation in S is flagged as either "safe" if classifying 3 k nearest neighbors knn can be done correctly, otherwise it's flagged as "noisy". For each $x_i \in l$ flagged as noise it creates "safe copies" and for each $x_i \in m$ marked noise it moves them to set l. The relabeling portion in SPIDER is optional and the creation of safe copies can be modified to accommodate more k nearest neighbors.

Adaptive Synthetic (ADASYN) Sampling Approach

Adaptive synthetic sampling shares similar properties to SMOTE with regard to over-sampling with one subtle difference. In oversampling it calculates the needed amount of minority samples to synthesize using a density distribution (He, Bai, Garcia, & Li, 2008).

For example, let D_{tr} be the training set of examples with m samples $\left\{(x_i, y_i) \mid 1 \le i \le m \wedge x_i \in \Re^k\right\}$, where $x_i \in \Re^k$ represents the i_{th} examples input space and $y_i \in \{-1,1\}$ represents the i_{th} examples class label. Let m_s represent the number of minority examples and m_l represent the number of majority examples. Which implies $m_s < m_l$ and $m_s + m_l = m$.

First ADASYN calculates the balance number of synthetic samples needed using (1.3)

$$G = (m_l - m_s) \cdot \beta \tag{1.3}$$

where the term $\beta \in [0,1]$ is the balance level specifier and $\beta = 1$ represents full balance. For each $x_i \in m_s$, find knn based on the Euclidean distance measure and calculate r_i as

$$r_i = \frac{\Delta i}{K}, i = 1, \cdots, m_s \tag{1.4}$$

where the term Δi is the number of examples that are knn of $x_i \in m_l$. The term r_i is then normalized as $\hat{r}_i = \frac{r_i}{\sum_i^{m_s} r_i}$ so that $\hat{r}_i$ is a density distribution thus $\sum_i^{m_s} r_i = 1$. The actual number of synthetic samples to create is then calculated $g_i = \hat{r}_i \cdot G$.

Next it iterates through each x_i in the minority group, randomly chooses one knn say x_j and generates a synthetic sample using

$$S_i = x_i + (x_j - x_i) \cdot \lambda, \lambda \in [0,1] \tag{1.5}$$

where the term $(x_j - x_i)$ is the difference between the two observations and λ represents a random number. This equation is the same form that smote uses for sample generation as shown further on.

Synthetic Oversampling Minority Technique (SMOTE)

SMOTE remains arguably one of the most commonly used over-sampling techniques used through literature. SMOTE performs over sampling although in its original published manuscript it was shown as a combination of under sampling on the over represented group and over sampling on the under-represented group. In under sampling observations are randomly removed based on a user defined threshold. The threshold is expressed as a percentage ratio. As an example, consider a data set containing an over represented group of 200 observations and an under represented group of 100 observations. Specifying a user defined threshold of 200% would reduce the over represented to 50 observations thus the under-represented group is now 200% greater.

For over sampling of the under-represented group SMOTE applies an iterative search and selection approach. Each observation from the under-represented group G_1 will be iterated through until the needed amount is reached. To generate new sample k are selected using Euclidean distance where k is user defined. One knn is then selected at random and then the process continues until all samples have been selected (Blagus & Lusa, 2013; Chawla, Bowyer, Hall, & Philip, 2011).

For example, if a ratio of 300% is specified then 3 knn will be selected. One will be chosen at random and a new instance N is generated from the features of the random sample x_j and the original x_i observation used to generate it. New features are generated by the feature difference of x_i and x_j multiplied by a random number r between 0 and 1.

$$N = x_i + r \cdot (x_j - x_i), 0 \le r \le 1 \tag{1.6}$$

Under-Sampling

Under sampling techniques remove majority examples to lessen the impact of bias. These approaches usually improve accuracy and prediction of the target concept but at the cost of increased misclassification of the negative examples. Empirical studies have shown that they tend to outperform over sampling techniques when the data is relatively small (Japkowicz, 2000). We discuss classical techniques that mostly focus on removal of just the members in the majority group (Batista, Carvalho, & Monard, 2000). There has been some proposed evolutionary under sampling approaches (S. García & Herrera, 2009; Orriols-puig & Bernad, 2008) but these fall outside the scope of our discussion. For a good explanation regarding those techniques the reader should review Garcia et al. for a taxonomy of evolutionary under-sampling strategies (García & Herrera, 2009).

Propensity Score Matching (PSM)

The propensity score is defined as the conditional probability of group membership to the under-represented group versus the over represented group based on its covariates, formally:

$$e(x) = P\{G = 1 \mid x\} \tag{1.7}$$

Propensity score matching (PSM) uses a matching metric in order to reduce observations of the over represented group to match the underrepresented group in both overall size and feature space. PSM is heavily used in the medical field to allow for statistical inferences between a control and treated group (Abadie & Imbens, 2009; Austin, 2011; Caliendo & Clement, 2012; Li, 2011; Rosenbaum & Rubin, 1983, 1985).

Common matching metric approaches include nearest neighbor (knn) matching on the logit of the estimated propensity score and the more commonly used Mahalanobis distance metric which includes all the features and the logit of the estimated propensity score (Austin, 2011; Rosenbaum & Rubin, 1983).

$$d(u,v) = (u - v)^T C^{-1}(u - v) \tag{1.8}$$

where the term u is the vector of features from the minority group G_j and v is the vector of features from the majority group G_i having covariance matrix C which is representative of the over represented group.

For example, in one to one propensity score matching without replacement a single score is assigned for each observation using the sigmoid function based on weighted features. Weighs can be estimated through use of either logistic regression or linear discriminant analysis (LDA).

$$f(X) = \frac{1}{1 + e^{-(X^T \beta + \alpha)}} \tag{1.9}$$

where $\beta = \{\beta_1, \beta_2, \cdots, \beta_n\}$ are the estimated weights, $X = \{x_1, x_2, \cdots, x_n\}$ are the covariates in the feature space and α is the intercept term. Observations from the over represented group G_i are selected based on a match criteria and removed from the pool of available candidates until all observations in the underrepresented group G_j have selecting the most closely matched pair.

PSM differs from other under sampling techniques mainly its purpose. That is it under-samples to perform statistical comparisons between groups not for predictive accuracy of future observations. This technique has only been used in our studies because it helped inspire our novel contribution OUPS which is fully discussed further on.

Random (RUS) and Cluster Based Under-Sampling

Random under sampling selects members of the majority group at random and then removes them from the examples in order to achieve balance. As an enhancement Garcia proposed cluster based sampling (CBUS) using K means clustering to partition majority group observations into similar groups. CBUS then picks the closest 2 subsets at random and combines them with all the minority group examples to create 1 combined set with full balance.

For example let S be the set of training data with $m, m \subseteq S$ representative of the examples that belong to the majority group and $l, l \subseteq S$ containing the members of the minority group. Set m is then split into k groups or clusters. Let the number of majority group members in the i_{th} cluster be nmi then the ratio of majority group items in each i_{th} cluster of k total clusters is defined as $r_i = \frac{nmi}{|m|}$. The number of selected majority group samples in the i_{th} cluster is thus $s_i = |l| \cdot r_i$ (García et al., 2012).

Tomek Links (TK) Re-Sampling

Tomek links is probably one of the oldest under-sampling schemes in literature. It attempts to eliminate noise generated from the majority group by finding bordered instances. Once found the majority group instance are removed (Dal Pozzolo, Caelen, Waterschoot, & Bontempi, 2013; Jeatrakul, Wong, Fung, & Takama, 2010).

For example let x represent an example from the over represented group and y represent an example from the underrepresented group and $d(a,b)$ be the distance between two points. The pair (x, y) is considered a Tomek link if no example z exists such that $d(x,z) < d(x,y)$ or $d(y,z) < d(x,y)$. Since these examples remain closer to each other than any other example they can be considered either noise or border line.

Condensed Nearest Neighborhood (CNN) Re-Sampling

The condensed nearest neighbor algorithm also referred to as the Hart algorithm was originally designed to improve *knn* classification by reducing the overall set.

For example, let X be the set of training examples and let U be an empty set. CNN will first choose one observation at random x_i known at the prototype from set X and place it in set U .Next it scans all neighbors of x_i in X that have a different label then x_i. CNN absorbs these other examples based on the following criteria:

$$\|x_i - q\| - \|x_i - p\| > 0 \tag{1.10}$$

where p resents an example with the same label as x_i and q represents an example with a different label. The procedure continues until there are no more prototype examples left to add to U (Chou, Kuo, & Chang, 2006).

One Sided Selection

One sided selection is one of the earliest attempts to improve upon random under sampling by intelligently removing majority samples that appear as noise or redundant. Conceptually it applies Tomek links followed by CNN re-sampling.

For example let S be the set of all training examples and $C \subseteq S$ all the examples from the minority group and one randomly selected negative examples. It then builds a model using 1 nearest neighbor from set C. The model is used to predict each member in S. Any member that is misclassified in S gets placed in C. Next it removes all Tomek links in C that belong to the over represented group. The resulting set is thus removed of all noisy and border line examples (S. García & Herrera, 2009; Kubat & Matwin, 1997).

Edited Nearest Neighborhood (ENN) and Neighborhood Cleaning Rule (NCR) Re-Sampling

Edited Nearest Neighborhood (ENN) is also referred to as Wilson's Edited Nearest Neighbor rule. This technique removes examples of the majority group that have different labels from two of its three nearest neighbors (Batista, Prati, & Monard, 2004; Koplowitz & Brown, 1981).

For each example x with a label belonging to the majority group in training set S select $3\,knn$ and perform classification. If the classification from more than 1 is incorrect it than removes those examples from S.

Neighborhood Cleaning Rule (NCR) modifies the ENN method by removing classified's negative examples by their three nearest neighbors. It then removes members of the majority group which are neighbors of each positive example found (Dal Pozzolo et al., 2013). The theory is that it performs a more thorough cleaning then ENN alone.

Ensemble Approaches

Some solutions to class imbalance offer a combination of data processing or algorithmic approaches. These often times are represented through the use of ensemble learning techniques that perform some combination of the two over many classifiers and then pick the best learners. Ensemble learning allows for multiple learners to be modeled at the same time. The structural form of an ensemble takes the following form,

$$F(x) = a_0 + \sum_{m}^{M} a_m \cdot f_m(x) \qquad (1.11)$$

where M is the size of the ensemble and each member $f_m(x)$ represents a unique prediction rule or ensemble member for input x and $F(x)$ represents the linear relationship for each ensemble member. Ensembles allow for many diverse models to be created thus allowing for maximum flexibility. Models can then be aggregated by combination or a voting scheme in where each model applies the prediction rule on an example and the majority prediction is used. Two of the most common approaches for ensembles is boosting and bagging.

Both approaches learn by taking subsets of the training data to learn and then combining them. For example in bagging the ensembles members are combined to create one predictive rule which uses an average of the entire ensemble. This is also termed boot strap aggregation (Junfei, Qingfeng, & Huailin, 2010; Mendes-Moreira & Soares, 2012).

Boosting employs a weighted average usually conducted over iterations that apply weights based on what it deems "hard examples", those examples most difficult to classify. The use of ensembles can be done with any learner but it is most commonly done with decision tree learners. Combining the use of sampling techniques, genetic algorithms and clustering have all been combined to form voting based ensembles (Akbani et al., 2004; Junfei et al., 2010; Mirza & Lin, 2013; Qian, Liang, Li, Feng, & Shi, 2014; Saha & Ekbal, 2013; Seiffert, Khoshgoftaar, Van Hulse, & Napolitano, 2010).

In 2009 Liu, Wu, and Zhou proposed easy ensemble and balanced cascade algorithms which utilized under sampled data to construct rules. Two approaches were offered, one where subsets are trained and later combined. The other included training the data which is used to drive the sampling of subsequent learners. Easy ensembles partitions the majority examples M_0 into s subsets then trains each S_1 along with the minority examples M_1 to from s learners which are later combined. An alternative view is that each learner is a feature in the final learner. Balance cascade only differs in that it will remove correctly classified examples from the training set so that it is not eligible to be used again (Liu, Wu, & Zhou, 2009).

In 2010 Junfei, Qingfeng and Wu proposed and explored improvements to an existing ensemble creation technique using genetic algorithms called GASEN. The GASEN technique was compared with under-sampling techniques which showed that the error rates using GASEN were higher (Junfei et al., 2010). Seiffert et al introduced improvements to AdaBoost by including random under sampling RUSBoost and SMOTE sampling SMOTEBoost. Both of which performed better than just using RUS, SMOTE or AdaBoost (Seiffert et al., 2010). In 2012 Huang et al. also performed experiments combining SMOTE and a random subspace sampling ensembles against boosting and bagging (Huang, Lin, Chen, & Lu, 2012).

OVER-SAMPLING USING PROPENSITY SCORES (OUPS)

Over-sampling using propensity score matching blends concepts from both SMOTE and propensity score matching by calculating the propensity score for use as a match criteria without the need to perform under sampling of the underrepresented group. We retained the approach SMOTE uses for creating the synthetic sample and removed the portion of selecting random neighbors. OUPS then performs over-sampling based on the needed amount. This is accomplished in a two stage approach.

1. Predict the probability of group membership.

Given a set of observations $X = \{x_1, x_2, \ldots, x_n\}, x_i \in \Re^k$ we calculate the linear coefficients for each k feature in x_i by minimizing the residuals between the actual and estimated value:

$$Min_\beta \sum_i^n (y_i - f(x_i))^2 \tag{1.12}$$

where $y_i \in \{0,1\}$ and $f(x_i)$ is the estimated value using the sigmoid function as previously described. Having obtained the weight vector β we then calculate the propensity score for each observation x_i as

$$f(\beta, x_i) = \frac{1}{1 + e^{-(x_i^T\beta + \beta_0)}} \tag{1.13}$$

Next order the entire set X by the propensity score. This should naturally produce the following subsets with the majority group as $MG = \{x_1, x_2, \ldots, x_n\}$ and the minority group $MN = \{x_{m+1}, x_{m+2}, \ldots, x_n\}$.

2. Re-sample using the propensity score.

We then calculate the needed amount to over-sample using the imbalance ratio $n = \frac{|MG|}{|MN|}$. For each observation in MN we select n examples based on propensity scores calculated in stage 1 and use the entire group to produce new observations using equation (1.6).

For example when an over-sampling of 300% is needed to match the over represented group size, 3 new cases are generated from 3 observations with the closest propensity score.

Over-Sampling Using Propensity Score Algorithm

Reducing the over represented group by under-sampling may not only impact accuracy but can introduce high variance into the classifier. We see no need to perform under-sampling provided we can achieve higher accuracy by just over-sampling of the underrepresented group. Another noticeable difference between SMOTE and OUPS is that OUPS does not pick a random neighbor from the group selected but rather just generates synthetic samples from the entire group.

This reduces redundant searching during the generation phase which is not needed since the features are also randomized. Switching to the propensity score for matching also allows for simple single metric matching that effectively removes matching on confounding variables.

Using the propensity score is more effective than using the *knn* approach because *knn* is often difficult to select particularly in data with a large feature size while the propensity score is calculated based on the probability of group membership.

Generated synthetic samples on closely matched propensity scores allows for similar observations to be created with the same likelihood thus effectively increasing the group amount and reducing the

Algorithm 1.

Procedure OUPS

$G_1 = \{(x, y) \mid y = 1\}$

$G_0 = \{(x, y) \mid y = 0\}$

$calcPscores(G_1, G_0)$

$k = \frac{|G_0|}{|G_1|}$

$j = |G_1| - 1$

$F = \{\ \}$

While $j \geq 0$

$g = G_{1j}$

$m = k$

$itm = findKnn(g)$

While $m > 0$

$r = rand(0,1)$

$F = F \cup \{g + r(itm - g)\}$

$m = m - 1$

EndWhile

$j = j - 1$

EndWhile

return $F \cup G_0 \cup G_1$

EndProcedure

bias. This can be seen as a way of applying costs to the minority observations that does not rely on any previous knowledge or distributional assumptions.

For example let's assume that we are given an observation $x_i \in X = \{x_1, x_2, \ldots, x_n\}$ where X represents examples in the minority group. When we apply equation (1.6) we see that a synthesized data is weighted

Approximately $n\left[x_i + \frac{x_i - \Delta x}{2}\right]$ where n is the number of synthesized samples to generate per i_{th} iteration and $\Delta x = \frac{1}{n}\sum_{j}^{n} x_j$. This weight applies to all original x_i members of X. Again we provide this rationale to support the concept that OUPS and any re-sampling technique for the matters shares similar properties to cost assignment approaches at a local level.

SAFE LEVEL OUPS

Safe Level OUPS draws its inspiration from recent improvements to SMOTE namely Safe-Level-SMOTE as well as taking into account prior knowledge offered through OUPS (Bunkhumpornpat, Sinapiromsaran, & Lursinsap, 2009; Rivera, Goel, & Kincaid, 2014). Safe Level OUPS combats data intrinsic properties of class imbalance data by selectively choosing the samples that do not appear as noise based on its propensity of minority group membership $P\{G=1 \mid X\}$.

In general there exist three regions for a given example safe, border line or noise. Given a negative example G_0 having k nearest neighbors we can define these regions using Table 2 (Han, Wang, & Mao, 2005).

The "safe" level (sl) is considered the number of minority group G_1 examples found in k nearest neighbors. Examples that have a small amount of similar membership in particular 0 are considered noise. In order to consider examples for candidates to be synthesized the "safe" level ratio (slr) is used. The "safe" level ratio is defined as

$$slr = \frac{slp}{s\ln} \quad (1.14)$$

where slp is the "safe level" for a given example x and $s\ln$ is the "safe level" for a k randomly selected neighbor of x which we call n. In general we consider only candidates that have minority group observations for both x and n. Those examples chosen to generate new samples are done according to the following:

$s = x + q(n-x)$ (1..15)

where the term s is new sample generated from the example x plus the percent difference g from example x and neighbor n. Percent g is calculated in one of three ways.

If $slr = 1$ then $g \in (0,1]$

If $slr > 1$ then $g \in \left(0, \frac{1}{slr}\right]$

If $slr < 1$ then $g \in [1-slr, 1]$

Table 2. Region description (Bunkhumpornpat et al., 2009; Han et al., 2005)

Region	Definition
Noise	$G_0 = k$
Border Line	$\frac{1}{2}k \le G_0 \le k$
Safe	$0 \le G_0 \le \frac{1}{2}k$

A ratio of 1 means that both x and n are equally safe thus the new example can be chosen at random. When the ratio is greater than 1 the newly synthesized data will be weighted in the positive direction which makes the newer set lie closer to example x. When the ratio is less than 1 it is weighted in the negative direction which makes the newer sample lie closer to example n. The algorithm for "safe level" OUPS is provided below.

In interesting characteristic of Safe Level OUPS is that it uses the prior knowledge to determine group membership propensity. Although the propensity score is similar for all the surrounding neighbors since we use this criterion for determining knn, there will still be local areas where there is noticeable overlap because probability of group membership does not consider the actual label. However, the stochastic nature of this approach only selects safe examples or randomly selected neighbor n. that have similar properties of a minority group member thus ensuring that a borderline example still may be eligible at lower probability.

Algorithm 2. Safe level OUPS algorithm

Procedure SL-OUPS
$F = \{\ \}$
$G_1 = \{(x, y) \mid y = 1\}$
$G_0 = \{(x, y) \mid y = 0\}$
$D = calcPscores(G_1, G_0)$
$OrderByPscore(D)$
ForAll $x \in D$
If $x = 0$
    Next
    EndIf
$n = findRandKnn(g)$
$slx = GetSL(x)$
$s\ln = GetSL(n)$
If $s\ln = 0$
    Next
    EndIf
$slr = \frac{slx}{s\ln}$
If $slr = 1$
$g = rand(0,1)$
ElseIf $slr > 1$
$g = rand(0, \frac{1}{slr})$
ElseIf $slr < 1$
$g = rand(1 - slr, 1)$
    EndIf
$F = F \cup \{x + g(n - x)\}$
    EndFor
return $F \cup G_0 \cup G_1$
EndProcedure

EXPERIMENTAL DESCRIPTION

We conducted a series of experiments evaluating the OUPS algorithm, "Safe Level" OUPS and the comparison of preprocessing approaches in general. This included comparing feature selection, under-sampling and over-sampling methods and combination of mixed approaches such as mixing over sampling with feature selection.

In all of the experiments four different machine learning algorithms were trained on the original and simulated data sets. The resulting model was then applied against a test set that was created from the original data set before any synthetic data was created in order to evaluate how well each classification model would work against a real data. To measure the effectiveness of each sampling approach the use of confusion matrix was used to evaluate each algorithm.

In the first set of experiments OUPS was compared to PSM and SMOTE. In the net set of experiments we compare the Safe Level OUPS technique against individual and combination approaches which included mix and match combinations of algorithms to evaluate how these approaches all fare in comparison. Followed by our last experiment which compared the preprocessing approaches as a whole.

For comparing under-sampling ENN and Tomek Link were included. For over-sampling SMOTE, Safe Level SMOTE and OUPS were included. For feature selection Correlation based Feature selection (CFS) and Consistency based subset evaluation were evaluated. We then created 3 different pre-processing approaches that combined over-sampling, under-sampling and feature selection which we refer to as combined imbalance processing methods (CIP).

Experimental Data Sets

Seven data sets were obtained from online repositories, six from the UCI Machine Learning Repository (http://archive.ics.uci.edu/ml) and one from the American Statistical Association (http://www.amstat.org) with varying class imbalance. New data sets where then synthesized using R statistical software. The DMwR package was used for SMOTE and the Matchit package for PSM. An algorithm for performing over-sampling using propensity scores (OUPS) was created. Table 3 summarizes the original data sets.

Table 3. Data summary

Data Set	Observations	Features	% Minority
Pima	768	8	35%
Bank	45211	16	12%
Adult	30721	14	25%
Readmit	100244	36	13%
Turkey	5820	33	11%
TA	151	6	32%
Us News	1134	11	34%

Algorithm Selection

Four different machine learning algorithms were used for testing against a test set generated from the original data set before performing any sampling. Each data set was then sampled to create a training set. This was done using k fold validation with 10 folds. The only test set used was the one generated from the original data set only, all other modified data set test sets were not used.

- **Logistic Regression:** The glm function was used to run logistic regression against each of the newly synthesized and original non altered test set. This algorithm has nice properties because it makes no distributional assumptions about the data.
- **Support Vector Machine:** The svm function was used to perform SVM classification. Although computationally expensive, SVM are among one of the more modern approaches that performs classification relatively well in comparison to the other approaches.
- **Neural Network:** The nnet function was used to generate a neural network with 5, 10 and 20 nodes in a hidden layer. The choice of nodes was used to reduce the complexity and to closely match number of inputs.
- **Linear Discriminant Analysis:** The lda function was used because this algorithm is a very simple and effective approach which performs relatively well with minimal computation effort in comparison to other approaches.

Evaluation Criteria

A confusion matrix similar to Table 4 was used to produce metrics of classification accuracy, sensitivity, specificity and F-measure. True positives (TP) are results that were correctly classified as belonging to the minority group while true negatives (TN) represent all the results correctly classified as belonging to the majority group. False positives (FP) are results that belonged to the majority group but were incorrectly classified as belonging to the minority group and false negatives (FN) are results that belonged to the minority group but were incorrectly classified as belonging to the majority group (Baldi, Brunak, & Chauvin, 2000; Batista et al., 2000).

For imbalanced data sets the traditional accuracy metric can seem misleading since the over represented group may be accurately classified and the underrepresented group being small will not impact the performance metric. For example assume there are 190 observations that belong to the over represented group and only 10 to the underrepresented group. If the classifier is able to identify 185 observations accurately from the over represented group and 0 from the underrepresented group you have a classifier with 93% accuracy and with no ability to identify the target concept correctly.

Table 4. Confusion matrix

	Predicted Positive	**Predicted Negative**
Actual Positive	(TP)	(FN)
Actual Negative	(FP)	(TN)

Therefor the sensitivity metric is preferred. Sensitivity, sometimes referred to as the hit rate or recall rate is the ability to identify a condition correctly $TP/(FN+FT)$. If the desire is to exclude a condition correctly instead of include then the specificity or true negative rate can be used as an evaluation metric $TN/(FP+TN)$. In a patient level setting specificity is the probability of a well patient testing negative while sensitivity is the probability of an ill patient testing positive.

In addition to the above metrics we used Receiving Operator Characteristic (ROC) curves along with the area under the curve (AUC) to measure the overall performance of each approach. The Receiving Operator Characteristic (ROC) is a common balanced metric between true positive TP and false positive FP error rates. On an ROC curve the X axis is the Specificity and the Y axis represents the Sensitivity. The ideal point in an ROC curve is the point (0,100) as this represent 100% of positive examples are classified correctly and that no negative examples misclassified as being positive. The ROC graph shows the tradeoff between classification accuracy of both the majority and minority group.

The Area Under the Curve (AUC) is the area under the ROC curve which too can be used as a performance measure. AUC is typically used to measure against competing learners but in this case we compare against other types of techniques.

RESULTS

The results from each run and machine learning algorithm were then averaged over each data set per sampling technique and also per sampling technique. Table 5 provides a summary of the performance measures by percentage along with the standard error. Overall OUPS outperformed SMOTE and PSM in terms of accuracy and sensitivity. In particular OUPS increased accuracy over SMOTE by about 5% and PSM by about 22%. OUPS increased sensitivity by about 10% compared to SMOTE and about 24% compared to PSM which was a considerable increase.

SMOTE outperformed the other techniques in terms of specificity and F measure although in comparison to OUPS it was about a 1% difference in both cases. Additionally it can be assumed that the confidence interval that would be produced for F measure falls within the range for OUPS so one may conclude that there is not a difference between using both if the performance measure under consideration is the F measure.

PSM was consistently outperformed by the other sampling techniques which suggest that for prediction purposes it is not as reliable as the others. We see this same trend when we review the individual data set results further on as well. The answer to this is not surprising considering that PSM keeps similar observations based on the feature space thus the overlap would be much higher but our results help shed light into how much of that difference is seen when compared to these other approaches.

Table 5. Results by technique

Technique	% Accuracy	% Sensitivity	% Specificity	% F Measure
OUPS	81.65 ± 0.23	57.63± 0.53	92.28 ± 0.13	55.95 ± 0.64
SMOTE	76.49 ± 0.27	47.54 ± 0.58	93.75 ± 0.11	56.79 ± 0.55
PSM	58.18 ± 0.66	33.48± 0.51	81.07 ± 0.35	35.01 ± 0.36

In context of accurately classifying membership in the underrepresented group, sensitivity remains the most relevant measure of interest. As an extreme example, assume that you are interested in predicting cancer in patients which are severely under represented group. Sensitivity would indicate the true positive rate or the accuracy that you identify a patient as positive for cancer. In other words we see that the imbalance skew shifted with OUPS to allow for more accuracy of prediction of the under represented by about 10 - 25% making OUPS a more reliable approach. Table 6 provides a summary of sensitivity using OUPS by data set.

Results by Classifier

We grouped the results by classifier in order to understand the impact of the classifier when using SMOTE OUPS and PSM re-sampling techniques. The data is shown in Table 7.

Regardless of the classifier the OUPS algorithm produced more accurate and sensitive predictions on average. For specificity and F measure performance it was considerably close to SMOTE which resulted in the highest performance. The F measure ranges, which includes standard error usually overlapped between SMOTE and OUPS which shows that there is not a significant difference between the two.

Results for Safe Level OUPS

Figure 1 shows the trade-off between specificity and sensitivity for over-sampling, under-sampling, Feature selection and CIP approaches. For under-sampling ENN and tomek link re-sampling were aggregated. For over-sampling OUPS, SMOTE and safe level SMOTE were aggregated. For feature selection CFS and consistency were aggregated. Three different CIP approaches were aggregated and discussed further on.

Overall CIP obtained an auc measure of 77.60% followed by over-sampling which totaled 76.00%. Under-sampling produced 70.38% followed by the use of feature selection techniques resulting in 67.93%. Using no technique results in an auc measure of 67.93%. With any classification scheme there is always a balance between sensitivity and specificity. In particular strategically combining three different approaches we are able to obtain a more balanced scheme as compared to under and over-sampling and feature selection alone. The obvious trade-off being specificity and sensitivity measures. Depending on the domain this may be highly desirable.

Table 6. Sensitivity measure by data set

Data Set	Observations	% Minority	% Sensitivity
Pima	768	35%	64.62 ± 0.36
Bank	45211	12%	40.91 ± 0.27
Adult	30721	25%	56.84 ± 0.66
Readmit	100244	13%	59.70 ± 1.15
Turkey	5820	11%	23.08 ± 0.35
TA	151	32%	60.53 ± 0.89
US News	1134	34%	97.94 ± 0.03

Table 7. Results by learner

	Learner	% Accuracy	% Sensitivity	% Specificity	% F Measure
OUPS	LDA	78.48 ± 0.64	50.51± 1.26	91.22 ± 0.32	52.78 ± 1.48
	Logistic Regression	78.81 ± 0.63	51.86 ± 1.25	91.26 ± 0.32	52.53 ± 1.54
	NN 5	79.16 ± 0.66	57.28± 1.46	91.77 ± 0.40	56.10 ± 1.56
	NN 10	83.80 ± 0.48	60.59± 1.28	92.98 ± 0.27	52.27 ± 1.60
	NN 20	86.33 ± 0.38	63.03± 1.20	93.62 ± 0.26	60.43 ± 1.39
	SVM	83.60 ± 0.46	62.55± 1.20	92.82 ± 0.26	57.50 ± 1.57
SMOTE	LDA	71.78 ± 0.73	44.15 ± 1.41	92.25 ± 0.29	53.98 ± 1.31
	Logistic Regression	72.43 ± 0.73	44.75 ± 1.42	92.20 ± 0.29	54.36 ± 1.32
	NN 5	75.19 ± 0.68	45.90 ± 1.47	93.58 ± 0.27	55.04 ± 1.38
	NN 10	78.88 ± 0.58	49.53 ± 1.45	94.18 ± 0.24	57.97 ± 1.38
	NN 20	82.04 ± 0.45	52.12 ± 1.46	94.92 ± 0.23	60.43 ± 1.39
	SVM	71.78 ± 0.73	44.15 ± 1.41	92.25 ± 0.29	53.98 ± 1.31
PSM	LDA	78.82 ± 0.55	48.90± 1.31	95.40 ± 0.20	58.98 ± 1.28
	Logistic Regression	54.77 ± 0.73	28.65± 1.01	78.39 ± 0.81	33.85 ± 0.79
	NN 5	56.97 ± 0.89	34.84± 1.40	1.38 ± 0.79	31.86 ± 0.86
	NN 10	59.55 ± 0.73	36.34± 1.42	81.61 ± 0.89	34.09 ± 0.92
	NN 20	61.35 ± 0.66	38.38± 1.46	82.69 ± 0.87	36.25 ± 0.93
	SVM	61.75 ± 0.64	34.12± 1.07	83.81 ± 0.94	40.17 ± 0.92

Figure 1. Sampling type comparison

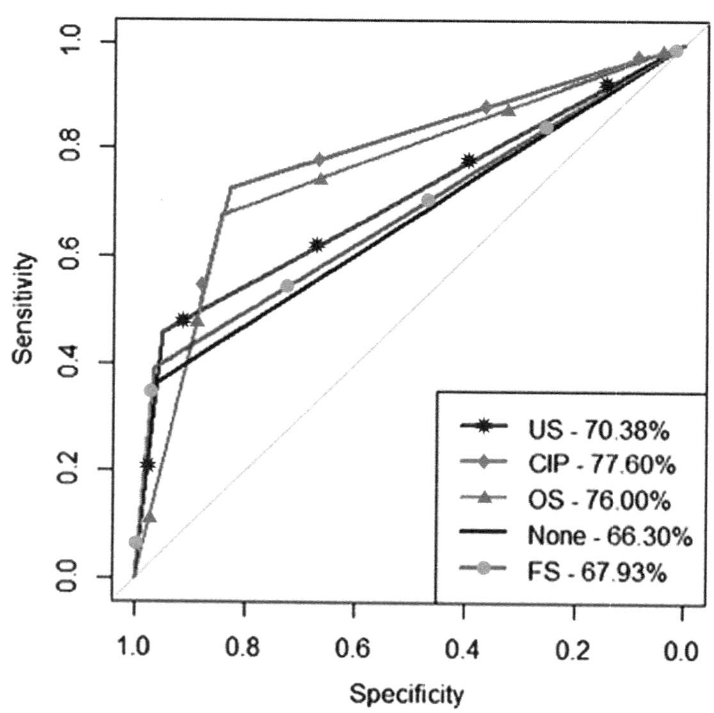

Figure 2 shows the results for combined techniques. CIP1 was comprised of the use of OUPS, consistency feature selection and tomek links. CIP2 consisted of safe level SMOTE, consistency feature selection and tomek links. CIP3 consisted of OUPS, CFS feature selection and ENN. They were then compared against combining OUPS and tomek links as well as combining CFS and tomek links. In general combining techniques seems to increase auc measures compared to not performing any pre-processing at all.

CIP1 resulted in high auc measures which were over 80% while CIP2 and CIP3 resulted in auc measures closer to 76%. Combining OUPS and tomek links resulted in an auc measure close to 79% which was higher than CIP2 and CIP3 but not higher than CIP1. This was not too surprising because CIP1 is the combination of that particular grouping with a feature selection technique as well. This provides some evidence that including feature selection into a pre-processing strategy provides more coverage than just using over and under sampling strategies alone.

Table 8 results by technique provides specificity and sensitivity measures for each technique individually. Safe level OUPS outperforms all other techniques in regards to sensitivity. The safe level SMOTE technique also performed better. In general the under sampling techniques perform better than not using any approach while most of the techniques seem to perform worse than doing nothing. The under sampling approaches remove noisy samples from the over represented group while both the safe level approaches increase the density of minority samples that are least likely to be considered noise. We can see the connection between the impact of noise on the learner as a result.

Figure 2. Mix and match comparison

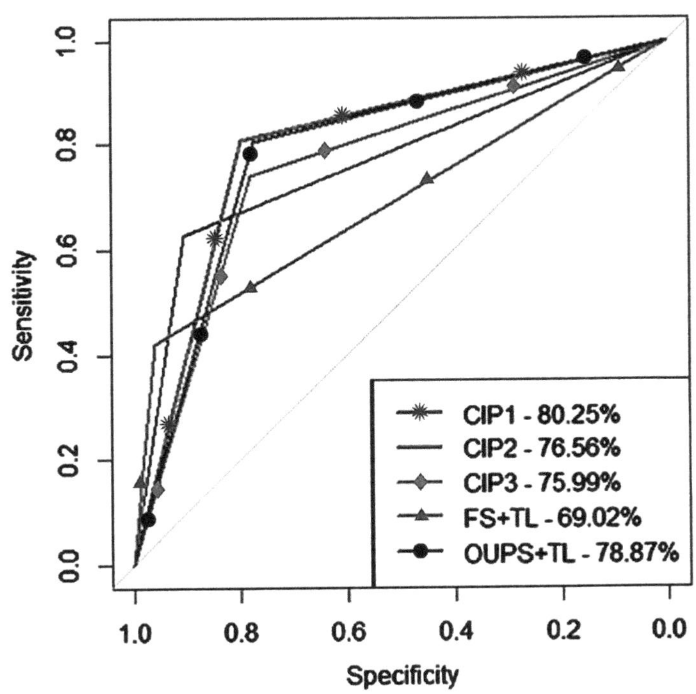

The CIP and mixed approaches were surprisingly worse than using no technique at all. What is also interesting is that the in some cases using a mixed approach resulted in degradation in sensitivity compared to just using a single approach alone.

All the techniques provided improvements in specificity which indicates that performing any of the above mentioned techniques is better than not doing anything at all if your desire is specificity. SMOTE and the combination of OUPS and tomek link re-sampling performs higher than the rest but at the cost of decreased sensitivity.

Out of all the sampling techniques that improved in both sensitivity and specificity "safe" level OUPS outperformed them all in both categories making it a reliable approach in improving prediction of imbalanced data. Using the CIP approaches did not offer remarkable improvements compared to just using an under-sampling or over-sampling scheme.

CONCLUSION

In this chapter we discuss the use of combined approaches in comparison to just using single techniques alone. We also introduced a new technique for increasing sensitivity and specificity aimed at combating noise, small disjuncts and class overlap called OUPS and its recent improvement called "safe" level OUPS.

We implemented a blended approach to sampling data with imbalanced classes (OUPS) that resulted in higher accuracy and sensitivity then SMOTE or propensity score matching. We conducted experiments using accuracy, specificity, sensitivity and F-measure performance measures and analyzed the results. The OUPS approach was found to improve the overall accuracy and sensitivity of the learner on average while SMOTE improved overall all F measures although this is arguable.

Table 8. Results by technique

Technique	% Sensitivity	% Specificity
SL-OUPS*	65.78 ± 0.68	90.32 ± 0.18
SL-SMOTE*	62.69 ± 0.84	90.18 ± 0.19
CIP1	46.85 ± 0.80	92.65 ± 0.29
CIP2*	59.30 ± 0.62	90.86 ± 0.29
CIP3	43.06 ± 0.73	91.36 ± 0.19
SMOTE	48.02 ± 0.85	94.32 ± 0.13
OUPS	58.36 ± 0.71	92.59 ± 0.16
ENN*	63.13 ± 0.72	90.23 ± 0.18
TOMEK LINK (TL)*	61.95 ± 0.86	90.31 ± 0.18
Consistency	50.96 ± 1.13	89.55 ± 0.19
CFS	49.23 ± 1.06	87.85 ± 0.15
CFS + TL	47.66 ± 1.02	88.56 ± 0.12
NONE	58.74 ± 0.94	86.93 ± 0.28

* indicates improvements in both measures above using nothing

OUPS and SMOTE consistently provided improvements for the performance measures as already mentioned for various levels of class imbalance and sample size. However, the lowest imbalanced set was 11%. It may be the case that performance measures may be different for extreme levels of imbalance closer to 1%, although we see no reason to believe that is the case.

Using propensity scores for generating synthetic data effectively retrieves the most likely neighbors with the most similar probabilities of occurrence. This provides a more reliable sample space that particularly when there is a large amount of variables in the input space.

The "safe" level OUPS approach out performed common data pre-processing techniques in regards to sensitivity. Specificity measures although higher than doing no processing were not the highest. However, in cases were specificity was high the usual trade off was sensitivity measures. Out of all the cases that improved both sensitivity and specificity measures over no pre-processing "safe" level OUPS provided the highest specificity measures.

The combined imbalanced preprocessing (CIP) approaches had the most coverage according to AUC measures but upon further review we see that there is a cost of misclassifying the target concept that was not detected until reviewing sensitivity and specificity measures. Combining approaches does not guarantee improvements to classification accuracy. In general focused techniques that target data intrinsic properties offer improvements.

REFERENCES

Abadie, A., & Imbens, G. W. (2009). *Matching on the estimated propensity score*. National Bureau of Economic Research. doi:10.3386/w15301

Akbani, R., Kwek, S., & Japkowicz, N. (2004). Applying support vector machines to imbalanced datasets. *Machine Learning: ECML, 2004*, 39–50.

Attenberg, J., & Ertekin, S. (2013). Class imbalance and active learning learning. In Imbalanced Learning: Foundations, Algorithms, and Applications (1st ed., pp. 101–147). John Wiley & Sons, Inc.

Austin, P. C. (2011). An Introduction to Propensity Score Methods for Reducing the Effects of Confounding in Observational Studies. *Multivariate Behavioral Research*, *46*(3), 399–424. doi:10.1080/00273171.2011.568786 PMID:21818162

Bahnsen, A. C., & Aouada, D. (2014). Example-Dependent Cost-Sensitive Logistic Regression for Credit Scoring. *Proceedings of the 2014 13th International Conference on Machine Learning and Applications*. doi:10.1109/ICMLA.2014.48

Baldi, P., Brunak, S., Chauvin, Y., Andersen, C. A. F., & Nielsen, H. (2000). Assessing the accuracy of prediction algorithms for classification: An overview. *Bioinformatics (Oxford, England)*, *16*(5), 412–424. doi:10.1093/bioinformatics/16.5.412 PMID:10871264

Batista, G. E., Carvalho, A. C., & Monard, M. C. (2000). Applying one-sided selection to unbalanced datasets. *MICAI 2000. Advances in Artificial Intelligence*, 2000, 315–325.

Batista, G. E., Prati, R. C., & Monard, M. C. (2004). A study of the behavior of several methods for balancing machine learning training data. *ACM SIGKDD Explorations Newsletter*, *6*(1), 20. doi:10.1145/1007730.1007735

Batuwita, R., & Palade, V. (2013). Class imbalance learning methods for support vector machines. In Imbalanced Learning: Foundations, Algorithms, and Applications (1st ed., pp. 83–99). John Wiley & Sons, Inc.

Blagus, R., & Lusa, L. (2013). SMOTE for high-dimensional class-imbalanced data. *BMC Bioinformatics*, *14*(1), 106. doi:10.1186/1471-2105-14-106 PMID:23522326

Bunkhumpornpat, C., Sinapiromsaran, K., & Lursinsap, C. (2009). Safe-Level-SMOTE : Safe-Level-Synthetic Minority Over-Sampling TEchnique. In *Advances in Knowledge Discovery and Data Mining* (pp. 475–482).

Caliendo, M., & Clement, M. (2012). Research Note-The Cost Impact of Spam Filters: Measuring the Effect of Information System Technologies in Organizations. *Information Systems Research*, *23*(June 2014).

Chawla, N. V. (2005). DATA MINING FOR IMBALANCED DATASETS : AN OVERVIEW. In In Data mining and knowledge discovery handbook (pp. 853–867). Springer.

Chawla, N. V., Bowyer, K. W., Hall, L. O., & Philip, W. (2011). SMOTE: synthetic minority over-sampling technique. *Journal of Artificial Intelligence Research, 16*, 321–357.

Chou, C., Kuo, B., & Chang, F. (2006). The Generalized Condensed Nearest Neighbor Rule as A Data Reduction Method. *Proceedings of the 18th International Conference on Pattern Recognition (ICPR'06)* (pp. 556–559). doi:10.1109/ICPR.2006.1119

D'Agostino, R. B. (1998). Tutorial in biostatistics: Propensity score methods for bias reduction in the comparison of a treatment to a non-randomized control group. *Statistics in Medicine*, *17*(19), 2265–2281. doi:10.1002/(SICI)1097-0258(19981015)17:19<2265::AID-SIM918>3.0.CO;2-B PMID:9802183

Dal Pozzolo, A., Caelen, O., Waterschoot, S., & Bontempi, G. (2013). Racing for unbalanced methods selection. *Proceedings of the Intelligent Data Engineering and Automated Learning–IDEAL 2013*.

Debowski, B., Areibi, S., Grewal, G., & Tempelman, J. (2012). A Dynamic Sampling Framework for Multi-class Imbalanced Data. *Proceedings of the 2012 11th International Conference on Machine Learning and Applications* (pp. 113–118). doi:10.1109/ICMLA.2012.144

Denil, M., & Trappenberg, T. (2010). Overlap versus imbalance. *Advances in Artificial Intelligence*.

Domingos, P. (1999). Metacost: A general method for making classifiers cost-sensitive. *Proceedings of the Fifth ACM SIGKDD International Conference on Knowledge Discovery and Data Mining*. doi:10.1145/312129.312220

Estabrooks, A., Jo, T., & Japkowicz, N. (2004). A Multiple Resampling Method for Learning from Imbalanced Data Sets. *Computational Intelligence*, *20*(1), 18–36. doi:10.1111/j.0824-7935.2004.t01-1-00228.x

Fan, Y. (2014). A revisit to the class imbalance learning with linear support vector machine. *Proceedings of the 2014 9th International Conference on Computer Science & Education* (pp. 516–521). doi:10.1109/ICCSE.2014.6926515

Fernández, A., García, S., & Herrera, F. (2011). Addressing the classification with imbalanced data: open problems and new challenges on class distribution. In *Hybrid Artificial Intelligent Systems* (pp. 1–10).

Friedman, J. H., & Popescu, B. (2008). Predictive Learning via Rule Ensembles. *The Annals of Applied Statistics*, *2*(3), 916–964. doi:10.1214/07-AOAS148

García, S., & Herrera, F. (2009). Evolutionary undersampling for classification with imbalanced datasets: Proposals and taxonomy. *Evolutionary Computation*, *17*(3), 275–306. doi:10.1162/evco.2009.17.3.275 PMID:19708770

García, V., Sánchez, J. S., & Mollineda, R. A. (2012). On the effectiveness of preprocessing methods when dealing with different levels of class imbalance. *Knowledge-Based Systems*, *25*(1), 13–21. doi:10.1016/j.knosys.2011.06.013

Ghazikhani, A. (2012). Class imbalance handling using wrapper-based random oversampling. *Proceedings of the 20th Iranian Conference on Electrical Engineering, (ICEE2012)* (pp. 611–616). doi:10.1109/IranianCEE.2012.6292428

Guo, H., & Viktor, H. L. (2004). Learning from imbalanced data sets with boosting and data generation: The DataBoost-IM approach. *ACM SIGKDD Explorations Newsletter*, *6*(1), 30–39. doi:10.1145/1007730.1007736

Guo, X., Yin, Y., Dong, C., Yang, G., & Zhou, G. (2008). On the Class Imbalance Problem. *Proceedings of the 2008 Fourth International Conference on Natural Computation* (pp. 192–201). doi:10.1109/ICNC.2008.871

Han, H., Wang, W., & Mao, B. (2005). Borderline-SMOTE : A New Over-Sampling Method in. *Advances in Intelligent Computing* (pp. 878–887).

Haro-garcia, A. De, & Garcia-Perajas, N. (2011). A scalable method for instance selection for class-imbalance datasets. *Proceedings of the Intelligent Systems Design and Applications (ISDA)* (pp. 1383–1390).

He, H., Bai, Y., Garcia, E. A., & Li, S. (2008). ADASYN: Adaptive synthetic sampling approach for imbalanced learning. *Proceedings of the 2008 IEEE International Joint Conference on Neural Networks (IEEE World Congress on Computational Intelligence)* (Vol. 3, pp. 1322–1328). doi:10.1109/IJCNN.2008.4633969

Huang, H.-Y., Lin, Y.-J., Chen, Y.-S., & Lu, H.-Y. (2012). Imbalanced data classification using random subspace method and SMOTE. *Proceedings of the 6th International Conference on Soft Computing and Intelligent Systems, and The 13th International Symposium on Advanced Intelligence Systems* (pp. 817–820). doi:10.1109/SCIS-ISIS.2012.6505155

Japkowicz, N. (2000). Learning from imbalanced data sets: a comparison of various strategies. *Proceedings of the AAAI Workshop on Learning from Imbalanced Data Sets.*

Jeatrakul, P., Wong, K. W., Fung, C. C., & Takama, Y. (2010). Misclassification analysis for the class imbalance problem. *Proceedings of the World Automation Congress (WAC).*

Junfei, C., Qingfeng, W., & Huailin, D. (2010). An empirical study on ensemble selection for class-imbalance data sets. *Proceedings of the 2010 5th International Conference on Computer Science & Education* (pp. 477–480). doi:10.1109/ICCSE.2010.5593573

Koplowitz, J., & Brown, T. (1981). On the relation of performance to editing in nearest neighbor rules. *Pattern Recognition*, *13*(3), 31–32. doi:10.1016/0031-3203(81)90102-3

Kotsiantis, S., Kanellopoulos, D., & Pintelas, P. (2006). Handling imbalanced datasets: A review. *GESTS International Transactions on Computer Science and Engineering, 30*(1).

Kretzschmar, R., Karayiannis, N. B., & Eggimann, F. (2005). Feedforward neural network models for handling class overlap and class imbalance. *International Journal of Neural Systems*, *15*(5), 323–338. doi:10.1142/S012906570500030X PMID:16278937

Kubat, M., & Matwin, S. (1997). Addressing the curse of imbalanced training sets: one-sided selection. *Proceedings of ICML, 4*.

Lakshmanan, B., Priscilla, A. J., Ponni, S., & Sankari, V. (2011). Evaluation of imbalanced datasets using fuzzy support vector machine-class imbalance learning (FSVM-CIL). *Proceedings of the IEEE-International Conference on Recent Trends in Information Technology* (pp. 1131–1136).

Li, L. (2011). Propensity Score Analysis with Matching Weights. *arXiv Preprint arXiv:1105.2917*, 1–17.

Ling, C. X., & Sheng, V. S. (2008). Cost-Sensitive Learning and the Class Imbalance Problem. In *Encyclopedia of Machine Learning*. Springer.

Liu, X., Wu, J., & Zhou, Z. (2009). Exploratory undersampling for class-imbalance learning. *IEEE Transactions on Systems, Man, and Cybernetics, Part B*, 39(2), 539-550.

Liu, X., & Zhou, Z. (2006). The Influence of Class Imbalance on Cost-Sensitive Learning: An Empirical Study. *Proceedings of the Sixth International Conference on Data Mining (ICDM'06)* (pp. 970–974). doi:10.1109/ICDM.2006.158

López, V., Fernández, A., García, S., Palade, V., & Herrera, F. (2013). An insight into classification with imbalanced data: Empirical results and current trends on using data intrinsic characteristics. *Information Sciences*, *250*, 113–141. doi:10.1016/j.ins.2013.07.007

Ma, H., Wang, L., & Shen, B. (2011). A new fuzzy support vector machines for class imbalance learning. *Proceedings of the 2011 International Conference on Electrical and Control Engineering* (pp. 3781–3784). doi:10.1109/ICECENG.2011.6056838

Mendes-Moreira, J., Soares, C., Jorge, A. M., & Sousa, J. F. D. (2012). Ensemble approaches for regression: A survey. *ACM Computing Surveys*, *45*(1), 1–40. doi:10.1145/2379776.2379786

Mirza, B., & Lin, Z. (2013). One-vs-all for class imbalance learning. *Proceedings of the 2013 9th International Conference on Information, Communications & Signal Processing*, 1–5. doi:10.1109/ICICS.2013.6782785

Orriols-puig, A., & Bernad, E. (2008). Mining imbalanced data with learning classifier systems. *Learning Classifier Systems in Data Mining*, *125*, 123–145. doi:10.1007/978-3-540-78979-6_6

Prati, R., Batista, G., & Monard, M. (2004). Learning with class skews and small disjuncts. *Advances in Artificial Intelligence–SBIA*, *LNCS* (Vol. 3171, pp. 296–306).

Prati, R. C., Batista, G. E., & Monard, M. C. (2004). Class imbalances versus class overlapping: An analysis of a learning system behavior. *MICAI 2004*. *Advances in Artificial Intelligence*, LNCS (Vol. 2972, pp. 312–321).

Qian, Y., Liang, Y., Li, M., Feng, G., & Shi, X. (2014). A resampling ensemble algorithm for classification of imbalance problems. *Neurocomputing*, *143*, 57–67. doi:10.1016/j.neucom.2014.06.021

Quinlan, J. R. (1991). Improved estimates for the accuracy of small disjuncts. *Machine Learning*, *6*(1), 93–98. doi:10.1007/BF00153762

Rivera, W. A., Goel, A., & Kincaid, J. P. (2014). OUPS : a combined approach using SMOTE and Propensity Score Matching. *Proceedings of the 2014 13th International Conference on Machine Learning and Applications*, *1*(2), 4–7. doi:10.1109/ICMLA.2014.106

Rosenbaum, P. R., & Rubin, D. B. (1983). The central role of the propensity score in observational studies for causal effects. *Biometrika*, *70*(1083), 41–55. doi:10.1093/biomet/70.1.41

Rosenbaum, P. R., & Rubin, D. B. (1985). Constructing a control group using multivariate matched sampling methods that incorporate the propensity score. *The American Statistician*, *39*(1), 33–38.

Saha, S., & Ekbal, A. (2013). Combining multiple classifiers using vote based classifier ensemble technique for named entity recognition. *Data & Knowledge Engineering*, *85*, 15–39. doi:10.1016/j.datak.2012.06.003

Seiffert, C., Khoshgoftaar, T., Van Hulse, J., & Folleco, A. (2014). An empirical study of the classification performance of learners on imbalanced and noisy software quality data. *Information Sciences*, 2014, 651–658.

Seiffert, C., Khoshgoftaar, T. M., Van Hulse, J., & Napolitano, A. (2010). RUSBoost: A Hybrid Approach to Alleviating Class Imbalance. *IEEE Transactions on Systems, Man, and Cybernetics. Part A, Systems and Humans*, *40*(1), 185–197. doi:10.1109/TSMCA.2009.2029559

Stefanowski, J. (2014). The Impact of Local Data Characteristics on Learning from Imbalanced Data. In *Rough Sets and Intelligent Systems Paradigms*, 1–13.

Stefanowski, J., & Wilk, S. (2008). *Selective pre-processing of imbalanced data for improving classification performance*. Data Warehousing and Knowledge Discovery. doi:10.1007/978-3-540-85836-2_27

Tan, D., & Liew, S. (2012). A feature selection model for binary classification of imbalanced data based on preference for target instances. *Data Mining and Optimization (DMO)*, (September), 2–4.

Thanathamathee, P., & Lursinsap, C. (2013). Handling imbalanced data sets with synthetic boundary data generation using bootstrap re-sampling and AdaBoost techniques. *Pattern Recognition Letters*, *34*(12), 1339–1347. doi:10.1016/j.patrec.2013.04.019

Tian, J., Gu, H., & Liu, W. (2011). Imbalanced classification using support vector machine ensemble. *Neural Computing & Applications*, *20*(2), 203–209. doi:10.1007/s00521-010-0349-9

Van Hulse, J., & Khoshgoftaar, T. M. (2002). Experimental Perspectives on Learning from Imbalanced Data. *Proceedings of the 24th International Conference on Machine Learning* (pp. 935–942).

Wasikowski, M., & Chen, X. (2010). Combating the small sample class imbalance problem using feature selection. *IEEE Transactions on Knowledge and Data Engineering*, *22*(10), 1388–1400. doi:10.1109/TKDE.2009.187

Weiss, G. M. (2010a). Data Mining and Knowledge Discovery Handbook. *Data Mining and Knowledge Discovery Handbook*, *1*, 747–757. doi:10.1007/978-0-387-09823-4

Weiss, G. M. (2010b). The impact of small disjuncts on classifier learning. In R. Stahlbock, S. F. Crone, & S. Lessmann (Eds.), *Data Mining* (Vol. 8, pp. 193–226). Boston, MA: Springer US; doi:10.1007/978-1-4419-1280-0_9

Wu, G., & Chang, E. Y. (2003). Class-boundary alignment for imbalanced dataset learning. *ICML 2003 Workshop on Learning from Imbalanced Data Sets II*, 49–56.

Wu, G., & Chang, E. Y. (2005). KBA: Kernel boundary alignment considering imbalanced data distribution. *IEEE Transactions on Knowledge and Data Engineering*, *17*(6), 786–795. doi:10.1109/TKDE.2005.95

Zadrozny, B., & Elkan, C. (2001). Learning and making decisions when costs and probabilities are both unknown. *Proceedings of the Seventh ACM SIGKDD International Conference on Knowledge Discovery and Data Mining - KDD '01* (pp. 204–213). doi:10.1145/502512.502540

Zhang, Y.-P., Zhang, L.-N., & Wang, Y.-C. (2010). Cluster-based majority under-sampling approaches for class imbalance learning. *Proceedings of the 2010 2nd IEEE International Conference on Information and Financial Engineering* (pp. 400–404). doi:10.1109/ICIFE.2010.5609385

Chapter 3
An Institution Wide Approach to Learning Analytics

Jennifer Heath
University of Wollongong, Australia

Eeva Leinonen
University of Wollongong, Australia

ABSTRACT

The desire to provide personalized learning support for students has been a strong driver of the development of learning analytics capabilities at the University of Wollongong (UOW), Australia. A case study approach is taken to explore the diverse challenges faced when adopting an institution wide approach to learning analytics. Aspects explored include: establishing a clear strategy and governance, implementing foundation technology, developing and applying analytics and visualizations, managing organizational culture change, understanding student expectations, and addressing ethical challenges associated with learning analytics. This chapter draws upon the results of a UOW student survey conducted in late 2013 that explored first year student expectations regarding privacy in relation to learning analytics, and their preferred approach to interventions. Throughout it is noted that the academic endeavor, rather than technology and data management, drives the UOW adoption of learning analytics.

INTRODUCTION

A case study approach has been taken in compiling this chapter, in order to share the experience of one Australian university in regard to the introduction of learning analytics. The specific objectives of the chapter are to share recent experience related to the many aspects of activity required for a successful learning analytics strategy, including "hard" technology aspects, governance and the "soft" aspects of culture change, all of which need to work in concert for the successful uptake of learning analytics across institutions to optimize student learning experiences. Throughout it is demonstrated that it is the academic endeavor, rather than technology and data management, that drives UOW's adoption of learning analytics, notwithstanding that both are of course the building blocks of a robust learning analytics system.

DOI: 10.4018/978-1-4666-9983-0.ch003

BACKGROUND

There is substantial peer reviewed literature available to inform the institution wide adoption of learning analytics, and the case study presented here has benefited from the willingness of colleagues world-wide to share such experiences. For the purposes of this chapter, preference is given to those background materials that wrestle with institution level initiatives, whereas works that focus on learning analytics activities focused on particular technical challenges are excluded from this discussion. However, concepts associated with the technology-enhanced learning (TEL) complex (Scanlon et al., 2013) are applied in this case study, to guide and structure the discussion. Each element of the TEL complex is important, and no hierarchy of priority has been assumed in compiling the case study material.

SETTING THE SCENE

An enduring challenge for higher education institutions is how to choose carefully where to invest limited resources in order to gain maximum benefit for students and staff. Technology in learning has brought with itself some big promises, and it has been suggested that institutional decision making has at times been based on "hype" and "faddism" (Beer, Tickner, & Jones, 2014), without the backing of strong evidence based practice. This is a reflection both of the fast moving field of technology and of the capacity of universities to adjust and change direction in a myriad of considerations such as infrastructure, staff, students and academic cultures. The decision at UOW to set up a unit to drive the university's learning analytics development and implementation was motivated by one overarching factor: our desire to maximize success for our diverse student population through supporting transition, personalized learning and an early identification of students at risk. To support these goals our learning analytics strategy was developed in consultation with the university community. We did not have evidence for the effectiveness of all of our decisions, but we were careful to build resilience and agility into our processes and to adopt a phased approach to implementation that could be adjusted as we learnt what worked well and what didn't.

Australian higher education has seen increased diversification in its student demographics, with more young people from non-traditional backgrounds entering universities, and with a greater range of academic capability at entry. This is partly a reflection of uncapped student numbers and, for a university such as UOW, the success of its regional campuses, which enable education in more remote communities. With this comes the challenge of how to support students who may not have the necessary academic and personal skills at entry, despite having the inherent capacity to succeed. This is a challenge that many countries share. The challenge is not simply student "performance", but knowing how our students engage with learning in its broadest sense throughout their studies, thus enabling us to adjust our teaching and support accordingly, whether students are struggling or not. If institutions can get that right, it serves to address issues relating to retention, progression and completion. The knack is not to lose sight of what is underneath the metrics, "the numbers", and to concentrate on the fundamentals that underpin good pedagogy and academic support. That is one of the key principles underpinning UOW learning analytics work: It is motivated by the academic endeavor rather than by technology and data management, notwithstanding that both are of course core building blocks of a robust learning analytics system.

Academic communities have long-established patterns of being—patterns that are comfortable and well rehearsed—and ways of doing, which have served, and may continue to serve, the community well. There is not necessarily any perceived imperative for change. Yet the world around us is changing, rapidly, not least because of the way technology connects with our everyday living, including learning. UOW, like many other universities, has observed changing patterns in student behavior, including their ever- increasing expectations to be digitally connected, and dropping class attendance numbers. Uncapped enrolment numbers have been accompanied by larger class sizes, without the necessary increase in the unit of resource, and therefore the need has arisen for academic and professional services staff to manage complexity in the student cohort in more effective and creative ways. The case for embracing different ways of being and doing was first made intellectually, and we found largely accepted by our academic communities. The challenge in our learning analytics work has centered on implementation, in doing things differently, in stopping doing some things to make space for new things, and in finding clarity about roles and responsibilities. The team leading this work needed to be sensitive to the challenges while remaining focused on the goals, finding ways of integrating learning analytics within different disciplinary and academic cultures, while never losing sight of the imperative of demonstrating the value added to students and staff. This dual approach was the key to what was achieved in a relatively short time period, and encouragement comes from the institution wide progress that continues to be made.

CASE STUDY PART 1: AN INSTITUTION WIDE STRATEGY

The University of Wollongong operates with a five faculty structure for Australian onshore operations, with the faculties being Business; Engineering and Information Sciences; Law, Humanities and the Arts; Science, Medicine and Health; and Social Sciences. From the outset an institution wide approach to the adoption of learning analytics has been followed, with early responsibilities lying within the portfolio of the Deputy Vice-Chancellor (Academic). None of the schools or faculties at UOW had explored the use of learning analytics on a significant scale: this enabled a "greenfields" approach to be taken, without such considerations as the need to scale up solutions previously developed at a school or faculty level (Ferguson et al., 2014; Lonn, Aguilar, & Teasley, 2013).

The literature regarding the technology-enabled learning (TEL) complex is very informative on the development of a multi-faceted strategic approach to learning analytics. The TEL complex approach includes many facets that go beyond the technology, as Scanlon et al. note "… it is a complex system, which includes communities, technologies and practices that are informed by pedagogy" (Scanlon, et al., 2013, p. 5). The UOW case study reinforces this view of a TEL complex, of many interconnecting elements required to work in concert towards a shared goal so as to enable the progress of the learning analytics strategy. The key interconnecting elements for the UOW learning analytics are depicted in Figure 1.

The strategy developed included each of these TEL complex components. Due to space limitations, this chapter is restricted to Students, Technology, Academics and Governance matters. The learning analytics information technology work at UOW began with consideration of the tools and resources already available to support the goal of offering learning analytics capabilities across the University. At the time that consideration of the available information technologies was initiated, a survey of student perspectives was undertaken; this is described in more detail in the next section. Ethical and privacy related matters were explored through the student survey, and two governance structures were put in place at the outset of the project, as described below. The role of academics, pedagogy and support staff is also addressed.

Figure 1. The TEL complex for learning analytics at UOW

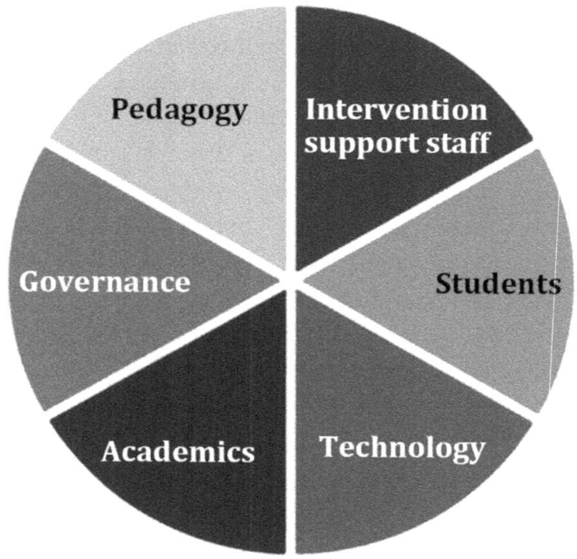

Existing data warehouse infrastructure and capable, skilled technical staff were rapidly identified and drawn into the interdisciplinary collaboration, along with policy makers, senior university administrators and leaders, academics and student support staff. UOW operates with a mature data warehouse infrastructure, with key institution wide transaction processing systems (TPS) contributing to the enterprise data warehouse, including the library (Cox & Jantti, 2012) and student administration systems. Additional TPS data was captured for the learning analytics data warehouse, including student usage of peer assisted study sessions (PASS) and Learning Development workshops and individual consultations. Challenges regarding disparate learning-related datasets and the need to bring them together into a consolidated location were faced at UOW, as they have been elsewhere (Arnold, 2010). The information technology adopted for learning analytics at UOW is not the sole innovation. The changes to the broader TEL complex are jointly responsible for the learning analytics innovation (Scanlon, et al., 2013). As earlier work has noted (Macfadyen & Dawson, 2012; Macfadyen, Dawson, Pardo, & Gasevic, 2014), policy and financial support are essential to success when embracing cultural change such as that offered through learning analytics. It was necessary for UOW to invest in the employment of additional staff with strong analytical skills, experience working with big data and statistics and a knowledge of education (preferably gathered through teaching experience) to help overcome the constraints arising from shortages of suitable data management staff, as highlighted in recent literature (Buerck, 2014).

Recent publications also describe the need to grow or scale up learning analytics solutions (Ferguson, et al., 2014). Often this relates to up-scaling technology employed simultaneously with the up-scaling of the other TEL complexes components. At UOW an approach was used that captured all institution wide data and held it in a suitably scalable data warehouse from the start. While the technology aspects do not need to be grown, growth does need to take place in other components of the TEL complex, with a continual increase in the number of academics adopting learning analytics as part of their "business as usual". Figure 2 is a conceptual representation of the traditional information system approach to up-scaling production solutions from prototypes, contrasted with the UOW LA approach of full scale technology

Figure 2. Contrasting approaches to LA implementation: phased up-scaling from prototype vs UOW "blossoming" on an institution wide technology foundation

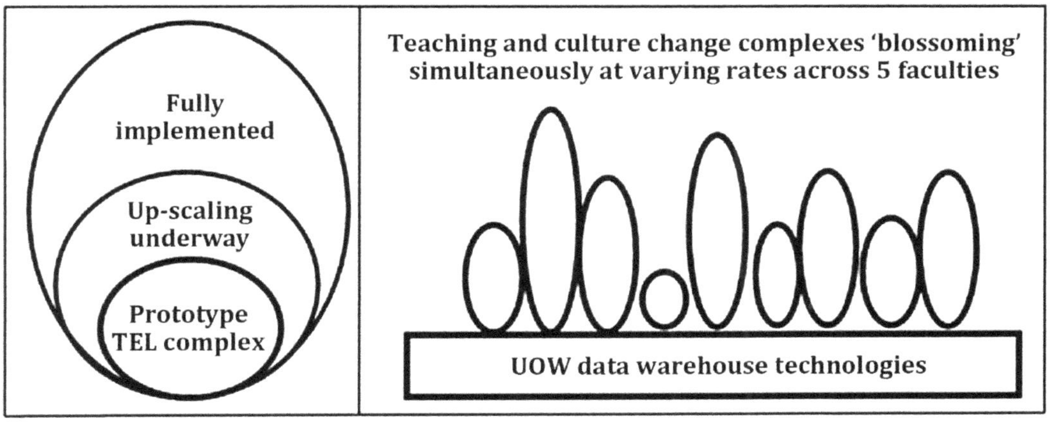

implemented, enabling the phased up-scaling (or "blossoming") of teaching and culture change aspects upon that solid technology platform.

Adoption of the use of learning analytics by academic staff members is optional at UOW. A very pleasing number of core first year subjects with high enrolment numbers (e.g. circa 800), were early adopters of the reports, visualizations and other learning analytic artifacts supporting the identification of students who may not be active with their studies. A largely online postgraduate subject was quick to engage in the use of the learning analytics reports and visualizations, as Moodle was a vital element of the subject delivery strategy: patterns in student usage of Moodle and the library, alerted the subject coordinator to cases where less use than expected was made of research resources. A broadcast message to all students directing their attention to the library resources for an upcoming assessment item appeared to be useful, with increased uptake of student resource access following the broadcast.

The approaches taken to academic staff engagement with learning analytics differ across the five UOW faculties. A community of practice approach is pursued in one faculty, and includes subjects across multiple schools and year levels. Other faculties have adopted the learning analytic artifacts as an additional source of business intelligence that is woven into the existing good practice in supporting students—particularly those in transition.

The following chapter sections will each consider the following TEL complex components: students, technology, academics and governance.

CASE STUDY PART 2: STUDENTS – HEARING THE STUDENT VOICE THROUGH UOW SURVEY

There is little published research regarding student perspectives on learning analytics: therefore, UOW undertook a survey to find out whether learning analytics were a function that students would find useful, and whether there would be any perceived barriers to adopting this approach.

Survey Deployment

The *Learning Analytics—Student Perspective Survey* was conducted online in late 2013. The survey was made available to the cohorts of five first year subjects, one from each UOW faculty. The sampling frame included a high proportion of equity students, as a goal of learning analytics is to support non-traditional students: an opportunity was sought to hear their views in a non-stigmatizing manner.

The survey received ethics approval from the Human Research Ethics Committee of the University of Wollongong (Ethics No. HE13/342). The Associate Deans (Education) in each Faculty provided assistance through: advice on the most suitable subjects for inclusion, liaison with students for focus groups, and liaison with subject coordinators. A low-value department store/supermarket voucher was provided as an incentive for student survey completion. The quantitative questions used a 5 point Likert scale with an additional "not applicable" option. Sample size calculations sought 270 student responses; the 326 valid responses received exceeded this target.

The survey investigated:

- Student preferences for learning analytics system functionality.
- Student preferences for intervention strategies and
- Student perceptions of privacy.

Table 1 includes all the survey questions, aligned to the appropriate construct.

Quantitative Results

This section presents an overview of the quantitative results for each of the above constructs, and then presents a selection of qualitative results.

System Functionality Results

The majority of the respondents (84%) indicated that they would like to be able to see their academic progress during the semester, both against the progress of their classmates and the learning outcomes of the subject. While the majority of the respondents (89%) also indicated that they would like personalized suggestions for improvement, fewer indicated they would like the use of "traffic lights" to indicate their progress (47%). This is an interesting result as, sector wide, there is much activity pursuing the implementation of traffic light systems as part of University learning analytic strategies. The majority of respondents (69%) indicated that they would like to have a choice about regarding their inclusion in learning analytic initiatives. Learning analytics can be scoped to include students providing feedback to academic staff during session; the survey respondents (69%) indicated a desire to be involved in providing such feedback.

Intervention Strategy Results

Overall, the majority of the respondents (65%) indicated that they would want to be contacted if the learning analytics system suggested that they were struggling with their studies. The most preferred form of intervention was a personalized email providing information about the academic support services

Table 1. Questions used in student perspective survey

Construct	Question	
Student preferences for LA system functionality	Q1	During semester I would like to know how I am progressing in a subject relative to my classmates.
	Q2	I would like to be able to see how well I am achieving the learning outcomes of a subject as I complete assignments during semester.
	Q3	Using traffic lights of green, amber and red to indicate how my learning is progressing within a subject during semester would be a useful tool for me.
	Q4	During the semester I would be pleased to receive personalized suggestions for learner activities or resources I could use to better achieve the learning outcomes of a subject.
	Q5	I would like to be able to choose for myself which learning analytics tools were available to me.
	Q11	I would like to be able to give feedback to academic staff on the quality of their teaching during semester rather than waiting until the end of semester.
Student preferences for intervention strategy	Q6	If the learning analytics system at UOW showed the staff that I was struggling with my studies I would like one of the academics from my Faculty to contact me.
	Q7	If the learning analytics system at UOW showed the staff that I was struggling with my studies I would like one of the specialist support staff to contact me.
	Q8	If the learning analytics system at UOW showed the staff that I was struggling with my studies I would like an email giving me information about the academic support services that could help me with my studies.
	Q9	If the learning analytics system at UOW showed the staff that I was struggling with my studies I would like a phone call from a senior student in my Faculty.
	Q10	If the learning analytics system at UOW showed the staff that I was struggling with my studies I would not want to be contacted.
Student Perceptions of Privacy	Q12	Within the context of studying a particular subject, I am happy for the subject coordinator to be able to use all available data about me to maximize my learning opportunity.
	Q13	Subject coordinators should only be able to see how I am progressing in the subject they are teaching.
	Q14	Once the university has gathered some anonymous data about me I don't really care what they do with it provided it stays anonymous.
	Q15	Knowing that the information gathered about me at UOW could be used for learning analytics feels like a "big brother" scenario and it makes me feel a little uncomfortable.
	Q16	There should be a way for students to choose NOT to be included in learning analytics activities at UOW.
	Q17	There should be a way for students to provide feedback on the effectiveness of the UOW learning analytics system.
	Q18	There should be a student representative on the UOW committee(s) addressing learning analytics.
	Q19	Information gathered in one context, say enrolment, should only be used for the original intended purpose and not become part of the learning analytics system.
	Q20	I am pleased that UOW are asking students about learning analytics.

available to help (84%), followed by contact from an academic from the student's faculty (74%), and contact from specialist support staff (61%). The least preferred intervention strategy was a phone call from a senior student, with only 27% indicating they would like this approach.

Privacy Results

While 78% of respondents were willing to have a subject (module) coordinator access all of their data to maximize their learning opportunity, 50% of respondents indicated that subject (module) coordinators should only be able to see how a student is progressing in the subject (module) they are teaching. In addition, 38% of respondents indicated that information gathered in one context (e.g. enrolment) should only be used for its original purpose and not become part of the learning analytics activities; however, the largest group (40%) indicated that they were neutral to this statement.

If the data were anonymous, respondents were more comfortable for it to be used for multiple purposes, with 69% of respondents indicating that once the university gathers anonymous data, they don't mind what it is used for, as long as it remains anonymous. Respondents were comfortable with the use of their data at UOW, with only 17% indicating that knowing the information gathered about them at UOW could be used for learning analytics felt like a "big brother" scenario, making them feel uncomfortable.

The data also suggest that respondents would like to have a say in how learning analytics is used at UOW, with 68% stating they should be able to choose not to be included in learning analytic activities, 91% of respondents stating that they would like to provide feedback about the effectiveness of the learning analytic system, and 68% believing there should be a student representative on the University of Wollongong committee addressing learning analytics. Overall, the students were pleased (87%) that UOW engaged with them at the outset of learning analytic initiatives at UOW.

Qualitative Results

Qualitative feedback was also elicited from the students through a single stimulus asking "Do you have any further comments?" *S*ample comments from the students, related to the dominant emergent themes of system requirements, data issues, intervention strategies, privacy, teaching and learning, are listed below:

- I think that the learning analytics activities should use results from everyone. That way, if you are not doing so well you can see where you are in the context of the whole year group, rather than only comparing yourself to the students with good marks that don't mind sharing their marks.
- Information regarding student progress within a subject should be disclosed quickly to allow for improvement.
- I believe that UOW should allow students to know how they are doing against other students and how they are going in terms of satisfying the learning objectives.
- More feedback regarding progress in my subjects would be useful, rather than just relying on 2–4 assessment task results before it comes to your exam.
- I think the more sharing of information and effective communication is extremely beneficial for students, especially if information gathered is used in a positive way to improve quality teaching and learning.
- If a student's learning analytics statistics indicated that they were struggling in a subject, rather than phoning the student and warning them about the problem it would be better for constructive feedback to be given. The student could be mentored by a figure with significance in their own faculty and guided back on course.
- If the uni could call and personally tell me my progress this would be most ideal but an email alert with a visual aid would also work, like a pie chart showing an average myself and the course requirement.
- I believe that a learning analytics systems at UOW would help student to get through subjects that they might find challenging (especially core subjects that students must do before they specialise the path of their degree). I believe consultation with students is crucial to the process and regular

monitoring of the system as I believe that students will feel that this sort of system is an intrusion by the University into their private study routines.

- Sometimes students find it difficult seeking help, I think it helps if sometimes the help comes to them, so being able to keep track of a student's progress or lack thereof is important. Thanks.
- It is easy to feel as though you are alone in large cohorts, especially when you feel you are struggling with a subject. Receiving information about where you fall in the cohort could be enormously reassuring, as would be knowing that the university has systems in place to support you even though you may not be prepared to admit that you need help.
- I feel as though a learning analytics system would benefit students and academics alike at UOW.
- I think that, based on the questions asked in this survey, the prospect of learning analytics holds some serious potential. Go for it!

These comments, as representative of student views, were generally supportive, showing insight into the learning process and acknowledging that responsibility for the successful use of learning analytics needs to be shared by staff and students alike.

The Student Voice Influencing Learning Analytics (LA) at UOW

The feedback provided by the students through completion of the survey clearly indicated that students are interested in knowing how they are progressing with their studies, compared to the other students in their cohort. The UOW LA Governance Committee considered this student perspective in approving the development of a student dashboard within the Moodle Learning Management System in use at UOW. The student dashboard displays simple visualizations, at a subject level, that display an individual student's utilization of Moodle compared to their subject cohort, and that also display individual student cumulative and progressive assessment results. Suitable anonymization is used to preserve the privacy of students, with a threshold minimum number of students being required to be engaged in subject activities to enable inclusion in the dashboard. The student dashboard was designed, developed and tested throughout 2014, and release to students is expected in 2015. Initial student testing of the dashboard, during development, has indicated very positive responses.

The Learning Analytics Governance Committee and the Learning Analytics Ethical Use of Data Advisory Groups debated, at length, the feedback from students regarding question 16: "There should be a way for students to choose NOT to be included in Learning Analytics activities at UOW". Diverse points of view were considered and debated. The ultimate position adopted was that a student could not choose to be excluded from learning analytics initiatives, because the University has a duty of care and a responsibility to optimize student success, and any attempt to exclude students from the capabilities offered through learning analytics would undermine these core University responsibilities. Student survey feedback also indicated a desire to have student representation on the Learning Analytics Governance Committee (LAGC) and as a result the governance committee has an undergraduate student representative.

CASE STUDY PART 3: TECHNOLOGY – DATA WAREHOUSE TECHNOLOGY

The use of data warehouse technologies was well established in the administrative operations of UOW prior to initiating the learning analytics activities. Previously, little work had been undertaken in the use of data warehouse technologies for learning and teaching, however. The Performance Indicator Unit (PIU) at the UOW was first established to focus on the deployment of data warehouse technologies to support finance and administrative operations more than a decade ago, and UOW was one of the earliest higher education institutions in Australia to shift towards the use of data warehousing approaches for performance indicators and other diverse purposes.

The Business Analysis & Learning Analytics (BALA) team, reporting directly to the Deputy Vice-Chancellor Academic, was formed at UOW in the third quarter of 2013 to lead the development of an institution wide approach to learning analytics. Close collaboration between the BALA and PIU teams enabled rapid progress to be made in the design of a data warehouse approach. Like many higher education institutions, UOW is awash with data from dozens of transaction processing systems (TPS) that support diverse student system needs throughout the entire student life cycle: from engagement prior to enrolment, through study, to graduation and beyond. Add to these the powerful Moodle learning management system, and there was plenty of data available to inform learning analytics at UOW! Sources for this data included the student management system, student support services systems (multiple in use), library resource use (without providing any information about the specific books and electronic resources used, so as to protect student privacy), inclusion in peer assisted study sessions and the use of Moodle learning management system resources (gleaned through use of logfile data).

The challenge was to bring the disparate datasets with conflicting data definitions together into a cohesive solution. This is typical of the type of scenario well suited to the deployment of data warehousing technologies, and while it was undertaken in a higher education environment, there are many successful precedents in other domains, including the retail, finance, transport and energy industries.

It is very interesting to note that it was not necessary to implement any new transaction processing systems to get learning analytics operationalized at UOW; no additional data were required. The challenges related to the coordinated development of a clean dataset that included as much information as possible from existing information systems. This facilitated the development of a student behavioral model that gives some sense of the breadth and depth of student utilization of the various student support services, electronic educational resources and technology-enhanced learning tools available at UOW.

There is much debate in the field of Learning Analytics regarding the use of the term "student engagement" as opposed to "student utilization" of services, resources etc. This debate is acknowledged here through the careful use of the phrase "student utilization" rather than engagement. It is unclear whether a student using a forum in Moodle is truly engaged. Similarly, if a student attends a one-on-one consultation with an academic staff member targeting academic literacy we are not entirely sure that the student has engaged with the opportunity presented. It is however clear that the student has sought to "utilize" the opportunity available.

Internal Design of the Learning Analytics Cube

The design of the fact table within the data warehouse reflects this learning opportunity aspect of the higher education environment. There are numerous opportunities available to students, including library electronic resources, academic literacy workshops, Peer Assisted Study Sessions (PASS), downloadable resources on Moodle, formative quizzes on Moodle, etc. Depending on the course and subjects a student is enrolled in, the opportunities available vary. However, there is a core set of opportunities, and these are captured in the learning analytics fact table, with numerous associated dimensions providing the detail needed to model teaching and learning scenarios in the UOW case study.

Careful analysis of teaching and learning needs, of the available data from TPS, of data quality, underlying infrastructure and sustainability issues is needed when arriving at a suitable learning analytics data warehouse solution. These considerations are context specific and best developed from well established, reliable data sources that are likely to be supporting varied aspects of an institution's operations. It is unlikely that a one-size-fits all warehouse solution could be expeditiously installed for a University without substantial interfaces to "feeder" systems.

CASE STUDY PART 4: ACADEMICS – INVOLVING THE ACADEMIC COMMUNITY

Making the case to the UOW academic community and to senior management that learning analytics is an area worth investing money and time in, was initially based on student performance and the need to embrace technology in supporting students' learning. The case was accepted, and continued to be reinforced in many different contexts, in the spirit of seeking advice and feedback on the developing strategy and its implementation, and showing how the feedback had shaped future steps. It was acknowledged that the LA team did not have all the answers, and reminders were sometimes necessary that the aim was to add value. Support and enthusiasm, criticism and resistance were encountered as well as it began to dawn in the academic community that this is an agenda that the university is serious about. With the latter, there has been increasing interest from staff wishing to find out more about the University's learning analytics plans and how they can be involved in them. An important change is always a journey, and one worth taking time and care over.

In order to build agility and resilience, as well as increasing sustainable buy-in from staff and students, a phased approach was adopted, with voluntary engagement by subjects (modules) in semester long pilots. Taking this approach allowed academics who were engaged and willing to work closely with the LA team, to provide valuable feedback and intelligence. This created a valuable early community of practice.

One area that was brought into focus by the pilots and early adopters is the need to have a clear understanding by all that with information provided by learning analytics comes the responsibility for action. Once a student is potentially at risk from, say, lack of engagement with learning materials, such information cannot be ignored. There is an imperative to know the options for action by staff, and who is responsible to take the desired action and follow it through. A particularly important question, what the role of the academic is in such situations, brings to the surface a much wider university issue: the role of the academic in the modern university context. Furthermore, an equally challenging question arises: the boundaries of academic and non-academic support in addressing issues highlighted by data. It is important to understand and agree, early in the implementation process, who is the right person to contact the student and provide continuing support.

CASE STUDY PART 5: GOVERNANCE – IMPLEMENTING GOVERNANCE STRUCTURES

Ethical and privacy challenges abound in the domain of learning analytics (Heath, 2014; Prinsloo & Slade, 2013; Slade & Prinsloo, 2013). In the very early weeks of the learning analytics activities at UOW two governance committees were formed to guide the project and wrestle with the ethical issues that inevitably arise. At times these groups pull in opposite directions; this creates a healthy debate! The

Learning Analytics Governance Committee's terms of reference focus on decision making and management of the project. The Deputy Vice-Chancellor (Academic) is the Chair of this committee. This sends a clear message to the University community that she considers the learning analytics activities to be priority areas for lending senior executive support, as recommended in other publications (Macfadyen, et al., 2014). The Ethical Use of Data Advisory Group's terms of reference are narrowly scoped, to focus on the student privacy and ethical issues that arise from stewardship of the potentially very sensitive learning analytics dataset. This committee includes senior members from the Legal and Administrative Services, Associate Deans (Education) from two Faculties and the Director, Business Analysis & Learning Analytics from the Deputy Vice Chancellor Academic's portfolio. The chair of the Advisory Group is an Associate Professor from the Faculty of Engineering and Information Sciences whose research focus is on surveillance and privacy matters arising from emerging technologies (Michael & Clarke, 2013; Michael & Miller, 2013). Contemporary privacy theories (Tavani, 2008; Tavani & Moor, 2001) have been useful in discussions undertaken by the Advisory Group, with the contextual integrity concepts proposed by Nissenbaum (Nissenbaum, 2009, 2014) proving particularly so.

Considering contextual integrity is informative when wrestling with the secondary use of data, such as enrolment and student demographics data, for learning analytics purposes. Can the view be taken that students provide this data to enable their successful completion of higher education learning? If learning analytics is to focus on enabling student success, should this be undertaken in a context quite separate to the context in which enrolment data is initially captured? Or is this one context where the actors, attributes and transmission principles (Nissenbaum, 2009) are unchanged? These matters are often considered and revisited by the UOW LA Governance committees.

The LA Ethical Use of Data Advisory Group provided guidance regarding the design of a student dashboard under development within the Moodle environment. It was the collective opinion of the Advisory Group that the initial design of the dashboard did not adequately protect the privacy of students. The dashboard operates at the subject (module) level, and gives students a set of visualizations that present their relative, progressive assessment marks and Moodle usage compared to the other students in the subject (module) cohort. As the previous section of this paper described our students indicated a strong interest in having access to this type of cohort comparative information. The changes suggested by the Advisory Group were adopted, and specifications for the dashboard were amended to ensure adequate protection of individual student privacy. Policy and procedures regarding the use of the learning analytics data held in the UOW data warehouse were endorsed by the University Education Committee, and strict governance measures were put in place regarding access to the student data. These limitations are particularly necessary for research purposes that are outside the scope of business as usual and within the scope of learning analytics as defined at UOW, where the focus is on near real-time provision of intelligence to academics and students.

SOLUTIONS AND RECOMMENDATIONS

The UOW case study demonstrates the benefits of adopting an enterprise wide approach to the information technology aspects of learning analytics. Adoption of an enterprise wide technology foundation delivered a solution in response to the need to consolidate the disparate teaching and learning related datasets necessary for learning analytics. In addition, solutions addressing academic and governance TEL complex elements have been described. These include a variety of approaches to adoption of learning analytics as "business as usual" by academic staff, including a community of practice approach. There are many suitable approaches to adopting learning analytics—including the up-scaling of prototypes. By taking an institution wide approach to developing the information technology aspects, a stable foundation was provided to support the other TEL complexes, as summarized in *Figure 1: The TEL Complex for Learning Analytics at UOW.*

FUTURE RESEARCH DIRECTIONS

The evolving role of academics in the technology rich higher education environment presents a future research direction. Future research directions need to be motivated by the academic endeavor, rather than by technology and data management. Even acknowledging this primary motivator, there are also many more technically oriented open research areas surrounding the data mining and modeling, and the predictive modeling to support student learning and identify, as early as possible, at risk students. In refining the metrics used for learning analytics the question of how to recognize whether a student is actually "engaged" in learning or simply "going through the motions" must be considered. The ethics and privacy aspects of working with higher education "big data" continue to be open areas of research within diverse legal jurisdictions and cultural contexts world-wide. Finally, optimizing the actions taken based on the evidence of learning analytics, in order to best support students, is an area for future multidisciplinary research.

CONCLUSION

Different institutional cultures and leadership styles call for different approaches to the adoption of learning analytics as an institution wide activity. The approach chosen at UOW is one that builds on a collegiate culture, on a goal orientated approach to change, and the appreciation that what we need to do is add value to our strategic imperatives and our students' success. Four key decisions have set us on a scalable path:

1. Start with common data warehouse and the underpinning technology.
2. Hear the student voice in all stages of development.
3. Engage early adopters in the development of the analytics framework and functionality as well as encourage the establishment of communities of practice.
4. Establish a robust governance framework for both strategic and ethical decisions.

The development at UOW has also been underpinned by a clear buy-in from senior management with appropriate resourcing and support, by a clear understanding that the drivers are academic rather than technological and by iterative communications that demonstrate responsiveness to feedback. The area where greater clarity could have been had earlier in the development cycle relates to the roles and responsibilities of staff and students in taking action on the basis of the information gathered through the analytics. This is an area which reflects complex cultural and procedural practices and one where the greatest challenges as well as opportunities can be encountered.

REFERENCES

Arnold, K. E. (2010). Signals: Applying Academic Analytics. *EDUCAUSE Quarterly*, *33*(1), n1.

Beer, C., Tickner, R., & Jones, D. (2014). Three paths for learning analytics and beyond: moving from rhetoric to reality. Paper presented at the *ASCILITE*, Dunedin, New Zealand.

Buerck, J. P. (2014). A Resource-Constrained Approach to Implementing Analytics in an Institution of Higher Education: An Experience Report. *Journal of Learning Analytics*, *1*(1), 129–139.

Cox, B. L., & Jantti, M. (2012). Capturing business intelligence required for targeted marketing, demonstrating value, and driving process improvement. *Library & Information Science Research*, *34*(4), 308–316. doi:10.1016/j.lisr.2012.06.002

Ferguson, R., Clow, D., Macfadyen, L. P., Essa, A., Dawson, S., & Alexander, S. (2014). Setting Learning Analytics in Context: Overcoming the Barriers to Large-Scale Adoption. *Paper presented at the LAK '14*, Indianapolis. doi:10.1145/2567574.2567592

Heath, J. (2014). Contemporary Privacy Theory Contribution to Learning Analytics. *Journal of Learning Analytics*, *1*(1), 140–149.

Lonn, S., Aguilar, S., & Teasley, S. D. (2013). Issues, challenges, and lessons learned when scaling up a learning analytics intervention. *Paper presented at the Third International Conference on Learning Analytics and Knowledge*. doi:10.1145/2460296.2460343

Macfadyen, L. P., & Dawson, S. (2012). Numbers Are Not Enough. Why e-Learning Analytics Failed to Inform an Institutional Strategic Plan. *Journal of Educational Technology & Society*, *15*(3), 149–163.

Macfadyen, L. P., Dawson, S., Pardo, A., & Gasevic, D. (2014). Embracing Big Data in Complex Educational Systems: The Learning Analytics Imperative and the Policy Challenge. *Research and Practice in Assessment*, *9*, 17–28.

Michael, K., & Clarke, R. (2013). Location and tracking of mobile devices: Überveillance stalks the streets. *Computer Law & Security Report*, *29*(3), 216–228. doi:10.1016/j.clsr.2013.03.004

Michael, K., & Miller, K. W. (2013). Big Data: New Opportunities and New Challenges (Guest editors' introduction). *Computer*, *46*(6), 22–24. doi:10.1109/MC.2013.196

Nissenbaum, H. (2009). *Privacy in context: Technology, policy, and the integrity of social life*. California: Stanford University Press.

Nissenbaum, H. (2014). Respect for Context as a Benchmark for Privacy Online: What it Is and Isn't. *Cahier de prospective*, 19.

Prinsloo, P., & Slade, S. (2013). *An evaluation of policy frameworks for addressing ethical considerations in learning analytics*.

Scanlon, E., Sharples, M., Fenton-O'Greevy, M., Fleck, J., Cooban, C., & Ferguson, R. et al.. (2013). *Beyond prototypes: Enabling innovation in technology-enhanced learning*. Milton Keynes: Open University.

Slade, S., & Prinsloo, P. (2013). Learning Analytics: Ethical Issues and Dilemmas. *The American Behavioral Scientist*, *57*(10), 1510–1529. doi:10.1177/0002764213479366

Tavani, H. T. (2008). Informational privacy: concepts, theories, and controversies. In The handbook of information and computer ethics (pp. 131-164).

Tavani, H. T., & Moor, J. H. (2001). Privacy protection, control of information, and privacy-enhancing technologies. *ACM SIGCAS Computers and Society*, *31*(1), 6–11. doi:10.1145/572277.572278

KEY TERMS AND DEFINITIONS

Community of Practice: A group of people engaged in collective learning in a particular domain.

Data Warehouse: A subject-oriented (in this chapter, learning related), time-variant and non-volatile (never over-written) collection of data that aids decision making within organizations.

Learning Analytics: A broadly inclusive umbrella term that includes measurement, collection, analysis and reporting of data about learners and their contexts for real-time, retrospective and predictive analysis to support learning and teaching.

Technology-Enhanced Learning (TEL) Complex: TEL is a complex system including but not limited to learning and teaching communities, technologies and pedagogy.

Chapter 4
Developing a Framework for the Effective Use of Learning Analytics:
A UK Perspective

Collette Gavan
Edge Hill University, UK

ABSTRACT

Research and experimentation is uncovering forms of best practice and possible factors on which to centre the analysis of students in an effective way, however learning analytics has yet to be comprehensively implemented country-wide in the United Kingdom. The chapter explores the current impact of learning analytics in higher education at mome discusses and observes the current vacancies with which a framework enabled to function with data visualisation could be utilised. The deliverable seeks to design an initial framework that has the potential to be utilised in a higher education setting for more effective and insightful decision making with regards to learner retention and engagement. This framework will combine the theory and scientific action of predictive analytics with a comparison of the most suitable data visualisation toolsets that are currently available in open-source software.

INTRODUCTION

Traditional approaches to teaching programming have encountered a number of issues. However when coupled with changes in both the demographic and political constitution of the student body it is clear that the strategies adopted to attain successful outcomes in relation to creating lifelong students need to re-evaluated. Clearly significant progress has been achieved, yet addressing the changing vision of higher education provision in relation to the Browne Report and the generational shift in technological demand places additional pedagogical requirements when designing implementing courses and assessment. This research investigates the extent to which the practical application of robotics affects undergraduate computing students' engagement in learning the Java programming language. The findings from this study have been interpreted using learning and academic analytics to derive meaning from the data gathered.

DOI: 10.4018/978-1-4666-9983-0.ch004

TEACHING PROGRAMMING TO UNDERGRADUATE STUDENTS

Teaching undergraduate students how to write code and develop their own programs has long proved a difficult task [Hagan and Markham, 2000; Kelleher and Pausch, 2005]. There are numerous hurdles that need to be overcome by the students in order to fully understand the concepts that underpin software development. Whilst syntax and semantics may be cited as issues [Hagan and Markham, 2000], these are specific details related to programming languages. It could be argued that the greatest challenge which face students when learning to program is the abstract nature involved in the processes of the software development cycle [Kölling, M et al, 2003]. An excellent example of this has been cited in the current trends to adopt object-oriented (OO) programming languages, such as Java and C++, as teaching languages [Sheard and Hagan, 1997; Xiaohui & Yaguan, 2010].

Whilst the selection of languages such as these can be justified by their widespread usage within the computing industry, thereby assisting the students in developing skills for employment following completion of their programmes of study, a significant issue lies in the theoretical underpinning for designing software using OO concepts. Within OO the classes, and related attributes and methods, are highly abstract. When learning to program using these languages students are not only facing the idiosyncrasies of the adopted programming language, but also the complexities of developing models of a software system which may or may not represent tangible objects in the real world [Azemi, 1995; Enzai et al, 2011; Sobrinho & Goncalves, 2011].

Addressing the issues faced by the students is hugely significant. Without the development of strategies and techniques to engage and assist students with their initial problems, then the students will soon become anxious and demotivated [Chan & Lee, 2005] and deem that programming is "too hard" or "not for them". However, computer programming can be a hugely creative and innovative subject. The importance of developing creativity within the teaching environment as a means of enhancing student engagement has been the focus of previous studies, with a positive impact being identified [Enzai, 2011; Gibson, 2011; Rinkevich, 2011; Sun, 2011]. Indeed computer programming can be considered as part art-form, and there have been successful efforts to engage traditional non-programmers, such as artists and musicians, with the development of computing technology through subjects such as physical computing [O'Sullivan &Igoe, 2004; Igoe, 2007].

The pedagogic approach to teaching programming must therefore be considered with care. Often there is a misalignment between the goals of materials and the approach that is taken [Fincher, 1999]. Alternative approaches which align with working practices in the industry have been reported, such as those that align with a cyclic approach to developing skills [Barnes et al, 1997] or utilise concepts such as peer programming [Nagappan et al, 2003]. Equally attempts to instil more reflective practices have been reported to achieve greater engagement with the subject [Lilley and Rollins, 1995][Sitthiworachart and Joy, 2008].

The different student behaviours in confronting a problematic situation can be recognized [Greyling et al, 2006]. Perkins et al (1989) named two main types: stoppers and movers. In problematic situations stoppers simply stop and abandon all hope of solving the problem on their own, while movers keep trying, modifying their code and use feedback about errors effectively. There are also extreme movers, "tinkerers", who cannot track their program, make changes more or less randomly, and like stoppers do not progress very much in their task.

TEACHING NOVICE PROGRAMMERS

Supporting the successful development of a higher cognitive understanding of conceptual, and practical, programming issues is a non-trivial problem for students. Not only are students faced with the problems of understanding the technical, or syntactical, complexities of writing code, but they are equally faced with the somewhat abstract nature of the underlying paradigms related to programming. Typically, case studies report on technical solutions with varied degrees of success, as discussed above. Within these projects, innovative ways of representing the underpinning conceptual features of code have been devised to support visualisation, or a tangible physical reaction, being generated as output from the code that the students have developed.

However, this addresses only part of the issues. The pedagogical approach that is employed when designing modules can also be highlighted from the studies. Typically employing team working, peer collaboration and review, and a high degree of creativity has been identified as key to increasing engagement, motivation and thereby attainment amongst student cohorts under study. Equally, a reported reduction in student drop out [Mota, 2007] also indicates that a change of approach to the teaching of programming promotes student belief that a successful outcome can be achieved.

Regardless of the technology deployed within the studies, there is clear evidence that the creative element bears significant benefit to the students. Whether the students are building games or movies in virtual worlds, or constructing robots to solve set problems, there exists a common theme of motivation in which students not only rise to the challenges, but also enjoy to compete within the classroom to attain better outcomes that their peers [Panadero et al, 2010].

These findings would suggest that, given support in both technical and group working aspects, developing coursework and assignments that make use of virtual worlds or robotics would lead to higher attainment amongst the students. The area of concern that arises relates to the pedagogical choices that educators adopt, the relevance of the technology to the concepts being taught, and the workload of the students. Cliburn (2006) identified that potential existed for the student workload to become excessive which would lead to a negating of the positive impacts that may otherwise be derived.

LEARNING ANALYTICS

Learning analytics have been adopted by educational institutions as a means of determining the effectiveness and quality of the learning experience for students [Brown, 2012; Greller & Drachsler, 2012]. Derived from the analytic processes that underpin much commercial activity [Larose, 2005; Han & Kamber, 2006; Cooper, 2012], higher education establishments quickly identified that mining and understanding the data that is collected through the breadth of university systems could facilitate the improvement in delivery of courses, particularly with the pervasive adoption of online systems to support teaching and learning that facilitated non-intrusive data collection [Savage & Burrows, 2007; Long & Siemens, 2011]. Implementing learning analytic initiatives is not without its issues [Buerk & Mudigonda, 2014], but the importance of implementing and enhancing such processes cannot be underestimated.

Associated to the field of Learning Analytics is the related study of Academic Analytics [Long & Siemens, 2011]. A clear distinction can be drawn between the two fields: learning analytics focuses on the study of data to benefit tutors and students, whereas academic analytics maintains a focus on supporting the administrative bodies related to institutions. Learning analytics is therefore more fine-grained in approach, treating courses and departments as central objects to a study, and is therefore more appropriate to consider in the context of the research to be undertaken.

The proliferation of data collected through online systems leads to a requirement to understand the dimensions to be monitors and evaluated through the analytic processes applied, alongside a requirement to understand the scope of such a study [Buerk & Mudigonda, 2014]. Greller and Drachsler (2012) identified six dimensions to ensure the effective mining of analytic data in an educational context (Figure 1).

The six dimensions (Stakeholders, Internal Limitations, External Constraints, Instruments, Data and Objectives) are each decomposed into sub-categories, called instantiations, and are designed to determine a holistic view of the learning process. The intention of the approach is to aid the construction of use-cases through the connection of one or more instantiations with a goal of defining clear analytical approaches through detailed specification of each use-case. That said, what is not clear is the influence that learning analytics has on the pedagogical approaches being adopted (or whether one pedagogical approach aligns to learning analytics more closely to others) [Duffy & Cunningham, 2001; Pardo & Kloos, 2011]. These instantiations are not definitive either, as they may also be decomposed further (for example, the further decomposition of students determined by Gray et al, 2014).

In relation to this research, the data will not be captured through online systems, but will be captured through a mixed method approach. The data captured will be digital in nature, but must be encoded for that data to be analysed in a meaningful way. To support the adoption of learning analytics, the encoding

Figure 1. Critical dimensions of learning analytics (Greller and Drachsler, 2012)

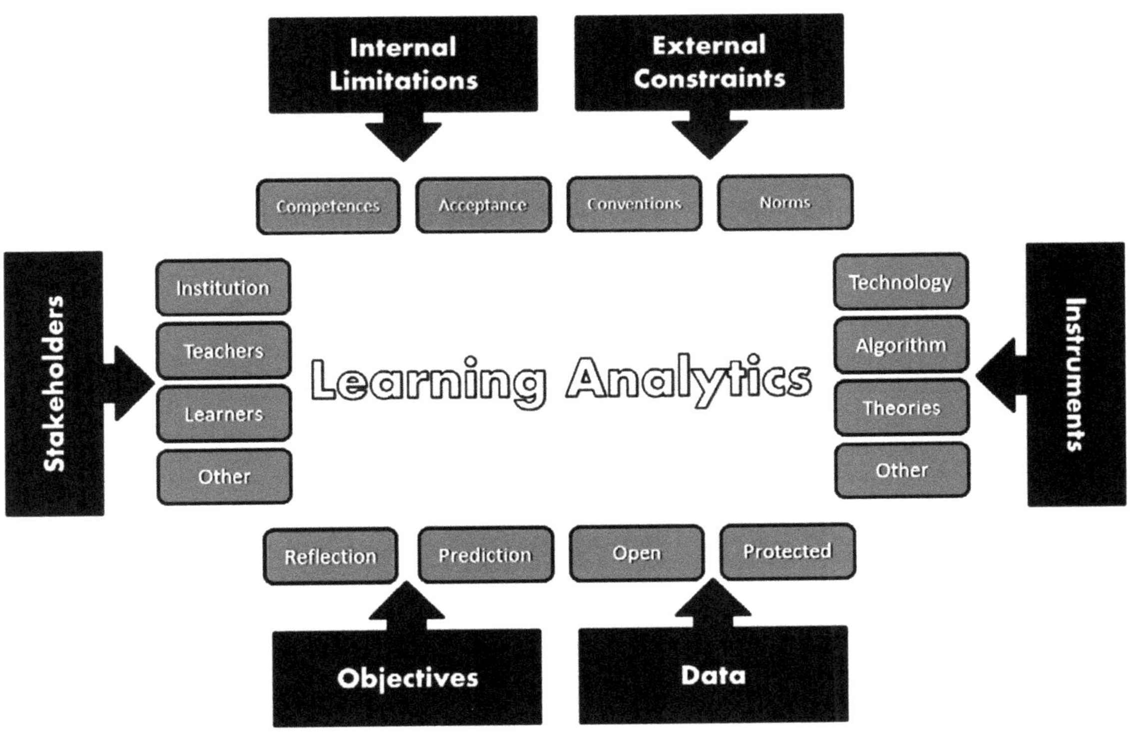

of the data shall be mapped onto the dimensions thereby enhancing the effectiveness of the analytics deployed in the research. In the context of this research, there is a single use-case that is being analysed for multiple groups of subjects. The table below (Table 1) outlines the details of this use-case.

Much weight has been placed on the product of an analytical process: the means by which the processed data can be examined and understood. A central element to the output of a number of studies is the visualisations that can be achieved to simplify or better depict the outcomes of the analytic process [Brown, 2012]. However, it has been argued that the production of visualisations may mask, or divert attention, away from underlying trends or determinant factors driving the pedagogical outcomes [Greller & Drachsler, 2012]. Essa and Ayad (2012) identify five indicators to underpin the foundation for modelling: preparation, attendance, participation, completion and social learning. These indicators support both dispositional and performance related factors that the subjects will demonstrate and assist in developing more accurate predictions. It is therefore proposed that these factors will be captured and visualised for the proposed study via the adoption of digital capture which facilitates the adoption of these indicators.

However, when implementing learning analytics one issue which must be addressed is that of the ethical considerations and management of the data [Slade & Prinsloo, 2013]. Of particular importance is in gaining the consent of the subjects of the study. Slade and Prinsloo (2013) expand upon this to identify six principles that should be implemented to construct an ethical framework in which a learning analytics study may take place. The research that is to be undertaken within this study builds upon the proposed framework and focuses upon cohorts of students learning programming rather than being an institution-wide and as such places a well-defined scope on the body of subjects to provide consent and participate in the study.

USING VIDEO AS A DATA SOURCE

One of the difficulties when adopting video as a data capture mechanism relates to the objectivity of the recording and the subsequent encoding process that the video evidence goes through. It is possible, in some situations, where the question of objectivity becomes a central concern. For example, studies that follow existing coding patterns related to a well-defined theoretical field [Berkhout et al, 2008].

Table 1. Use case and sample values for analysis

Dimension	Values
Stakeholders	*Subjects:* Groups of students
Objective	*Reflection:* Analyse the interactions between groups of students undertaking project work, and identify the engagement and building knowledge of students through the work undertaken
Data	*Dataset:* Student video recordings of the project completion, videos of reflective elements *Indicators:* Verbal interactions, body language *Time scale:* 6 week time frame with 2x2hr recordings per week
Instruments	*Pedagogic theory:* Hypothesis that practical engagement drives better understanding of subject *Technology:* Video analytics, statistics *Presentation:* Visualisation of coded findings
External limitations	*Conventions:* Consider whether privacy, ethics and norms have been identified and appropriate action taken
Internal limitations	*Competencies:* Can the data captured be interpreted, visualised and analysed in a meaningful and effective manner

In these cases the researcher must demonstrate that there interaction in the process has been minimal, and the concerns will focus on objectivity and quality of the evidence gathered and the interpretations derived from processing the evidence. In situations such as this, it is likely that the video evidence may be a valid data source from the point of capture.

To address this issue, this research considers the video recordings as sources of data rather than as data in themselves. The processing of the video to determine the underlying patterns shall make use of Learning Analytics practices and tools to derive the data for analysis. Domain knowledge to aid coding of the video and understand the social context of the interactions between the subjects is held by the researcher. Therefore the coding of the video will provide a rich medium from which the essential data to analyse and understand the outcomes can be determined. The critical factor in determining accurate observations and findings will lie in the coding of the participant behaviours within the captured video.

CODING AND GESTURE RECOGNITION

Within this study, each session would result in many hours of video recording which will require analysis. However, there is a risk that videos might be viewed in an unsynchronized order or may be inadvertently missed. To overcome this issue then the captured evidence will be carefully managed and maintained to ensure that sufficient triangulation of evidence occurs. The methodology makes use of a semiotic approach to capture the elements which are contained within each segment of video and determine the key "signs" of an event occurring [Geertz, 1988; Barron & Engle, 2007]. Furthermore, to ensure that each event is captured in a holistic form necessary for the study, then multiple video cameras will be deployed. Each student group will record their own coursework with a video camera and additional cameras will capture the broader classroom environment during sessions. The importance of this step lies in contextualizing each action within a video segment with those actions which are occurring simultaneously [DuFon, 2002].

A further significant issue lies in the interpretation of the evidence captured. There is a rich set of data that will be captured during the process of undertaking the research. Some of the evidence will be represented through audio and behavioural presentations which will be captured in the video evidence. Capturing these elements, and their significance, needs to be consistently applied to all the evidential video material which will be captured. There are concepts which can be applied from ethnographic studies to assist in overcoming these issues. For example, there have been previous studies which have considered the modelling of video events to determine the order in which events have occurred in a collected data source [Hibino & Rundensteiner, 1994]. Other evidence can be derived from the student assessment and student feedback which is gathered at the end of the module. Initial investigations in a related pilot study have demonstrated the effectiveness of this evidence as a tool that can be deployed for triangulating the focal ethnographic elements of the study [Gavan & Anderson, 2012].

Furthermore, the body of work in learning analytics has failed to focus on the complex combinations of factors that drive deeper engagement in learning [Buckingham Shum & Deakin Crick, 2012]. The engagement of students in the process is central to building effective learning experiences and, as such, is a key driver of this research. Indeed, this is not a new concept and has been applied to educational theory throughout the years [Dewey, 1933 p 30; Yazzie-Mintz, 2009]. One approach to addressing this issue, and also offering a means through which effective visualisations can be developed, has been research focussed on Learning Power. Created using the hypothesis of identifying the "power to learn"

[Deakin Crick et al, 2004], the multi-dimensional construct is underpinned by seven identified dimensions that lead to learning. These have been evaluated using the Effective Lifelong Learning Inventory (ELLI) [Claxton, 1999]. Buckingham Shum and Deakin Crick (2012) define the seven dimensions as:

- **Changing and Learning:** Recognising that learning skills are learnable
- **Critical Curiosity:** Maintaining a wish to discover
- **Meaning Making:** Linking know facts with what is being learnt
- **Dependence and Fragility:** Encountering problems or making mistakes when learning cause the learner to become averse to risk taking and limit opportunities
- **Creativity:** Identifying new opportunities and potential when learning
- **Learning Relationships:** Maintaining an effective balance between social and private learning
- **Strategic Awareness:** The most effective students a fully aware of their own learning

The dimensions can then be mapped onto categorisations of students (see Table 2). The classification relates to a holistic view of the behaviours of the students. This is not to determine that a student will only exhibit behaviours within a single category, but the visualisation techniques applied to Learning Power determine the ever changing profile that students may exhibit as they develop through the learning process. This is particularly pertinent in relation to the research study, as an ELLI profile captures

Table 2. Seven learning dimensions [Vital Partnership, 2010]

Changing and Learning	Being like....... **'The Explorer'** Changing and Learning versus being stuck and static	Seeing learning as a positive experience. Seeking out new learning opportunities. Accepting responsibility for learning and having belief in personal capacity to learn/ change.
Critical Curiosity	Being like....... **'The Investigator'** Critical Curiosity versus passivity	Enjoying a challenge and confronting perplexity. Learning by working things out, problem-solving, seeking out information and better understanding. Enjoying questioning, finding out, self-directed research; refusing to accept things at face value.
Meaning Making	Being like....... **'The Integrator'** Meaning Making versus data accumulation	Seeking to make connections, integrate ideas, and make a 'whole' from separate parts. Relating new learning to relevant past and current personal experience. Pulling learning from different sources.
Creativity	Being like....... **'The Inventor'** Creativity versus being rule-bound	Exploring possibilities, enjoying Novelty and uncertainty. Using creative imagination; 'playing' with ideas and concepts. Willing to let go of control and take risks, seeing mistakes as opportunities for learning.
Resilience	Being like....... **'The Builder'** Resilience versus fragility and dependence	Enjoying problem-based learning. Being willing to 'wrestle' with difficult concepts and persistent in achieving personal goals. Good at accepting and managing negative emotions, fears and frustrations related to learning.
Strategic Awareness	Being like....... **'The Navigator'** Strategic Awareness versus being robotic	Being thoughtful about intentions and making conscious choices about how to learn. Planning and applying effective learning strategies; reflecting upon personal learning experiences and taking responsibility for own learning development.
Learning Relationships	Being like....... **'The Networker'** Positive Learning Relationships versus isolation or dependence	Having good social resources to learn through; knowing how to work with others. Benefits from pooled learning and shared expertise, enjoying collaboration but confident and capable when required to work alone.

the key attributes related to engagement and lifelong learning; most notably self-awareness, the strive to evolve knowledge and the building of relationships between students to help develop understanding [Small & Deakin Crick, 2008]. This categorisation of learning skills maps well onto the problem-based approach that has been adopted within the study, and therefore lends itself well as an initial focus for the visualisation of data gathered through the video evidence. This table shall inform the selection of appropriate coding to apply to the video evidence for the analysis phase of the project.

ANALYSING THE DATA

One of the key benefits of using video technology is the richness and depth of reliable data that can be captured [Edwards & Westgate, 1987; Gonzalez, 2012]. The opportunity thereby exists for the video captured to be analysed for quantitative data (such as the time spent by the students in performed tasks] and also for qualitative data (such as the nature of interactions between the students, or the strategies being adopted by the teams in performing tasks). In terms of the analysis of data from the video capture, a semiotic approach may therefore be taken [Geertz, 1988] in which words, actions and phrases may be encoded and linked into sequences for analysis [Barron & Engle, 2007]. Data visualisation techniques will be explored as a means of parsing and mining the encoded data sets which result from the video analysis [Fry, 2007]. Visualisation techniques will assist in dealing with the large amounts of data that will be captured through a video source. When analysing the data, an inductive approach will be taken. The will enable the full exploitation of one advantage of video; its ability for a reliable and full data capture to be reviewed [Derry et al., 2010]. The result of reviewing the entire is that the frequency of events can be identified and confirmed, and that unusual or unexpected events can also be included in the analysis.

Whilst video capture will provide a rich level of information for analysis, there is an associated issue with this process that the amount of footage captured can be overwhelming and the boundaries of individual events can be difficult to determine [Plowman, 1999; DuFon, 2002], although this will be addressed through the adoption of an inductive approach. To this extent, it will be important to develop a framework through which the captured video streams can be reviewed [Bowman, 1994; Derry et al., 2010]. The significance in creating such a framework for analysis is to ensure that the subtle gestures and actions of the members of the student team are appropriately captured for analysis to determine any significance in the context within which they occur.Determining the effectiveness of teaching and the progression that student's make on introductory programming courses has been a problem that has been studies over a long period of time [Watson, Li and Godwin, 2013]. Whilst studies have considered a wide range of indicators to determine the factors that may assist student success in the subject, there has been some research in the adoption of predictive analytics to assess the learning outcomes achieved by students [Ventura, 2005; Bennedsen & Caspersen, 2006].

In order to derive meaning from the captured data to understand the effect that the approach is having upon the student learning, then tools can be adopted from the broader field of data processing and applied to the large data sets that have been collated. Specifically, tools from the fields of Data Mining and Predictive Analysis can be applied to assist in developing a deeper understanding of the emerging patterns. Data mining techniques can be applied to the raw encoded data to identify emergent patterns within the data sets [McCue, 2006]. Predictive Analytics, on the other hand, will facilitate the projection of trends in data to determine the most likely outcomes [Geerdink, 2013]. These may then be used to determine the most appropriate action that would lead to the desired outcome, should this not be evident. Applying these concepts within a learning context has been identified as a means of producing 'actionable intelligence' [Campbell et al., 2007].

This approach can be validated as the technique has been utilised in a different context with success. Nebot et al. (2010) determine that research on the effectiveness of e-learning courses can be evaluated by analysing the behaviour patterns of students as they progress through an online system. Equally, Serrano et al (2012) identify the use of similar metrics when evaluating educational games. In both cases, these studies embody the emerging fields of Learning Analytics [Brown, 2010] and Educational Data Mining (EDM) [Abdous et al, 2012]. The current focus in the field lies in the capture and analysis of data collated from online resources, such as websites or games, and aims to lead to understanding of student engagement and behaviour in order to make predictions regarding future student learning [Buerk & Mudigonda, 2014].

However, there have been studies that make use of this approach in the analysis of data captured through video streams. Abdous et al (2012) report upon a study in which the participants were distance students who communicated through a live video stream. The methodology has been underpinned by earlier research [Garcia et al, 2011] and relies on stages of pre-processing, mining and post-processing to undertake multimodal discourse analysis [Erickson, 2006]. The stages can be decomposed into the following processes as defined by Chan (2013):

- **Perceiving (Pre-Processing):** To identify which data is important
- **Comparing (Pre-Processing):** To initially identify similarities
- **Contrasting (Mining):** Consider differences in data or emerging patterns
- **Aggregating (Mining):** Add structure to the finding and categorise
- **Ordering (Mining):** Higher level analysis to determine hierarchies of categories
- **Establishing Linkages and Relationships (Post-Processing):** To identify the links between the categories and sub-categories
- **Speculating (Post-Processing):** To identify theses in the context of the research.

Clearly in relation to this research the seven stages of the analysis phase will rely on the data coding phase of the data collection process as coding should assist in the alignment of similarities within the observed recordings. Linking to the ELLI dimensions discussed earlier places the observations into context of the students' journey through the project work undertaken. It is envisaged that the ELLI dimensions that be further decomposed through the coding process to relate to the dimensions of Learning Analytics [Greller & Drachsler, 2012], and the associated instantiations. In doing so, the relationship between the initial use-case and the research findings shall be retained and the impact of the study aligned to the experimental design of the coursework undertaken.

The Student Context

Students are requested at the commencement of the academic year to indicate their programming experience due to the variety of educational backgrounds presented to the Department. One of the indicators of experience is the prior knowledge of a recognised programming language. The academic year 2014-2015 saw 147 students join the Department of Computing, of which 117 complied with the request.

In determining the level of experience that the students had gained prior to joining the degree programme, the qualitative comments that the students returned was analysed. The key criteria indicated by the students in this regard related to the number of languages that the students had been exposed to, and also the number of programs that the students had developed. For those students who could confidently identify a number of languages, or relate programming theoretical concepts to the code that they had developed, then the student was judged to have extensive experience in relation to the cohort. If a student could identify one language or one concept, or identify that they had developed a single program, then that student was identified as having minimal experience.

THE COURSEWORK CONTEXT

The coursework task that was designed for this study adopted a PBL approach. Building upon the Little et al (2009) definition of student engagement, the students are challenged in the assessment to solve problems through the design, construction and programming of a small robot using Lego Mindstorms NXT 2 kits. Through this the students are empowered to develop their own designs as they interpret the problems that must be solved. In addressing the problems that may be faced through the use of a problem-based, or active, learning approach, the assessment requires students to work in small teams of up to four students. The limit on the number of students in a group was determined through experience when teaching other modules; larger group sizes often would result in some students becoming disengaged and subsequently not participating fully in the activity.

The study utilised evidence that has been gathered from four groups of students who are undertaking a first year programming course. Groups of students undertake the exercise utilising the robots and working closely within teams. Further groups of students complete an equivalent exercise which does not utilise the robots but uses a more traditional programming exercise for the coursework to implement a game, thereby providing a control set. The students completing the coursework using the robots work within teams of 3 or 4 students to design, build and program a robot that will complete a series of predefined tasks. To complete the work, the groups of students meet for 4 hours per week (as two 2 hours sessions per week) over a period of five weeks. Selection to the groups will be randomised, with this study utilising a post-test only randomised design. Each session is observed. Comparative data is collected from the cohort to determine the impact that introducing the robots into the curriculum has had. Following the completion of the exercises, interviews are conducted to gather further data from the participants. One group of students within the study provides historical data from a previous year who did not make use of robots in an equivalent coursework exercise will also be used in the study to support empirical results.

Student Participation

The coursework also required the students to maintain video diaries of their progress throughout each of the challenges within the coursework. The purpose of recording video diaries being two-fold. Firstly the diaries encourage the students to be reflective practitioners as they discuss the work that they have undertaken in the previous week; with the importance of reflection being identified as a significant driver to aid engagement [Lilley & Rollins, 1995; Sitthiworachart & Joy, 2008]. Secondly as all group members are required to participate in the recording of the diaries and discuss their involvement, then the issues surrounding the assessment of individuals within the teams [Hahn, Mentz & Meyer, 2009] is also addressed.

The Interpretative Process

Once qualitative data has been collected, which for this study largely refers to transcribed video recordings, questionnaires and interview responses, the problem that arises is how to use the data to develop conjectures, hypotheses, and ultimately knowledge that will contribute to the field of study.

To facilitate the analysis and interpretation of the data that has been captured, a coding system is applied to all transcripts. Whilst coding data may be a highly subjective process, the implementation of codes that are hierarchical and applied to sentences within the transcripts supports the identification of the underlying themes that emerge through the data available. These themes are then to be triangulated with facial encoding, questionnaires and interviews to verify the coding in support of an interpretation of the data. For this study four key themes are identified: student engagement, conceptual understanding, student attainment, learning to program.

PRE-COURSE EXPERIENCE

Programming is a key skill in the subject area of Computing and demonstrable knowledge of the guiding practices and principles underpins the future careers of professionals irrespective of career choice; analysts, software testers, or software developers. It is therefore essential that all students achieve a level of competence in computer programming to evidence their understanding of the relevant principles, to discuss or communicate appropriate theories with their peers and establish the appropriate analysis and problem solving skills required to practice in the industry. Therefore Programming: Concepts to Construction is a compulsory module that all students must undertake at level 4.

During their first programming session students are posed the question "What is your level of programming experience?" No definition or elaboration of the question is deliberately provided in order to gain a full sense of where the students own knowledge and their perceptions of their knowledge is positioned and a starting point gained. The rationale for posing this question is to gain an understanding of the level of exposure that a student has gained in computer programming, potentially and understanding of the languages or paradigms that the students have encountered and, most importantly, to determine whether misconceptions may exist in a student's interpretation of programming. The students are required to email their responses to the tutor.

Of the 147 students that are enrolled, 117 replied. The replies received indicated that 73 students stated that they had no programming experience, 37 students stated that they had minimum experience (Figure 2) and qualified their answers with comments such as;

"I did one unit of programming in college but still have little knowledge of programming" (Student 4)

"Well I had a few lessons in college on object oriented programming however, i still don't know most of the basics of programming and i have no experience in any language." (Student 73)

"Visual Basic to create small programs" (Student 114)

Only 1 student considered themselves with extensive experience having undertaken Basic for 2 years and a further 6 cited experiences of using HTML as their knowledge of programming;

Figure 2. Programming experience

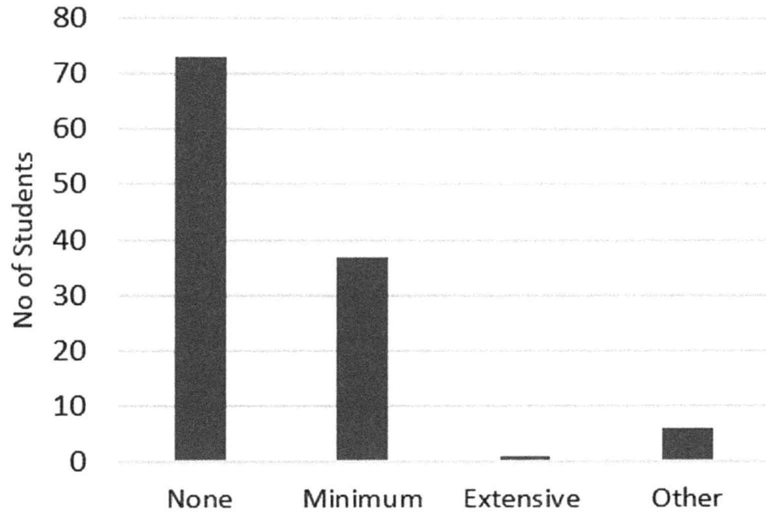

"The main languages used were HTML, CSS, JavaScript and PHP" (Student 3)

"I have done some programming with HTML Code in A-level and that is all." (Student 97)

Using the definition of programming for this study those students who indicated that their knowledge is based primarily from a scripting language, or even a mark up language, and to no significant depth other than an aspect of the course they were undertaking, are deemed as having no experience (figure 3).

Further enquires were made of the students who categorised themselves as having minimum experience via tutor questioning during the following session. This entailed a discourse of their anonymised responses to the initial question followed by a further open question "In what context have you gained your programming experience?" This also afforded an opportunity for those who had not previously

Figure 3. Programming experience

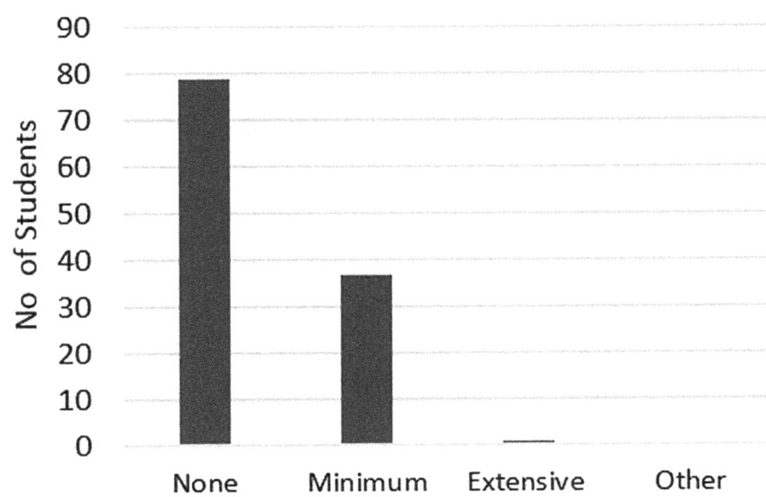

responded to the initial question to provide an indication of the group experience level. The elicited group discussion indicated that the students obtained their experiences via the classroom through the application of Visual Basic software for a specific coursework element with the coding constructs provided by the tutor. The students indicated that little or no work was required outside of the classroom as answers were provided in areas of complexity.

INTERPRETATION / SUMMARY

An initial indication from the 80% of students that responded, 54% are considered to have no programming experience, 25% have a minimum level of experience and 1% has extensive experience. However, as illustrated in Figure 2, following the further discussions with the student cohort it became evident that 79% of the student cohort can be categorised as having no experience.

IN-COURSE EXPERIENCE

Prior to undertaking the construction and implementation of the Lego Mindstorms robots a baseline of programming experience needed to be established. In order to begin the practical and theoretical underpinning of programming concepts that are essential for undertaking coding coursework, students were required to undertake the construction of a portfolio of small Java programs using the Eclipse IDE that increased in complexity throughout the portfolio. The activities were delivered by a virtual learning environment during a timetabled laboratory session. Each activity consisted of a number of smaller exercises / activities with each building from the preceding tasks, thereby enabling the students to continuously develop upon their growing experience throughout the activities. Students were encouraged to discuss with their peers and tutors each of the activities to ensure understanding and resolve problems. Tutors would not provide direct answers to problems but would guide students through the theoretical underpinning of the problem.

PROGRAMMING ACTIVITY

The coursework being investigated for this research requires students to utilise the skills that they have developed through the preceding activities. This might require the students to utilise concepts that they encountered earlier, or to extend their knowledge through the enhancement of their skill sets.

In the completion of this coursework the student teams were required to record blogs each week at the end of the levels to discuss what they had done, what the challenges were that they had faced and what actions they had taken to resolve any issues. The videos were to be no longer than 10 minutes in duration.

VIDEO ANALYSIS: PRELIMINARY FINDINGS

An initial analysis has been undertaken through the examination of the transcripts of the video evidence provided by the student teams. The teams were required to record blogs each week at the end of the levels to discuss what they had done, what the challenges were that they had faced and what actions they had taken to resolve any issues. To understand the content of the transcripts, the frequency of the words used by the students has been represented using word clouds. As a visualisation technique, a word cloud is a useful representation for uni-variate data; in this case the word frequency, to gain a holistic view of the language being used by the students in the teams. The purpose for this is to test the premise that as students' knowledge and confidence increases, then their use of language and terminology will change to reflect the understanding of the subject that they have gained. Whilst this representation provides a high-level viewpoint and there are additional features that could be mined (for example, the distance between words that make up phrases), word frequency as an analysis measure is adequate for the purposes of this study as the student transcripts demonstrate that the students typically make very short statements in turn on the video, resulting in word distance becoming relatively meaningless.

Presented here are the visualisations of transcripts for four of the teams. The transcripts are presented in level order (i.e. level one to five), and are broadly representative of the visualisations developed for all the teams. The colour of the words presented is immaterial, but the size of the words corresponds directly to the frequency as captured in the transcripts; that is, the larger the word the more often it has been used in the discussions (figures 4-7).

Figure 4. Control Group 1

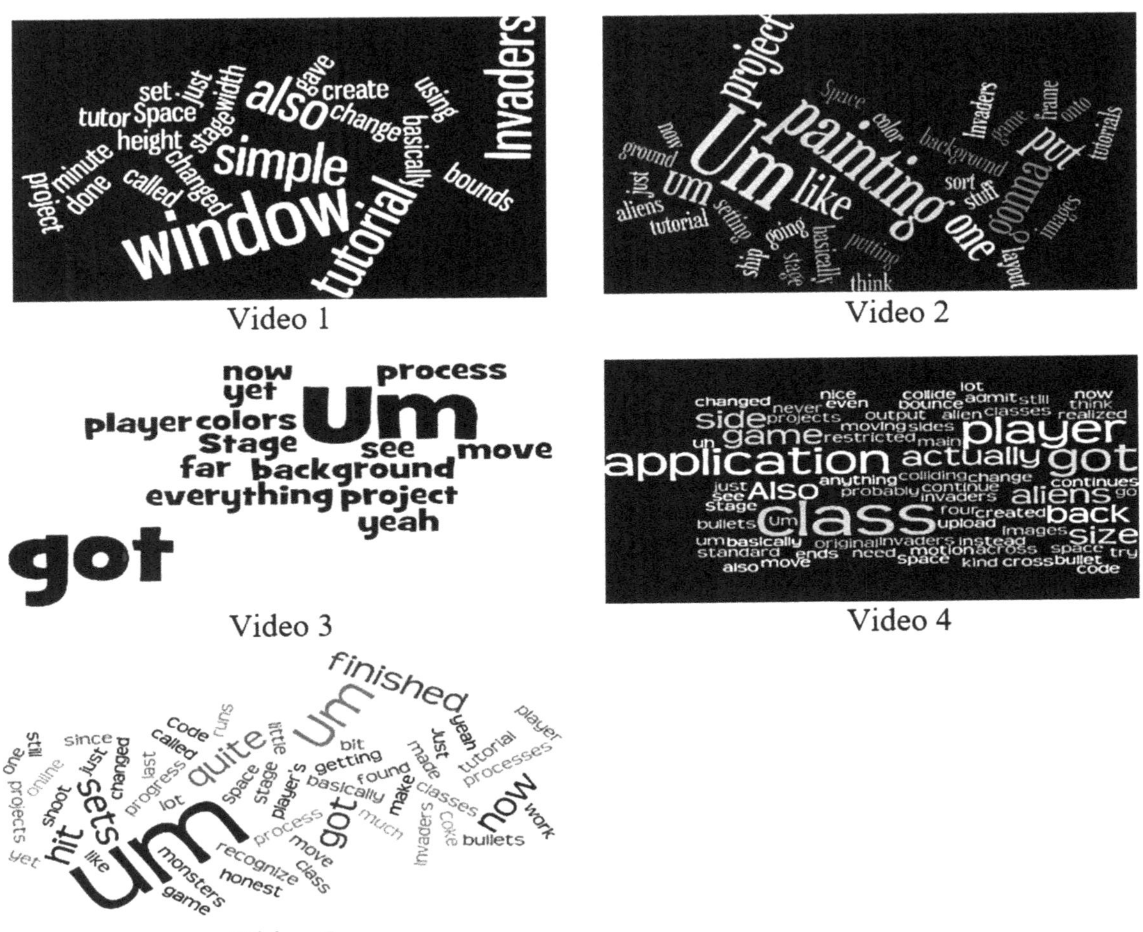

Video 1 Video 2 Video 3 Video 4 Video 5

Figure 5. Team A: Level 1 - 5

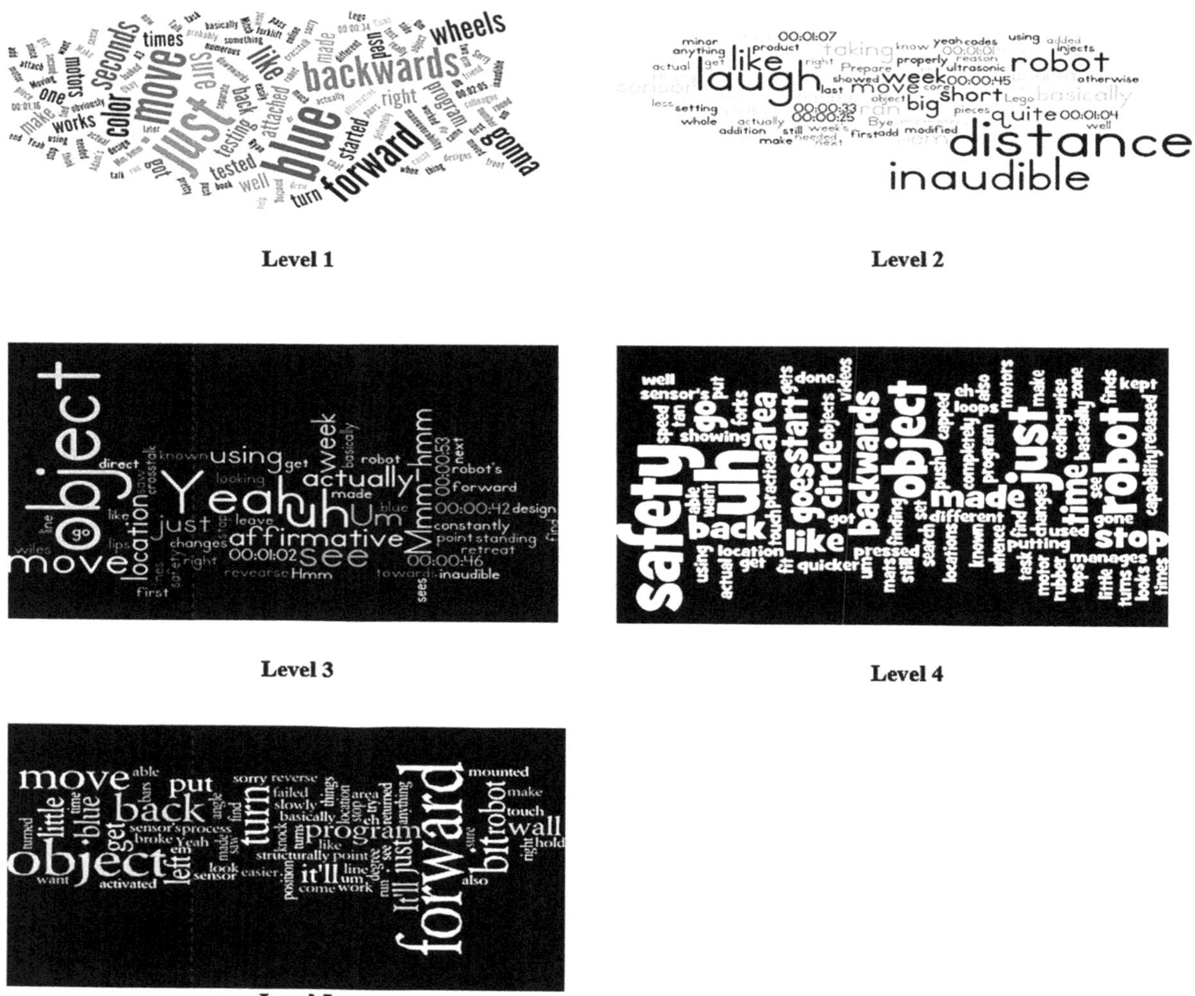

Level 1 Level 2 Level 3 Level 4 Level 5

Word clouds are insightful representations of the transcripts in that they provide a clear visualisation of the language that has been used by the students. It is evident from the word clouds that there are a number of words used that might be considered irrelevant or meaningless; "words" such as "um". The analysis of the word clouds will therefore focus upon those words that can be linked to desired behaviours or approaches adopted by the students, such as the development of technical competence or the building of employability skills that can be evidenced through the language and terms being used.

VIDEO ANALYSIS: INCLUSIVE

The conversations between group members were transcribed verbatim. From the transcriptions it was possible to determine the category or categories that the conversations could best be assigned to. Table

Figure 6. Team B: Level 1 - 5

1 indicates the number of occurrences of the coded key words. It is important to note that not all of the categories will appear within every transcript. In fact, it is vital to acknowledge this as it is directly representative of how student behaviour and attitudes move throughout the course (tables 2-3).

Robot Groups

The results that have been presented in Table 1, have been normalised to facilitate direct comparison between the levels. The resultant figures are presented in Table 2 below.

The tables above present the code words and their holding category. As a result, each of the four categories (Engagement, Employability, Technical and Attainment) can be presented independently to determine the impact that the students vocalise through the transcriptions of the video diaries. As identified earlier, engagement is representative of the students' wish to participate. Attainment, on the other

Figure 7. Team C: Level 1 - 5

hand, is a representation of the students' desire to achieve improved outcomes or grades. The final two categories relate to the skills that the students develop throughout the coursework. Technical skills are typically indicated by the students' appropriate use of terminology when discussing implementation details. Employability skills manifest through the students discussing broader recognised concepts, such as working together to the more holistic learning experience.

Throughout the period in which the coursework ran, video and data evidence has been captured for the purposes of undertaking an emotion FACS analysis. In relation to this study, the purpose of the FACS analysis is to provide a point of triangulation between the beliefs that the students have expressed through their video logs, and the pre-course data that was captured through the questionnaires that were completed. The importance of embedding this data into the analysis is that it provides evidence of the emotional state of the students as they undertake the tasks that were set. The data was collated through

Table 1. Control group

		Level 1	Level 2	Level 3	Level 4	Level 5
Engagement	Peer Interaction					
Employability	Reflection		1			
Engagement	Problem Solving					
Engagement	Pride		1			1
Technical	Concepts	3	2		1	1
Attainment	Belief					
Technical	Strategy	4	3	1	1	1
Technical	Creativity					
Technical	Design	2			1	
Technical	Implementation					
Technical	Application				1	
Employability	Collaboration	3		1		
Engagement	Extra-Curricular					
Attainment	Competence					

Table 2. Code word frequency

		Level 1	Level 2	Level 3	Level 4	Level 5
Engagement	Peer Interaction	174	106	120	74	74
Employability	Reflection	6	6	2	3	10
Engagement	Problem Solving	35	23	24	15	28
Engagement	Pride	17	11	9	9	14
Technical	Concepts	4	3	5	2	3
Attainment	Belief	10	15	10	7	12
Technical	Strategy	17	11	13	4	5
Technical	Creativity	6	1	0	2	1
Technical	Design	45	32	19	27	17
Technical	Implementation	15	11	15	7	19
Technical	Application	27	16	13	11	14
Employability	Collaboration	13	10	3	4	7
Engagement	Extra-Curricular	0	0	1	2	3
Attainment	Competence	4	4	3	10	19

each of the assignments within the coursework (level 1 to 5 challenges), and the expressions aligned with the emotion FACS coding system discussed in the previous chapter. As such, this evidence will provide an opportunity not only to understand the student emotional journey throughout the coursework, but also as a means of underpinning the interpretations of student engagement captured in the other stages of data gathering.

Table 3. Normalised code frequency

		Level 1	Level 2	Level 3	Level 4	Level 5
Engagement	Peer Interaction	47	43	51	42	33
Employability	Reflection	2	2	1	2	4
Engagement	Problem Solving	9	9	10	8	12
Engagement	Pride	5	4	4	5	6
Technical	Concepts	1	1	2	1	1
Attainment	Belief	3	6	4	4	5
Technical	Strategy	5	4	5	2	2
Technical	Creativity	2	0	0	1	0
Technical	Design	12	13	8	15	8
Technical	Implementation	4	4	6	4	8
Technical	Application	7	6	5	6	6
Employability	Collaboration	3	4	1	2	3
Engagement	Extra-Curricular	0	0	0	1	1
Attainment	Competence	1	2	1	6	8

As the video and photographic evidence was analysed, incidents of differing emotions were logged relative to the level that the students were undertaking. It should be noted that not all videos that were analysed resulted in the recognised emotions being identifiable. However, those that were recorded are presented in Table 4.

IN-COURSE INTERPRETATION / SUMMARY

There are clearly patterns that emerge through the visualisation of the transcripts as represented by word clouds. Despite the limitation highlighted, that this representation is best suited to uni-variate data, the students use of terminology can be seen to change throughout the coursework.

Table 4. Recorded emotions

Emotion FACS Expressions	Level 1	Level 2	Level 3	Level 4	Level 5
Joy	11	12	12	12	13
Sadness / Disappointment	8	6	7	6	2
Anger / Frustration	9	6	2	4	1
Fear					
Disgust					
Contempt	2		1		
Surprise	9	13	13	10	12
Neutral		3	9	9	10

As an example, team A spend most of the level one recording discussing the task rather than the solution that they have developed. This is demonstrated by their use of terms such as "backwards", "forwards" and "blue" that are directly linked to the task (where blue represents the colour of the line that the team have selected to determine when the robot had reached the end of its movement. However, increasingly through subsequent levels the students begin to discuss implementation details. They refer to "objects" (linked to the programming language / terminology used in Java) and "program".

A similar pattern emerges through the discussions of team B. However whilst they also focus on the task in level 1, their subsequent discussions not only reveal a growing technical competence but also developing soft skills, problem-solving and increased engagement. By week 3, the students are considering collaboration in the team through "discussion". In level 4 the conversation is focussed heavily on problem-solving as they discuss issues related to the surface on which the robot is operating. In level 5, the students are discussing video "conferences" and also extra-curricular work over the "Easter" period (when there are no laboratory sessions).

Equally for team C, there is evidence throughout the visualisations that their focus moves from discussing the problem that has been set towards considering the technical solution they are developing. Perhaps most interesting in team C's discourse is that they demonstrate pride in the output they achieve. As an example of this, they discuss how much they "like" their robot.

When considering the coded transcripts, the developing patterns that emerge are indicative of the student experience and supportive of other data collected through this study. In relation to the engagement factors, the most significant code identifies that the students maintain a high level of engagement with their team members as peer interaction remains consistently high. Outside of this area, the students demonstrate broadly increasing through their problem-solving, pride and discussion of extra-curricular work. Whilst there is an apparent dip in pride for levels 2 and 3, this could be attributed to the students feeling a sense of accomplishment on completing the first level (leading to a higher score) that stabilises at levels two and three, and then then rises again as the more challenging levels are completed.

In the area of attainment, the students' belief in their abilities rises considerably after completing level one. This falls a little through levels three and four which are more technically challenging, but increases back towards its peak levels by level five as the students complete the challenge. Accompanying this, the students' levels of competence, and ability to discuss problems or solutions in technical terminology, rises consistently and considerably through the coursework. Indeed, the students possess more understanding of programming than they believe they do by level 4 of the challenge.

In the technical coding, the students' creativity and design discussions are clearly linked as both reach peak values around levels one and four. These link directly to the points in the coursework in which the teams must build or adapt their robots. The students focus their creativity around the implementation of the physical device. This is perhaps understandable, as the conceptual or abstract nature of designing code requires a level of experience before creativity or alternative designs can be employed. There would also appear to exist a link between the students considering strategy and the conceptual understanding of the tasks. As student understanding of concepts grow, then they are more able to apply the concepts to maximise the output and minimise the additional effort in successfully completing tasks. Concept and strategy discussion reduce towards the level five logs, but this is understandable as the students are completing the final level of the coursework. The level of application, or discussion of testing results, remains consistent throughout the coursework, but the discussions around implementing coding solutions peak at levels three and five. This aligns perfectly with the discussions of design and creativity. Where the levels required the students to evaluate the design of the devices, then this became the major focus of the discussion. In the other levels the students centred their discussion on the coding elements. What is particularly notable is that the students are discussing the code elements of their coursework as the key priority by level five.

In relation to employability, there is a more obvious link between reflection and collaboration throughout the coursework. In earlier stages collaboration is very important to the students as the teams are forming and team roles becoming established. However, by level five it is the reflective elements that become more significant to the students. They have the experience of both developing a device/application, and also the experience of working with peers, to discuss and reflect upon.

The results that have been presented relating to FACS coding appear to demonstrate key trends in the student emotional experience that is presented throughout the coursework. The initial observation to note is that start at a high level and increase slightly over the length of the coursework as each level is completed. It might therefore be suggested that the students' engagement with the coursework, leads to a satisfaction amongst the cohort and that this rises as the students successfully complete increasingly difficult challenges.

In relation to negative emotional expressions, there is also an identifiable trend of these decreasing between levels 1 to 5. The student disappointment and frustration would appear to diminish as their ability builds through the challenges. This also leads to greater resolve, hence the students become less disappointed and more capable and engaged in developing solutions to meet the challenges that they face.

Perhaps the most interesting outcome that can be observed in the FACS analysis is the apparent rise and then fall in the levels of surprise expressed by the students. A possible explanation may lie in the students developing enhanced skills. The level 1 challenge that the students complete places limited demands on the abilities of the students, and it might therefore be expected that the students do not express much surprise when they complete this level. However, the next two challenges are more complex and, whilst they build upon the preceding level, do demonstrate step changes in the level of technical skill that the students must possess to successfully complete those levels. The final two levels continue the learning process of incrementally building skills and, having successfully completed the second and third challenge, it might also be expected that the students are not surprised that they can successfully complete increasingly difficult levels. This is equally underpinned by the neutral expressions that the students develop; as the skill level increases the students will begin to develop belief in their abilities.

POST-COURSE EXPERIENCE

Student Questionnaires

Quantitative primary data was gathered from questionnaires aimed at the students own perception of their participation with the coursework. The questions were categorised into the Cognitive; Emotional; Participation/Interaction and Performance factors of engagement.

The design of the questionnaires is such that it explores the students' personal experience in such a way that this can be aligned with the analysis undertaken using in-course data captured through video evidence. Significant links can be drawn between

1. Transcript analysis and cognitive, participation and performance factors
2. FACS analysis and emotional factors
3. Code word analysis and interaction and cognitive factors.

The questionnaire thereby provides a key indication of the student perception of the experience that they have gained through the module.

Questionnaire Mean Summary

The following table shows the mean values of the quantitative data gathered. The mean value is on a Likert scale of 1 – 5 (3 being neutral) (Table 5).

The Table 6 shows the lowest, highest and median value of the engagement factors measured.

As the scoring of the questionnaires can be considered across four central categories (cognitive, emotional, participation and performance), it is useful to determine the underlying trends in scoring by the students across the categories. To achieve this, the number of submissions for each ranking (1-5) has been calculated for each category and the data has been normalised to effectively show the percentage weighting of each score within a given category. The resultant values are presented in the graph below (Figure 8).

STUDENT EVALUATIONS

Following the completion of the coursework each student in the cohort completes an evaluation form which gathers both qualitative and quantitative data relating to the student experience on the module. The evaluation form is a generic form used by the department. The paper based form is given out in

Table 5. Questionnaire individual mean values

Question	Engagement Type	Mean Value (1-5)
Ensure that you study on a regular basis	Cognitive	4
Put forth effort into the programming activities	Cognitive	4
Complete all homework tasks	Cognitive	4
Look over course material between classes	Cognitive	4
Listen carefully during classes	Cognitive	4
Attend every class	Cognitive	5
Apply what you learn in class to other aspects of your life	Emotional	3
Think about the programming module in between classes	Emotional	4
Desire to learn the course material	Emotional	4
Find ways to make the course more interesting	Emotional	4
Ask questions when you do not understand concepts	Participation / Interaction	4
Have fun in class	Participation / Interaction	4
Participation in group activities	Participation / Interaction	4
Contact your tutor outside of class about the programming module	Participation / Interaction	3
Help fellow students on the programming module	Participation / Interaction	4
Feel like you will get a good grade	Performance	4
Feel confident that you can learn and do well in class	Performance	4

Table 6. Questionnaire overall mean values

Lowest Mean	3	Q 14 Contact your tutor outside of class about the programming module Q7 Apply what you learn in class to other aspects of your life
Highest Mean	5	Q 6 Attend every class
Cognitive Mean Value	4	Cognitive engagement factors
Emotional Mean Value	4	Emotional engagement factors
Participation/Interaction Mean Value	4	Participation/Interaction engagement factors
Performance Mean Value	4	Performance engagement factors
Total Mean	4	Total engagement factors

Figure 8. Normalised average scores

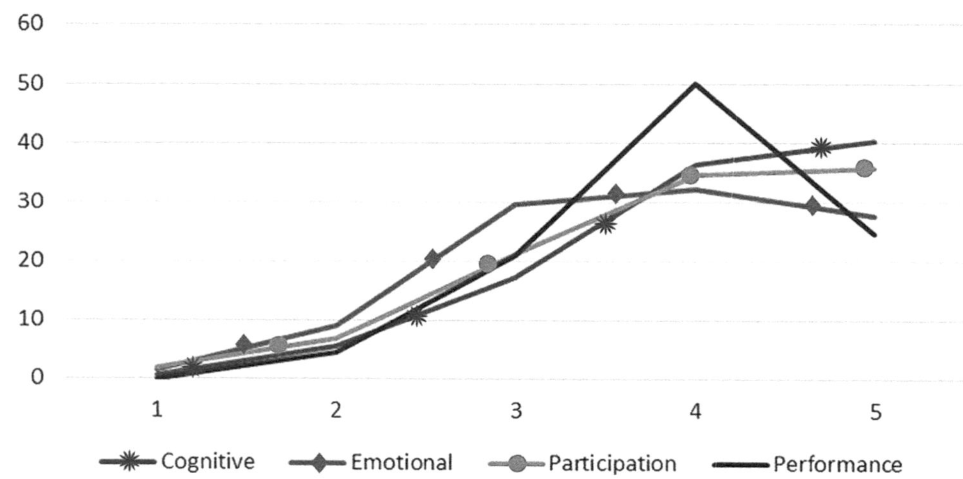

class and students are given 15-20 minutes to complete it. In order to preserve anonymity students are not required to provide names but a head count and paper count are conducted to ensure that as many completed forms are submitted as possible. The evaluation is based on a Likert scale of 1 to 5; 1 indicating that the students strongly agree; 2 = students are likely to agree; 3 = students are non-committal; 4 = indicating that they disagree and 5 = indicating that the statement is not applicable in their opinion. The results presented in figure 20 relate to the 2014/2015 cohort. Of the 147 students 123 responses were obtained which reflect the experiences of the students within the confines of this module.

How students perceive their overall satisfaction with the module is illustrated in figure 9. The results indicated a mean of 2 suggesting that students are fairly positive. While 1 student appeared dissatisfied with the quality of the module; 7 students remained undecided with 69 students indicating satisfaction. The remaining 46 students were very satisfied with the quality of the module. Dissatisfaction and uncertainty can be attributed to a number of factors; students may not like the subject and as such respond negatively irrespective of what approach is tried; the students own academic background, coming from school or college where the level of support afforded by teachers is of a greater level than they now encounter combined with their immature level of social skills, inexperience of working with others and

Figure 9. Student satisfaction

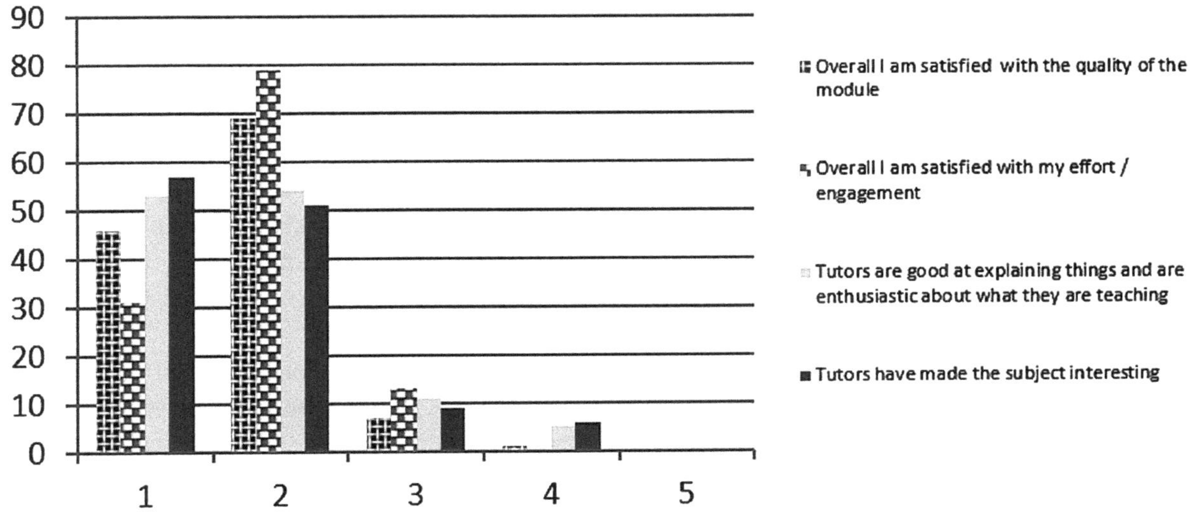

reluctance to become an autonomous learner, can produce a persona of negativity that will impact upon their engagement with a course. The overall indication however is that 93% of the returning students were satisfied with the course.

The students were also asked how they rated their own level of effort and engagement with the course (Figure 20). It is less than surprising that no student responded negatively; 13 were undecided; 79 students indicated that they were happy with their level of performance and a further 31 students were very happy with their level of effort and engagement. A high personal satisfaction rate may be attributed to the students perceiving consistent attendance and completion of required activities by due dates as an indicator. In addition marks and feedback may serve to build confidence with regards to their developing skills and knowledge thereby creating a cycle of positive reinforcement.

Commentary on the tutors' performance regarding how they felt the tutor explained things and whether they were enthusiastic about what they were teaching was also asked. The results indicated that 5 students were dissatisfied; 13 were non-committal; 54 were satisfied and 53 very satisfied with their tutors' performance. The module delivery was conducted by a team of tutors – from a PHd Student to a Senior Lecturer. Dissatisfaction may have occurred because the students perceived that they were not receiving the same experience from a PHd student as they would receive from a Senior Lecturer despite the teaching team adopting the same strategy for every class. Nevertheless 87% of the student responses indicate that the students were more than satisfied with the tutors' performance.

How students perceive whether the subject has been made interesting is illustrated in figure 20. The results indicate that 6 students disagree; 9 students are non-committal; 51 students agree and a further 57 are very happy with the techniques the tutors have utilised in order to make the subject interesting. Achieving complete cohort satisfaction with regards to adopting a teaching strategy is unlikely to be achieved due to the diverse nature of the students. Dissatisfaction for students can again be attributed to factors such as non-acceptance of alternative teaching methods; personal learning styles not being specifically addressed; to merely not liking the subject matter.

Module Results

The overall module results from the introductory programming module for four iterations are shown below in Table 7.

The grade boundaries correlate to degree classifications in the institution. A student is required to attain 40% or greater to pass the module. The Mean column shows the average student mark achieved within the module in that academic year. It must be noted that the regulations regarding student reassessment was amended during the academic year 2014/2015 (table 8). The change meant that level 4 students could no longer undertake an in module reassessment; which occurred 2 weeks after they were notified of a fail. Reassessment for all years, with the exception of final year students in semester one would revert, to August.

The results which are shown for 2011/12 are those which have been produced prior to the reassessment period, and hence the module pass rate appears lower in this year than in previous years.

The use of the NXT kits was first introduced into the curriculum in 2009/10. In this academic year, all students were required to make use of the robots for their final programming coursework. However, the department only had a limited number of kits for the students to use therefore the students were provided with a pre-built robots in order to complete the challenges.

In the following academic year 2010/11 the use of the robots was optional. The student teams were able to select between a coursework to program the NXT robots, or alternatively to write a game in Java using Swing. Due to the wider availability of kits the teams were able to design and build their own robots.

In the academic year 2011/12 the use of the Mindstorms has been extended so that the majority of students would work in teams to design, build and program their own devices to resolve the challenges they were set. A small number of students (8) who had not engaged in earlier teamwork exercises, either out of choice or for personal reasons, were set an alternative programming coursework. Each team

Table 7. Overall module results

	70-100%	60-69%	50-59%	40-49%	<40%	Pass Rate (%)	No Students	No of Boys	No of Girls	Mean	SD
2011/12	40(48%)	18(21%)	12(14%)	2(1%)	10(13%)	84%	82	73	9	62.82	19.96
2012/13	48(53%)	28(31%)	5(6%)	5(6%)	4(4%)	96%	90	75	15	69.54	14.09
2013/14	50 (39%)	59(46%)	10 8%	7(6%)	2(1%)	99%	128	105	23	67.35	11.25
2014/15	19	52	52	17	7	95.%	147	127	20	58.24	11.25

Table 8. Coursework 3 results

	A	B	C	D	Fail	CW Pass Rate	No Students	Mean	SD
2011/12	43	10	16	2	11	87%	82	63.68	26.67
2012/13	60	17	4	2	7	92%	90	72.16	21.64
2013/14	45	60	14	2	7	95%	128	65.38	13.33
2014/15	33	52	31	18	13	91%	147	57.85	14.51

was allocated their own kit and was given a brief introduction to programming using leJOS. Again, the teaching team noted high levels of engagement with the teams using the NXT devices. This has been reflected in the results profile for the module. The innovation and creativity which the students have demonstrated has led to over two-thirds of the students achieving an 'A' or 'B' grade. It is also noted that the average grade on the module has increased significantly. If the results for the coursework's in 2011/12 are examined in further detail it can be observed that the student's had achieved a consistent level of improved outcome and following this the coursework has continued for a further 3 academic years to establish a underpinning pattern of improved achievements by the students who participate in the module.

POST-COURSE INTERPRETATION / SUMMARY

The post course evaluation demonstrates that the student experience is enhanced through the adoption of the robotics coursework's in the programming module.

The student questionnaires underpin this notion as the majority of the participants rank their experience as, at least, with a score of 4 in all the categories. It is noted that in two categories, cognitive and participation, the ranking for scores of 5 is even higher, where as in the remaining categories (emotional and performance) the ranking of a score of 5 dips below that of a score of 4. This is a feature that shall be considered in further detail through the holistic analysis and triangulation of the results presented in this chapter. Nevertheless, the indication is that students perceive the robot coursework to lead to significant developmental benefits for their skills and abilities.

There is clear evidence that the students not only felt that their technical skills had developed to meet the requirements of the task, but that there was a sense of invigoration to explore the subject of programming in more detail. Furthermore, the students identified benefits in relation to the development of so-called soft skills; those skills essential for the broader requirements of academic progression and future employability, such as team-working and presentation skills.

SUMMARY

Teaching programming to novices is often cited as a difficult process with a range of challenges facing both tutors and students. Equally, there are drives in the United Kingdom to demonstrate that programmes not only equip students with course-related competencies, but also with more generic employability skills. The purpose of this study has been to understand the impact of introducing a physical computing element into the curriculum, and the effect that this would have upon the student experience. In order to evaluate the study, an analytical approach adopting both learning and academic analytics has been taken.

The findings of this study have revealed that student engagement is significantly enhanced when a problem-based learning strategy encompasses physical computing in the form of robotics. Equally, the analysis of data that has been collated also highlights the student appreciation of the holistic experience. The analytics facilitated both direct and indirect data capture, with triangulation of this evidence supporting the findings that have been reached.

Therefore the introduction of a captivating physical object (a robot) that can inspire the imagination of students while motivating and engaging them simultaneously into a subject that has a pre-disposition of being known as difficult and complex must not be ignored.

REFERENCES

Abdous, M., He, W., & Yen, C.-J. (2012). Using Data Mining for Predicting Relationships between Online Question Theme and Final Grade. *Journal of Educational Technology & Society*, *15*(3), 77–88.

Azemi, A. 1995. Teaching Computer Programming Courses in a Computer Laboratory Environment. *Proceedings of the Frontiers in Education Conference FIE '95* (Vol. 1). doi:10.1109/FIE.1995.483036

Barnes, D. J., Fincher, S., & Thompson, S. (1997) Introductory Problem Solving in Computer Science. In G. Daughton, & P. Magee (Eds.), *Proceedings of the 5th Annual Conference on the Teaching of Computing* (pp. 36-39). Centre for Teaching Computing, Dublin City University, Dublin, Ireland.

Barron, B., & Engle, R. A. (2007) Analyzing Data Derived from Video Records. In S.J. Derry (Ed.), Guidelines for Video Research in Education: Recommendations from an Expert Panel (White paper) (pp. 24-33). Retrieved from http://drdc.uchicago.edu/what/video-research-guidelines.pdf#page=1&view=fitV,0

Bennedsen, J., & Caspersen, M. E. (2006, June). Abstraction ability as an indicator of success for learning object-orientated programming? *SIGCSE Bulletin*, *38*(2), 39–43. doi:10.1145/1138403.1138430

Berkhout, L., Hoekman, J., & Goorhuis-Brouwer, S. M. (2011). Observation instrument of play behaviour in a classroom setting. *Early Child Development and Care*. doi:10.1080/03004430.2011.608429

Bowman, M. (1994). *Using Video in Research. SCRE Spotlights 45*. Scottish Council for Research in Education.

Brown, M. (2010). *Learning analytics*. Learning Circuits.

Brown, M. (2012) Learning Analytics: Moving from Concept to Practice. EDUCAUSE Learning Initiative, July 2012

Buerk, J. P., & Mudigonda, S. P. (2014). A Resource-Constrained Approach to Implementing Analytics in an Institution of Higher Education: An Experience Report. *Journal of Learning Analytics*, *1*(1), 129–139.

Campbell, J. P., DeBlouis, P. B., & Oblinger, D. G. (2007). Academic analytics: A new tool for a new era. *Educause Review Online*, *42*(4), 40–57.

Chan, A., & Lee, M. J. W. (2005). An MP3 a day keeps the worries away: Exploring the use of podcasting to address preconceptions and alleviate pre-class anxiety amongst undergraduate information technology students. In D.H.R. Spennemann & L.Burr (Eds.), *Good Practice in Practice: Proceedings of the Student Experience Conference* (pp.58-70). Wagga Wagga, NSW

Chan, S. (2013). Using videos and multimodal discourse analysis to study how students learn a trade. *International Journal of Training Research*, *11*(1), 69–78. doi:10.5172/ijtr.2013.11.1.69

Cliburn, D. C. (2006, October 28-31). Experiences with the LEGO Mindstorms throughout the Undergraduate Computer Science Curriculum. *Proceedings of the 36th ASEE/IEEE Frontiers in Education Conference*, San Diego, CA, USA (pp. 1-6).

Cooper, A. (2012). *A Brief History of Analytics, JISC CETIS Analytics Series 1(9)*. University of Bolton.

Deakin Crick, R., Broadfoot, P., & Claxton, G. Developing an Effective Lifelong Learning Inventory: The ELLI Project. *Assessment in Education*, 11(3), 248-272.

Derry, S. J., Pea, R. D., Barron, B., Engle, R. A., Erickson, F., Goldman, R., & Sherin, B. L. et al. (2010). Conducting Video Research in the Learning Sciences: Guidance on Selection, Analysis, Technology and Ethics. *Journal of the Learning Sciences*, *19*(1), 3–53. doi:10.1080/10508400903452884

Dewey, J. (1933). *How We Think: A Restatement of the Relation of Reflective Thinking to the Educative Process*. Boston: Heath and Co.

Duffy, T. M., & Cunningham, D. J. (2001). Constructivism: Implications for the design and delivery of instruction. In D. H. Jonassen (Ed.), *Handbook of Research for Educational Communications and Technology*. New York, NY: Simon and Schuster.

DuFon, M. A. (2002). Video recording in Ethnographic SLA Research: Some issues of validity in data collection. *Language Learning & Technology*, *6*(1), 40–59.

Edwards, A. D., & Westgate, D. P. G. (1987). *Investigating Classroom Talk*. Lewes: Falmer Press.

Enzai, N. I. M., Kar, S. A. C., Husni, H., & Ahmed, N. 2011. Harnessing Creativity in Teaching and Learning Introductory Programming. *Proceedings of 2011 IEEE Student Conference on Research and Development*, Putrajaya, Selangor, Malaysia doi:10.1109/SCOReD.2011.6148778

Erickson, F. (2006). Definition and analysis of data from videotape: Some research procedures and their rationales. In J. L. Green, G. Camili, & P. B. Elmore (Eds.), *Handbook of complementary methods in educational research* (pp. 177–191). Mahwah, NJ: Lawrence Erlbaum Associates.

Essa, A., & Ayad, H. (2012, April 29–May 2). Student Success System: Risk Analytics and Data Visualization using Ensembles of Predictive Models. *Paper presented at the Learning Analytics and Knowledge Conference*, Vancouver, British Columbia.

Fincher, S. (1999). What are we doing when we teach programming? *Proceedings of the 29th ASEE/IEEE Frontiers in Education Conference*.

Fry, B. (2007). *Visualizing Data*. Sebastapol, CA: O'Reilly.

Gavan, C., & Anderson, M. (2012, October 10-14). Engaging Undergraduate Programming Students: Experiences using Lego Mindstorms NXT. *Proceedings of ACM Special Interest Group for Information Technology Education Conference (SIGITE)*, Calgary, Canada.

Geertz, C. (1988). *Works and Lives: The Anthropologist as Author*. Cambridge: Polity Press.

Gibson, R. (2010). The 'art' of creative teaching: Implications for higher education. *Teaching in Higher Education*, *15*(5), 607–613. doi:10.1080/13562517.2010.493349

Goldman, R. (2007). Video Representations and the Perspectivity Framework: Epistemology, Ethnography, Evaluation, and Ethics. In R. Goldman, R. Pea, B. Barron, & S. J. Derry (Eds.), *Video Research in the Learning Sciences* (pp. ix–xiii). New York: Lawrence Erlbaum Associates.

Gonzalez, M. J. F. (2012) Advantages and Limits of Video Recording as a Tool for Students, Teachers and Researchers in Music Conservatoires. *Proceedings of International Conference on The Future of Education*, Florence, Italy.

Gray, G., McGuiness, C., Owende, P., & Carthy, A. (2014). A Review of Psychometric Data Analysis and Applications. *Journal of Learning Analytics*, *1*(1), 75–106.

Greller, W., & Drachsler, H. (2012). Translating Learning into Numbers: A Generic Framework for Learning Analytics. *Journal of Educational Technology & Society*, *15*(3), 42–57.

Greyling, J. H., Cilliers, C. B., & Calitz, A. P. (2006, July 10-13) B#: The Development and Assessment of an Iconic Programming Tool for Novice Programmers. *Proceedings of the 7th International Conference on Information Technology Based Higher Education and Training ITHET '06*, Ultimo, NSW (pp. 367-375).

Hagan, D., & Markham, S. (2000). Teaching Java with the BlueJ environment. *Proceedings of Australian Society for Computers in Learning in Tertiary Education Conference ASCILITE 2000.*

Hahn, J. H., Mentz, E., & Meyer, L. (2009). Assessment Strategies for Pair Programming. *Journal of Information Technology Education*, *8*, 273–284.

Han, J., & Kamber, M. (2006). *Data mining concepts and techniques*. Burlington, MA: Morgan Kaufmann.

Hibino, S., & Rundensteiner, E. A. (1994) A Graphical Query Language for Identifying Temporal Trends in Video Data (Technical Report). University of Michigan. Retrieved from http://citeseerx.ist.psu.edu/viewdoc/download?doi=10.1.1.50.1145&rep=rep1&type=pdf&ei=VTE7UZGwCuaM7Qag3YGwCg&usg=AFQjCNFf_jWvyoA5h_L9qvoPS-bd06VsiQ&si

Igoe, T. (2007). *Making Things Talk: Practical Methods for Connecting Physical Objects*. Make Books.

Kelleher, C., & Pausch, R. (2005). Lowering the Barriers to Programming: A Taxonomy of Programming Environments and Languages for Novice Programmers. *ACM Computing Surveys*, *37*(2), 83–137. doi:10.1145/1089733.1089734

Kölling, M., Quig, B., Patterson, A. and Rosenberg, J. (2003). The BlueJ System and its pedagogy. *Journal of Computer Science Education, Special Issue on Learning and Teaching Object Technology*, 13(4), Dec 2003.

Krause, K., & Coates, H. (2008). Students' Engagement in First-Year University. *Assessment and Evaluation in Higher Education*, 33(5), 493–505.

Larose, D. T. (2005). *Discovering knowledge in data: An introduction to data mining*. Hoboken, NJ: John Wiley and Sons, Inc.

Lilley, J., & Rollins, B. (1995) Using undergraduates as teaching assistants in introductory programming courses: an update on the Stanford experience. *Proceedings of the twenty-sixth SIGCSE technical symposium on Computer science education SIGCSE '95* (pp. 48-52).

Little, B., Locke, W., Scesa, A., & Williams, R. (2009). Report on Student Engagement (February 2009). HEFCE by the Centre for Higher Education Research and Information (Open University). Retrieved from http://www.hefce.ac.uk/pubs/rdreports/2009/rd03_09/

Long, P., & Siemens, G. (2011). Penetrating the Fog: Analytics in Learning and Education. *EDUCAUSE Review*, September/October, 31–40.

McCue, C. (2006). Data Mining and Predictive Analysis in Public Safety and Security. IT Professional, 8(4), 12-18.

Mota, M. I. G. (2007, October 10-13) Work In Progress - Using Lego Mindstorms and Robolab as a mean to lowering dropout and failure rate in programming course. *Proceedings of the 37th ASEE/IEEE Frontiers in Education Conference*, Milwaukee, WI, USA (pp. F4A-1 – F4A-2).

Nagappan, N., Williams, L., Ferzli, M., Wiebe, E., Yang, K., Miller, C., & Balik, S. (2003). Improving the CS1 Experience with Pair Programming. *Proceedings of the 34th SIGCSE technical symposium on Computer science education SIGCSE '03* (pp. 359-362). doi:10.1145/611892.612006

Nebot, A., Mugica, F., & Castro, F. (2010, July 18-23) Fuzzy Predictive Models to Help Teachers in e-Learning Courses. *Proceedings of the 2010 International Joint Conference on Neural Networks (IJCNN)*, Barcelona, Spain. doi:10.1109/IJCNN.2010.5596582

O'Sullivan, D., & Igoe, T. (2004). *Physical Computing: Sensing and Controlling the Physical World with Computers*. Course Technology.

Panadero, C. F., Roman, J. V., & Kloos, C. D. (2010). Impact of learning experiences using LEGO Mindstorms in engineering courses. [IEEE.]. *Proceedings of Education Engineering EDUCON, 2010*, 503–512.

Pardo, A., & Kloos, C. D. (2011). Stepping out of the box: Towards analytics outside the learning management system. *Proceedings of the 1st International Conference on Learning Analytics and Knowledge* (pp. 163–167). New York, NY: ACM. doi:10.1145/2090116.2090142

Perkins, D., Hancock, C., Hobbs, R., Martin, F., & Simmons, R. (1989). Conditions of learning in novice programming. In *Studying the Novice Programmer* (pp. 261–279). New Jersey: Lawrence Erlbaum Associates.

Plowman, L. (1999). *Using video for observing interaction in the classroom. SCRE Spotlights 72*. Edinburgh: Scottish Council for Research in Education.

Rinkevich, J.L. (2011). Creative Teaching: Why it matters and Where to Begin. *The Clearing House: A Journal of Educational Strategies, Issues and Ideas*, *84*(5), 219–223.

Savage, M. & Burrows, R. (2007). The coming crisis of empirical sociology. *The Journal of the British Sociological Association*, *41*(5), 885–899. doi:10.1177/0038038507080443

Sheard, J., & Hagan, D. 1997. Experiences with Teaching Object-oriented Concepts to Introductory Programming Students using C++. *Proceedings of the Technology of Object-Oriented Languages and Systems (TOOLS'97)*.

Shum, B., Simon & Deakin Crick, Ruth (2012, April 29 - May 2). Learning dispositions and transferable competencies: pedagogy, modelling and learning analytics. *Proceedings of the 2nd International Conference on Learning Analytics & Knowledge*, Vancouver, British Columbia, Canada. doi:10.1145/2330601.2330629

Sitthiworachart, J., & Joy, M. (2008). Computer support of effective peer assessment in an undergraduate programming class. *Journal of Computer Assisted Learning*, *24*(3), 217–231. doi:10.1111/j.1365-2729.2007.00255.x

Slade, S., & Prinsloo, P. (2013). Learning analytics: Ethical issues and dilemmas. *The American Behavioral Scientist*, *57*(10), 1509–1528. doi:10.1177/0002764213479366

Small, T., & Deakin Crick, R. (2008). Learning and Self-Awareness: An Enquiry into Personal Development in Higher Education. Vital Partnership and Bristol University, Bristol. Retrieved from http://www.northumbria.ac.uk/sd/central/ar/lts/ltselli/

Sobrinho, W. T., & Goncalves, R. S. (2011, October 1-4). Study of Robotics Singularities using LEGO Mindstorms Kit. *Proceedings of 2011 IEEE IX Latin American and IEEE Colombian Conference on Automatic Control and Industry Applications LARC*, Bogota, Columbia. doi:10.1109/LARC.2011.6086792

Sun, L.-P., Lv, T.-q., & Pan, L.-w. (2011). Reinforcing Practice Teaching of Software Engineering for Fostering the Creative Talent. *Proceedings of the International Conference on Consumer Electronics, Communications and Networks* (pp. 1548-1551).

Ventura, P. R. Jr. (2005, September). Identifying predictors of success for an objects-first CS1. *Computer Science Education*, *15*(3), 223–243. doi:10.1080/08993400500224419

Watson, C., Li, F. W. B., & Godwin, J. L. (2013). Predicting Performance in an Introductory Programming Course by Logging and Analyzing Student Programming Behavior. *Proceedings of 2013 IEEE 13th International Conference on Advanced Learning Technologies* (pp. 319-323). doi:10.1109/ICALT.2013.99

Xiaohui, G., & Yaguan, Q. (2010, May 7-9). The Exploration of Teaching about Java Programming. *Proceedings of the International Conference on E-Business and E-Government ICEE 2010*, Guangzhou, China. doi:10.1109/ICEE.2010.1397

Yazzie-Mintz, E. (2009). *Charting the Path from Engagement to Achievement: A Report on the 2009 High School Survey of Student Engagement*. Center for Evaluation & Education Policy, Indiana University.

Chapter 5
Developing a Framework for the Visualisation of Learning Analytics in UK Higher Education

Jack Halliday
Edge Hill University, UK

Mark Anderson
Edge Hill University, UK

ABSTRACT

Learning analytics has vast potential as a tool to further unlock the effectiveness of education in a digital age. The amount of data that can be gathered from varying access points can provide new insight and knowledge into how learners are interacting with course materials, learning systems and even fellow classmates. Research and experimentation is uncovering forms of best practice and possible factors on which to centre the analysis of students in an effective way, however learning analytics has yet to be comprehensively implemented country-wide in the United Kingdom.

The chapter explores the current impact of learning analytics in higher education at moment. This chapter also discusses and observes the current vacancies with which a framework enabled to function with data visualisation could be utilised. The eventual deliverable seeks to design an initial framework that has the potential to be utilised in a higher education setting for more effective and insightful decision making with regards to learner retention and engagement. This framework will combine the theory and scientific action of predictive analytics with a comparison of the most suitable data visualisation toolsets that are currently available in open-source software. The opportunity for further development and refinement of the framework, as well as the validity of deeper investigation into key concepts of data visualisation will also be elaborated on.

DOI: 10.4018/978-1-4666-9983-0.ch005

INTRODUCTION

This purpose of this research project is to explore the current usage of learning analytics in UK higher education institutions. Furthermore, the project intends to offer the foundations of a viable learning analytic framework that could enable a deeper understanding of student engagement and retention. Examples of recently or previously implemented learning analytic function have been evaluated.

Background

This research looks to significantly build upon previous work conducted by the author in which the presence of learning analytics across the United Kingdom, United States and Australia. Previous research concluded that although learning analytic adoption is present in the United Kingdom and advancements are being made, the concept remains up and coming. Some of the absences discovered prompted further investigation into a way for learning analytic and predictive analytic practice could be further explored for the UK higher education environment.

This research document will firstly explore the current literature and landscape of learning analytics and predictive analytics whilst developing an understanding of how to define learner behaviour so that analytics can be effectively analysed.

Aims and Objectives

The overall aim is to propose the design of a framework within which learning analytics can be applied and used beneficially by UK higher education institutions to make meaningful predictions. The individual objectives assigned to achieve this aim are as follows:

- To learn and evaluate current learning analytic methodology and how it can be utilised in a UK higher education institution.
- To explore and understand the presence of big data and data analytics in the UK higher education sector at the time of conducting the research.
- To learn about and evaluate predictive analytic methodology and how it can be utilised in a UK higher education institution.
- To critically evaluate and compare open source data visualisation tools and assess any advantages that one has over another.
- To design and propose a framework that could combine learning analytics, predictive analytics and data visualisation for effective insight.

Scope

This research currently exists within the scope of the United Kingdom higher education landscape. In addition, the research and project will be developed with a specific focus on Edge Hill University. Within this scope, the research will be directed towards the Computing Department at Edge Hill University. The sample data used during the development of the framework theory will be taken from first year undergraduate students within the Computing Department. In further work and research, this framework could be expanded to cover different departments within Edge Hill University or even other higher education institutions in the United Kingdom. The other factor to be considered in the scope is the visualisation tools that are to be critically compared. These software tools are open source and the framework will be optimised for use with these programs. Once the underpinning theory of framework has been established, other visualisation tools can be experimented with. Nevertheless, the aforementioned scope parameters currently exist for the research at present.

CURRENT ENVIRONMENT

Technological advancements and their gradual integration into academic practice means that the modern classroom is no longer restricted to the existence of a physical room. The classroom has become a multi-dimensional space that seamlessly blends the physical and the digital aspects of learning together (Phillips et al. 2012). Although many technologies are now established within the educational sector, the application of learning analytics [LA] into higher education is considered a relatively new and exciting field of practice and research (van Barneveld et al 2012). Nevertheless, evidence regarding the impact of LA on study behaviours and learning outcomes is still considered to be lacking (Phillips et al. 2011). The purpose of this review is to develop deeper understanding of learning analytics and predictive analytics as concepts and how they are being applied in research and practice currently. In addition, there will be an exploration of learner behaviour as quantifiable factors and how they can be best applied to a framework for predictive analytics in education.

Learning and Predictive Analytics

Two of the most vital components for the proposed model of this research is learning analytics and predictive analytics. Here the two concepts will be defined and contrasted with further exploration into the concepts of learning analytics and predictive analytics in practice.

Firstly, learning analytics uses masses of data captured on learners as they interact with online learning systems. As suggested by Long and Siemens (2011) learning analytics is related to educational data mining and is considered to be usable at higher education course and higher education department level. In addition, van Harmelen and Workman (2012) explain that the priority of learning analytics is to address the challenge of improving and optimising the availability and benefits of online learning. These methods allow educational institutions to further understand student engagement, progress and performance as defined by Phillips et al (2012). The foundational concepts of learning analytics are not newly founded. Analytics and the accompanying tools were first utilised in a business environment. The application of these tools were already showing significant benefits within the Fortune 500 and as stated by Luan (2002) the only alterations required for effective analytics within academia would be to ask different questions. However, modern day learning analytics is not merely a mirror image or translation of business analytics. Chatti et al. (2012) suggests that LA is a merging of several other related areas, such as personalised adaptive learning, academic analytics and action research. As stated by Siemens & Baker (2012) there are currently two major researching bodies that are exploring the purpose and effectiveness of data mining and analytics in education - Learning Analytics and Knowledge [LAK] and the Educational Data Mining [EDM]. Nevertheless, the EDM held their first workshop in 2005 and the first LAK conference occurred in 2010, which further highlights the current infancy of this research. In addition, numerous countries are actively encouraging the development and experimentation with learning analytics in higher education United Kingdom, United States and Australia.

Predictive analytics, although related to learning analytics, is a different collection of technologies. As defined by Eduventures (2013), the purpose of predictive analytics is to "uncover relationships and patterns within large volumes of data that can be used to predict behaviour and events".

Having gauged learner engagement through the use of learning analytics, predictive analytics allows for the development of foresight in relation to institutions acting for the betterment of students. This is particularly true when using predictive analytics for the benefit of 'at-risk' learners. Eduventures (2013) explain that predictive analytics can be utilised to pin-point learners who are most at-risk of failing a class or withdrawing from the institution entirely.

The application of predictive analytics in education has been explored by some researchers at present. This research has led to several hypotheses and theories on how to correctly and effectively apply data-based predictions in the academic environment; particularly with regards to student withdrawal. In order to effectively use learning analytics to anticipate and counteract student disengagement or withdrawal, predictive analytic methods and practices will be required. Predictive analytics has been defined by Shmueli and Koppius (2011) as the application of data mining and empirical statistical methodology in order to develop near or distant future predictions. In addition, Hair. Jr (2007) considers predictive analytics to be the use of existing relationships between variables to determine future outcomes. At this stage, it is also important to highlight that, although often believed to be a singular entity, predictive analytics and data mining are not the same. However, the two methods are directly related in practice, as data mining is the method used to extract the aforementioned relationships between variables. Data mining alone does not give basis for predictive analytics as it operates at machine level, is largely anonymous and exists without meaningful context.

At the forefront of learning analytic research in the United Kingdom is the Joint Information Systems Committee [JISC]. Formed in 1993, JISC are a registered charity that develops and funds research and implementation of learning analytic theory and practices in partnership with companies and educational establishments. Collaborative efforts from JISC have seen some pioneering research emerge from the United Kingdom, including a learning analytic project from the University of Huddersfield that looks to develop university library analytics. The eventual model looks to bring the standard learner data together with library data to bring an additional dimension to how student engagement can be measured.

For the United States, the Office of Education Technology is responsible for the management and introduction of technological advancements into the education system. The Office of Education Technology is a department contained within the U.S. Department of Education. The adoption of learning analytic technology at government level has been extremely beneficial for experimentation with analytic method in the US education system. A study compiled by Campbell et al. (2007) observed a variety of institutions that had begun modelling, developing and incorporating learning analytics at various levels for various purposes. For example, Baylor University implemented a model for predicting student enrolment and the University of Alabama had installed a predictive learning analytic model for the improvement of student retention. Additional implemented models in US institutions includes assessing at-risk students in the first year of study as well as observing how career advising could be incorporated into the analytic model to enhance student retention.

Australian learning analytic research and implementation is also handled by government bodies. The Australian Government have supported the development of learning analytic technology to enable improvements in student access, student attainment and student engagement (Commonwealth of Australia, 2009). The discussion, sharing and collation of learning analytic research in Australia is greatly encouraged amongst the Australian higher education institutions. A research body known as the Society of Learning Analytics Research created the Australian Learning Analytics Summer Institute convention. This convention provides an avenue for the demonstration of evidence and research outcomes in relation to the application of learning analytic research in Australian education. Furthermore, Phillips et al (2011) has observed the frequency at which students engage with distance learning and external study in Australia. As such, the Australian education system makes significant use of virtual learning environments and web-based lecture capture software. This factor has seen valuable research movements for learning analytics and external study. However, it is important to collate the currently available research to extract the importance of learning analytics, establish which methods are used within the term learning analytics and to further understand how these methods can be combined with predictive analytics.

Experimentation and implementation with learning analytics has been considerably active across the world. Efforts are being made to find best practices in a number of different ways ranging from integration with web-based lecture capture to combining learning analytics with other facets of university education, such as library analytics. Learning analytics in education is handled by the state governmental bodies like in the United States and Australia or by independent bodies in others such as JISC in the United Kingdom. This could perhaps be indicative of the pace at which learning analytics is being adopted as an expected standard in countries where governmental bodies are encouraging its implementation. Campbell et al (2007) demonstrated the immediate efforts being made throughout the United States with learning analytics in areas. Furthermore, learning analytics in Australia appear significant with both governmental and independent discussion and research existing in parallel, with a considerable focus on integration with distance learning (Phillips et al, 2011). In contrast, the JISC annual report from 2014 demonstrated the infancy of learning analytics in the United Kingdom; illustrated through inconsistent market share of learning analytic software systems in the United Kingdom (Sclater, 2014).

Learner Behaviours

An important predicament posed to research communities on this topic is the definition of student behaviours and how this investigate analysis can arrive at the core of any given issue (Duval, 2011). One of the primary behaviours that a predictive learning analytic model would look to address is student interaction. This could include student interaction with learning materials, learning systems (such as a virtual learning environment), communication with lecturers and tutors as well as attendance in lectures and seminars. A study conducted by Phillips et al. (2012) suggests that student learning behaviour categories can be established to help lend context to data analysis. In this example, categories were established through the use of lecture capture applications. This application captured student interaction and activity with lecture materials and educational resources. Research focused on the weekly activity of students in order to establish learning behaviour categories. For example, a student that regular reviewed the lecture material more than once in the week would be considered a "high achiever". However, students that were only recorded as viewing the material in the last two weeks of the semester would be classed as "cramming." These behaviours providing significant insight into how students are interacting with learning materials which in turn could be used to intervene accordingly with students displaying distance or disregard for a particular module. These data and their relevance to learning analytic measurements have been applied elsewhere as well. Whilst studying the Student Activity Monitor, Duval (2011) observing applied analytic measurement values such total time spent on the course, average time spent within a document, number of documents accessed and the average time of the day that a student is working.

Although these behaviours are key indicators of student engagement, a lack of student engagement could also represent the potential for student withdrawal behaviour. It is this ambiguity that continues to plague existing research into student withdrawal by producing contradictory findings. Tinto (1975) describes how "failure to distinguish academic failure from voluntary withdrawal" has contributed towards sporadic evidence that attempts to link and unlink student ability to student withdrawal. Furthermore, Tinto (1975) describes a longitudinal model that attempts to observe the reasons for student withdrawal. This initial schema incorporates several points of communication between the student and the institution, both academically and socially. This includes standard indicators such as grade performance, but also includes how a student is interacting with a peer group or with the faculty at the institution. In addition to this, an acknowledgement of family background, individual attributes and previous education are considered indicators for predicting student withdrawal. All of these factors revolve around two student commitments that Tinto believes are considered before the decision to withdraw arrives. The first is the goal commitment, which in this case would be the commitment to succeed academically and progress to the intended next career step. The second is the institutional commitment, which looks at the connections between a student and a peer group or tutor and the social environment of the institution. These factors need to be considered for a predictive framework to be established as without them, the model will fail to observe the multi-dimensional aspects of higher education study.

Conversely, a theoretical model requires application to understand if it is viable in practice. Pascarella and Terenzini (1980) conducted a research study that used the concepts of the Tinto model and applied previously established measurable variables to it. These variables including individual attributes such as sex and race, family history in education and household income. In addition, goal commitments such as how important a student perceived graduating to be and how confident a student was in their choice of university. Finally, students are asked about how many hours they spend in extracurricular activities and how much time they anticipate to have informal communications with faculty. Pascarella and Terenzini (1980) used thirty-four "institutional integration items" from which predictive scales were extracted and used for the statistical analysis. The questions were posed to 763 subjects in two sample groups who then give scores against each question and the findings from each group were collected and cross-referenced. The conclusion found that the various integration scales such as pre-higher education characteristics, extracurricular involvement and first year academic performance "increased correct identification of persisters and dropouts in a cross-validation sample" (Pascarella & Terenzini, 1980: 72). This saw an improvement on prediction from 58.2 per cent to 81.4 per cent for persisters and 34.5 percent to 75.8 percent for withdrawals. In addition, 75.8 per cent of the students who withdrew that participated in the cross-validation sample of participants were also correctly identified.

Overall, the outcome of the study supported the "predictive validity" of the Tinto model.

Furthermore, Pascarella and Terenzini (1980) found that the "quality and impact of student-faculty informal contacts" is extremely valuable to student persistence. A more recent study from Mazza and Dimitrova (2004) saw student behaviour being tracked through a more academic context with some incorporation of social aspects. Within this study, student behaviour was defined through access to web-based lecture software and included measurements centred on student attendance, interaction with reading materials, discussion participation and general course progression. In addition, students were also assessed cognitively through quiz performance as well as socially through interaction with a student community message board which tracked contributions to discussion. These contributions were measured on the date they were posted, the topic they centred on and any following up that occurred after the post had been made. All of these elements were tracked, visualised and combined into a complete visualisation through a system known as CourseVis. The eventual aim of these visualisations was to enable instructors to critically reflect on how courses were run based on the comprehensive analysis they were presented with. This is further supported by research from Naps et al (2004) that incorporated factors such as learner satisfaction, learning time, course progression and learner understanding. This study incorporated a scale referred to as Bloom's taxonomy scale to assess the varying levels of student understanding so it can be used comprehensively as a measurement of engagement. This included six levels that vary from a base level factual recall to a fully developed evaluative and critical understanding of a topic. These factors were measured through the assignment of tasks to learners and the results of these tasks were measured against expected outcomes.

Whilst understanding ambiguities surrounding the definition of student learning behaviours, some research suggests that a significant obstacle in learning analytic adoption is the lack of approachability for educators. When researching how learning analytics fails to adequately support educational strategy, Macfayden and Dawson (2012) describe how current research does not factor in the cultural and social requirements of educational establishments to promote them to accept change. A further illustration of this comes from the JISC report (Sclater, 2014) that reported on findings of a survey on learning analytic tool adoption in thirteen higher education institutions in the United Kingdom. Findings displayed fifteen different technologies being implemented across the institutions that were questioned, including one in-house developed system. Furthermore, learning analytic buzzwords appeared to be in need of clarification for some of the institutions interviewed as a part of the same report (Sclater, 2014). Wagner and Ice (2012) consider that the most effective place to integrate learning analytic practices is with the educators that are dealing with students on a regular basis. Without the understanding and willingness of these "front-line educators" as defined by Wagner & Ice, learning analytics will seemingly struggle to be unanimously installed. This research proposes that a key way in which to bring about a clear understanding of how to gain insight from learning analytic data is data visualisation.

Data Visualisation

The concept of data visualisation long predates the modern era of technology. The practice of graphically representing measurement first emerged in the 17th Century with statistical practice breakthroughs from Michael Florent van Langren in 1644 (Friendly, 2005: 3). Since then visualisation in data analysis has persisted and evolved within the data technology era. Visualisations were reportedly first adopted in the 1980s and have since grown in capability and integration (Naps et al., 2002: 132). Ware (2004: 3) explains how modern data visualisation now has the capacity to demonstrate and reveal the importance of millions of measurements. The visualisation process is defined by Ware (2004: 4) as having four stages. The first involves the act of collecting and storing the data that is to be visualised. Once the data has been stored, it must be pre-processed to allow for it to be correctly understood by the people perceiving it. Data is then fed into the hardware and pushed through the relevant algorithms to allow for it to be physically visualised on a screen. The final stage involves the actual perception of the visualisation by the end user, whereupon action can be taken. Modern visualisation gives the capacity to understand patterns, meaning and even problems with the data itself on a variety of scales (Ware, 2004:3). This includes a number of approaches to analysis with multiple variables, therefore multivariate analysis (Friendly, 2005: 14). Effective use of visualisation for business decisions revolves around two main goals – an explanatory objective and an exploratory objective (Fusion Charts, n.d.). Explanatory objectives seek to deliver description of the patterns that are stored within the data. This purpose provides clarity in instances where a question has been asked or a decision has to be supported as it explains current trends of the data that is analysed (Fusion Charts, n. d.). Exploratory objectives are alternatives to explanatory as they do not require a specific end goal. Where explanatory works at finding a definitive solution to a specific goal, exploratory looks to generate new questions. Exploratory is typically more multivariate in nature as it may often compare data sets against each other rather than explaining a specific data set (Fusion Charts, n. d.). Keim (2002:100) explains that the exploratory objective of data visualisation can often be viewed as a way to generate a hypothesis. This could then lead to explanatory objectives to seek confirmation on the hypothesis that has been generated.

Although primarily used in the business environment, data visualisation has proven to be a valuable tool in the education sector as well. Knowles (2014) demonstrates some of the visualisation formats and tools for visualisation that can be used for certain scenarios such as attendance monitoring and academic performance through grade fluctuation. Research from Mazza and Dimitrova also incorporated student comprehensive of subject matter as a measurement to be visualised which was obtained through web logs of student interaction with web-based distance learning applications. Experimentation has been undertaken in the effective use of visualisation in education and results are assisting in the craft of future best practice. However, research from Naps et al (2003) suggests that visualisation can only be truly effective in the educational setting when paired with an accurate taxonomy that can be correctly representative of student engagement. The taxonomy proposed throughout this study focused on student comprehensive of the subject matter of the course. Therefore it can be determined that the accuracy and insight of the data accrued through the use of learning analytic methodology is directly influential on the potential impact that visualisations can provide.

DESIGN AND DEVELOPMENT

Methodology

Various methodologies have been employed for different elements of this project. The overall methodology has been selected and will be described, justified and critically analysed here. An additional methodology has been adopted for the research activity and the design sections of the project. The research methodology would represent the undertaking of research and the completion of the literature review segment of project development. It is important to note that these segmented methodologies are explained and utilised within a master methodology that represents the entire development and delivery of the project as a whole.

The waterfall methodology has been selected for the overall development of the project. Typically, the waterfall methodology will see the project segmented into significant milestones. The methodological approaches requires that each milestone is completed in its entirety rather than the employment of iterative design. The primary justification for the selection of this methodology is its simplicity of use and its suitability for smaller scale projects (ISTQB Exam Certification, n. d.). Furthermore, the linear nature of the waterfall methodology is deemed suitable for this project considering the manageable and rigid structure (Centers for Medicare & Medicad Services, 2005). The only alterations made to the methodology is with regards to the coding stage and the operation support stages. This is due to the actual deliverable being a theoretical framework rather than a physical piece of software.

The following describes each stage of the waterfall methodology and how it is applied within the context of this project:

- Initial investigation

The initial investigation represents the gathering and evaluation of the current landscape with regards to learning analytics, predictive analytics and data visualisation within the United Kingdom and additional countries for the purpose of cross comparison. This investigation will be represented by the contents of the literature review. This investigation will provide the foundational understanding of where to begin with the development of the theoretical framework. Data gathering has already been completed at this stage and will then be used later during the design and implementation stages of the project. Data sets that are to be used include coded transcripts, questionnaires completed by students and end of module evaluation forms completed by students. The aim here is to provide a multivariate approach to the development of the theoretical framework.

As discussed, the data sets that are to be used for the development of the framework are considerably varied. The variation exists both in the data itself as well as the variables that exist within the data. For example, the coded transcripts span the course of several weeks and there are also transcripts to represent separate groups. Considering the multivariate nature of the data set, experimentation with visualisation techniques can take an iterative approach. To begin, core visualisations that represent a single outcome, such as the frequency at which words were used within a transcript can be analysed. From here, the analysis can become more variable, by adding an additional group or additional time frame into the analysis. This iterative development process will eventually end with a multivariate approach that incorporates all elements of the data, therefore providing a concept to the framework and a demonstrated outcome that can be cross referenced through the module evaluation forms.

Research Methodology

During the research process of this project, a methodology for research was important to the establishment of a sound foundation for further development. The grounded theory methodology was selected for the research. Considering the deliverable of the project is a theoretical framework, any research undertaken must focus on directly aiding the underpinning theory of the deliverable. Savin-Baden and Major (2013:182) describe the grounded theory methodology as an approach with a precise purpose of establishing theory from the back of research. Grounded theory also requires a significant amount of comparison to be made between the foundation of research and the consequential practical application. In this instance, comparisons are being made between open-source visualisation tools. In addition, the project will be making many comparisons between existing research and the associated measurement values when analysing learning analytics. Furthermore, these comparisons will be the basis for the newly established theoretical framework that emerges as part of the project deliverable. Grounded theory will also be applied in the process of converting between qualitative and quantitative data that is analysed throughout the course of the implementation of this framework.

IMPLEMENTATION

As outlined in the methodology section of the report, the implementation and experimentation of design will be iterative. The employment of each data set and the variations within each data set will build up as experimentation and observation take place. The following section of the report will document each iteration, with discussion and justification for chosen visualisation outcomes as well as a discussion of what conclusions can be drawn at each stage. The employment of iterative experimentation in this intended to improve the insight gained for the eventual deliverable outcome or collection of theoretical concepts.

There are various sources from which data can be analysed in this experiment. Much of the data originates from a Programming module undertaken by first year undergraduate students. More specifically, the data comes from a particular coursework that students completed during the module. This coursework involved the construction and design of a Lego robot that required students to build and program specific actions at each stage. The first data source are transcripts from student video diaries recorded over the duration of the coursework at the completion of each stage. The second data source is an assessment of student experience with programming concepts prior to the course beginning. Finally, a number of module reviews submitted by students are also available for analysis. This data comes in the form of a questionnaire that asks for feedback on several components of the course content, course tutoring and student development.

Level 1: Word Clouds

The base level of this experimentation looks a single variable of frequency within a portion of the dataset. The data set for this will be a single transcript taken from a first year undergraduate student video log where they are reflection on a specific section of coursework. The first visualisation will be creating a word cloud that will demonstrate the frequency of word choice in the video log and can be seen in Figure 1. The transcript is taken from the second task of the coursework and therefore represents not only the early stages of the course but also the early stages of the first year of undergraduate study.

Figure 1. Word cloud representing single transcript from a single team at the beginning of the course (Level One)

Observing the word cloud does give the viewer an output to some degree, namely the variety of language used in the transcript as well as which word choices were made more. However, with a singular output such as this, it can be difficult to derive the significant insight that is required for informed action. Therefore, this method needs to be built upon further by including an additional variant. For example, taking the transcript from the last task of the coursework and creating another word cloud. Now the output can represent language choice, word choice frequency and a cross-comparison between the two world clouds could indicate language change. This change in language could be considered as one way of demonstrating how a student has progressed throughout the course. The second word cloud will be generated from a transcript of the same team of students but during a video log reflection of the last coursework task. This word cloud can be viewed in Figure 2.

Although this method can paint the raw beginning of a picture, there are several vital elements that this sort of visualisation has not given us access to. For example, outside of a previous description of the context, this visualisation has not provided any form of context. In addition, without a defined model for assessing language change, attempting to define how the language has changed over time can be difficult. An observer could suggest that the word "problem" appears to feature quite frequently in the first word cloud but has become considerably less frequent in the second. It could be argued that is shows some indication of progress, but without a specified and objective scale, this information is not enough for insightful action. It is merely an assistive tool in the reflection of progress rather than a way in which to proactively respond to a situation. In addition, this visualisation has not provided any indication of student ability before or after the direct instances from which the transcripts where recorded. The univariate nature of this form of analysis can provide a solid starting point, however it requires further and deeper development.

Figure 2. Word cloud representing a single transcript from a single team at the end of the course (Level 1)

Level 2: Coded Transcript Analysis

The next level to providing significant insight into the data that has been gathered will use a system of coding the transcript responses. The general context or theme of the remark being made is categorised to give a semi-qualitative way of manipulating the available data. The categories created for defining student language within these transcripts are as follows:

- **Peer Interaction:** An instance where another student joins the discussion after the initial speaker.
- **Fear:** An instance where the students appear fearful, worried or apprehensive about an element of the work.
- **Reflection:** An instance where students are recalling events in order to analyse or assess them.
- **Problem Solving:** A subset of the reflection category in which students describe how a problem they identified was resolved.
- **Pride:** An instance where a student is pleased, proud or happy in the outcome of something they have done.
- **Concept:** An instance where students are explaining the concept and background information of what is being discussed.
- **Belief:** An instance where a student has displayed confidence in their ability to achieve or overcome something.
- **Strategy:** An instance where students are discussing the approach they intend to take or displays the strategic approach they did take.
- **Desire:** An instance where students are discussing the desire to succeed at the task.
- **Creativity:** An instance where students are discussing when and how they had to be creative.
- **Design:** An instance where students assess or describe the design of the work that they carried out.

As with the word clouds, the frequency at which these categories appear is where the analysis is centred here. In doing this, the analysis is provided with semi-qualitative data which provides qualitative indication with quantitative formatting.

The first step is to take a single transcript that represents one video log reflection from one level of the coursework, in this instance Stage 2. Stage 2 in this context is the first significant piece of work that the students have to design and build themselves, therefore it can be considered as the starting point. It is important to note that not all of the categories will appear within every transcript. In fact, it is vital to acknowledge this as it is directly representative of how student behaviour and attitudes move throughout the course. To begin, the findings from this coded transcript can be placed within a simple table, displayed here in Table 1.

However, as described by Spence (2007:17) tabular presentation is not the most useful format when the observer is not looking for specific measurement. Furthermore, this sort of table does not accommodate for the additional variables that are to be added in to give the scope of progression. Multiple tables would be required to represent the additional video logs and at that time, the analysis will only have a collection of tables and no immediate visual representation of the pathway or progression or change. This is where visualisation can provide insight on the surface level. To give an example of this,

Table 1. Simple table containing the frequency at which certain predetermined categories appear within a transcript.

Category	Frequency
Fear	*1*
Reflection	*4*
Problem Solving	*3*
Pride	*5*
Concept	*1*
Belief	*2*

the same data can be represented in a visualised format. Instead of representing the data within a table, the data can be better displayed within a bar gram. The generated bar gram for this specific data range can be found in Figure 3.

Although without a numbered axis like that of a graph or the numbers appearing within a table, this form of visualisation allows for immediate awareness of scale. As argued by Spence (2007: 18) the representation of range can be significantly informative in the initial stages of analysis and can help in the formation of a "mental model" just from the first observation. Furthermore, this sort of visualisation can accommodate the passage of time within the course and give visual representation of each log altogether, as shown in Figure 4.

Figure 3. Bar gram to represent a single coded transcript from the beginning of a course.

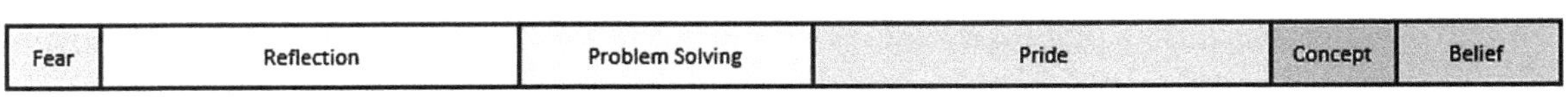

Figure 4. Bar gram to represent all four transcripts from video logs recorded after each milestone within the coursework

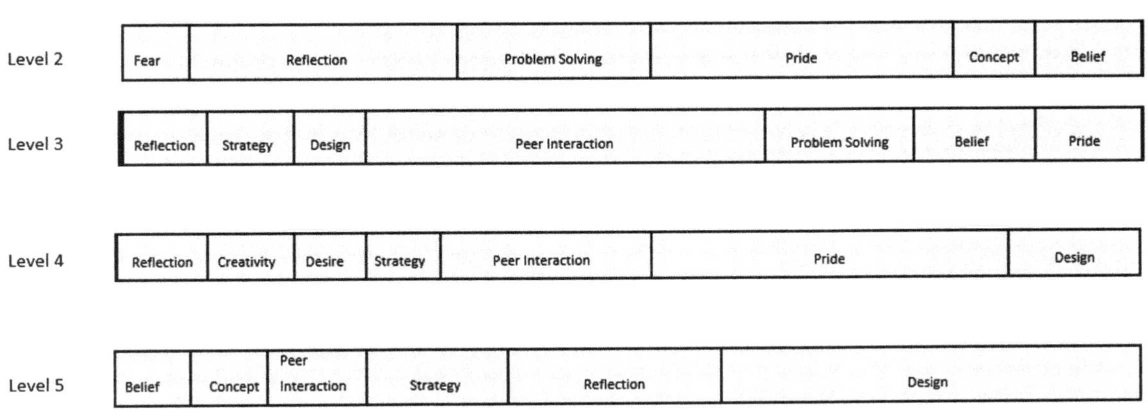

From various surface level observations of this visualisation, there are several points that could be made. Firstly, the only time in which fear is present is at the beginning of the coursework process.

Furthermore, from this visualisation we can observe the movement of student behaviour, which in this case is apparent. Students begin largely reflecting on the core problems they encountered and reporting happiness and pride at the completion. As the students move through the coursework, elements of strategy and design begin appearing. Personal responses to the coursework such as pride, desire and belief do feature throughout. However, upon arrival at Level 5, the students are reporting on more technical level throughout their video logs. A significant portion of the language used within the video log is dedicated to design and strategic elements of the work rather than the emotional responses to that work. At this stage, observers are able to gain additional insight into how student behaviour moved during the course. It could be proposed that this is indicative of student progression, as the students become more aware and focused on discussing the tasks and the functional requirements of those tasks. Cross-comparing these outcomes with a coded video log from other students could display different movement. Furthermore, if these observations could be compared against the eventual grades that were earned by the students, this would deliver insight into how these behaviours correlate with academic performance.

Level 3: Visualising Student Learning Background

As stated during the introduction of this chapter, one of the data sources available for this analysis are questionnaires relating to the background knowledge of a collection of students. These questions were asked before the students began the course to give an indication into the previous experiences they have had with programming languages. When analysing the language use in the word clouds earlier, one of the criticisms levelled at the visualised output was the absence of context before or after the word cloud. That is to say that the student background, expectation or ability is not present and therefore cannot be taken into account. Here, data that establishes a starting point for the student journey is available and can be incorporated.

When presenting the bar gram in the previous level of this experimentation, the first avenue for analysis would often be a table. In the interest of presenting the core data to begin, and to provide labels and context to the data, firstly it will be represented in a simple table. This is to enable the eventual comparison between the effectiveness of tabular representation and visualised representation. The data comes 117 first year undergraduate students and asks about their previous experience with any form of programming. The parameters for answers are displayed in Table 2.

This data can then be rearranged into a visualisation. Spence (2007: 36) describes scatterplot visualisation as standard representation for bivariate data. Although in this instance, the additional variable of gender does exist, this can still be represented on two axis with an additional line that is defined through

Table 2. Tabular representation of first year undergraduate student background in programming before programming module

Gender	Minimum Experience	Extensive Experience	No Experience	Experience with Scripting Languages
Male	29	1	69	0
Female	8	0	10	0

the chart legend. The scatterplot for this data set is displayed in Figure 5. Upon observing this scatterplot, numerous questions can be posed that have the capacity to unveil further insight for analysis. Firstly, what is the main attraction to a computer science course for people who have had no previous experience with programming, arguably one of the core components of computer science? Furthermore, why does only a single male student express having extensive programming experience out of 99 male students? On the surface, it could be suggested that this is the only student who has had significant experience prior to attending the course. However it could also be suggested that lower confidence or belief could also be a factor affecting student self-assessment.

At this stage, a contextualisation of where students are coming from in relation to course subject matter has been established. This now provides the starting point to understand more of how students feel about their competency moving into the subject matter. Contrasting these findings with the bar gram representing progress throughout the coursework is a way in which further insight could be gained about student performance. For example, acknowledging that the vast majority of students report no previous programming experience, the potential for student disengagement or anxiety could be considered a significant possibility, especially during the beginning of the course. Indeed, the earlier findings within the bar gram in Figure 5 do exhibit the appearance of fear.

Level 4: Analysis of Module Evaluations

The process has already observed the beginning of the path in forms of student background as well as observing the progression through the course and how behaviours change. This is where an observation and analysis of the end of the movement through the course can be obtained. Upon completion of the course, students were asked to assess how they believed the module had performed against numerous criterion. The assessment covers the module in its entirety, including the quality of teaching, availability and quality of resources, management and scheduling of the module itself and how a student feels they

Figure 5. Scatterplot representation of student background experience in programming before beginning the course

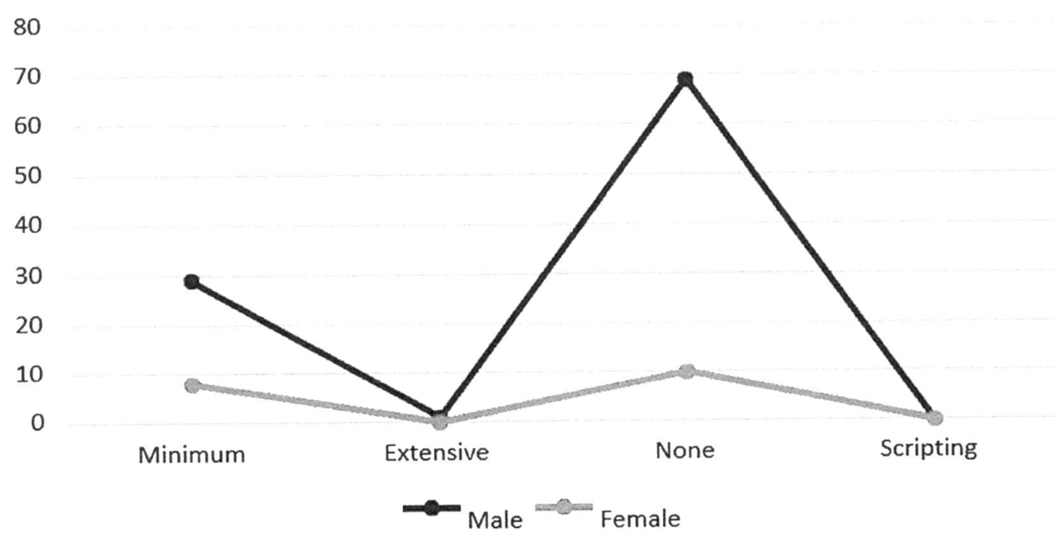

have personally developed as a result of partaking in the module. These scores are gathered quantitatively on a typical questionnaire scale with one (5) representing 'Strongly Agree' and (1) representing 'Strongly Disagree'. Sixteen questionnaires in total were completed. For the purpose of context and visualisation, the scores have been assigned in semantic groups, as were the breakdowns of student language in the transcript analysis. The semantic groups are as follows:

- **Teaching:** Involves questions specifically related to how the staff deliver the content. This includes staff enthusiasm, ability at explaining or making content interesting.
- **Assessment & Feedback:** Involves questions relating specifically to feedback on assignments. This includes the quality of feedback, the speed of feedback and how the feedback helped students understand their mistakes.
- **Academic Support:** Involves questions relating to the support received throughout the studying of the module. This includes an assessment of the quality of opportunities to contact academic staff and the support provided during studies.
- **Organisation & Management:** Involves questions relating to how the course is organised against student schedules. This includes an assessment of how the module is running against a schedule and how changes to the schedule are communicated to students.
- **Learning Resources:** Involves questions relating to the quality of the resources available to students. This includes an assessment of academic resources as well as physical resources such as library or IT resources.
- **Personal Development:** Involves questions about how the students feel they have developed upon completion of the course. This includes an assessment of student confidence and communication skills.

All of the answers given within each semantic section were totalled, to provide a running total for that semantic group. Therefore each of the 16 questionnaires will have 6 scores that each represent all the questions within that group. There are several ways in which we can attempt to visualise this data to gain insight. Firstly, each of the 16 questionnaires can be compiled into a clustered bar graph. This enables us to visualise the responses of each of the 16 individuals to assess any points where the module is excelling or failing. The clustered bar graph is pictured in Figure 6.

Upon surface level evaluation of this visualisation, several conclusions can be drawn. Firstly, the assessment & feedback scores received from students appear to be the highest across the six groups. Furthermore, academic support and learning resource scores appear to be amongst the lowest throughout the average. This suggests areas that would be considered in need of improvement throughout the multiple dimensions of the student experience. However, it is also vital to consider how a visualisation at this stage is misleading. This is because the semantic grouping of the questions do not have an even spread of questions within them. As a result of this, some scores will be typically lower than others as the number of questions asked within those groups are lower. Considering this, a new approach needs to be taken in order to give more valuable and reliable insight through visualisation.

A suggest approach for this would to be use a star plot or radar graph. Spence (2007: 60) suggests an advantage of a star plot visualisation lies within the effective representation through a single shape, especially when representing multivariate data. In order to plan onto the star plot, the data needs to be reformed into two variables. The first variable is a total score for each of the 6 semantic groups that the

Figure 6. Cluster graph representation of 16 module reviews

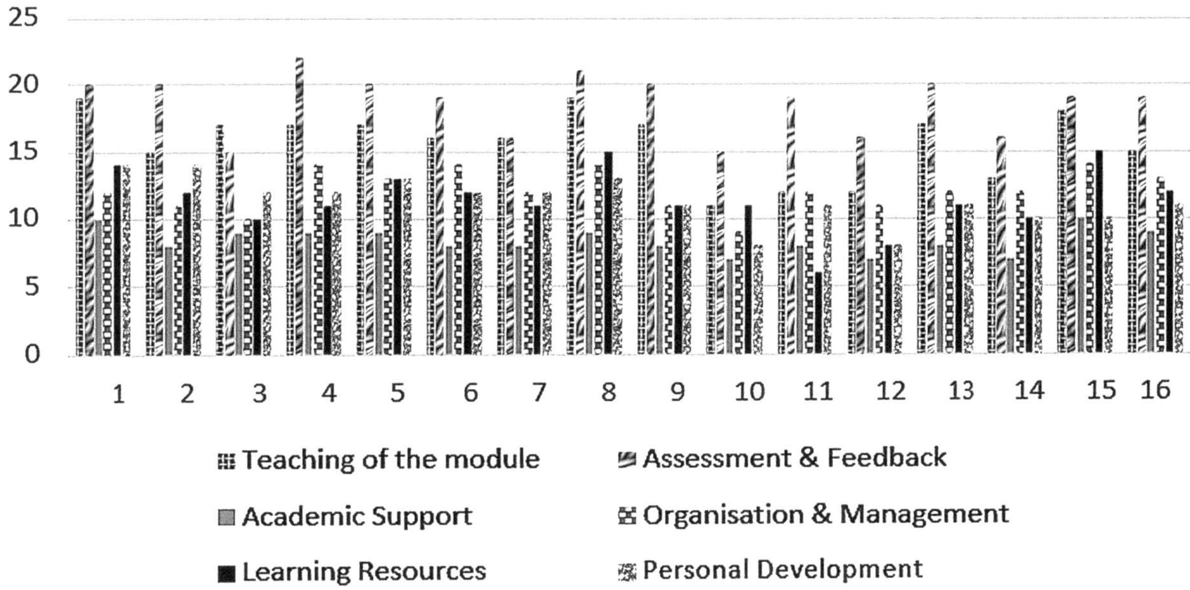

answer scores have been collected within. The second is a figure to represent the maximum possible score that is attainable within each semantic group. Compiling this into a star plot visualisation would appear as in Figure 7.

Reviewing the star plot graph now represents something entirely different to that of the clustered bar graph created earlier. Observing the shapes on display within this visualisation shows that some of the

Figure 7. Radar or starplot graph to represent the total scores given by students and compare them to the total possible score attainable

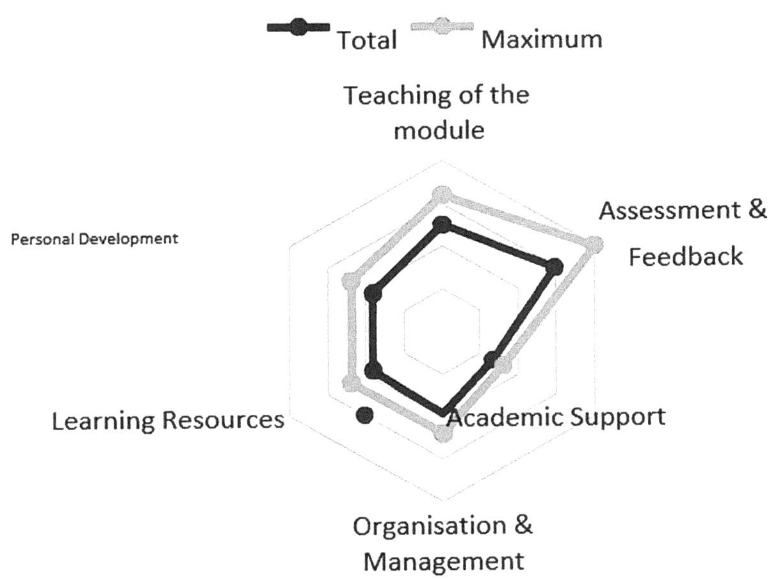

conclusions drawn from the previous conclusion actually misrepresent the data. From here, it is clear that academic support is in fact one of the closest points to the potential maximum. In addition, assessment and feedback would appear to be furthest away from its equivalent potential maximum value.

This technique is also relevant for use with individual students. Taking one single sample of scores given by one student and applying the same visualisation can assist in personalising the analysis.

Doing this would have particular benefit in assisting "at-risk" students through the establishment of problem areas. Furthermore, the application of this approach in relation to the social and cultural aspects of university may be worthwhile to deliver an additional dimension of analysis.

CONCLUSION

Through experimentation, several suggestions for the design of an effective framework have become apparent. Firstly, observations throughout the passage is time is vitally important. Analysing student backgrounds before the course as well as gathering data upon course completion can provide considerable insight that allow for action to be taken for future course design. However, tracking student behaviour and attitudes as they progress through the course content is especially important. Gauging attitudes towards course content and observing the changing of behaviour as time passes can allow the possibility of more catered education delivery in the future. Furthermore, employing the use of visualisation in understanding patterns and movements in behaviour more clearly is a valuable tool. Not only is the tool valuable in itself for providing immediately recognisable patterns but it is also approachable to the educators that are interacting with students on a regular basis. Permitting those who are the primary source of contact to generate these insights is an approach worthwhile investigating more. This is because it has the potential to allow for more widespread integration of learning analytic techniques. It is also important to consider the vast array of visualisation techniques that are available and how best to use them. As displayed in some of the experimentation, the choice of certain visualisations over others do not demonstrate the same outcome, therefore the outcomes and insight are counter-productive. Ensuring the accurate understanding of data and what it represents is just as important as understanding the techniques used to harvest that data.

In summary, a suggested framework would consider observing and collecting data from students at the beginning and the end of the course, as well as throughout the duration. Elements outside of the regularly inspected elements such as availability of resources and contact time with lecturers are particularly valuable. In addition, it may not be of the upmost importance to apply exact quantified measurements onto data, especially when it is visualised. As demonstrated with the bar grams representing student behaviours throughout the course, the most important element of that visualisation is the pattern more so than the frequency. Of course, the frequency is necessary to create the visualisation in the first place, but the visualisation itself should focus on the patterns and movement of the shapes more so than exact figures. These methods can be contrasted and combined with more quantitatively focused representations as featured in some of the other visualisations throughout the course of experimentation. However, ensuring the capture of data outside the traditional is what would be considered the biggest breakthrough in furthering the effectiveness of learning analytics. Expanding data gathering beyond the confines of a specific course and its relevant materials could offer entirely new insights. The module evaluation section of a proposed framework should look to explore the academic side of this further. As demonstrated in the experimentation, elements like student perceived personal development and the scheduling of modules are interesting avenues for exploration. However, factors outside of academic practice are especially interesting when considering the social and cultural effects that students can endure and how that can positively or negatively impact performance. Elements such as social integration into university life, availability of activities and events existing outside of the classroom setting can provide an extra dimension in the complete picture.

One of the primary known problems associated with this study is the data set. Although the data set is valuable and has led towards a series of experimentations within this project, the data was not gathered specifically for the purpose of this study. As a result, experimentation was conducted ad-hoc to the data set and crossing over the data effectively proved difficult. The quantity of data was vastly different across samples. The inconsistency in sample sizes also proved difficult when considering a compounded multivariate analysis of all samples together. However, the iterative implementation of each sample in stages throughout the experimentation as well as establishing links after individual analysis of samples did compensate for this. Additional elements of critical reflection will be discussed in more detail in a later chapter of this report.

FURTHER WORK

Opportunities for further work to expand on this project are extensive. Firstly, experimentation with social and cultural elements of university outside of the specifically academic data gathering would be of great interest. Gathering and collating this additional data with findings from this project would assist in the deeper exploration of student behaviour and engagement causation. A student may be academically bright however external mitigating circumstances have not been accounted for in analysis, therefore academic-focused analysis cannot explain, understand or predict it. In addition, taking the theoretical framework established here and implementing it further has the potential to deepen development. Collecting sample data specifically for the purpose of further learning analytic research would be invaluable in furthering understanding of theoretical concepts. In addition, the inclusion of data from other university-related functions such as library analytics would provide an opportunity to attempt further exploration of alternative dimensions in university study and how that can influence behaviour.

CRITICAL EVALUATION

The following section this report will reflect on the overall execution of the project. This includes reflecting on the outcome. It will begin with an assessment of the fulfilment of the original objectives posed at the beginning of the project; factoring in anything that changed during the course of the completion of the project. This will be followed by an evaluation of how the project performed against the project plan that was devised at the early stages of the project. Then an assessment of how the project was designed will be undertaken and evaluated. Finally, the ways in which the project was executed will also be critically evaluated.

Objective Evaluation

Firstly, the outcome of the project is to be evaluated against the aims and objectives that were established at the point of conception. For the purpose of the evaluation, each objective will be critically evaluated individually and the overall satisfaction of the project objective will also be evaluated.

- To learn and evaluate current learning analytic methodology and how it can be utilised in a UK higher education institution. Throughout the course of this project, various forms of learning analytic methodology has been researched. Methods and studies were compiled, explained contrasted in the literature review. In addition, several learning analytic methods for data gathering were utilised in the experimentation phase of this project. This includes the use of student surveys and transcripts from video logs. However, the inclusion of more advanced techniques and the use of specifically gathered data would have certainly improved the attainment of this objective. Nevertheless, the overall achievement and demonstration of the contents of this objective does appear throughout the project.
- To explore and understand the presence of big data and data analytics in the UK higher education sector at the time of conducting the research.

Extensive research was conducted in the presence of big data and data analytics within higher education. This includes specifically within the United Kingdom, but also in other major countries. This included observations and evaluations of data analytic methodology that is utilised in countries such as the United States of America and Australia. The overall presence of data analytics and big data usage in UK higher education was also contrasted with the activity in the aforementioned countries. Overall, this objective was attained to an acceptable level.

- To learn about and evaluate predictive analytic methodology and how it can be utilised in a UK higher education institution.

Significant research was conducted in the interest of understanding predicative analytics and some of the methodologies behind it. However, the inclusion of predictive analytics into the overall design of the theoretical framework is considered lacking. Some indication as to how predictions could be made based on the experiments were touched upon but no explicit methodology was employed. Instead, the focus moved more towards the observation and experimentation with visualisation techniques.

- To critically evaluate and compare open source data visualisation tools and assess any advantages that one has over another.

This objective changed as the project progressed. The original focus was to use open source tools such as Lumify and Nodebox and compare the two in terms of functionality. However, these source tools were later considered unsuitable in application. Lumify was largely in a demo stage at the point of undertaking this project and Nodebox did not align with the overall objective of the project. The focus no longer centred on the tools themselves; more the visualisation techniques that could be utilised in the various scenarios featured during the implementation. Therefore, the original objective was not fulfilled, however the alternative objective was met. Several visualisation methods were explored and developed during the implementation stage of the project. However, additional and significantly more advanced visualisation techniques were not experimented with during the course of this project. The implementation of more advanced techniques would be considered as a part of further work.

Project Plan Evaluation

The original project plan for this project was deviated away from significantly at several points during the project life cycle. This deviation was due to unforeseen personal circumstances that had to be accommodated for in a way that could not be accounted for previously to the project beginning. The preliminary work in submitting a project proposal and project progress report were in time with the originally established project plan. The work entailed in producing the final report did not remain in keeping with the original project plan. Nevertheless, the order in which the project objectives were completed remained the same and the equivalent timescale was afforded to the work completed were possible.

Design Evaluation

Numerous design decisions were made throughout the course of this project and the following section will look to elaborate on those decisions further. The first element to address is the application of grounded theory methodology for the research proportion of this project. As explained within the relevant sections of the documentation, the grounded theory method operates with the desire to generate theory through research and observation (Savin-Baden & Major, 2013:182) and was therefore relevant to the work undertaken here. Furthermore, the requirements for comparison and observation employed through the grounded theory methodology was believed to be extremely applicable. Working within this methodology for research has been considered largely appropriate and successful.

Secondly, the application of the waterfall method for the overall execution of the project has been applied in this instance. The justification for this method lies specifically with its rigidity and linearity as a methodology. Conducting a debut project with a generally smaller scale meant that using the waterfall method felt most appropriate. In addition, aside from the implementation stage of the project, which uses a separate methodology of its own, the project naturally flowed in a more linear fashion. Using a linear methodology in the approach to overall structure helped keep the flow of progress moving and established a clear pathway to travel during development. However, through researching the waterfall methodology and its correct usage, it became clear that an alternative approach should be taken for the implementation and experimentation segment of the project. The decision was made to use an iterative approach to the experimentation and general design of the theoretical framework to enable the continuous building of theory with the opportunity to revisit elements during progression. In that way, elements of exploration and new discovery remained entirely possible with that form of systematic approach. Generally speaking, the application of this method during experimentation proved useful and lent itself to the way in which experimentation moved along.

Implementation Evaluation

Various elements of implementation changed from the original proposal. The explanation and justification surrounding these changes are to be elaborated on in the following section. One of the primary changes that occurred from the proposal stages of the project came in the form of a shift of focus in the objectives. As previously discussed, the element of predictive analytics and predictive analytic method was researched and evaluated as outlined in the original objectives. However, the application of these methods were not as prominent as they were intended to be. Instead of this, a focus on the application and use of visualisation techniques became much more of a central focal point. Furthermore, the original implementation objective of comparing and contrasting open-source visualisation software was no longer considered an objective of the project. Instead, these changes resulted in a new objective that sought to compare visualisation techniques when used with learning analytic data to assess their suitability for the theory of a framework. The reason the original objective of open source tool comparison was disregarded was due to the selected software tools being deemed unsuitable for the tasks and data sets that were to take place as a part of this project. One of the open source tools was prefaced to be existing within a demo state and therefore the functions were significantly limited in comparison to the aspirations of the project and its objectives. Furthermore, the other open source tool originally proposed for comparison did not appear to have the necessary features that the project wished to employ. However, the comparison of visualisation techniques and demonstrating how different visualisations techniques can represent learning analytic data felt like a more suitable and relevant substitute approach.

An additional component of the project which should be critically evaluated is the data sets used against the original project aspirations. Although extremely useful for the experimentation and suggested theory that manifested during the course of this project, the project had to be redesigned around the data rather than the data being designed as a part of the project. The data sets used during the course of this project had already been gathered before the project had begun. In addition, the quantity of data from each set used varied significantly and therefore does not provide the greatest degree of consistency. As a result, the combination of these data sets to create more in-depth multivariate visualisations proved considerably difficult. In future work, it would be extremely beneficial to design data gathering requirements and gather data specifically collected for the purpose of the research taking place. Nevertheless, the overall analysis, insight and understanding derived from this project with the data set was substantial. In addition, the use of previously gathered data made for a higher degree of simplicity in relation to ethical practice, as data had already been gathered, anonymised and secured.

REFERENCES

Campbell, J. F., DeBlois, P. B., & Oblinger, D. G. (2007). Academic Analytics: A New Tool for a New Era. *EDUCASE Review*, *42*(4), 40–57.

Centers for Medicare & Medicad Services. (2005). *Selecting a Development Approach.* Retrieved from http://www.cms.gov/Research-Statistics-Data-and-Systems/CMS-Information-Technology/XLC/Downloads/SelectingDevelopmentApproach.pdf

Chatti, M. A., Dyckhoff, A. L., Schroeder, U., & Thüs, H. (2012). A Reference Model for Learning Analytics. *International Journal of Technology Enhanced Learning*, *4*(5/6), 318–331. doi:10.1504/IJTEL.2012.051815

Commonwealth of Australia. (2009). *Transforming Australia's Higher Education System.* Retrieved from http://planipolis.iiep.unesco.org/upload/Australia/Australia_TransformingAusHigherED.pdf

Duval, E. (2011) Attention please! Learning Analytics for Visualization and Recommendation. *Proceedings of LAK11 1st International Conference on Learning Analytics and Knowledge 2011* (pp. 9-17). New York, ACM

Eduventures. (2013). *Predictive Analytics in Higher Education: Data-Driven Decision-Making for the Student Life Cycle* (White Paper). Retrieved from http://www.eduventures.com/wp- content/uploads/2013/02/Eduventures_Predictive_Analytics_White_Paper1.pdf

Friendly, M. (2005). *Milestones in the History of Data Visualization: A Case Study in Statistical Historiography.* Retrieved from http://www.datavis.ca/papers/gfkl.pdf

Fusion Charts. (n. d.). *Principles of Data Visualization - What We See in a Visual.* Available: http://www.fusioncharts.com/whitepapers/downloads/Principles-of-Data-Visualization.pdf

Hair, J. F. Jr. (2007). Knowledge creation in marketing: The role of predictive analytics. *European Business Review*, *19*(4), 303–315. doi:10.1108/09555340710760134

ISTQB Exam Certification. (n. d.). *What is Waterfall model- advantages, disadvantages and when to use it?* Retrieved from http://istqbexamcertification.com/what-is-waterfall-model-advantages-disadvantages-and-when-to-use-it/

Keim, D. A. (2002). Information Visualisation and Visual Data Mining. *IEEE Transactions on Visualization and Computer Graphics*, *7*(1), 100–107.

Knowles, J. (2014). *Data Visualisation for Education.* Retrieved from jaredknowles.com/s/KnowlesS-DPTalk2014.html

Luan, J. (2002). Data Mining and Its Applications in Higher Education. *New Directions for Institutional Research*, *2002*(113), 17–36. doi:10.1002/ir.35

Macfadyen, L. P., & Dawson, S. (2012). Numbers Are Not Enough. Why e-Learning Analytics Failed to Inform an Institutional Strategic Plan. *Journal of Educational Technology & Society*, *15*(3), 149–163.

Mazza, R., & Dimitrova, V. (2004). Visualising Student Tracking Data to Support Instructors in Web-Based Distance Education. *WWW Alt. '04 Proceedings of the 13th International World Wide Web Conference on Alternate Track Papers & Posters* (pp. 154-161).

Naps, T. L., Robling, G., Almstrum, V., Dann, W., Fleischer, R., Hundhausen, C., & Velazquez-Iturbide, J. A. et al. (2003). Exploring the role of visualization and engagement in computer science education. *ACM SIGCSE Bulletin*, *35*(2), 131–152. doi:10.1145/782941.782998

Pascarella, E., & Terenzini, P. (1980). Predicting Freshman Persistence and Voluntary Dropout Decisions from a Theoretical Model. *The Journal of Higher Education*, *51*(1), 60–75. Retrieved from http://www.jstor.org/stable/1981125?seq=13#page_scan_tab_contents doi:10.2307/1981125

Phillips, R., Maor, D., Preston, G., & Cumming-Potvin, W. (2012). Exploring Learning Analytics as Indicators of Study Behaviour. In: T. Amiel, & B. Wilson (Eds.), *Proceedings of World Conference on Educational Multimedia, Hypermedia and Telecommunications 2012* (pp. 2861-2867).

Phillips, R., Maor, D., Cumming-Potvin, W., Roberts, P., Herrington, J., Preston, G., . . . Perry, L. (2011, December 4–7). Learning analytics and study behaviour: A pilot study. Proceedings of ASCILITE 2011, Wrest Point, Hobart, Tasmania (pp. 997-1007).

Savin-Baden, M., & Major, C. H. (2013). *Qualitative Research: The essential guide to theory and practice* (pp. 182–192). Oxon: Routledge.

Sclater, N. (2014). *Learning analytics - The current state of play in UK higher and further education.* Retrieved from http://repository.jisc.ac.uk/5657/1/Learning_analytics_report.pdf

Siemens, G., & Baker, R. S. J. d (2012) Learning Analytics and Educational Data Mining: Towards Communication and Collaboration. *Proceedings of the 2nd international conference on learning analytics and knowledge*. doi:10.1145/2330601.2330661

Shmueli, G., & Koppius, O. R. (2011). Predictive Analytics in Information Systems Research. *Management Information Systems Quarterly*, *35*, 553–572.

Spence, R. (2007). Information Visualization Design for Interaction (2nd ed., pp. 17–60). Harlow: Pearson Education Limited.

Tinto, V. (1975). Dropout from Higher Education: A Theoretical Synthesis of Recent Research. *Review of Educational Research*, *45*(1), 89–125. Retrieved from http://www.jstor.org/stable/1170024

van Barneveld, A., Arnold, K. E., & Campbell, J. P. (2012). Analytics in Higher Education: Establishing a Common Language. Educase Learning Initiative, 1, 1-11.

Wagner, E., & Ice, P. (2012). Data Changes Everything: Delivering on the Promise of Learning Analytics in Higher Education. EDUCASE Review, 47(4), 33–42.

Ware, C. (2004). Information Visualization: Perception for Design (2nd ed., pp. 3–4). San Francisco: Morgan Kaufmann.

Chapter 6
Effective Learning Strategies for the 21st Century: Implications for the E-Learning

Catherine Chen
Ball State University, USA

ABSTRACT

Due to the ubiquity of technology use in today's society, 21st century workers are likely to be knowledge workers who can use computer technologies to perform non-routine tasks. Students in this century are also likely to learn computer skills online. A robust instrument to investigate effective strategies while learning computer skills is needed. Although the Motivated Strategy for Learning Questionnaire (MSLQ) have been used widely in a conceptual learning environment, it has limitation in assessing students' use of learning strategies in computer software courses. In addition, there have been concerns about the latent factor structure of the MSLQ. This chapter presents a revised learning strategies section of the MSLQ for assessing learning strategies used in a hands-on, computer-skill learning environment. The new instrument contains five learning strategy subscales and exhibits validity and reliability. This revised instrument can be used to assess learning computer skills online.

INTRODUCTION

The 21st century is a digital century. Not only a great deal of information have been digitalized, new data and information are being collected daily in an astonishing rate. This transformation has impacted and will continue to impact the occupations in demand and the skills needed to be successful in the 21st century. In response, countries and organizations have identified competencies that the 21st century workers would need to be successful professionals and as citizens.

In the meantime, instructional theories have shifted from viewing students as reactive learners in the mid-1980s to the current view of students as active participants in their own learning process (Perkins, 1992; Zimmerman, 2001). Students monitor their progress and adjust their learning strategies to achieve their learning goals; this type of action is regarded as self-regulated learning (SRL). Interestingly, there

DOI: 10.4018/978-1-4666-9983-0.ch006

are significant overlap between the identified 21st century competencies and the characteristics associated with SRL (Pellegrino & Hilton, 2013; Wolters, 2010). With the wealth of research on SRL in the past 25 years, Wolters (2010) suggested to utilize SRL research to improve the understanding of the 21st century skills.

This chapter presents core 21st century competencies, SRL, and the commonality between the two. In addition, the chapter reviews online learning and explain MSLQ's limitations, both in assessing students' use of learning strategies in a hands-on learning environment and in the instrument's latent factor structure. Finally, this chapter presents a study that explored the latent factor structure of the learning strategy subscales in a revised MSLQ, which was designed to assess students'. This study also addresses validity and reliability of this revised MSLQ.

BACKGROUND

To provide the background and the rationale for the study, this section reviews literature on 21st century skills and competencies, SRL, online learning, learning computer skills, and the MSLQ.

21st Century Skills and Competencies

The advances in technology and the use of computers in all aspects of business operation have altered the demands in job skills. After analyzing data from 1960 to 1998, Autor, Levy, and Murnane (2003) found that computers have replaced workers who performed routine tasks, those tasks that could be programmed to and performed by computers. A research conducted by Goos, Manning, and Salomons (2009) had reached similar conclusion after analyzing occupational and wage data in Europe. Twenty-first century workers will more likely to be knowledge workers, and the jobs would likely to require them to perform non-routine problem-solving. The skills to use information and communications technologies (ICT) are crucial to their success (Ananiadou & Claro, 2009; Autor, Levy, & Murnane, 2003).

In response to the realization that the technological changes had shifted the skills in demand in the 21st century, many countries go through curriculum reforms in the first decade of the new century, such as the Knowledge Promotion curriculum reform in 2006 in Norway and the new national core curriculum introduced in Poland in 2009 (Ananiadou & Claro, 2009). Ananiadou and Claro (2009) compiled a comprehensive list of competencies as part of a survey, which was then sent to all Organization for Economic Co-operation and Development (OECD) members. These competencies were rooted in three dimensions: information, communication, and ethics and social impact. The specific competencies listed in the survey included critical thinking, problem solving, decision making, communication, collaboration, research and inquiry, flexibility and adaptability, initiative and self-direction, among others. The survey results showed that the majority of skills listed in the survey were covered in the curricula in majority of countries that participated in the survey. Another key finding was that while most competencies were integrated across the curriculum, ICT-related skills were more likely taught as a separate subject. The reason that the authors provided for this findings was that ICT-related skills were considered different in nature. Unlikely many skills needed in the past century, most of these skills in knowledge management are supported by ICT and are learned only in schools (Ananiadou & Claro, 2009).

In the United States, the National Research Council (NRC) was charged, among other tasks, to define the set of 21st century skills that would enable higher-order thinking and would prepare students to be college and career ready (Pellegrino & Hilton, 2013). Competencies in three domains were identified: cognitive, interpersonal, and intrapersonal. The competencies in the cognitive domain included thinking, reasoning, problem solving, and memory. The intrapersonal competencies included emotions, feelings, and the ability to manage one's emotions and set goals. The interpersonal competencies were the ability to "express information to others and to interpret others' messages...and respond appropriately" (Pellegrino & Hilton, 2013, p. 22). The common themes between the OECD survey results and the report released from the NRC were (1) using technologies to search, analyze, and interpret information and then (2) communicating this information to others. This information is mainly used for problem solving or decision making, which would require critical thinking. Reflection, elaboration, collaboration, self-regulation, and adaptability were all important competencies for the 21st century, according to the OECD survey results and the NRC report.

The competencies identified by the survey and by NRC were for K-12 education. Although many competencies identified were in the information- and media-related technology, they tend to focus on general ICT skills, which may not be sufficient for careers after the completion of a bachelor degree. To prepare students for employment upon graduation, universities and colleges are incorporating software skills in their curricula to prepare students to be proficient in using the 'tools of the trade' upon graduation. These could be computer-aided design tools, accounting software, econometric software, enterprise resource planning software, database design software, multimedia software, statistical analysis software, or many other tools specific to particular career fields and areas of study.

Self-Regulated Learning

Parallel to the advances in technologies was the shift in instructional theories. Current learning theories view students as active participants in their own learning process and regard learners as self-regulated (Schuck, 2008, Zimmerman, 2001). Self-regulated learners set their learning goals and monitor and control their efforts to achieve the goals, including regulate physical and social environment, attention, emotions, as well as time management (Pintrich, 1995; Zimmerman & Risemberg, 1997). To be able to achieve this type of regulation, students must have metacognition skill, which is defined as the ability to self-assess and self-correct based on the assessment by Dobrovolny (2006). In other words, metacognition referred to the awareness, knowledge, and control of cognition.

SRL is regarded as an event as opposed to an aptitude. When viewed as an aptitude, learners have relatively stable approaches to selecting and managing the strategies they use in learning. Viewed as an event, on the other hand, learners monitor their engagement and learning outcomes and dynamically adjust their use of strategies as the task proceeds (Butler & Winne, 1995; Pintrich, Smith, Garcia, & McKeachie, 1991). More importantly, when viewed as an event, the skills can be taught and learned (Coppola, 1995; McCombs, 1989). Many studies in self-regulated learning have been conducted to identify effective learning strategies with the objective of recommending instructors to teach these strategies to help students reach their learning goals.

There are many commonalities between SRL and the competencies identified in both the 21st competencies survey results and the NRC's recommendations (Pellegrino & Hilton, 2013; Wolters, 2010). The initiation and self-direction competencies in the 21st century competencies are similar to the goal-setting and 'managing one's achievement of these goals' in SRL. The activities of monitoring and reflection of the SRL are similar to the adaptability and the ability to incorporate feedback effectively listed as part of the 21st century competencies, as well as the intrapersonal competencies in the NRC list. To achieve one's learning goal, self-regulated learners seek help and engage in collaboration (Newman, 2008). This interpersonal aspect of SRL is very similar to both the communication and collaboration competencies in the 21st century competencies and the interpersonal competencies in the NRC recommended list. Although critical thinking is a less discussed aspect of SRL, it is regarded as a skill that self-regulated learners use to be effective in regulating their learning. Indeed, critical thinking is a subscale in a popular instrument, MSLQ, developed by Pintrich and his colleagues (Pintrich, Smith, Garcia, & McKeachie, 1991) to assess students' SRL. MSLQ will be discussed in detail in the next section.

SRL has been an important framework in student learning for decades due to the wealth of empirical research relating the use of SRL to many measurements, including grades and performance (Chen & Chalupa, 2003; Donker, De Boer, Kostons, Dignath van Ewijk, & van der Werf, 2014; Puzziferro, 2008; VanZile-Tamsen & Livingston, 1999; Pintrich & DeGroot, 1990), better understanding of complex concepts (Greene & Azevedo, 2009), student engagement (Sun & Rueda, 2012; Wang & Lin, 2007; Whipp & Chiarelli, 2004), and lower dropout rate (Lee & Choi, 2011). With the similarity between the 21st century competencies and SRL, Wolters (2010) recommended to apply the findings on SRL "as a guide for conducting future work intended to further establish the theoretical foundations of the 21CC [21st century competencies] framework" (p. 18).

E-Learning and Self-Regulated Learning

Online learning has gained immense popularity and attention. According to the Education Department, 5.5 million students took at least one online course in 2012 (Kolowich, 2014). Yet, the attrition rate of online courses was higher than that of face-to-face courses (Angelino, Williams & Natvig, 2007; Lee & Choi, 2011; Patterson & McFadden, 2009; Street, 2010).

In an online environment, students need to be more autonomous because the instructors may not be present to provide immediate support (Rake & Dunn, 2010) and students may feel lost or socially isolated (Cho, Shen, & Laffey, 2010; Sun & Rueda, 2012). While SRL is especially important for online learning (Zimmerman, 2008), it is challenging for many students to exercise self-regulation (Cho & Shen, 2013). Unlike in a traditional learning environment where attendance is likely to be required and the class progresses in a steady pace, it is the online students' responsibility to complete learning activities and assignments on time, although activities are assigned due date. Not surprisingly, the lack of time management was found consistently related to online dropout rate (Nash, 2005; Street, 2010; Willging & Johnson, 2004), but yet interestingly, Elvers, Polzella, and Graetz (2003) found that procrastination was negatively correlated with exam scores in the online sections but not in face-to-face sections of the same course.

Research found that online students' lack of ability to self-regulate their learning is a significant reason for high dropout rate (Lee & Choi, 2011), although other variables, such as personal reasons or job-related factors, were also found related to online dropout rate (Dembo, Junge, & Lynch, 2006; Nichols, 2010; Street, 2010; Willging & Johnson, 2004). In addition to the negative relationship found between the lack of self-regulation to high dropout rate, research also showed that SRL was an important factor in determining students' success in online learning environments (Artino, 2008; Dabbagh & Kitsantas, 2005; Puzziferro, 2008; Whipp & Chiarelli, 2004; Wolters, Pintrich & Karabenick, 2005). These findings suggested a compelling need to establish self-regulated guidelines for online learning (Wang & Lin, 2007).

Effective Learning Strategies and MSLQ

One of the most widely used instruments to assess students' use of learning strategies is the MSLQ. Based on a self-regulatory perspective on student motivation and learning, the questionnaire assesses student motivation and SRL in college students (Pintrich, Smith, Garcia, & McKeachie, 1991). There are two sections in the MSLQ: a motivational section and a learning strategies section. The MSLQ was designed with the flexibility to allow researchers to select sub-section or sub-scales for their research projects. This chapter focuses on the learning strategies section, which consists of nine subscales: rehearsal, elaboration, organization, critical thinking, metacognitive self-regulation, time and study environment, effort regulation, peer learning, and help seeking.

The learning strategies section mainly assesses students' use of strategies for processing information from "texts and lectures" (Duncan & McKeachie, 2005, p. 3). As aforementioned, many 21st century competencies are ICT-related or computer software skills. Learning to use software is applied learning that requires frequent practice and experimentation with different software functionality. Research showed that when hands-on learning was involved in a computer course, peer learning (Niemczyk & Savenye, 2001), critical thinking (Chalupa, Chen, & Charles, 2001; Niemczyk & Savenye, 2001), and organization (Chalupa, Chen, & Charles, 2001) all had an inverse relationship with course grade. These findings contradict the general belief that if students use these learning strategies, they are more cognitively engaged; therefore, the use of these strategies should not have hindered their grades. In Chen's research (2002) to investigate students' use of SRL strategies and grades, two normal probability plots were created to evaluate the variate for the assumptions of regression analysis (Hair, Black, Babin, Anderson, & Tatham, 2010). When test scores were used as the dependent variable and the Effort Regulation subscale in the MSLQ was used as the independent variables in a lecture-learning environment, the plotted values fell closely along the diagonal line as shown in Figure 1. This plot illustrated that the residuals were considered to represent a normal distribution; therefore, the regression variate met the assumption of normality.

Unlike the normal probability plot with Test scores as dependent variable, the normal probability plot for computer hands-on lab assignments showed substantial departures from the diagonal line, as shown in Figure 2.

These plots suggested that MSLQ had its limitation in investigating effective learning strategies in hands-on, computer software courses. Citing others' work in learning strategies used in different subject areas, Wolters and Pintrich (1998) concluded that "the level of SRL in terms of strategy use can very as a function of subject area differences in classroom context" (p. 43). This statement implied the need to development different versions of the instrument to assess effective learning strategies in different classroom context.

In addition, research had revealed concerns about the latent factor structure of the MSLQ. According to Hilpert, Stemien, van der Hoeven Kraft, and Husman (2013), the confirmatory factor analysis (CFA) did not produce a good fit in MSLQ's first development in 1990. An attempted was made to improve the fit in 1993 without success. Dunn, Lo, Mulvenon, and Sutcliffe, (2012) suggested further investigation to explore the latent factor structure of both motivation and learning strategies scales.

Figure 1. Normal probability plot of regression standardized residuals: test (adapted from Chen, 2002)

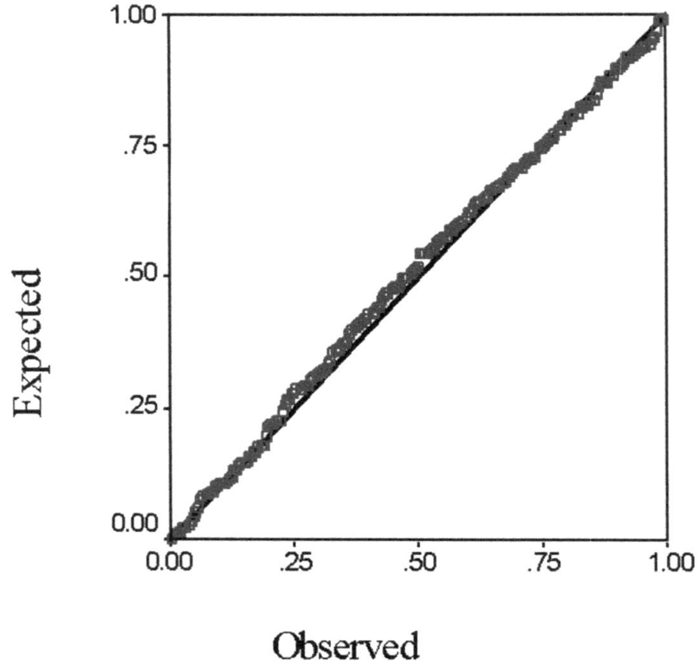

Figure 2. Normal probability plot of regression standardized residuals: lab assignments (adapted from Chen, 2002)

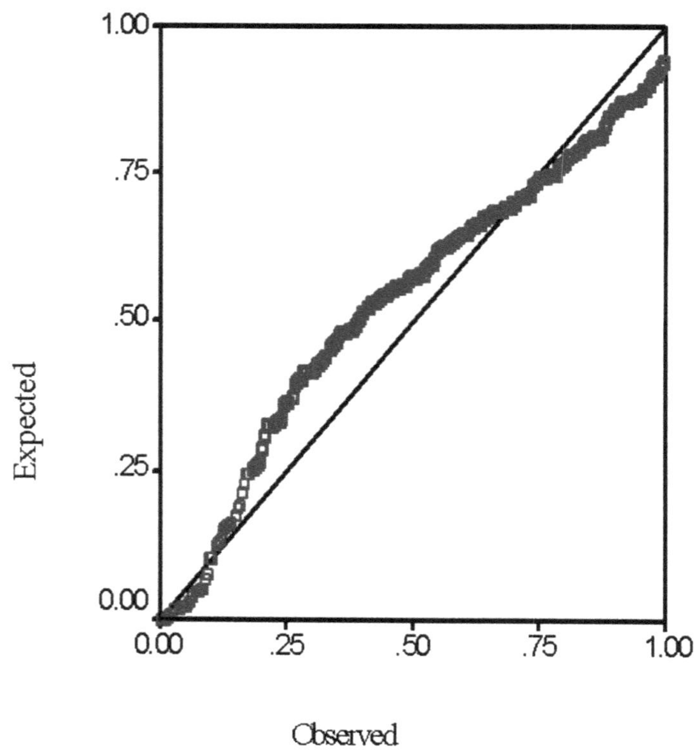

VALIDITY AND RELIABILITY ANALYSES OF A REVISED MSLQ

The purpose of this study was to revise the learning strategies section of the MSLQ to reflect the unique learning strategies involved in learning computer skills. Then, data was collected from college students to analyze the latent factor structure, as well as establishing validity and reliability.

Method

This section describes the procedures used in learning strategies revision and in data collection. It also describes the analysis methods used.

The Revisions of the Learning Strategies Items

The original learning strategies section in the MSLQ consisted of 50 items, numbered from 32 to 81. These items were renumbered to 1 to 50. Then, the statements were revised to be more applicable to learning computer skills. For example, item 8, "I ask the instructor to clarify concepts I don't understand well," was rewritten to incorporate using Help. The new item reads "I frequently use the software Help function or online Help when the instructor is not readily available." Using Help is also incorporated into item 37 by adding "or use the software Help feature" at the end of the statement.

One senior instructor with 20 years of teaching computer software experience revised the instrument, and the second senior instructor with 10 years of teaching experience reviewed the revision. Minor changes were made. This first draft of the revision was then reviewed by two junior instructors. Suggestions and clarifications were discussed and changes were made. For example, the original item 6 stated that "I often feel so lazy or bored when I study for this class that I quit before I finish what I planned to do." The junior instructors thought that the words "so lazy" had negative connotation and suggested to remove them. The authors agreed that it was not necessary to keep the expression and removed them.

This second draft was then administered to two graduate and two undergraduate, one female and three male, students. These four students were interviewed individually to discuss the items. Minor wording changes were made. Feedback from these students showed concern about some items sounding very similar, so items 8 and 27 were exchanged and items 13 and 31 were exchanged to move similar sounding items farther from each other. Appendix 1 lists the original items from MSLQ and the revisions made to the items. The words with strikethrough lines were removed from the original items, and the italicized text was added.

Subjects

Students enrolled in seven sections of an Introduction to Microcomputer Applications course in a large Midwestern university were invited and 201 students participated in the study. Responses were scored using a 7-point Likert type scale, from 1 (*not at all true of me*) to 7 (*very true of me*). The Introduction to Microcomputer Applications course was a required course for all business students. All instructors used the same textbook.

Data Collection Procedures

The data was collected in the week prior to the last week of a semester. Consent to collect data was obtained from each of the instructors who taught the course. On the prearranged day, one of the authors used the last 20 minute of the class to collect the data after the instructor who taught the class had left the classroom. Students were presented with a consent form and the revised learning survey. The participation was voluntary based and instructors did not have access to the data.

Analysis Approach

Exploratory factor analysis (EFA) using principal components factor extraction was used to determine if the learning strategies items correspond to the learning strategies scales. To ensure that it was appropriate to perform factor analysis on the data, measure of sample adequacy (MSA) statistics were calculated prior to performing the factor analysis (Hair et al., 2010). Then, a path model was created and CFA was used to investigate the fit of the model. In other words, both convergent and discriminant evidence were sought to test validation (Messick, 1990). In addition, the internal consistency of reliability was computed using Cronbach's coefficient alphas (Cronbach & Shavelson, 2004).

Findings

This section reports the MSA statistics and the findings on factor analysis, EFA, CFA, and reliability.

Exploratory Factor Analysis

All but five survey items were found to have a MSA exceeding .7. The items that had strictly inadequate MSA statistics were items 2 (.589), 14 (.692), 21 (.694), 30 (.446), and 46 (.676). Since three of these MSA statistics were very close to the cut-off value, it was determined that the MSA criterion was almost completely satisfied. Then, an EFA using principal components factor extraction was conducted. Nine factors were arbitrarily extracted, because there were nine learning strategy scales. The factor loadings reported in the following tables were the correlation coefficients between the variables (rows) and factors (columns), and a factor loading of lower than .4 was not presented in the tables. The tables also provide the communality values, which were the variance explained for each item. A low communality suggests that the factor model was not working well for that indicator, and a communality of lower than .5 was considered inadequate.

The results showed that the factor loadings did not correspond well to the pre-specified learning strategies scale definitions. In most cases, each factor contained items from several different scales. The loadings for the Elaboration scale were scattered across five different factors as shown in Table 1; therefore, the exploratory analysis clearly did not correspond to the Elaboration scale.

Items associated with other scales exhibited the same problem: the Metacognitive Self-Regulation scale loaded on six different factors (Factors 1, 2, 3, 5, 8, and 9), the Time and Study Environment Management scale loaded on three different factors (Factors 1, 2 and 6), and the Effort Regulation scale loaded on three factors (Factors 2, 6, and 8).

Table 1. Factor loadings for elaboration scales

		Factors									
Scale	**Item**	**1**	**2**	**3**	**4**	**5**	**6**	**7**	**8**	**9**	**Communality**
Elaboration	13			.621							.543
	22	.432						.458			.535
	33					.476					.556
	36	.723									.590
	38							.567			.646
	50									-.403	.588

Although Factor 3 loaded relatively well on the Critical Thinking scale, as shown in Table 2, the problem was that several items from other scales loaded on this factor as well, such as item 13 (Elaboration), item 10 and 24 (Metacognitive Self-Regulation), and item 9 (Help Seeking). Item 9 loaded on both Factor 3 and Factor 4.

The Peer Learning scale was another scale that relatively clearly identified as Factor 4 in the EFA, although item 19 had multiple loadings (Factors 1 and 4). The main problem was that the Help Seeking scale was also fairly clearly identified as Factor 4, with three of the four items were loaded on Factor 4, as illustrated in Table 3. There seemed to be no difference between Peer Learning and Help Seeking in the data.

Confirmatory Factor Analysis

As discussed in the EFA section, it appeared that Peer Learning and Help Seeking were indistinguishable; therefore, they were combined into one factor when construct the path model. Figure 3 shows the model. This model included all items in the learning strategies scales with one exception. When item

Table 2. Factor loadings for factor 3

		Factors									
Scale	**Item**	**1**	**2**	**3**	**4**	**5**	**6**	**7**	**8**	**9**	**Communality**
Elaboration	13			.621							.512
Critical thinking	7			.697							.624
	16			.582							.538
	20			.590							.504
	35			.710							.681
	40			.699							.566
Metacognitive Self-regulation	10			.579							.619
	24			.510							.505
Help seeking	9			.442	-.485						.664

Table 3. Factor loadings for peer learning and help seeking scales

		Factors									
Scale	Item	1	2	3	4	5	6	7	8	9	Communality
Peer learning	3				.627						.555
	14				.793						.699
	19	.561			.483						.598
Help seeking	8							.601			.603
	9			.442	-.485						.664
	37				.645						.645
	44				.738						.711

28 was included in the model, an admissible solution could not be obtained. After an examination of the correlation coefficients between the items in the Rehearsal scale, item 28 was removed due to the existence of a negative correlation coefficient between that item and another item in the scale.

Generally, if the comparative fit index (CFI) of a model is above.9 and the goodness-of-fit index (GFI) is above.9, the model is considered a good fit (Hair et al., 2010). For this model, the CFI was .619 and the GFI was .632. Although the fit of the model fell well short of the satisfying fit criteria, convergent validity was conducted.

Convergent Validity

Convergent validity shows items in the same learning strategy were correlated if convergent validity existed in the collected data. Two tests were used for convergent validity. The first was to test if the unstandardized regression weights (path coefficients) were statistically significant. The second was to test if the factor loadings (standardized regression weights) were .5 or higher. Table 4 lists the estimates of the path coefficients for the model and the factor loadings.

As shown in Table 4, none of the items in the Metacognitive Self-regulation scale passed the first test. In addition, item 8 failed to pass the first test in the Peer Learning/Help Seeking scale. Many items failed the second test. The only scale exhibiting convergent validity based on the second test was the Critical Thinking scale.

Discriminant Validity

Discriminant validity refers to the ability of measurement scales to measure the concept or construct they are intended to measure rather than some other related concept or construct. Discriminant validity is measured by comparing the square root of the average variance explained for each scale with the correlations between the scales. The discriminant validity tests showed that Rehearsal, Organization, Metacognitive Self-regulation, and Peer Learning/Help Seeking exhibited discriminant validity. Elaboration was confounded with Critical Thinking and Critical Thinking was confounded with Elaboration. Effort Regulation was confounded with Time and Study Environment management and vice versa.

Figure 3. Path model of the original learning strategies
Note: ORG: Organization, ELAB: Elaboration, REH: Rehearsal, ER: Effort Regulation, TSE: Time and Study Environment, PLHS: Peer Learning and Help Seeking, MSR: Metacognitive Self-Regulations

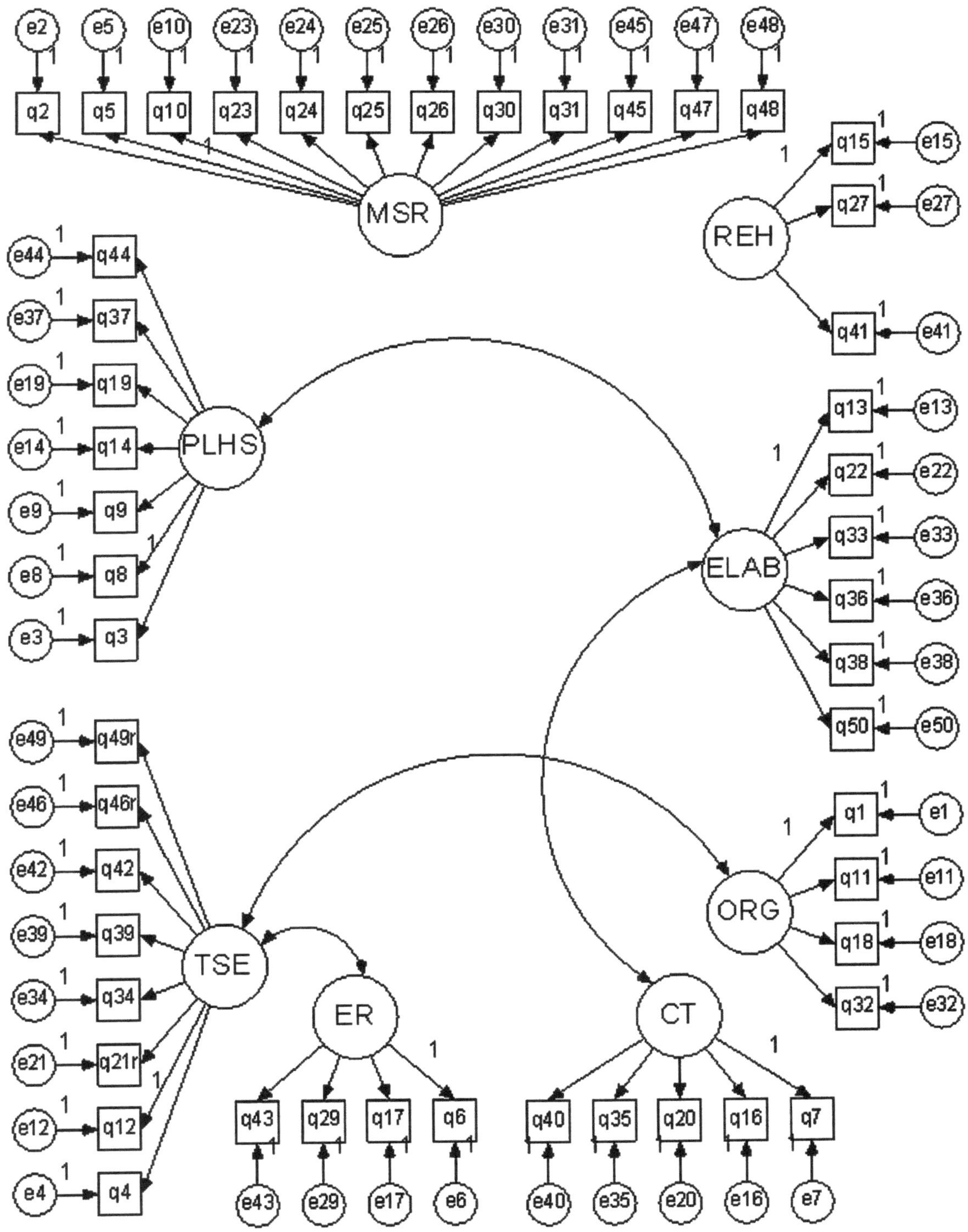

Table 4. Estimates of path coefficients and factor loadings

Scale	Item	Estimate	Standard Error	Critical Ratio	p-value	Factor Weight
Rehearsal	15	1.000				.736
	27	0.783	0.218	3.588	.000	.592
	41	0.580	0.164	3.537	.000	.417[b]
Elaboration	13	1.000				.475[b]
	22	1.333	0.261	5.106	.000	.547
	33	1.204	0.231	5.217	.000	.570
	36	0.363	0.171	2.115	.034	.175[b]
	38	1.580	0.283	5.577	.000	.657
	50	1.547	0.279	5.549	.000	.649
Organization	1	1.000				.814
	11	0.592	0.103	5.745	.000	.490[b]
	18	0.574	0.096	5.954	.000	.512
	32	0.649	0.100	6.471	.000	.571
Critical thinking	7	1.000				.670
	16	0.949	0.121	7.869	.000	.673
	20	0.821	0.118	6.979	.000	.582
	35	1.045	0.127	8.254	.000	.717
	40	0.953	0.012	7.842	.000	.670
Effort regulation	6	1.000				.285[b]
	17	-2.457	0.683	-3.599	.000	-.736
	29	1.344	0.429	3.129	.002	.410[b]
	43	-2.395	0.665	-3.600	.000	-.739
Time-study environment management	4	1.000				.543
	12	1.182	0.177	6.678	.000	.683
	21	0.737	0.170	4.325	.000	.369[b]
	34	1.051	0.200	5.255	.000	.474[b]
	39	1.231	0.202	6.096	.000	.587
	42	0.678	0.158	4.292	.000	.366[b]
	46	0.577	0.155	3.724	.000	.310[b]
	49	0.743	0.165	4.496	.000	.387[b]
Metacognitive self-regulation	2	1.000				.001[b]
	5	345.200	21651.8	0.016	.987[a]	.446[b]
	10	220.391	13823.5	0.016	.987[a]	.323[b]
	23	598.274	37525.8	0.016	.987[a]	.651
	24	432.429	27123.0	0.016	.987[a]	.513
	25	579.757	36363.7	0.016	.987[a]	.672
	26	209.534	13142.7	0.016	.987[a]	.213[b]
	30	49.008	3074.4	0.016	.987[a]	.066[b]
	31	329.169	20646.3	0.016	.987[a]	.432[b]
	45	487.049	30548.8	0.016	.987[a]	.609
	47	651.969	40893.0	0.016	.987[a]	.701
	48	482.179	30243.4	0.016	.987[a]	.549

continued on following page

Table 4. Continued

Scale	Item	Estimate	Standard Error	Critical Ratio	p-value	Factor Weight
Peer learning/Help seeking	3	1.000				.613
	8	0.236	0.131	1.803	.071[a]	.143[b]
	9	-0.441	0.117	-3.776	.000	-.309[b]
	14	1.205	0.160	7.523	.000	.731
	19	0.763	0.013	5.804	.000	.507
	37	0.983	0.146	6.745	.000	.616
	44	1.182	0.156	7.591	.000	.744

[a]Path coefficients not statistically significant
[b]Factor loadings < .5

Development of Refined Scales

The original learning strategies scales did not confirm to the latent factor structure and failed all validity tests, so it was decided to remedy these deficiencies. The items that did not have factor loadings of .5 or higher in the initial factor loading (as listed in Table 4) were eliminated with the exception of item 34. In the initial test, item 34 had an inadequate factor weight of .474 (< .5), but it was left in the model due to estimation problems with the new model if it was omitted. The fit statistics for the refined confirmatory factor model showed that the ratio of the chi-square statistic to the degrees of freedom was adequate (2.437), but the GFI statistic was .742, which does not meet the criterion of .9.

To test validity, the same comparison of root average variance explained and inter-scale correlation was produced for the refined model. The only scale clearly exhibiting discriminant validity was Peer Learning/Help Seeking. The convergent validity statistics showed that all regression coefficients were statistically significant, and all factor scores were at least .5 with the exception of item 34. Although the scales in the refined model exhibit convergent validity, this information should be considered in light of the knowledge that the overall model fit was poor. In addition, EFA was carried out on the reduced set of variables and the number of factors was restricted to eight in order to reflect the combination of the Peer Learning and Help Seeking scales. The results showed that most factors contain items from several different scales, and most scales loaded into more than one factor.

Decisions were then made to drop the items that did not have a loading of .4 or more and those items that were loaded on multiple factors. An EFA was carried out on the remaining items. Only five factors were extracted as shown in Table 5. Unlike that of previous models, the EFA showed that each factor contains only items from one single scale, and each scale can be identified to only one factor, with the exception of item 15.

Convergent Validity

Figure 4 shows the path model based on the five factors extracted in the EFA.

The fit statistics of the model included the following: CMIN/DF= 1.551, df=240, p=.000, GFI= .866, CFI=.913, RMSEA= .052. The GFI was close to the desired .9, and the CFI met the desired .9. In addition, RMSEA was within the range of a good fit (< .07) (Hair, et al., 2010).

Table 5. Results of exploratory factor analysis on reduced scale variables

		Factors					
Scale	**Item**	**1**	**2**	**3**	**4**	**5**	**Communality**
Rehearsal/Organization	1				.746		.625
	15				.525	.427	.559
	18				.713		.584
	32				.762		.603
Elaboration	22					.753	.700
	38					.652	.679
Critical thinking	7		.790				.645
	16		.648				.582
	20		.615				.431
	24		.597				.456
	35		.744				.635
	40		.702				.567
Metacognitive self-regulation/ Effort Regulation/ Time and study environment management	4	.597					.425
	12	.561					.566
	17	.737					.609
	25	.456					.450
	34	.507					.340
	39	.620					.566
	43	.798					.687
	45	.609					.556
Peer learning/Help seeking	3			.690			.583
	14			.784			.640
	37			.672			.576
	44			.792			.728

Note. Factor loadings of less than 0.4 have been omitted. The plot indicated that the correct number of factors was five. Five factors explain 57.5% of the variation in the items.

Table 6 lists the estimates of path coefficients and factor scores. All path coefficients were statistically significant, which satisfied the first test of convergent validity. The second test of convergent validity was mostly confirmed since all but two items in the Metacognitive Self-regulation/Effort Regulation/Time and Study Environment Management scale (item 25 and 34) had satisfactory factor loadings of higher than .5.

Discriminant validity. As shown in Table 7, the average variance explained in each scales was larger than any correlation coefficient with another scale; therefore, the combined scales appeared to exhibit discriminant validity

Figure 4. Path model of the modified learning strategies
Note: REHORG: Rehearsal/Organization, ELAB: Elaboration, CT: Critical Thinking, MSRERTSE: Metacognitive Self-regulation/ Effort Regulation/Time-study Environment Management, HSPL: Peer Learning/Help Seeking

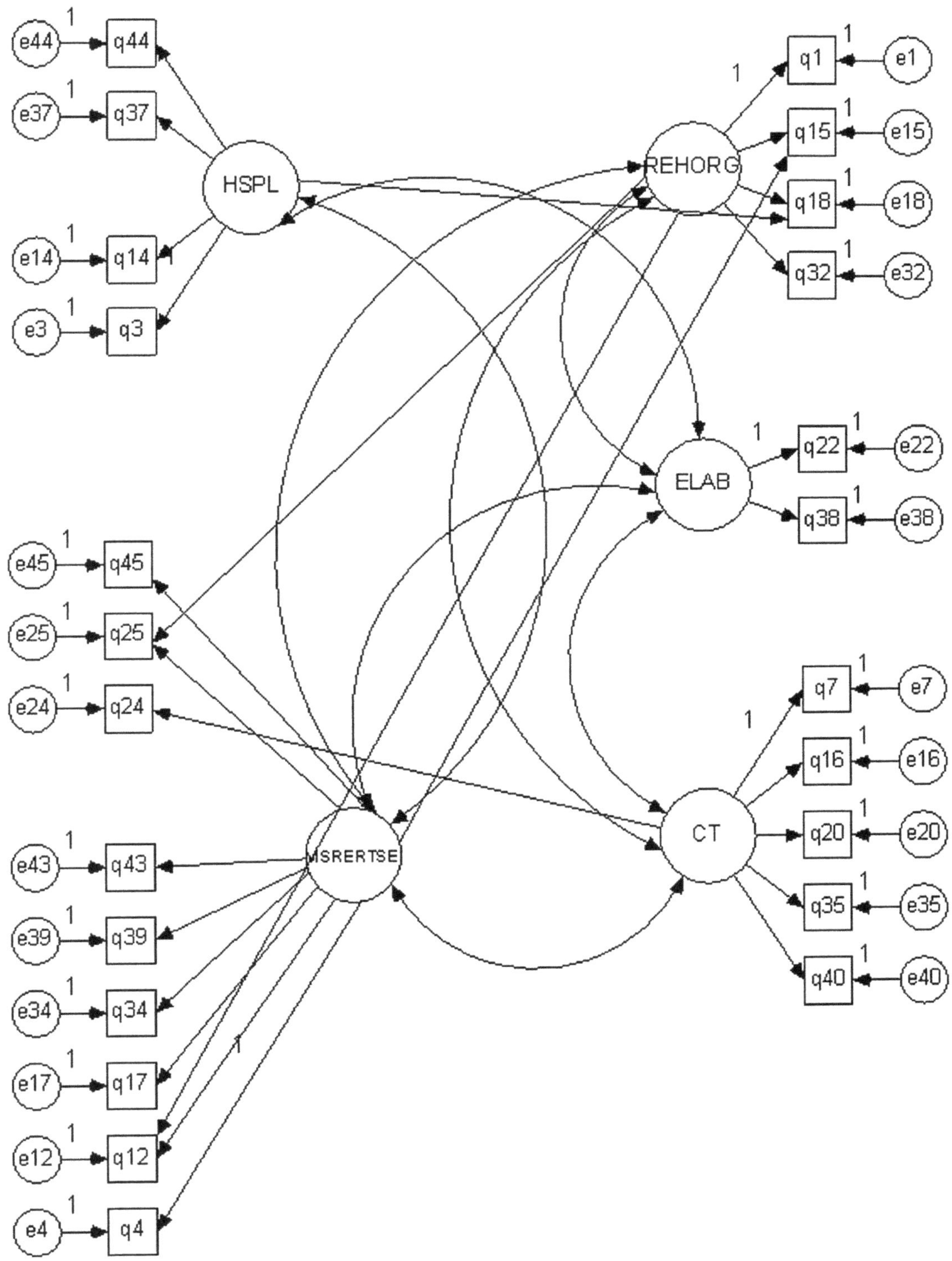

Table 6. Estimates of path coefficients and factor scores for the combined-scale confirmatory factor model

Scale	Item	Estimate	Standard Error	Critical Ratio	p-value	Factor Weight
Rehearsal / Organization	1	1.000				.684
	15	0.737	0.114	6.475	.000	.558
	18	0.741	0.116	6.384	.000	.561
	32	0.897	0.127	7.055	.000	.662
Elaboration	22	1.000				.660
	38	1.137	0.159	7.132	.000	.759
Critical thinking	7	1.000			.000	.673
	16	0.942	0.118	7.993	.000	.671
	20	0.806	0.115	7.003	.000	.575
	24	0.895	0.119	7.489	.000	.621
	35	1.054	0.124	8.508	.000	.726
	40	0.917	0.118	7.758	.000	.647
Metacognitive self-regulation/Effort regulation/ Time-study environment management	4	1.000				.546
	12	0.970	0.155	6.236	.000	.564
	17	1.146	0.168	6.807	.000	.686
	25	0.867	0.162	5.361	.000	.460[a]
	34	1.074	0.198	5.435	.000	.487[a]
	39	1.257	0.200	6.293	.000	.602
	43	1.144	0.165	6.912	.000	.705
	45	1.103	0.170	6.483	.000	.632
Peer learning/Help seeking	3	1.000				.545
	14	1.186	0.185	6.425	.000	.639
	37	1.166	0.180	6.489	.000	.650
	44	1.523	0.214	7.111	.000	.852

[a]Factor loadings < .5

Table 7. Comparison of root average variance explained and inter-scale correlations, combined-scale model

Scale	Rehearsal/ Organization	Elaboration	Critical thinking	Metacognitive self-regulation/ Effort regulation/Time-study environment management	Peer learning/ Help seeking
Rehearsal/ Organization	0.654	0.466	0.316	0.122	0.000
Elaboration		0.711	0.567	0.588	0.330
Critical thinking			0.654	0.474	0.000
Metacognitive self-regulation/Effort regulation/ Time-study environment management				0.625	0.437
Peer learning/Help seeking					0.681

Reliability

The combined scales were subjected to item analysis to assess the reliability; results are shown in Table 8. With the exception of Elaboration (.679), all scales met the minimum reliability criterion of .7.

As shown in Table 9, no deletion of any item would increase the alpha of any scale, including Elaboration.

There were 24 learning strategies items in the revised questionnaire. Appendix 2 lists the items and their new numbers. Table 10 shows the item numbers and the learning strategies scales. The new scale that consisted of Metacognitive Self-regulation, Effort Regulation, and Time and Study Environment management was shortened to Self-Regulation scale. The combined Rehearsal and Organization scale was labeled Organization since the items were about organization studying materials.

Table 8. Results of item analysis on combined scale items

Scale	Alpha	Item	Alpha if Item Deleted
Rehearsal / Organization	.731	1	.637
		15	.690
		18	.679
		32	.674
Elaboration	.679	22	-----
		38	-----
Critical thinking	.816	7	.776
		16	.786
		20	.800
		24	.797
		35	.773
		40	.785
Metacognitive self-regulation/Effort regulation/ Time-study environment management	.820	4	.805
		12	.792
		17	.791
		25	.806
		34	.814
		39	.801
		43	.789
		45	.794
Peer learning / Help seeking	.767	3	.743
		14	.712
		37	.728
		44	.661

Table 9. Comparison of Cronbach's alpha before and after combining of scales

Original Scale	Alpha	Combined Scale	Alpha
Rehearsal	.607	Rehearsal/Organization	.731
Organization	.690		
Elaboration	.727	Elaboration	.679
Critical thinking	.797	Critical thinking	.816
Effort regulation	.655	Effort regulation/ Metacognitive self-regulation/ Time-study environment management	.820
Time study environment management	.709		
Metacognitive self-regulation	.758		
Peer learning/Help seeking	.776	Peer learning/Help seeking	.767

Discussion

MSLQ was developed to assess students' learning in a conceptual environment using text and lectures, not for an applied learning environment such as learning computer skills. In addition, latent factor structure of the instrument has been a concern. The purposes of this study were to revise the learning strategies section of the MSLQ to reflect valid computer skill learning strategies and to conduct a pilot test of the latent factor structure, as well as testing the initial validity and reliability of the revised MSLQ.

The first revision of the revised learning strategies scales failed both convergent and discriminant validity tests. To remedy the deficiencies, items with a factor loading of less than .5 were removed to construct a refined model. Nonetheless, the refined model did not satisfy the goodness-of-fit criterion, nor did it exhibit discriminant validity when the original scales were maintained. A decision was made to exclude items with a loading of lower than .4 and those items that were loaded on multiple factors. An EFA revealed that only five factors were extracted. In addition, each factor contained only items from one single scale, and each scale can be identified to only one factor, with the exception of one item. The analysis showed that Effort Regulation, Time and Study Environment, and Metacognitive Self-regulation were identified as one scale, which confirmed to the theory that time management and regulating one's effort and learning environment were different aspects of self-regulation. Rehearsal and Organization were clearly identified as one scale in the EFA.

Table 10. New learning strategies and item numbers

Scale	Item
Organization	1, 7, 10, 15
Elaboration	12, 19
Critical thinking	4, 8, 11, 13, 17, 21
Self-regulation	3, 5, 9, 14, 16, 20, 22, 24
Peer Learning / Help Seeking	2, 6, 18, 23

A path model, based on these five factors, exhibited satisfactory goodness-of-fit. The revised questionnaire exhibited construct validity because both convergent validity and discriminant validity were confirmed. Most of the scales exhibited reliability as well with a higher Cronbach's alpha than the scales in the learning section of the original MSLQ.

This pilot test of the computer skills learning strategies questionnaire suggested that only 24 of the original 50 items were relevant and they contributed to only 5 learning strategies scales. In the original learning strategies section of the MSLQ, Metacognitive Self-Regulation, Effort Regulation, and Time and Study Environment Management were separate scales. In this study, however, the latent factor structure and construct validity of the revised MSLQ showed that items in Metacognitive Self-Regulation, Effort Regulation, and Time and Study Environment Management scales were correlated and they measure the construct they were intended to measure. In other words, this pilot test showed that items in the combined scale measure similar construct: self-regulation.

Limitations

Several limitations need to be considered. Validity and reliability testing are best served with large amounts of data collection, so it is important to note that one of the limitations of this study was the small number of students (N= 201) participated in the study. The second limitation was that only the learning strategies section of the MSLQ was examined. The third limitation was that it was not the intention of this study to analyze if certain learning strategies were more effective in learning computer skills. Therefore, data was not collected in students' course grades, and it is unknown which learning strategies may help students excel in learning computer skills.

FUTURE RESEARCH DIRECTIONS

SRL is an established learning theory that is supported by rich empirical research. It has been linked to grade, depth of understanding, student engagement, and dropout rate. A widely used instrument to assess students' SRL is the MSLQ; however, prior research revealed concerns about its latent factor structure and its limitation in assessing learning hands-on, software skills.

This study took the first step of revising the MSLQ to be used for assessing students' learning strategies in a traditional, hands-on learning environment. The next step will be to test its validity and reliability in an e-learning environment. To develop a robust survey instrument, many iterations of data collection are needed to refine the instrument. Therefore, future research on the validity and reliability of this revised MSLQ in a wide variety of online classes is needed. Further, this study revised only the learning strategies section of the MSLQ. Future research to revise and validate the motivation section of the instrument for e-learning will also be helpful.

After a robust instrument is developed, research on how each learning strategy is related to learning will be needed to identify effective learning strategies. The results, in turn, provide valuable information for instructors when they teach online classes, in both instructional design and the inclusion of teaching the effective strategies to students to help them reach their learning goals.

CONCLUSION

With the advances in ICT, most skills needed in the 21st century are in knowledge management and are supported by technology. Since most 21st century skills are learned only in schools, the opportunity for the future generations to enter 21st century occupations would be limited if they are unable to obtain the competencies through education. One of the new learning environments makes education accessible to those for whom the education would have been otherwise unobtainable due to distance, financial, or other factors is e-learning. Yet, e-learning presents its own challenges. Students must be autonomous and take charge of their own learning; in other words, they must be self-regulated learners. Research investigating effective computer-skill related learning strategies in an e-learning environment will reveal strategic tools that online students can learn to use to reach their learning goals.

The data gathered in the study presented in this chapter revealed that there were five scales, not the original nine scales, in the learning strategies section of the MSLQ for learning computer skills. Items in the Metacognitive Self-Regulation, Effort Regulation, and Time and Study Environment Management scales were correlated; this conformed the theory that all these are different aspects of SRL. This revised instrument exhibited reliability and construct validity with both convergent validity and discriminate validity confirmed.

As revealed in the OECD survey, ICT skills were taught as a separate subject, while other competencies were integrated across curriculum. Research revealed that learning computer skills was different in nature. To improve the learning of computer skills that are essential for the 21st century workers and citizens, instructors need to know effective strategies in learning computer skills, in both tradition and e-learning environments, so that they can incorporate these strategies in their instruction. Continued research is needed to develop a robust instrument to provide this information.

REFERENCES

Ananiadou, K., & Claro, M. (2009). 21st Century Skills and Competences for New Millennium Learners in OECD Countries (OECD Education Working Papers, No. 41). OECD.

Angelino, L. M., Williams, F. K., & Natvig, D. (2007). Strategies to engage online students and reduce attrition rates. *Journal of Educators Online*, *4*(2), n2.

Artino, A. R. (2008). Motivational beliefs and perceptions of instructional quality: Predicting satisfaction with online training. *Journal of Computer Assisted Learning*, *24*(3), 260–270. doi:10.1111/j.1365-2729.2007.00258.x

Autor, D., Levy, F., & Murnane, R. (2003). The skill content of recent technological change: An empirical exploration. *The Quarterly Journal of Economics*, *118*(4), 1279–1333. doi:10.1162/003355303322552801

Butler, D. L., & Winne, P. H. (1995). Feedback and self-regulated learning: A theoretical synthesis. *Review of Educational Research*, *65*(3), 245–281. doi:10.3102/00346543065003245

Chalupa, M., Chen, C., & Charles, T. (2001). An analysis of college students' motivation and learning strategies in computer courses: A cognitive view. *Delta Pi Epsilon Journal*, *43*(4), 185–199.

Chen, C. (2002). Self-regulated learning strategies and achievement in an introduction to information systems course. *Information Technology, Learning and Performance Journal*, *20*(1), 11–25.

Chen, C., & Chalupa, M. (2003). The role of motivation and use of learning strategies in computer courses: Early and late in the semester. *Delta Pi Epsilon Journal*, *45*(2), 98–117.

Cho, M.-H., Shen, D., & Laffey, J. (2010). Relationships between self-regulation and social experiences in asynchronous online learning environments. *Journal of Interactive Learning Research*, *21*, 297–316.

Coppola, B. P. (1995). Progress in practice: Using concepts form motivational and self-regulated learning research to improve chemistry instruction. In P. R. Pintrich (Ed.), *Understanding self-regulated learning* (pp. 8787–8796). San Francisco, CA: Jossey-Bass Publishers. doi:10.1002/tl.37219956310

Cronbach, L. J., & Shavelson, R. J. (2004). My current thoughts on coefficient alpha and successor procedures. *Educational and Psychological Measurement*, *64*(3), 391–418. doi:10.1177/0013164404266386

Dabbagh, N., & Kitsantas, A. (2005). Using web-based pedagogical tools as scaffolds for self-regulated learning. *Instructional Science*, *33*(5-6), 513–540. doi:10.1007/s11251-005-1278-3

Dembo, M. H., Junge, L. G., & Lynch, R. (2006). Becoming a self-regulated learner: implications for web-based education. In H. O' Neil (Ed.), *Web-based learning: theory, research, and practice* (pp. 185–202). Mahwah, NJ: Lawrence Erlbaum Associates.

Dobrovolny, J. (2006). How adults learn from self-paced, technology-based corporate training: New focus for learners, new focus for designers. *Distance Education*, *27*(2), 155–170. doi:10.1080/01587910600789506

Donker, A. S., De Boer, H., Kostons, D., Dignath van Ewijk, C. C., & van der Werf, M. P. C. (2014). Effectiveness of learning strategy instruction on academic performance: A meta-analysis. *Educational Research Review*, *11*, 1–26. doi:10.1016/j.edurev.2013.11.002

Duncan, T., & McKeachie, W. J. (2005). The making of the motivated strategies for learning questionnaire. *Educational Psychologist*, *40*(2), 117–128. doi:10.1207/s15326985ep4002_6

Dunn, K. E., Lo, W.-J., Mulvenon, S. W., & Sutcliffe, R. (2012). Revisiting the motivated strategies for learning questionnaire: A theoretical and statistical reevaluation of the metacognitive self-regulation and effort regulation subscales. *Educational and Psychological Measurement*, *72*(2), 312–331. doi:10.1177/0013164411413461

Elvers, G. C., Polzella, D. J., & Graetz, K. (2003). Procrastination in online courses: Performance and attitudinal differences. *Teaching of Psychology*, *30*(2), 159–162. doi:10.1207/S15328023TOP3002_13

Goos, M., Manning, M., & Salomons, A. (2009). Job polarization in Europe. *The American Economic Review*, *99*(2), 58–63. doi:10.1257/aer.99.2.58

Greene, J. A., & Azevedo, R. (2009). A macro-level analysis of SRL processes and their relations to the acquisition of a sophisticated mental model of a complex system. *Contemporary Educational Psychology*, *34*(1), 18–29. doi:10.1016/j.cedpsych.2008.05.006

Hair, J. F., Black, W. C., Babin, B. J., Anderson, R. E., & Tatham, R. (2010). *Multivariate Data Analysis*. Upper Saddle River, New Jersey: Pearson Education.

Hilpert, J., Stemien, J., van der Hoeven Kraft, K., & Husman, J. (2013). Evidence for the latent factor structure of the MSLQ: A new conceptualization of an established questionnaire. *SAGE Open*. Retrieve from http://classic.sgo.sagepub.com/content/3/4/2158244013510305.short

Kolowich, S. (2014, January 16). Exactly know many students take online courses? *The Chronicle of Higher Education*. Retrieved from http://chronicle.com/blogs/wiredcampus/exactly-how-many-students-take-online-courses/49455

Messick, S. (1990). Validity of test interpretation and use (Report No. ETS-RR-90-11). Princeton, NJ: Educational Testing Service.

Newman, R. (2008). Adaptive and nonadaptive help seeking with peer harassment: An integrative perspective of coping and self-regulation. *Educational Psychologist*, *43*(1), 1–15. doi:10.1080/00461520701756206

Nichols, M. (2010). Student perceptions of support services and the influence of targeted interventions on retention in distance education. *Distance Education*, *31*(1), 93–113. doi:10.1080/01587911003725048

Niemczyk, M. C., & Savenye, W. C. (2001). The relationship of student motivation and self-regulated learning strategies to performance in an undergraduate computer literacy course. (ED 470107)

Patterson, B., & McFadden, C. (2009). Attrition in online and campus degree programs. *Online Journal of Distance Learning Administration*, *12*(2).

Pellegrino, J. W., & Hilton, M. L. (Eds.). (2013). *Education for life and work: Developing transferable knowledge and skills in the 21st century*. National Academies Press.

Perkins, D. N. (1992). Technology meets constructivism: Do they make a marriage? In T. M. Duffy & D. H. Jonassen (Eds.), *Constructivism and the technology of instruction: A conversation* (pp. 45–55). Hillsdale, NJ: Lawrence Erlbaum Associates.

Pintrich, P. R. (1995). Understanding self-regulated learning. In P. R. Pintrich (Ed.), *Understanding self-regulated learning* (pp. 3–12). San Francisco, CA: Jossey-Bass Publishers.

Pintrich, P. R., & DeGoot, E. V. (1990). Motivational and self-regulated learning components of classroom academic performance. *Journal of Educational Psychology*, *82*(1), 33–40. doi:10.1037/0022-0663.82.1.33

Pintrich, P. R., Smith, D., Garcia, T., & McKeachie, W. J. (1991). *A manual for the use of the motivated strategies for learning questionnaire*. Ann Arbor, MI: University of Michigan.

Puzziferro, M. (2008). Online technologies self-efficacy and self-regulated learning as predictors of final grade and satisfaction in college-level online courses. *American Journal of Distance Education*, *22*(2), 72–89. doi:10.1080/08923640802039024

Street, H. D. (2010). Factors influencing a learner's decision to drop-out or persist in higher education distance learning. *Online Journal of Distance Learning Administration*, *13*(4).

Sun, J. C. Y., & Rueda, R. (2012). Situational interest, computer self-efficacy and self-regulation: Their impact on student engagement in distance education. *British Journal of Educational Technology*, *43*(2), 191–204. doi:10.1111/j.1467-8535.2010.01157.x

VanZile-Tamsen, C., & Livingston, J. A. (1999). The differential impact of motivation on the self-regulated strategy use of high- and low-achieving college students. *Journal of College Student Development*, *40*(1), 54–60.

Wang, S. L., & Lin, S. S. J. (2007). The application of social cognitive theory to web-based learning through NetPorts. *British Journal of Educational Technology*, *38*(4), 600–612. doi:10.1111/j.1467-8535.2006.00645.x

Whipp, J. L., & Chiarelli, S. (2004). Self-regulation in a web-based course: A case study. *Educational Technology Research and Development*, *52*(4), 4, 5–22. doi:10.1007/BF02504714

Willging, P. A., & Johnson, S. D. (2009). Factors that Influence Students' Decision to dropout of online courses. *Journal of Asynchronous Learning Networks*, *13*(3), 115–127.

Wolters, C. A. (2010). Self-regulated learning and the 21st century competencies. *Artikel Online*. Retrieved from http://www.hewlett.org/uploads/Self_Regulated_Learning__21st_Century_Competencies.pdf

Wolters, C. A., & Pincrich, P. R. (1998). Contextual differences in student motivation and self-regulated learning in mathematics, English, and social studies classrooms. *Instructional Science*, *26*, 27–47.

Wolters, C. A., Pintrich, P. R., & Karabenick, S. A. (2005). Assessing academic self-regulated learning. In K. A. Moore & L. Lippman (Eds.), *What do children need to flourish? Conceptualizing and measuring indicators of positive development* (pp. 251–270). New York: Springer. doi:10.1007/0-387-23823-9_16

Zimmerman, B. J. (2001). Theories of self-regulated learning and academic achievement: An overview and analysis. In B. J. Zimmerman & D. H. Schunk (Eds.), *Self-regulated learning and academic achievement: Theoretical perspectives* (2nd ed., pp. 1–37). Hillsdale, NJ: Erlbaum.

Zimmerman, B. J. (2008). Investigating self-regulation and motivation: Historical background, methodological developments, and future prospects. *American Educational Research Journal*, *45*(1), 166–183. doi:10.3102/0002831207312909

Zimmerman, B. J., & Risemberg, R. (1997). Self-regulatory dimensions of academic learning and motivation. In G. D. Phye (Ed.), *Handbook of academic learning: Construction of knowledge* (pp. 105–125). San Diego, CA: Academic Press. doi:10.1016/B978-012554255-5/50005-3

KEY TERMS AND DEFINITIONS

Applied Learning: The learning of practical skills that often requires the use of tools to practice and experiment to gain practical skills.

Competency: The ability to draw on skills and attitudes to meet complex demands in a particular context.

Conceptual Learning: The learning of concepts and theories by attending lectures, taking notes, and studying notes and textbooks.

Information Communication Technology (ICT): The use of technology to gather, manipulate, transmit, receive, store, and communicate information.

Metacognition: The cognition about cognition; knowing what one knows and does not know, planning, ahead, efficiently apportioning one's time and attentional resources, and monitoring and adjusting one's efforts in the process of learning or problem-solving.

Self-Regulated Learning (SRL): A process of taking control of one's own learning by using metacognition to assess, evaluate, and adjust one's learning environment and behavior to reach learning goals.

APPENDIX 1

1. When I study the ~~readings~~ *material* for this course, I outline the material to help me organize ~~my thoughts~~ *the concepts and computer functions.*
2. During class time I often miss important points because I'm ~~thinking of~~ *distracted by* other things.
3. When studying for this course, I often try to *learn by* explain*ing* the material to a classmate or friend.
4. I usually study in a place where I can concentrate on my course work.
5. When reading for this course, I make up questions to help focus my ~~reading~~ *studying.*
6. I often feel ~~so lazy or~~ bored when I study for this class ~~that I~~ *and* quit before I finish what I planned to do.
7. I often find myself ~~questioning things I hear or read in this course to decide if I find them convincing~~ *experimenting on the computer to find the most efficient way to complete a task.*
8. ~~I ask the instructor to clarify concepts I don't understand well.~~ *I frequently use the software Help function or online Help when the instructor is not readily available.*
9. Even if I have trouble learning the material in this class, I try to do the work on my own, without help from anyone.
10. When I become confused about something I'm ~~reading~~ *learning* for this class, I go back and try to figure it out.
11. When I study for this class, I go through the readings and my ~~class notes~~ *lab exercises* ~~and try~~ to find the most important ~~ideas~~ *points.*
12. I make good use of my study time for this course.
13. I try to relate ~~ideas~~ *the computer skills* in this ~~subject~~ *class* to those in other courses whenever possible.
14. I try to work with other students from this class to complete the course assignments.
15. When studying for this course, I read my class notes and ~~the course readings~~ *practice on my computer* over and over again.
16. When a ~~theory, interpretation, or conclusion~~ *concept* is presented in class or in the readings, I try to ~~decide if there is good supporting evidence~~ *test it using the software.*
17. I work hard to do well in this class even if I don't like what we are doing.
18. I make simple ~~charts,~~ diagrams~~, or tables~~ to help me *remember how to navigate through the software that I am learning*. ~~organize course material.~~
19. When studying for this course, I often set aside time to ~~discuss course material~~ *go over the material and work out computer problems* with a group of students from the class.
20. I treat the course material as a starting point and try to ~~develop~~ *experiment with the software and solve* my own ~~ideas about it~~ *problems.*
21. I find it hard to stick to a study schedule *for this course.*
22. When I study for this class, I pull together information from different sources, such as lectures, readings, ~~and~~ *or* ~~discussions~~ *computer exercises.*
23. Before I study new course material thoroughly, I often skim *over* it to see how it is organized.
24. I ~~ask myself questions~~ *often experiment on the computer* to make sure *that* I *thoroughly* understand the ~~material I have been studying in this class~~ *software functions.*

25. I try to change the way I study in order to fit the course requirements and the instructor's teaching style.
26. ~~I often find that~~ I have been *trying to understand the materials* ~~reading for~~ *covered in* this class but ~~don't know what it was all about~~ *I still have trouble getting it.*
27. When I study for this class, I practice ~~saying the material to myself~~ *the computer functions* ~~over and over~~ *more than once to make sure I understand them.*
28. I ~~memorize key words to remind me of important concepts~~ *try to remember the steps to perform important computer functions learned* in this class.
29. When course work is difficult, I either give up or only study the easy parts.
30. I try to ~~think through a topic and decide what I am supposed~~ *focus on the software functions that are important* to learn ~~from it rather than just reading it over when studying for this course~~ *instead of looking at all the information equally.*
31. If course readings are difficult to understand, I ~~change the way I read the material~~ *try approaching the material in new ways.*
32. When I study for this course, I go over my class notes and make an outline of ~~important concepts~~ *the most important parts.*
33. When ~~reading~~ *studying* for this class, I try to relate the material to what I already know.
34. I have a regular ~~place~~ location set aside for studying.
35. I try to play around with *different software functions* ~~ideas of my own~~ related to what I am learning in this course.
36. When I study for this course, I write brief summaries of the ~~main ideas~~ *computer functions* from the readings and my ~~class notes~~ *lab exercises.*
37. When I can't understand the material *or cannot solve the computer problems* ~~in this course~~, I ask another student in this class for help *or use the software Help feature.*
38. I try to understand the material in this class by making connections between the ~~readings and the~~ concepts from the lectures *and the lab exercises/assignments.*
39. I make sure that I keep up with the weekly readings and assignment for this course.
40. Whenever I ~~read or~~ *hear* ~~an assertion or conclusion in this class,~~ or *have a computer problem,* I think about possible ~~alternatives~~ *solutions.*
41. I make lists of important *computer functions* ~~items~~ for this course ~~and memorize the lists~~.
42. I attend this class regularly.
43. Even when course materials ~~are dull~~ and uninteresting, I manage to keep working until I finish.
44. I try to identify students in this class ~~whom~~ *that* I can ask for help if necessary.
45. When studying for this course I try to determine which concepts I don't understand well.
46. I often find that I don't spend very much time on this course because of other activities.
47. When I study for this class, I set goals ~~for myself in order to direct my activities in each study period~~ *to complete during each study period.*
48. If I get confused taking notes in class, I make sure I sort it out afterwards.
49. I rarely find time to review my notes or ~~readings~~ *to practice on computer* before an exam.
50. I try to apply *concepts learned* ~~ideas~~ from ~~course readings in other class activities such as~~ lectures ~~and discussion~~ *to computer assignments/projects.*

APPENDIX 2

1. When I study the material for this course, I outline the material to help me organize the concepts and computer functions.
2. When studying for this course, I often try to learn by explaining the material to a classmate or friend.
3. I usually study in a place where I can concentrate on my course work.
4. I often find myself experimenting on the computer to find the most efficient way to complete a task.
5. I make good use of my study time for this course.
6. I try to work with other students from this class to complete the course assignments.
7. When studying for this course, I read my class notes and practice on my computer over and over again.
8. When a concept is presented in class or in the readings, I try to test it using the software.
9. I work hard to do well in this class even if I don't like what we are doing.
10. I make simple diagrams to help me remember how to navigate through the software that I am learning.
11. I treat the course material as a starting point and try to experiment with the software and solve my own problems.
12. When I study for this class, I pull together information from different sources, such as lectures, readings, or computer exercises.
13. I often experiment on the computer to make sure that I thoroughly understand the software functions.
14. I try to change the way I study in order to fit the course requirements and the instructor's teaching style.
15. When I study for this course, I go over my class notes and make an outline of the most important parts.
16. I have a regular location set aside for studying.
17. I try to play around with different software functions related to what I am learning in this course.
18. When I can't understand the material or cannot solve the computer problems, I ask another student in this class for help or use the software Help feature.
19. I try to understand the material in this class by making connections between the concepts from the lectures and the lab exercises/assignments.
20. I make sure that I keep up with the weekly readings and assignments for this course.
21. Whenever I hear or have a computer problem, I think about possible solutions.
22. Even when course materials are uninteresting, I manage to keep working until I finish.
23. I try to identify students in this class that I can ask for help if necessary.
24. When studying for this course I try to determine which concepts I don't understand well.

Chapter 7
Here Be Dragons:
Mapping Student Responsibility in Learning Analytics

Paul Prinsloo
Unisa, South Africa

Sharon Slade
The Open University, UK

ABSTRACT

Learning analytics is an emerging but rapidly growing field seen as offering unquestionable benefit to higher education institutions and students alike. Indeed, given its huge potential to transform the student experience, it could be argued that higher education has a duty to use learning analytics. In the flurry of excitement and eagerness to develop ever slicker predictive systems, few pause to consider whether the increasing use of student data also leads to increasing concerns. This chapter argues that the issue is not whether higher education should use student data, but under which conditions, for what purpose, for whose benefit, and in ways in which students may be actively involved. The authors explore issues including the constructs of general data and student data, and the scope for student responsibility in the collection, analysis and use of their data. An example of student engagement in practice reviews the policy created by the Open University in 2014. The chapter concludes with an exploration of general principles for a new deal on student data in learning analytics.

INTRODUCTION

It is easy to be seduced by the lure of our ever-increasing access to student data to address and mitigate against the myriad of challenges facing higher education institutions (HEIs) (Greenwood, Stopczynski, Sweat, Hardjono & Pentland, 2015; Stiles, 2012; Watters, 2013; Wishon & Rome, 2012). Challenges include, inter alia, changes in funding regimes and regulatory frameworks necessitating greater accountability to a widening range of stakeholders such as national governments, accreditation and quality assurance bodies, employers and students (Altbach, Reisberg, & Rumbley, 2009) (also see Bowen & Lack,

DOI: 10.4018/978-1-4666-9983-0.ch007

2013; Carr, 2012; Christensen, 2008; Hillman, Tandberg, & Fryar, 2015; New Media Consortium, 2015; Shirky, 2014). Though anything but a recent development (see e.g., Hartley, 1995), funding increasingly follows performance rather than preceding it (Hillman et al., 2015). The continuous decrease of public funding for higher education increases the pressures on higher education institutions to not only be accountable to an increasing number of stakeholders, but also to ensure the effectiveness of their teaching and student support strategies. There are also increasing concerns that HEIs have not solved, nor done enough to attempt to solve, the 'revolving door' syndrome whereby many students either fail to complete their courses or programmes or take much longer than planned (Subotzky & Prinsloo, 2011; Tait, 2015).

As teaching and learning increasingly move online and digital, the amount of digital data available for harvesting, analysis and use increases. HEIs' access to and use of student data is thought to have the potential to revolutionise learning (Van Rijmenam, 2013) with the expectation that it will change 'everything' (Wagner & Ice, 2012), that student data is the *new black* (Booth, 2012) and the *new oil* (Watters, 2013). The current emphasis on the 'potential' of learning analytics without (as of yet) definitive evidence that learning analytics does indeed provide appropriate and actionable evidence (Clow, 2013a, 2013b; Essa, 2013; Feldstein, 2013; Selwyn, 2014), can produce and sustain a number of 'blind spots' (Selwyn & Facer, 2013).

In a climate of expectation then that the increased collection and analysis of student data can provide much needed intelligence to both increase our understanding of the challenges and issues facing HEIs and may further assist in formulating more effective responses; there are also concerns that data1 and increasingly Big Data, is not an unqualified good (Boyd and Crawford, 2012, 2013; Kitchen, 2014a). The harvesting, analysis and use of student data must also be seriously considered amidst the discourses surrounding privacy, student surveillance, the nature of evidence in education, and so forth (Biesta, 2007, 2010; Eynon, 2013; Prinsloo & Slade, 2013; Selwyn & Facer, 2013; Wagner & Ice, 2012).

In much of the current discussions around learning analytics, the emphases are on the institution, the potential of data, modelling and algorithms and on students as producers of data, modelling and algorithms. Though student data is central in learning analytics, the role of students is mostly limited to the production of intelligence for more effective teaching and resource allocation. Students are seen as (merely) generators of data, objects of surveillance, customers and recipients of services (Kruse & Ponjasapan, 2012).

A further concern is a view that for most sites involving the use of personal data, the Terms and Conditions (TOC) of use are generally considered to be ineffective in providing users with informed control over their own data. More seriously though, many users simply do not take the time nor have the necessary technical or legal expertise to engage with those TOCs and make informed and rational decisions (Antón & Earp, 2004; Bellman, Johnson, & Lohse, 2001; Earp, Antón, Aiman-Smith, & Stufflebeam, 2005; Lane, Stodden, Bender, & Nissenbaum, 2014; Miyazaki & Ferenandes, 2000). Higher education is no exception to this dire state of affairs. Analyses of the Terms and Conditions (TOCs) for three major providers of Massive Open Online Courses (MOOCs) found that students' role in the data exchange is severely limited to the sole responsibility to ensuring that the information provided by them is correct and current (Prinsloo & Slade, 2015a). Once students accept such TOCs, they have very little control over what data is collected, used and shared; the persons or entities with whom their data is shared; the governance and storage of their data; and even access to their own digital profiles.

In the light of the asymmetrical power relationship between students and HEIs, where students have little choice but to accept the TOCs, there is a need to think differently with regard to the ethical issues in the collection, analysis and use of student data (Slade & Prinsloo, 2013). If one accepts that higher education is, amongst other things, a moral practice based on a social contract between students and their institutions, it is impossible to ignore the fiduciary duty of HEIs to re-think the student role in the value chain of data exchange.

The rationale for rethinking the role and responsibilities of students in this context is found in an awareness of the *ethical* implications and considerations in learning analytics. Although there are promising signs of increasing attention paid to issues surrounding privacy and ethics in learning analytics (Eynon, 2013; Pardo & Siemens, 2014; Siemens, 2013), the practical challenges associated with adopting institutional policy and frameworks to address those issues are complex (Prinsloo & Slade, 2013). It is believed that the Open University (UK) policy on the *Ethical use of student data* (Open University, 2014) is the first of its type within the context of higher education.

This chapter argues that ignoring the role of students in the context of the value exchange of their data is seriously underestimated and under-theorised. We propose that students' responsibility in the data exchange is much more than just ensuring that the information provided is correct and current. Students can and should actively collaborate in the institution's collection, analysis and use of that data. Students' agency is much more than just opting in or out of having data collected, analysed and used. We therefore position students as *agents* in a student-centric approach (e.g., Kruse & Pongsajapan, 2012; Slade & Prinsloo, 2013; Prinsloo & Slade, 2015a) to learning analytics.

In times past, ancient maps were used to record what was already known and to guide exploration into areas which were not yet familiar. Such maps were informed and shaped by the cartographers' skills, knowledge and understanding of the areas they were trying to map. Areas unknown to the cartographer were often accompanied with warnings, such as 'here be dragons.'

In the new world of learning analytics, this chapter attempts to map some of the current approaches to student data and more specifically the potential of student-centric learning analytics. The authors are aware that the simple binary of opting in or out is does not provide an effective nor sufficiently nuanced approach (Prinsloo & Slade, 2015a). In exploring and mapping the unknown areas of student responsibility in the context of learning analytics, it is perhaps pertinent to suggest that 'here be dragons.'

ENGAGING WITH DATA AS *CONSTRUCT*

Data in a variety of formats has always been essential to scientific research, commercial enterprises and higher education, but it is also fair to say that *[d]ata have traditionally been time-consuming and costly to generate, analyse and interpret, and generally provided static, often course, snapshots of phenomena* (Kitchen, 2014a, p. xv). The production and availability of data have overtaken our understanding of the complexities and ethical challenges of data as phenomenon (Barnes, 2013; Diakopoulos, 2014a; Eubanks, 2015; Koponen, 2015; Mehta, 2015). *While many analysts may accept data at face value, and treat them as if they are neutral, objective, and pre-analytics in nature, data are in fact framed technically, economically, ethically, temporally, spatially and philosophically. Data do not exist independently of the ideas, instruments, practices, contexts and knowledges used to generate, process and analyse them* (Kitchen, 2014a, p. 2) (Also see Boellstorff, 2013; De Zwardt, 2014; Pasquale, 2015; Uprichard, 2015).

This is illustrated by the fact that unless a dataset can be considered complete, that data remains *inherently partial, selective and representative, and the distinguishing criteria used in their capture has consequence* (Kitchen, 2014a, p. 3). While data, in the social imaginary, has become to be understood as representative of the total sample, objective and neutral, data is *different in nature to facts, evidence, information and knowledge* (Kitchen, 2014a, p. 3). Except for the fact that we can frame data technically and ethically, data also needs to be framed politically and economically that are used to discriminate against individuals, classes of people and geopolitical entities (Kitchen, 2014a, p. 15). (Also see Crawford, 2013; Henman, 2004; Selwyn & Facer, 2013; Uprichard, 2015).

DATA, BLACK BOXES AND ALGORITHMS

At the intersection of the deluge of data shared and collected by a variety of stakeholders and a growing reliance on predictive models are growing concerns about the ways in which algorithms now appear to shape our existence. As the reach, impact and downstream impacts of those algorithms become clearer (Eubanks, 2015; Henman, 2004; Kalhan, 2013; Pasquale, 2015), so too does the unease around accuracy, reliability and inherent biases (Bozdag, 2013; Diakopoulous, 2014a, 2014b; Friedman & Nissenbaum, 1996; Kitchen, 2014b; Pariser, 2011; Pasquale, 2011). While it falls outside of the scope of this chapter to fully explore this more fully, it is crucial that we again warn that 'here be dragons.'

Amidst the concerns regarding *algorithmic regulation* (Morozov, 2013, par.15) the *algorithmic turn*, (Napoli, 2013, p. 1), and the *threat of algocracy* (Danaher, 2014), scholars, researchers and policymakers are beginning to engage in debate around how best to control and regulate *automated authority* (Diakopoulous, 2014b, p. 12). Current strategies include (but are not limited to) data and algorithmic transparency, accountability and due process (Crawford & Schultz, 2014; Diakopoulous, 2014a; Koponen, 2015; Lohr, 2015; Seaver, 2013).

Given that many higher education institutions increasingly rely on algorithms to determine access, inform policy, personalise learning and support, and determine at-risk student populations (e.g., Cabral, Castolo, & Gallardo, 2015; Daniel, 2015; Prinsloo & Slade, 2013), we suggest a growing need to engage with the construct of student data.

ENGAGING WITH *STUDENT* DATA AS CONSTRUCT

Kitchen states that *data are a means by which political agendas and work can be legitimated, conducted and contested by enabling the construction of evidence-information narratives and counter-discourses that have great rhetorical value than anecdote or sentiment* (2014a, p. 16). If we accept this, we also accept that collecting and analysing is directly related to and in service of, inter alia, prevailing beliefs regarding student learning, policy frameworks as well as funding and regulatory regimes.

In the light of the accountability regimes and cost of funding for higher education as public good *[student] data can thus be understood as an agent of capital interests* (Kitchen, 2014a, p. 16). How then does this influence and shape our practices of selecting and analysing student data? If this data does not represent the whole reality of students' life and learning worlds, what does this mean for our analyses and interventions? If we accept that student data is not benign (Shah as cited in Kitchen, 2014a, p. 21) but should be understood as *framed and framing* (Gitelman & Jackson, as cited in Kitchen, 2014a, p. 21) – why are we so complacent about the analyses and the predictability models which flow from those analyses? The construct of student data therefore raises, inter alia, two important issues - namely our assumptions regarding student digital (non)activity and the 'situatedness' of that data.

Within higher education, students' digital footprints combined with their demographic details collected through registration and funding applications processes are often believed to represent the total picture of student potential and risk. Further, there is a belief that more data will, necessarily, provide a more holistic picture and result in better and more effective interventions (Prinsloo, Archer, Barnes, Chetty, & Van Zyl, 2015).

Indeed, it would seem that many theoretical frameworks and practices relating to learning analytics assume that the learning management system (LMS) provides a sufficient picture of student learning and that measuring activity, such as the number of clicks, time-on-task, or page views provides a direct correlation to student retention and success. (See Guillaume & Khachikian, 2011; Kovanović, Gašević, Dawson, Joksimović, Baker, & Hatala, 2015; Tempelaar, Rienties, & Giesbers, 2014). However, Kruse and Pongsajapan (2012) question this assumption that evidence of student activity on the LMS is a valid proxy for learning. (See also Godwin-Jones, 2012; Pardo & Kloos, 2011; Slade & Prinsloo, 2013).

Moreover, the notion that student digital data represents a total or holistic picture of the complexities of *students' learning* continues to gain acceptance, although surely questionable in the context of education as an open and recursive ecosystem. Not only is such data abstracted but also decontextualised - resulting in a loss of contextual integrity. Considering that *[c]ontexts are structured social settings characterised by canonical activities, roles, relationships, power structures, norms (or rules), and internal values (goals, ends, purposes)* (Nissenbaum, 2010, p. 132), there is a need to seriously question assumptions around student digital data as a reliable proxy or as fully representative. In a world seeking the elusive n=all data set, we should not accept that data showing student (dis)engagement on the LMS is sufficiently complete (Mayer-Schönberger & Cukier, 2013). (Also see Campbell, Chang, & Hosseinian-Far, 2015; Harford, 2014).

When we look at students' trajectories in higher education as *heterotopic spaces* (Foucault, 1984, p. 1), the notion of the LMS as representative of the total student journey becomes even more problematic. For researchers, the clear boundaries between public and private spaces are disappearing as we inhabit various spaces simultaneously (Rymarczuk & Derksen, 2014). Students concurrently live in physical worlds and digital worlds where their private (digital and non-digital) and public (digital and non-digital) lives intersect and become mutually constitutive. Our notions of synchronous and asynchronous, past and present lose their heuristic value and fundamentally contradict our assumptions and analyses. The assumption that student digital data collected from the LMS represents the 'reality' and allocate values to time-on-task, number of clicks, etc., disregards the LMS as a socially constructed space with its own norms, rules and activities (see Nissenbaum, 2010).

STUDENT DATA AND STUDENT RESPONSIBILITY

The *potential* benefits of learning analytics for increasing the effectiveness of learning are well-documented (Diaz & Brown, 2012; McKeown & Ayson, 2013; Oblinger, 2012; Siemens & Long, 2011). Durall & Gros (2014) state that analytics in education can be used to identify students at risk, provide recommendations to students to help personalise resources, reading and support, to *detect the need for, and measure the results of, pedagogic improvements*, to *identify teachers who are performing well, and teachers who need assistance with teaching methods* and to *assist in the student recruitment process*

(p. 380). (For a discussion on the difference between academic and learning analytics and their different potential, see Siemens & Long, 2011). We should remember and keep on reminding ourselves, that learning analytics is, primarily, about learning (Gašević, Dawson, & Siemens, 2015).

Central to a great deal of the literature highlighting the potential benefits of learning analytics is the notion of students and their learning trajectories as data *objects*. Students are portrayed in the main as *producers* of data and *recipients* of services and personalised learning journeys based on the availability of their digital data, the assumptions made and understanding of the complexities of learning, and analyses conducted. In addition, there is often also a worrying absence of concern regarding students' (lack of) knowledge of the collection of their data and any possible impact on their learning journeys. The only apparent requirement of students to engage in their role as data objects is to ensure that the demographic data which they provide is correct and current.

The current thinking about the scope of student responsibility may be influenced by the complexities of conceptualising student retention and success. Many models place the responsibility for student success on the ability of students to *fit into* the processes, epistemologies and pedagogical strategies of higher education (Prinsloo, 2009). This view of student involvement and responsibility stands in stark contrast to the conceptual model proposed by Subotzky and Prinsloo (2011) who suggest that students are not mere recipients of services, but active agents in a reciprocal social contract with higher education.

The underlying notion of students as passive recipients of services and as objects of interventions is amplified when the *constant language of 'intervention' perpetuates an institutional culture of students as passive subjects – the targets of a flow of information – rather than self-reflective learners given the cognitive tools to evaluate their own learning processes* (Kruse & Pongsajapan, 2012, p. 2) (Also see Gašević et al., 2015). If instead we see student success as *the outcome of the mutually influential activities, behaviours, attitudes, and responsibilities of students and the institution, which are viewed in the sociological perspective of situated agents* (Subotzky & Prinsloo, 2011, p. 184), it is clear that any assumptions of students as (just) producers of data must be revised. (Also see Slade & Prinsloo, 2013; Prinsloo & Slade 2015a, 2015b).

STUDENT-CENTRED LEARNING ANALYTICS

While the notion of student-centred analytics has not gained wide traction in the discourses on educational mining and learning analytics, a number of authors (Kruse & Pongsajapan, 2012; Slade & Prinsloo, 2014; Prinsloo & Slade, 2015a, 2015b) point to students not only making more informed choices regarding the information that they share, but also in holding their higher education institutions accountable for any subsequent analysis, and interpretation.

Engaging with the possibility and potential of students in learning analytics, Kruse and Pongsajapan (2012) propose that higher education needs to move from an *intervention-centric* approach to learning analytics and to reimagine analytics *in the service of learning [and] transform it into a practice characterised by a spirit of questioning and inquiry*. In this way, students become participants in the identification and gathering of their data as well as co-interpreters of their own data (p. 4). Durall and Gros (2014) support this view, stating that *very rarely are students considered the main receivers of the learning analytics data or given the opportunity to use the information to reflect on their learning activity and self-regulate their learning efficiently* (p. 382). Indeed, not only should students be given the possibility to verify their digital dossiers, but HEIs *should [also] provide mechanisms for learners to interact with these systems explicitly* (Durall & Gros, 2014, p. 382). (Also see Kump, Seifert, Beham, Lindstaedt, & Ley, 2012; Slade and Prinsloo (2013) go on to suggest that *valuing students as agents, making choices and collaborating with the institution in constructing their identities* is a positive approach *in the context of the impact of skewed power relations, monitoring, and surveillance* (p. 1520).

STUDENT DATA, AGENCY AND PRIVACY SELF-MANAGEMENT

It falls outside of the scope of this chapter to engage with the various definitions and regulatory frameworks which set out the protection of privacy. See for example, Gurses (2014), Marx (2001), Nissenbaum (2010), Tene and Polonetsky (2012) and Solove (2001, 2004, 2013) for discussion of the general context and specifically geopolitical and institutional contexts. However, it is possible to surmise that due to, inter alia, technological developments and changing social and cultural norms, the notion of privacy is *fluid* (Solove, 2013, p. 61).

Our discussion so far has suggested that users are in an asymmetrical power relationship to those different entities who collect, analyse and increasingly combine different sources of information. It would seem then that one of the few remaining ways for users to exercise their admittedly limited control over the collection and use of their data is by engaging with an organisation's Terms of Conditions (TOCs). Even so, it is broadly accepted that those TOCs are not particularly effective in ensuring either transparency or user control of that data, as those TOCs may be overly complex and/or lengthy (see, e.g., Bellman, Johnson, & Lohse, 2001, Prinsloo & Slade, 2015a). Furthermore, users must engage with separate TOCs on a case to case basis to an extent that the engagement becomes anything rational (Solove, 2013). The result is that users will often exchange their personal data for limited benefits.

Despite increasing sensitivity regarding surveillance and the use and sharing of personal data (PewResearchCenter, 2014) many users have become digitally promiscuous (Brian, 2015; Murphy, 2014). Against this backdrop, Prinsloo and Slade (2015a) present consent as a fragile concept. Despite this, Solove (2013) states that *Providing people with* notice, access, *and the* ability *to control their data is key to facilitating some autonomy in a world where decisions are increasingly made about them with the use of personal data, automated processes, and clandestine rationales, and where people have minimal abilities to do anything about such decisions* (p. 1899; emphasis added).

While we may think consent options as a straight binary choice between of opting in or opting out, Miyazaki and Fernandez (2000) suggest that there is a broader range of choice. *Possibilities of disclosure range from never collecting data or identifying customers when they access a site; customers opting in by explicitly agreeing to having their data collected, used and shared; customers explicitly opting out; the constant collection of data without consumers having a choice (but with their knowledge); to the collection, use and sharing of personal data without the user's knowledge* (Prinsloo & Slade, 2015a, par. 13). Despite this, it is also clear that once consent is provided in a particular context, however consensual and well understood, current legal frameworks do not protect user data when it is repurposed and reused in other contexts (Ohm, 2010, 2015).

Taking into account the fluidness of the notion of privacy and the fragility of the notion of consent, Greenwood et al.(2015) propose a *new deal on data* (p. 192) while Gurses (2014) suggests a *palette of 'privacy solution'* to allow individuals the agency to make more informed choices (Kerr & Barrigar, 2012).

A CASE STUDY OF OPEN UNIVERSITY POLICY

While the ethical considerations of research on students are covered extensively in research policies with ample consideration of 'doing no harm' there is very little or no consideration of the ethical or harm considerations in the use of learning analytics within higher education (Prinsloo & Slade, 2013).

Many learning analytics strategies focus on informing students of the uses of their data, but as Solove (2013) indicates, privacy policies are not always read or well understood. Indeed, there is little formal evidence that students are explicitly consulted or even loosely aware of the broader uses of their data beyond research. The Open University in the UK is an open, distance learning university supporting over 200,000 students each year. Like many other HEIs, the Open University is making increasing use of its student data and became aware that this position was not adequately described within existing policy. To that end, the development of a new institutional policy was commissioned to address ethical issues relating to its approach to learning analytics.

A thorough review of the literature and of existing external practice within the higher education sector was conducted which indicated little evidence of other new policy development beyond that required under national legislation. Themes and issues from the review were used to develop a set of eight broad guiding principles, describing key tenets and values of the University's approach to student support and of the use of data to guide and shape that support.

The creation of any new institutional policy, of necessity, requires considerable consultation combined with a formal and iterative approval process. A small working group of staff with expertise and authority in relevant areas met frequently taking shared ownership of tasks. Key stakeholders were consulted at an early stage on the eight principles. This initial consultation specifically included a few elected student representatives to ameliorate concerns that broader inclusion of students might introduce disquiet at a point when issues had not been thoroughly appraised. Once a coherent draft was agreed, the policy was circulated to a larger group of students via a formal consultation process to uncover student attitudes to their data, and specific issues such as privacy and scope.

The student perspective was crucial, offering both direct insight and understanding of the need for transparency and informed consent. Capturing the student voice clarified key issues and emphasised a need to consider seriously the issue of opt-out. However, this particular issue was not easily resolved. Opt-out introduces significant systems issues, but also unearths a specific moral conflict. Some staff felt strongly that opt-out would render the University unable to act in students' best interests (considered unethical in itself), whilst others felt that students, as active and adult learners, should have rights to determine their own support. As a result, the policy was approved in July 2014, with the condition that the specific issue of consent be reviewed within a year.

The new policy has been clearly communicated to all stakeholder groups. For many students, the emergence of the policy has highlighted for the first time the uses being made of their data. The formal consultation yielded insight that many were unaware that any of their data was collected and used for monitoring or tracking purposes, and it has been clear that there is significant unease regarding the ways in which personal data might be used. Managing the communication process has required a sensitive balance - with the need to both reveal longstanding and ongoing practices, and, at the same time, to clarify and reassure students of the purposes, boundaries and potential benefits. Alongside the publication and communication of the policy, further staff resources were provided to ensure a practical understanding of how existing and planned activities might be impacted.

In retrospect, the emergence of the new policy has been both more straightforward and more complex than anticipated. Key to its creation and implementation has been the emergence of a high level champion, the input of a fully representative set of stakeholders and the awareness that the very creation of a policy flagging the activities undertaken is akin to opening a Pandora's box. Whilst the existence of the policy offers some sense of moral comfort for the University, it is clear that ongoing work will be needed to ensure that the changing legislative environment is adhered to and that the student voice continues to be heard and reflected.

GENERAL PRINCIPLES FOR A NEW DEAL ON STUDENT DATA IN LEARNING ANALYTICS

So far we have attempted to open up the constructs of student data, student responsibility and their involvement in learning analytics and to look at a case study of an institutional response to the complexities and practicalities of the use of student data in teaching and learning contexts.

If HEIs are to successfully rethink students' roles and participation in learning analytics, they must accept a new dispensation where students are no longer (only) the producers of data and data objects, but *participating* agents. Prinsloo and Slade (2015a) propose a number of principles for HEIs to move beyond a paternalistic approach to the collection, analysis and use of student data, to a discursive-disclosive approach (Stoddart, 2012). In discussing Prinsloo and Slade's (2015a) suggested principles, we specifically focus on the *agency* and *responsibility* of students.

The Duty of Reciprocal Care

The asymmetrical power relationship between students and HEIs necessitates that we seriously consider the *ethical* dimensions and impact of this asymmetry. With HEIs currently cast in the role of provider, it is clear that the imperative for an ethical approach to the use of student data lies within the locus of control of HEI. As students become increasingly aware of and concerned about the collection and use of their data (Slade & Prinsloo, 2013), we argue that HEIs have a fiduciary duty to respond.

HEIs can, amongst other things, make their TOCs more accessible and understandable; make clear the scope, timing, use, governance and conditions of sharing student data and information; and provide students with recourse in case of privacy breaches. The TOCs should, however, also reimagine the role and responsibility of students to not only empower students with actionable information, but also allow them to verify data, provide context, and provide additional information.

The Contextual Integrity of Student Data

Earlier we established the importance of context in considering the collection, analysis and use of student data. Student engagement on an institutional LMS does not represent a holistic picture of students' learning and/or progress. Any measure of LMS activity such as students' sharing of data and their time-on-task, number of clicks and page views should also consider the embedded rules, conventions and norms of engagement.

Should data from students' activity *outside* of the LMS be collected and analysed, it is crucial to remember that information shared in one context and for a specific context-specific purpose may not be transferable to other contexts (see Nissenbaum, 2010). While there are increasing claims regarding the potential of combining different sources and databases, and for the repurposing of data sets (Long, 2014), we cannot and should not disregard the social contract between higher education and its students.

Rethinking Student Agency and Consent

In seeking to move toward students as active agents, we should first rethink the ways in which students are more practically able to become involved in their HEIs' approaches to learning analytics. One perspective on this might be to examine how students are able to grant consent to their involvement. We suggest that effective privacy self-management requires a more nuanced approach to that of the simple binary of opting in or out. Students may, for example, agree to share data in specific contexts or may agree to share specific aspects of their learning experiences if they are given a clear understanding of the details of data collection, e.g., the scope of data collected, who will have access, under which conditions, for how long and for what purpose (Prinsloo & Slade, 2015a). (Also see Solove, 2013). Prinsloo and Slade (2015a) suggest that, despite some residual concerns, nudging students to share their data with clear guidance on the purpose and benefits of such sharing would be an improvement on current practice in learning analytics where students largely don't know and have no choice.

Adjusting Privacy's Timing and Focus

Accepting the importance of contextual integrity and guarding against context-collapse (Nissenbaum, 2010), we suggest that students should be informed regarding aspects such as how long their data will be kept in personalised forms, for what purposes their data may be used and shared downstream. While students may provide consent at the time of the collection of their data, they may have legitimate concerns regarding other uses of their data outside of the original context and timing of the initial collection. Prinsloo and Slade (2015) therefore suggest that HEIs should provide students with a range of options *such as outright restrictions, partial consent which may depend on the scope, context and timing, and permission to harvest and use data, with an option to later revoke consent or change the scope of consent depending on the context or circumstances* (p. 90).

Moving Toward Substance Over Neutrality

Amidst tensions between paternalistic or rule-based considerations of user data privacy and discursive-disclosive approaches (Stoddart, 2012), there is a need for clear and enforceable legislation and regulatory frameworks to prevent gross misuse and unfair practices. Alongside this, it might be argued, there is also a need for flexible, case-by-case and context-appropriate guidelines. Given that ordinary users are unlikely to have the resources or access to legal advice to enforce due process if feeling aggrieved or if rights to privacy and data protection are breached, the introduction of institutional guidelines offers some protection against the potential for harm.

From Quantified Selves to Qualified Selves

In the broader context of a *quantification fetish* (Prinsloo, 2014) in higher education, there is greater potential to collect, analyse and use student data, it is crucial that we keep in mind that students are more than their data (e.g., Carney, 2013). The danger is that students become quantified selves based on the number of their log-ins, clicks, downloads, time-on-task and various other data points (Prinsloo & Slade, 2015b). Ideally we should aim to move from quantified selves to qualified selves (e.g., Boam & Webb, 2015; Davies, 2013; Li, Dey, & Forlizzi, 2011; Lupton, 2014a, 2014b; Prinsloo & Slade, 2015b). *Where the quantified self gives us the raw numbers, the qualified self completes our understanding of those numbers* (Boam & Webb, 2015, par. 8). Our students are therefore much more than just conglomerates of quantifiable data (e.g., Lupton, 2014b) and it is important that we take into account *the contexts in which numbers are created* (Lupton, 2014b, p. 6).

CONCLUSION

There is a danger that amidst the hype regarding Big Data in general, and specifically learning analytics in the context of higher education, we don't acknowledge a number of blind spots (Selwyn & Facer, 2013). In this chapter we have attempted to highlight some of these and to warn that 'here be dragons.' Despite those dragons, the blind spots and a myriad of as yet unresolved issues with regard to privacy and the ethical implications of learning analytics, we are of the firm opinion that higher education cannot afford (often literally) *not* to collect, analyse and to use student data (Slade & Prinsloo, 2014).

Given that higher education is a moral endeavour and that higher education has a fiduciary duty towards caring for students, it is clear that the issue is not whether higher education should collect, analyse and use student data, but *under what conditions*.

Although we would suggest that there are some clear principles which may be considered in involving students in the collection, analysis and use of their data, we would also acknowledge that there are a number of remaining uncertainties and practicalities that deserve exploration and further investigation. Some of these include consideration of the implications and scalability of allowing students to opt in to some data collection and analyses, while opting out of others. What are the implications when students opt in, and then after a period of time, decide to opt out?

Students' digital dossiers are only a part of their learning trajectories and provide but glimpses of their activities in an increasingly open and recursive system where their engagement or disengagement flows from mutually constitutive and interdependent variables. It is clear that our assumptions about time-on-task, their number of clicks and page views are nothing more than peeks into the unknown and that there are still many unchartered territories in student learning.

REFERENCES

Altbach, P. G., Reisberg, L., & Rumbley, L. E. (2009). Trends in global higher education: tracking an academic revolution. A report prepared for the UNESCO World Conference on Higher Education. Paris: UNESCO. Retrieved from http://atepie.cep.edu.rs/public/Altbach,_Reisberg,_Rumbley_Tracking_an_Academic_Revolution,_UNESCO_2009.pdf

Antón, A. I., & Earp, J. B. (2004). A requirements taxonomy for reducing web site privacy vulnerabilities. *Requirements Engineering*, *9*(3), 169–185. doi:10.1007/s00766-003-0183-z

Barnes, T. J. (2013). Big Data, little history. *Dialogues in Human Geography*, *3*(3), 297–302. doi:10.1177/2043820613514323

Bellman, S., Johnson, E. J., & Lohse, G. L. (2001). On site: to opt-in or opt-out?: it depends on the question. *Communications of the ACM*, *44*(2), 25–27. Retrieved from http://dl.acm.org/citation.cfm?id=359241 doi:10.1145/359205.359241

Biesta, G. (2007). Why "what works" won't work: Evidence-based practice and the democratic deficit in educational research. *Educational Theory*, *57*(1), 1–22. doi:10.1111/j.1741-5446.2006.00241.x

Biesta, G. (2010). Why 'what works' still won't work: From evidence-based education to value-based education. *Studies in Philosophy and Education*, *29*(5), 491–503. doi:10.1007/s11217-010-9191-x

Boam, E., & Webb, J. (2015). The qualified self: going beyond quantification [Blog comment]. Retrieved from http://designmind.frogdesign.com/articles/the-qualified-self-going-beyond-quantification.html

Boellstorff, T. (2013). Making big data, in theory. *First Monday*, *18*(10). http://firstmonday.org/ojs/index.php/fm/article/view/4869 doi:10.5210/fm.v18i10.4869

Booth, M. (2012, July 18). Learning analytics: the new black. *EDUCAUSEreview*. Retrieved from http://www.educause.edu/ero/article/learning-analytics-new-black

Bowen, E. G., & Lack, K. A. (2013). *Higher education in the digital age*. Princeton, N.J.: Princeton University Press. doi:10.1515/9781400847204

Boyd, D., & Crawford, K. (2012). Critical questions for Big Data. *Information Communication and Society*, *15*(5), 662–679. doi:10.1080/1369118X.2012.678878

Boyd, D., & Crawford, K. (2013). Six provocations for Big Data. Retrieved from http://papers.ssrn.com/sol3/papers.cfm?abstract_id=1926431

Bozdag, E. (2013). Bias in algorithmic filtering and personalization. *Ethics and Information Technology*, *15*(3), 209–227. doi:10.1007/s10676-013-9321-6

Brian, S. 2015. The unexamined life in the era of big data: toward a UDAAP for data. Retrieved from http://papers.ssrn.com/sol3/papers.cfm?abstract_id=2533068

Cabral, S. R., Castolo, J. C. G., & Gallardo, S. C. H. (2015, January). Algorithm to optimize a fuzzy model of students' academic achievement in higher education. In *Congreso Virtual sobre Tecnología. Education et Sociétés*, *1*(4).

Campbell, J., Chang, V., & Hosseinian-Far, A. (2015). Philosophising data: A critical reflection on the 'hidden' issues. [IJOCI]. *International Journal of Organizational and Collective Intelligence*, *5*(1), 1–15. doi:10.4018/IJOCI.2015010101

Carney, M. (2013). You are your data: the scary future of the quantified self movement [Blog comment]. Retrieved from http://pando.com/2013/05/20/you-are-your-data-the-scary-future-of-the-quantified-self-movement/

Carr, N. (2012). The crisis in higher education. *Technology Review*. Retrieved from http://www.technologyreview.com/featuredstory/429376/the-crisis-in-higher-education/

Christensen, C. (2008). Disruptive innovation and catalytic change in higher education. Forum for the Future of Higher Education. *EDUCAUSE*. Retrieved from https://net.educause.edu/ir/library/pdf/ff0810s.pdf

Clow, D. (2013a). An overview of learning analytics. *Teaching in Higher Education*, *18*(6), 683–695. doi:10.1080/13562517.2013.827653

Clow, D. (2013b, November 13). Looking harder at Course Signals [Blog comment]. Retrieved from http://dougclow.org/2013/11/13/looking-harder-at-course-signals/

Crawford, K. (2013, April 1). The hidden biases in big data. [Web log comment]. Harvard Business Review. Retrieved from http://blogs.hbr.org/cs/2013/04/the_hidden_biases_in_big_data.html

Crawford, K., & Schultz, J. (2014). Big data and due process: Toward a framework to redress predictive privacy harms. *BCL Rev.*, *55*, 93–128.

Danaher, J. (2014). Rule by algorithm? Big data and the threat of algocracy. Institute for Ethics and Emerging Technologies. [Blog comment]. Retrieved from http://philosophicaldisquisitions.blogspot.com/2014/01/rule-by-algorithm-big-data-and-threat.html

Daniel, B. (2015). Big Data and analytics in higher education: Opportunities and challenges. *British Journal of Educational Technology*, *46*(5), 904–920. doi:10.1111/bjet.12230

Davies, J. (2013, March 13). The qualified self [Blog comment]. Retrieved from http://thesocietypages.org/cyborgology/2013/03/13/the-qualified-self/

De Zwart, H. (2014, May 5). During World War II, we did have something to hide. (Translated by Benjamin van Gaalen). Retrieved from https://www.bof.nl/2015/04/30/during-world-war-ii-we-did-have-something-to-hide/

Diakopoulos, N. (2014a). Algorithmic Accountability Reporting: On the Investigation of Black Boxes. Tow Center. Retrieved from http://www.nickdiakopoulos.com/wp-content/uploads/2011/07/Algorithmic-Accountability-Reporting_final.pdf

Diakopoulos, N. (2014b). Algorithmic Accountability: Journalistic investigation of computational power structures. *Digital Journalism*.

Diaz, V., & Brown, M. (2012). Learning analytics. A report on the ELI focus session. Retrieved from http://net.educause.edu/ir/library/PDF/ELI3027.pdf

Durall, E., & Gross, B. (2014). Learning analytics as a metacognitive tool. Retrieved from https://files.ifi.uzh.ch/stiller/CLOSER_2014/CSEDU/CSEDU/Information_Technologies_Supporting_Learning/Short Papers/CSEDU_2014_152_CR.pdf

Earp, J. B., Antón, A. I., Aiman-Smith, L., & Stufflebeam, W. H. (2005). Examining Internet privacy policies within the context of user privacy values. *Engineering Management. IEEE Transactions on*, *52*(2), 227–237.

Essa, A. (2013). Can we improve retention rates by giving students chocolates? [Blog comment]. Retrieved from http://alfredessa.com/2013/10/can-we-improve-retention-rates-by-giving-students-chocolates/

Eubanks, V. (2015, April 30). The policy machine. Slate Magazine. Retrieved from http://www.slate.com/articles/technology/future_tense/2015/04/the_dangers_of_letting_algorithms_enforce_policy.html

Eynon, R. (2013). The rise of Big Data: What does it mean for education, technology, and media research? *Learning, Media and Technology*, *38*(3), 237–240. doi:10.1080/17439884.2013.771783

Feldstein, M. (2013, November 6). Purdue's non-answer on Course Signals [Blog comment]. Retrieved from http://mfeldstein.com/purdues-non-answer-course-signals/

Foucault, M. (1984). Of other spaces. Utopias and heterotopias. In *Architecture/Mouvement/Continuité, Des Espace Autres* (1967, March). (trans. by J. Miskowiec). Retrieved from http://web.mit.edu/allanmc/www/foucault1.pdf

Friedman, B., & Nissenbaum, H. (1996). Bias in computer systems. *ACM Transactions on Information Systems*, *14*(3), 330–347. doi:10.1145/230538.230561

Gašević, D., Dawson, S., & Siemens, G. (2015). Let's not forget: Learning analytics are about learning. *TechTrends*, *59*(1), 64–71. doi:10.1007/s11528-014-0822-x

Godwin-Jones, R. (2012). Challenging Hegemonies in Online Learning. *Language Learning & Technology*, *16*(2), 4.

Greenwood, D., Stopczynski, A., Sweat, B., Hardjono, T., & Pentland, A. (2015). The new deal on data: a framework for institutional controls. In J. Lane, V. Stodden, S. Bender, & H. Nissenbaum (Eds), Privacy, big data, and the public good (pp. 192-210). New York, NY: Cambridge University Press.

Guillaume, D. W., & Khachikian, C. S. (2011). The effect of time on task on student grades and grade expectations. *Assessment & Evaluation in Higher Education*, *36*(3), 251–261. doi:10.1080/02602930903311708

Gurses, S. (2014). Privacy and security. Can you engineer privacy? Viewpoints. *Communications of the ACM*, *57*(8), 20–23. Retrieved from http://dl.acm.org/citation.cfm?id=2632661.2633029 doi:10.1145/2633029

Harford, T. (2014). Big data: are we making a big mistake. *Financial Times*, 28, 1-5.

Hartley, D. (1995). The 'McDonaldization' of higher education: Food for thought? *Oxford Review of Education*, *21*(4), 409–423. doi:10.1080/0305498950210403

Henman, P. (2004). Targeted! Population segmentation, electronic surveillance and governing the unemployed in Australia. *International Sociology*, *19*(2), 173–191. doi:10.1177/0268580904042899

Hillman, N. W., Tandberg, D. A., & Fryar, A. H. (2015). Evaluating the impacts of "new" performance funding in higher education. *Educational Evaluation and Policy Analysis*.

Kalhan, A. (2013). Immigration policing and federalism through the lens of technology, surveillance, and privacy. *Ohio State Law Journal*, *74*, 1105–1165.

Kerr, I., & Barrigar, J. (2012). Privacy, identity and anonymity. In K. Ball, K. D. Haggerty, & D. Lyon (Eds.), *Routledge Handbook of Surveillance Studies* (pp. 386–394). Abingdon, UK: Routledge. doi:10.4324/9780203814949.ch4_1_c

Kitchen, R. (2014a). *The data revolution. Big data, open data, data infrastructures and their consequences*. London, UK: SAGE. doi:10.4135/9781473909472

Kitchen, R. (2014b). Thinking critically about and research algorithms. The Programmable City Working Paper 5. Retrieved from http://eprints.maynoothuniversity.ie/5715/

Koponen, J. M. (2015, April 18). We need algorithmic angels [Blog comment]. *TechCrunch*. Retrieved from http://techcrunch.com/2015/04/18/we-need-algorithmic-angels/

Kovanović, V., Gašević, D., Dawson, S., Joksimović, S., Baker, R. S., & Hatala, M. (2015, March). Penetrating the black box of time-on-task estimation. *Proceedings of the Fifth International Conference on Learning Analytics and Knowledge* (pp. 184-193). ACM. doi:10.1145/2723576.2723623

Kruse, A., & Pongsajapan, R. (2012). Student-centered learning analytics. Retrieved from https://cndls.georgetown.edu/m/documents/thoughtpaper-krusepongsajapan.pdf

Kump, B., Seifert, C., Beham, G., Lindstaedt, S. N., & Ley, T. (2012, April). Seeing what the system thinks you know: visualizing evidence in an open learner model. *Proceedings of the 2nd International Conference on Learning Analytics and Knowledge* (pp. 153-157). ACM. doi:10.1145/2330601.2330640

Lane, J., Stodden, V., Bender, S., & Nissenbaum, H. (Eds.). (2014). *Privacy, big data, and the public good*. New York, NY: Cambridge University Press. doi:10.1017/CBO9781107590205

Li, I., Dey, A. K., & Forlizzi, J. (2011, September). Understanding my data, myself: supporting self-reflection with ubicomp technologies. *Proceedings of the 13th international conference on Ubiquitous computing* (pp. 405-414). ACM. doi:10.1145/2030112.2030166

Lohr, S. (2015, April). How much should humans intervene with the wisdom of algorithms [Blog comment]. Retrieved from http://www.afr.com/technology/how-much-should-humans-intervene-with-the-wisdom-of-algorithms-20150407-1mfqiw

Long, S. (2014, February 20). 'Re-purposing data' in the digital humanities [Blog comment]. Retrieved from https://technaverbascripta.wordpress.com/2014/02/20/re-purposing-data-in-the-digital-humanities/

Lupton, D. (2014a, July 28). Beyond the quantified self: the reflexive monitoring self [Blog comment]. Retrieved from https://simplysociology.wordpress.com/2014/07/28/beyond-the-quantified-self-the-reflexive-monitoring-self/

Lupton, D. (2014b). You are your data: self-tracking practices and concepts of data. Retrieved from http://papers.ssrn.com/sol3/papers.cfm?abstract_id=2534211

Marx, G. T. (2001). Murky conceptual waters: The public and the private. *Ethics and Information Technology*, *3*(3), 157–169. doi:10.1023/A:1012456832336

Mayer-Schönberger, V., & Cukier, K. (2013). *Big data. A revolution that will transform how we live, work, and think*. New York, N.Y.: Houghton Miffling Harcourt Publishing Company.

McKeown, T., & Ayson, S. (2013, December 4-6). *Unleashing the potential of learning analytics: A project outline and a model to put the student first*. Paper presented at the Australian and New Zealand Academy of Management (ANZAM) Conference, Hobart, Australia. Retrieved from http://funrun.gcc.tas.gov.au/anzam/content/pdfs/anzam-2013-398.pdf

Mehta, P. (2015, March 12). Big Data's radical potential. *Jacobin Magazine*. Retrieved from https://www.jacobinmag.com/2015/03/big-data-drones-privacy-workers/

Miyazaki, D., & Ferenandez, A. (2000). Internet privacy and security: An examination of online retailer disclosures. *Journal of Public Policy & Marketing*, *19*(1), 54–61. doi:10.1509/jppm.19.1.54.16942

Morozov, E. (2013a, October 23). The real privacy problem. *MIT Technology Review*. Retrieved from http://www.technologyreview.com/featuredstory/520426/the-real-privacy-problem/

Murphy, K. (2014, October 4). We want privacy, but can't stop sharing. The New York Times [Blog comment]. Retrieved from http://www.nytimes.com/2014/10/05/sunday-review/we-want-privacy-but-cant-stop-sharing.html

Napoli, P. (2013). The algorithm as institution: Toward a theoretical framework for automated media production and consumption. *Proceedings of the Media in Transition Conference* (pp. 1–36). DOI: doi:10.2139/ssrn.2260923

New Media Consortium. (2015). Horizon report higher education edition. Retrieved from https://net.educause.edu/ir/library/pdf/HR2015.pdf

Nissenbaum, H. (2010). *Privacy in context. Technology, policy, and the integrity of social life*. Stanford, CA: Stanford Law Books.

Oblinger, D. G. (2012). Let's talk analytics. *EDUCAUSEreview*. Retrieved from http://www.educause.edu/ero/article/lets-talk-analytics

Ohm, P. (2010). Broken promises of privacy: Responding to the surprising failure of anonymisation. *UCLA Law Review. University of California, Los Angeles. School of Law*, *57*, 1701–1777. Retrieved from http://heinonline.org/HOL/Page?handle=hein.journals/uclalr57&div=48&g_sent=1&collection=journals

Ohm, P. (2015). Changing the rules: general principles for data use and analysis. In J. Lane, V. Stodden, S. Bender, & H. Nissenbaum (Eds.), *Privacy, big data, and the public good* (pp. 96–111). New York, NY: Cambridge University Press.

Open University. (2014). Policy on ethical use of student data for learning analytics. Retrieved from http://www.open.ac.uk/students/charter/essential-documents/ethical-use-student-data-learning-analytics-policy

Pardo, A., & Kloos, C. D. (2011, February). Stepping out of the box: towards analytics outside the learning management system. *Proceedings of the 1st International Conference on Learning Analytics and Knowledge* (pp. 163-167). ACM. doi:10.1145/2090116.2090142

Pardo, A., & Siemens, G. (2014). Ethical and privacy principles for learning analytics. *British Journal of Educational Technology*, *45*(3), 438–450. doi:10.1111/bjet.12152

Pariser, E. (2011). *The filter bubble. What the Internet is hiding from you*. London, UK: Viking.

Pasquale, F. (2015). *The black box society: the secret algorithms that control money and information*. London, UK: Harvard University Press. doi:10.4159/harvard.9780674736061

Pasquale, F. A. (2011). *Restoring Transparency to Automated Authority*. Seton Hall Research Paper, (2010-28).

PewResearchCenter. (2014). Public perceptions of privacy and security in the post-Snowden era. Retrieved from http://www.pewinternet.org/2014/11/12/public-privacyperceptions/

Prinsloo, P. (2009). Modelling Throughput at Unisa: The key to the successful implementation of ODL. Retrieved from http://uir.unisa.ac.za/handle/10500/6035

Prinsloo, P. (2014). *A brave new world: student surveillance in higher education*. Presentation at the Annual Conference of the Southern African Association for Institutional Research (SAAIR) Conference 16-18 October, Pretoria, South Africa. Retrieved from http://www.slideshare.net/prinsp/a-brave-new-world-student-surveillance-in-higher-education

Prinsloo, P., Archer, E., Barnes, G., Chetty, Y., & Van Zyl, D. (2015). Big (ger) data as better data in open distance learning. *The International Review of Research in Open and Distributed Learning*, *16*(1), 284–306.

Prinsloo, P., & Slade, S. (2013, April). An evaluation of policy frameworks for addressing ethical considerations in learning analytics. *Proceedings of the Third International Conference on Learning Analytics and Knowledge* (pp. 240-244). ACM. doi:10.1145/2460296.2460344

Prinsloo, P., & Slade, S. (2014). Educational triage in open distance learning: Walking a moral tightrope. *The International Review of Research in Open and Distributed Learning*, *15*(4), 306–331.

Prinsloo, P., & Slade, S. (2015, b). *Student vulnerability, agency and learning analytics: an exploration*. Presented at the EP4LA workshop during the Fifth International Conference on Learning Analytics and Knowledge.

Prinsloo, P., & Slade, S. (2015a, March). Student privacy self-management: implications for learning analytics. *Proceedings of the Fifth International Conference on Learning Analytics and Knowledge* (pp. 83-92). ACM. doi:10.1145/2723576.2723585

Rymarczuk, R., & Derksen, M. (2014). Different spaces: Exploring Facebook as heterotopia. *First Monday*, *19*(6). Retrieved from http://firstmonday.org/ojs/index.php/fm/article/view/5006/4091 doi:10.5210/fm.v19i6.5006

Seaver, N. (2013). Knowing Algorithms. *Media in Transition*, *8*, 1–12.

Selwyn, N. (2015). Data entry: Towards the critical study of digital data and education. *Learning, Media and Technology*, 40(1).

Selwyn, N., & Facer, K. (Eds.). (2013). *The politics of education and technology*. New York: Palgrave Macmillan. doi:10.1057/9781137031983

Shirky, C. (2014, January 29). The end of higher education's golden age. [Blog comment}. Retrieved from http://www.shirky.com/weblog/2014/01/there-isnt-enough-money-to-keep-educating-adults-the-way-were-doing-it/

Siemens, G. (2013). Learning analytics: The emergence of a discipline. *The American Behavioral Scientist*, *57*(10), 1380–1400. doi:10.1177/0002764213498851

Siemens, G., & Long, P. (2011). Penetrating the fog: Analytics in learning and education. *EDUCAUSE Review*. Retrieved from http://www.educause.edu/ero/article/penetrating-fog-analytics-learning-and-education

Slade, S., & Prinsloo, P. (2013). Learning analytics ethical issues and dilemmas. *The American Behavioral Scientist*, *57*(10), 1510–1529. doi:10.1177/0002764213479366

Solove, D. J. (2001). Privacy and power: Computer databases and metaphors for information privacy. *Stanford Law Review*, *53*(6), 1393–1462. doi:10.2307/1229546

Solove, D. J. (2004). *The digital person. Technology and privacy in the information age*. New York, NY: New York University Press.

Solove, D. J. (2013). Introduction: Privacy self-management and the consent dilemma. *Harvard Law Review* 1880 GWU Legal Studies Research Paper No. 2012-141. Retrieved from http://ssrn.com/abstract=2171018

Stiles, R. J. (2012). Understanding and managing the risks of analytics in higher education: A guide. *EDUCAUSE*. Retrieved from https://net.educause.edu/ir/library/pdf/EPUB1201.pdf

Stoddart, E. (2012). A surveillance of care. Evaluating surveillance ethically. In K. Ball, K. D. Haggerty, & D. Lyon (Eds.), *Routledge Handbook of Surveillance Studies* (pp. 369–376). Abindgon, UK: Routledge. doi:10.4324/9780203814949.ch4_1_a

Subotzky, G., & Prinsloo, P. (2011). Turning the tide: A socio-critical model and framework for improving student success in open distance learning at the University of South Africa. *Distance Education*, *32*(2), 177–193. doi:10.1080/01587919.2011.584846

Tait, A. (2015). Student success in open, distance and e-learning. ICDE Report Series. Retrieved from http://icde.org/admin/filestore/Resources/Studentsuccess.pdf

Tempelaar, D. T., Rienties, B., & Giesbers, B. (2014). In search for the most informative data for feedback generation: Learning Analytics in a data-rich context. *Computers in Human Behavior*. Retrieved from http://www.sciencedirect.com/science/article/pii/S0747563214003240

Tene, O., & Polonetsky, J. (2012). Big data for all: Privacy and user control in the age of analytics. *Northwestern Journal of Technology and Intellectual Property, 239*, 1–36. Retrieved from http://papers.ssrn.com/sol3/papers.cfm?abstract_id=2149364

Uprichard, E. (2015, February 12). Philosophy of data science - Most big data is social data – the analytics need serious interrogation. *Impact of Social Sciences*. Retrieved from http://blogs.lse.ac.uk/impactofsocialsciences/2015/02/12/philosophy-of-data-science-emma-uprichard/

Van Rijmenam, M. (2013, April 30). Big data will revolutionise learning [Blog comment]. Retrieved from http://smartdatacollective.com/bigdatastartups/121261/big-data-will-revolutionize-learning

Wagner, E., & Ice, P. (2012, July 18). Data changes everything: delivering on the promise of learning analytics in higher education. *EDUCAUSEreview*. Retrieved from http://www.educause.edu/ero/article/data-changes-everything-delivering-promise-learning-analytics-higher-education

Watters, A. (2013, October 13). Student data is the new oil: MOOCs, metaphor, and money [Blog comment]. Retrieved from http://www.hackeducation.com/2013/10/17/student-data-is-the-new-oil/

Wishon, G. D., & Rome, J. (2012, 13 August). Enabling a data-driven university. *EDUCAUSE review*. Retrieved from http://www.educause.edu/ero/article/enabling-data-driven-university

ENDNOTES

1 Though *data* as the plural of *datum* have traditionally been treated as plural, data is increasingly used as a phenomenon and therefore *singular*. In this chapter we therefore refer to data as singular unless used as plural in quotations.

Chapter 8
Outstanding Student Achievement:
A Journey of Pedagogy Informed and Confirmed by Analytics

Richard J. Self
University of Derby, UK

ABSTRACT

This chapter will describe, evidence and critically evaluate a pedagogical journey which takes the reader from a traditional position of the "academic as a domain expert" to what turns out to be a far more effective position as the "academic as a Learning to Learn expert". The evidence used to confirm the value and effectiveness of this changed approach by the author over a period of 5 years or so is based on Learning Analytics which demonstrate significantly improved academic results and achievements. It also demonstrates that the author's teaching styles have a dramatic impact on the so-called BME Achievement Deficit, compared to many modules at the institution. It has also had a significant impact in terms of improving student satisfaction. The confirmatory evidence derived from the Learning Analytics is now being used to make informed choices by other colleagues to change their own pedagogical choices to also develop excellent achievement in their own modules and programmes

INTRODUCTION

Learning Analytics can be of great value in helping academics to evaluate the impact of different pedagogic choices. It should, therefore, be considered a standard part of academic continuous professional development practice, an aid to reflection, a guide to the continuous development of teaching practice and materials. If this is to be the case, then it is vital that the analytics techniques and tools and data employed do not impose an unnecessary burden on the practitioners themselves.

This chapter uses a case study evaluation of the author's recent practice to demonstrate how changes to pedagogy have been shown to have unexpected and powerful consequences in terms of student achievement using very simple forms of analysis and data collection which imposed minimal workload on the author.

DOI: 10.4018/978-1-4666-9983-0.ch008

The pedagogic practice change that is evaluated for effectiveness is a change from the comparatively traditional perspective of the "Academic as Source of all Knowledge" to an approach of the "Academic as source of Learning to Learn Skills". A consequence of this changed perspective is that the, so-called, teaching approach is no longer to concentrate on delivering the domain knowledge, facts and answers but on clarifying domain concepts, relationships and sets of important questions that the learners must be aware of and understand. This provides great freedom to use as much of the allocated contact time as possible or necessary for one-to-one and very small group formative discussion and feedback, there is little or no need to dedicate much time to delivering the domain facts which can be easily researched and read by the students, provided that suitable signposting is provided. It is an approach that stops trying to fill leaky buckets with information and replaces it with lighting the fires of inspiration and enquiry (to amend Plutarch (100 A.D.)).

The Learning Analytics demonstrate conclusively the significant increase in average marks achieved by the cohorts as a result of the change. More interestingly, it also demonstrates that over the ten year period between 2004 and 2013, the BMEI (Black, Minority Ethnic and International) students did not display the problematic grade deficit that appears to pervade much of the UK HE landscape.

Comparison between different approaches to generating the analytics is presented to illustrate the value of simple Microsoft XL based analytics in aiding the understanding the basic messages of the data, and illustrating the additional insights that can be obtained through the use of more complex analytics based on using the SAS® statistical methods.

Key academic research based literature is introduced in the section entitled 'academic as "learning-to-learn" expert', where justification for researched and problem based pedagogy is introduced.

Objectives

There are three objectives for this chapter:

1. Outline and evaluate the pedagogic choices and implications.
2. Identify and critically evaluate lessons from the application of Learning Analytics.
3. Demonstrate the ease of applying relevant Learning Analytics to evaluating the consequences and impact of pedagogical choices.

ACADEMIC CONTEXT

This section of the chapter provides an understanding of the context in which the pedagogic choices were being evaluated and the nature of the modules that were taught by the author in both styles of teaching. The application of Learning Analytics was an almost accidental side effect of providing information for the end of semester module report but became very important in terms of selling the changes to skeptical colleagues, as will be seen in this section.

Background

The author started teaching at the University of Derby in 2002, following a thirty year career in industry.

This case study draws on the recent experience of the author, as the School Learning and Teaching Advisor (SLTA) for the School of Computing and Maths in academic years 2011/2013, during a period when Student Satisfaction scores in the National Student Survey (NSS) had to be improved rapidly for one particular BSc Programme. In addition, in common with many UK Higher Education (HE) institutions, there was the significant BMEI grade gap, which averages some 10 to 15% less than the White grade average (Alltree et.al., 2010, Berry and Loke, 2011 and HEA, 2011)).

The role of the SLTA was to identify new ways of engaging the students, delivering the academic content and introducing ways of assessing the students and to gather examples of great practice that were capable of being implemented across the programme and the School. At the same time, it was clearly necessary to build the most persuasive case for change.

In order to build this case for change, measures other than the NSS questions needed to be identified. One set of the metrics that needed to be developed was clearly the measurable impact on achievement in terms of grades and grade profiles. This is because changing teaching and assessment philosophies is often considered to be risky and colleagues need to have some re-assurance that achievement results will not be worse than before and should be improved.

In addition, they may also need to convince their external examiners of the validity of the proposed changes, particularly if significant changes are made to the assessment approaches and that the dramatic improvement in marks is not just a result of grade inflation attempts but, rather, is fully grounded in achievement of the required learning outcomes for the module and the programme. This latter aspect can be a concern in the UK HE environment, given the constantly rising numbers of high achieving students (grade inflation).

The Metrics

A critical consideration in choosing the set of metrics was that the data was already being generated, in large part, during the assessment marking process, thus delivering the data "for free", a factor that figures significantly in all academics' minds when new metrics are suggested. End of Semester and End of Year module and programme reports are a normal part of academic quality systems and will, if best practice is followed, consist of a reflection on all aspects of Teaching, Learning and Assessment, including objective evidence to support the reflection.

Achievement profiles and metrics are one of the most persuasive ways of proving the merit of new approaches. In other words, Learning Analytics is key to the persuasive case for change.

Pedagogical Approaches

The journey starts with traditional "Academic as source of all knowledge" approach, with long seminar / lectures, students who did not read or research, who only worked the minimum necessary to write the assessments. Grade profiles were similar to other modules across the respective programmes.

The journey then changes gear to the current "Academic as source of Learning-to-Learn skills", with a research intensive approach, little direct teaching and outstanding quality of writing. Grade profiles were fundamentally changed for the better.

The Modules

Seven different modules provide the data for this case study which span a period from 2004 to 2014. The basic data for each module is given in Table 1. All the 15 credit modules were taught using the Didactic approach and the new 20 credit modules were taught using the Socratic approach.

The 20 credit modules were designed as part of the diet for a fully re-designed BSc IT programme, which was necessary as a result of an institution wide change from 15 credit modules to 20 credit modules. The opportunity was taken at this point to take advantage the new validation process and very supportive academic management to change pedagogic philosophy to take advantage of some evidence which suggested that a different approach might be very beneficial.

All the module instances that form the basis of this analysis were taught and assessed by the author. This this controls for variations in teaching style or marking standards between different tutors which might perturb the clarity of the analysis. All the results in this evaluation have been both internally and externally moderated according to the institutional quality systems.

The following sub-sections will provide some details about the individual modules, so that the reader understands the context of the discussion in the following two major sections. The entire portfolio of programmes and modules was revised for the start of the 2012 autumn semester, with a change from 15 credit modules (150 hours nominal study time) to 20 credit modules (200 hours nominal study time).

Information Systems Management

This 15 credit module was one of the first modules that the author delivered after starting at the University of Derby. It was a module that was studied by students from many of the different programmes offered by the School of Computing, together with students enrolled on the Joint Honours programme. Data from one of the early years (2005) and the last year that the module was taught (2012) are used for this analysis. The Learning Outcomes were:-

1. Discuss the issues relating to, and implications for information systems management.
2. Understand and be able to apply critically the concepts of, and approaches to information systems management.

Table 1. Case study modules

Course Code	Credits	Course Title	Dates	Year of Degree
5CC006	15	Information Systems Management (ISM)	2005, 2012	Second year
6CC036	15	Systems Methods for Problem Solving (SMPS)	2004, 2005, 2006	Final Year
6CC044	15	IT Law and Governance (ITL&G)	2007, 2008, 2011, 2012	Final Year
5CC521	20	IT Services Management (ITSM)	2012, 2013,	Second Year
6CC506	20	Enterprise Systems (ES)	2012, 2013	Final year
6CC508	20	Information Security and Assurance (ISA)	2012, 2013	Final Year
6CC517	20	Sustainable Information and Corporate Governance (SI&CG)	2012, 2013,	Final Year

The module was assessed by a 2000 word assignment and an exam, each with a 50:50 weighting for the overall module grade. The assignment, based on learning outcome 1, identified 11 broad topics across the domain, from which the students chose a single topic and carried out relevant research in the academic literature in order to write a suitable critical evaluation of an area of the topic. The exam focused on learning outcome 2. The analytics presented relate to the assignment.

Systems Methods for Problem Solving

The author inherited this 15 credit module from a previous academic and re-wrote much of the teaching materials and re-focused the assignment. It was a module that was studied by students from many of the different programmes offered by the School of Computing, together with students enrolled on the Joint Honours programme. The Learning Outcomes of the module were:-

1. Prepare a critical analysis of methodologies.
2. Critically evaluate methods and methodologies for their suitability to particular problem contexts.
3. Apply their understanding of the development, and synthesis, of systems methods in a specific context.

The module was assessed by a single 3000 - 4000 word assignment, based on a single, provided case study which was sourced from the National Audit Office and Public Accounts Committee reports into government systems.

IT Law and Governance

This 15 credit module was created by the author and was first taught in 2007. It was a module that was studied by students from many of the different programmes offered by the School of Computing, together with students enrolled on the Joint Honours programme. The Learning Outcomes of the module were:-

1. Critically evaluate issues of good governance in the context of the deployment and operation of Information Systems.
2. Critically evaluate and apply, in appropriate contexts, the relevant legal issues that impact on the design, provision and operation of Information Systems.

The module was assessed by a single 3000 - 4000 word assignment, based on a single, provided case study which was constructed, in the early years from National Audit Office reports, and in the last two years, to relate to important business IT scenarios targeted at the SME business sector. During the last two years when this module was presented (2011 and 2012) a mandatory, mid-semester, individual formative review with each student of their approach and progress was introduced.

IT Services Management

This 20 credit module was inherited by the author and first presented in the autumn semester of 2012. It is only available to the BSc IT students. The Learning outcomes are:-

1. Demonstrate an understanding of the role of IT Services management in enabling a business, recognising the difference between a Technology Service and a Technology Product and the impact of the ways that technology services can be to an organisation.
2. Critically evaluate a number of options for the delivery of an IT Service and make an appropriate recommendation.
3. Design, with clear justification of the choices made, an IT Service using multiple technology products from different sources to meet a defined business need.

The module is assessed by a single, approximately 2500 word assignment addressing all learning outcomes. The topic was very broadly specified to critically evaluate the introduction of a new IT based service for students. There was a mandatory, late-semester individual formative review with each student of their approach and progress, based on their final draft report. In order to develop skills for employability, they are required to adhere to a document template (currently the Springer LNCS template) and meet a range of presentation requirements, such as they will meet when employed.

The best reports (achieving 65% and above) are edited by a volunteer student into an e-journal issue which is published on the school OJS web site.

Sustainable Information and Corporation Governance

This 20 credit module was designed by the author and first presented in the autumn semester of 2012 It is only available to the BSc IT students. The Learning outcomes are:-

1. Critically evaluate issues of sustainable governance in the context of the development and evaluation of information strategies.
2. Critically evaluate the impact, sustainability and risks related to the introduction of emerging technologies and business practices, including questions of ethics and compliance.
3. Develop and justify an appropriate sustainable information governance strategy for an organisation.

The module is assessed by a single approximately 3000 word assignment addressing all learning outcomes. The topic is very broadly specified to critically evaluate critical strategic Information Governance issues relating to the introduction of new information technologies into the portfolio of organisations. There is a mandatory, late-semester individual formative review with each student of their approach and progress, based on their final draft report. In order to develop skills for employability, they are required to adhere to a document template (currently the Springer LNCS template) and meet a range of presentation requirements, such as they will meet when employed.

The best reports (achieving 70% and above) are edited by a volunteer student into an e-journal issue which is published on the school OJS web site.

Enterprise Systems

This 20 credit module was not designed by the author but has since been modified to meet the Socratic approach and was first presented in the autumn semester of 2012 as a Capstone module. It is now (2014) only available as an option to the BSc IT students, although for 2012 and 2013 (the period of this study) it was also mandatory for the BSc Computer Science students. The Learning outcomes are:-

1. Demonstrate a comprehensive and critical familiarity with available enterprise application implementation options, and demonstrate the ability to make objective, rational decisions – and defend them – about enterprise application development issues, implementation and operation.
2. Be able to design and implement key features of enterprise applications from a strategic perspective.

The module is assessed by a portfolio of an infographic poster (30% of the module grade), which is peer assessed, and an approximately 2500 word assignment (70% of module grade) addressing all learning outcomes. The topic is very broadly specified to critically evaluate critical strategic issues relating to the *"questions of opportunities, challenges, benefits and operations"* associated with a specified leading edge technology. There is a mandatory, late-semester individual formative review with each student of their approach and progress, based on their final draft report. In order to develop skills for employability, they are required to adhere to a document template (currently the Springer LNCS template) and meet a range of presentation requirements, such as they will meet when employed.

The best reports (achieving 70% and above) are edited by a volunteer student into an e-journal issue which is published on the school OJS web site.

Information Systems and Assurance

This 20 credit module was not designed by the author but has since been modified to meet the Socratic approach and was first presented in the autumn semester of 2012 as a Capstone module. It is available to BSc IT students (as an option) and is mandatory for BSc Computer Forensics Investigation students. The Learning outcomes are:-

1. Critically evaluate and apply the available techniques to secure, manage and investigate an information system in a corporate environment, taking account of the risks and compliance issues relating to the security of an information system.
2. Develop and justify appropriate strategic and operational policies that are relevant to specific situations and organisations.

The module is assessed by a portfolio of an infographic poster (30% of the module grade), which is peer assessed, and an approximately 2500 word assignment (70% of module grade) addressing all learning outcomes. The topic is very broadly specified to critically evaluate critical strategic issues relating to the *"questions of ethics, trust, governance, security, audit and provenance"* associated with a specified leading edge technology. There is a mandatory, late-semester individual formative review with each student of their approach and progress, based on their final draft report. In order to develop skills for employability, they are required to adhere to a document template (currently the Springer LNCS template) and meet a range of presentation requirements, such as they will meet when employed.

The best reports (achieving 70% and above) are edited by a volunteer student into an e-journal issue which is published on the school OJS web site.

ACADEMIC AS "DOMAIN" EXPERT

This section evaluates the first three 15 credit modules in Table 1. It is based on the application of Didactic approach to learning and teaching. The academic tutor "knows" everything about the domain and clearly knows more than his pupils and will continue to, even at the end of the teaching and assessment cycle.

Didactic Teaching Approach

A very traditional approach of formal lectures, seminars and tutorials was applied to all three of these modules with very comprehensive sets of slides containing all the necessary knowledge that needed to be transferred to the students about each topic each week. The presentations tended to be very information heavy and served the function of both *aide-memoir* for the lecturer and also as a repository of the key information that needed to be committed to memory and to be used as a source for revision by the students. Much of the information on the slides was quoted or cut and pasted from the various source textbooks and other, relevant documents (such as key paragraphs of ISO 27002), which were cited as the source in the slides, which also functioned as the electronic handouts, through the LMS (Learning Management System) in use in the School.

Use of Contact Time

The following sections identify the teaching patterns and general approaches to using the scheduled contact time for each of the three 15 credit, didactic modules.

Information Systems Management

This second year module was presented as a 1 hour lecture followed by 1 hour tutorials with approximately 20 students per tutorial.

The lecture was a very traditional presentation of the facts, illustrated by extempore illustrations from recent reports in the professional press and the lecturer's own personal experience of thirty years in the IT world to provide the context and consequences of the theory.

The tutorial would serve two purposes; first to provide small scenarios relating to the previous lecture and questions to develop critical analysis; second, towards the end of the semester, to use worked examples of exam questions from previous academic years, in order to develop their skills to interpret exam questions and to identify the key topics and issues that should be addressed in the answer to an exam question together with practice in structuring the answer.

It was a very traditional form of presentation and was very similar to the approach used by most colleagues.

Systems Methods for Problem Solving and IT Law and Governance

These modules were presented as a traditional three hour lecture/seminar. The overall structure of the three hours was a short review of the previous week's topic aimed at gathering together the threads of the previous topic and the results of any work carried out by the students during the week following the seminar, followed by an extended lecture/seminar presentation of a range of "critical" new knowledge interspersed with small group and plenary discussions at relevant points during the period. The intention being that the students would be able to contribute based on their preparation for the seminar prior to the seminar. The final part of the three hour period provided a review of the session, offered a few significant questions to form the basis of consolidation work during the independent study during the following week and indicated preparatory work for the following week's seminar. During the final two years when ITL&G was presented (2011 and 2012), a mandatory mid-semester individual formative review was introduced in order to help the students to be sure that they had not missed critical information provided in the case study (Brown and Wilson, 2013).

Defining Assessments and Marking Criteria

All three modules were assessed against "holistic" criteria, as was the standard for the institution. In 2005, the author, drawing on experience from working in the School of Business, introduced the use of the overall holistic criteria applied to different aspects or components of the work with identification of which elements would be most significant in forming the overall judgment of the final grade for the assignment, there was no explicit use of weighting factors. Examples are presented in the following tables.

Information Systems Management

The standard form of indication of the grade levels was shown in Table 2. There was some discussion of the criteria during the lecture which introduced the students to the assignment.

Superimposed on these criteria was a Business interpretation of the overall impact of the report as can be seen in Table 3, which is provided to give the students an understanding of the worth and impact of their reports in a business environment.

Systems Methods for Problem Solving

This module uses a similar approach to ISM, with similar assessment grids and Business Impact equivalence very similar to those in Tables 2 and 3.

Table 2. ISM 2005 and 2012 criteria

		A	B	C	D	Fm	F
1	Purpose of assignment achieved						
2	Writing and presentation style						
3*	Scope, depth and currency of the research						
4*	Quality and accuracy of analysis						
5*	Demonstration of understanding and application of the research						
6*	Clear representation of ideas and structured argument						
7	Referencing						
	* these criteria are particularly important in forming an opinion of the overall **grade**						

Table 3. Business impact grade A

To achieve an *Excellent Pass (A)* you will have:- o Shown excellent evidence of research and will have many relevant citations that examine the current limits of the topic field. o There is strong evidence of clear understanding, comprehensive analysis and effective application of the researched materials. Ideas are well represented and the arguments are presented in a clear, well-structured fashion.

IT Law and Governance

During 2007 and 2008, assessment grids similar to Tables 2 and 3 were used. By 2011 and 2012 they had been changed to the form in Table 4, with the individual criteria being closely aligned to aspects and sections of the assignment specification.

In addition, in order to reflect the strategic nature of the assignment and the fact that this was a final year module, the Business Impact equivalence statements were strengthened for the overall holistic grade, see Table 5.

Place of Research and Reading

All modules were provided with extensive reading lists of appropriate academic books and academic journal articles which provided a wide range of perspectives on the domain areas of the three modules.

Table 4. 2011 version of assessment grid for ITL&G

		A	B	C	D	MP	F
1*	Purpose of Assignment Addressed						
2	Writing and Presentation Style						
3*	Justification of need and basis of ISMS						
4*	Justification of chosen Compliance Risks						
5*	Critical evaluation of legislative impact						
6*	Use of relevant examples from case study						
7*	Conclusions and Recommendations						
8	Use of additional supporting examples from other literature						
9*	Referencing						
10*	Evidence of research and Bibliography						
	* these criteria are particularly important in forming an opinion of the overall grade						

Table 5. ITL&G A grade business impact equivalence

An *Excellent Pass* **(A)** will have the following characteristics:- • The paper is highly persuasive and answers all the questions that the Board of Directors is likely to ask. • There is an excellent balance between the business and legal issues and the impact of relevant technical issues that are presented in a manner which can be easily understood by the Board of Directors. • The Board of Directors will accept your strategic recommendations and proposals with minimal debate.

The students were strongly advised to make good use of the sources which were categorised into "Required" and "Additional" reading lists which were included in the module handbooks.

The 2 third year modules also strongly encouraged the students to make wide use of the computing weekly and monthly press, using sources such as Computer Weekly and Computing (the monthly journal from the British Computer Society) and subscriptions to the daily, weekly and monthly on-line sources, because these sources would provide up-to-date perspectives on current issues, that were of importance to senior IT managers, in the domain.

However, as is common in many modules, it was generally apparent that, whilst the best students researched comparatively widely for the assignments, as could be seen from the quality of bibliographies, very little reading or preparation was done on a weekly basis for seminars. This had the effect that discussions during seminars was very short and of little value, resulting in seminars becoming didactic lectures.

LEARNING ANALYTICS OF DIDACTIC TEACHING

The Learning Analytics presented for the 15 credit modules taught using didactic pedagogy is based on the assignment grades. The exam grades for ISM are not included in this analysis for simplicity of comparison.

Grade Profiles

Grade profiles are presented for each cohort and, where the data is available from the older modules, separately for the Black, Minority Ethnic and International students and the White UK students. This presentation allows a characterisation of the overall achievement levels resulting from the didactic approach, which were generally similar to many other modules taught in the School at that time. In addition, it provides a baseline for the BMEI grade deficit on modules taught by the author.

The initial data presented in Table 6 and Table 7 and Figure 1 was created very easily and quickly in MS Excel.

Information Systems Management

The simplified analytics presented in Table 6 are suggestive that there may be a difference between the BMEI and White UK cohorts, but the small size of the groups means that the statistics are not conclusive. More complex statistical tests are indicated. These will be considered towards the end of this chapter.

Systems Methods for Problem Solving

Figure 1 illustrates the grade profiles for 2004; the overall cohort profile was considered fairly normal for the School. Table 7 clearly demonstrates that whilst there are changes in overall achievement levels, there is some evidence of a BMEI grade deficit in the 2005 instance but not for 2004 and 2006. Figure 1 is inconclusive and suggests that more complex analytics should be applied to the data, in order to provide a clearer story.

Table 6. Information systems management analytics data

	Academic Year	2005	2012
Cohort	Average for Cohort	56.2%	58.8%
	Standard Deviation	17.5%	15.3%
	Good Honours	46%	42%
	Number in Group	35	77
BMEI	Average for Cohort	54.1%	58.2%
	Standard Deviation	15.3%	17.7%
	Good Honours	42%	38%
	Number in Group	24	29
UK White	Average for Cohort	60.9%	59.2%
	Standard Deviation	20.8%	13.6%
	Good Honours	55%	44%
	Number in Group	11	48

Table 7. SMPS analytics data

	Academic Year	2004	2005	2006
Cohort	Average for Cohort	56.5%	64.7%	59.0%
	Standard Deviation	13.5%	17.6%	13.8%
	Good Honours	35%	65%	58%
	Number in Group	60	51	33
BMEI	Average for Cohort	55.5%	61.6%	59.9%
	Standard Deviation	10.6%	18.4%	12.7
	Good Honours	27%	62%	67%
	Number in Group	30	29	18
UK White	Average for Cohort	58.8%	68.8%	57.9%
	Standard Deviation	14.9%	15.7%	13.8
	Good Honours	43%	68%	47%
	Number in Group	30	22	15

Figure 1. SMPS grade profiles

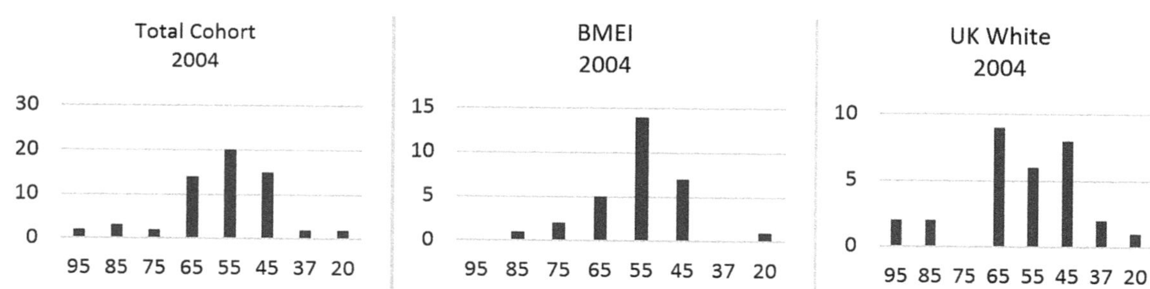

IT Law and Governance

Table 8 illustrates a different facet of the BMEI vv White UK story, which is that although the average grades are very similar in 2008, the proportion of good honours is, apparently quite different for the two groups in 2008. As with Figure 1 profiles, part of the explanation is related to small groups and un-even distributions of individual grades.

ACADEMIC AS "LEARNING-TO-LEARN" EXPERT

This approach is based on the Socratic idea of posing questions and guiding research, debate and strongly engenders critical thinking and analysis of multiple perspectives to obtain a good answer in a specific context. It concentrates on developing the communication skills that are necessary to allow the persuasive presentation of the problem understanding, the existing knowledge that contributes to developing a relevant, context based solution and the persuasive presentation of the recommended solution itself.

Socratic Teaching Approach

Foundation

The fundamental approach is that 'I do not teach; rather, I facilitate, catalyse and guide learning. I pose questions rather than present answers' contrasting with 'if I give you answers then you stop learning', a deeply Socratic approach to learning and teaching.

To modify Plutarch's words, the new approach is based on a view that successful education is about lighting fires, rather than filling leaky buckets. Experience with this approach shows that getting students

Table 8. ITL&G analytics data

	Academic Year	2007	2008	2011	2012
Cohort	Average for Cohort	59.0%	54.0%	57.8%	59.9%
	Standard Deviation	17.5%	17.5%	15.5%	14.0%
	Good Honours	50%	35%	40%	52%
	Number in Group	52	43	50	81
BMEI	Average for Cohort	57.4%	53.0%	53.4%	58.9%
	Standard Deviation	16.5%	18.2%	15.4%	15.4%
	Good Honours	47%	22%	26%	50%
	Number in Group	32	23	23	34
UK White	Average for Cohort	61.6%	55.0%	61.6%	60.6%
	Standard Deviation	18.6%	10.0%	14.6%	13.0%
	Good Honours	55%	50%	52%	53%
	Number in Group	20	20	27	47

to fill their own buckets mysteriously and magically repairs all the leaks as they learn by exploration and research and application. It is, in essence, an extreme flipped teaching concept (Educause, 2012) but does not use the video presentation aspect for self-study prior to seminars and workshops.

This approach leads to intense engagement in the subject during the supervised learning periods of seminars or workshops or tutorials. It draws on the ideas of experiential learning and the "learn by exploring" (Kolb 1984) variant of "learn by doing" which explicitly employs elements of problem-based learning (Hmelo-Silver 2004) and enquiry-based learning (Edelson et al. 1999). It also leads to high student achievement and satisfaction.

Seminars and Workshops

In this learning model, seminars in computer labs provide the students with the opportunity to research and explore, within a relevant, defined context, for academic and industry sources which identify, explain and justify relevant theories and analytical frameworks. Students are expected to find at least five strong sources (which must be added to their module Working Bibliography using the Harvard referencing standard) for each part of the activities. The workshop that follows, then provides the students with the opportunity to apply their new-found knowledge of theories and frameworks to suitable case studies during the first week or two of the semester or, once the assignment has been launched, to their developing assignment, with regular, weekly opportunities to obtain appropriate feed-back and feed-forward in relation to the developing drafts.

An additional aspect of the teaching philosophy and reflected in the design of the curriculum and activities is that continual prompt and instant feed-back and feed-forward during the seminars and workshops is vital and generates very positive results, including high attainment levels, very low failure rates and can also reverse the BME&I to White UK attainment level ratios. This can be seen in all the data presented in this section where the relevant statistics show that on some occasions BME&I students achieve better results than White UK.

The continuous exploration, researching and application that this approach requires the students to undertake, combined with the weekly feed-back and feed-forward provided on an individual level during the seminars and workshops also develops strong research and assignment bibliographies, as is shown in many of the module reports, with average bibliographies achieving around 15 to 20 sources for second and third year students, with the best assignments containing up to 40 or 80 sources.

Assessment Criteria

The final element of the Teaching and Learning Philosophy is to ensure that the assessments are strongly related to current, leading edge business issues and that the assessment criteria are extremely clear, are related to each task that is set within the assessment (building on the 2011/2012 ITL&G approach), and can be understood by the students (in language that they understand *and* feel) and that show the incremental nature of the assessment criteria, as the students attempt to achieve the higher level bands.

A further innovation in the 20 credit modules is the introduction of employability relevant criteria related to excellence of presentation and meeting professional levels of compliance with report writing standards. Such standards are normally set by professional and business organisations for internal and external business reports. This innovation was introduced in response to the oft repeated criticisms from business leaders about the lack of communication skills seen in many graduates.

This has been set at 20% of the overall grade and is based on a set of criteria, which, if not achieved, have specified deductions from the presentation portion of the grade. An example is given in Table 9, the 6 page limit relates to the main content and excludes front page, table of contents and references sections. The minimum mark for the presentation is 0% and cannot be negative. The page length criterion is a limit that many academics meet in submissions to conference and journal papers, above the page limit, additional fees are often charged.

Use of Contact Time

The approach to the IT Service Management and Sustainable Information & Corporate Governance is somewhat different to that for Enterprise Systems and Information Security and Assurance. The former pair of modules are designed to introduce new domain areas to the students, whereas the latter pair, as capstone modules, concentrate on research, integration and deepening of existing knowledge, understanding and application to novel contexts.

As a result, the learning materials for ITSM and SI&CG are structured to provide research materials relating to critical concept areas of the domain, whereas the learning materials for ES and ISA structured around research and presentation concepts in order to develop a strong culture of researching the latest knowledge that is necessary to solve a current business problem and to develop a strongly justified and very well communicated solution.

The impact of this difference drives different approaches to the use of the contact time in the seminars, whilst the workshops use the same approach for all four modules.

For ITSM and SI&CG, the semester provides weekly time to explore critical questions and frameworks relating to 8 or 9 of the most important aspects of the domains. Each seminar (composed of 20 students) will consist of no more than 15 to 20 minutes of tutor input, using no more than 6 to 8 slides which cover the context of the topic, two or three critical questions and guidance on what research is required, the topics of small group discussions and regular reminders to continue building their research bibliographies. After each small group discussion, time is taken for a short summary, plenary discussion. The workshops for these two modules are a continuation of the seminar but with the emphasis on applying the newly acquired frameworks and questions to developing the relevant section of their assignment. During this time, the tutor is actively involved with individuals and small groups in challenging ideas, offering advice in terms of the direction to develop ideas and analysis and reviewing presentation standards.

Because the primary focus of the pedagogy is towards learning to learn, mentoring and coaching in employability skills (Pegg et. Al., 2012), the decision was taken to dedicate all contact time in two or

Table 9. 20 credit module presentation standards criteria (20% of grade)

Perfect adherence to the Springer LNCS template is worth **100%** Your mark will be reduced for each type of error from the following list by the specified amount • Errors on each line of the Title and Affiliation section – 5% each (maximum 30% deduction) • Formatting errors with the Heading styles - 5% each broken style level (maximum 15% deduction) • Failure to use a consistent Harvard standard for citations – 20% (-10% for too few citations) • Failure to use a consistent Harvard formatting of the References – 20% (-10% for too few references) • Failure to use the body-text style - 15% • Failing to meet the specified **six page** length requirement - 50% (+zero lines, -10 lines) • Failure to use the template - 100% deduction

three weeks to individual formative (Brown & Wilson, 2013) and summative review and assessment of each student's final draft and final submission based on a published 15 minute review schedule. This is typically in week 9 or 10 for the formative review using the summative rubric, with discussion of the work, with a view to improving the strength and quality of the report. All relevant comments are recorded electronically and provide the basis for the improvement of the final draft, prior to final submission. The summative marking is typically performed, to a similar schedule, in week 12 or the first week of the exam period. This ensures that the students have instant feedback

For ES and ISA, large cohort based seminars are used with the weekly topics relating to aspects of communication, including topics such as understanding the intended audience, structuring ideas and reports. Much of the seminar time is used in small group activities designed to reinforce the learning and also, in some cases to develop the concept of group-work to improve overall achievement, thus duplicating the real world of employment in teams. The workshops are dedicated to working on the two components of their assessment and using the time for individual tutor review and feedback.

For similar reasons as above, 3 weeks of contact time are dedicated to formative and summative assessment. In week 5, the infographic posters are peer assessed; in week 9 or 10, the same scheduled, individual formative review and in week 12 or the first week of exams, the final scheduled individual summative assessment.

Defining Assessments and Marking Criteria

The assessments are based on broad topics which address current issues challenging CIOs of SMEs and large organisations. They provide opportunities for the students demonstrate high level skills and attainment levels in the IT industry's various skills frameworks, such as SFIA. The criteria are designed so that students can critically evaluate their approach to ensure that their work meets the highest possible band, see Table 10. This particular example indicates the need for novelty of approach as compared to the rather basic approach needed for the basic pass level of 45%.

Place of Research and Reading

Research and reading forms the foundation of this set of modules, the students obtain guidance in relation to context and analytical frameworks relevant to the modules. There are no reading lists for the modules. There are, however, often comprehensive bibliographies on the closing slide(s) for each week's seminar materials for ITSM and SI&CG which support the learning materials.

Table 10. Example of 95% and 45% band criteria (SI&CG)

95% Criteria	**Critically and comprehensively evaluates and justifies** the choice of governance frameworks and issues and the impact on the incorporation of location services. There is a **clear and logical** structure to the analysis and justification. Shows **professional level** of knowledge and understanding of the topic. **Provides a novel approach with clear synthesis of a wide range of perspectives**
45% Criteria	**Justifies** the relevant governance issues and the impact on the incorporation of location services

LEARNING ANALYTICS RELATING TO SOCRATIC TEACHING

This section will illustrate the use of more complex statistical analyses from the SAS system to demonstrate the more significant insights that can be derived from the use of more complex analytical environments. The author has imported all the grade data from all the subject modules into the SAS system from the original Excel spreadsheets.

Grade Profile Impact of Change from Didactic to Socratic

The following statistics in Table 11 demonstrate a highly significant improvement in both mean score and in a reduction in the standard deviation.

As can be seen in Figure 2, observing the differences in the kernel profiles (which represents the distribution of the actual data), there is clear evidence of significantly improved achievement for the new 20 credit modules, with a strong skewing of achievement into the >= 70% marks

The impact of the changing approach can be better seen in Table 12 and Figure 3 which contrasts achievements in 2004 with that in 2013 and demonstrates with a high degree of confidence that the two cohorts have different mean grades of 56% and 71%, an improvement of 15%.

Table 11a. Impact of Changing from didactic to socratic approach

Pedagogy	N	Mean	Std Dev	Std Err	Minimum	Maximum
D	573	60.3380	17.0730	0.7132	20.0000	96.0000
S	270	68.8604	15.2298	0.9269	5.0000	96.0000
Diff (1-2)		-8.5223	16.5058	1.2184		

Table 11b.

Method	Variances	DF	t Value	Pr > |t|
Pooled	Equal	841	-6.99	<.0001
Satterthwaite	Unequal	585.38	-7.29	<.0001

Table 12a. Mean achievement 2004 compared to 2013

Year	N	Mean	Std Dev	Std Err	Minimum	Maximum
2004	60	56.1083	14.7252	1.9010	20.0000	95.0000
2013	183	70.9563	13.9882	1.0340	5.0000	96.0000
Diff (1-2)		-14.8480	14.1722	2.1083		

Figure 2. Change in mark distribution profiles

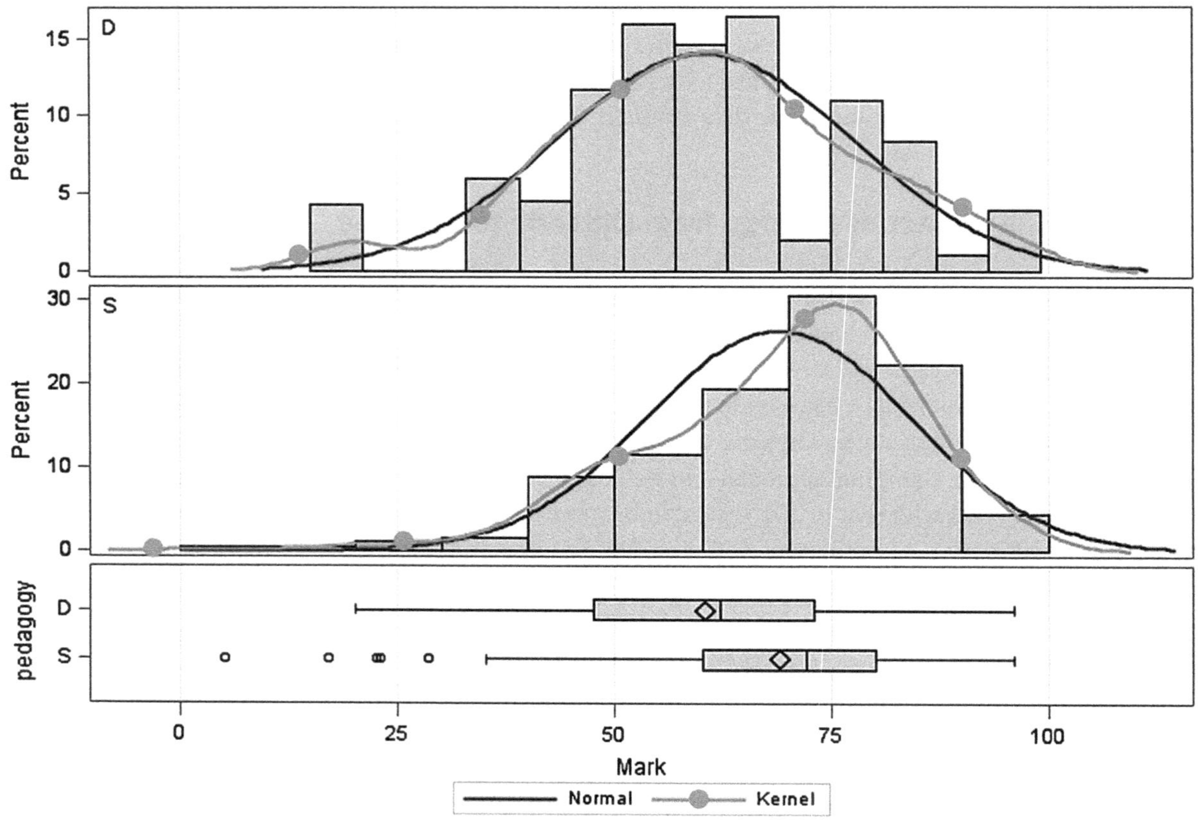

Table 12b.

Method	Variances	DF	t Value	Pr > |t|
Pooled	Equal	241	-7.04	<.0001
Satterthwaite	Unequal	96.343	-6.86	<.0001

Grade Impact on Ethnicity Profiles

Comparing the profiles for 2004 and 2013 above we can see clear evidence of a significant change but Table 13, Table 14, Figure 4 and Figure 5 demonstrate little evidence of a difference between the ethnic groups.

2004

The above statistics strongly suggest that there is no significant difference between the two populations, as can also be seen in the strong similarity between the two graphical profiles in Figure 4.

Figure 3. Mean achievement 2004 compared to 2013

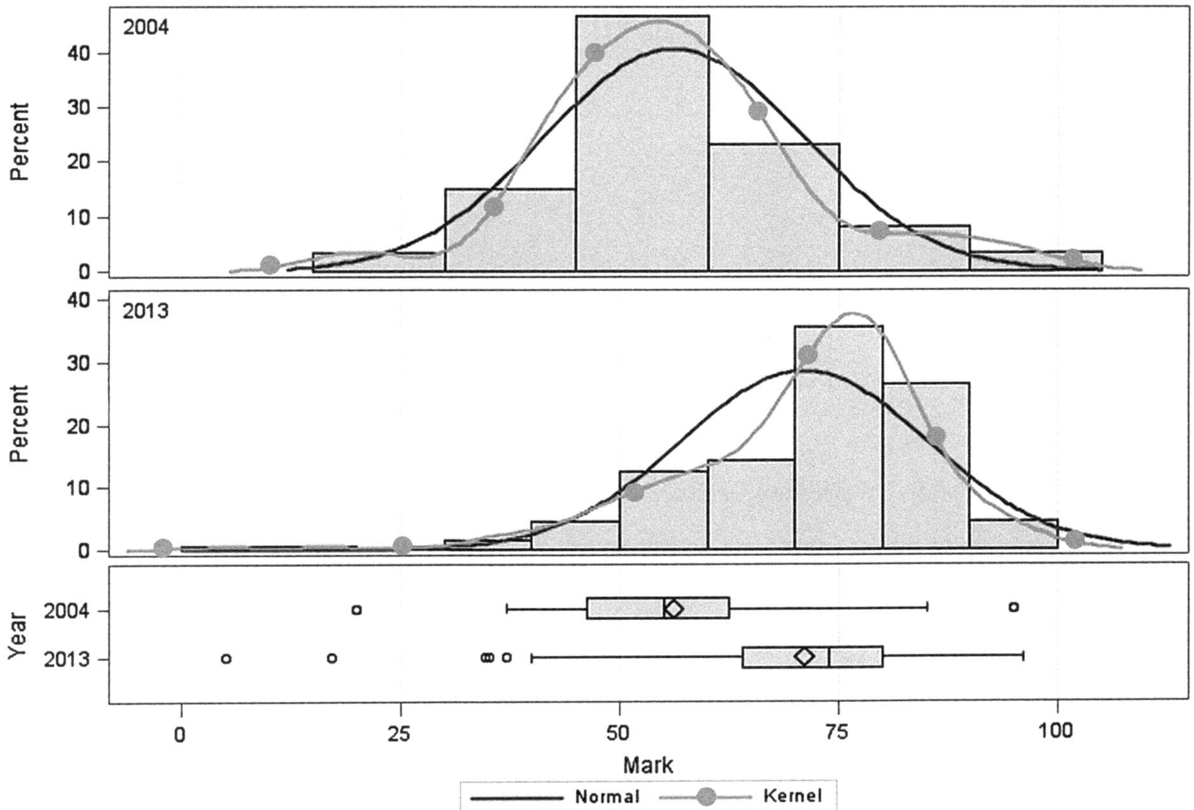

Table 13a. Significance of ethnicity in achievement - 2004

BMEI	N	Mean	Std Dev	Std Err	Minimum	Maximum
B	30	55.0833	12.2384	2.2344	20.0000	85.0000
W	30	57.1333	17.0055	3.1048	20.0000	95.0000
Diff (1-2)		-2.0500	14.8150	3.8252		

Table 13b.

Method	Variances	DF	t Value	Pr > |t|
Pooled	Equal	58	-0.54	0.5941
Satterthwaite	Unequal	52.686	-0.54	0.5943

Table 14a. Significance of ethnicity in achievement - 2013

BMEI	N	Mean	Std Dev	Std Err	Minimum	Maximum
B	95	69.7916	12.4321	1.2755	34.6000	96.0000
W	88	72.2136	15.4680	1.6489	5.0000	96.0000
Diff (1-2)		-2.4221	13.9739	2.0675		

Table 14b.

Method	Variances	DF	t Value	Pr > |t|
Pooled	Equal	181	-1.17	0.2429
Satterthwaite	Unequal	166.95	-1.16	0.2470

Figure 4. BMEI vs. white UK profiles for 2004

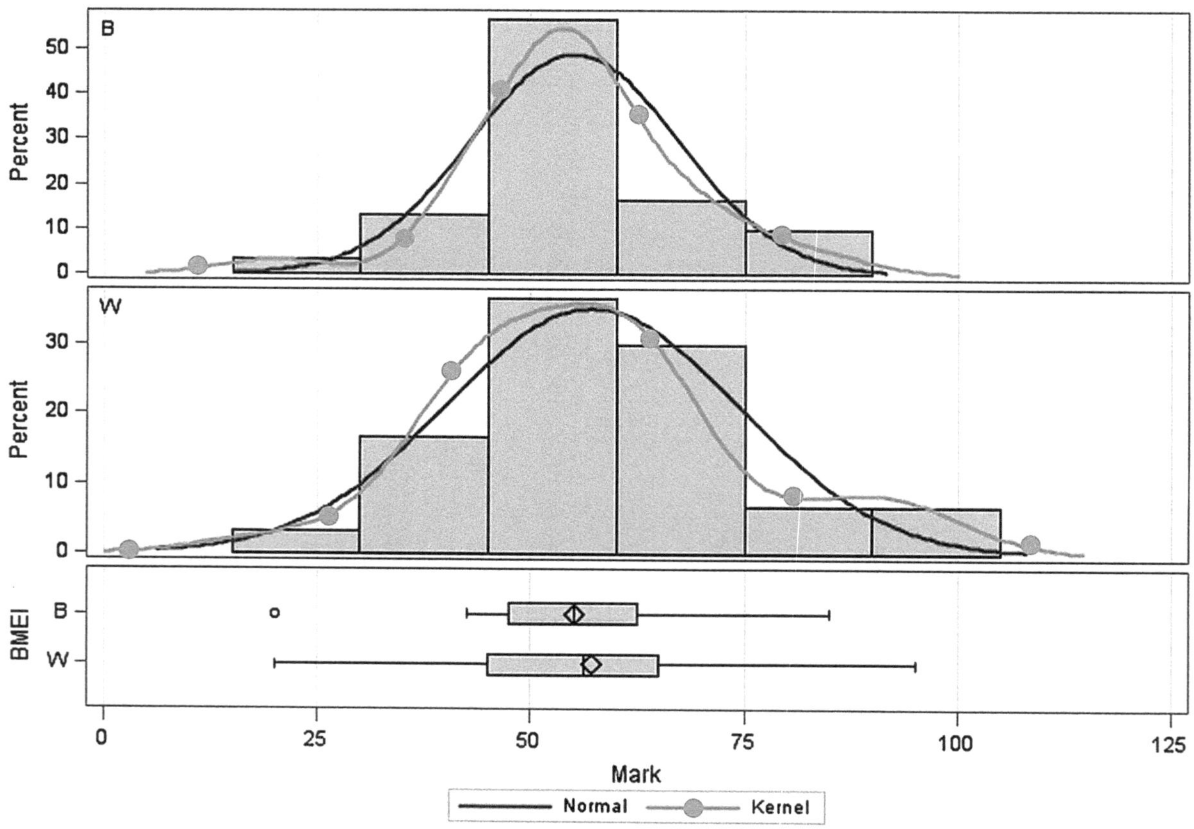

Figure 5. BMEI vs. white UK profiles for 2013

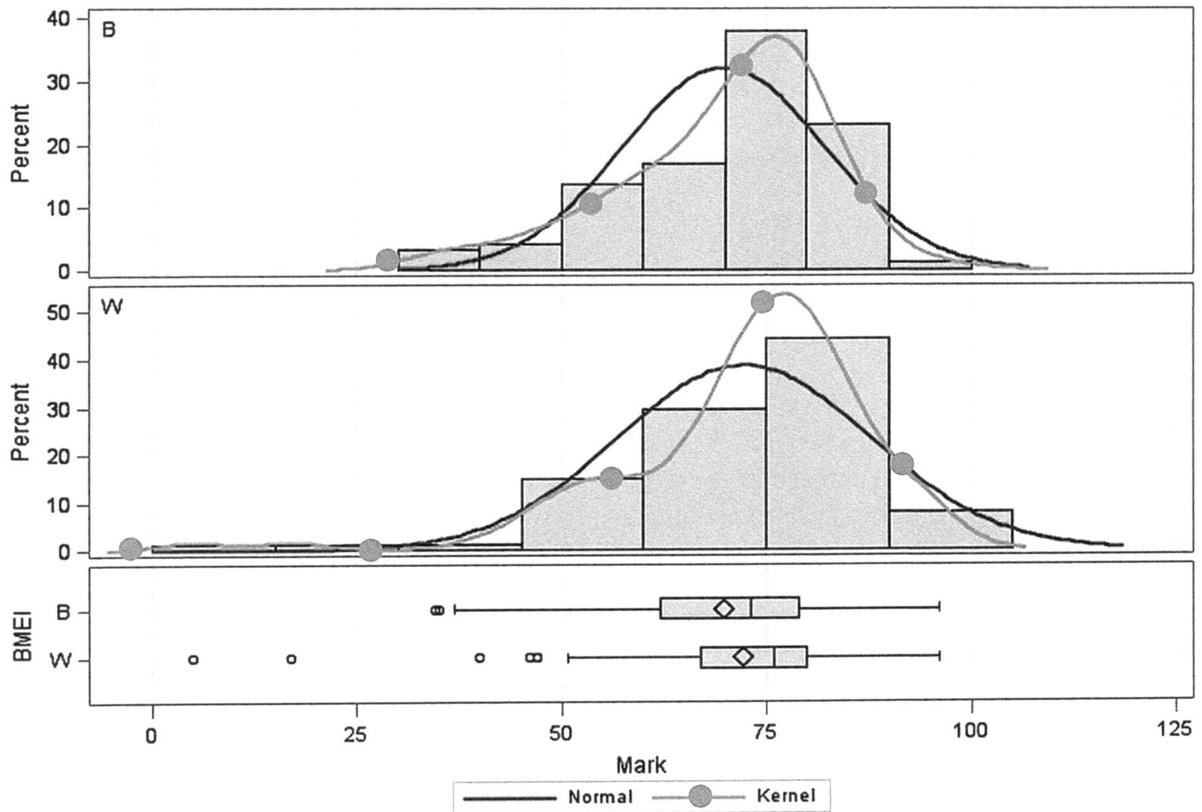

2013

The statistics suggest that the 2.4% difference in the means for the two populations is not very significant. The kernel and normal curves in Figure 4 also illustrate this. Figure 4 and the statistics above also identify the fact that in 2013, there were several very low achievers in the white UK group, whereas the BMEI group all achieved above 35%. The difference between the location of the mead (the diamond) and the median (the vertical bar) demonstrates the skewing of the data towards high achievement and the impact of the outliers in the White UK population.

Figure 5. does, however, illustrate one of the idiosyncrasies of the default settings for SAS in creating different bin sizes for the comparative plots which can cause some confusion in interpreting the plots.

CRITICAL APPLICATION OF LEARNING ANALYTICS RESULTS

This section summarises the key changes in achievement that can be seen from the Learning Analytics presented above. It identifies two critical impacts on the academic landscape. The first section is devoted to the impact on the levels of student achievement; the second section considers the impact on the academic.

Primary Impact

This section provides the comparison and commentary relating to the Learning Analytics data presented above, identifying the issues that are apparent in the 15 credit Didactic modules and the significant improvements at cohort level with the change to the Socratic process in the 20 credit modules. This is followed by a commentary on the impact of the change from Didactic to Socratic learning.

Impact on Overall Grade Profiles

For the purposes of this section, whilst the graphical output in figures 2, 3 and 4 were actually generated in SAS, they could have been just as easily created in Excel from the basic data and the messages would be just the same.

Table 11. demonstrates with a high degree of confidence based on the pooled variance t test that there is a significant difference between the mean achievement levels between the old style of teaching and assessing and the new approach of the order of 8.5%. Comparing the changes between 2004 and 2012 using Tables 12 and 13, it can be seen that whilst there is inconclusive evidence that there is any significant difference between the achievements of BMEI and White UK groups in either 2004 or 2013, there is a highly significant improvement in overall achievement between the two years.

BMEI Grade Changes

Overall, that data does not demonstrate that there is any significant difference in achievements levels between the BMEI and White UK groups on a year by year basis.

Secondary Impact

This section provides a short commentary on the clear value of the change to the academic workload of the change to Socratic philosophy, followed by some observations relating to the value of Learning Analytics as a means of clearly demonstrating the impact of changes in teaching and learning strategies in terms of that most important metric of student achievement.

Academic Workload

There two very significant consequences on the academic's workload as a result of the Socratic approach incorporated in the 20 credit modules that form the basis of this case study.

The first is large reduction in the amount of preparation for the weekly set of slides, from between 50 to 70 very information dense slides that were required for the didactic, 15 credit modules to between 8 to 10 sparse slides for the weekly material for the Socratic 20 credit modules. The weekly material for the 20 credit modules was typically created in approximately 30 minutes, compared to the 3 to 5 hours per weekly set of material for the 15 credit modules.

In addition, because the Socratic approach identifies critical questions within the topic and, in the field of Computer Science, where the fundamental questions and issues change very slowly whilst the specifics of the technology change very quickly. The critical business issues and questions relating to the operation of IT today are very similar to those which exercised CIOs and IT managers 20 or 30 years ago. The consequence is that the seminar slides will not need to be reviewed or changed for several years. The only requirement is that the academic remains fully up-to-date with the current situation of the domain, through regular review of the business, IT and academic press, as is expected of all academics as part of their scholarly activity.

The second and very significant impact is that all assessment is carried out during contact/office hours or the exam period, on the university premises. There is no requirement to mark assignments at home, out of working hours, etc. This has a very significant impact on work/life balance, especially over the Christmas holiday. Learning Analytics conclusively demonstrates that the improvement in achievement is worth the time dedicated to individual mentoring, challenging and coaching students in the research process necessary for successful employment

Selling the Changes

During the academic year 2013/2014, the role of the SLTA was to lead by example and demonstrate the value of changes to pedagogy and forms of assessment that would enable students to achieve to their limits and also improve the NSS scores for all of the programmes in the School.

The Learning Analytics results were a powerful illustration of the benefits of the suggested developments to colleagues, who were able to feel more confident about beginning the journey of change to a more Socratic teaching style.

CRITICAL EVALUATION OF LEARNING ANALYTICS IMPACT

This section summarises two key factors in the deployment of Learning Analytics.

KISS Principle

Most of the Learning Analytics data incorporated in this chapter were collected during the assessment process in the usual spreadsheets that academics construct for recording marks, prior to entry into the formal institutional Student Records systems. The basic statistics and the charts were created as part of the process to create the post semester, module evaluation reports, which form part of the institutional quality processes for continuous improvement.

In this respect, the Keep-It-Simple-Stupid (KISS) principle was the guide. There is little apparent need to develop any additional, more complicated metrics, if significant impact can be demonstrated with a simple set.

It is of interest that the simple graphical outputs that can be achieved from Excel generally provide a quick and easy way of gaining an overall picture of the impact of a change.

However, in order to gain deeper insight and a full appreciation of the degree of confidence in the graphs, it is necessary to develop some of the statistics, as has been done with the SAS® system.

Objective Analysis of Achievement Results

A review of journal articles covering academic research into pedagogic practice and theory seems too often to be based on qualitative research into student preferences and satisfaction, a highly subjective approach. There is often little connection between student preferences and achievement. However, students are the first to complain if they do not get a high enough grade to qualify them for jobs.

The use of Learning Analytics on achievement data provides clear, objective results which, in this case study, shows significant benefits for the changes made to pedagogy.

The use of the graphical output can provide a quick understanding of the attainment levels and impact of pedagogic choices. These can easily be developed with minimal effort in Excel by most academics.

Use of the more technical statistics, developed for this paper in SAS®, provides greater insights and confidence in the significance, or otherwise, of the data.

It should also be noted that once the data has been imported into a database, it is very much faster and easier to carry out a wide range of different analyses, which can be very tedious and difficult in spreadsheets unless macros can be used (a little known skill for most academics).

CONCLUSION

This final section summarises the key conclusions of this chapter, following which are a few recommendations, relating to implementing Learning Analytics and using them to quickly and objectively evaluate experiments in changing learning, teaching and assessment strategies and pedagogies.

There are several conclusions that can be drawn about both the changing pedagogy choices and about the use of Learning Analytics.

1. The use of simple histograms can provide a quick means of evaluating learning achievements for individual modules and providing comparisons between modules.
2. The use of more complex statistics within an analytical system, such as SAS®, provides greater opportunities for more wide ranging comparisons between different modules and cohorts and between different categorisations, such as were used here with the BMEI / White UK, Year and Pedagogy criteria were used in different t-Test comparisons.
3. Use of Learning Analytics can clearly be used to evaluate the impact of changes in all aspects of pedagogy and to provide confidence to colleagues that the change is valid and worthwhile.

REFERENCES

7 Things You Should Know About Flipped Classrooms. (2012). *Educause*. Retrieved from http://www.educause.edu/library/resources/7-things-you-should-know-about-flipped-classrooms

Alltree, J., Barefoot, H., Flynn, S., Haddleton, F., Weston, K., & Wright, M. (2010). *The University of Hertfordshire's Higher Education Academy (HEA) and Equality Challenge Unit's (ECU's) Black and Minority Ethnic (BME) Summit project – Report April* 2010. University of Hertfordshire. Retrieved from http://www.heacademy.ac.uk/resources/detail/Hertfordshireethnicitysummit

Berry, J., & Loke, J. (2011). *Improving the degree attainment of Black and minority ethnic students (Final Report)*. HEAcademy. Retrieved from http://www.heacademy.ac.uk/resources/detail/inclusion/Ethnicity/BMEProgramme_FinalReport

Brown, M., & Wilson, C. (2013, October 1). *Formative assessment: getting to know your students* (Presentation). University of Derby APP. Retrieved from http://prezi.com/rxevkq1gdr3e/?utm_campaign=share&utm_medium=copy

Edelson, D., Gordin, D., & Pea, R. (1999). Addressing the Challenges of Inquiry-Based Learning Through Technology and Curriculum Design. *Journal of the Learning Sciences*, *8*(3), 391–450. doi:10.1207/s15327809jls0803&4_3

Hmelo-Silver, C. E. (2004). Problem-Based Learning: What and How Do Students Learn? *Educational Psychology Review*, *16*(3), 235–266. doi:10.1023/B:EDPR.0000034022.16470.f3

Improving the degree attainment of Black and minority ethnic students. (2011, March 17). UK Higher Education Academy, http://www.heacademy.ac.uk/news/detail/2011/improving_BME_degree_attainment

Kolb, D. (1984). *Experiential Learning as the Science of Learning and Development*. Englewood Cliffs, NJ: Prentice Hall.

Pegg, A., Waldock, J., Hendy-Isaac, S., & Lawton, R. (2012). *Pedagogy for employability*. HEA.

Plutarch. (100 AD) On Listening to Lectures (De auditu), in Moralia (Vol 1, 3), http://penelope.uchicago.edu/Thayer/E/Roman/Texts/Plutarch/Moralia/De_auditu*.html

ADDITIONAL READING

Gunn, V., & Fisk, A. (2013). *Considering teaching excellence in higher education: 2007-2013*. HEA.

Miller, K., Weyers, J., Cross, S., Walsh, L., & Monaghan, E. (2009). *A toolkit for enhancing personal development planning strategy, policy and practice in higher education institutions*. HEA Scotland.

Ottewil, R. (2005). Integrating Personal Development Planning (PDP) into a module for 1st Year Sociology students. HEA case Study.

QAA. (2009). *Personal development planning: guidance for institutional policy and practice in higher education, Quality Assurance Agency for Higher Education.*

Rees, C., Forbes, P., & Kubler, B. (2006). *Student employability profiles: A guide for higher education practitioners*. HEA.

Senior, N. (2013) Exploring the retention and attainment of black and minority ethic (BME) students on Social Policy pathways in higher education. Retrieved from http://www.heacademy.ac.uk/resources/detail/disciplines/hsc/Social-Work-and-Social-Policy/retention-and-attainment-senior

Stevenson, J. (2010). Enhancing BME student success through staff-student collaboration, Summit Programme to Promote Student Success: Improving the Degree Attainment of Black and Minority Ethnic Students. Retrieved from http://www.heacademy.ac.uk/resources/detail/inclusion/Leedsethnicitysummit

University of Northampton. (2009). The University of Northampton - Improving the degree attainment of Black and minority ethnic students. Retrieved from http://www.heacademy.ac.uk/resources/detail/inclusion/northampton_ethnicity_summit

Chapter 9
Personalising the Pathway:
Learning Analytics for Leveraging Pedagogically Purposeful Indicators of Academic Performance

Donna M. Velliaris
Eynesbury Institute of Business & Technology, Australia

ABSTRACT

The Eynesbury Institute of Business and Technology (EIBT) is one of a growing number of private providers partnering with universities to establish pre-university pathway programs worldwide. As a second chance for prospective students who do not meet initial Australian Higher Education (HE) entrance requirements, pathway providers attract students early in their tertiary lifecycle to secure their destination. EIBT has an abundance of empirically-rich and 'big' data that may be used to find pedagogically useful indicators, predictors and recommendations for teaching and learning advancement by careful evaluation of the findings. The work of 'researchers' often resides in isolation from that of 'educators', whereby the 'gap' may reflect a poor-cycle of communication and interaction between empirical studies and praxis. This chapter is limited to a select and somewhat brief discussion of specific uses of Learning Analytics (LA) in the context of EIBT and related sense-making and predicting of student performance.

INTRODUCTION

In the Higher Education (HE) sector, learning quality assurance data are typically derived from *Student Experience Surveys* (Lockyer, Heathcote, & Dawson, 2013) alongside measures of attrition, progression and assessment scores (Monson, Bunney, & Lawrence, 2013). The adoption of education technologies—such as Learning Management Systems (LMS)—has resulted in a vast set of accessible data. These data, however, are commonly used 'retrospectively' to improve future iterations of program delivery, to determine impact on learning outcomes, and to provide a benchmark on overall institutional performance. Digital footprints can, however, be collected and analysed to establish indicators of teaching quality and provide a more proactive assessment of student learning and engagement.

DOI: 10.4018/978-1-4666-9983-0.ch009

This chapter employs the definition of Learning Analytics (LA) set out in the first International Conference on Learning Analytics and Knowledge (LAK 2011) and adopted by the Society for Learning Analytics Research (SoLAR) that says, 'LA is the measurement, collection, analysis and reporting of data about learners and their contexts, for purposes of understanding and optimising learning and the environments in which it occurs' (Siemens, 2011). Indeed, the educational 'context' plays a key role as 'an in-depth understanding of the institution and how it functions will include knowledge of its operational and strategic objectives and direction' (Prinsloo, Archer, Barnes, Chetty, & Van Zyl, 2015). As it stands, this definition is usually coupled with two underlying assumptions: (1) that LA make use of pre-existing and machine-readable data; and (2) that LA techniques are used to handle 'big data' i.e., large data sets that would not be practicable to deal with manually.

The Eynesbury Institute of Business and Technology (EIBT) has an abundance of empirically-rich and 'big' data that may be used to find pedagogically useful indicators, predictors and recommendations for teaching and learning advancement by careful evaluation of the findings. In agreement with Slade and Prinsloo (2013, p. 5), '[h]igher education institutions have always analyzed data to some extent, but the sheer volume of data continues to rise along with institutions' computational capacity...' EIBT is conceptually bridging technical and educational domains (Lockyer, et al., 2013, p. 1446). EIBT's LMS is embedded within a 'wider network of platforms and systems' involved in supporting its institutional teaching and learning mission, and is increasingly viewed as a core component of the EIBT's educational infrastructure (L. Macfadyen & Dawson, 2012, p. 150). That is, EIBT is increasing its focus on data-driven decision-making and the integration of the technical with social/pedagogical dimensions of HE (Romero & Ventura, 2013, p. 13). Added to this, however, is the need to utilise such analytical tools to reduce the timeframe between (a) *analysis* and (b) *action*. Ideally, effective tools can promptly explore real-time user feedback, as well as enable manipulation/visualisation based on the interests of researchers, practitioners and stakeholders.

EIBT is successfully using its data for many and varied purposes, among which includes linking available datasets with its fellow pathway colleges and partner universities in order to implement more learner-oriented services and thus improve student performance. With analytical tools growing more powerful and their reach increasing, the aim is to assist EIBT educators to interpret *instructor-* and *learner*-centric data for informing future pedagogical decisions. Objectives related to EIBT's motivation to pursue LA include, for example:

- *To develop* a deep(er) understanding of student learning at an individual-level to support the personalisation of their educative experiences;
- *To embed* emergent feedback on student learning into practices through enabling adaptations to EIBT's teaching and learning in a timely manner; and
- *To identify* Students-At-Risk (STAR) of poor learning experiences/outcomes, in real-time and with insight to allow for meaningful intervention.

Amid a long list of measurable factors, some data are strong indicators of positive academic outcomes, while others are not (Anirban, 2014; Brown, 2011). Specific examples of LA that help personalise the pathway experience for EIBT students are presented. This chapter examines developing areas of LA utilisation and research within EIBT and distinguishes a series of processes, limitations, recommendations and future challenges. Since the potential uses for LA are varied, this chapter is limited to a select and somewhat brief discussion of uses; important topics of sense-making and predicting of student performance from the perspective of a first-generation LA researcher-practitioner and *not* a data analyst. For confidentiality purposes, a *backward-looking* discussion on the use of LA to drive EIBT's pedagogic agendas are presented. Relatedly, precautions have been taken to ensure that the data collections of students, lecturers and/or institutional performance is not abused in ways that could be potentially damaging i.e., data is anonymised as far as possible and individual identifiers have been removed.

Importantly, the term 'international students' or simply 'students' is specific to individuals enrolled at 'Eynesbury' (pre-university institution) on temporary student visas and who are almost exclusively Non-English Speaking Background (NESB).

BACKGROUND

The Eynesbury Institute of Business and Technology

The Eynesbury Institute of Business and Technology (EIBT) is one of a growing number of private providers partnering with universities to establish pre-university pathway programs worldwide. As a second chance for prospective students whose academic results and/or English language proficiency were marginally below the requirements for direct entry into Australian undergraduate programs, EIBT offers pathways to either (a) *The University of Adelaide* or (b) *University of South Australia* with Diplomas in (1) Business—DB; (2) Information Technology—DIT; and (3) Engineering—DIPE (Fiocco, 2006; Velliaris & Breen, 2014; Velliaris & Willis, 2014; Velliaris, Willis, & Breen, 2015).

Though EIBT is accessible to local students, recruitment is predominantly directed towards full fee-paying international students who: (a) have completed Year 11 high school in Australia and would prefer to continue their studies in a different academic context; (b) have completed Year 12 high school in Australia, but did not obtain an ATAR [Australian Tertiary Admission Rank] sufficient for direct entry into university; (c) have graduated from high school abroad, but whose English language proficiency did not meet the minimum requirement for direct entry into university; or (d) are above 20 years of age with a relevant employment history (Velliaris & Willis, 2014; Velliaris, et al., 2015).

EIBT has established a strong profile as a pre-university pathway provider in South Australia where students benefit from the discipline-specific expertise and academic rigour the universities apply to their own curriculum (Velliaris & Willis, 2014; Velliaris, et al., 2015). Cross-institutional lecturers—from other pathway and partner institutions—deliver approximately 40 courses across three back-to-back trimesters (-01, -02, -03). EIBT has an agreement to use the partner university's intellectual property and is contractually obliged to deliver courses with equivalent outcomes (Velliaris, et al., 2015). As articulation and credit transfer agreements are well documented, programs (and each course within) are consistently monitored to ensure that the validity of contractual arrangements are maintained.

The pathway university moderates diploma program delivery and grants advanced standing for first-year courses if students achieve an overall minimum entry-level average grade or Grade Point Average (GPA) upon graduation. In greater detail, EIBT's agreement specifies a range of quality assurance measures (adapted Velliaris, et al., 2015, pp. 221-222) that include:

- *Assessing EIBT* students in the equivalent form to those conducted for the same units at the partner university. In most cases, assessment items (e.g., final examination) are provided by the partner university's Course Coordinator, but where they are not, EIBT lecturers submit sample questions for approval;
- *Benchmarking,* internally and externally, program and course results and presenting final grades to EIBT's Academic Broad for approval, which includes partner university academic staff;
- *Collecting* student evaluations at the end of each trimester. The individual results—reviewing the instructor and the coursework—are summarised and provided to the partner university's Course Coordinator and as feedback to the EIBT lecturer. Evaluations are analysed and influence subsequent employment and final summaries are presented to EIBT's Academic Board for review;
- *Delivering* courses/units that comprise the first-year undergraduate degree in the partner university. EIBT's curriculum, texts and teaching resources are identical/comparable to those prescribed/provided by the relevant School for its own students;
- *Limiting* class size to less than 25 students and one consistent lecturer, enabling rapport to develop among EIBT lecturers and students, and thus enhancing interaction and aiding in identification of a student's area(s) of weakness;
- *Meeting* the standards required for appointment to the partner university. That is, only lecturers approved by the relevant Heads of School can teach a course(s). Generally this implies a minimum qualification of a first degree in a specialist area, together with relevant teaching and/or professional experience in the discipline; and
- *Offering* EIBT students more contact time per week than the equivalent course at the partner university. This equates to approximately 10-20% more face-to-face time to allow EIBT lecturers to affirm terminology/principles, to consolidate concepts before moving on through course content, and to better develop students' tertiary skills over the duration of their diploma program.

All EIBT programs are university approved and moderated, and the final award is accredited through the Australian Department of Further Education, Employment, Science and Technology (DFEEST).

LITERATURE REVIEW

'Institutions of HE are increasingly called upon to measure, demonstrate, and improve student performance' (Mattingly, Rice, & Berge, 2012, p. 241). Learning Analytics (LA) is a generic all-encompassing term to describe a Technology-Enhanced Learning (TEL) research area that focuses on the development of methods for analysing and detecting *patterns* within data collected from educational settings, and leveraging those findings to support different stakeholders. Stakeholders include: administrators; counsellors; educators; executive officers; faculty decision-makers; industry; instructors; legislators; mentors; moderators; parents; public authorities; regulatory agencies; researchers; students; system designers; tutors; and institutions as a whole, all of whom have their own perspective(s) and/or goal(s). The choice of target audience (i.e., stakeholder), therefore, 'affects how researchers conceptualise problems, capture data, report findings, act on their findings and refine their models' (Chacon, Spicer, & Valbuena, 2012; Ferguson, 2012). In other words, data integration can improve the accuracy of a learner's profile and subsequent adaptation and 'personalisation' of the curriculum.

Defining Learning Analytics

The applications discussed in this chapter focus on teaching and learning and, hence, specifically examine LA. LA is a fast-growing area of TEL research, whereby the data silos that often exist(ed) in HE, including EIBT, present a challenge for researchers, practitioners and stakeholders (Siemens, 2012). The emerging popularity of LA—represented by a tsunami of publications and conferences etcetera—is articulated in the extant literature. As listed in Table 1, a plethora of terms suggesting synonyms and/or terminological confusion are presented (e.g., Barber & Sharkey, 2012; Dyckhoff, 2011; Dyckhoff, 2014; Dyckhoff, Zielke, Bültmann, Chatti, & Schroeder, 2012; Essa & Ayad, 2012; Ferguson, 2012; Gulbahar & Ilgaz, 2014; Piety, Hickey, & Bishop, 2014).

The emergent field is 'multidisciplinary' and draws on artificial intelligence, business intelligence, computer science, psychology, social network analysis, and statistics related to Educational Data-Mining (EDM) (Lockyer, et al., 2013, p. 1441). Its connections to these fields have meant that researchers, practitioners and stakeholders have approached it from a range of perspectives, but should now work collaboratively to identify not only the goals that *can be* achieved using LA, but equally important, *how to* attain those goals.

With reference to the literature, ten definitions/explanations of LA are presented below using a chronological and alphabetical framework to chart its evolution:

- LA is an emerging field in which sophisticated analytic tools are used to improve learning and education. It draws from, and is closely tied to, a series of other fields of study including business intelligence, web analytics, academic analytics, educational data-mining, and action analytics (Elias, 2011, p. 2).
- LA deals with the development of methods that harness educational data sets to support the learning process. LA is a multi-disciplinary field involving machine learning, artificial intelligence, information retrieval, statistics, and visualization (Chatti, Dyckhoff, Schroeder, & Thüs, 2012, p. 318).

Table 1. Terms in the associated literature used interchangeably with Learning Analytics (LA)

Action analytics	Information retrieval
Adaptive learning analytics	Information visualisation
Advanced learning technologies	Institutional analytics
Analytics for achievement	Intelligent tutoring
Analytics tools	Interpretable models
Data-disaggregation	Knowledge discovery
Data-driven analytics	Learner analytics
Data-driven decision-making	Learner-focused analytics
Data-mining	Learning & knowledge analytics
Data-processing	Machine learning
Data-visualisation	Predictive analytics
Data-warehousing	Predictive modelling
Disposition analytics	Process mining
Education analytics	Risk analytics
Educational data-mining	Systemic instructional improvement
E-science	Technology-enhanced learning

- LA offers the possibility of tracking and researching these associations in real-time, and—most importantly—using them to enhance the learner's experience before they come to the end of their study (Clow, 2012, p. 136).
- LA can provide powerful tools for lecturers in order to support them in the iterative process of improving the effectiveness of their courses and to collaterally enhance their students' performance (Dyckhoff, et al., 2012, p. 58).
- LA is a fast-growing area of Technology-Enhanced Learning (TEL) research. It has strong roots in a variety of fields, particularly business intelligence, web analytics, educational data-mining and recommender systems... LA are distinguished by their concern for providing value to learners, whether in formal, informal or blended settings (Ferguson, 2012, p. 304).
- Colleges and universities are increasingly aggregating and analyzing once disparate sources of data, such as a student's admissions records, academic history, and use of campus information technologies, all under the rubric of 'LA' ... At its core, LA is about using data to inform decision-making... (Krumm, Waddington, Lonn, & Teasley, 2012, pp. 1 & 3).
- LA and Academic Analytics (AA) in HE are used to predict student success by examining how and what students learn and how success is supported by academic programs and institutions (Mattingly, et al., 2012, p. 237).
- LA... the collection, analysis, and reporting of data associated with student learning behavior... offers a passive method of gathering information on how learners are interacting with learning resources, each other, and their lecturers. Unlike traditional surveys or focus groups, which rely on participants both opting to provide feedback and accurately remembering and reporting past events, LA captures data on specific, observable behavior in real-time (Lockyer, et al., 2013, pp. 1439-1440).
- LA offer the possibility of implementing real-time assessment and feedback systems and processes at scale that are focused on improvement of learning, development of self-regulated learning skills, and student success (L. P. Macfadyen, Dawson, Pardo, & Gasevic, 2014, p. 17).
- Building on ideas from process mining, data processing, information retrieval, technology-enhanced learning, educational data-mining, and visualisation LA is a multi-disciplinary research field that now forms its own domain... Making use of LA can benefit learners as well as educators (Scheffel, Drachsler, Stoyanov, & Specht, 2014, p. 124).

Characteristics and Processes of High Quality Learning Analytics

Growing interest in LA in HE teaching and learning raises the priority for increased, high-quality research into large collections of detailed data to detect patterns that can be sourced from data-mining techniques e.g., recommendations can be made for activities, staffing and resources likely to be relevant. The data can then be processed—tabular form and/or visually—in ways that may enable educators to make real-life and authentic 'sense' of trends/patterns and thus, increase the potential for '...timeliness and granularity of student data related to learning and interaction' (Chacon, et al., 2012, p. 6).

In general/generic terms, Few (adapted 2009) listed eight traits of *meaningful* data collection: (1) *clean*—accurate, free-of-error and complete; (2) *clear*—expressed in familiar and understandable terms; (3) *consistent*—when change occurs, data remains consistent; (4) *dimensionally-structured/richly-segmented*—data is pre-sorted into meaningful groups and organised into dimensions such as departments, regions or year; (5) *high volume*—increases the likelihood that there will be sufficient data to explore questions being pursued; (6) *historical*—understanding of how information changes with time often provides valuable insight; (7) *known pedigree*—how the data came to be, where it came from, and what calculations may have been used to draw conclusions; and (8) *multivariate*—more variables at hand when trying to make sense of data increases the likelihood of discovering meaningful patterns.

With specific reference to LA, Campbell, DeBlois and Oblinger (2007, p. 50) described the characteristics of successful projects as having: (1) leaders who are committed to evidence-based decision-making; (2) administrative staff who are skilled at data analysis; and (3) a flexible technology platform that is available to collect, mine, and analyse data. In the same year, Campbell and Oblinger (2007) summarised the process of LA as an engine with five stages: (1) capturing; (2) reporting; (3) predicting; (4) acting; and (5) refining. Campbell and Oblinger (2007, p. 15) also reported that the EDUCAUSE Advisory Committee for Teaching and Learning (ACTL) identified ten important issues associated with LA, namely: (1) establishing and supporting a culture of evidence; (2) demonstrating improvement of learning; (3) translating learning research into practice; (4) selecting appropriate models and strategies for e-learning; (5) providing tools to meet growing student expectations; (6) providing professional development and support to new audiences; (7) sharing content, applications and application development; (8) protecting institutional data; (9) addressing emerging ethical challenges; and (10) understanding the evolving role of academic technologists.

Several years late, Brown (2011) acknowledged five key concerns associated with LA, namely: (1) data collection; (2) analysis; (3) student learning; (4) audience; and (5) interventions. The following year, Clow (2012, p. 134) conceptualised successful LA as having four linked steps: (1) learners; (2) generating data; (3) data is used to produce metrics, analytics or visualisations; and (4) data is fed back to learners through one or more interventions. Diaz and Brown (2012, p. 2) delineated LA in terms of three primary goals: (1) to facilitate the analysis of many kinds of learner-produced and learner-related data; (2) to monitor learner activity and progress and to predict learner outcomes; and (3) to enable interventions and decision-making about learning by instructors and students.

As evidenced above, while the field of LA continues to evolve and the diversity of data sources increases, there has been/will be an associated escalation in the number and accuracy of predictive models for advancing academic performance, thus raising the opportunity to leverage analytical tools and visualisations to establish pedagogical recommendations (Dyckhoff, 2011).

Leveraging Learning Analytics to Advance Teaching and Learning Design

Making sound data-informed decisions and becoming less reliant on 'guess-timates' regarding critical issues facing EIBT are worthy pursuits for increasing institutional LA (Stiles, 2012). An understanding of *learning design*, however, is imperative for establishing accurate predictive models *alongside* pedagogical recommendations. Moreover, any data should be analysed in relation to the specific education context from which it is derived. With this in mind, EIBT is attempting to cover all bases by utilising LA to:

- *Advance* research initiatives to identify those practices, curricular structures and pedagogies that best support achievement of selected learning outcomes;
- *Ascertain* from the LMS the strongest drivers of diploma student success;
- *Build* models for early prediction of study outcomes using student enrolment data;
- *Develop* a complexity index for an outcome(s) that allows focus on areas of greatest challenge for students and correlate that data with specific learner data;

- *Employ* techniques to identify supporting relations among learning outcomes in order to define data-evidenced curricular sequencing (e.g., course pre-requisites) to maximise student success within diploma offerings;
- *Enable* the potential of benchmarking between/among HE institutions in which the same course (i.e., subject) is offered;
- *Ensure* curricular and instructional policies and procedures are aligned to findings in the data;
- *Facilitate* a planning of cycle of reviews whereby there is continuous engagement with HE pathways/partners to build institutional capacity and familiarity with evaluation;
- *Furnish* evidence of the effectiveness of institutional quality assurance practices;
- *Highlight* matters for HE advancement at the institutional, statewide and national levels;
- *Identify* targeted points of intervention to better support student achievement and which strongly correlates to transition, retention, and graduation;
- *Present* comparative information to leaders on issues such as academic standards across institutions;
- *Provide* an overall picture of the state-of-health of a discipline and/or course at a particular time;
- *Source* data to identify Students at Risk (STAR) and support targeted interventions across the institution that are informed at the level of student learner characteristics;
- *Suggest* small-scale pilot exercises to test new processes before wider implementation; and
- *Use* testing, demographics, learning styles, outcome achievement (i.e., from previous courses), surveys, and other LMS activity data to attach a probability-scoring to student achievement of an individual outcome(s) prior to entering a diploma program.

Among the various strategies and techniques Australian HE has developed to monitor and improve teaching and learning performance, benchmarking has emerged as a popular tool (Stella & Woodhouse, 2007, p. 5). Effectual benchmarking can yield information to underpin curriculum evaluation and is an essential component of efforts to raise academic standards across schools (Muijtjens, Schuwirth, Cohen-Schotanus, Thoben, & van der Vleuten, 2008, p. 83). Benchmarking involves questioning how processes are performed, seeking out best practices, and implementing new models of operation. With recent changes in the Australian HE environment from the *Australian Universities Quality Agency* (AUQA) to the *Tertiary Education, Quality and Standards Agency* (TEQSA), benchmarking has become a pragmatic tool for comparing discipline standards across the sector as an approval mechanism for registration/re-registration of providers, and the accreditation/re-accreditation of their programs and courses (Australian Government, 2012).

EIBT AND LEARNING ANALYTICS: CHALLENGES AND OPPORTUNITIES

Collection and analysis of data for LA does not necessarily have a 'natural beginning or end' (Siemens, 2012, p. 2). '[A]nalytics applications have the potential to provide a predictive view of upcoming challenges, both for the institution and for students' (Elias, 2011, pp. 6-7). LA activity can feed into practice, and each EIBT practitioner/student can serve as a new data point. There are, however, factors or dispositions brought to EIBT's learning context by learners before their diploma program begins and that may provide some indication of how they will be *predisposed to* and/or *prepared for* their studies.

First, in relation to 'new' EIBT students, factual and readily quantifiable demographics include, but are not limited to: admissions details; age; agent; contact information; country of origin; date of birth; diagnostic test results in literacy and numeracy; English-language proficiency level; financial status; gender; health history; learning disabilities; orientation participation; passport number/expiry dates; primary/mother-tongue language; prior academic results; program/course selection; recruitment; religion; residency/citizenship; sponsorship; student identification number; and student visa number and conditions. Second, in relation to 'continuing' EIBT students, factual and readily quantifiable demographics include, but are not limited to: assignments/assessment tasks submitted; attendance rates; case notes; completion of online quiz; counselling sessions; course and overall program grades; current/past course instructors; files viewed and occurrence; forum participation; frequency of logins; learning activity; mail messages sent; number of downloads; program progression; retrieval of reading materials; risk levels; site engagement; subject loading; and test/examination results. LA is important for bringing fresh insights into educational settings by making *invisible* data *visible* (Gulbahar & Ilgaz, 2014).

Student Demographics

In agreement with McKenzie and Schweitzer (2001, p. 3), the challenge for Australian HE and EIBT more specifically, is to 'recognise this diversity of needs and cater for this changing and heterogeneous population of students'. Indeed, greater understanding of the diversity of EIBT students, including *where they come from*, *their interests* and *their aspirations*, can help facilitate a (more) student-centred approach to teaching and learning. EIBT educators should be demonstrating pedagogical practices that have relevance and meaning to students' social, cultural, educational and professional realities (Crosling, Heagney, & Thomas, 2009, p. 16). 'Inclusive' teaching recognises the explicit connection between culture and learning, and sees students' cultural capital as an asset and *not* a detriment to their intellectual success.

EIBT students are typically between the ages of 17-27 years. As shown in Tables 2, 3 and 4, in trimester 3, 2014 (2014-03), the population was 374 student with only one pupil a 'new' local student and most likely an 'international student' with Australian Permanent Residence (PR), but not citizenship. The vast majority of EIBT students were, and still remain, 'international'. As evidenced in the data (Table 5), EIBT enrolls international students from across the globe, albeit with a majority from two countries/regions i.e., mainland China and Hong Kong. Students from different social and cultural backgrounds—diverse experiences and varying standards of education—bring with them unique needs and academic potential.

Discipline and Class Size

With reference to Tables 6 and 7, the number of students in a class has the potential to affect how much is learned in a number of ways. Class size may affect the lecturer's allocation of time concerning the

Table 2. Student heads across all diploma offerings in 2014-03

Local			International			
New	Continuing	Total	New	Continuing	Total	All Total
1	7	8	134	232	366	374

Table 3. Student heads in individual diploma offerings in 2014-03

EIBT Program	New Students	Continuing Students	Total Students
DB	93	146	239
DIT	8	16	24
DIPE	21	59	80
Total	*135*	*239*	*374*

Table 4. Student intake and student heads over a two-year period 2012-03 to 2014-03

	2012-03	2013-01	2013-02	2013-03	2014-01	2014-02	2014-03
Diploma of Business							
Local	4	1	X	2	3	X	1
International	43	77	34	57	95	58	92
Total	*47*	*78*	*34*	*59*	*98*	*58*	*93*
Diploma of Information Technology							
Local	X	X	X	X	X	X	X
International	2	7	6	3	6	9	8
Total	*2*	*7*	*6*	*3*	*6*	*9*	*8*
Diploma of Engineering							
Local	1	2	X	1	2	X	X
International	7	16	7	19	31	13	21
Total	*8*	*18*	*7*	*20*	*33*	*13*	*21*
Total							
Total New	68	143	62	104	176	90	135
Total Continuing	138	143	187	141	165	225	239
Total Students	*206*	*286*	*249*	*245*	*341*	*315*	*374*

Notes:

- Continuing students = continuing from previous trimester.
- EIBT students are typically between the ages of 17-27 years.
- Local students = Australian citizen or Permanent Residents (PR status).

amount, depth and breadth of material that can be covered. Exposure to a particular learning environment may affect how students interact with each other e.g., the level of social engagement. This may result, for example, in more or less noise and disruptive behaviour, which in turn may affect the kinds of activities the lecturer is able to undertake and/or promote. Lecturers may choose diverse methods of teaching and assessment when they have smaller classes. They may assign more writing, provide more feedback on students' work, use open-ended assessments and/or encourage more discussions; activities that are feasible with smaller numbers of students (Ehrenberg, Brewer, Gamoran, & Willms, 2001, p. 1). Certainly, class size could affect how much time the lecturer is able to focus one-to-one with individual students and better understand and cater for their specific needs.

Table 5. Student diversity in alphabetical order over a two-year period 2012-03 to 2014-03

Country/Region	Offers	Accepted	Commenced	Graduated
Afghanistan	1	0	0	0
Australia	34	13	12	3
Azerbaijan	1	0	0	0
Bahrain	1	0	0	0
Bangladesh	9	4	4	0
Bhutan	2	0	0	0
Bolivia	1	0	0	0
Brazil	1	0	0	0
Burundi	1	0	0	0
Cambodia	4	3	3	3
Cameroon	1	0	0	0
Canada	1	0	0	0
China	1311	795	791	227
East Timor	4	4	4	0
Egypt	5	1	1	1
Fiji	1	0	0	0
France	1	0	0	0
Gambia	1	0	0	0
Hong Kong	278	153	153	83
Hungary	1	0	0	0
India	64	31	31	2
Indonesia	20	10	10	6
Iran	1	1	1	0
Japan	5	2	2	1
Kenya	30	13	13	1
Lebanon	1	1	1	1
Liberia	1	0	0	0
Macao	7	3	3	2
Malaysia	147	73	72	24
Mauritius	1	0	0	0
Myanmar	1	0	0	0
Nepal	26	3	3	0
New Zealand	1	0	0	0
Nigeria	8	0	0	0
Oman	2	1	1	0
Pakistan	38	11	11	0
Papua New Guinea	1	0	0	0
Russian Federation	2	0	0	0
Saudi Arabia	36	10	8	1

continued on following page

Table 5. Continued

Country/Region	Offers	Accepted	Commenced	Graduated
Singapore	15	4	4	1
South Korea	22	12	12	5
Sri Lanka	8	1	1	1
Sweden	1	1	1	0
Taiwan	14	10	10	1
Tanzania	1	0	0	0
Thailand	1	0	0	0
Turkey	1	1	1	0
Uganda	1	1	1	0
United Arab Emirates	4	0	0	0
United Kingdom	5	4	4	0
Vietnam	112	65	69	13
Zambia	2	0	0	0
Zimbabwe	4	0	0	0

Notes:
- Majority of students from 'mainland' China.
- Total of 53 different countries/regions listed.

Table 6. Average class size across all three diploma offerings over a two-year period 2012-03 to 2014-03

Trimester	2012-03	2013-01	2013-02	2013-03	2014-01	2014-02	2014-03
DB	26.8	32.7	27.6	26.9	29.4	30.2	33.0
DIT	3.5	5.2	5.4	4.2	5.0	7.0	9.2
DIPE	7.0	10.2	13.0	12.7	16.4	14.5	16.4
Total	*10.9*	*15.3*	*14.0*	*13.6*	*16.4*	*15.8*	*16.9*

Attendance Rates and Student Engagement

Internationally, there is a considerable body of literature supporting the general notion that absence from school affects a student's academic achievement (e.g., Cleary-Holdforth, 2007; Massingham & Herrington, 2006; Rodgers, 2001), particularly at the first-year level (Moore et al., 2003; Thatcher, Fridjhon, & Cockcroft, 2007). Studies have shown that students who have high attendance rates outperform those with a poor attendance record (e.g., Purcell, 2007). Absences can predict both current and future academic performance—independent of previous achievement—that pose a risk to the successful completion of EIBT studies. Indeed, the availability of quality data is central to understanding the links between attendance and achievement.

The simplest expression of students' motivation is class attendance, particularly for those with poor English-language proficiency and/or poor previous academic standing. Although class attendance is not the only ingredient for success, it is essential for the vast majority of EIBT students. Additionally,

Table 7. Diploma of Business average course class size (2013-03)

Diploma of Business Course [alphabetical]	No. Classes	Average Size %	Average International %	Average Local %
1. Accounting for Business	2	27.5	26.5	1
2. Business & Society	1	35	34	1
3. Communication & Info. Systems in Business	2	29.5	29	0.5
4. Foundations of Business Law	2	25	24.5	0.5
5. Management Principles	2	27	26	1
5. Marketing Principles: Trading & Exchange	2	30.5	30.5	0
6. Principles of Economics	2	17	17	0
7. Quantitative Methods for Business	2	27	26.5	0.5
Total	*61*	*14.1*	*13.7*	*0.4*

Notes:
- Class size may affected by classroom capacity.
- Different pathways have slightly different course selection requirements.
- Diploma of Business comprises 8-courses.
- Diploma of Business is the most popular diploma offering in EIBT.
- Number of classes is not predetermined, but depends on number of students enrolled in course.
- Students can undertake a maximum of 4-courses per trimester.
- University admission is dependent upon overall GPA and not just a 'Pass'.

and in accordance with attendance requirements prescribed within the *National Code of Practice for Registration Authorities and Providers of Education and Training to Overseas Students 2007, Standard 11 – Monitoring Attendance* (Australian Government: Department of Education Employment and Workplace Relations, 2010), EIBT must keep thorough attendance records across all diploma programs for EIBT students who possess temporary 'student' visas. As such, EIBT routinely collects data to monitor the attendance and progress of its students (A=Approved, M=Medical Certificate, H=Half Absent, and N=No Reason). The richness and depth of such data has been a valuable resource for informing the development of EIBT's student attendance policy, as well as identifying those students who may be experiencing 'other' non-academic personal issues preventing them from coming on campus. Records are maintained on a course basis and calculated over an identified timetabling period (refer to Tables 8, 9 and 10). Typically, records are kept in both hard-copy (teacher copies) and electronic (computer database) form. Students at risk of breaching attendance requirements are swiftly identified.

Table 8. Anonymous student's summary of absence over a one-year period 2013-01 to 2014-01

Trimester	Weekly Sessions	Semester Sessions	Total Absences	Unapproved Absences	Unapproved %
2013-01	6	84	19	12	85.71
2013-02	5	70	20	13	81.43
2013-03	4	56	8.5	6	89.29
2014-01	5	70	38.5	26	62.86
2014-02	4	56	27	23	58.93
2014-03	3	45	12.5	7	84.44

Table 9. Random five students and summary of poor overall attendance (2014-03 based on 14 weeks)

Student ID	Name	Classes Per Week	Total Absent	Absent %	Weighted Total	Weighted %	Average Per Week
X	Student 1	4	25	44.6	23.0	41.1	1.6
X	Student 2	3	17	40.5	17.0	40.5	1.2
X	Student 3	3	17	40.5	16.0	38.1	1.1
X	Student 4	3	16	38.1	16.0	38.1	1.1
X	Student 5	5	28	40.0	26.5	37.9	1.9

Notes:

- Total absent is the total number of recorded absences (regardless of the recorded reason).
- Weighted total is the total number of absences counted, where absences of reason N (no Reason) count as 1, H (Half Absent) count as 0.5, and other absences are not counted.

Table 10. Random five students with at least three absences in a single week during 2014-03

ID	Name	Diploma of Business	Week 1	Week 2	Week 3	Week 4	Week 5	Week 6	Week 7	Week 8	Week 9	Week 10	Week 11	Week 12	Week 13
ID-1	Student 1	DB	1	1	1	2	3	1					1		
ID-2	Student 2	DB	2	1	1		3			1	1	1	2		
ID-3	Student 3	DB	3						1	1	1		1	2	
ID-4	Student 4	DB	2									1	1	3	1
ID-5	Student 5	DB			1		2		2		1	3	1	1	1

In terms of student engagement, it could be expected that EIBT students who are actively engaged in Moodle would visit the 'Student Portal' more frequently and for longer periods of time than students who are less engaged (Beer, Clark, & Jones, 2010, p. 80). At best, LA applications can identify factors that are unexpectedly associated with course completion. It would seem reasonable to expect that students who are more actively engaged in LMS courses should receive higher grades than students who are less engaged. LA can generate reports of student log-in behaviours (refer to Figures 1 and 2); indicators of when students have commenced the learning sequence (Lockyer, et al., 2013). Additionally, LA tools can track far more data than an instructor can alone and such monitoring may offer timely guidance to students whose academic (under)performance may otherwise pass unnoticed. The opportunity then exists for automatic or teacher-generated alerts that can be incorporated to prompt late-starters to initiate learning activity. This information is immensely valuable to (a) faculty—*in how they structure curricula*; and (b) students—*in how they approach learning*.

In agreement with Jayaprakash et al., (2014, p. 20), workload varies across instructors and their courses. For example, one instructor may be more demanding and/or post materials more frequently onto the portal depending on the characteristics of their subject. This may have an impact on the ability of predictive models to capture behavioural patterns of students across different courses, such as: average time spent on a document; number of documents accessed; page views and page posts; percentage

Figure 1. Activity by an individual on EIBT's Moodle with dates, timings and views

EIBT MOODLE 2.0

Home▶ My profile▶ Activity reports▶ Today's logs

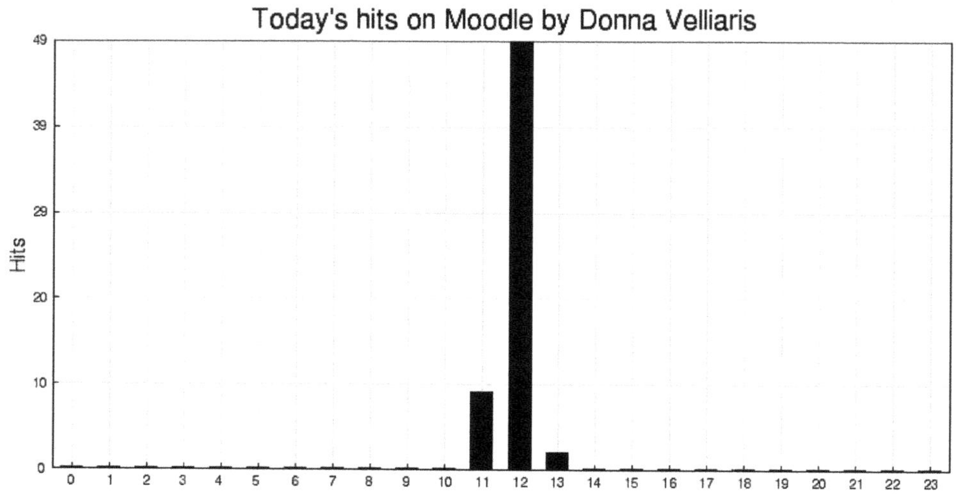

Displaying 60 records

Course	Time	IP address	User full name	Action	Information
Moodle	Mon 16 March 2015, 01:00 PM	10.8.158.15	Donna Velliaris	course user report	Donna Velliaris
Moodle	Mon 16 March 2015, 01:00 PM	10.8.158.15	Donna Velliaris	course report log	EIBT Moodle 2.0
Moodle	Mon 16 March 2015, 12:59 PM	10.8.158.15	Donna Velliaris	course report log	EIBT Moodle 2.0
Moodle	Mon 16 March 2015, 12:56 PM	10.8.158.15	Donna Velliaris	course report log	EIBT Moodle 2.0
Moodle	Mon 16 March 2015, 12:55 PM	10.8.158.15	Donna Velliaris	course report log	EIBT Moodle 2.0
Moodle	Mon 16 March 2015, 12:55 PM	10.8.158.15	Donna Velliaris	course user report	Donna Velliaris

of on-time or late submissions; status of assignments; time of the day student enters the portal; and total time spent on a single or all courses. Thus, certain patterns may inaccurately portray differences in behaviour of the same student or among students of similar characteristics.

Students at Risk

Student engagement is generally acknowledged as a key factor in student retention and enhancing engagement is a fundamental strategy for improving transition, retention and graduation (Crosling, et al., 2009, p. 10). The commitment of institutions to their students is a critical factor in retention, particularly for students who face the greatest challenges e.g., EIBT students who are predominantly Non-English Speaking Background (NESB) pathway students. LA tools can leverage information that is embedded in student records to show that monitoring is done on a routine basis and that the institution has consistently taken action to support their efforts (Piety, et al., 2014). For example, '[v]arious data are used to make predictions about Students-At-Risk (STAR)... analytics may be used to initiate an intervention designed to change student behavior and improve learning' (Mattingly, et al., 2012, p. 139).

Figure 2. Activity by individual person on EIBT's Moodle at the end of each week throughout a trimester

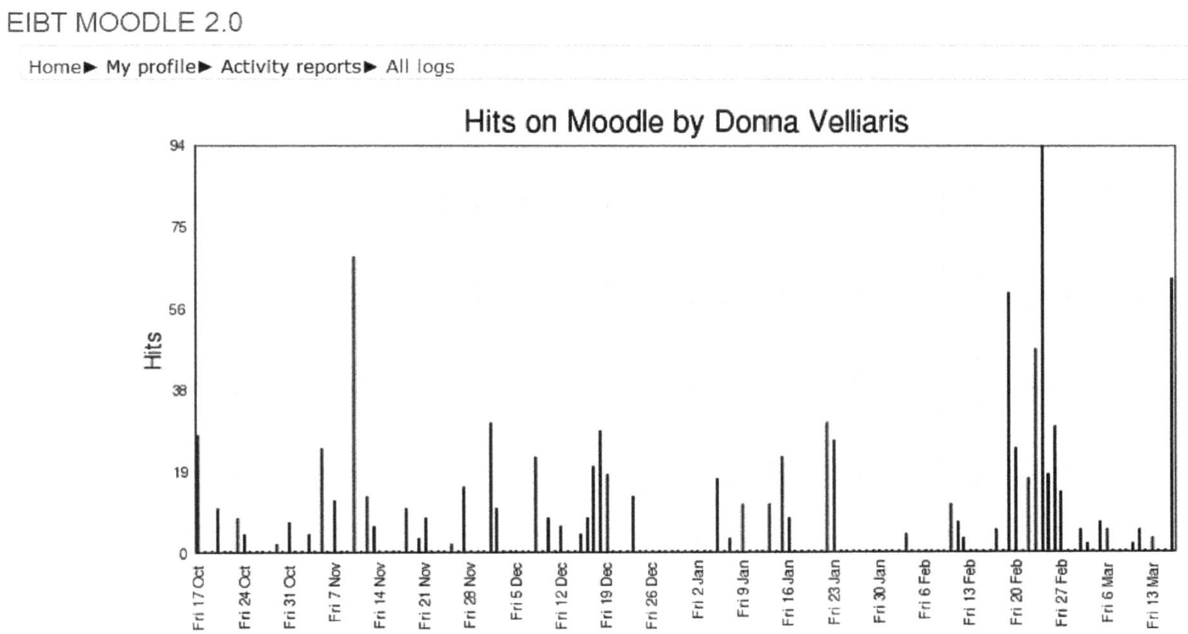

EIBT students identified as being at risk are counselled—depending upon their results and assigned a Risk Level 1, 2 or 3—and are required to enter into a *Student Performance Contract* for the proceeding trimester. This contract is a mandatory intervention and support strategy that a 'student' visa holder must undertake to maintain their enrolment (i.e., an underperforming international student has implications on their expected completion date as specified on their visa's Confirmation of Enrolment (CoE)). The contract outlines a study plan that includes a reduced workload (maximum 75% = three courses) to suit the individual student and their likelihood of success, as well as a compulsory Tertiary Skills Development (TSD) session held weekly. The TSD course is designed to help at-risk students understand the challenges associated with studying at the HE level and to improve their confidence in undertaking self-directed learning. Recently, the effectiveness of this 'free' course has been monitored using LA data before, during and after TSD delivery and intervention as shown in Figure 3.

Attrition and Retention Rates

The importance of student retention in EIBT is underscored by its inclusion via institutional statistics as a key 'performance indicator' in educational quality (Crosling, et al., 2009, p. 9). Student attrition and retention rates are defined as '... the percentage of students in a particular year who neither graduate nor continue studying in an award course at the same institution in the following year' (Department of Education, Science and Training, 2005). Student attrition and retention are not simple phenomena and involve a host of variables related to the academic and social integration/acculturation of learners into their diplomas. Notably, the literature suggests that the most vulnerable students at institutions of HE are first-years who are at the greatest risk of dropping or not completing their program on time (e.g., Kovacic, 2010). Therefore, studies oftentimes address the early identification of first-year students who

Figure 3. Results before, during and after TSD intervention for at-risk students

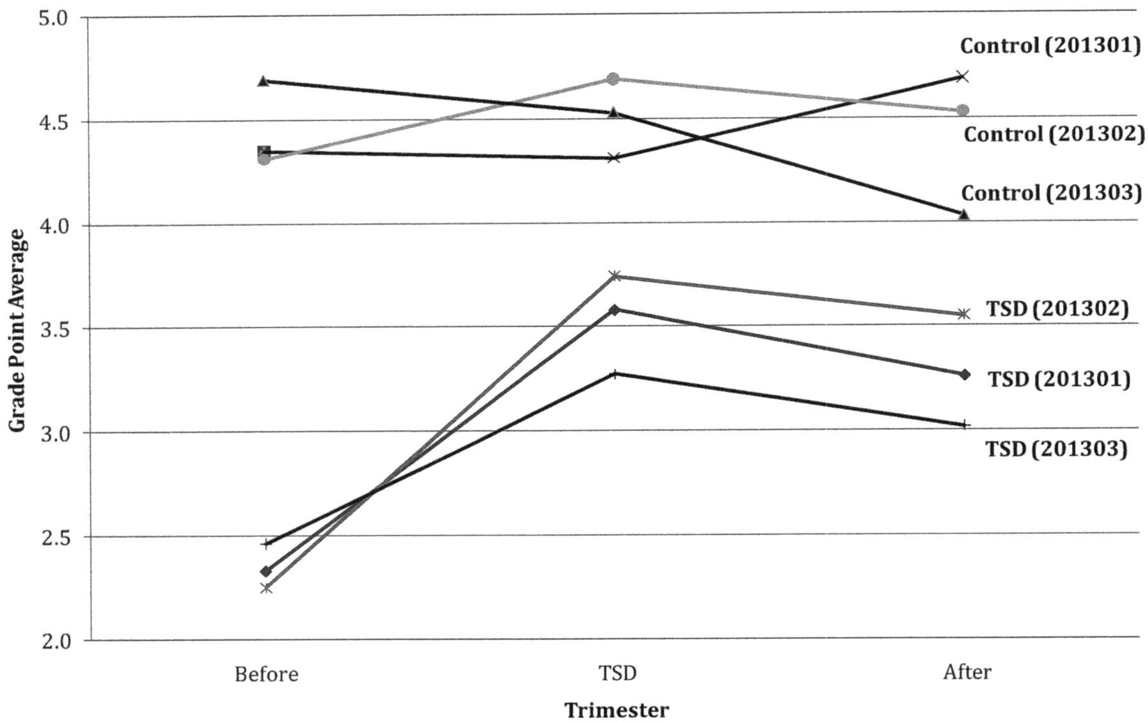

may be prone to drop-out. Once identified, these 'at-risk' students can be targeted with administrative and academic support to increase the chance of them staying on track. Associated LA allows educational institutions to undertake timely and pro-active measures. Table 11 shows some information related to the retention of EIBT students in 2014-03.

Intra-Institutional Tracking

LA can help with course (re)design. Traditionally, educators draw on their past experience when they teach a course or are designing a new course. For many educators this may be an informal process derived from student surveys, and/or teacher notes recorded during or after teaching sessions, but probably through recall. Revisiting the LA collected during a course supports EIBT educators when they are planning to teach the same course the following trimester and/or when the learning design is being applied

Table 11. EIBT retention rates between trimester comparisons

2014-03 – 2013-03 Comparison Data All Students	2014-03 Budgeted	2014-03 Current	2014-03 Max Enrolments	2013-03 Enrolments	2013-03 to 2014-03 Increase	2013-03 to 2014-03 Increase %
Diploma (Local)	10	8	8	5	3	60.0%
Diploma (Int'l)	293	342	375	204	138	67.6%

to a different cohort. Tables 12, 13 and 14 present the results distribution of (a) 'all' EIBT diplomas, (b) Diploma of Business students across three trimesters or one calendar year, as well as (c) the results of one single Diploma of Business course chosen in isolation.

EIBT students are required to complete and 'PASS' eight courses to graduate with a diploma, but can only undertake a maximum of four courses per trimester (=100% load). Grade allocations and percentage scores are in line with EIBT's partner universities i.e., High Distinction = HD = 85-100% = GPA 7; Distinction = D = 75-84% = GPA 6; Credit = C = 65-74% = GPA 5; Pass Level 1 = P1 = 55-64% = GPA 4.5; Pass Level 2 = P2 = 50-54% = GPA 4; Fail Level 1 = F1 = 40-49% = GPA 1.5; Fail Level 2 = F2 = > 40% = GPA 1; Withdraw Fail = WF = GPA 1.5; and Withdraw No Fail = WNF = GPA n/a.

Inter-Institutional Benchmarking

EIBT is aware of the risks involved in not maintaining academic standards and has robust processes of assessment and moderation in place to ensure that its standards are aligned with those of its partner institutions. To identify and refine key indicators for measuring the extent to which EIBT is realising its *Educational Objectives* in relation to student outcomes, EIBT remains committed to collecting data to:

Table 12. Average pass rate percentages in each diploma program over a two-year period 2012-03 to 2014-03

Program	2012-03	2013-01	2013-02	2013-03	2014-01	2014-02	2014-03
DB	78.7	75.1	81.0	79.6	72.4	73.4	71.1
DIT	56.5	52.6	53.5	54.5	53.3	59.5	65.2
DIPE	77.3	74.3	72.1	70.8	71.8	79.3	66.3
Total	*69.5*	*67.7*	*70.5*	*71.0*	*64.4*	*71.9*	*68.4*

Table 13. Diploma of Business (DB) student cohort overall pass rates/grade distributions in 2013

Trimester + Grade	2013-01	Total %	2013-02	Total %	2013-03	Total %
F2	69	11.5	36	7.5	42	10.1
F1	85	14.1	46	9.6	33	8.0
Total Fail	*154*	*25.6*	*82*	*17.0*	*75*	*18.1*
CP	3	0.5	0	0.0	1	0.2
P2	50	8.3	30	6.2	22	5.3
P1	158	26.2	128	26.6	107	25.8
C	145	24.1	163	33.9	125	30.1
D	74	12.3	61	12.7	63	15.2
HD	18	3.0	17	3.5	22	5.3
Total Pass	*448*	*74.4*	*399*	*83.0*	*340*	*81.9*
Total	*602*		*481*		*415*	

Table 14. Diploma of Business (DB) single course overall pass rates/grade distributions in 2013

Trimester + Grade	2013-01	Total %	2013-02	Total %	2013-03	Total %
F2	15	16.1	5	8.9	5	9.3
F1	15	16.1	11	19.6	8	14.8
Total Fail	*30*	*32.3*	*16*	*28.6*	*13*	*24.1*
CP	X	0.0	X	0.0	X	0.0
P2	3	3.2	6	10.7	1	1.9
P1	16	17.2	9	16.1	12	22.2
C	21	22.6	15	26.8	8	14.8
D	16	17.2	7	12.5	8	14.8
HD	7	7.5	3	5.4	12	22.2
Total Pass	*63*	*67.7*	*40*	*71.4*	*41*	*75.9*
Total	*93*		*56*		*54*	

Notes:
- A 'Pass' result requires a 'minimum score' in coursework + 'minimum score' in examination.
- CP = Conceded Pass was stopped in 2015.

(1) track the performance of EIBT students over time, as well as compare this performance with other appropriate education providers i.e., Navitas pathway colleges and especially partner universities; and (2) track the exit of students from EIBT into the university and their progress once at university.

Benchmarking performance has strengthened relationships between/among partners and engendered trust in EIBT's ability to deliver programs where students—who would not have otherwise had the chance to attend university—are achieving both short-term (graduation from diploma program) and long-term (graduation from bachelor degree) success. Effective measuring and monitoring has enabled EIBT to identify areas in course delivery and student satisfaction to make adjustments and continuous improvements that ensure continued achievement of its educational 'vision and mission', coupled with the ability to maintain cultural and organisational integrity (Bender, 2002, p. 116).

With reference to Tables 15, 16 and 17, EIBT students' results—pass rates and grade distributions—are externally benchmarked twice per year against equivalent courses delivered at Navitas partner institutions in South Australia and nationally, as well as its partner universities. EIBT tracks the GPAs of student cohorts through longitudinal studies. Data relating to the progress of graduates within a particular intake and without identifying individual students is reported annually to ensure admissions requirements are suitable and standards are maintained (Australian Universities Quality Agency, 2010).

Table 15. Diploma of Business course benchmarking across pathway institutions (2007-01)

Diploma of Business	School	No. Pupils	Pass Rate %	HD	D	C	P1	P2	F1	F2
Course 1	EIBT	35	97	0	20	40	32	7	0	3
	Institution 1	140	73	0	6	31	18	18	19	5

Table 16. Diploma of Business benchmarking across pathway and partner institutions in a single trimester (2009-03)

Institution	EIBT						Pathway Institution 1						Partner Institution 1					
Diploma of Business	Enrolment	Pass	%	Fail	%	Average %	Enrolment	Pass	%	Fail	%	Average %	Enrolment	Pass	%	Fail	%	Average %
Course 1	105	79	75%	26	25%	55	155	93	60%	62	40%	47	615	402	65%	213	35%	NA
Course 2	116	78	67%	38	33%	52	136	88	65%	48	35%	48	378	296	78%	82	22%	NA

Table 17. Diploma of Business benchmarking across pathway and partner institutions over two trimesters (2010-02 and 2010-03)

Diploma of Business		2010-02		2010-03	
		Total	Pass Rate %	Total	Pass Rate %
Course 1	EIBT	104	69	110	66
	Institution 1	170	56	107	47
	Institution 2	725	74	414	58
Course 2	EIBT	59	76	104	84
	Institution 1	141	77	120	77
	Institution 2	881	78	719	83

Completion, Graduation, and Articulation

Analysis of diploma completion and graduation data provides another lens and level of granularity on student retention. EIBT's Diploma of Business leads to nine undergraduate degree programs at *The University of Adelaide* (e.g., Bachelor of Commerce, Bachelor of Economics, Bachelor of Finance). EIBT's Diploma of Business also leads to 13 undergraduate degree programs at the *University of South Australia* (e.g., Bachelor of Business Administration, Bachelor of International Relations, Bachelor of Management). EIBT's Diploma of Information Technology leads to one undergraduate degree programs at *The University of Adelaide* (i.e., Bachelor of Computer Science) and eight undergraduate degree programs at the *University of South Australia* (e.g., Bachelor of Information Technology in Cloud Computing). EIBT's Diploma of Engineering leads to 24 undergraduate degree programs at *The University of Adelaide* (e.g., Bachelor of Engineering - Chemical, Bachelor of Engineering - Mechanical, Bachelor of Engineering - Techtronic) and eight undergraduate degree programs at the *University of South Australia* (e.g., Bachelor of Engineering - Civil, Bachelor of Engineering - Electrical & Electronic, Bachelor of Engineering - Mechanical & Advanced Manufacturing). Hence, EIBT graduation data (Tables 18-22), are available for analysis and reporting purposes to a range of stakeholders.

Summary: Personalising the Pathway

Graphical/visual presentations of LA data are already moving towards (more) compelling, dynamically-generated views available in real-time to EIBT academic staff and students. As new types of data are

Table 18. Local and international student division of graduated and withdrawn students in Diploma of Business over a two-year period 2012-01 to 2014-01

Local Students					
Start Trimester	**Student Nos.**	**Graduated**	**Graduated %**	**Withdrew**	**Withdrew %**
2012-01	1	1	100.00	0	0.00
2012-03	5	4	80.00	1	20.00
2013-01	3	0	0.00	3	100.00
2013-02	1	0	0.00	1	100.00
2013-03	3	3	100.00	0	0.00
2014-01	5	4	80.00	1	20.00
International Students					
Start Trimester	**Student Nos.**	**Graduated**	**Graduated %**	**Withdrew**	**Withdrew %**
2012-01	89	56	62.92	33	37.08
2012-02	52	32	61.54	20	38.46
2012-03	68	55	80.88	13	19.12
2013-01	106	71	66.98	35	33.02
2013-02	55	36	65.45	19	34.55
2013-03	95	62	65.26	33	34.74
2014-01	146	66	45.21	80	54.79

Table 19. Diploma of Business number of graduated and withdrawn students over a two-year period 2012-01 to 2014-01

Start Trimester	Student Nos.	Graduated	Graduated %	Withdrew	Withdrew %
2012-01	90	57	63.33	33	36.67
2012-02	52	32	61.54	20	38.46
2012-03	73	59	80.82	14	19.18
2013-01	109	71	65.14	38	34.86
2013-02	56	36	64.29	20	35.71
2013-03	98	65	66.33	33	33.67
2014-01	151	70	46.36	81	53.64

added, systems are becoming more sophisticated and robust in their ability to predict EIBT students' success. Data gathering across the EIBT environment allows a student's probability of success to be measured against a 'broad' base, resulting in further 'reliability' pertaining to the *interplay of factors* that are associated with different learning outcomes and effective strategies for helping pathway students get back-on-track.

Table 20. Graduands and university articulation of 'all' students between 2006-01 and 2008-03

Start Trimester	No. of Graduands	University of Adelaide	University of South Aust.	Other University	Total Articulated	Progression %
Feb-06	17	0	13	2	15	88.24
Jun-06	20	3	15	1	19	95.00
Oct-06	20	8	9	0	17	85.00
Feb-07	21	3	12	1	16	76.19
Jun-07	19	3	13	2	18	94.74
Oct-07	10	5	4	1	10	100.00
Feb-08	48	10	27	10	47	97.92
Jun-08	73	23	37	10	70	95.89
Oct-08	36	6	26	3	35	97.22

LIMITATIONS AND FUTURE RECOMMENDATIONS

As a pathway provider to mainstream HE in Australia, EIBT is continually and increasingly seeking ways to make available to students the assistance they need in order to progress socially, culturally, linguistically and educationally. Although a number of static triggers (e.g., attendance monitoring) exist to monitor students for signs of trouble, there is interest in improving the availability of information in order to better address/direct interventions. It is important, however, to consider several limitations and recommendations.

Limitations

- Student recruitment and admissions processing may favour certain student populations and attributes that may affect, to varying degrees, the teaching and learning environment and subsequent results.
- Although LA produces a prediction based on data available, no forecast can take into account all the possible causes of student success or lack of success. It is reasonable to be sceptical of the ability of a 'number' to account for all the interpersonal relationships and personal growth that comes from attending a particular institution.
- Differences in teacher performance/experience and student's demographic details may create invalid forecasts leading to inefficient decisions and unforeseen problems. A misalignment of English-language proficiency, level/previous academic standing, and course progression, as examples, could increase the late identification of learners at risk.

Recommendations

- Besides the analysis of numerical data, a qualitative analysis of semantically rich data (e.g., content of discussion forums, responses to open-ended questionnaires) will enable better understanding of learners' knowledge and needs.

Table 21. Top 5 Diploma of Business students to articulate to The Adelaide University in 2012-02 (July 2012)

ID	Birthdate	Citizenship	Overseas O Local L	Course	Final Semester	Mark Average %	Final GPA (Total = 7)	University Business Program + Stream
X	29/03/1989	China	O	DB	201201	86.75	6.63	Bachelor of Commerce
X	04/03/1992	Hong Kong	O	DB	201201	77.38	6	Bachelor of Commerce (Accounting)
X	04/10/1993	Hong Kong	O	DB	201201	77.25	6	Bachelor of Economics
X	24/05/1992	Hong Kong	O	DB	201201	77.63	5.88	Bachelor of Commerce (Corporate Finance)
X	21/06/1992	Hong Kong	O	DB	201201	78.63	5.88	Bachelor of Commerce (Marketing)

Table 22. EIBT's database hosts a vast array of student details related to diploma progression and graduation

ID	Proper Name	Preferred Name	Gender	Country	Contact Details	State	Country	Post Code	Diploma	Parchment No.	Local or Overseas	DOB	Graduated	University Offer	GPA	Degree Program
ID-1	X	Lee	M	CHN	X	SA	Aust.	5034	DB	201401076	O	30/12/1994	201401	Adel.	6.63	B. Commerce
ID-2	X	Lulu	F	SIN	X	SA	Aust.	5000	DB	201401029	O	10/11/1994	201401	UniSA	4	B. Commerce (Accounting)
ID-3	X	Paul	M	CHN	X	SA	Aust.	5037	DB	201401013	O	22/10/1992	201401	UniSA	4	B. Commerce (Accounting)
ID-4	X	Sam	M	JPE	X	SA	Aust.	5069	DB	201401015	O	09/02/1993	201401	Adel.	5.88	B. Commerce (Accounting)
ID-5	X	John	M	HKG	X	SA	Aust.	5000	DP	201401009	O	11/08/1993	201401	Adel.	5.88	B. Business (Tourism & Event Management)

- In order to solve problems faced by learners, EIBT needs to further investigate what those problems are and what success looks like from the perspective of learners. Thus, EIBT needs to keep abreast of future trends in LA and the implications it will/may have for informing teaching and learning outcomes. This may, however, require a new generation of LA experts with unique inter/multidisciplinary competences in order to accelerate such understanding.
- Not all educational data is relevant and/or equivalent. Therefore, the validity of future data collection, extraction, and analyses is critical for generating useful formative, real-time and predictive insights within the context of EIBT.

CONCLUSION

During the last decade, LA has emerged as a significant area of research in TEL. LA are distinguished by their concern for providing 'value to learners'—whether in formal, informal and/or blended settings—to understand and optimise learning and the environments within which it takes place. In other words, LA has the potential to generate new insights into what works and what does not work pedagogically. Meeting the challenge, however, will require the tools and techniques to capture data and improve the connections among related fields in order to translate findings into practice. The task is significant, but well worth embracing given the potential benefit of an integrated and holistic LA researcher-practitioner model. It is essential that LA developments and innovations draw on *and* energise educational research *and* praxis. EIBT is committed to finding pedagogically useful indicators for teaching and learning advancement and although contemplation and planning for further LA collection has not been addressed here, the possibilities abound and EIBT's future 'pathway' certainly looks clearer and brighter.

REFERENCES

Anirban, S. (2014). Big data analytics in the education sector: Needs, opportunities and challenges. *IJRCCT*, *3*(11), 1425–1428.

Australian Government. (2012). Tertiary Education Quality and Standards Agency (TEQSA). Retrieved from http://www.teqsa.gov.au/

Australian Government: Department of Education Employment and Workplace Relations. (2010). National Code of Practice for Registration Authorities and Providers of Education and Training to Overseas Students.

Australian Universities Quality Agency. (2010). Report of an Audit of Eynesbury Institute of Business and Technology Retrieved from http://teqsa.gov.au/sites/default/files/auditreport_eibt_2010.pdf

Barber, R., & Sharkey, M. (2012). Course correction: Using analytics to predict course success. *Paper presented at the 2nd International Conference on Learning Analytics and Knowledge*. doi:10.1145/2330601.2330664

Beer, C., Clark, K., & Jones, D. (2010). Indicators of engagement. *Paper presented at the Ascilite 2010*, Sydney.

Bender, B. E. (2002). Benchmarking as an administrative tool for institutional leaders. *New Directions for Higher Education*, *2002*(118), 113–120. doi:10.1002/he.60

Brown, M. (2011). Learning analytics: Moving from concept to practice. Retrieved http://net.educause.edu/ir/library/pdf/ELIB1203.pdf

Campbell, J. P., DeBlois, P. B., & Oblinger, D. G. (2007). Academic analytics: A new tool for a new era. *EDUCAUSE Review*, *42*(4), 41–57.

Campbell, J. P., & Oblinger, D. G. (2007). Top-ten teaching and learning issues. *EDUCAUSE Quarterly*, *30*(3), 15–22.

Chacon, F., Spicer, D., & Valbuena, A. (2012). Analytics in support of student retention and success. *EDUCAUSE: Center for Applied Research. Research Bulletin (Sun Chiwawitthaya Thang Thale Phuket)*, *3*, 1–9.

Chatti, M. A., Dyckhoff, A. L., Schroeder, U., & Thüs, H. (2012). A reference model for learning analytics. *International Journal of Technology Enhanced Learning*, *4*(5), 318–331. doi:10.1504/IJTEL.2012.051815

Cleary-Holdforth, J. (2007). Student non-attendance in higher education: A phenomenon of student apathy or poor pedagogy. *Dublin Institute of Technology*. Retrieved from http://level3.dit.ie/html/issue5/cleary-holdforth/cleary_holdforth.pdf

Clow, D. (2012). The learning analytics cycle: Closing the loop effectively. *Paper presented at the 2nd International Conference on Learning Analytics and Knowledge*. doi:10.1145/2330601.2330636

Crosling, G., Heagney, M., & Thomas, L. (2009). Improving student retention in higher education: Improving teaching and learning. *Australian Universities Review*, *51*(2), 9–18.

Diaz, V., & Brown, M. (2012). Learning analytics: A report on the ELI focus session. EDUCAUSE Learning Initiative. Retrieved from https://net.educause.edu/ir/library/PDF/ELI3027.pdf

Dyckhoff, A. L. (2011). Implications for learning analytics tools: A meta-analysis of applied research questions. *International Journal of Computer Information Systems and Industrial Management Applications*, *3*, 594–601.

Dyckhoff, A. L. (2014). *Action research and learning analytics in higher education*. Doctor of Philosophy, Universitätsbibliothek. Retrieved from http://darwin.bth.rwth-aachen.de/opus3/volltexte/2014/5208/pdf/5208.pdf

Dyckhoff, A. L., Zielke, D., Bültmann, M., Chatti, M. A., & Schroeder, U. (2012). Design and implementation of a learning analytics toolkit for teachers. *Journal of Educational Technology & Society*, *15*(3), 58–76.

Ehrenberg, R. G., Brewer, D. J., Gamoran, A., & Willms, J. D. (2001). Class size and student achievement. *Psychological Science in the Public Interest*, *2*(1), 1–30. doi:10.1111/1529-1006.003 PMID:26151146

Elias, T. (2011). Learning analytics: Definitions, processes and potential. Retrieved 20 February 2015 http://learninganalytics.net/LearningAnalyticsDefinitionsProcessesPotential.pdf

Essa, A., & Ayad, H. (2012). Improving student success using predictive models and data visualisations. *The Journal of the Association for Learning Technology (ALT). Research in Learning Technology*, 2012, 20.

Ferguson, R. (2012). Learning analytics: Drivers, developments and challenges. *International Journal of Technology Enhanced Learning*, *4*(5), 304–317. doi:10.1504/IJTEL.2012.051816

Few, S. (2009). *Now you see it: Simple visualization techniques for quantitative analysis*. US: Analytics Press.

Fiocco, M. (2006). An evaluation of a pathway program: The students' view. Paper presented at the Australian International Education Conference. Perth, Western Australia: Perth Convention Exhibition Centre. Retrieved from www.idp.com/aiec

Gulbahar, Y., & Ilgaz, H. (2014). Premise of learning analytics for educational context: Through concept to practice. *International Journal of Informatics Technologies*, *7*(3), 12–20.

Jayaprakash, S. M., Moody, E. W., Lauría, E. J. M., Regan, J. R., & Baron, J. D. (2014). Early alert of academically at-risk students: An open source analytics initiative. *Journal of Learning Analytics*, *1*(1), 6–47.

Kovacic, Z. (2010). Early prediction of student success: Mining students' enrolment data. *Paper presented at the Informing Science & IT Education Conference InSITE '10.*

Krumm, A. E., Waddington, R. J., Lonn, S., & Teasley, S. D. (2012). Increasing academic success in undergraduate engineering education using learning analytics: A design-based research project. Retrieved from http://deepblue.lib.umich.edu/bitstream/handle/2027.42/106032/aera2012_krumm_learning_analytics.pdf?sequence=1

Lockyer, L., Heathcote, E., & Dawson, S. (2013). Informing pedagogical action: Aligning learning analytics with learning design. *The American Behavioral Scientist*, *57*(10), 1439–1459. doi:10.1177/0002764213479367

Macfadyen, L., & Dawson, S. (2012). Numbers are not enough: Why e-learning analytics failed to inform an institutional strategic plan. *Journal of Educational Technology & Society*, *15*(3), 149–163.

Macfadyen, L. P., Dawson, S., Pardo, A., & Gasevic, D. (2014). Embracing big data in complex educational systems: The learning analytics imperative and the policy challenge. *Research & Practice in Assessment*, *9*(2), 17–28.

Massingham, P., & Herrington, T. (2006). Does attendance matter? An examination of student attitudes, participation, performance and attendance. *Journal of University Teaching & Learning Practice*, *3*(2), 82–103.

Mattingly, K. D., Rice, M. C., & Berge, Z. L. (2012). Learning analytics as a tool for closing the assessment loop in higher education. *Knowledge Management & E-Learning: An International Journal*, *4*(3), 236-247.

McKenzie, K., & Schweitzer, R. (2001). Who succeeds at university? Factors predicting academic performance in first year Australian university students. *Higher Education Research & Development, 20*(1), 21–33. doi:10.1080/07924360120043621

Monson, R., Bunney, D., & Lawrence, T. (2013). MOOCs, learning analytics and learning advisors. *eCULTURE, 6*, 1-14.

Moore, R., Jensen, M., Hatch, J., Duranczyk, I., Staats, S., & Koch, L. (2003). Showing up: The importance of class attendance for academic success in introductory science courses. *The American Biology Teacher*, *65*(5), 325–329. doi:10.2307/4451508

Muijtjens, A. M. M., Schuwirth, L. W. T., Cohen-Schotanus, J., Thoben, A. J. N. M., & van der Vleuten, C. P. M. (2008). Benchmarking by cross-institutional comparison of student achievement in a progress test. *Medical Education*, *42*(1), 82–88. doi:10.1111/j.1365-2923.2007.02896.x PMID:18181848

Piety, P. J., Hickey, D. T., & Bishop, M. J. (2014, March 24-28). Educational data sciences: Framing emergent practices for analytics of learning, organizations, and systems. *Paper presented at the 4th International Conference on Learning Analytics & Knowledge*, Indianapolis, IN. doi:10.1145/2567574.2567582

Prinsloo, P., Archer, E., Barnes, G., Chetty, Y., & Van Zyl, D. (2015). Big(ger) data as better data in open distance learning. *The International Review of Research in Open and Distributed Learning*, *16*(1).

Purcell, P. (2007, September 3-7). Engineering student attendance at lectures: Effect on examination performance. *Paper presented at the International Conference on Engineering Education (ICEE)*, Coimbra, Portugal.

Rodgers, J. R. (2001). A panel-data study of the effect of student attendance on university performance. *Australian Journal of Education*, *45*(3), 284–295. doi:10.1177/000494410104500306

Romero, C., & Ventura, S. (2013). Data mining in education. *Wiley Interdisciplinary Reviews: Data Mining and Knowledge Discovery*, *3*(1), 12–27.

Scheffel, M., Drachsler, H., Stoyanov, S., & Specht, M. (2014). Quality indicators for learning analytics. *Journal of Educational Technology & Society*, 2014, 124–140.

Siemens, G. (2011). 1st International Conference on Learning Analytics and Knowledge LAK '11. Retrieved from https://tekri.athabascau.ca/analytics/

Siemens, G. (2012). Learning analytics: Envisioning a research discipline and a domain of practice. *Paper presented at the Proceedings of the 2nd International Conference on Learning Analytics and Knowledge*. doi:10.1145/2330601.2330605

Slade, S., & Prinsloo, P. (2013). Learning analytics ethical issues and dilemmas. *The American Behavioral Scientist*, *57*(10), 1510–1529. doi:10.1177/0002764213479366

Stella, A., & Woodhouse, D. (2007). *Benchmarking in Australian higher education: A thematic analysis of AUQA audit reports*. Citeseer.

Stiles, R. J. (2012). Understanding and managing the risks of analytics in higher education: A guide. *EDUCAUSE*.

Thatcher, A., Fridjhon, P., & Cockcroft, K. (2007). The relationship between lecture attendance and academic performance in an undergraduate psychology class. *South African Journal of Psychology. Suid-Afrikaanse Tydskrif vir Sielkunde*, *37*(3), 656–660. doi:10.1177/008124630703700316

Velliaris, D. M., & Breen, P. (2014, December 2-5). Tailoring graduate attributes to meet the needs of international students in a pathway program. *Paper presented at the Conference Proceedings of the 25th ISANA International Education Conference*, Adelaide, South Australia.

Velliaris, D. M., & Willis, C. R. (2014). Getting personal: An autoethnographic study of the professional identit(ies) of lecturers in an Australian pathway institution. In P. Breen (Ed.), Cases on teacher identity, diversity, and cognition in higher education (pp. 87–110). Hershey, PA, USA: IGI Global. doi:10.4018/978-1-4666-5990-2.ch004

Velliaris, D. M., Willis, C. R., & Breen, P. (2015). Academic reflections: Disciplinary acculturation and the first year pathway experience. In P. N. Shrestha (Ed.), *Current developments in English for academic and specific purposes: Local innovations and global perspectives* (pp. 217–235). Reading, UK: Garnet Publishing Ltd.

KEY TERMS AND DEFINITIONS

Acculturation: In its simplest sense, this includes the changes that arise following contact between/among individuals from a different cultural background. This may lead to progressive adoption of elements of the other culture (e.g., ideas, words, values and/or behaviours).

Course: Refers to one subject leading to an EIBT diploma award.

Diploma: An EIBT diploma comprises 8-courses that take between 6-months and 2-years to complete. Diplomas are generally considered equivalent to first-year at the degree level. Such diplomas in Australia are delivered by universities, technical colleges and other private Registered Training Organisations (RTOs).

EIBT: The *Eynesbury Institute of Business and Technology* is one of a growing number of private providers linking up with partner universities to establish programs that create opportunities to promote Australian HE globally. EIBT offers pathways to a Bachelor of Business, Information Technology, or Engineering at one of two South Australian HE institutions: *The University of Adelaide*; or the *University of South Australia*.

International Student: Within the context of this chapter, they are individuals enrolled in EIBT on temporary student visas and who are exclusively from a Non-English Speaking Background (NESB).

Pathway Provider: Educational institutions that offer students alternative forms of entry into university programs. Applicants may include: early school leavers; those that have not achieved the academic and/or English requirements to obtain direct entry; or students looking to return to study after a period of absence.

Chapter 10
Post-Course Survey Development:
A Practical Approach with Valid and Reliable Results

Scott Frasard
University of Illinois - Chicago, USA

ABSTRACT

Evaluating workplace training often involves using participant surveys to gather information about effectiveness. Unfortunately, how well these surveys are designed will play a major role in the information quality used to make conclusions. Following a proper survey design method will improve data quality and help trainers better understand what these data truly mean. Additionally, as a first step in a chain of evidence, properly designed post-course surveys will play a key role in connecting training with any on-the-job changes. This chapter will describe in detail a survey design process adapted from Spector (1992) to yield key insights about training's design, trainer and participants' interactions during training, and participants' perceived value of attending.

INTRODUCTION

Training employees is a critical part of any corporate organization. Keeping staff up to date on the latest information is necessary in order to operate effectively and not become obsolete. To determine trainings' worth or value, trainers must evaluate the outcomes (Fitzpatrick, Sanders & Worthen, 2011) and collect evidence to show training was a proximate cause for change. Making a convincing case, however, that training was the cause for any change versus some other cause can be quite challenging. Most organizations do this by using surveys following training to gain insights into how effective the training was perceived by the participants (Caffarella, 2002; Morrison, Ross, Kalman & Kemp, 2011; Phillips & Stone, 2002), but this isn't necessarily sufficient evidence to connect training with change. Unfortunately, many organizations do not conduct training evaluations beyond post-course surveys and

DOI: 10.4018/978-1-4666-9983-0.ch010

more problematic are the surveys themselves. Poorly designed surveys may provide some insights into what effect training may have, but in such situations, decisions made from poorly-designed surveys will be flawed (Kraut, 1996).

This chapter will provide trainers and training leaders with a practical survey-building approach, adapted from Spector (1992), which will yield valuable training insights. These insights will help demonstrate training effectiveness related to the training design, trainers' interactions with the participants, and participants' perceived outcome value. Additionally, specific elements of the organizational context known to impact training success and transfer of training will be identified, all of which help support claims of training's impact on change.

TRAINING EVALUATION

Evaluating training programs can be simple or complex and range from gathering information on participants' satisfaction to determining a precise financial return attributable to training efforts. Regardless, the primary purpose of any evaluation is "to render judgments about the value of whatever is being evaluated" (Fitzpatrick, Sanders & Worthen, 2011), which can take place at one or more of many levels. While many evaluation models exist, two models are foundational to the field: Kirkpatrick and Kirkpatrick's "four levels" model and Phillips' five-level ROI model.

Kirkpatrick and Kirkpatrick (2007) espouse a four-level evaluation hierarchy. The first level involves measuring customer satisfaction, or the reaction to the training. This involves determining how participants felt about the training and typically involves conducting surveys. The second level involves measuring how much participants learned as a result of attending the training. This level typically involves conducting tests of knowledge or skills to determine if participants know information or are able to do something taught in the training. The third level assesses changes in behaviors on the job following training. A measure of transfer of learning, this evaluation level helps to determine if training is a proximal cause, provided the opportunities to use the new knowledge or skill exist within the organization following training. Finally, the fourth level seeks to determine what, if any, business results are attributable to training. These results can take the form of business metrics or other indications of a "return on expectations" (Kirkpatrick & Kirkpatrick, 2007).

Phillips' (1991) training evaluation model is very similar to Kirkpatrick and Kirkpatrick's model. Level one measures participants' reaction to the training, level two measures learning achievement in training, level three measures implementing lessons learned from training to the job, and level four measures changes on specific business impacts, such as various performance metrics. Where the two models differ is that Phillips differentiates a mere return on expectations with a return on investment in financial terms in a fifth level. This fifth level measures the monetary value of business results and costs for the program expressed as a percentage. Phillips' approach to evaluation relies heavily on a "logical, systematic process that flows from one step to another" (p. 66) and requires planning early within the training development process to execute properly. While potentially more intricate than Kirkpatrick & Kirkpatrick's approach, Phillips' evaluation model effectively isolates training's impact on the business through proper evaluation design, data collection, data analysis, and stakeholder involvement.

A key concept in training evaluation is connecting the training event to post-training effects at each evaluation level desired. When training is measured, starting with the first level (participant satisfaction) and includes each evaluation level up to the desired level, a chain of evidence is created. This chain of evidence provides support for claims that training was a cause of changes following training (Phillips & Stone, 2002). This requires a solid evaluation plan in order to provide credible evaluation results (Wang & Wilcox, 2006). As Simons (2004) notes, "Practice settings and the complexity of professional judgments they entail call for a range of evaluation evidence" (p. 420). Thus, to have a stronger connection of any realized outcomes to training, as opposed to some non-training source, it is critical to understand how participants felt about the training, which means capturing key data at the conclusion of the training event.

Using surveys to collect key training evaluation data has advantages and disadvantages (Johnson & Turner, 2003). A sound evaluation strategy will make full use of survey's advantages while minimizing the inherent disadvantages with a robust survey development process. On the positive side, surveys are good for measuring attitudes of a large number of participants in a short amount of time. With a perceived level of anonymity, participants will feel more comfortable sharing their true thoughts. Closed-ended survey items (those where participants select from a range of possible responses) provide relevant data that is easy to analyze with minimal useless information.

Despite these advantages, surveys have their disadvantages. A primary disadvantage is that to be certain the survey provides intended information, the instrument must be validated. Additionally, to get the most useful information, the survey needs to be short, which may results in missing data. Providing an opportunity for participants to share their thoughts with open-ended survey items may result in useless or vague information, which must be analyzed; a time-consuming endeavor. Additionally, how one responds to a survey may reflect social desirability where answers provided do not reflect the participant's actual feelings. Finally, non-response and responding in a set pattern may confuse the results. These disadvantages can be overcome to a certain degree with proper survey development practices.

SURVEY DEVELOPMENT METHOD

Building a post-course survey is not as simple as drafting a series of questions and providing a mechanism for training participants to answer them. To be meaningful, valid, and reliable, this instrument must be carefully planned, developed, and tested to ensure it is performing as intended and able to yield results that are both accurate and practical. This section will outline a practical approach to developing such an instrument to include: (1) developing an appropriate measurement framework, (2) survey item generation and reduction, (3) prototype instrument testing, and (4) instrument validation and pilot testing.

Post-Course Survey Measurement Framework

Quantifying training effectiveness is a challenging task without distilling this broad construct into its component parts. Fortunately, this has been the focus of much research for many years and these component parts are well-known, to include: (1) the course design, (2) the interaction between the trainer and participants, (3) the learners' perceived outcomes, and (4) the context (Alshare & Lane, 2011; Caffarella, 2002; Cornelius-White, 2007; Gagné, Wager, Golas & Keller, 2005; Klein, Noe, & Wang, 2006; Morrison, Ross, Kalman, & Kemp, 2011; Swan, 2001;). Drawing on what is already known from the adult education literature about effective training, a foundational measurement framework would be built (See figure 1). This framework sets a consistent stage, which is used to answer an overarching, collaboratively designed evaluation question, "Did the training effectively prepare participants for success?" With this overarching question guiding the rest of the measurement, each of the four components is defined with

Figure 1. Post-course measurement framework

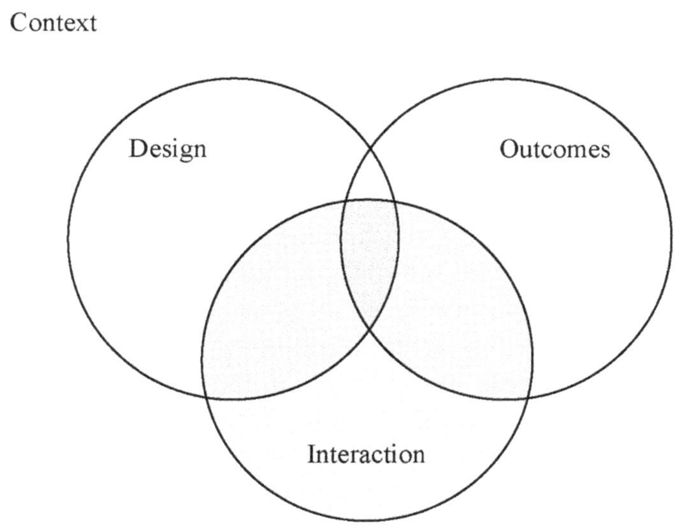

an evaluation question of their own. Having these guiding questions for the overall framework and each individual component allows for a very clear purpose for the post-course survey and ensures that every survey item developed is specific as to what data it will provide.

The first component of the post-course survey measurement framework is the course *design*. A training course must be well-developed in order to contribute to meaningful, purposive learning. Asking participants about course elements provides some indication as to how well the instruction performed (Gagné, Wager, Golas & Keller, 2005). This will also provide evidence to potential design problems. Questions on the post-course survey measuring this construct center on elements related to the learning activities, relating training topics to job performances, and ways of solving problems in the classroom. Data from this construct helps to answer the question, "Did the course design ensure participants will be successful?"

The second component of the post-course survey measurement framework is the *interaction* between the trainer and training participants. In the learner-centered classroom, "person-centered teacher variables have an above average finding-level association with positive student outcomes" (Cornelius-White, 2007, p. 130). These variables include empathy, warmth, genuineness, encouraging, adaptable to differences, and having learning-centered beliefs. Further, Swan (2001) found a significant and meaningful relationship between learner-teacher interactions and learning outcomes. Thus, asking participants about these construct elements provides a profound insight into the trainer's performance as a separate, yet correlated, construct from the course design. Data from this construct helps to answer the question, "Did the trainer help prepare participants to be successful in their role?"

The third component of the post-course survey measurement framework is the training participants' perceived *outcomes* from attending the training. Training participants must feel they got something valuable from the training in order to feel it was worth their time to attend and provide them with something practical for job performance. This perceived learning outcome is, in part, affected by the course structure (Alshare & Lane, 2011). What's more, Klein, Noe, and Wang (2006) found that the relationship between how training is delivered and the learning outcome is mediated by active learning states, demonstrating a relationship between this *outcomes* construct and the *interaction* construct. Thus, asking participants about perceived outcome elements provides significant insights into both trainer performance and course design. Data from this construct helps to answer the question, "Did participants learn new knowledge, skills, and/or attitudes to be successful on the job?

The fourth component of the post-course survey measurement framework is the *context*, which is recognized as one of the critical variables in learning (Caffarella, 2002). Understanding the context surrounding learning, both as a component of the learning space itself as well as the work environment, provides valuable information to trainers and course designers about training effectiveness. Additionally, this context allows for increased interpretability of the other three constructs (*design*, *outcomes*, and *interaction*) in order to understand the role each construct may play in effective training. One of the context-oriented elements Morrison, Ross, Kalman, and Kemp (2011) suggest to measure is the learner characteristics. In this study's business setting, this takes the form of participants' confidence to use the knowledge and skills taught. Thus, asking about confidence in applying concepts, using skills, and helping others with the concepts are central to understanding training effectiveness and are a separate, yet correlated construct to the course design, interaction, and outcomes. Data from this construct helps to answer the question, "How might participants' environment help him/her successfully implement training concepts?"

The single biggest advantage to taking a measurement framework approach to post-course survey development in a global learning context is that multiple survey instruments can be developed to measure these four constructs in a way to account for different ways of learning/making meanings, language, culture, and what's important to people regionally. While the four constructs stay constant globally, the actual questions asked may be slightly or very different regionally, but when scores for each construct are summated, they can be compared across regions. This comparison provides global and regional managers with a powerful tool to evaluate performance and make decisions about regional practices.

Item Generation and Reduction

With a well-defined measurement framework, which included overarching questions, survey items were generated. Items were generated from three primary sources: (1) previous post-course surveys, (2) existing literature on training evaluations, and (3) trainers and instructional designers. All items represented each construct in terms of how that construct may manifest in the classroom setting. A total of 128 items were generated, potentially representing each of the four constructs. Table 1 contains the total number of items in the item pool by construct.

Table 1. Total number of items in item pool by construct

Construct	Total Items
Design	33
Interaction	62
Outcomes	21
Context	12
Total Items	128

To reduce the number of potential survey items, a validity sort was conducted to determine how clear each question or statement was in terms of which construct it purported to measure. First, all items were reviewed to ensure they adhered to proper survey writing guidelines so they provide "answers that provide meaningful information about what we are trying to describe" (Fowler, 1995, p. 1). Next, all items were loaded into an online survey tool. This tool allowed trainers, instructional designers, and their supervisors to categorize each into one of the following: (1) design construct, (2) interaction construct, (3) outcomes construct, (4) context construct, (5) more than one construct, or (6) none of these constructs. All those who participated in the validity sort activity were given an introduction as to its purpose and process with any needed clarification given. Additionally, the survey itself included instructions and definitions of each construct to increase confidence in consistent categorization.

A total of 22 (88%) participants completed the validity sort. Items were analyzed to determine the degree of construct agreement for each item using frequencies and ranked means. First, items with 80% or better agreement (n=56) were considered written clearly as to the construct in which the respondent perceived they were measuring and were retained for potential inclusion on the prototype survey instrument. Next, the frequencies of each item's agreement were analyzed; those with 100% agreement were retained for potential inclusion. Items for the *Interaction* and *Design* constructs had a sufficient number of items with 100% agreement; however, there were insufficient numbers of items with 100% agreement for the *Outcomes* and *Context* constructs. Additional items with the next highest agreement level were selected until a sufficient number of potential items were retained. Given the large number of potential items for the *Interaction* and *Design* constructs with 100% agreement (n=20 and n=18, respectively), an additional sorting activity took place. All potential items were presented to all training supervisors and each were asked to identify their top three most important items, which would yield the most valuable information regarding trainer and instructional designer performance. Lastly, the final list of potential items (n=30) was presented to the trainers, instructional designers, and supervisors for approval. Table 2 contains the total number of items retained for the prototype instrument by construct.

Each of the retained survey items were assigned a measurement scale. All *design*, *interaction*, and *outcomes* construct items were assigned an agreement scale (1=strongly disagree, 2=disagree, 3=agree, 4=strongly agree). Four *context* items were assigned a confidence scale (0% confident to 100% confident) while the remaining three were assigned a length of time scale. These items were loaded into an online survey tool for prototype testing.

In addition to these closed-ended survey items, four carefully crafted open-ended items were included to collect qualitative data. Just like the closed-ended items, these open-ended items followed the same measurement framework. The *design* construct item asks the participant to complete the statement, "The thing that helped me learn the most in this class was:" The *interaction* construct item asks the

Table 2. Total number of items retained for prototype instrument by construct

Construct	Total Items
Design	10
Interaction	8
Outcomes	5
Context	7
Total Items	30

participant to respond to the statement, "Please provide an example of something the trainer did to help you learn in this class. The *outcomes* question asks respondents, "What was the most important thing you learned from this class?" Finally, the *context* construct question asks the respondent, "What support would you need from your workplace to successfully implement the concepts taught in this class? These open-ended items were generated, reduced, revised, and finalized through an iterative process with all training leaders and some of the instructional designers and trainers.

One may notice that in the open-ended items, there is nothing that asks participants to identify anything that needs improvement. This is because this instrument was built upon an appreciative inquiry (AI) philosophy. As David Cooperrider, one of the leading pioneers of AI, notes, "AI begins by identifying what is positive and connecting to it in ways that heighten energy, vision, and action for change" (Cooperrider, 2008, p. *xv*). Following this simple precept of change, in order to get the most out of post-course survey data, one should look for what is working well and make attempts to replicate those successes rather than focusing on what is broken and make attempts to correct them. Simply put, there will never be a lack of suggestions for training improvements; however, an AI approach is a more powerful approach to positive change and can impact change on a systems level, something that is necessary for effective change in training initiatives.

Prototype Testing

Once the prototype instrument was developed, it was tested concurrently with the current post-course survey instrument of the time. Prior to leaving the classroom, training participants access the online post-course survey instrument and are greeted with a welcome message. After reading the welcome message, participants enter a unique 6-digit alphanumeric survey code assigned to the specific course offering and its trainer (See Figure 2). Next, participants select one of six "Pick me!" options, which randomly assigns each person to either the current post-course survey or the prototype survey. Finally, the participants take the post-course survey. Half of the "Pick me!" options directed the participant to the current post-course survey and the other half to the prototype.

During the prototype testing period, the current post-course survey was used alongside the prototype survey for two purposes. First, prior to changing post-course instruments, the organization wanted to continue collecting and reporting performance data and was comfortable, but not satisfied with, the cur-

Figure 2. Survey code and randomization

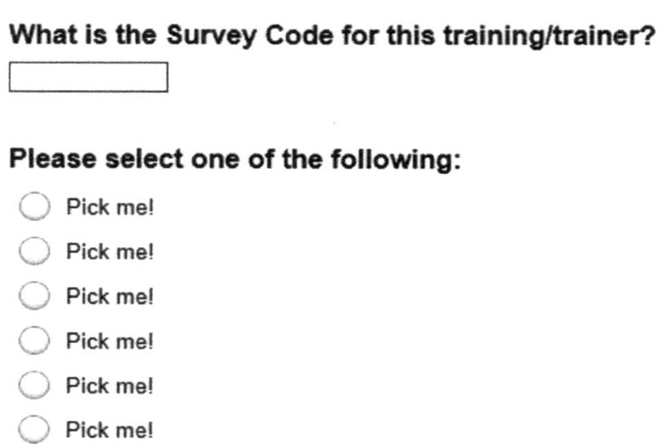
What is the Survey Code for this training/trainer?

Please select one of the following:

- Pick me!
- Pick me!
- Pick me!
- Pick me!
- Pick me!
- Pick me!

rent post-course survey scores. By continuing to use the current post-course survey, normal reporting practices could remain until the prototype post-course survey was fully tested and the final items identified. Additionally, measuring the same course with both instruments allowed for comparisons between the two surveys, serving two purposes: (1) from a measurement perspective, differences in scores could be analyzed to determine instrument performance strengths and weaknesses, and (2) the training leadership could see side-by-side the benefits of a properly-designed post-course survey.

Analysis of the prototype instrument took place after collecting a sufficient number of post-course responses. This analysis included a principle components analysis to explore the instrument's ability to measure distinctly different theorized constructs, a reliability analysis for each construct to ensure the items retained for each construct is appropriate, and regression analysis to determine the relative contributions of each item within each construct to an overall construct score. According to Mundfrom, Shaw, & Ke (2005), "absolute minimum necessary sample sizes are probably unrealistic (p. 166), but offer a sample size of 500 for an instrument with between three and six factors. Given that the post-course survey measurement framework contains four theoretical constructs, 500 responses was selected as the minimum needed for an adequate analysis with a total of 513 collected.

First, a principle components analysis with Oblimin rotation of the 23 *design, interaction*, and *outcomes* was conducted to confirm the theoretical constructs. Using this oblique rotation method provide greater interpretability and allows the factors to correlate (Osborne, 2015). Items from these three constructs were selected as these are direct measures of instructional designer and trainer performance and the *context* items were excluded to ensure this clarity. The analysis yielded a three-factor solution explaining 76.2% of the variance. Seven items loaded onto Factor 1 and all were related to the *interaction* construct. Nine items loaded onto Factor 2, eight of which were related to the *design* construct and one related to the *outcomes* construct. Finally, seven items loaded onto Factor 3, four of which were related to the *outcomes* construct, two related to the *design* construct and the remaining one related to the *interaction* construct.

Next, a reliability analysis of items from each factor was conducted individually. Within each factor, Chronbach's alpha and alpha if deleted were obtained to identify items that should be retained for the final pilot post-course survey. The *design* construct consisted of 10 items ($\alpha = .787$), but had three items, which if deleted, increased the Chronbach's alpha to .833. The *interaction* construct consisted of eight items ($\alpha = .892$), but had two items, which if deleted, increased the Chronbach's alpha to .910. Finally, the *outcomes* construct consisted of 5 items ($\alpha = .856$), but had one item, which if deleted, increased the Chronbach's alpha to .919.

A multiple regression analysis was used to test if each *design, interaction*, and *outcomes* variables significantly predict participants' confidence to apply the concepts taught. The results of the regression indicated that four of the seven *design* items were significantly related to confidence to apply concepts taught ($R^2=.927$, $F(4,510)=2514.38$, $p<.001$). The results of the regression indicated that four of the six *interaction* items were significantly related to confidence to apply concepts taught ($R^2=.908$, $F(4,510)=2961.96$, $p<.001$). Finally, the results of the regression indicated that three of the four *outcomes* items were significantly related to confidence to apply concepts taught ($R^2=.951$, $F(3,511)=3815.19$, $p<.001$).

The items were retested for Chronbach's alpha scores prior to being included in the final pilot post-course survey (*design* $\alpha=.801$; *interaction* $\alpha=.898$; *outcomes* $\alpha=.910$). Once item reliabilities were recalculated, items weights were obtained from the regression analysis. Table 3 contains the final items and contribution weights to their respective construct.

Table 3. Final items and item weights for pilot instrument by construct

Construct	Item Weight	Item
Design	18%	This class provided me the opportunity to solve a problem on my own.
	41%	This class provided me what I need to know to perform my job.
	20%	This class was designed similar to how my job is actually performed.
	21%	This class was arranged in a way that makes sense to me.
Interaction	28%	The trainer for this class provided me with understandable instructions.
	16%	The trainer for this class gave me useful feedback.
	30%	The trainer for this class respected me as a learner.
	26%	The trainer for this class appeared to care about my learning.
Outcomes	40%	From this class, I learned something to be better prepared to do my job.
	26%	From this class, I learned something of practical value.
	34%	From this class, I learned something important for my current job.

Lastly, the online post-course survey tool was revised to include those items identified from the analysis as being the proper ones to retain and to remove the concurrent administration of the previously current post-course survey. The same process of participant access to the survey and indicating the course and trainer with a survey code remained the same. All training leaders were informed of the analysis results and its impact on score reporting practices. Additionally, all training members (leaders, instructional designers, and trainers) were given training on reading and interpreting the new instrument as well as how to use these results to inform practice.

Validation and Pilot Testing

As with the prototype testing, the final post-course pilot survey was tested after being used for six months. A total of 821 post-course survey responses were used in the analysis. A principle components analysis with Oblimin rotation of the 11 *design, interaction*, and *outcomes* was conducted to confirm the theoretical constructs. The analysis confirmed a three-factor solution explaining 81.5% of the variance. Four items loaded onto Factor 1, and all were related to the *interaction* construct. This factor explained 61.1% of the variance. Four items loaded onto Factor 2, all of which were related to the *design* construct. This factor explained 12.9% of the variance. Finally, three items loaded onto Factor 3, all of which were related to the *outcomes* construct. This factor explained 7.5% of the variance.

Next, a reliability analysis of items from each factor was conducted individually. The *design, interaction*, and *outcomes* constructs have Chronbach alphas of .887, .929, and .917, respectively. Additionally, these alphas were similar to the alphas obtained in the prototype instrument analysis, providing support for the construct structures. All items within each construct were examined to determine if deletion of any would have an impact on the overall reliability of the construct. In all cases, deletion of any item would reduce the alphas, thus all were retained.

Finally, a multiple regression analysis tested the *design, interaction,* and *outcomes* variables' ability to predict participants' confidence to apply the concepts taught. The results of the regression indicated that all four *design* items were significantly related to confidence to apply concepts taught (R^2=.967, $F(4,510)=3690.40$, $p<.001$). The results of the regression indicated that all four *interaction* items were significantly related to confidence to apply concepts taught (R^2=.960, F(4,514)=3100.97, p<.001). Finally, the results of the regression indicated that all four *outcomes* items were significantly related to confidence to apply concepts taught (R^2=.964, F(4,510)=4601.18, p<.001).

With all items retested, items weights were obtained from the regression analysis. Table 4 contains the final items and contribution weights to their respective construct. These item weights were similar to original prototype weights, providing additional evidence of reliability.

Finally, these item weights were programmed into a purpose-built post-course survey reporting tool to calculate metrics for each of the three constructs. Details of this reporting are discussed next.

SUMMARY REPORTING

All participants of every training course were asked to take part in a post-course survey prior to leaving the classroom. Trainers provided participants with a link to an online survey, which used Survey Monkey (www.surveymonkey.com), to collect data. Additionally, trainers provided participants with a unique 6-digit alphanumeric number to identify the trainer and training course. This number was generated by a purpose-built post-course data administration database.

Course-by-Course Data Analysis

At the conclusion of each course, post-course survey data were downloaded from the online survey into the post-course survey database. This database housed all post-course and course offerings data and generates various reports, to include a *Course Feedback Summary Report* (see Appendix). The *Course Feedback Summary Report* and the calculations described in the previous section are automatically generated for the specific trainer/course offering and distributed to the individual trainer and his or her supervisor.

The report has three main sections: (1) course offering information and score summary, (2) detailed item analysis, and (3) comments. The first section includes basic course information such as:

Table 4. Final items and item weights for final instrument by construct

Construct	Item Weight	Item
Design	15%	This class provided me the opportunity to solve a problem on my own.
	48%	This class provided me what I need to know to perform my job.
	18%	This class was designed similar to how my job is actually performed.
	19%	This class was arranged in a way that makes sense to me.
Interaction	29%	The trainer for this class provided me with understandable instructions.
	16%	The trainer for this class gave me useful feedback.
	26%	The trainer for this class respected me as a learner.
	29%	The trainer for this class appeared to care about my learning.
Outcomes	41%	From this class, I learned something to be better prepared to do my job.
	30%	From this class, I learned something of practical value.
	29%	From this class, I learned something important for my current job.

- The course title;
- Date(s) taught;
- Start time, which is important when multiple offerings of the same course take place on the same date;
- Trainer;
- Survey code;
- Training location;
- Number of post-course surveys sent/returned;
- Return rate are included.

Finally, the first section includes a score summary box with the three accountability metrics and confidence scores displays. The *interaction* score is informative regarding primarily the trainer's performance while the *design* score is informative regarding primarily the instructional designer's performance. The *outcomes* score, while a distinct construct, is a shared performance indicator of both the trainer and instructional designer. The three confidence scores reflect participants' perceived confidence levels in applying the concepts, using the skills, and helping others with the concepts taught and provide some contextual understanding when compared with other scores/indicators.

The second section provides an item-level analysis of the three constructs measured using item means from all post-course surveys completed. Additionally, the report indicates the weight of each item within each construct, which provides the trainer and instructional designer information about the relative impact each item has on the final score. Having item weights displayed allows the trainer and instructional designer to make better decisions about his or her performance and potential areas of weaknesses, which may need improvement. If, for example, two item means in the *interaction* construct were low, using the item weights, the trainer would know which of the two items he or she should focus on for improvement efforts – the item with the highest item weighting. Additionally, the item means for the three *course length* items provides information regarding the time spent in each of the three learning domains – cognitive, psychomotor, and affective. Like the confidence scores in the section one summary box, these three scores provide context to help understand other scores when the trainer or instructional designer is reading and interpreting the report. Finally, there is white space available for the trainer or instructional designer to make notes regarding their experiences in the specific course offering. This has been helpful in capturing otherwise lost data regarding the course, which may help explain ratings.

The third section provides the trainer and instructional designer with comments connected to each of the four areas of the measurement framework. For the *design* construct, the question asks the training participant, "The thing that helped me learn most in this class was:" For the *interaction* construct, the question asks the training participant, "Please provide an example of something the trainer did that helped you learn in this class." For the *context* construct, the question asks the training participant, "What support would you need from your workplace to successfully implement the concepts taught in this class?" Finally, for the *outcomes* construct, the question asks the training participant, "What is the most important thing you learned from this class?" These comments provide trainers, instructional designers, and their supervisors with additional detail about trainer and instructional design performance, what participants learned, and workplace context influencing transfer of training, the latter of which can be forwarded to the workplace as a proactive measure to increase training's impact on the business. Decisions around best practices to maintain and potential opportunities for instructional design changes or trainer practice changes can be made and implemented.

CONCLUSION AND RECOMMENDATIONS

Building a proper post-course survey is not insurmountable, even in a face-paced business context. The intersection of an academic approach within a global corporate training organization yielded a post-course survey that not only provided valuable information to the entire training organization, but also provided statistical evidence to support validity and reliability claims. While claims that evaluating training is a challenging and mysterious process (Phillips, 1997) may exist, developing and following a sound measurement framework will result in useful and defensible results.

Training leaders now collect data from every training class delivered. Given the robust process used to build and validate the post-course survey, trainers, instructional designers, and leaders alike are able to see for the first time where strengths and opportunities for improvement exist without taking a best guess based on potentially irrelevant information. Follow-up meetings with trainers and instructional designers to examine post-course survey results and scores revealed something quite interesting and desired – the *design*, *outcomes*, and *interaction* scores matched their personal experiences during the individual training sessions. Specifically, trainers recalled training sessions where they felt the instructional designers' learning activities were less than desired for the topic, which were reflected in lower *design* scores and slightly decreased *outcome* scores while their *interaction* scores remained higher, a clear indication that the constructs being measured were independent. Knowing this, corrective actions could be taken to address the actual cause rather than something completely unrelated.

Given the global nature of the subject organization, multiple post-course surveys were built using the same process and same measurement framework. The item generation process yielded different survey items to measure each construct, yet some remained the same or similar across multiple countries. Doing so allows for appropriate localization of item wording to account for language, cultural, and learning differences while measuring the same constructs and enabling cross-regional comparisons of training based on a common measurement. This enables trainers, instructional designers, and leaders an unprecedented ability to examine training practice effects globally to identify appropriate adjustments necessary when training in multiple regions. Further, different performance levels in each region become crystal clear when normal score ranges are calculated regionally, allowing leaders to make better decisions about trainers and instructional designer performances and setting appropriate performance expectations.

In order to clearly articulate training's importance and worth to the organization, training leaders should start by exploring their current evaluation practices. Beginning with learner reaction/satisfaction will provide information about training value at its most basic level, but will serve as the key connection between training efforts and organizational impact. The ubiquitous post-course survey should not be taken for granted, but rather raised to a higher stature by becoming purposeful and rigorous in its development. The process outlined in this chapter will provide training leaders with the necessary insights to replicate the steps and implement a valuable post-course survey.

Future work in this area could extend these results further. Specifically, more work is needed to test the process and results utility in different contexts. This was a global corporate training environment, but would other settings be more or less accepting? Are the challenges corporate trainers face similar enough to other settings and would those training leaders see similar value? In the current context, can the *design*, *outcomes*, and *interaction* scores provide useful insights into transfer of learning (level 3 evaluation) or impact on business performance metrics (level 4 evaluation) with enough predictive validity to support claims that training would have contributed to tangible results before a meaningful higher-order evaluation could take place? Further study into the relationships between post-course survey scores and higher-order evaluation outcomes are necessary to establish a causal link, potentially lending more credibility to the post-course survey practice. Finally, there are other potential constructs available, which indicate corporate training success; course design, perceived learner outcomes, and trainer/participant interaction are merely three such constructs. Future work should explore other meaningful constructs and any potential relationships between those and the constructs presented in this chapter (figure 4 in Appendix).

REFERENCES

Alshare, K. A., & Lane, P. L. (2011). Predicting student-perceived learning outcomes and satisfaction in ERP courses: An empirical investigation. *Communications of the Association for Information Systems*, *28*(24), 571–584.

Babbie, E. (1990). *Survey research methods* (2nd ed.). Belmont, CA: Wadsworth Publishing Company.

Caffarella, R. S. (2002). *Planning programs for adult learners: A practical guide for educators, trainers, and staff developers*. San Francisco, CA: Jossey-Bass.

Cooperrider, D. L., Whitney, D. K., & Stavros, J. M. (2008). *Appreciative inquiry handbook: For leaders of change* (2nd ed.). Brunswick, OH: Crown Custom Publishing, Inc.

Cornelius-White, J. (2007). Learner-centered teacher-student relationships are effective: A meta-analysis. *Review of Educational Research*, *77*(1), 113–143. doi:10.3102/003465430298563

Driscoll, A., & Wood, S. (2007). *Developing outcomes-based assessment for learner-centered education: A faculty introduction*. Sterling, VA: Stylus Publishing, LLC.

Fitzpatrick, J. L., Sanders, J. R., & Worthen, B. R. (2011). *Program evaluation: Alternative approaches and practical guidelines* (4th ed.). Upper Saddle River, NJ: Pearson Education, Inc.

Fowler, F. J. Jr. (1995). *Improving survey questions: Design and evaluation*. Thousand Oaks, CA: SAGE Publications.

Gagné, R. M., & Wager, W. W. >, Golas, K. C., & Keller, J. M. (2005). Principles of instructional design (5th ed.). Belmont, CA: Thompson Wadsworth.

Johnson, B., & Turner, L. A. (2003). Data collection strategies in mixed methods research. In A. Tashakkori & C. Teddlie (Eds.), *Handbook of mixed methods in social & behavioral research* (pp. 297–319). Thousand Oaks, CA: SAGE Publications, Inc.

Kirkpatrick, D. L., & Kirkpatrick, J. D. (2007). *Implementing the four levels: A practical guide for effective evaluation of training programs*. San Francisco, CA: Berrett-Koehler Publishers, Inc.

Klein, H. J., Noe, R. A., & Wang, C. (2006). Motivation to learn and course outcomes: The impact of delivery mode, learning goal orientation, and perceived barriers and enablers. *Personnel Psychology*, *59*(3), 665–702. doi:10.1111/j.1744-6570.2006.00050.x

Kraut, A. I. (1996). Planning and conducting the survey: Keeping strategic people in mind. In A. I. Kraut (Ed.), *Organizational surveys: Tools for assessment and change* (pp. 149–176). San Francisco, CA: Jossey-Bass Publishers.

Mager, R. F. (1997). *Preparing instructional objectives: A critical tool in the development of effective instruction* (3rd ed.). Atlanta, GA: CEP Press.

Morrison, G. R., Ross, S. M., Kalman, H. K., & Kemp, J. E. (2011). *Designing effective instruction* (6th ed.). Hoboken, NJ: John Wiley & Sons, Inc.

Mundfrom, D. J., Shaw, D. G., & Ke, T. L. (2005). Minimum sample size recommendations for conducting factor analyses. *International Journal of Testing*, *5*(2), 159–168. doi:10.1207/s15327574ijt0502_4

Osborne, J. W. (2015). What is rotating in exploratory factor analysis? *Practical Assessment, Research & Evaluation*, *20*(2), 1–7. Retrieved from http://pareonline.net/getvn.asp?v=20&n=2

Phillips, J. J. (1997). *Handbook of training evaluation and measurement methods* (3rd ed.). Houston, TX: Gulf Publishing Company.

Phillips, J. J., & Stone, R. D. (2002). *How to measure training results: A practical guide to tracking the six key indicators*. New York, NY: McGraw-Hill.

Simons, H. (2004). Utilizing evaluation evident to enhance professional practice. *Evaluation*, *10*(4), 410–429. doi:10.1177/1356389004050284

Spector, P. E. (1992). *Summated scale construction: An introduction*. Newbury Park, CA: SAGE Publications, Inc. doi:10.4135/9781412986038

Swan, K. (2001). Virtual interaction: Design factors affecting student satisfaction and perceived learning in asynchronous online courses. *Distance Education*, *22*(2), 306–331. doi:10.1080/0158791010220208

Wang, G. G., & Wilcox, D. (2006). Training evaluation: Knowing more than is practiced. *Advances in Developing Human Resources*, *8*(4), 528–539. doi:10.1177/1523422306293007

KEY TERMS AND DEFINITIONS

Construct: A deliberate idea, drawn from theory, which typically cannot be measured directly.

Context: Refers to environmental elements associated with the training and workplace, which may have direct or indirect influences on and can be used to explain changes in training effectiveness.

Design: Refers to the instructional design elements of training, such as learning activities, materials, and presentations.

Evaluation: A process of collecting evidence used to demonstrate the value or effect of an intervention, such as training.

Interaction: Refers to the engagement and actions between trainers and training participants.

Outcomes: Refers to training participants' perceived value gained by attending training.

Post-Course Survey: An instrument used to collect data from participants regarding their perspective about the training.

Reliable: Consistently measuring something over several administrations with similar results.

Valid: Measuring what is intended and conclusions based on the measurements accurately reflect reality.

APPENDIX: POST-COURSE FEEDBACK SUMMARY REPORT

Figure 3.

ABC Company

Global Learning Organization

Course Feedback Summary Report

Score Summary	
Interaction:	3.86
Outcomes:	4.00
Design:	3.83
Confidence (0%-100%):	
- Apply concepts:	94%
- Use skills:	94%
- Help others:	94%

Course: Teaching Strategies I

Course Date: 5/14/2013 through 5/14/2013 Start Time: 1:00 AM Sent: 8

Trainer/Designer: Frasard, Scott Returned: 7

Survey Code: 328C7C Location: Location A Return Rate: 88%

Notes

INTERACTION	Item AVG
[29%] The trainer for this class provided me with understandable instructions.	3.86
[16%] The trainer for this class gave me useful feedback.	3.86
[26%] The trainer for this class respected me as a learner.	3.86
[29%] The trainer for this class appeared to care about my learning.	3.86

OUTCOMES	Item AVG
[41%] From this class, I learned something to be better prepared to do my job.	4.00
[30%] From this class, I learned something of practical value.	4.00
[29%] From this class, I learned something important for my current job.	4.00

DESIGN	Item AVG
[15%] This class provided me the opportunity to solve a problem on my own.	3.86
[48%] This class provided me what I need to know to perform my job.	3.86
[18%] This class was designed similar to how my job is actually performed.	3.71
[19%] This class was arranged in a way that made sense to me.	3.86

Scale: 4=Strongly agree, 3=Agree, 2=Disagree, 1=Strongly disagree

COURSE LENGTH	Item AVG
The amount of time spent in this class learning key knowledge (cognitive domain) was...	5.00
The amount of time spent in this class practicing key tasks (psychomotor domain) was...	5.00
The amount of time spent in this class understanding the value (affective domain) was...	5.00

Scale: 0 1 2 3 4 5 6 7 8 9 10
Too short About Right Too Long

Report printed on 4/29/2014 6:35:47 AM

Figure 4.

Design *The thing that helped me learn the most in this class was:*	Interaction *Please provide an example of something that helped you learn in this class.*	Context *What support would you need from your workplace to successfully implement the concepts taught in this class?*	Outcomes *What is the most important thing you learned from this class?*
The rubric we filled out on our own was great.	The juxtaposition of the initial activity and the last activity was great!		
Doing the activities and then discussing as a group.	Came prepared with handouts for us to use, learning objectives, and a guide.	Everything about my workplace will help me implement the concepts. I constantly analyze what training strategy to use and everything we learned can be applied.	The breakdown of teaching strategies and the advantages and disadvantages to each.
The activities applied directly to what we were learning.	Gave examples specific to what we do everyday which was really helpful	It would be great if someone came in to observe the class and it was discussued prior so you can practice each of the strategies and receive feedback on them.	Try different strategies and tailor them to your learners.
Great activity and discussion. Everything linked and labled back to the class objectives.	Loved the activities. At the end of the class you mentioned "which felt longer? The 2 minute activity or the 5 minute activity?" We all knew what the answer was and could tell that we learned a ton from the excercise.	Being part of the SOP team, this class helps me in keeping my audience in mind when designing SOPs. And most importantly how to colaborate with LOBs.	3 different strategies when approaching a class as a facilitator. Thank you so much Scott!
Understanding the basic layouts of what the different teaching strategies are and how to use them within different ways.	I loved how we were constantly engaged as participants. We were always learning or working on an activity, it always felt like a group effort and I loved it!		I learned that I need to adapt more to my learners needs and also step out of my comfort zone at times.
I loved the discussions as well as the group activities. It was great to hear different points of view to come up with our "skits".	Gave us the points but allowed us to discuss as a group to get additional insights from each other.		To look at things out of my comfort zone and reach out for other ideas/concenpt from my peers that have worked for them. Or discuss what hasn't worked in some cases.
Both of the learning activities	Taught in the different styles as he discussed them	We have the freedom to adjust our training as we need to, this will help me to practice the knowledge I obtained	details on the different teaching strategies

Report printed on 5/2/2014 6:03:39 AM

Chapter 11
Role of Learning Analytics in Enhancing Teaching and Learning

Amir Manzoor
Bahria University, Pakistan

ABSTRACT

Data analytics, tools and techniques are no more confined to research organizations. These tools are being adopted by many organizations to generate business intelligence for improving decision making. Higher education institutions (HEIs) are beginning to use data analytics for improving their services and for increasing student grades and retention. Educational learning analytics are used to research and build models in several areas that can influence online learning systems. While use of analytics and data mining in education is increasing, sorting out fact from fiction and identifying research possibilities and practical applications are not easy. This chapter intends to help policymakers and administrators of HEIs understand how learning analytics have been used and can be applied for educational improvements.

INTRODUCTION

Increasing use of online learning offers opportunities to integrate assessment and learning. With this integration, information needed to improve future instruction can be gathered in real time. With online learning, students get multiple opportunities to exploit the power of technology for assessment. The same technology can be used to support learning activities and for assessment. An online system can collect much more and detailed information about how students learn. The system can capture students input and collect evidence of their problem-solving sequences, knowledge, and strategy use. This input can be in the form of inputs selected by student, the number of attempts made by the student, the number of hints and feedback given, and the time spent across various parts of the problem solved. Besides students, this detailed learning data also has potential value for the broad education community. With increasing number of activities occurring over the web, the amount of data online activities generate is increasing exponentially. Commercial companies have pioneered in developing techniques for harvest-

DOI: 10.4018/978-1-4666-9983-0.ch011

ing insights from this mass data. These insights are being used to identify likely consumers of products, refining products to better fit consumer needs, and tailor marketing and user experiences to the preferences of the individual. More recently, educational institutions offering online learning have begun to explore the same techniques for gaining insights from the learner's online activities (U.S. Department of Education, 2012)..

In a broader sense, analytics programs evaluate large data sets to provide decision makers with information that can help determine the best course of action for an organization. Learning analytics (LA) uses similar approach but with specific goal of improving learning outcomes. This improvement could be measured by student grades, retention, or completion. LA collects and analyzes various connected pieces of digital information that students leave as they interact with various information systems. The purpose of this analysis is to find any correlations between student activities and learning outcomes. To do so, LA compares a student's activity with their peers in the class to create a model for how each student is likely to behave. In this way, by analyzing the vast quantities of data that mot HEIs already collect, LA attempts to find patterns that can be used to improve learning. The most common use of learning analytics is to identify academically weak students. And to enable targeted interventions to help them achieve better outcomes. LA tools can also be used to identify specific units of study in a course that course students' difficulty generally and to modify learning activities to improve learning of all students (U.S. Department of Education, 2012).

The objective of this chapter is to explore data analytics in the commercial world and how data analytics techniques are being applied in education. The chapter will examine the challenges being encountered and the potential of such efforts for improving student outcomes and the productivity of higher education systems. This contribution will be helpful for education policymakers and administrators to understand how analytics work and how they can be applied within online learning systems to support education-related decision making.

LEARNING ANALYTICS: CONCEPT, TOOLS, AND TECHNIQUES

Companies historically have used data for decision making. Business intelligence (BI). BI techniques can help discover historical patterns and trends from data and can create models that that predict future trends and patterns. In broad sense, analytics comprises applied techniques from computer science, mathematics, and statistics for extracting usable information from very large datasets.

Organizations now face data from multiple sources with unstructured text and image data. New techniques are needed to work on this vast amount of data (also called big data). Big data is defined relative to current or typical capabilities of technology. For example, Manyika et al. (2011) defines big data as "Datasets whose size is beyond the ability of typical database software tools to capture, store, manage, and analyze." Big data captured from users' online behaviors can provide important insights about the users' knowledge, intentions, and interests and to create models for predicting future behaviors and interests (U.S. Department of Education, 2012).

Educational Data Mining (EDM) and Learning Analytics (LA)

Specifically, big data have two applications in the education i.e. educational data mining and learning analytics. These two fields have had different research histories and are developing as distinct research areas. In general, educational data mining aims to find new patterns in data and develops new models. This data can be collected during education administration and services, teaching, and learning. LA, on the other hand, applies existing predictive models in instructional systems.

Educational Data Mining (EDM)

EDM develops models and uses techniques from statistics, machine learning, and data mining to analyze data. EDM can be used to test learning theories and inform educational practice. LA applies techniques from information science, sociology, psychology, statistics, machine learning, and data mining to analyze data (U.S. Department of Education, 2012). According to Romero and Ventura (2010, p.601), "Educational data mining…exploits statistical, machine-learning, and data-mining…algorithms over...different types of educational data. … EDM is concerned with developing methods to explore the unique types of data in educational settings and, using these methods, to better understand students and the settings in which they learn. ... EDM seeks to...develop computational approaches that combine data and theory to transform practice….". The data used in EDM and LA, irrespective of the sources of data, generally has multiple levels of meaningful hierarchy. This hierarchy can be determined by using data properties.

EDM is an emerging research area. EDM comprises computational and psychological methods and research approaches to understand how students learn. New computer-supported interactive learning methods and tools (such as intelligent tutoring, simulations, and games) have provided opportunities to collect and analyze student data, to discover patterns and trends, make new discoveries and test hypotheses about students learning. Online learning systems provide vast amounts of student data containing many variables that EDM techniques can explore for model building (U.S. Department of Education, 2012).

Early efforts at EDM involved mining website log data (Baker & Yacef, 2009). The current online learning systems are more integrated, instrumental, and sophisticated and provide more kinds of data. EDM's general emphasis is to reduce learning into small components. These components can then be analyzed and influenced by software that adapts to the student (Siemens & Baker, 2012). The enormous amount of student data provided by online learning systems are being explored to develop predictive models. EDM methods classify data or find relationships to develop these models. These models play a key role in building adaptive learning systems. In these models, interventions based on the model's predictions can be used to modify students' experience and to recommend other outside academic services to support student learning (U.S. Department of Education, 2012). Educational data is important and unique because they are hierarchal and different levels of data hierarchy (such as answer level, the session level etc.) are nested inside one another (Baker 2011; Romero and Ventura 2010). Other important features of educational data are time, sequence, and context. Time is important to capture data, such as time to learn. Sequence represents how concepts build on one another and how practice and tutoring should be ordered. Context is important for explaining results and applicability of a model.

According to Baker (2011) and Baker and Yacef (2009), there exist few goals of EDM. First goal of EDM is to predict students' future learning behavior by creating student models that incorporate such detailed information as students' knowledge, motivation, metacognition, and attitudes. The second goal of EDM is to discover or improve domain models that characterize the content to be learned and optimal instructional sequences. The third goal of EDM is to study the effects of different kinds of pedagogical support that can be provided by learning software. The fourth goal of EDM is to advance scientific knowledge about learning and learners through building computational models that incorporate models of the student, the domain, and the software's pedagogy.

To accomplish these four goals, EDM uses five categories of technical methods (Baker, 2011). The first technique is prediction. In prediction, a model is developed that can infer a single aspect of the data (predicted variable) from some combination of other aspects of data (predictor variables). One example of the use of this technique is detecting student behavior (e.g. when they are gaming the system. Predictive models can be used to understand what student behaviors in an online learning environment (e.g. taking practice tests) will predict which students might fail a class. Predictive models can be used to develop domain models and forecasting and understanding educational outcomes (Baker, Gowda, and Corbett 2011). The second technique is clustering. This technique involves finding data points that naturally group together and can be used to split a full dataset into categories. One example of application of clustering technique is grouping students based on their learning difficulties and interaction patterns (e.g. how they use tools in a learning management system) (Amershi & Conati, 2009) and grouping users for purposes of recommending actions and resources to similar users. Data to be analyzed can come from many sources such as online learning resources. This data is analyzed using unstructured data analysis techniques to extract characteristics of the data and then clustering the results. Clustering can be used in any domain that involves classification. Clustering can even be used to determine how much collaboration users exhibit based on postings in discussion forums (Anaya & Boticario, 2009). The third technique is relationship mining. This technique involves discovering relationships between variables in a dataset and encoding them as rules for later use. One example of the application of this technique is to identify the relationships among products purchased in an online shopping environment (Romero & Ventura, 2010). Another sub-technique is association rule mining. This technique can be used e.g. to find students mistakes that co-occur to develop content-user association to build recommendations for content that interest users and to make changes to teaching approaches (Merceron & Yacef, 2010). These techniques can be used to associate student activity with student grades or to investigate certain trend such as students' use of practice tests decreases over a semester of study. Sequential pattern mining is another sub-technique of relationship mining. This technique is used to build rules that could capture the connections between occurrences of sequential events. One example of such sequential events is students' mistakes followed by help seeking. Capturing these connections can help detect events such as students' interaction in online discussion forums. Relationship mining can also be used to discover association between student performance and course sequences and discover which pedagogical strategies lead to more effective learning. This later application is called learning analytics (LA). LA is growing in importance and is intended to help researchers build automated systems that model how effective teachers operate by mining their use of educational systems. Fourth technique is distillation for human judgment. This technique involves representing data in a form so that the data features could be quickly identified. This technique intends to improve machine-learning models. This is because humans can identify patterns /features of student learning actions/behaviors. This approach overlaps with visual data analytics. The fifth technique is discovery with models. In this technique, validated model of a phenomenon is developed as a component to be used in further analysis. This model can be developed using prediction, clustering, or manual knowledge engineering (Jeong & Biswas, 2008). Discovery with models supports can help discover relationships between student behaviors and student characteristics (i.e. contextual variables). These methods can also be used to analyze research questions across contexts and to investigate psychometric modeling frameworks into machine-learning models (U.S. Department of Education, 2012).

Learning Analytics (LA)

According to Johnson et al. (2011, p. 28), "Learning analytics refers to the interpretation of a wide range of data produced by and gathered on behalf of students in order to assess academic progress, predict future performance, and spot potential issues……. The goal of learning analytics is to enable teachers and schools to tailor educational opportunities to each student's level of need and ability……. Learning analytics need not simply focus on student performance. It might be used as well to assess curricula, programs, and institutions. It could contribute to existing assessment efforts on a campus, helping provide a deeper analysis, or it might be used to transform pedagogy in a more radical manner. It might also be used by students themselves, creating opportunities for holistic synthesis across both formal and informal learning activities."

LA is a research and application area related to academic analytics, action analytics, and predictive analytics. LA covers a broader array of academic disciplines and incorporate concepts and techniques from information science and sociology, computer sciences, statistics, psychology, and the learning sciences. While educational data mining focuses on reducing learning into components, the focus of LA is to understand the entire systems and to support decision making. Learning analytics emphasizes that institutions should undertake and understand data measurement and collection activities and focus on the analysis and reporting of the data. While EDM generally address the development of new computational methods for data analysis, LA addresses the application of known methods and models to answer important questions that affect student learning and organizational learning systems. According to Johnson et. al., (2011) the goal of LA is to enable teachers and schools to tailor educational opportunities to each student's level of need and ability. While EDM focused on system-generated and automated responses to students, LA provides human tailoring of responses such as through feedback (U.S. Department of Education, 2012).

LA uses many technical methods used by EDM. Additionally, LA may employ social network analysis (e.g., analysis of student-to-teacher relationships and interactions to identify disconnected students, influencers, etc.) and social metadata to determine what a user is engaged with. LA provides visual analytics (e.g. display of information in dashboards) to generate actionable analyses. One important application of LA is monitoring and predicting students' learning performance and spotting potential issues. Early identification of these issues is important so that interventions can be provided to identify students at risk of failing a course of study (EDUCAUSE 2010; Johnson et al. 2011). These exist several LA models to help identify student risk level in real time to increase the students' likelihood of success. One example of such system is Purdue University's Course Signals system (Arnold 2010). The other example is the Moodog system at the University of California, Santa Barbara, and the University of Alabama (EDUCAUSE 2010). Higher education institutions today face calls for more transparency and greater scrutiny of their student recruitment and retention practices. As such, LA provides a great opportunity to help recruit and retain students. Data mining models of students' behavior in online courses have been developed. These models revealed differences between successful and unsuccessful students. The difference is measured in terms of such variables as level of participation in discussion boards, number of emails sent, and number of quizzes completed (Macfayden and Dawson 2010; U.S. Department of Education, 2012)). Analytics based on these student behavior variables is very useful. This feedback can be used to provide more fluid and flexible curricula and to support immediate course alterations (e.g., sequencing of examples, exercises, and self-assessments) based on analyses of real-time learning data.

APPLICATION AREAS OF LEARNING ANALYTICS

LA researchers are facing increasingly complex questions about what a student knows and whether a student is engaged. For example, questions may concern what a short-term boost in performance in reading a word says about overall learning of that word. There exist new techniques for model building and new kinds of learning system data that have shown promise for predicting student outcomes. The applications areas of LA represent the broad categories in which analytics can be applied to student activity (Manyika et al. 2011).

These application areas are a) modeling of user knowledge, user behavior, and user experience; b) user profiling; c) modeling of key concepts in a domain and modeling a domain's knowledge components, and d) and trend analysis. Another application area is the use of analytics to personalize the user's experience. Each of these application areas uses different sources of data and answers different questions (U.S. Department of Education, 2012).

User Knowledge Modeling (UKM)

Researchers and developers build and tune user models. These models are representation of user-specific data. These user models can be customized and personalized to users' specific needs (Gerhard 2001). Inferring what a user knows i.e. user knowledge modelling looks at accumulated data. This data represents the interactions between learners and the learning system. User knowledge modeling is used to build adaptive hypermedia, recommender systems, expert systems, and intelligent tutoring systems. Intelligent tutoring systems direct key tasks such as selecting problems to be solved by the students. There exist many methods for estimating students' knowledge. One such popular method is Corbett and Anderson's knowledge tracing model (Corbett and Anderson 1994). This method is based on Bayesian-network-based model. This method estimates the probability that a student knows a skill. This estimation is based on observations of student attempting to perform the skill. Another method of knowledge tracing has been proposed by (Baker, Corbett, & Aleven, 2008). This method uses a machine learning approach and makes contextual estimations of the probability that a student guessed or not. According to Baker, Corbett, and Aleven (2008), models of guessing and slipping can predict student future performance more accurately. Knowledge can be inferred from such interactions as repetition of wrong answers. Predictive models can help faculty make these inferences (U.S. Department of Education, 2012).

Commercial learning products typically include student knowledge modeling. How these models are used to adapt instruction varies. For example, one company can build dynamic student models for ascertaining whether student is ready to move to new learning content. The student then advances automatically. The models of other companies may not provide automatic advancement. These models offer suggestions to teachers after detecting as student's performance. Some examples of data collected by learning software include how many minutes a student spent on a unit, how many hints he/she used, and common errors made. The data for an individual student can then be compared against a model built from a large number of students. Faculty can use this data to distinguish between students who are not trying and students who are trying but struggling. With this information, faculty can come up with different instructional strategies for those two groups of students (U.S. Department of Education, 2012). Learning software such as the one provided by the Onsophic Inc. can collect data at per topic level for each student. The software can detect student mastery at topic level rather than at the course level. The software can provide students with detailed feedback.

User Behavior Modeling (UBM)

UBM in education can be used as a proxy for student engagement. UBM relies on the same kinds of learning data used in UKM software to predict user knowledge. UBM can also be used to measure e.g. how much time a student has spent online. UBM can also measure a student's level of knowledge. This measurement is based on e.g. data sources such as standardized test scores. In a series of studies on detecting and adopting to students' off-task behaviors in adaptive learning systems that teach algebra (Baker et al., 2004, 2006), researchers found that gaming behaviors were strongly associated with less learning for students with below-average academic achievement levels. Similar studies have been done in learning environments that are more open-ended. For example, Blikstein (2011) developed an automatic technique and a case study. The purpose was to assess, analyze, and visualize behaviors of students learning. Online learning systems log student data that can be mined to detect student behaviors that correlate with learning. Macfayden and Dawson (2010) analyzed such data from a learning management system. They found variables that correlated with student final grade. Their model was able to predict the student failure with an accuracy level of 81% (U.S. Department of Education, 2012). Generally, UBM is adopted by those learning software that collect and provide data to faculty to help them diagnose student learning issues. Carnegie Learning software used user behavior modeling. The software could detect shifts in the classroom (such as the use of a substitute teacher). Social gaming software, such as one developed by Zynga can predict what users want and will do next in a game. This information helps determine how to make games more fun and increase use reengagement. Other software, such as one developed by Onsophic Inc. can capture on and off-task behaviors to help understand online learning.

User Experience Modeling (UEM)

UEM is used to establish student's satisfaction level with the learning experience. This can be ascertained by knowing students' responses to follow-up surveys or questionnaires. UEM is most popular in web-based applications such as online shopping. Some of the software model user experience through methods other than data mining. Zynga uses surveys, user studies, and conduct postmortem analyses. Another experimental approach is to analyze free-text responses given by users responding to a survey. This technique is especially useful when sample of users is large (U.S. Department of Education, 2012). While there exist many commercial software for experience modeling, few applications are available for educational analytics to improve students' learning experience and foster their success and retention rate. Dawson, Heathcote, and Poole (2010) examined effectiveness of higher education institutions in harnessing the data-capture mechanisms from different sources for improving student learning experiences. They found that by considering multiple means of student engagement with university systems, individual activity can be tracked throughout the entire student life cycle. The combined data captured by various systems build a detailed picture of the overall activities in the university and can be used to improve relevance, efficiency, and effectiveness in a higher education institution.

Commercial online course providers such as Kaplan, also use UEM. Kaplan, Inc. uses retention to judge whether its product is meeting customer needs. Kaplan has experimented with course redesigns using analytics where they changed courses on topics such as nutrition. The students in old courses followed a classic online learning sequence and the new courses followed more active learning sequence. The redesigned courses offered opportunities for students to get help when the need it. These courses had built-in assessments and quick surveys for self-efficacy and perceived value. These courses also provided much more structured support for faculty. Kaplan used multiple measures such as periodic surveys of students' motivation state during the course and faculty feedback. Through A/B testing, Kaplan ascertained that the new course was better overall. It is interesting to note that students still reported that they liked the old version more (U.S. Department of Education, 2012).

User Profiling

A user profile is a collection of personal data. This data describes essential characteristics of a user. User profiling is a process using data mining and machine learning to construct and apply student or group profiles. Students differ in their preferences, interests, backgrounds and goals of learning. As such, one common long-term objective of use profiling is to provide personalized learning environments for individual or group of students to maximize learning effectiveness and efficiency. User profiling can be used for a variety of purposes. In commercial firms, it is used to get knowledge about customer behavior and preferences. Commercial firms use profiling to predict the behavior of different types of consumers. These firms can than tailor their marketing strategies (such as personalized advertising). Educational institutions often use data mining techniques (such as classification and clustering) to profile students based on personal learning data or student demographic data or both. Kardan and Conati (2011) proposed a user modeling framework. This framework relies on interaction logs and identify different types of learners and their characteristic interactions with the learning system. A new classification of learners can then be developed based on this information. Game developer companies cluster users into groups. This grouping is done by using behavioral data. Different strategies are used with each group to increase engagement. These groups emerge from the data and often are named on human interpretations of the emergent patterns (e.g. causal players) (U.S. Department of Education, 2012).

Domain Modeling

A domain model is a representation of key concepts that make up a subject or topic area (e.g. mathematics) and also identifies the relationships among all the key concepts or units of study. Research in domain modeling in education investigates how learning is affected by differences in how a topic is divided into key concepts at a particular level of generalization. One example is a case where an HEI wants to specify that students in a class must learn data analysis, statistics, and probability. A more granular requirement could be that students understand data representation techniques. In education, domain modeling is used as an approach to fine-tune learning systems to better serve learning and instruction. Martin et al., (2011) demonstrated how learning curves can be used to drive changes in the user model for personalized learning environments. Martin showed that learning curves for subsets of the domain model yielded insight into the appropriateness of the model's structure and granularity. In the education industry, some learning software companies collect data on objects that teach one concept that cannot be decomposed. They create relationships among topics based on user tags or other actions. This technique can be combined with a feature that enables users to improve on any automatically built relationships or to create their own taxonomies (U.S. Department of Education, 2012).

Learning System Components and Instructional Principle Analysis

Instructional principle analysis examines components of a learning system and types of instructional practices adopted at various time points or for various student groups to address different questions. These questions may include the learning components needed for effective learning, whether the new or old curriculum provides more learning, and the types of instructional practices that are more effective. To get answers to these questions, data collection is needed. This data includes data such as student input and response correctness and student actions on learning system components over time.

Study of the effectiveness of different learning system components and instructional practices can result in better learning systems and improved student learning. As such, it is a key area of research in data analytics (Baker & Yacef, 2009). At Carnegie Mellon, researchers developed cognitive models of mathematics that incorporated the Cognitive Tutor, an intelligent tutoring system. This system decomposed complex tasks into individual knowledge components. Then, a model followed students' actions and diagnosed their strategy in solving a problem (Ritter et al. 2007). Beck and Mostow (2008) proposed learning decomposition to discover most effective pedagogical support. This decomposition, a type of relationship mining, was proposed as an alternative to traditional A/B testing.In this learning decomposition, exponential learning curves were fitted to student performance data and student access to the amount of each type of pedagogical support a student received. A weightage was assigned to each type of support to indicate how effective each type of pedagogical support is for improving learning. Software applications are available that attempt to identify the pedagogical patterns of effective teachers. Here effective teachers are those whose students learn the most. The software can than attempt to predict what happens in the learning system when these other teachers adopt those patterns (U.S. Department of Education, 2012).

Trend Analysis

In general, trend analysis is the practice of collecting information and attempting to discover trend in the information over time which might be partly or nearly completely hidden by data that does not contribute to the pattern (i.e., noise). Commercial online firms use trend analysis to predict what users might be searching for or be interested in. In education, trend analysis is used to answer such questions as what changes have occurred in the student learning over time. Trend analysis can be used to examine test scores and other student indicators over time. Trend analysis can help HEIs determine the impact of policies. Typically longitudinal data from at least three points in time are required to perform a trend analysis. On example of educational trend analysis is the trend analysis of tool provided by Postsecondary Education Commission of California. This tool can examine the commission's database tables to identify trends and discover anomalies with the data (such as gaps when no data were reported) and generate customized reports (such as on enrolment and degree completion) (U.S. Department of Education, 2012).

Adaptation and Personalization

Personalization indicates adaptive pacing, styling instruction to learning preferences, and tailoring content to learners' interest (U.S. Department of Education, 2010a). Adaptation indicates the changes a system or instructor makes in response to students. Adaptation helps personalize students' experience and altering user experience to best serve individual users in real time. User classification techniques and trend analyses are often applied to create models for adapting instruction to students' needs. These adaptations may include feedback to students about their best next actions (U.S. Department of Education, 2012).

A user profile is often created to adapt instruction or personalize student learning experience. This user profile is based on data such as student demographic information. Köck and Paramythis (2011) investigated the monitoring and interpretation of sequential learning activities by analyzing student problem-solving data from a tutoring system (VanLehn et al. 2005).They first converted the activity sequences in the raw data into chain-like models. They then clustered these sequences to detect problem-solving styles.

This section described various application areas of educational data mining and learning analytics techniques to adapt and personalize learning and improve teaching. These applications show the promise of educational data mining and learning analytics. The next section examines challenges and considerations to bring these techniques into higher education.

CHALLENGES AND BARRIERS TO SUCCESSFUL APPLICATION OF LEARNING ANALYTICS

Commercial firms offering learning analytics products are optimistic to personalize their learning systems for a personalized learning experience. Online service providers, such as Yahoo!, Google and Facebook store enormous amounts of personal data. These service providers supported open-source big-data software. One example is Hadoop developed by Adobe Corporation. These service providers also supported collective learning through public gatherings of developers (U.S. Department of Education, 2012).

Educational institutions need to consider many implementation challenges and potential barriers while planning to implement a learning analytics solution. These may include technical challenges, institutional capacity, legal, and ethical issues. Successful implementation of educational learning analytics would require effort and developing an organizational data-driven culture for decision making (U.S. Department of Education 2010). Looking at implementation gaps of learning analytics in commercial and education sectors, it is evident that wide-spread adoption of learning analytics will take few more years (New Media Consortium, 2012; U.S. Department of Education, 2012)).

Technical Challenges

Researchers and developers can use online learning technologies to create personalized learning environments. These learning environments would be based on large datasets that can be analyzed to support continuous improvement. However, the success of such learning environments would be based on the amount of data that can be captured in real time for all the students. There exist many challenges for successful implementation of educational learning analytics techniques. One of them is insufficient technical resources for using big data. Another challenge is the large expenses associated with software services and storage. Research is being conducted to reduce the computer memory requirements needed to support advanced algorithms of learning analytics. However, this is a project that would probably not be successful in near future. In response to these challenges, every learning analytics implementation must consider few issues including the choice of data collection, the questions to be answered, and aligning data with the questions. Developers need to a strategic vision while deciding what data to collect and study the analytic techniques needed to answer the most pressing questions (U.S. Department of Education, 2012).

There are many challenges for data analytics that rely on diverse and distributed data. One such challenge is lack of data interoperability among different data systems. A haphazard approach to procure software can lead to significant decentralization of the source of education data. The US National Center for Education Statistics (NCES) is working to create interoperability among data sources at state level. NCES developed Common Education Data Standards to create and encourage the use of voluntary standards for student data. Adoption of these standards is an important first step to moving data across disparate data systems, and across institutions and education levels.

Student's interaction with an online learning system is commonly used by educational learning analytics to make claims about a student's learning topics. A comparison of scores on assessments and course grades can be used to validate these claims. To provide an integrated view of a student's progress, we need to combine multiple sources of data (e.g., multiple tests). This is not a straightforward task. One problem is that design of existing datasets may not support creating profiles of student behaviors. Another problem is that making claims about student learning based on disparate data sources must meet appropriate standards for valid student assessment (U.S. Department of Education, 2012).

Limitations in Institutional Capacity

Educational institutions can overcome technical challenges research, development, and testing but there are additional costs involved beyond technical challenges. Significant human resources are needed for data preparation, processing, and analysis and integrating various disparate data sources can be expensive and pose requirements beyond the capabilities of the IT department of a single educational institution. It is estimated that 70-85% of the effort in data analytics is devoted to data cleaning, formatting, and alignment (U.S. Department of Education, 2012).

Even when technical challenges are overcome and data is prepared, only smart consumers can use this data. Educators and leadership of educational institutions is overburdened by the amount of data available and need to sort out the useful data. Researchers and developers need to understand the user's challenges for adoption and implementation of analytics in classrooms, schools, and other institutions. With this understanding, developers can pose relevant and important questions to users of learning analytics system and frame their thoughtful and doable recommendations.

We often underemphasize the role of human judgment while adapting, personalizing, and recommending new technologies. People can play key role in many steps of the analytics process and smart consumers can help develop important questions, suggest what data to collect, provide recommendations to make reports meaningful and actionable, help interpret data, discover patterns, and help in model building. Learning analytics helps in human effort of making meaning out of experience. User approach the problem in an informed way, considering what can be acted on, what evidence can came from data analysis, and what early pilots of the analytics applications reveal (U.S. Department of Education, 2012). Learning analytics can provide findings different from the opinions of data consumers (e.g. beliefs about student knowledge, abilities, and effort). As such, the data consumers must use learning analytics with an open mind-set.

Privacy and Ethics Issues

For many years personalized interaction and user modeling have significant privacy implications (Kobsa, 1990). This is because customizing software for individuals need collection of personal information of user. There exists many weaknesses in online companies' privacy protection. For example one can search a social network site for registered email addresses on a large scale (Balduzzi et al., 2010). Balduzzi et al. (2010) used a list of about 10.4 million email addresses and was able to automatically identify more than 1.2 million user profiles associated with the addresses. By performing a quick search on these profiles, they collected publicly available personal information about each user. Online consumer value online content but they also value their privacy (ChoiceStream, 2005). Privacy versus personalization is not a simple trade-off and requires consideration of many factors such as the level of disclosure and personal attitudes (Kobsa 2007; U.S. Department of Education, 2012).

Any effort of collection, storage, analysis, and disclosure of personally identifiable information from students' education records for analytics must consider privacy, policy and legal issues. In US, a federal law called The US Family Educational Rights and Privacy Act (FERPA) protects the privacy of students' education records while generally allowing disclosure of personally identifiable information from a student's education record without consent to officials of educational institution provided there is a legitimate education interest. FEPRA also provides guidelines for institutions; use of detailed and longitudinal student data for research, accountability, and school improvement while maintaining student privacy and parents' rights. It is possible that the institution purchases an externally hosted analytics-based solution from a third party. In that case, the institution would use de-identified student and teacher data to fine-tune predictive models or build models to generate actionable intelligence. Analyses based on large datasets can provide more accurate and valuable predictions when more features of the data are included in the analysis (U.S. Department of Education, 2012).

Since learning analytics predictions are based on the level of access to the student data, there can be a number of social and ethical concerns. It is argued that the learning analysts have an ethical obligation when they gain knowledge about students through data mining. The insights gained should be shared with those who can benefit from them (for example, students, teachers, and parents) and the insights must be presented in a way that benefits than harm. For example, an insight should be shared if it helps improve teaching practices but an insight that tells a student has only 10% chance of success should not be shared. Policymakers have an ethical responsibility to validate any predictive model used to make consequential decisions about students and understand the evidence predictive models use to make predictions. Predictive models may reveal some previously unknown patterns or associations that may involve sensitive data (such as student's family information). These associations and patters should be validated with external observations and more data collection (U.S. Department of Education, 2012).

PRACTICAL/MANAGERIAL IMPLICATIONS AND RECOMMENDATIONS

Early adopters of educational learning analytics are realizing the payoff in terms of improved learning and student retention (Koedinger, McLaughlin, and Heffernan 2010). According to Hamilton et al. (2009), educators can use student data to both track students' performance and decide which instructional practices to adopt for making their teaching more effective. According to Hamilton et al. (2009), students can also use their own assessment data to analyze their strengths/weaknesses and make adjustment in their learning goals accordingly. A clear strategy for developing a data-driven culture and a focus on building infrastructure that provide visualization of aggregated data trends should be the prime target for the educational institutions. Doing so educational institutions will not only get timely and meaningful information but also introduce ethical and privacy considerations in their student learning strategy

(Hamilton et al., 2009). According to Wayman (2005), use of assessment data by educators and students to drive learning improvement is not a new concept but the feasibility of this practice increases when detailed and granular learning data is generated using newly available tools for data mining and analytics. This data-driven approach to learning can be further enhanced by increasing awareness of how these data and tools can be used for product improvement and evidence of their practical application and utility in higher education (Manyika et al. 2011; U.S. Department of Education, 2012).

Commercial firms know the power of using data for rapid improvement of their practices. By experimentation and measurement of change that is understandable this data can lead to actionable future plan. The most important thing for data analysis in education sector is the data presentation in a way that clearly answers a question being asked and point toward a doable action.

Role of Educators

Stakeholders in the higher education should increase the use of educational learning analytics. A prerequisite for this is development of a culture of using data for making instructional decisions. We need a mind-set that more strategic use of data can drive educational improvement (U.S. Department of Education, 2010). Educators need real-time access to easy-to-understand visual representations of student learning data. This data should be detailed enough to guide them in developing useful and actionable strategies for teaching and learning. The educators need to analyze this learning data with a different mind-set. Their purpose is to seek improvement and not the accountability. (U.S. Department of Education, 2012).

IT Department is Part of Learning Analytics Effort

Higher education institutions should understand that their information technology (IT) department is their partner in the effort to improve learning and instruction but this department cannot be held completely responsible for this effort. Establishing a data-driven culture goes beyond having a strong IT department. IT staff should join hands with educators and decision makers in an iterative cycle of improving data collection, processing, analysis, and dissemination. Higher education institutions can establish this data-driven culture by start asking themselves which instructional materials or approaches have been most effective in promoting student learning. Answer to this question would lead them investigate any differences in students success rates and discovering any existing best teaching practices that can be used as a model (U.S. Department of Education, 2012).

Gain Full Understanding of a Proposed Solution

One important thing educational systems should pay attention to when acquiring a learning analytics application is the kinds of learning analytics provided by the application. Educational institutions should ensure that learning analytics application provides information that school leaders and educators could use for learning and instruction improvement. Educational institutions should analyze the sources of data on which the analytics is based, the mechanism of validation of the analytics, the level of data visualization, and the authentication/access mechanism of this analytics. Educators should be involved in the selection process of learning analytics application so they could probe the value that the analytics system will bring to them and the steps they can take in response to the data the system will give them. Educational institutions may adopt predictive models for consequential use (for example for qualifying students for advanced courses). In this case, educational institutions should ensure that these predictive models are transparent and their results are based on solid empirical evidence based on data from similar institutions (U.S. Department of Education, 2012).

Start Small and Leverage the Work of Others

Educational institutions should understand that there are no easy turnkey solutions in educational learning analytics that can integrate all data systems to support powerful learning analytics (Hamilton et al. 2009). The data available to higher education institutions reside in multiple systems in different formats and is typically more than what higher education institutions can use to inform their actions. Many things are still in developing stage such as standards for education information systems, software to facilitate data integration from multiple systems, and easy-to-use data dashboards for different data systems. As such, higher education institutions typically incur significant costs when trying to integrate data across different systems. They also incur additional costs for developing staff capacity for using data in smart ways. Higher education institutions should take adoption of learning analytics as a set of processes and ongoing investments and should start with a small-scale application to build a receptive culture for data use and continuous improvement. This would help educational institution prepare to make the best use of more powerful, economical systems as they become available (U.S. Department of Education, 2012).

Help Students and Parents Understand the Source and Usefulness of Learning Data

Higher education institutions should help students understand the data sources used in learning analytics, how the data are used by learning systems, and how they can use the data to inform their own choices and actions. Feedback is an important variable in changing behavior. Understandable feedback increases students' appropriate response. By providing parents access to assessment data, educational institutions can give parents a chance help their children make smarter choices.

Align Government Policy to Support Learning Analytics

The changes required to adopt an analytics-focused approach to education can be greatly facilitated by the appropriate government policies. For example, the state-level supporting policies can help adoption of online and digital learning at the educational institutions. Digital Learning Now and Data Quality Campaign are two such initiatives to reform implementations. These initiatives highlights the importance of many important things for adoption of learning analytics such as better data systems, faster Internet connections, interoperable and portable electronic student records, and professional development for educators and administrators (U.S. Department of Education, 2012).

To realize full potential of this kind of digital data infrastructure educational institutions will require research to develop and validate new techniques for efficient extraction of evidence of the effectiveness of specific instructional approaches. Learning and education research can help identify potential predictors (or variables) of students' learning and educational attainment. If data analytics techniques can capture these variables in connected data systems then educators can determine the extent to which there are relationships between them and desired outcomes. This can provide educators the evidence both for improving and for choosing among instructional products and practices (U.S. Department of Education, 2012).

Role of Researchers and Developers

Both educational institutions and commercial firms are involved in learning analytics research and development. R&D in learning analytics seeks to understand basic processes of data interpretation, decision making, and learning and to use those insights to develop better systems.

Research of Usability and Impact of Alternative Ways of Data Presentation

There can be alternate ways to present fine-grained learning data to instructors, students, and parents. R&D efforts are needed to analyze the usability and probable impact of these alternate ways of presenting data. Data visualizations can act as a bridge between the information systems and data analytics. As such, an easy-to-understand design of data visualizations is extremely important area for R&D in learning analytics. To do so, R&D efforts need to identify various choices that learning analytics users can make with fine-grained learning data, and the time pressure and cognitive load factors present when different kinds of decisions are made (U.S. Department of Education, 2012).

Decision Supports and Recommendation Engines

R&D efforts should also be focused on building decision support and recommendation engines for educators. Diagnostic real-time assessment tools combined with this additional support, would help educators easily interact with automated systems to make real-time quick decisions to improve instruction for all students (Crawford et al. 2008). To provide further support to educators in their teaching, decision support and recommendation engines should link student learning profiles to recommended instructional actions and learning resources (U.S. Department of Education, 2012).

Anonymization of Data and Tools for Data Aggregation and Disaggregation

R&D face a big challenge of protecting individual's privacy while ensuring advancements in the use of educational data. This requires focus of R&D efforts to anonymize data and tools for data aggregation and disaggregation. In US, The Family Educational Rights and Privacy Act (FERPA) was amended to provide clarification on the legality of states and schools disclosing student data for audit, evaluation, or study purposes. Still, work needs to be done to support aggregation and disaggregation of student data at different levels of the education system. In this aggregation and disaggregation, we also need to combine data from different sources while protecting student privacy in compliance with applicable law.

Develop Models That Help Adopt and Repurpose Learning Analytics and Recommendation Systems in Different Contexts

Currently, learning analytics and recommender system developed in one educational context are difficult to be adapted efficiently in other educational contexts. Different educational models pose serious challenges to develop and implement standard predictive models across different educational contexts. Students, administrative policies, course programs, and/or adopted learning systems often vary among institutions. As such there can be variations in the collected students' data. Therefore, a model that works in one institutions may directly and efficiently applied in another institution without researching the changes required to implement it (Lauría and Baron 2011). Understanding how this process can become more efficient will be key to scaling up the use of learning analytics (U.S. Department of Education, 2012).

Collaborations across Sectors

Capacity building of educational institutions for meaningful use of analytics is a daunting task that can be aided by collaboration among educational institutions and research community. Commercial designers of educational products/systems, educators, and learning specialist can all be part of this collaboration. Commercial designers need knowledge developed by academic research community. Policy makers need these academic research findings and some clear guidelines for effective student learning (O'Neil 2005). With a move towards digital classrooms, learning products are expected to change rapidly. Academic institutions and policy makers need preparation to adapt to these changes. Next five years are expected to bring a wave of new models of collaboration among commercial designers, researchers, and educators. Following are some such models of collaboration (U.S. Department of Education, 2012):

Learning Labs

Learning labs are very helpful for commercial designers of educational products. Commercial designers can use these labs to provide access to data in their learning systems to the researchers. One example is Pittsburgh Science of Learning Center's DataShop based in USA (Koedinger et al. 2010).

Partnerships between Research Organizations and Education Organizations

Strategic Education Research Partnership (SERP) is a US-based organization devoted to simulate innovation in research. SERP provides sustained collaboration among various researchers, designers, and educators in a bid to improve research-based educational products. Researchers work with SERP and partners to develop tools and interventions (U.S. Department of Education, 2012).

Organizational Structures to Attract Human Capital

To improve learning systems, we need sustained interactions among people who have required expertise. These people may come from industry and academia. To do so, we need suitable organizational structures. Digital Promise (digitalpromise.org) is a US-based program. The objective of this program is to foster investments in building strategic partnerships among various stakeholders in order improve learning systems.

FUTURE RESEARCH DIRECTIONS

One area that needs further research is the data collection for learning analytics use. It is important to know the appropriate amount of data needed for analysis. While a top-down approach may be favored here it is important that the data collection and analysis is based on answers of meaningful questions. A targeted strategy for the right data collection should be the pre-requisite of data collection. A bottom-up approach may also be used as it allows collection of more inclusive data collection that allows not the analysis of the main questions but also helps explain some unexpected patterns that may come up during analysis (U.S. Department of Education, 2012).

Another area of research is the selection of the right data structure. Educational data can have many sources and many levels. As such, it is challenging to determine the data structure and data formats that provides accurate representation of the event under consideration. The type of problem to be solved derives the choice of data structure analytic technique to be used. This choice is very important because analysis of focused questions require significant data cleaning and extraction.

CONCLUSION

Use of analytics for working with big data has become a common practice of commercial firms. Sophisticated tools and techniques are now available to both industries and educational institutions. Educational institutions are using analytics as a tool for detecting areas of service improvement (such as policy setting and results measurement) and to make their targets (such as student grades and student retention) more visible and measureable.

Adaptive learning systems have developed to an advanced level. It is now possible to leverage the feedback at individual teacher and student level. Educational institutions are now in the position to measure and make visible student learning and assessment. This, in turn, allows students to monitor their own learning and see where they can improve their performance. Faculty can analyze students' performance to identify appropriate interventions and to modify their teaching styles. Adaptive learning systems provides faculty the ability to quickly observe the results of their interventions and changes in teaching methodologies. Faculty can also provide their continuous feedback to students so that students could improve their performance. It is also possible to quickly compare various approaches of teaching and learning. This allows faculty to keep abreast of the latest developments and adopt latest teaching and learning practices.

There are various factors that are causing fundamental shifts in teaching and learning systems. We see rapidly emerging open-source and commercial tools for adaptive learning systems. Faculty is now better able to draw inferences from the data available. We see that more and more content is moving to the net and mobile technology is becoming common to access this online content. As such, we can forecast that future will be always on and educational data mining and learning analytics will enable learning to be always assessed.

REFERENCES

Alexander, B. (2006). Web 2.0: A new wave of innovation for teaching and learning? *EDUCAUSE Review*, *41*(2), 32.

Amershi, S., & Conati, C. (2009). Combining Unsupervised and Supervised Classification to Build User Models for Exploratory Learning Environments. *Journal of Educational Data Mining*, *1*(1), 18–71.

Anaya, A. R., & Boticario, J. G. (2009). A Data Mining Approach to Reveal Representative Collaboration Indicators in Open Collaboration Frameworks. In T. Barnes, M. Desmarais, C. Romero, & S. Ventura (Eds.), *Proceedings of the 2nd International Conference on Educational Data Mining* (pp. 210–219).

Arnold, K. E. (2010). Signals: Applying Academic Analytics. *EDUCAUSE Quarterly*, *33*(1). Retrieved from http://www.educause.edu/EDUCAUSE+Quarterly/EDUCAUSEQuarterlyMagazineVolum/SignalsApplyingAcademicAnalyti/199385

Arnold, K. E., & Pistilli, M. D. (2012, April). Course Signals at Purdue: Using learning analytics to increase student success. *Proceedings of the 2nd International Conference on Learning Analytics and Knowledge* (pp. 267-270). ACM. doi:10.1145/2330601.2330666

Baepler, P., & Murdoch, C. J. (2010). Academic analytics and data mining in higher education. *International Journal for the Scholarship of Teaching and Learning*, *4*(2), 17.

Bajzek, D., Brooks, J., Jerome, W., Lovett, M., Rinderle, J., Rule, G., & Thille, C. (2008). Assessment and Instruction: Two Sides of the Same Coin. In G. Richards (Ed.), *Proceedings of World Conference on E-Learning in Corporate, Government, Healthcare, and Higher Education 2008*, (pp. 560–565). Chesapeake, VA.

Baker, R. S., Corbett, A. T., Koedinger, K. R., & Wagner, A. Z. (2004). Off-Task Behavior in the Cognitive Tutor Classroom: When Students 'Game the System. *Proceedings of the SIGCHI Conference on Human Factors in Computing Systems (CHI '04)* (pp. 383–390) New York, NY: Association for Computing Machinery. doi:10.1145/985692.985741

Baker, R. S. J. d. (2011). Data Mining for Education. In B. McGaw, P. Peterson, & E. Baker (Eds.), *International Encyclopedia of Education* (3rd ed.). Oxford, UK: Elsevier.

Baker, R. S. J. d., Corbett, A. T., & Aleven, V. (2008). More Accurate Student Modeling Through Contextual Estimation of Slip and Guess Probabilities in Bayesian Knowledge Tracing. *Proceedings of the 9th International Conference on Intelligent Tutoring Systems* (pp. 406–415). Berlin, Heidelberg: Springer-Verlag. doi:10.1007/978-3-540-69132-7_44

Baker, R. S. J. d., Corbett, A. T., Koedinger, K. R., & Roll, I. (2006). Generalizing Detection of Gaming the System across a Tutoring Curriculum. *Proceedings of the 8th International Conference on Intelligent Tutoring Systems* (pp. 402–411). Berlin, Heidelberg: Springer-Verlag.

Baker, R. S. J. d., Gowda, S. M., & Corbett, A. T. (2011). Automatically Detecting a Student's Preparation for Future Learning: Help Use Is Key. In M. Pechenizkiy, T. Calders, C. Conati, S. Ventura, C. Romero, & J. Stamper (Eds.), *Proceedings of the 4th International Conference on Educational Data Mining* (pp. 179–188).

Baker, R. S. J. D., & Yacef, K. (2009). The State of Educational Data Mining in 2009: A Review and Future Visions. *Journal of Educational Data Mining*, *1*(1), 3–17.

Balduzzi, M., Platzer, C., Holz, T., Kirda, E., Balzarotti, D., & Kruegel, C. (2010). Abusing Social Networks for Automated User Profiling (Research Report RR-10-233). EURECOM, Sophia Antipolis; Secure Systems Lab, TU Wien and UCSB.

Bass, R. (2012). Disrupting ourselves: The problem of learning in higher education. *EDUCAUSE Review*, *47*(2), 23–33.

Beck, J. E., & Mostow, J. (2008). How Who Should Practice: Using Learning Decomposition to Evaluate the Efficacy of Different Types of Practice for Different Types of Students. *Proceedings of the 9th International Conference on Intelligent Tutoring Systems* (pp. 353–362). Berlin, Heidelberg: Springer-Verlag . doi:10.1007/978-3-540-69132-7_39

Bienkowski, M., Feng, M., & Means, B. (2012). Enhancing teaching and learning through educational data mining and learning analytics: An issue brief. US Department of Education, Office of Educational Technology.

Blikstein, P. (2011, February). Using learning analytics to assess students' behavior in open-ended programming tasks. *Proceedings of the First International Conference on Learning Analytics and Knowledge* (pp. 110-116). ACM. doi:10.1145/2090116.2090132

Brown, W., Lovett, M., Bajzek, D., & Burnette, J. (2006). Improving the Feedback Cycle to Improve Learning in Introductory Biology Using the Digital Dashboard. In G. Richards (Ed.), *Proceedings of World Conference on E-Learning in Corporate, Government, Healthcare, and Higher Education 2006I*, (pp. 1030–1035) Chesapeake, VA. AACE.

ChoiceStream Personalization Survey: Consumer Trends and Perceptions. (2005). Retrieved from dfshttp://www.choicestream.com/pdf/ChoiceStream_PersonalizationSurveyResults2005.pdf

Corbett, A. T., & Anderson, J. R. (1994). Knowledge Tracing: Modeling the Acquisition of Procedural Knowledge. *User Modeling and User-Adapted Interaction*, *4*(4), 253–278. doi:10.1007/BF01099821

Crawford, V., Schlager, M., Penuel, W. R., & Toyama, Y. (2008). Supporting the Art of Teaching in a Data-Rich, High-Performance Learning Environment. In E. B. Mandinach & M. Honey (Eds.), *Data-Driven School. Improvement* (pp. 109–129). New York, NY: Teachers College Press.

Dawson, S., Heathcote, L., & Poole, G. (2010). Harnessing ICT Potential: The Adoption and Analysis of ICT Systems for Enhancing the Student Learning Experience. *International Journal of Educational Management*, *24*(2), 116–128. doi:10.1108/09513541011020936

Drachsler, H., & Greller, W. (2012, April). The pulse of learning analytics understandings and expectations from the stakeholders. *Proceedings of the 2nd International Conference on Learning Analytics and Knowledge* (pp. 120-129). ACM. doi:10.1145/2330601.2330634

Dyckhoff, A. L., Zielke, D., Bültmann, M., Chatti, M. A., & Schroeder, U. (2012). Design and Implementation of a Learning Analytics Toolkit for Teachers. *Journal of Educational Technology & Society*, *15*(3), 58–76.

Elias, T. 2011. Learning Analytics: Definitions, Processes and Potential. Retrieved from http://learninganalytics.net/LearningAnalyticsDefinitionsProcessesPotential.pdf

Feng, M., Heffernan, N. T., & Koedinger, K. R. (2009). User Modeling and User-Adapted Interaction: Addressing the Assessment Challenge in an Online System That Tutors as It Assesses. *The Journal of Personalization Research*, *19*(3), 243–266.

Fournier, H., Kop, R., & Sitlia, H. (2011). The value of learning analytics to networked learning on a personal learning environment.

Gerhard, F. (2001). User Modeling in Human-Computer Interaction. *User Modeling and User-Adapted Interaction*, *11*(1/2), 65–86. doi:10.1023/A:1011145532042

Goldstein, P. J. 2005. Academic Analytics: The Use of Management Information and Technology in Higher Education. EDUCAUSE Center for Applied Research. Retrieved from http://net.educause.edu/ir/library/pdf/ECM/ECM0508.pdf

Graf, S., & Kinshuk. (in press). Dynamic Student Modeling of Learning Styles for Advanced Adaptivity in Learning Management Systems. *International Journal of Information Systems and Social Change.*

Hamilton, L., Halverson, R., Jackson, S., Mandinach, E., Supovitz, J., & Wayman, J. (2009). *Using Student Achievement Data to Support Instructional Decision Making (NCEE 2009-4067).* Washington, DC: U.S. Department of Education, Institute of Education Sciences, National Center for Education Evaluation and Regional Assistance.

Jeong, H., & Biswas, G. (2008). Mining Student Behavior Models in Learning-by-Teaching Environments. *Proceedings of the 1st International Conference on Educational Data Mining*, (pp. 127–136). Montréal, Québec, Canada.

Johnson, L., Adams Becker, S., Cummins, M., Estrada, V., Freeman, A., & Ludgate, H. (2013). Horizon report (2013 higher education ed.).

Johnson, L., Levine, A., Smith, R., & Stone, S. (2010). The 2010 Horizon Report. Austin, TX: The New Media Consortium. Retrieved from http://wp.nmc.org/horizon2010/

Johnson, L., Smith, R., Willis, H., Levine, A., & Haywood, K. (2011). The 2011 Horizon Report. Austin, TX: The New Media Consortium. Retrieved from http://net.educause.edu/ir/library/pdf/HR2011.pdf

Kardan, S., & Conati, C. 2011. A Framework for Capturing Distinguishing User Interaction Behaviours in Novel Interfaces. In M. Pechenizkiy, T. Calders, C. Conati, S. Ventura, C. Romero, & J. Stamper (Ed.), *Proceedings of the 4th International Conference on Educational Data Mining* (pp. 159–168).

Kim, K., & Bonk, C. J. (2006). The future of online teaching and learning in higher education: The survey says. *EDUCAUSE Quarterly*, *29*(4), 22.

Kobsa, A. (1990). User Modeling in Dialog Systems: Potentials and Hazards. *AI & Society*, *4*(3), 214–231. doi:10.1007/BF01889941

Köck, M., & Paramythis, A. (2011). Activity Sequence Modeling and Dynamic Clustering for Personalized E-Learning. *Journal of User Modeling and User-Adapted Interaction*, *21*(1-2), 51–97. doi:10.1007/s11257-010-9087-z

Koedinger, K., McLaughlin, E., & Heffernan, N. (2010). A Quasi-experimental Evaluation of an On-line Formative Assessment and Tutoring System. *Journal of Educational Computing Research*, *4*(4), 489–510. doi:10.2190/EC.43.4.d

Koedinger, K. R., Baker, R., Cunningham, K., Skogsholm, A., Leber, B., & Stamper, J. (2010). A Data Repository for the EDM Community: The PSLC DataShop. In C. Romero, S. Ventura, M. Pechenizkiy, & R. S. J. d. Baker (Eds.), *Handbook of Educational Data Mining* (pp. 43–55). Boca Raton, FL: CRC Press. doi:10.1201/b10274-6

Lauría, E. J. M., & Baron, J. (2011). Mining Sakai to Measure Student Performance: Opportunities and Challenges in Academic Analytics. Retrieved from http://ecc.marist.edu/conf2011/materials/LauriaECC2011-%20Mining%20Sakai%20to%20Measure%20Student%20Performance%20-%20final.pdf

Lockyer, L., & Dawson, S. (2011, February). Learning designs and learning analytics. *Proceedings of the 1st international conference on learning analytics and knowledge* (pp. 153-156). ACM. doi:10.1145/2090116.2090140

Long, P., & Siemens, G. (2011). Penetrating the Fog: Analytics in Learning and Education. *EDUCAUSE Review*, *46*(5).

Lovett, M., O. Meyer, & C. Thille. (2008). The Open Learning Initiative: Measuring the Effectiveness of the OLI Statistics Course in Accelerating Student Learning. *Journal of Interactive Media in Education* (Special Issue: Researching Open Content in Education).

Macfadyen, L., & Dawson, S. (2012). Numbers Are Not Enough. Why e-Learning Analytics Failed to Inform an Institutional Strategic Plan. *Journal of Educational Technology & Society*, *15*(3), 149–163.

Macfayden, L. P., & Dawson, S. (2010). Mining LMS Data to Develop an 'Early Warning' System for Educators: A Proof of Concept. *Computers & Education*, *54*(2), 588–599. doi:10.1016/j.compedu.2009.09.008

Manyika, J., Chui, M., Brown, B., Bughin, J., Dobbs, R., Roxburgh, C., & Byers, A. H. (2011). Big Data: The Next Frontier for Innovation, Competition, and Productivity. McKinsey Global Institute. Retrieved from http://www.mckinsey.com/Insights/MGI/Research/Technology_and_Innovation/Big_data_The_next_frontier_for_innovation

Martin, B., Mitrovic, A., Koedinger, K., & Mathan, S. (2011). Evaluating and Improving Adaptive Educational Systems with Learning Curves. *User Modeling and User-Adapted Interaction*, *21*(3), 249–283. doi:10.1007/s11257-010-9084-2

Means, B., Chelemer, C., & Knapp, M. S. (Eds.). (1991). *Teaching Advanced Skills to at-Risk Students: Views from Research and Practice*. San Francisco, CA: Jossey-Bass.

Merceron, A., & Yacef, K. (2010). Measuring Correlation of Strong Symmetric Association Rules in Educational Data. In C. Romero, S. Ventura, M. Pechenizkiy, & R. S. J. d. Baker (Eds.), *Handbook of Educational Data Mining* (pp. 245–256). Boca Raton, FL: CRC Press. doi:10.1201/b10274-20

New Media Consortium. 2012. NMC Horizon Project Higher Ed Short List. Austin, TX: New Media Consortium. Retrieved from http://www.nmc.org/news/download-horizon-project-2012-higher-ed-short-list

Next Generation Learning Challenges: Learner Analytics Premises. (2010). Retrieved from http://www.educause.edu/Resources/NextGenerationLearningChalleng/215028

O'Neil, H. F. (2005). *What Works in Distance Learning: Guidelines*. Greenwich, CT: Information Age Publishing.

Pardo, A., & Kloos, C. D. (2011, February). Stepping out of the box: towards analytics outside the learning management system. *Proceedings of the 1st International Conference on Learning Analytics and Knowledge* (pp. 163-167). ACM. doi:10.1145/2090116.2090142

Picciano, A. G. (2012). The Evolution of Big Data and Learning Analytics in American Higher Education. *Journal of Asynchronous Learning Networks*, *16*(3), 9–20.

Reese, D. D., Seward, R. J., Tabachnick, B. G., Hitt, B., Harrison, A., & McFarland, L. (in press). Timed Report Measures Learning: Game-Based Embedded Assessment. In D. Ifenthaler, D. Eseryel, & X. Ge (Eds.), *Assessment in Game-Based Learning: Foundations, Innovations, and Perspectives*. New York, NY: Springer. doi:10.1007/978-1-4614-3546-4_9

Ritter, S., Anderson, J., Koedinger, K., & Corbett, A. (2007). Cognitive Tutor: Applied Research in Mathematics Education. *Psychonomic Bulletin & Review*, *14*(2), 249–255. doi:10.3758/BF03194060 PMID:17694909

Romero, C. R., & Ventura, S. (2010). Educational Data Mining: A Review of the State of the Art. *IEEE Transactions on Systems, Man and Cybernetics. Part C, Applications and Reviews*, *40*(6), 601–618. doi:10.1109/TSMCC.2010.2053532

Siemens, G. (2010). What are learning analytics.

Siemens, G. (2011, January). Learning analytics: A foundation for informed change in Higher Education. *Proceedings of EDUCAUSE Conference*.

Siemens, G. (2012, April). Learning analytics: Envisioning a research discipline and a domain of practice. *Proceedings of the 2nd International Conference on Learning Analytics and Knowledge* (pp. 4-8). ACM. doi:10.1145/2330601.2330605

Siemens, G., & d Baker, R. S. (2012, April). Learning analytics and educational data mining: towards communication and collaboration. *Proceedings of the 2nd international conference on learning analytics and knowledge* (pp. 252-254). ACM. doi:10.1145/2330601.2330661

Siemens, G., & Baker, R. S. J. d. (2012). Learning Analytics and Educational Data Mining: Towards Communication and Collaboration. *Proceedings of LAK12: 2nd International Conference on Learning Analytics & Knowledge* (pp. 252–254). New York, NY: Association for Computing Machinery. doi:10.1145/2330601.2330661

Siemens, G., & Gasevic, D. (2012). Guest Editorial-Learning and Knowledge Analytics. *Journal of Educational Technology & Society*, *15*(3), 1–2.

Siemens, G., Gasevic, D., Haythornthwaite, C., Dawson, S., Shum, S. B., Ferguson, R., ... & Baker, R. S. J. D. (2011). Open Learning Analytics: an integrated & modularized platform. Proposal to design, implement and evaluate an open platform to integrate heterogeneous learning analytics techniques.

Siemens, G., & Long, P. (2011). Penetrating the fog: Analytics in learning and education. *EDUCAUSE Review*, *46*(5), 30–32.

Slade, S., & Prinsloo, P. (2013). Learning Analytics Ethical Issues and Dilemmas. *The American Behavioral Scientist*, *57*(10), 1510–1529. doi:10.1177/0002764213479366

Taibi, D., & Dietze, S. (2013). Fostering analytics on learning analytics research: the LAK dataset.

U.S. Department of Education. (2010). National Education Technology Plan. Retrieved from http://www.ed.gov/technology/netp-2010

Van Barneveld, A., Arnold, K. E., & Campbell, J. P. (2012). *Analytics in higher education: Establishing a common language*. EDUCAUSE Learning Initiative.

VanLehn, K., Lynch, C., Schulze, K., Shapiro, J. A., Shelby, R. H., Taylor, L., & Wintersgill, M. et al. (2005). The Andes Physics Tutoring System: Lessons Learned. *International Journal of Artificial Intelligence in Education*, *15*(3), 147–204.

Verbert, K., Duval, E., Klerkx, J., Govaerts, S., & Santos, J. L. (2013). Learning analytics dashboard applications. *The American Behavioral Scientist*.

Viégas, F. B., Wattenberg, M., McKeon, M., Van Ham, F., & Kriss, J. (2008). Harry Potter and the Meat-Filled Freezer: A Case Study of Spontaneous Usage of Visualization Tools. *Proceedings of the 41st Annual Hawaii International Conference on System Sciences* (p. 159). doi:10.1109/HICSS.2008.188

Wagner, E., & Ice, P. (2012). Data Changes Everything: Delivering on the Promise of Learning Analytics in Higher Education. *EDUCAUSE Review*, *47*(4), 32.

Wayman, J. C. (2005). Involving Teachers in Data-Driven Decision Making: Using Computer Data Systems to Support Teacher Inquiry and Reflection. *Journal of Education for Students Placed at Risk*, *10*(3), 295–308. doi:10.1207/s15327671espr1003_5

Chapter 12
The Role of Learning Analytics in Global Higher Education

Kijpokin Kasemsap
Suan Sunandha Rajabhat University, Thailand

ABSTRACT

This chapter presents the role of learning analytics in global higher education, thus illustrating the theoretical and practical overview of learning analytics; learning analytics and educational data mining (EDM); learning analytics and learning management system (LMS); learning analytics and Course Signals; learning analytics and knowledge perspectives; learning analytics and social networking sites; and the significance of learning analytics in global higher education. The application of learning analytics is critical in global higher education that seeks to serve the school administrators and students, increase educational performance, sustain competitiveness, and fulfill expected accomplishment in global higher education. The chapter argues that applying learning analytics has the potential to improve educational performance and reach strategic goals in the information age.

INTRODUCTION

Learning analytics is a new field that grows at the confluence of learning technologies, educational research, and data science (Ochoa, Suthers, Verbert, & Duval, 2014). Learning analytics aims at using the collected information to improve the quality of a learning experience (Pardo & Siemens, 2014). Learning analytics enables a new level of data-driven decision making for the purpose (Diaz & Fowler, 2012). Learning analytics and educational data mining introduce a number of new techniques and frameworks for learning (Worsley & Blikstein, 2014). Agudo-Peregrina et al. (2014) stated that learning analytics is the analysis of electronic learning data which allows teachers, course designers, and school administrators of virtual learning environments to search for unobserved patterns in the learning processes.

Learning analytics is an emerging research discipline that occupies the middle space between the learning educational research and the use of computational techniques to capture and analyze data (Suthers & Verbert, 2013). Learning analytics needs to better connect with the existing body of research

DOI: 10.4018/978-1-4666-9983-0.ch012

knowledge about learning and teaching (Gašević, Dawson, & Siemens, 2015). Learning analytics can provide the powerful tools for teachers in order to support them in the iterative process of improving the effectiveness of their courses and to enhance their students' performance (Dyckhoff, Zielke, Bültmann, Chatti, & Schroeder, 2012). Learning analytics can help learners to better plan and reflect these learning activities by becoming aware of their actions and learning processes (Scheffel, Drachsler, Stoyanov, & Specht, 2014). The use of technologies has enabled researchers to tackle and study educational challenges in the modern ways (Worsley & Blikstein, 2014).

The strength of this chapter is on the thorough literature consolidation of learning analytics. The extant literature of learning analytics provides a contribution to practitioners and researchers by describing a comprehensive view of the functional applications of learning analytics to appeal to the different segments of learning analytics in order to maximize the educational impact of learning analytics in global higher education.

BACKGROUND

The growth of data surpasses the ability of organizations to make sense of it. This concern is particularly pronounced in relation to knowledge, teaching, and learning. In an age where educational institutions are under growing pressure to reduce costs and increase efficiency, analytics promises to be an important method through which to plan for change at the course and institutions levels. Corporations face pressure for increased competitiveness and productivity, a challenge that requires important contributions in organizational capacity building from both workplace learning and informal learning. Learning analytics can play a role in highlighting the development of employees through their learning activities. The massive adoption of technology in the learning processes comes with an equally large capacity to track the learners (Pardo & Siemens, 2014).

In enterprise settings, information flow and social interactions can yield novel insights into organizational effectiveness and capacity to address new challenges when unanticipated event arise. Advances in knowledge modeling and representation, the semantic web, data mining, analytics, and open data form a foundation for new models of knowledge development and analysis. The technical complexity of this growing field is paralleled by a transition within the complete perspectives of learning (e.g., education, workplace learning, and informal learning) to the networked learning. These technical, pedagogical, and social domains must be brought into dialogue with each other to ensure that the interventions and organizational systems can effectively serve the stakeholders' requirements.

ROLE OF LEARNING ANALYTICS IN GLOBAL HIGHER EDUCATION

This section illustrates the theoretical and practical overview of learning analytics; learning analytics and EDM; learning analytics and LMS; learning analytics and Course Signals; learning analytics and knowledge perspectives; learning analytics and social networking sites; and the significance of learning analytics in global higher education.

Overview of Learning Analytics

The field of learning analytics is concerned with the collection and analysis of data traces related to learning in order to improve learning processes and their outcomes. A distinction can be made between classes of analytics based on the types of data collected and the kinds of decision making targeted (Ferguson, 2012). At a macro level, administrators, and policymakers have the opportunity to use learning analytics to make legislative decisions. In such situations, data on the past learning events is used to make decisions about future perspectives (Clow, 2012), affects the large numbers of people, and involves the outcome data such as summative assessments and performance indicators (Shum & Ferguson, 2012).

Analytics is a field of research and practice that aims to reveal the new patterns of information through the aggregation of large sets of data held in previously distinct sources drawing on a number of informing disciplines (Clarke & Nelson, 2013). Learning analytics emerges from the two converging trends (i.e., the increasing use of virtual learning environment in the educational institutions and the application of data mining techniques to the business intelligence processes in organizational information systems) (Agudo-Peregrina et al., 2014). Learning analytics can be recognized as the information production from the data collected at the course level and at the departmental level (Abhyankar & Ganapathy, 2014). From the course level perspective, the objects of the analysis are social networks, conceptual development, discourse analysis, and intelligent curriculum (Siemens & Long, 2011). The departmental level analysis focuses on the predictive modeling-related patterns of success or failure (Abhyankar & Ganapathy, 2014).

Learning analytics can help managers learn from business changes in global business (Kasemsap, 2015a). Data mining bridges the gap from applied statistics and artificial intelligence to database management by utilizing the process that data is stored and indexed in databases to manipulate the actual learning and discovery algorithms more competently, allowing such data mining methods to be utilized in the larger data sets (Kasemsap, 2015b). Learning analytics is an area of research related to business intelligence, web analytics, academic analytics, action analytics and predictive analytics (Papamitsiou & Economides, 2014). Learning analytics can advance the new research methodologies in education, help educators better assess their pedagogical practices, and arrange innovative educational methods toward improving educational performance (Elias, 2011; Pardo & Delgado, 2011; Siemens, 2012).

Learning analytics can leverage improvement through the improved educational decision making (Arnold, 2010; Norris, Baer, Leonard, Pugliese, & Lefrere, 2008; Vatrapu, Tplovs, Fujita, & Bull, 2011), more timely and frequent feedback for students and teachers (Hamalainen, Suhonen, Sutinen, & Toivonen, 2004; Merceron & Yacef, 2005; Suthers, Ravi, Medina, Joseph, & Dwyer, 2008), the individualization of teaching and learning (Lu, 2004; Talavera & Gaudioso, 2004), and the generation of a richer set of data on student behavior and learning (Baker & Yacef, 2009; Mazza & Dimitrova, 2004; Pavlik, Cen, & Koedinger, 2009).

The emerging conversation goes beyond technologists to include researchers in education, policymakers, educational practitioners, organizational administrators, instructional designers, product vendors, and the learners who are the first adopters of new cloud applications, many of which make data available, and who are the primary consumers of certain kinds of learning analytics (Shum, 2012). Learning analytics derived from the semantically interlinked data can provide a more comprehensive picture of students learning experiences and outcomes, and support the personalization of student's learning process (Ali, Asadi, Gašević, Jovanović, & Hatala, 2013). Siemens (2010) defined learning analytics as the use of intelligent data, learner-produced data, and analysis models to discover the information.

Learning analytics is defined as the measurement, collection, analysis, and reporting of data about learners and their contexts, for the purposes of understanding and optimizing learning and the environments in which it occurs (Siemens & Long, 2011). The effective use of big data can offer the education sector the potential to enhance its systems and outcomes. Norris and Baer (2013) stated that data expands the organizational ability to make sense of complex environments. Learning analytics offers the capacity to investigate the rising tide of learner's data with the goal of understanding activities and behaviors correlated with effective learning, and to leverage knowledge in optimizing educational systems (Bienkowski, Feng, & Means, 2012; Campbell, DeBlois, & Oblinger, 2007). Increasing populations of the increasingly diverse learners focuses on quality and accountability (Macfadyen & Dawson, 2012).

Learning analytics is a collective institutional effort in every way in terms of identifying data, developing analytic models, collaborating with people of diverse skill sets, and determining actionable steps to use the information gathered. Taking action is the critical step and requires the most collaboration and leadership (Diaz & Fowler, 2012). Interactions between students and teachers, as well as interaction among students, may lead to effective learning by means of the intellectual stimulation and the exchange of ideas (Agudo-Peregrina et al., 2014). Successful institutional adoption demands the comprehensive development and the implementation of policies to address the learning analytics challenges of learning design, leadership, institutional culture, data access and security, data privacy and ethical dilemmas, technology infrastructure, and a gap in the institutional learning analytics skills and capacity (Siemens, Dawson, & Lynch, 2013).

In order to be able to understand and optimize the learning processes in virtual learning environment, it is necessary to know which data are stored by the system and to integrate them in a context which gives them a useful meaning for analysis (Agudo-Peregrina et al., 2014). Serrano-Laguna et al. (2012) stated that learning interactivity increases compared to traditional activities (e.g., reading a document), which can be a powerful source of data to support the learning analytics systems that infer knowledge about the effectiveness of the educational process. Learning analytics programs evaluate large data sets to provide decision makers with information that can help determine the best course of action for an organization.

Teachers increasingly use the computer-supported learning in their classrooms to facilitate challenging activities such as collaboration among students (van Leeuwen, Janssen, Erkens, & Brekelmans, 2014). Learning analytics software compares a student's activity with others in the class, with students who previously took the course, and other rubrics to create a model for how each student is likely to fare. In order to improve the learning design of a course and be able to assess its efficiency, teachers should know the real flow of learning activities that students have followed during the course (Fernández-Gallego, Lama, Vidal, & Mucientes, 2013).

In order to support students within a course, teachers should be aware of what the students are doing, how they are interacting with the course material, where comprehension problems arise. If the number of students in the course is high, teachers may need assistance for keeping track of the students' activities with the help of activity-based learner-models (Florian, Glahn, Drachsler, Specht, & Fabregat, 2011). Zinn and Scheuer (2006) conducted a survey among teachers trying to identify requirements for student tracking tools. The built-in student tracking functionality is far from satisfaction (Hijon & Carlos, 2006). Data for learning analytics applications can come from divergent sources and must be converted to the consistent formats and structures to allow the suitable learning analysis.

Learning analytics capitalizes on the vast quantities of data that most universities collect to find patterns that can be utilized to improve learning. Learning analytics seeks to capitalize on the modeling capacity of learning analytics toward predicting behavior, acting on predictions, and feeding those results back into the learning process (Eckerson, 2006) as it relates to the learning practices. Learners are encouraged to think about the context, reliability, validity, certainty, and connectedness of knowledge (Knight, Shum, & Littleton, 2014). The most common use of learning analytics is to indicate students who appear less likely to educationally succeed and to enable the targeted interventions to help them achieve better learning outcomes. Many university faculties practically adopt the learning analytics tools to demonstrate the specific units of study in a course that cause students difficulty. Instructors can modify the learning activities to improve learning on the part of all students.

The adoption of a specific tool for practice is based on how its learning analytics are perceived by educators to support their pedagogical and organizational goals (Ali et al., 2013). Educators who adopt online learning systems are often required to constantly adapt and evolve their online courses to assure high performance and learning efficiency of their students (Gašević, Jovanović, & Devedzic, 2007). Effective adaptation requires a comprehensive and insightful awareness of student's learning experiences, comprehension, and their interactions in the learning systems. By having access to the learning analytics on student's completion status of lessons, educators should have a better sense of students' ability to understand the course contents, the students' social interactions, and knowledge contributions.

Educators require a learning system that provides learning analytics on their online courses that are both comprehensive and informative (Ali et al., 2013). The new field of learning analytics is predicated on the ability of school administrators, instructors, and students to apply technology to mine data in order to improve the student's learning and performance. Such data can be drawn from course management systems, e-portfolios, library systems, student's information systems, clicker systems, external publishers, and other educational sources. Ferguson and Shum (2012) have introduced the concept of social learning analytics to provide mechanisms for identifying patterns and behaviors at both individual level and group level.

Learning Analytics and Educational Data Mining

Educational data mining (EDM) has become a useful method for research in other educational paradigms, with the potential to offer both richness and rigor (Berland, Baker, & Blikstein, 2014). Early research in EDM involved the structured learning environments such as intelligent tutoring systems (Merceron & Yacef, 2004). Within educational technology, there has been a recent expansion of analytical approaches such as EDM (Romero & Ventura, 2010) and academic analytics (van Barneveld, Arnold, & Campbell, 2012). EDM involves the modern research to take educational data and to apply data mining techniques such as prediction, the discovery of latent structure (e.g., clustering and q-matrix discovery), relationship mining (e.g., association rule mining and sequential pattern mining), and discovery with models to understand the learning and learner's individual differences (Romero & Ventura, 2010).

EDM methods and related learning analytics methods have been utilized to study programming and the development of programming skills, including the learners' patterns in program construction, compilation, and debugging (Berland, Martin, Benton, Smith, & Davis, 2013), modeling programmers' trajectories within an assignment using Hidden Markov Models (Piech, Sahami, Koller, Cooper, & Blikstein, 2012), the inference of what a student is trying to program (Vee, Meyer, & Mannock, 2006), and the prediction of whether the student is at risk of failing to acquire the programming skill (Dyke, 2011). Access to the extension of data has been central to the development and proliferation of both the learning analytics and EDM communities (Baker & Yacef, 2009).

EDM is related to the development of methods for analysis of learning data (Baker & Yacef, 2009). EDM practically supports the educational institutions in developing, researching, and applying computerized methods in order to detect patterns in the collection of educational data (Romero & Ventura, 2013). EDM is used to model the student's strategies (Amershi & Conati, 2009), student's behaviors related to disengagement (Baker, Corbett, Roll, & Koedinger, 2008), student's emotions (D'Mello, Lehman, & Person, 2010), longer-term student's learning (Baker, Gowda, & Corbett, 2011), and participation in future learning (Arnold, 2010). EDM can support the real-time assessment on student's process and progress, in which the amount of formative feedback is fundamentally increased (Berland et al., 2014).

EDM promotes the learning progress (Shute, 2008), supports opportunity for the teacher's insight into the student's learning (Roschelle, Penuel, Yarnall, Shechtman, & Tatar, 2005), and provides a constructive foundation for continuous learning evaluation. EDM can support teachers in learning, which owing to the reasons of practicality is found in more affluent schools (Warschauer & Matuchniak, 2010), by providing access to more data to support the students' progress monitoring and teachers' continual assessment of progress. EDM techniques can help organize the work of analytical type (Sherin, 2012). By combining EDM with qualitative analysis, it is possible to strengthen the qualitative arguments that use the discourse analysis by exploring regularities and similarities (Duncan & Berland, 2012).

Learning Analytics and Learning Management System

Learning management system (LMS) is broadly utilized and has become part of the educators' toolkits (Schroeder, 2009). The effort of researchers from a broad range of disciplines (e.g., science, education, linguistics, neuroscience, and psychology) can provide an influential impetus toward understanding complex learning processes through the combination of analytical methods (Mirriahi, Gašević, Long, & Dawson, 2014). Educational institutions have placed a high degree of importance on their reputations rather than on improving academic performance of their students (Norris et al., 2008). Much of the data on which learning analytics applications depend comes from the LMS, the rates of participation in specific activities, and time that students spend interacting with online resources in the class.

One of the major goals of the integration of traditional teaching methods with technology enhancement is the improvement of teaching and learning quality in the university courses with many students (Dyckhoff et al., 2012). Applications that perform data analysis are either built into or added onto the LMS from which they draw primary data. LMS vendors increasingly offer the analytics tools linked to their software, while other learning analytics applications are built by universities or by third parties to work with the LMS. Researchers have used the tracking data of student's activities in LMS to examine student's learning, they emphasize the student as the analysis unit, ignoring the instructor's role and the relationship between student and instructor (Ma, Han, Yang, & Cheng, 2015).

Student information systems and learner's interactions with various technologies such as LMS and social media leave a trail of digital perspectives that are accessible for data mining and analysis (Duval, 2011; Fournier, Kop, & Sitlia, 2011; Shum & Ferguson, 2012). Data analysis derived from these technologies has captured the attention of politicians, education leaders, researchers, and education practitioners. This is partly due to the expectation that these relatively new forms of learning analytics can address more pressing concerns confronting the education sector. These concerns include increasing completion rates, addressing basic curriculum standards, student's questionnaire overload, accountability, and measuring teaching effectiveness.

Recent research has explored the students' social networks by obtaining data from the instructors and students' activities in the online discussion forums (Cambridge & Perez-Lopez, 2012; Rahman & Dron, 2012; Wise, Zhao, & Hausknecht, 2013). As for the analysis unit of researches using the tracking data to examine teaching and learning, most of previous studies have employed the student as the unit in a course to analyze the correlation between student's activities and their academic achievement (Agudo-Peregrina et al., 2014). Macfadyen and Dawson (2010) employed 118 students as the sample, capturing their LMS tracking data in the online undergraduate course to study which variables can predict the student's achievement.

Smith et al. (2012) conducted the research about the engagement perspective. In the research, 539 students were selected as the sample in the online freshman-level course. The researchers tried to identify if the key variables of students' activities can be used to predict the students' course outcome. Morris et al. (2005) used 354 students enrolled in three courses to evaluate the relationship between student's online participation behavior and their achievement. Falakmasir and Habibi (2010) ranked the online learning activities of 824 students in 11 courses based on their impact on students' final grades. Instructor's activity tracking data records cannot be employed as the variables to examine the relationship between the instructors and students. Dawson et al. (2008) acknowledged the instructors' engagement in the context of the whole institution level and faculty management level.

Learning Analytics and Course Signals

There are the notable exceptions including the Course Signals project (Course Signals, 2013), initially developed at Purdue University, which has gathered the worth of evidence, and from which a commercial product has been created (Arnold & Pistilli, 2012). Using the trace data collected by the Blackboard LMS and data from the institutional student information system, Course Signals uses a data-mining algorithm to indicate the students at risk of academic failure in a course (Gašević et al., 2015). While Course Signals is a recognized example, there have been many other predictive algorithms aimed toward the identification of students at risk of failure or retention (Jayaprakash, Moody, Lauria, Regan, & Baron, 2014).

Course Signals illustrates the three main outcome types (i.e., a student at a high risk, moderate risk, and not at risk of failing the course) (Gašević et al., 2015). The three outcomes are symbolically represented as traffic light where each light represents one of the three levels of risk (i.e., red, orange, and green). The traffic lights serve to provide an early warning signal to both instructor and student. This signal is designed to prompt a form of intervention that is aimed at improving the progression of the student identified as at risk of failure. Early studies of Course Signals showed the high levels of predictive precision and important benefits in the retention of the students who took at least one course adopting the early alert software versus those who took a course without the Course Signals tool (Arnold & Pistilli, 2012).

Course Signals software incorporates the student's past academic performance, demographics with LMS activity, and engagement to provide a statistical assessment of an individual learner's probability for success (Arnold, 2010). In the instance of Course Signals, learning success is measured by an individual's overall assessment score. The direction of the Course Signals software is to provide the early warning indicators to learners and instructors regarding an individual's risk of the course failure. The examples of Course Signals are the exception rather than the rule and considerable work is still required to translate the current research into the application of learning analytics approaches to teaching and learning. Any predictive model is accompanied by a dashboard to support the sense-making perspective by visualizing the trace data and prediction results (Ali, Hatala, Gašević, & Jovanović, 2012).

Learning Analytics and Knowledge Perspectives

Learning analytics and knowledge perspectives are broadly recognized on the research areas. Verbert et al. (2012) stated that the learning analytics and knowledge perspectives include the six major items (e.g., predicting learner's performance and modeling learners, suggesting relevant learning resources, increasing reflection and awareness, enhancing social learning environments, detecting undesirable learner behaviors, and detecting effects of learners).

1. Predicting learner's performance and modeling learners. The prediction of learner's performance and modeling of learners have been researched by the educational data mining, educational user modeling, and educational adaptive hypermedia communities. The aim of this perspective is to evaluate the unknown value of a variable that explains the learner in terms of performance, knowledge, scores, and learner's grades (Romero & Ventura, 2007). The predictions are employed by the intelligent tutoring systems to provide suggestion when a learner is solving a problem.

Predicting student's learning success and providing proactive feedback have been two of the most frequently adopted tasks related to learning analytics (Dawson, Gašević, Siemens, & Joksimovic, 2014). Several data sets are available that can support the research on prediction of learner's performance and discovery of learner models (Verbert et al., 2012). Romero et al. (2008) compared the different data mining techniques to classify learners based on the LMS data and the final grade obtained for courses. Data sets that have been captured from the personal learning environments effectively offer the interesting perspectives to elaborate the research in the open learning environments (Verbert et al., 2012). Dynamic learner models are implemented to support the adjustment in the educational hypermedia systems (Brusilovsky & Millan, 2007).

2. Suggesting relevant learning resources. In the field of education, the term technology-enhanced learning (TEL) gets special focus due to the utilization and consumption of modern technology to assist learning (Abhyankar & Ganapathy, 2014). The need for better measurement, collection, analysis, and reporting of data about learners has been described by several researchers in TEL field (Duval, 2011). Recommender systems for learning have gained the increased interest in recent years. Manouselis et al. (2011) developed the survey of TEL recommender systems. Recommender systems analyze the learner's data to suggest the relevant learning resources, peer learners, and learning paths (Verbert et al., 2012).
3. Increasing reflection and awareness. Several researchers emphasize the analysis and visualization of different learning indicators to promote awareness and reflection about learning processes. These indicators involve the resource access, time spending, and knowledge level indicators (Mazza & Milani, 2005). Other data sets contain timestamp information that can be applied to derive the indicators of the time that users were active (Verbert et al., 2012).
4. Enhancing social learning environments. The visualization of social interaction is investigated to make people aware of their social context and to enable them to explore this context (Heer & Boyd, 2005). In TEL, this is relevant for the computer-supported collaborative learning (CSCL) (Stahl, 2009), where the interactions with peer learners are an influential aspect of how learning is organized. In CSCL, much research has focused on the analysis of networks of learners with a social network analysis approach (Reffay & Chanier, 2003).

5. Detecting undesirable learner behaviors. The objective of detecting undesirable learner behavior is to discover those learners who have many types of problem such as erroneous actions, misuse, cheating, dropping out, and academic failure (Romero & Ventura, 2007). Data sets derived from the personal learning environments provide a rich source of data to detect unusual behavior, as these data sets record the learners' actions with various tools that they were utilizing during the classes (Verbert et al., 2012).
6. Detecting affects of learners. Researchers in TEL refer to the affective states determined by D'Mello et al. (2007). The affective states are categorized as boredom, confusion, frustration, eureka, engagement, versus neutral. The adoption of emoticons and affective words is investigated in social interaction data sets (Reffay, Teplovs, & Blondel, 2011). Conati and Maclaren (2005) conducted the research in building a user model of affect from real data. The detection of affects is analyzed to adjust the pedagogical strategies during the learning of complex material (Verbert et al., 2012).

Learning Analytics and Social Networking Sites

Information technology applied in higher education has influenced the teaching strategies, learning methods, activities, and the way that students are engaging with their study (Coates, 2007). The degree to which students have been actively engaged in their academic task considerably affects the level of their learning outcomes, cognitive development, and educational quality (Kuh, 2003). Discussing the engagement issues can help examine the students' online learning activities, and evaluate the quality of online teaching and learning in order to help the instructors design the appropriate online courses and implement the necessary support strategies to improve the quality of online learning (Robinson & Hullinger, 2008). Learning analytics can capture the direct data of online activities, thus providing more authentic, objective, and evidence in the modern educational world (Lockyer, Heathcote, & Dawson, 2013).

A vast proliferation of data has forced the modern organizations to use information technology as a platform for a more analytical approach to management and decision making (LaValle, Lesser, Shockley, Hopkins, & Kruschwitz, 2011). Business analytics, data mining, and knowledge discovery have become the major trends in the application of information technology toward increasing organizational performance (Hostmann, Rayner, & Herschel, 2009). Computers, tablets, and mobile devices offer the technological tools to support learning, both inside and outside the classroom (Monroy, Rangel, & Whitaker, 2014). Web-based learning systems are built under the promise to make the anywhere and anytime learning vision possible by transcending the time and space boundaries inherent to the traditional classroom-based teaching and learning (Ali et al., 2012).

It is commonplace to perceive the learning and knowledge building as the related activities on the Web 2.0 (Halatchliyski, Hecking, Göhnert, & Hoppe, 2014). Knowledge creation as a social product (Scardamalia & Bereiter, 2006) effectively bounds the learning environments, networks, and communities of people. Exploring how many posts students read has been found to be informative (Gunnarsson & Alterman, 2012). The traditional classroom is changing, with devices (e.g., laptop and smartphone) that access the Internet, connecting the classroom to the modern educational world (Gunnarsson & Alterman, 2014). Blogs are widely used for various educational purposes (Ducate & Lomicka, 2005). Blogs are recognized as an open journal (Zagal & Bruckman, 2007) and a tool of reflection (Deng & Yuen, 2011).

Student's blogging has been reported to have the positive effects on higher order thinking skills (Philip & Nicholls, 2009), knowledge sharing (Du & Wagner, 2006), the learning process beyond the classroom (Ferdig & Trammell, 2004), sense of ownership (Hong, 2008), sense of community as measured by the community dimension (Deng & Yuen, 2011), and identity development (Luehmann, 2008). Social networking sites help support the technological connection to the data and video information in the knowledge-based organizations (Kasemsap, 2014a). Leaders of global businesses should effectively adjust information and communications technology skills to improve their knowledge of social networking sites (Kasemsap, 2014b).

Blogging is a simple activity requiring technical skills (e.g., click buttons to write, publish, browse, read, and comment). Different methods of measuring content quality have been applied to blogs (Huang, Cheng, & Huang, 2009) such as automated methods based on various quality measures (Kargar & Azimzadeh, 2009), classification of different types of blog posts using machine learning techniques (Ni, Xue, Ling, Yu, & Yang, 2007), and using natural language processing (Rubin & Liddy, 2006). New features are added to blogs toward enhancing the learning methods such as the dynamic learning maps (Wang, Huang, Jeng, & Wang, 2008).

Meta-data (e.g., promotions and tags) produced by the students can increase the students' involvement (Gunnarsson & Alterman, 2014). Counting comments, counting external links, login data, load time, and other features (Kargar & Azimzadeh, 2009) can help make sense of the online community. The blogosphere gives students the opportunity to collaborate outside of class in a loosely coordinated manner (Alterman & Larusson, 2013). Multiple conversations emerge on a single topic, thus enabling greater coverage and diversity with reduced coordination costs (Gunnarsson & Alterman, 2014). Students publish to the rest of the class, providing the examples of work (Benkler & Nissenbaum, 2006).

Significance of Learning Analytics in Global Higher Education

Higher education institutions are a superb example of complex adaptive systems (MacLennan, 2007) and exist in a state that some have characterized as the organized anarchy (Cohen & Marsh, 1986). Universities have focused on increasing the number of online courses and program offered (Meyer, 2014). The urge for higher education expansion has placed the undue pressures on the state of quality enhancement and autonomy of universities (Akalu, 2014). The goal of first-generation learning analytics is intervention for at-risk students toward helping them educationally succeed. Students who are having difficulties are not certain what action they should take or how they should approach their instructors.

Despite the depth and range of data available and its ability to inform a diversity of end-users, to date there has been the limited application of data in global higher education (Dawson, Heathcote, & Poole, 2010). Educators often lack the specific information that they need to identify the important performance issues. Learning analytics is positioned to provide the insights and information to directly support the student's success, as defined by increasing retention and completion rates among the first-generation and underrepresented students (Diaz & Fowler, 2012). Learning analytics looks at student's behavior that can be indicative of learning. An instructor's course preparation is positively related to the student's viewing activities, while instructor's guidance has a significant impact on the student's learning tasks (Ma et al., 2015).

Learning analytics offers the modern ways for learners to improve and develop while a course is in progress (Ferguson, 2014). Results of learning analytics can be used to foster the awareness and reflection (Verpoorten, Westera, & Specht, 2011) and to give recommendations for further steps in a current learning scenario (Greller & Drachsler, 2012). Reflection can promote the insight into something that previously went unnoticed (Bolton, 2010) and lead to a change in learning behavior. Awareness and reflection support for students are the highly important aims of learning analytics (Scheffel et al., 2014).

Learning analytics takes the specific goal of improving the learning outcomes which can be measured by grades, retention, and completion. Using digital communication is relatively new in learning (Gunnarsson & Alterman, 2014). Common communication methods are e-mail, forum posts, blog posts, and chat rooms. Creating sense-making visualizations for instructors and school administrators (Dawson, 2010), exploring knowledge building in online social settings (Ferguson & Shum, 2012), and data mining institution-sized data sets (Smolin & Budakov, 2012) are the examples of work done in the learning analytics.

In the learning analytics environment, students collaborate in a blogging environment throughout the semester, thus distributing knowledge and building skills (Alterman & Larusson, 2013). Giving students access to each other's contributions is the foundation for a knowledge community (Scardamalia & Bereiter, 1994), with each contribution representing a different perspective that provides scaffolding for others to improve. Individual perspectives are shared, developed (Stahl, 2003), and composed (Suthers, 2006). Different contributions and examples on the same subject are the multiple representations, which are valuable for learning (Ainsworth, 2006), and can lead to higher order thinking (Ellison & Wu, 2008). Depending on the technology that mediates peer collaboration, there will be different benefits. For example, a blogosphere is valuable as a resource for co-reflection among the students, which is helpful for learning (Deng & Yuen, 2011).

Although to date the field of learning analytics has focused on learner progression and developing lead indicators of student attrition (Campbell et al., 2007; Fritz, 2011), there is much potential in using student's interaction data to establish the indicators of more complex concepts such as knowledge construction (Pozzi, Manca, Persico, & Sarti, 2007), sense of community (Dawson, 2006), creativity (Dawson, 2010; Dawson, McWilliam, & Tan, 2011), and self-regulated learning (Biswas, Jeong, Kinnebrew, Sulcer, & Roscoe, 2010; Winne & Hadwin, 2013). Regarding learning analytics, data gathering across such an environment allows a student's probability of success to be measured against a broader base, resulting in more reliable assessments of the interplay of factors that are associated with the different learning outcomes and in more effective strategies for helping at-risk students get back on track to succeed. Watson and Gemin (2008) defined at-risk as students with a high probability of withdrawing from the course as a result of academic failure, dropping out, and expulsion for behavioral reasons.

Learning analytics uses the data related to a learner's interactions with content, other learners, and the educational institution to make decisions and evaluations about teaching practices, personalized content, and required interventions for learner's success. Learning analytics practically integrates research and methodology related to data mining, social network analysis, data visualization, machine learning, learning sciences, psychology, semantics, artificial intelligence, e-learning, and educational theory and practice. Learning analytics emphasizes the interpretation of the educational data from a learner and teacher orientation. Learning analytics places emphasis on understanding the pedagogical context from where the data is derived as developing predictive models.

Regarding learning analytics, the types of analyses performed vary, but one approach involves the evaluation of historical student data to create predictive models of successful and at-risk students. Reports can take various forms, but most feature data visualizations designed to facilitate the quick understanding of which students are likely to succeed. Learning analytics applications can provide this information to students and faculty. Many systems progressively inform users. Other systems require users to take some actions to evaluate the reports. Learning analytics offers colleges and universities an effective way to use data, predict student success, and improve the tailoring of student's services to meet the student's requirements.

Learning analytics tools can track far more data than an instructor can alone. Learning analytics provides a support structure that monitors student's progress and offers guidance to students. The applications of learning analytics can indicate the learning factors related to the student's learning and course completion. This information can be valuable to students, in how they approach learning, and to faculty, in how they structure curricula. Learning analytics can provide data to instructors who can measure whether a class understands the concepts in the coursework and make changes in real time to remove the barrier to learning. In the area of institutional accountability, learning analytics tools can leverage information attached in student's records to show that student's monitoring is done on a routine basis.

When conducted within the boundaries of how an educational institution approaches the privacy of student's data and in alignment with an educational institution's philosophy about academic interventions and student's self-direction, learning analytics can help acknowledge how a student might be veering off track in academic progress in ways that suggest interventions to improve the educational performance. The interest in the learning analytics is energized by increasing the calls for accountability, the quest for evidence, and the demonstration of what counts as learning and teaching quality. The accessibility to student's learning data from various information systems has contributed to the use of learning analytics as a tool for informing the strategic decision-making process within educational institutions (Macfadyen & Dawson, 2012).

Although the concept of using the patterns of analytics for informing educational practice has been received, the majority of educational institutions seldom make optimal use of their available data and analytical resources (Norris et al., 2008). As a result of the relative infancy of the field of learning analytics, the level and sophistication of the data analysis performed has been limited (Dawson et al., 2014). The low-level analysis (e.g., the reporting of student's login times), the number of posted messages in a discussion forum, and total time online are the learning analytics approaches.

FUTURE RESEARCH DIRECTIONS

The strength of this chapter is on the thorough literature consolidation of learning analytics. The extant literature of learning analytics provides a contribution to practitioners and researchers by describing a comprehensive view of the functional applications of learning analytics to appeal to the different segments of learning analytics in order to maximize the educational impact of learning analytics in global higher education. The classification of the extant literature in the domain of learning analytics will provide the potential opportunities for future research.

Practitioners and researchers should recognize the applicability of a more multidisciplinary approach toward research activities in implementing learning analytics in terms of cloud computing and social media. It will be useful to bring additional disciplines together (e.g., strategic management, marketing, finance, and human resources) to support a more holistic examination of learning analytics in order to combine or transfer existing theories and approaches to inquiry in this area.

CONCLUSION

This chapter presented the role of learning analytics in global higher education, thus illustrating the theoretical and practical overview of learning analytics; learning analytics and EDM; learning analytics and LMS; learning analytics and Course Signals; learning analytics and knowledge perspectives; learning analytics and social networking sites; and the significance of learning analytics in global higher education. Learning analytics is an educational application of web analytics, a science that is broadly utilized by businesses to analyze commercial activities, identify spending trends, and predict consumer behavior. Learning analytics applies techniques from information science, sociology, psychology, statistics, machine learning, and data mining to analyze the data collected during education services, teaching, and learning.

Education is embarking on a similar pursuit into data science with the aim of learner profiling, a process of gathering and analyzing large amounts of detail about student's interactions in online learning activities. The goals of learning analytics are to build better pedagogies, empower student to take an active part in their learning, target at-risk student populations, and evaluate factors affecting completion and student's success. Learning analytics can gather data, analyze data, generate reports, and enable interventions in the modern educational world. The type of data gathered varies by institution and by application, but it includes information about the frequency with which students access online materials and the educational results of assessments from student's exercises and activities conducted online.

The application of learning analytics is critical in global higher education that seeks to serve the school administrators and students, increase educational performance, sustain competitiveness, and fulfill expected accomplishment in global higher education. Using information gathered from learning analytics, the higher education institutions can improve its early detection of risk factors for student's failure in order to improve student's persistence toward educational course completion. The process of learning analytics can enable students, faculty, and school administrators to recognize the student's problems and risks earlier and respond more effectively. Learning analytics can lead to the crucial interventions that can help students complete their educational programs. The higher education institutions can apply lessons drawn from learning analytics to deepen student's learning and engagement by pedagogy.

To be successful in learning analytics, more education is required among school administrators, faculty, and other stakeholders about what learning analytics is and how it can help advance the educational goals for student's academic success and degree completion in global higher education. It is required for the higher education institutions to apply their learning analytics, develop a strategic plan to regularly check their practical advancements, and immediately respond to the learning analytics needs of the school administrators and students in global higher education. Applying learning analytics in global higher education has the potential to improve educational performance and gain sustainable competitive advantage in the information age.

REFERENCES

Abhyankar, K., & Ganapathy, S. (2014). Technology-enhanced learning analytics system design for engineering education. *International Journal of Information and Education Technology*, *4*(4), 345–350. doi:10.7763/IJIET.2014.V4.427

Agudo-Peregrina, A. F., Iglesias-Pradas, S., Conde-Gonzalez, M. A., & Hernandez-Garcia, A. (2014). Can we predict success from log data in VLEs? Classification of interactions for learning analytics and their relation with performance in VLE–supported F2F and online learning. *Computers in Human Behavior*, *31*, 542–550. doi:10.1016/j.chb.2013.05.031

Ainsworth, S. (2006). DeFT: A conceptual framework for considering learning with multiple representations. *Learning and Instruction*, *16*(3), 183–198. doi:10.1016/j.learninstruc.2006.03.001

Akalu, G. A. (2014). Higher education in Ethiopia: Expansion, quality assurance and institutional autonomy. *Higher Education Quarterly*, *68*(4), 394–415. doi:10.1111/hequ.12036

Ali, L., Asadi, M., Gašević, D., Jovanović, J., & Hatala, M. (2013). Factors influencing beliefs for adoption of a learning analytics tool: An empirical study. *Computers & Education*, *62*, 130–148. doi:10.1016/j.compedu.2012.10.023

Ali, L., Hatala, M., Gašević, D., & Jovanović, J. (2012). A qualitative evaluation of evolution of a learning analytics tool. *Computers & Education*, *58*(1), 470–489. doi:10.1016/j.compedu.2011.08.030

Alterman, R., & Larusson, J. A. (2013). Participation and common knowledge in a case study of student blogging. *International Journal of Computer-Supported Collaborative Learning*, *8*(2), 149–187. doi:10.1007/s11412-013-9167-2

Amershi, S., & Conati, C. (2009). Combining unsupervised and supervised classification to build user models for exploratory learning environments. *Journal of Educational Data Mining*, *1*(1), 18–71.

Arnold, K. E. (2010). Signals: Applying academic analytics. *EDUCAUSE Quarterly*, *33*(1), n1.

Arnold, K. E., & Pistilli, M. D. (2012). *Course Signals at Purdue: Using learning analytics to increase student success.* Paper presented at the Second International Conference on Learning Analytics and Knowledge LAK '12, Vancouver, Canada. doi:10.1145/2330601.2330666

Baker, R., Corbett, A. T., Roll, I., & Koedinger, K. R. (2008). Developing a generalizable detector of when students game the system. *User Modeling and User-Adapted Interaction*, *18*(3), 287–314. doi:10.1007/s11257-007-9045-6

Baker, R., Gowda, S., & Corbett, A. T. (2011). Towards predicting future transfer of learning. In G. Biswas, S. Bull, J. Kay, & A. Mitrovic (Eds.), *Artificial intelligence in education* (pp. 23–30). Berlin, Germany: Springer–Verlag. doi:10.1007/978-3-642-21869-9_6

Baker, R., & Yacef, K. (2009). The state of educational data mining in 2009: A review and future visions. *Journal of Educational Data Mining*, *1*(1), 3–17.

Benkler, Y., & Nissenbaum, H. (2006). Commons-based peer production and virtue. *Journal of Political Philosophy*, *14*(4), 394–419. doi:10.1111/j.1467-9760.2006.00235.x

Berland, M., Baker, R., & Blikstein, P. (2014). Educational data mining and learning analytics: Applications to constructionist research. *Technology. Knowledge and Learning*, *19*(1/2), 205–220. doi:10.1007/s10758-014-9223-7

Berland, M., Martin, T., Benton, T., Smith, C. P., & Davis, D. (2013). Using learning analytics to understand the learning pathways of novice programmers. *Journal of the Learning Sciences*, *22*(4), 564–599. doi:10.1080/10508406.2013.836655

Bienkowski, M., Feng, M., & Means, B. (2012). *Enhancing teaching and learning through educational data mining and learning analytics: An issue brief.* Washington, DC: U.S. Department of Education Office of Educational Technology.

Biswas, G., Jeong, H., Kinnebrew, J., Sulcer, B., & Roscoe, R. (2010). Measuring self-regulated learning skills through social interactions in a teachable agent environment. *Research and Practice in Technology-Enhanced Learning*, *5*(2), 123–152. doi:10.1142/S1793206810000839

Bolton, G. (2010). *Reflective practice: Writing and professional development*. London, UK: Sage Publications.

Brusilovsky, P., & Millan, E. (2007). User models for adaptive hypermedia and adaptive educational systems. In P. Brusilovsky, A. Cobsa, & W. Nejdl (Eds.), *The adaptive web: Methods and strategies of web personalization* (pp. 3–53). Berlin, Germany: Springer–Verlag. doi:10.1007/978-3-540-72079-9_1

Cambridge, D., & Perez-Lopez, K. (2012). First steps towards a social learning analytics for online communities of practice for educators. *Paper presented at the Second International Conference on Learning Analytics and Knowledge LAK '12*, Vancouver, Canada. doi:10.1145/2330601.2330622

Campbell, J., De Blois, P. B., & Oblinger, D. (2007). Academic analytics: A new tool for a new era. *EDUCAUSE Review*, *42*(4), 42–57.

Clarke, J., & Nelson, K. (2013). Perspectives on learning analytics: Issues and challenges. Observations from Shane Dawson and Phil Long. *The International Journal of the First Year in Higher Education*, *4*(1), 1–8. doi:10.5204/intjfyhe.v4i1.166

Clow, D. (2012). *The learning analytics cycle: Closing the loop effectively.* Paper presented at the Second International Conference on Learning Analytics and Knowledge LAK '12, Vancouver, Canada. doi:10.1145/2330601.2330636

Coates, H. (2007). A model of online and general campus-based student engagement. *Assessment & Evaluation in Higher Education*, *32*(2), 121–141. doi:10.1080/02602930600801878

Cohen, M. D., & Marsh, J. G. (1986). *Leadership and ambiguity: The American college president*. New York, NY: McGraw–Hill.

Conati, C., & Maclaren, H. (2005). Data-driven refinement of a probabilistic model of user affect. In L. Ardissono, P. Brna, & A. Mitrovic (Eds.), *User modeling 2005* (pp. 40–49). Berlin, Germany: Springer–Verlag.

Course Signals. (2013). *Course signals*. Retrieved from http://www.itap.purdue.edu/learning/tools/signals/

D'Mello, S. K., Lehman, B., & Person, N. (2010). Monitoring affect states during effortful problem solving activities. *International Journal of Artificial Intelligence in Education*, *20*(4), 361–389. doi:10.3233/JAI-2010-012

D'Mello, S. K., Picard, R. W., & Graesser, A. (2007). Towards an affect-sensitive AutoTutor. *IEEE Intelligent Systems, 22*(4), 53–61. doi: 10.1109/MIS.2007.79

Dawson, S. (2006). Relationship between student communication interaction and sense of community in higher education. *The Internet and Higher Education*, *9*(3), 153–162. doi:10.1016/j.iheduc.2006.06.007

Dawson, S. (2010). "Seeing" the learning community: An exploration of the development of a resource for monitoring online student networking. *British Journal of Educational Technology*, *41*(5), 736–752. doi:10.1111/j.1467-8535.2009.00970.x

Dawson, S., Gašević, D., Siemens, G., & Joksimovic, S. (2014). *Current state and future trends: A citation network analysis of the learning analytics field.* Paper presented at the Fourth International Conference on Learning Analytics and Knowledge LAK '14, Indianapolis, IN. doi:10.1145/2567574.2567585

Dawson, S., Heathcote, L., & Poole, G. (2010). Harnessing ICT potential: The adoption and analysis of ICT systems for enhancing the student learning experience. *International Journal of Educational Management*, *24*(2), 116–128. doi:10.1108/09513541011020936

Dawson, S., McWilliam, E., & Tan, J. P. L. (2008). Teaching Smarter: How mining ICT data can inform and improve learning and teaching practice. *Paper presented at the ASCILITE 2008*, Melbourne, Australia.

Dawson, S., McWilliam, E., & Tan, J. P. L. (2011). Measuring creative potential: Using social network analysis to monitor and develop learners' creative capacity. *Australasian Journal of Educational Technology*, *27*(6), 924–942.

Deng, L., & Yuen, A. H. K. (2011). Towards a framework for educational affordances of blogs. *Computers & Education*, *56*(2), 441–451. doi:10.1016/j.compedu.2010.09.005

Diaz, V., & Fowler, S. (2012). *Leadership and learning analytics*. Retrieved from https://net.educause.edu/ir/library/pdf/ELIB1205.pdf

Du, H. S., & Wagner, C. (2006). Weblog success: Exploring the role of technology. *International Journal of Human-Computer Studies*, *64*(9), 789–798. doi:10.1016/j.ijhcs.2006.04.002

Ducate, L. C., & Lomicka, L. L. (2005). Exploring the blogosphere: Use of web logs in the foreign language classroom. *Foreign Language Annals*, *38*(3), 410–421. doi:10.1111/j.1944-9720.2005.tb02227.x

Duncan, S., & Berland, M. (2012). *Triangulating learning in board games: Computational thinking at multiple scales of analysis.* Paper presented at the Games + Learning + Society (GLS) Conference 8.0, Madison, WI.

Duval, E. (2011). *Attention please! Learning analytics for visualization and recommendation.* Paper presented at the First International Conference on Learning Analytics and Knowledge LAK '11, Banff, Canada. doi:10.1145/2090116.2090118

Dyckhoff, A. L., Zielke, D., Bültmann, M., Chatti, M. A., & Schroeder, U. (2012). Design and implementation of a learning analytics toolkit for teachers. *Journal of Educational Technology & Society*, *15*(3), 58–76.

Dyke, G. (2011). *Which aspects of novice programmers' usage of an IDE predict learning outcomes.* Paper presented at the 42nd ACM Technical Symposium on Computer Science Education SIGCSE '11, Dallas, TX.

Eckerson, W. W. (2006). *Performance dashboards: Measuring, monitoring, and managing your business*. Hoboken, NJ: John Wiley & Sons.

Elias, T. (2011). *Learning analytics: Definitions, processes, and potential*. Retrieved from http://learninganalytics.net/LearningAnalyticsDefinitionsProcessesPotential.pdf

Ellison, N., & Wu, Y. (2008). Blogging in the classroom: A preliminary exploration of student attitudes and impact on comprehension. *Journal of Educational Multimedia and Hypermedia*, *17*(1), 99–122.

Falakmasir, M. H., & Habibi, J. (2010). *Using educational data mining to study the impact of virtual classroom in e-learning*. Paper presented at the Third Annual Conference on Educational Data Mining, Pittsburgh, PA.

Ferdig, R. E., & Trammell, K. D. (2004). Content delivery in the "blogosphere.". *T.H.E. Journal*, *31*(7), 12–20.

Ferguson, R. (2012). Learning analytics: Drivers, developments and challenges. *International Journal of Technology Enhanced Learning*, *4*(5/6), 304–317. doi:10.1504/IJTEL.2012.051816

Ferguson, R. (2014). *Learning analytics don't just measure students' progress – They can shape it*. Retrieved from http://www.theguardian.com/education/2014/mar/26/learning-analytics-student-progress

Ferguson, R., & Shum, S. B. (2012). *Social learning analytics: Five approaches*. Paper presented at the Second International Conference on Learning Analytics and Knowledge LAK '12, Vancouver, Canada. doi:10.1145/2330601.2330616

Fernández-Gallego, B., Lama, M., Vidal, J. C., & Mucientes, M. (2013). Learning analytics framework for educational virtual worlds. *Procedia Computer Science*, *25*, 443–447. doi:10.1016/j.procs.2013.11.056

Florian, B., Glahn, C., Drachsler, H., Specht, M., & Fabregat, R. (2011). *Activity-based learner-models for learner monitoring and recommendations in Moodle*. Paper presented at the Sixth European Conference on Technology Enhanced Learning EC–TEL '11, Palermo, Italy. doi:10.1007/978-3-642-23985-4_10

Fournier, H., Kop, R., & Sitlia, H. (2011). *The value of learning analytics to networked learning on a personal learning environment*. Paper presented at the First International Conference on Learning Analytics and Knowledge LAK '11, Banff, Canada. doi:10.1145/2090116.2090131

Fritz, J. (2011). Classroom walls that talk: Using online course activity data of successful students to raise self-awareness of underperforming peers. *The Internet and Higher Education*, *14*(2), 89–97. doi:10.1016/j.iheduc.2010.07.007

Gašević, D., Dawson, S., & Siemens, G. (2015). Let's not forget: Learning analytics are about learning. *TechTrends*, *59*(1), 64–71. doi:10.1007/s11528-014-0822-x

Gašević, D., Jovanović, J., & Devedzic, V. (2007). Ontology-based annotation of learning object content. *Interactive Learning Environments*, *15*(1), 1–26. doi:10.1080/10494820600968203

Greller, W., & Drachsler, H. (2012). Translating learning into numbers: A generic framework for learning analytics. *Journal of Educational Technology & Society*, *15*(3), 42–57.

Gunnarsson, B. L., & Alterman, R. (2012). *Predicting failure*. Paper presented at the Second International Conference on Learning Analytics and Knowledge LAK '12, Vancouver, Canada. doi:10.1145/2330601.2330665

Gunnarsson, B. L., & Alterman, R. (2014). Peer promotions as a method to identify quality content. *Journal of Learning Analytics*, *1*(2), 126–150.

Halatchliyski, I., Hecking, T., Göhnert, T., & Hoppe, H. U. (2014). Analyzing the main paths of knowledge evolution and contributor roles in an open learning community. *Journal of Learning Analytics*, *1*(2), 72–93. doi: 10.1145/2460296.2460311

Hamalainen, W., Suhonen, J., Sutinen, E., & Toivonen, H. (2004). *Data mining in personalizing distance education courses*. Paper presented at the 21st ICDE World Conference on Open Learning and Distance Education, Hong Kong.

Heer, J., & Boyd, D. (2005). *Vizster: Visualizing online social networks*. Paper presented at the IEEE Symposium on Information Visualization InfoVis '05, Minneapolis, MN. doi:10.1109/INFOVIS.2005.39

Hijon, R., & Carlos, R. (2006). *E-learning platforms analysis and development of students tracking functionality*. Paper presented at the 18th Annual World Conference on Educational Multimedia, Hypermedia, and Telecommunications ED–MEDIA '06, Orlando, FL.

Hong, W. (2008). Exploring educational use of blogs in us education. *US–China Education Review*, *5*(10), 34–38.

Hostmann, B., Rayner, N., & Herschel, G. (2009). *Gartner's business intelligence, analytics and performance management framework*. Stamford, CT: Gartner.

Huang, T. C., Cheng, S. C., & Huang, Y. M. (2009). A blog article recommendation generating mechanism using an SBACPSO algorithm. *Expert Systems with Applications*, *36*(7), 10388–10396. doi:10.1016/j.eswa.2009.01.039

Jayaprakash, S. M., Moody, E. W., Lauria, E. J. M., Regan, J. R., & Baron, J. D. (2014). Early alert of academically at-risk students: An open source analytics initiative. *Journal of Learning Analytics*, *1*(1), 6–47.

Kargar, M. J., & Azimzadeh, F. (2009). A framework for ranking quality of information on a weblog. *World Academy of Science, Engineering and Technology*, *56*, 690–695.

Kasemsap, K. (2014a). The role of social media in the knowledge-based organizations. In I. Lee (Ed.), *Integrating social media into business practice, applications, management, and models* (pp. 254–275). Hershey, PA, USA: IGI Global. doi:10.4018/978-1-4666-6182-0.ch013

Kasemsap, K. (2014b). The role of social networking in global business environments. In P. Smith & T. Cockburn (Eds.), *Impact of emerging digital technologies on leadership in global business* (pp. 183–201). Hershey, PA, USA: IGI Global. doi:10.4018/978-1-4666-6134-9.ch010

Kasemsap, K. (2015a). The role of business analytics in performance management. In M. Tavana & K. Puranam (Eds.), *Handbook of research on organizational transformations through big data analytics* (pp. 126–145). Hershey, PA, USA: IGI Global. doi:10.4018/978-1-4666-7272-7.ch010

Kasemsap, K. (2015b). The role of data mining for business intelligence in knowledge management. In A. Azevedo & M. Santos (Eds.), *Integration of data mining in business intelligence systems* (pp. 12–33). Hershey, PA, USA: IGI Global. doi:10.4018/978-1-4666-6477-7.ch002

Knight, S., Shum, S. B., & Littleton, K. (2014). Epistemology, assessment, pedagogy: Where learning meets analytics in the middle space. *Journal of Learning Analytics*, *1*(2), 23–47.

Kuh, G. D. (2003). What we're learning about student engagement from NSSE. *Change*, *35*(2), 24–31. doi:10.1080/00091380309604090

LaValle, S., Lesser, E., Shockley, R., Hopkins, M. S., & Kruschwitz, N. (2011). Big data, analytics and the path from insights to value. *MIT Sloan Management Review*, *52*(2), 21–31.

Lockyer, L., Heathcote, E., & Dawson, S. (2013). Informing pedagogical action: Aligning learning analytics with learning design. *The American Behavioral Scientist*, *57*(10), 1439–1459. doi:10.1177/0002764213479367

Lu, J. (2004). *Personalized e-learning material recommender system*. Paper presented at the International Conference on Information Technology for Application ICITA '04, Harbin, China.

Luehmann, A. L. (2008). Using blogging in support of teacher professional identity development: A case study. *Journal of the Learning Sciences*, *17*(3), 287–337. doi:10.1080/10508400802192706

Ma, J., Han, X., Yang, J., & Cheng, J. (2015). Examining the necessary condition for engagement in an online learning environment based on learning analytics approach: The role of the instructor. *The Internet and Higher Education*, *24*, 26–34. doi:10.1016/j.iheduc.2014.09.005

Macfadyen, L. P., & Dawson, S. (2010). Mining LMS data to develop an "early warning system" for educators: A proof of concept. *Computers & Education*, *54*(2), 588–599. doi:10.1016/j.compedu.2009.09.008

Macfadyen, L. P., & Dawson, S. (2012). Numbers are not enough: Why e–learning analytics failed to inform an institutional strategic plan. *Journal of Educational Technology & Society*, *15*(3), 149–163.

MacLennan, B. (2007). Evolutionary psychology, complex systems, and social theory. *Soundings: An Interdisciplinary Journal*, *90*(3/4), 169–189.

Manouselis, N., Drachsler, H., Vuorikari, R., Hummel, H., & Koper, R. (2011). Recommender systems in technology enhanced learning. In F. Ricci, L. Rokach, B. Shapira, & P. Kantor (Eds.), *Recommender systems handbook: A complete guide for research scientists & practitioners* (pp. 387–415). Berlin, Germany: Springer–Verlag. doi:10.1007/978-0-387-85820-3_12

Mazza, R., & Dimitrova, V. (2004). *Visualizing student tracking data to support instructors in web-based distance education*. Paper presented at the 13th International Conference on World Wide Web WWW '04, New York City, NY. doi:10.1145/1013367.1013393

Mazza, R., & Milani, C. (2005). *Exploring usage analysis in learning systems: Gaining insights from visualisations*. Paper presented at the Workshop on Usage Analysis in Learning Systems at the 12th International Conference on Artificial Intelligence in Education AIED '05, Amsterdam, The Netherlands.

Merceron, A., & Yacef, K. (2004). Mining student data captured from a web-based tutoring tool: Initial exploration and results. *Journal of Interactive Learning Research*, *15*(4), 319–346.

Merceron, A., & Yacef, K. (2005). TADA-Ed for educational data mining. *Interactive Multimedia Electronic Journal of Computer-Enhanced Learning*, *7*(1), 267–287.

Meyer, K. A. (2014). Student engagement in online learning: What works and why. *ASHE Higher Education Report*, *40*(6), 1–114. doi:10.1002/aehe.20018

Mirriahi, N., Gašević, D., Long, P., & Dawson, S. (2014). Scientometrics as an important tool for the growth of the field of learning analytics. *Journal of Learning Analytics*, *1*(2), 1–4.

Monroy, C., Rangel, V. S., & Whitaker, R. (2014). A strategy for incorporating learning analytics into the design and evaluation of a K–12 science curriculum. *Journal of Learning Analytics*, *1*(2), 94–125.

Morris, L. V., Finnegan, C., & Wu, S. S. (2005). Tracking student behavior, persistence, and achievement in online courses. *The Internet and Higher Education*, *8*(3), 221–231. doi:10.1016/j.iheduc.2005.06.009

Ni, X., Xue, G. R., Ling, X., Yu, Y., & Yang, Q. (2007). *Exploring in the weblog space by detecting informative and affective articles*. Paper presented at the 16th International Conference on World Wide Web WWW '07, Banff, Canada. doi:10.1145/1242572.1242611

Norris, D. M., & Baer, L. L. (2013). *Building organizational capacity for analytics*. Louisville, CO: EDUCAUSE.

Norris, D. M., Baer, L. L., Leonard, J., Pugliese, L., & Lefrere, P. (2008). Action analytics: Measuring and improving performance that matters in higher education. *EDUCAUSE Review*, *43*(1), 42–67.

Ochoa, X., Suthers, D., Verbert, K., & Duval, E. (2014). Analysis and reflections on the third learning analytics and knowledge conference (LAK 2013). *Journal of Learning Analytics*, *1*(2), 5–22.

Papamitsiou, Z., & Economides, A. (2014). Learning analytics and educational data mining in practice: A systematic literature review of empirical evidence. *Journal of Educational Technology & Society*, *17*(4), 49–64.

Pardo, A., & Delgado, C. (2011). *Stepping out of the box: Towards analytics outside the learning management system*. Paper presented at the First International Conference on Learning Analytics and Knowledge LAK '11, Banff, Canada. doi:10.1145/2090116.2090142

Pardo, A., & Siemens, G. (2014). Ethical and privacy principles for learning analytics. *British Journal of Educational Technology*, *45*(3), 438–450. doi:10.1111/bjet.12152

Pavlik, P., Cen, H., & Koedinger, K. (2009). *Learning factors transfer analysis: Using learning curve analysis to automatically generate domain models*. Paper presented at the Second International Conference on Educational Data Mining EDM 09, Cordoba, Spain.

Philip, R., & Nicholls, J. (2009). Group blogs: Documenting collaborative drama processes. *Australasian Journal of Educational Technology*, *25*(5), 683–699.

Piech, C., Sahami, M., Koller, D., Cooper, S., & Blikstein, P. (2012). *Modeling how students learn to program.* Paper presented at the 43rd ACM Technical Symposium on Computer Science Education (SIGCSE 2012), Raleigh, NC. doi:10.1145/2157136.2157182

Pozzi, F., Manca, S., Persico, D., & Sarti, L. (2007). A general framework for tracking and analyzing learning processes in computer-supported collaborative learning environments. *Innovations in Education and Teaching International, 44*(2), 169–179. doi:10.1080/14703290701240929

Rahman, N., & Dron, J. (2012). *Challenges and opportunities for learning analytics when formal teaching meets social spaces.* Paper presented at the Second International Conference on Learning Analytics and Knowledge LAK '12, Vancouver, Canada. doi:10.1145/2330601.2330619

Reffay, C., & Chanier, T. (2003). *How social network analysis can help to measure cohesion in collaborative distance learning.* Paper presented at the International Conference on Computer–Supported Collaborative Learning CSCL '03, Bergen, Norway. doi:10.1007/978-94-017-0195-2_42

Reffay, C., Teplovs, C., & Blondel, F. M. (2011). *Productive re-use of CSCL data and analytic tools to provide a new perspective on group cohesion.* Paper presented at the International Conference on Computer–Supported Collaborative Learning CSCL '11, Hong Kong.

Robinson, C. C., & Hullinger, H. (2008). New benchmarks in higher education: Student engagement in online learning. *Journal of Education for Business, 84*(2), 101–109. doi:10.3200/JOEB.84.2.101-109

Romero, C., & Ventura, S. (2007). Educational data mining: A survey from 1995 to 2005. *Expert Systems with Applications, 33*(1), 135–146. doi:10.1016/j.eswa.2006.04.005

Romero, C., & Ventura, S. (2010). Educational data mining: A review of the state of the art. *IEEE Transactions on Systems, Man and Cybernetics, Part C: Applications and Reviews, 40*(6), 601–618. doi:10.1109/TSMCC.2010.2053532

Romero, C., & Ventura, S. (2013). Data mining in education. *Wiley Interdisciplinary Reviews: Data Mining and Knowledge Discovery, 3*(1), 12–27. doi:10.1002/widm.1075

Romero, C., Ventura, S., Espejo, P. G., & Hervs, C. (2008*). Data mining algorithms to classify students.* Paper presented at the First International Conference on Educational Data Mining EDM '08, Montreal, Canada.

Roschelle, J., Penuel, W. R., Yarnall, L., Shechtman, N., & Tatar, D. (2005). Handheld tools that "informate" assessment of student learning in science: A requirements analysis. *Journal of Computer Assisted Learning, 21*(3), 190–203. doi:10.1111/j.1365-2729.2005.00127.x

Rubin, V. L., & Liddy, E. D. (2006). *Assessing credibility of weblogs.* Paper presented at the AAAI Spring Symposium: Computational Approaches to Analyzing Weblogs AAAI–CAAW '06, Stanford, CA.

Scardamalia, M., & Bereiter, C. (1994). Computer support for knowledge-building communities. *Journal of the Learning Sciences, 3*(3), 265–283. doi:10.1207/s15327809jls0303_3

Scardamalia, M., & Bereiter, C. (2006). Knowledge building: Theory, pedagogy, and technology. In R. K. Sawyer (Ed.), *The Cambridge handbook of the learning sciences* (pp. 97–115). Cambridge, UK: Cambridge University Press.

Scheffel, M., Drachsler, H., Stoyanov, S., & Specht, M. (2014). Quality indicators for learning analytics. *Journal of Educational Technology & Society*, *17*(4), 117–132.

Serrano-Laguna, A., Torrente, J., Moreno-Ger, P., & Fernández-Manjóna, B. (2012). Tracing a little for big improvements: Application of learning analytics and videogames for student assessment. *Procedia Computer Science*, *15*, 203–209. doi:10.1016/j.procs.2012.10.072

Sherin, B. (2012). *Using computational methods to discover student science conceptions in interview data.* Paper presented at the Second International Conference on Learning Analytics and Knowledge LAK '12, Vancouver, Canada. doi:10.1145/2330601.2330649

Shum, S. B. (2012). *Learning analytics.* UNESCO Policy Brief. Retrieved from http://iite.unesco.org/pics/publications/en/files/3214711.pdf

Shum, S. B., & Ferguson, R. (2012). Social learning analytics. *Journal of Educational Technology & Society*, *15*(3), 3–26.

Shute, V. J. (2008). Focus on formative feedback. *Review of Educational Research*, *78*(1), 153–189. doi:10.3102/0034654307313795

Siemens, G. (2010). *What are learning analytics?* Retrieved from http://www.elearnspace.org/blog/2010/08/25/what-are-learning-analytics/

Siemens, G. (2012). *Learning analytics: Envisioning a research discipline and a domain of practice.* Paper presented at the Second International Conference on Learning Analytics and Knowledge LAK '12, Vancouver, Canada. doi:10.1145/2330601.2330605

Siemens, G., Dawson, S., & Lynch, G. (2013). *Improving the productivity of the higher education sector: Policy and strategy for systems–level deployment of learning analytics.* Sydney, Australia: Society for Learning Analytics Research for the Australian Government Office for Learning and Teaching.

Siemens, G., & Long, P. (2011). Penetrating the fog: Analytics in learning and education. *EDUCAUSE Review*, *46*(5), 30–32.

Smith, V. C., Lange, A., & Huston, D. R. (2012). Predictive modeling to forecast student outcomes and drive effective interventions in online community college courses. *Journal of Asynchronous Learning Networks*, *16*(3), 51–61.

Smolin, D., & Butakov, S. (2012). *Applying artificial intelligence to the educational data: An example of syllabus quality analysis.* Paper presented at the Second International Conference on Learning Analytics and Knowledge LAK '12, Vancouver, Canada. doi:10.1145/2330601.2330644

Stahl, G. (2003). *Meaning and interpretation in collaboration.* Paper presented at the International Conference on Computer Support for Collaborative Learning CSCL '03. Bergen, Norway.

Stahl, G. (2009). *Studying virtual math teams.* New York, NY: Springer–Verlag. doi:10.1007/978-1-4419-0228-3

Suthers, D. D. (2006). Technology affordances for intersubjective meaning making: A research agenda for CSCL. *International Journal of Computer-Supported Collaborative Learning*, *1*(3), 315–337. doi:10.1007/s11412-006-9660-y

Suthers, D. D., Ravi, V., Medina, R., Joseph, S., & Dwyer, N. (2008). Beyond threaded discussion: Representational guidance in asynchronous collaborative learning environments. *Computers & Education*, *50*(4), 1103–1127. doi:10.1016/j.compedu.2006.10.007

Suthers, D. D., & Verbert, K. (2013). *Learning analytics as a "middle space."* Paper presented at the Third International Conference on Learning Analytics and Knowledge LAK '13, Leuven, Belgium. doi:10.1145/2460296.2460298

Talavera, L., & Gaudioso, E. (2004). *Mining student data to characterize similar behavior groups in unstructured collaboration spaces*. Paper presented at the 16th European Conference on Artificial Intelligence ECAI '04), Valencia, Spain.

van Barneveld, A., Arnold, K. E., & Campbell, J. P. (2012). *Analytics in higher education: Establishing a common language*. Boulder, CO: EDUCAUSE Learning Initiative.

van Leeuwen, A., Janssen, J., Erkens, G., & Brekelmans, M. (2014). Supporting teachers in guiding collaborating students: Effects of learning analytics in CSCL. *Computers & Education*, *79*, 28–39. doi:10.1016/j.compedu.2014.07.007

Vatrapu, R., Teplovs, C., Fujita, N., & Bull, S. (2011). *Towards a visual analytics for teachers' dynamic diagnostic pedagogical decision-making*. Paper presented at the First International Conference on Learning Analytics and Knowledge LAK '11, Banff, Canada. doi:10.1145/2090116.2090129

Vee, M. H. N. C., Meyer, B., & Mannock, K. L. (2006). *Understanding novice errors and error paths in object-oriented programming through log analysis*. Paper presented at the Workshop on Educational Data Mining at the Eighth International Conference on Intelligent Tutoring Systems ITS '06, Jhongli, Taiwan.

Verbert, K., Manouselis, N., Drachsler, H., & Duval, E. (2012). Dataset-driven research to support learning and knowledge analytics. *Journal of Educational Technology & Society*, *15*(3), 133–148.

Verpoorten, D., Westera, W., & Specht, M. (2011). Infusing reflective practice in eLearning courses: Can widgets help? *International Journal of Technology Enhanced Learning*, *3*(1), 93–109. doi:10.1504/IJTEL.2011.039066

Wang, K. T., Huang, Y. M., Jeng, Y. L., & Wang, T. I. (2008). A blog-based dynamic learning map. *Computers & Education*, *51*(1), 262–278. doi:10.1016/j.compedu.2007.06.005

Warschauer, M., & Matuchniak, T. (2010). New technology and digital worlds: Analyzing evidence of the equity in access, use and outcomes. *Review of Research in Education*, *34*(1), 179–225. doi:10.3102/0091732X09349791

Watson, J., & Gemin, B. (2008). Using online learning for at-risk students and credit recovery. Washington, DC: International Council for K–12 Online Learning.

Winne, P. H., & Hadwin, A. F. (2013). nStudy: Tracing and supporting self-regulated learning in the Internet. In R. Azevedo, & V. Aleven (Eds.), International handbook of metacognition and learning technologies (pp. 293–308). Amsterdam, The Netherlands: Springer–Verlag.

Wise, A. F., Zhao, Y., & Hausknecht, S. N. (2013). *Learning analytics for online discussions: A pedagogical model for intervention with embedded and extracted analytics.* Paper presented at the Third International Conference on Learning Analytics and Knowledge LAK '13, Leuven, Belgium. doi:10.1145/2460296.2460308

Worsley, M., & Blikstein, P. (2014). Analyzing engineering design through the lens of computation. *Journal of Learning Analytics*, *1*(2), 151–186.

Zagal, J. P., & Bruckman, A. (2007). *GameLog: Fostering reflective gameplaying for learning.* Paper presented at the 2007 ACM SIGGRAPH Symposium on Videogames, San Diego, CA. doi:10.1145/1274940.1274950

Zinn, C., & Scheuer, O. (2006). *Getting to know your student in distance learning contexts.* Paper presented at the First European Conference on Technology Enhanced Learning EC–TEL '06, Crete, Greece. doi:10.1007/11876663_34

ADDITIONAL READING

Abdous, M., He, W., & Yen, C. J. (2012). Using data mining for predicting relationships between online question theme and final grade. *Journal of Educational Technology & Society*, *15*(3), 77–88.

Chatti, M. A., Dyckhoff, A. L., Schroeder, U., & Thüs, H. (2012). A reference model for learning analytics. *International Journal of Technology Enhanced Learning*, *4*(5), 318–331. doi:10.1504/IJTEL.2012.051815

Chaudhuri, S., Dayal, U., & Narasayya, V. (2011). An overview of business intelligence technology. *Communications of the ACM*, *54*(8), 88–98. doi:10.1145/1978542.1978562

Chrysafiadi, K., & Virvou, M. (2013). Student modeling approaches: A literature review for the last decade. *Expert Systems with Applications*, *40*(11), 4715–4729. doi:10.1016/j.eswa.2013.02.007

Cook, D. J., & Das, S. K. (2012). Pervasive computing at scale: Transforming the state of the art. *Pervasive and Mobile Computing*, *8*(1), 22–35. doi:10.1016/j.pmcj.2011.10.004

Ellis, C. (2013). Broadening the scope and increasing the usefulness of learning analytics: The case for assessment analytics. *British Journal of Educational Technology*, *44*(4), 662–664. doi:10.1111/bjet.12028

Giesbers, B., Rienties, B., Tempelaar, D., & Gijselaers, W. (2013). Investigating the relations between motivation, tool use, participation, and performance in an e-learning course using web-video conferencing. *Computers in Human Behavior*, *29*(1), 285–292. doi:10.1016/j.chb.2012.09.005

He, W. (2013). Examining students' online interaction in a live video streaming environment using data mining and text mining. *Computers in Human Behavior*, *29*(1), 90–102. doi:10.1016/j.chb.2012.07.020

Heer, J., & Shneiderman, B. (2012). Interactive dynamics for visual analysis. *Communications of the ACM*, *55*(4), 45–54. doi:10.1145/2133806.2133821

Huang, S., & Fang, N. (2013). Predicting student academic performance in an engineering dynamics course: A comparison of four types of predictive mathematical models. *Computers & Education*, *61*, 133–145. doi:10.1016/j.compedu.2012.08.015

Kwon, O., & Sim, J. M. (2013). Effects of data set features on the performances of classification algorithms. *Expert Systems with Applications*, *40*(5), 1847–1857. doi:10.1016/j.eswa.2012.09.017

Leong, C. K., Lee, Y. H., & Mak, W. K. (2012). Mining sentiments in SMS texts for teaching evaluation. *Expert Systems with Applications*, *39*(3), 2584–2589. doi:10.1016/j.eswa.2011.08.113

Levy, S. T., & Wilensky, U. (2011). Mining students' inquiry actions for understanding of complex systems. *Computers & Education*, *56*(3), 556–573. doi:10.1016/j.compedu.2010.09.015

Lin, C. F., Yeh, Y., Hung, Y. H., & Chang, R. (2013). Data mining for providing a personalized learning path in creativity: An application of decision trees. *Computers & Education*, *68*, 199–210. doi:10.1016/j.compedu.2013.05.009

Lust, G., Elen, J., & Clarebout, G. (2013). Students' tool-use within a web enhanced course: Explanatory mechanisms of students' tool-use pattern. *Computers in Human Behavior*, *29*(5), 2013–2021. doi:10.1016/j.chb.2013.03.014

Manouselis, N., Drachsler, H., Verbert, K., & Duval, E. (2013). *Recommender systems for learning*. New York, NY: Springer–Verlag. doi:10.1007/978-1-4614-4361-2

Nandagopal, K., & Ericsson, K. A. (2012). An expert performance approach to the study of individual differences in self-regulated learning activities in upper–level college students. *Learning and Individual Differences*, *22*(5), 597–609. doi:10.1016/j.lindif.2011.11.018

Peña-Ayala, A. (2014). Educational data mining: A survey and a data mining-based analysis of recent works. *Expert Systems with Applications*, *41*(4), 1432–1462. doi:10.1016/j.eswa.2013.08.042

Roll, I., Aleven, V., McLaren, B. M., & Koedinger, K. R. (2011). Improving students' help-seeking skills using meta-cognitive feedback in an intelligent tutoring system. *Learning and Instruction*, *21*(2), 267–280. doi:10.1016/j.learninstruc.2010.07.004

Siemens, G. (2013). Learning analytics the emergence of a discipline. *The American Behavioral Scientist*, *57*(10), 1380–1400. doi:10.1177/0002764213498851

Siemens, G., & Gašević, D. (2012). Special issue on learning and knowledge analytics. *Journal of Educational Technology & Society*, *15*(3), 1–163.

Slade, S., & Prinsloo, P. (2013). Learning analytics: Ethical issues and dilemmas. *The American Behavioral Scientist*, *57*(10), 1510–1529. doi:10.1177/0002764213479366

Sun, J. C. Y., & Rueda, R. (2012). Situational interest, computer self-efficacy and self-regulation: Their impact on student engagement in distance education. *British Journal of Educational Technology*, *43*(2), 191–204. doi:10.1111/j.1467-8535.2010.01157.x

Tanes, Z., Arnold, K. E., King, A. S., & Remnet, M. A. (2011). Using signals for appropriate feedback: Perceptions and practices. *Computers & Education*, *57*(4), 2414–2422. doi:10.1016/j.compedu.2011.05.016

Terzis, V., & Economides, A. A. (2011). The acceptance and use of computer based assessment. *Computers & Education*, *56*(4), 1032–1044. doi:10.1016/j.compedu.2010.11.017

Verbert, K., Duval, E., Klerkx, J., Govaerts, S., & Santos, J. L. (2013). Learning analytics dashboard applications. *The American Behavioral Scientist*, *57*(10), 1500–1509. doi:10.1177/0002764213479363

Wise, A. F., Zhao, Y., & Hausknecht, S. N. (2014). Learning analytics for online discussions: Embedded and extracted approaches. *Journal of Learning Analytics*, *1*(2), 48–71.

KEY TERMS AND DEFINITIONS

Educational Data Mining: An emerging discipline, concerned with developing methods for exploring the unique types of data that come from the educational settings.

Higher Education: An education beyond high school provided by graduate schools and professional schools.

Information Technology: The development, installation, and implementation of computer systems and applications.

Learning: The knowledge acquired by systematic study in any field of educational application.

Learning Analytics: An educational application of web analytics used by businesses to analyze commercial activities, identify spending trends, and predict consumer behavior.

Learning Management System: A software application or web-based technology used to plan, implement, and evaluate a specific learning process.

Social Networking Sites: The websites that enable users to create public profiles within that websites and form relationships with other users of the same websites who access their profile.

Web Analytics: The measurement, collection, analysis, and reporting of Internet data for the purposes of understanding website traffic and optimizing web usage.

Compilation of References

7 Things You Should Know About Flipped Classrooms. (2012). *Educause*. Retrieved from http://www.educause.edu/library/resources/7-things-you-should-know-about-flipped-classrooms

Abadie, A., & Imbens, G. W. (2009). *Matching on the estimated propensity score*. National Bureau of Economic Research. doi:10.3386/w15301

Abdous, M., He, W., & Yen, C.-J. (2012). Using Data Mining for Predicting Relationships between Online Question Theme and Final Grade. *Journal of Educational Technology & Society*, *15*(3), 77–88.

Abhyankar, K., & Ganapathy, S. (2014). Technology-enhanced learning analytics system design for engineering education. *International Journal of Information and Education Technology*, *4*(4), 345–350. doi:10.7763/IJIET.2014.V4.427

Agudo-Peregrina, A. F., Iglesias-Pradas, S., Conde-Gonzalez, M. A., & Hernandez-Garcia, A. (2014). Can we predict success from log data in VLEs? Classification of interactions for learning analytics and their relation with performance in VLE–supported F2F and online learning. *Computers in Human Behavior*, *31*, 542–550. doi:10.1016/j.chb.2013.05.031

Ainsworth, S. (2006). DeFT: A conceptual framework for considering learning with multiple representations. *Learning and Instruction*, *16*(3), 183–198. doi:10.1016/j.learninstruc.2006.03.001

Akalu, G. A. (2014). Higher education in Ethiopia: Expansion, quality assurance and institutional autonomy. *Higher Education Quarterly*, *68*(4), 394–415. doi:10.1111/hequ.12036

Akbani, R., Kwek, S., & Japkowicz, N. (2004). Applying support vector machines to imbalanced datasets. *Machine Learning: ECML*, *2004*, 39–50.

Akoumianakis, D., & Alexandraki, C. (2010). Understanding Networked Music Communities through a Practice-Lens: Virtual "Tells" and Cultural Artifacts. *Proceedings of the 2010 2nd International Conference on Intelligent Networking and Collaborative Systems (INCOS)* (pp. 62–69). doi:10.1109/INCOS.2010.65

Alexander, B. (2006). Web 2.0: A new wave of innovation for teaching and learning? *EDUCAUSE Review*, *41*(2), 32.

Ali, L., Asadi, M., Gašević, D., Jovanović, J., & Hatala, M. (2013). Factors influencing beliefs for adoption of a learning analytics tool: An empirical study. *Computers & Education*, *62*, 130–148. doi:10.1016/j.compedu.2012.10.023

Ali, L., Hatala, M., Gašević, D., & Jovanović, J. (2012). A qualitative evaluation of evolution of a learning analytics tool. *Computers & Education*, *58*(1), 470–489. doi:10.1016/j.compedu.2011.08.030

Alltree, J., Barefoot, H., Flynn, S., Haddleton, F., Weston, K., & Wright, M. (2010). *The University of Hertfordshire's Higher Education Academy (HEA) and Equality Challenge Unit's (ECU's) Black and Minority Ethnic (BME) Summit project – Report April* 2010. University of Hertfordshire. Retrieved from http://www.heacademy.ac.uk/resources/detail/Hertfordshireethnicitysummit

Alshare, K. A., & Lane, P. L. (2011). Predicting student-perceived learning outcomes and satisfaction in ERP courses: An empirical investigation. *Communications of the Association for Information Systems*, *28*(24), 571–584.

Altbach, P. G., Reisberg, L., & Rumbley, L. E. (2009). Trends in global higher education: tracking an academic revolution. A report prepared for the UNESCO World Conference on Higher Education. Paris: UNESCO. Retrieved from http://atepie.cep.edu.rs/public/Altbach,_Reisberg,_Rumbley_Tracking_an_Academic_Revolution,_UNESCO_2009.pdf

Alterman, R., & Larusson, J. A. (2013). Participation and common knowledge in a case study of student blogging. *International Journal of Computer-Supported Collaborative Learning*, *8*(2), 149–187. doi:10.1007/s11412-013-9167-2

Amershi, S., & Conati, C. (2009). Combining unsupervised and supervised classification to build user models for exploratory learning environments. *Journal of Educational Data Mining*, *1*(1), 18–71.

Amershi, S., & Conati, C. (2009). Combining Unsupervised and Supervised Classification to Build User Models for Exploratory Learning Environments. *Journal of Educational Data Mining*, *1*(1), 18–71.

Ananiadou, K., & Claro, M. (2009). 21st Century Skills and Competences for New Millennium Learners in OECD Countries (OECD Education Working Papers, No. 41). OECD.

Anaya, A. R., & Boticario, J. G. (2009). A Data Mining Approach to Reveal Representative Collaboration Indicators in Open Collaboration Frameworks. In T. Barnes, M. Desmarais, C. Romero, & S. Ventura (Eds.), *Proceedings of the 2nd International Conference on Educational Data Mining* (pp. 210–219).

Anderson, E. W. (2012). Evaluating scientific visualization using cognitive measures. *Paper presented at the2012 BELIV Workshop: Beyond Time and Errors - Novel Evaluation Methods for VisualizationBELIV '12*. doi:10.1145/2442576.2442581

Anderson, T., & Dron, J. (2011). Three Generations of Distance Education Pedagogy. *International Review of Research in Open and Distance Learning*, *12*(3), 1–18.

Angelino, L. M., Williams, F. K., & Natvig, D. (2007). Strategies to engage online students and reduce attrition rates. *Journal of Educators Online*, *4*(2), n2.

Anirban, S. (2014). Big data analytics in the education sector: Needs, opportunities and challenges. *IJRCCT*, *3*(11), 1425–1428.

Antón, A. I., & Earp, J. B. (2004). A requirements taxonomy for reducing web site privacy vulnerabilities. *Requirements Engineering*, *9*(3), 169–185. doi:10.1007/s00766-003-0183-z

Arnold, K. E., & Pistilli, M. D. (2012). Course signals at Purdue: using learning analytics to increase student success. *Paper presented at the2nd International Conference on Learning Analytics and KnowledgeLAK '12* (pp. 267–270). doi:10.1145/2330601.2330666

Arnold, K. E. (2010). Signals: Applying academic analytics. *EDUCAUSE Quarterly*, *33*(1), n1.

Arnold, K. E. (2010). Signals: Applying Academic Analytics. *EDUCAUSE Quarterly*, *33*(1), n1.

Artino, A. R. (2008). Motivational beliefs and perceptions of instructional quality: Predicting satisfaction with online training. *Journal of Computer Assisted Learning*, *24*(3), 260–270. doi:10.1111/j.1365-2729.2007.00258.x

Attenberg, J., & Ertekin, S. (2013). Class imbalance and active learning learning. In Imbalanced Learning: Foundations, Algorithms, and Applications (1st ed., pp. 101–147). John Wiley & Sons, Inc.

Austin, P. C. (2011). An Introduction to Propensity Score Methods for Reducing the Effects of Confounding in Observational Studies. *Multivariate Behavioral Research*, *46*(3), 399–424. doi:10.1080/00273171.2011.568786 PMID:21818162

Australian Government. (2012). Tertiary Education Quality and Standards Agency (TEQSA). Retrieved from http://www.teqsa.gov.au/

Australian Government: Department of Education Employment and Workplace Relations. (2010). National Code of Practice for Registration Authorities and Providers of Education and Training to Overseas Students.

Australian Universities Quality Agency. (2010). Report of an Audit of Eynesbury Institute of Business and Technology Retrieved from http://teqsa.gov.au/sites/default/files/auditreport_eibt_2010.pdf

Autor, D., Levy, F., & Murnane, R. (2003). The skill content of recent technological change: An empirical exploration. *The Quarterly Journal of Economics*, *118*(4), 1279–1333. doi:10.1162/003355303322552801

Azemi, A. 1995. Teaching Computer Programming Courses in a Computer Laboratory Environment. *Proceedings of the Frontiers in Education Conference FIE '95* (Vol. 1). doi:10.1109/FIE.1995.483036

Babbie, E. (1990). *Survey research methods* (2nd ed.). Belmont, CA: Wadsworth Publishing Company.

Baepler, P., & Murdoch, C. J. (2010). Academic analytics and data mining in higher education. *International Journal for the Scholarship of Teaching and Learning*, *4*(2), 17.

Bahnsen, A. C., & Aouada, D. (2014). Example-Dependent Cost-Sensitive Logistic Regression for Credit Scoring.*Proceedings of the 2014 13th International Conference on Machine Learning and Applications*. doi:10.1109/ICMLA.2014.48

Bajzek, D., Brooks, J., Jerome, W., Lovett, M., Rinderle, J., Rule, G., & Thille, C. (2008). Assessment and Instruction: Two Sides of the Same Coin. In G. Richards (Ed.), *Proceedings of World Conference on E-Learning in Corporate, Government, Healthcare, and Higher Education 2008*, (pp. 560–565). Chesapeake, VA.

Baker, R. S. J. d. (2011). Data Mining for Education. In B. McGaw, P. Peterson, & E. Baker (Eds.), *International Encyclopedia of Education* (3rd ed.). Oxford, UK: Elsevier.

Baker, R. S. J. d., Corbett, A. T., & Aleven, V. (2008). More Accurate Student Modeling Through Contextual Estimation of Slip and Guess Probabilities in Bayesian Knowledge Tracing.*Proceedings of the 9th International Conference on Intelligent Tutoring Systems* (pp. 406–415). Berlin, Heidelberg: Springer-Verlag. doi:10.1007/978-3-540-69132-7_44

Baker, R. S. J. d., Corbett, A. T., Koedinger, K. R., & Roll, I. (2006). Generalizing Detection of Gaming the System across a Tutoring Curriculum.*Proceedings of the 8th International Conference on Intelligent Tutoring Systems* (pp. 402–411). Berlin, Heidelberg: Springer-Verlag.

Baker, R. S. J. d., Gowda, S. M., & Corbett, A. T. (2011). Automatically Detecting a Student's Preparation for Future Learning: Help Use Is Key. In M. Pechenizkiy, T. Calders, C. Conati, S. Ventura, C. Romero, & J. Stamper (Eds.), *Proceedings of the 4th International Conference on Educational Data Mining* (pp. 179–188).

Baker, R. S. J. D., & Yacef, K. (2009). The State of Educational Data Mining in 2009: A Review and Future Visions. *Journal of Educational Data Mining*, *1*(1), 3–17.

Baker, R. S., Corbett, A. T., Koedinger, K. R., & Wagner, A. Z. (2004). Off-Task Behavior in the Cognitive Tutor Classroom: When Students 'Game the System.*Proceedings of the SIGCHI Conference on Human Factors in Computing Systems (CHI '04)* (pp. 383–390) New York, NY: Association for Computing Machinery. doi:10.1145/985692.985741

Baker, R., Corbett, A. T., Roll, I., & Koedinger, K. R. (2008). Developing a generalizable detector of when students game the system. *User Modeling and User-Adapted Interaction*, *18*(3), 287–314. doi:10.1007/s11257-007-9045-6

Baker, R., Gowda, S., & Corbett, A. T. (2011). Towards predicting future transfer of learning. In G. Biswas, S. Bull, J. Kay, & A. Mitrovic (Eds.), *Artificial intelligence in education* (pp. 23–30). Berlin, Germany: Springer–Verlag. doi:10.1007/978-3-642-21869-9_6

Baker, R., & Yacef, K. (2009). The state of educational data mining in 2009: A review and future visions. *Journal of Educational Data Mining*, *1*(1), 3–17.

Bakharia, A. (2011). SNAPP Presentation. Paper presented at the *Learning Analytics and Knowledge Conference*. Retrieved from http://www.slideshare.net/aneeshabakharia/snapp-learning-analytics-and-knowledge-conference-2011

Bakharia, A., & Dawson, S. (2011). SNAPP: a bird's-eye view of temporal participant interaction. *Paper presented at the1st International Conference on Learning Analytics and KnowledgeLAK '11*, New York, NY. doi:10.1145/2090116.2090144

Baldi, P., Brunak, S., Chauvin, Y., Andersen, C. A. F., & Nielsen, H. (2000). Assessing the accuracy of prediction algorithms for classification: An overview. *Bioinformatics (Oxford, England)*, *16*(5), 412–424. doi:10.1093/bioinformatics/16.5.412 PMID:10871264

Balduzzi, M., Platzer, C., Holz, T., Kirda, E., Balzarotti, D., & Kruegel, C. (2010). Abusing Social Networks for Automated User Profiling (Research Report RR-10-233). EURECOM, Sophia Antipolis; Secure Systems Lab, TU Wien and UCSB.

Barber, R., & Sharkey, M. (2012). Course correction: Using analytics to predict course success. *Paper presented at the2nd International Conference on Learning Analytics and Knowledge*. doi:10.1145/2330601.2330664

Barnes, D. J., Fincher, S., & Thompson, S. (1997) Introductory Problem Solving in Computer Science. In G. Daughton, & P. Magee (Eds.), *Proceedings of the5th Annual Conference on the Teaching of Computing* (pp. 36-39). Centre for Teaching Computing, Dublin City University, Dublin, Ireland.

Barnes, T. J. (2013). Big Data, little history. *Dialogues in Human Geography*, *3*(3), 297–302. doi:10.1177/2043820613514323

Barron, B., & Engle, R. A. (2007) Analyzing Data Derived from Video Records. In S.J. Derry (Ed.), Guidelines for Video Research in Education: Recommendations from an Expert Panel (White paper) (pp. 24-33). Retrieved from http://drdc.uchicago.edu/what/video-research-guidelines.pdf#page=1&view=fitV,0

Bass, R. (2012). Disrupting ourselves: The problem of learning in higher education. *EDUCAUSE Review*, *47*(2), 23–33.

Batista, G. E., Carvalho, A. C., & Monard, M. C. (2000). Applying one-sided selection to unbalanced datasets. *MICAI 2000. Advances in Artificial Intelligence*, 2000, 315–325.

Batista, G. E., Prati, R. C., & Monard, M. C. (2004). A study of the behavior of several methods for balancing machine learning training data. *ACM SIGKDD Explorations Newsletter*, *6*(1), 20. doi:10.1145/1007730.1007735

Batuwita, R., & Palade, V. (2013). Class imbalance learning methods for support vector machines. In Imbalanced Learning: Foundations, Algorithms, and Applications (1st ed., pp. 83–99). John Wiley & Sons, Inc.

Beck, J. E., & Mostow, J. (2008). How Who Should Practice: Using Learning Decomposition to Evaluate the Efficacy of Different Types of Practice for Different Types of Students.*Proceedings of the 9th International Conference on Intelligent Tutoring Systems* (pp. 353–362). Berlin, Heidelberg: Springer-Verlag . doi:10.1007/978-3-540-69132-7_39

Beer, C., Clark, K., & Jones, D. (2010). Indicators of engagement. *Paper presented at theAscilite 2010*, Sydney.

Beer, C., Tickner, R., & Jones, D. (2014). Three paths for learning analytics and beyond: moving from rhetoric to reality. Paper presented at the *ASCILITE*, Dunedin, New Zealand.

Bell, F. (2010). Network theories for technology-enabled learning and social change: Connectivism and actor network theory. *Proceedings of theInternational Conference on Networked Learning*. doi:10.1109/ITHET.2013.6671027

Bellman, S., Johnson, E. J., & Lohse, G. L. (2001). On site: to opt-in or opt-out?: it depends on the question. *Communications of the ACM*, *44*(2), 25–27. Retrieved from http://dl.acm.org/citation.cfm?id=359241 doi:10.1145/359205.359241

Bender, B. E. (2002). Benchmarking as an administrative tool for institutional leaders. *New Directions for Higher Education*, *2002*(118), 113–120. doi:10.1002/he.60

Benkler, Y., & Nissenbaum, H. (2006). Commons-based peer production and virtue. *Journal of Political Philosophy*, *14*(4), 394–419. doi:10.1111/j.1467-9760.2006.00235.x

Bennedsen, J., & Caspersen, M. E. (2006, June). Abstraction ability as an indicator of success for learning object-orientated programming? *SIGCSE Bulletin*, *38*(2), 39–43. doi:10.1145/1138403.1138430

Berkhout, L., Hoekman, J., & Goorhuis-Brouwer, S. M. (2011). Observation instrument of play behaviour in a classroom setting. *Early Child Development and Care*. doi:10.1080/03004430.2011.608429

Berland, M., Baker, R., & Blikstein, P. (2014). Educational data mining and learning analytics: Applications to constructionist research. *Technology. Knowledge and Learning*, *19*(1/2), 205–220. doi:10.1007/s10758-014-9223-7

Berland, M., Martin, T., Benton, T., Smith, C. P., & Davis, D. (2013). Using learning analytics to understand the learning pathways of novice programmers. *Journal of the Learning Sciences*, *22*(4), 564–599. doi:10.1080/10508406.2013.836655

Berry, J., & Loke, J. (2011). *Improving the degree attainment of Black and minority ethnic students (Final Report)*. HEAcademy. Retrieved from http://www.heacademy.ac.uk/resources/detail/inclusion/Ethnicity/BMEProgramme_FinalReport

Bienkowski, M., Feng, M., & Means, B. (2012). Enhancing teaching and learning through educational data mining and learning analytics: An issue brief. US Department of Education, Office of Educational Technology.

Bienkowski, M., Feng, M., & Means, B. (2012). *Enhancing teaching and learning through educational data mining and learning analytics: An issue brief.* Washington, DC: U.S. Department of Education Office of Educational Technology.

Biesta, G. (2007). Why "what works" won't work: Evidence-based practice and the democratic deficit in educational research. *Educational Theory*, *57*(1), 1–22. doi:10.1111/j.1741-5446.2006.00241.x

Biesta, G. (2010). Why 'what works' still won't work: From evidence-based education to value-based education. *Studies in Philosophy and Education*, *29*(5), 491–503. doi:10.1007/s11217-010-9191-x

Biswas, G., Jeong, H., Kinnebrew, J., Sulcer, B., & Roscoe, R. (2010). Measuring self-regulated learning skills through social interactions in a teachable agent environment. *Research and Practice in Technology-Enhanced Learning*, *5*(2), 123–152. doi:10.1142/S1793206810000839

Blagus, R., & Lusa, L. (2013). SMOTE for high-dimensional class-imbalanced data. *BMC Bioinformatics*, *14*(1), 106. doi:10.1186/1471-2105-14-106 PMID:23522326

Blikstein, P. (2011, February). Using learning analytics to assess students' behavior in open-ended programming tasks.*Proceedings of the First International Conference on Learning Analytics and Knowledge* (pp. 110-116). ACM. doi:10.1145/2090116.2090132

Boam, E., & Webb, J. (2015). The qualified self: going beyond quantification [Blog comment]. Retrieved from http://designmind.frogdesign.com/articles/the-qualified-self-going-beyond-quantification.html

Boellstorff, T. (2013). Making big data, in theory. *First Monday*, *18*(10). http://firstmonday.org/ojs/index.php/fm/article/view/4869 doi:10.5210/fm.v18i10.4869

Bolton, G. (2010). *Reflective practice: Writing and professional development*. London, UK: Sage Publications.

Bonsignore, E. M., Dunne, C., Rotman, D., Smith, M., Capone, T., Hansen, D. L., & Shneiderman, B. (2009). First Steps to Netviz Nirvana: Evaluating Social Network Analysis with NodeXL. *Proceedings of the 2009 IEEEInternational Conference on Computational Science and Engineering* (Vol. 4, pp. 332–339). doi:10.1109/CSE.2009.120

Booth, M. (2012, July 18). Learning analytics: the new black. *EDUCAUSEreview*. Retrieved from http://www.educause.edu/ero/article/learning-analytics-new-black

Bowden, E. M., & Jung-Beeman, M. (2003). Aha! Insight experience correlates with solution activation in the right hemisphere. *Psychonomic Bulletin & Review*, *10*(3), 730–737. doi:10.3758/BF03196539 PMID:14620371

Bowen, E. G., & Lack, K. A. (2013). *Higher education in the digital age*. Princeton, N.J.: Princeton University Press. doi:10.1515/9781400847204

Bowman, M. (1994). *Using Video in Research. SCRE Spotlights 45*. Scottish Council for Research in Education.

Boyd, D., & Crawford, K. (2013). Six provocations for Big Data. Retrieved from http://papers.ssrn.com/sol3/papers.cfm?abstract_id=1926431

Boyd, D., & Crawford, K. (2012). Critical questions for Big Data. *Information Communication and Society*, *15*(5), 662–679. doi:10.1080/1369118X.2012.678878

Bozdag, E. (2013). Bias in algorithmic filtering and personalization. *Ethics and Information Technology*, *15*(3), 209–227. doi:10.1007/s10676-013-9321-6

Brian, S. 2015. The unexamined life in the era of big data: toward a UDAAP for data. Retrieved from http://papers.ssrn.com/sol3/papers.cfm?abstract_id=2533068

Brown, M. (2011). Learning analytics: Moving from concept to practice. Retrieved http://net.educause.edu/ir/library/pdf/ELIB1203.pdf

Brown, M. (2012) Learning Analytics: Moving from Concept to Practice. EDUCAUSE Learning Initiative, July 2012

Brown, M. (2012, July). Learning Analytics: Moving from Concept to Practice. *EDUCAUSE Learning Initiative*.

Brown, M., & Wilson, C. (2013, October 1). *Formative assessment: getting to know your students* (Presentation). University of Derby APP. Retrieved from http://prezi.com/rxevkq1gdr3e/?utm_campaign=share&utm_medium=copy

Brown, W., Lovett, M., Bajzek, D., & Burnette, J. (2006). Improving the Feedback Cycle to Improve Learning in Introductory Biology Using the Digital Dashboard. In G. Richards (Ed.), *Proceedings of World Conference on E-Learning in Corporate, Government, Healthcare, and Higher Education 2006I*, (pp. 1030–1035) Chesapeake, VA. AACE.

Brown, M. (2010). *Learning analytics*. Learning Circuits.

Brusilovsky, P., & Millan, E. (2007). User models for adaptive hypermedia and adaptive educational systems. In P. Brusilovsky, A. Cobsa, & W. Nejdl (Eds.), *The adaptive web: Methods and strategies of web personalization* (pp. 3–53). Berlin, Germany: Springer–Verlag. doi:10.1007/978-3-540-72079-9_1

Bry, F., Gehlen-Baum, V., & Pohl, A. (2011). Promoting awareness and participation in large class lectures: The digital backchannel backstage.*Proceedings of the International Conference on Information Systems.*

Buerck, J. P., & Mudigonda, S. P. (2014). A Resource-Constrained Approach to Implementing Analytics in an Institution of Higher Education: An Experience Report. *Journal of Learning Analytics*, *1*(1), 129–139.

Buerk, J. P., & Mudigonda, S. P. (2014). A Resource-Constrained Approach to Implementing Analytics in an Institution of Higher Education: An Experience Report. *Journal of Learning Analytics*, *1*(1), 129–139.

Bull, S., Cooke, N., & Mabbott, A. (2007). Visual Attention in Open Learner Model Presentations: An Eye-Tracking Investigation. *Paper presented at the11th International Conference on User ModelingUM '07*, Springer-Verlag. doi:10.1007/978-3-540-73078-1_21

Bull, S., Ahmad, N., Johnson, M., Johan, R., Mabbott, A., & Kerly, A. (2008). Adaptive Navigation Support, Learner Control and Open Learner Models.*Proceedings of the 5th international conference on Adaptive Hypermedia and Adaptive Web-Based Systems, LNCS (Vol.* 5149, pp. 275–278). Berlin, Heidelberg: Springer-Verlag. doi:10.1007/978-3-540-70987-9_33

Bunkhumpornpat, C., Sinapiromsaran, K., & Lursinsap, C. (2009). Safe-Level-SMOTE : Safe-Level-Synthetic Minority Over-Sampling TEchnique. In *Advances in Knowledge Discovery and Data Mining* (pp. 475–482).

Butler, D. L., & Winne, P. H. (1995). Feedback and self-regulated learning: A theoretical synthesis. *Review of Educational Research*, *65*(3), 245–281. doi:10.3102/00346543065003245

Cabral, S. R., Castolo, J. C. G., & Gallardo, S. C. H. (2015, January). Algorithm to optimize a fuzzy model of students' academic achievement in higher education. In *Congreso Virtual sobre Tecnología. Education et Sociétés*, *1*(4).

Caffarella, R. S. (2002). *Planning programs for adult learners: A practical guide for educators, trainers, and staff developers*. San Francisco, CA: Jossey-Bass.

Caliendo, M., & Clement, M. (2012). Research Note-The Cost Impact of Spam Filters: Measuring the Effect of Information System Technologies in Organizations. *Information Systems Research, 23*(June 2014).

Calvani, A., Fini, A., Molino, M., & Ranieri, M. (2010). Visualizing and monitoring effective interactions in online collaborative groups. *British Journal of Educational Technology*, *41*(2), 213–226. doi:10.1111/j.1467-8535.2008.00911.x

Cambridge, D., & Perez-Lopez, K. (2012). First steps towards a social learning analytics for online communities of practice for educators. *Paper presented at theSecond International Conference on Learning Analytics and Knowledge LAK '12*, Vancouver, Canada. doi:10.1145/2330601.2330622

Campbell, J. F., DeBlois, P. B., & Oblinger, D. G. (2007). Academic Analytics: A New Tool for a New Era. *EDUCASE Review*, *42*(4), 40–57.

Campbell, J. P., DeBlois, P. B., & Oblinger, D. G. (2007). Academic analytics: A new tool for a new era. *EDUCAUSE Review*, *42*(4), 41–57.

Campbell, J. P., DeBlouis, P. B., & Oblinger, D. G. (2007). Academic analytics: A new tool for a new era. *Educause Review Online*, *42*(4), 40–57.

Campbell, J. P., & Oblinger, D. G. (2007). Top-ten teaching and learning issues. *EDUCAUSE Quarterly*, *30*(3), 15–22.

Campbell, J., Chang, V., & Hosseinian-Far, A. (2015). Philosophising data: A critical reflection on the 'hidden' issues. [IJOCI]. *International Journal of Organizational and Collective Intelligence*, *5*(1), 1–15. doi:10.4018/IJOCI.2015010101

Card, S. K., Mackinlay, J. D., & Shneiderman, B. (1999). *Readings in information visualization - using vision to think*. Academic Press.

Carmean, C., & Mizzi, P. (2010). The Case for Nudge Analytics. *EDUCAUSE Quarterly*, *33*(4), 1–8.

Carney, M. (2013). You are your data: the scary future of the quantified self movement [Blog comment]. Retrieved from http://pando.com/2013/05/20/you-are-your-data-the-scary-future-of-the-quantified-self-movement/

Carr, N. (2012). The crisis in higher education. *Technology Review*. Retrieved from http://www.technologyreview.com/featuredstory/429376/the-crisis-in-higher-education/

Centers for Medicare & Medicad Services. (2005). *Selecting a Development Approach*. Retrieved from http://www.cms.gov/Research-Statistics-Data-and-Systems/CMS-Information-Technology/XLC/Downloads/SelectingDevelopmentApproach.pdf

Cerezo, R., Suarez, N., Núñez, J. C., & Sánchez-Santillán, M. (2014). eGraph tool. *Paper presented at theFourth International Conference*, New York, NY (pp. 273–274). doi:10.1145/2567574.2567596

Chacon, F., Spicer, D., & Valbuena, A. (2012). Analytics in support of student retention and success. *EDUCAUSE: Center for Applied Research. Research Bulletin (Sun Chiwawitthaya Thang Thale Phuket)*, *3*, 1–9.

Chalupa, M., Chen, C., & Charles, T. (2001). An analysis of college students' motivation and learning strategies in computer courses: A cognitive view. *Delta Pi Epsilon Journal*, *43*(4), 185–199.

Chan, A., & Lee, M. J. W. (2005). An MP3 a day keeps the worries away: Exploring the use of podcasting to address preconceptions and alleviate pre-class anxiety amongst undergraduate information technology students. In D.H.R. Spennemann & L.Burr (Eds.), *Good Practice in Practice:Proceedings of the Student Experience Conference* (pp.58-70). Wagga Wagga, NSW

Chang, R., Ziemkiewicz, C., Pyzh, R., Kielman, J., & Ribarsky, W. (2010). Learning-based evaluation of visual analytic systems. *Proceedings of BELIV* (pp. 29–34). doi:10.1145/2110192.2110197

Chan, S. (2013). Using videos and multimodal discourse analysis to study how students learn a trade. *International Journal of Training Research*, *11*(1), 69–78. doi:10.5172/ijtr.2013.11.1.69

Chatti, M. A., Dyckhoff, A. L., Schroeder, U., & Thüs, H. (2012). A reference model for learning analytics. *International Journal of Technology Enhanced Learning*, *4*(5/6), 318–331. doi:10.1504/IJTEL.2012.051815

Chawla, N. V. (2005). DATA MINING FOR IMBALANCED DATASETS : AN OVERVIEW. In In Data mining and knowledge discovery handbook (pp. 853–867). Springer.

Chawla, N. V., Bowyer, K. W., Hall, L. O., & Philip, W. (2011). SMOTE: synthetic minority over-sampling technique. *Journal of Artificial Intelligence Research, 16*, 321–357.

Chen, B. (2014). Visualizing semantic space of online discourse: the knowledge forum case. *Paper presented at the-Fourth International Conference on Learning Analytics And KnowledgeLAK '14*. ACM. doi:10.1145/2567574.2567595

Chen, C. (2002). Self-regulated learning strategies and achievement in an introduction to information systems course. *Information Technology, Learning and Performance Journal*, *20*(1), 11–25.

Chen, C., & Chalupa, M. (2003). The role of motivation and use of learning strategies in computer courses: Early and late in the semester. *Delta Pi Epsilon Journal*, *45*(2), 98–117.

ChoiceStream Personalization Survey: Consumer Trends and Perceptions. (2005). Retrieved from dfshttp://www.choicestream.com/pdf/ChoiceStream_PersonalizationSurveyResults2005.pdf

Cho, M.-H., Shen, D., & Laffey, J. (2010). Relationships between self-regulation and social experiences in asynchronous online learning environments. *Journal of Interactive Learning Research*, *21*, 297–316.

Chou, C., Kuo, B., & Chang, F. (2006). The Generalized Condensed Nearest Neighbor Rule as A Data Reduction Method. *Proceedings of the18th International Conference on Pattern Recognition (ICPR'06)* (pp. 556–559). doi:10.1109/ICPR.2006.1119

Christensen, C. (2008). Disruptive innovation and catalytic change in higher education. Forum for the Future of Higher Education. *EDUCAUSE*. Retrieved from https://net.educause.edu/ir/library/pdf/ff0810s.pdf

Clarke, J., & Nelson, K. (2013). Perspectives on learning analytics: Issues and challenges. Observations from Shane Dawson and Phil Long. *The International Journal of the First Year in Higher Education*, *4*(1), 1–8. doi:10.5204/intjfyhe.v4i1.166

Cleary-Holdforth, J. (2007). Student non-attendance in higher education: A phenomenon of student apathy or poor pedagogy. *Dublin Institute of Technology*. Retrieved from http://level3.dit.ie/html/issue5/cleary-holdforth/cleary_holdforth.pdf

Cliburn, D. C. (2006, October 28-31). Experiences with the LEGO Mindstorms throughout the Undergraduate Computer Science Curriculum. *Proceedings of the 36th ASEE/IEEE Frontiers in Education Conference*, San Diego, CA, USA (pp. 1-6).

Clow, D. (2012). The learning analytics cycle: Closing the loop effectively. *Paper presented at the2nd International Conference on Learning Analytics and Knowledge*. doi:10.1145/2330601.2330636

Clow, D. (2013b, November 13). Looking harder at Course Signals [Blog comment]. Retrieved from http://dougclow.org/2013/11/13/looking-harder-at-course-signals/

Clow, D. (2013a). An overview of learning analytics. *Teaching in Higher Education*, *18*(6), 683–695. doi:10.1080/13562517.2013.827653

Coates, H. (2007). A model of online and general campus-based student engagement. *Assessment & Evaluation in Higher Education*, *32*(2), 121–141. doi:10.1080/02602930600801878

Cohen, M. D., & Marsh, J. G. (1986). *Leadership and ambiguity: The American college president*. New York, NY: McGraw–Hill.

Collins, C., Carpendale, S., & Penn, G. (2009). Docuburst: visualizing document content using language structure. *Computer Graphics Forum*, *28(3)*, 1039–1046. doi:10.1111/j.1467-8659.2009.01439.x

Commonwealth of Australia. (2009). *Transforming Australia's Higher Education System*. Retrieved from http://planipolis.iiep.unesco.org/upload/Australia/Australia_TransformingAusHigherED.pdf

Conati, C., & Maclaren, H. (2005). Data-driven refinement of a probabilistic model of user affect. In L. Ardissono, P. Brna, & A. Mitrovic (Eds.), *User modeling 2005* (pp. 40–49). Berlin, Germany: Springer–Verlag.

Consolvo, S., Markle, K., Patrick, K., & Chanasyk, K. (2009). Designing for persuasion: mobile services for health behavior change. *Paper presented at the4th International Conference on Persuasive TechnologyPersuasive '09*, New York: NY. doi:10.1145/1541948.1541964

Cook, R., & Kay, J. (1994). The Justified User Model: A Viewable, Explained User Model. *Proceedings of theFourth International Conference on User Modeling* (pp. 145–150).

Cooper, A. (2012). *A Brief History of Analytics, JISC CETIS Analytics Series 1(9)*. University of Bolton.

Cooper, A. (2012). *A Brief History of Analytics. JISC CETIS Analytics Series, 1(9)*. University of Bolton.

Cooperrider, D. L., Whitney, D. K., & Stavros, J. M. (2008). *Appreciative inquiry handbook: For leaders of change* (2nd ed.). Brunswick, OH: Crown Custom Publishing, Inc.

Coppola, B. P. (1995). Progress in practice: Using concepts form motivational and self-regulated learning research to improve chemistry instruction. In P. R. Pintrich (Ed.), *Understanding self-regulated learning* (pp. 8787–8796). San Francisco, CA: Jossey-Bass Publishers. doi:10.1002/tl.37219956310

Corbett, A. T., & Anderson, J. R. (1994). Knowledge Tracing: Modeling the Acquisition of Procedural Knowledge. *User Modeling and User-Adapted Interaction*, *4*(4), 253–278. doi:10.1007/BF01099821

Cornelius-White, J. (2007). Learner-centered teacher-student relationships are effective: A meta-analysis. *Review of Educational Research*, *77*(1), 113–143. doi:10.3102/003465430298563

Course Signals. (2013). *Course signals*. Retrieved from http://www.itap.purdue.edu/learning/tools/signals/

Cox, B. L., & Jantti, M. (2012). Capturing business intelligence required for targeted marketing, demonstrating value, and driving process improvement. *Library & Information Science Research*, *34*(4), 308–316. doi:10.1016/j.lisr.2012.06.002

Crawford, K. (2013, April 1). The hidden biases in big data. [Web log comment]. Harvard Business Review. Retrieved from http://blogs.hbr.org/cs/2013/04/the_hidden_biases_in_big_data.html

Crawford, K., & Schultz, J. (2014). Big data and due process: Toward a framework to redress predictive privacy harms. *BCL Rev.*, *55*, 93–128.

Crawford, V., Schlager, M., Penuel, W. R., & Toyama, Y. (2008). Supporting the Art of Teaching in a Data-Rich, High-Performance Learning Environment. In E. B. Mandinach & M. Honey (Eds.), *Data-Driven School. Improvement* (pp. 109–129). New York, NY: Teachers College Press.

Cronbach, L. J., & Shavelson, R. J. (2004). My current thoughts on coefficient alpha and successor procedures. *Educational and Psychological Measurement*, *64*(3), 391–418. doi:10.1177/0013164404266386

Crosling, G., Heagney, M., & Thomas, L. (2009). Improving student retention in higher education: Improving teaching and learning. *Australian Universities Review*, *51*(2), 9–18.

D'Agostino, R. B. (1998). Tutorial in biostatistics: Propensity score methods for bias reduction in the comparison of a treatment to a non-randomized control group. *Statistics in Medicine*, *17*(19), 2265–2281. doi:10.1002/(SICI)1097-0258(19981015)17:19<2265::AID-SIM918>3.0.CO;2-B PMID:9802183

D'Mello, S. K., Lehman, B., & Person, N. (2010). Monitoring affect states during effortful problem solving activities. *International Journal of Artificial Intelligence in Education*, *20*(4), 361–389. doi:10.3233/JAI-2010-012

Dabbagh, N., & Kitsantas, A. (2004). Supporting Self-Regulation in Student-Centered Web-Based Learning Environments. *International Journal on E-Learning*, *3*(1), 40–47.

Dabbagh, N., & Kitsantas, A. (2005). Using web-based pedagogical tools as scaffolds for self-regulated learning. *Instructional Science*, *33*(5-6), 513–540. doi:10.1007/s11251-005-1278-3

Dal Pozzolo, A., Caelen, O., Waterschoot, S., & Bontempi, G. (2013). Racing for unbalanced methods selection. *Proceedings of the Intelligent Data Engineering and Automated Learning–IDEAL 2013*.

Danaher, J. (2014). Rule by algorithm? Big data and the threat of algocracy. Institute for Ethics and Emerging Technologies. [Blog comment]. Retrieved from http://philosophicaldisquisitions.blogspot.com/2014/01/rule-by-algorithm-big-data-and-threat.html

Daniel, B. (2015). Big Data and analytics in higher education: Opportunities and challenges. *British Journal of Educational Technology*, *46*(5), 904–920. doi:10.1111/bjet.12230

Davies, J. (2013, March 13). The qualified self [Blog comment]. Retrieved from http://thesocietypages.org/cyborgology/2013/03/13/the-qualified-self/

Dawson, S., Gašević, D., Siemens, G., & Joksimovic, S. (2014). *Current state and future trends: A citation network analysis of the learning analytics field.*Paper presented at the Fourth International Conference on Learning Analytics and Knowledge LAK '14, Indianapolis, IN. doi:10.1145/2567574.2567585

Dawson, S., McWilliam, E., & Tan, J. P. L. (2008). Teaching Smarter: How mining ICT data can inform and improve learning and teaching practice. *Paper presented at the ASCILITE 2008*, Melbourne, Australia.

Dawson, S. (2006). Relationship between student communication interaction and sense of community in higher education. *The Internet and Higher Education*, *9*(3), 153–162. doi:10.1016/j.iheduc.2006.06.007

Dawson, S. (2010). "Seeing" the learning community: An exploration of the development of a resource for monitoring online student networking. *British Journal of Educational Technology*, *41*(5), 736–752. doi:10.1111/j.1467-8535.2009.00970.x

Dawson, S., Bakharia, A., & Heathcote, E. (2010). SNAPP: Realising the affordances of real-time SNA within networked learning environments.*Proceedings of the International Conference on Networked Learning* (pp. 125–133).

Dawson, S., Heathcote, L., & Poole, G. (2010). Harnessing ICT Potential: The Adoption and Analysis of ICT Systems for Enhancing the Student Learning Experience. *International Journal of Educational Management*, *24*(2), 116–128. doi:10.1108/09513541011020936

Dawson, S., McWilliam, E., & Tan, J. P. L. (2011). Measuring creative potential: Using social network analysis to monitor and develop learners' creative capacity. *Australasian Journal of Educational Technology*, *27*(6), 924–942.

de Laat, M., Lally, V., & Lipponen, L. (2004). In J. Nall & R. Robson (Eds.), *Proceedings of World Conference on E-Learning in Corporate, Government, Healthcare, and Higher Education* (pp. 1846-1853). Chesapeake, VA: Association for the Advancement of Computing in Education. Retrieved from http://www.editlib.org/p/11592

de Laat, M. (2011). Bridging the Knowledge Gap: Using Social Network Methodology for Detecting, Connecting and Facilitating Informal Networked Learning in Organizations.*Proceedings IEEE International Conference on System Sciences* (pp. 1–8). doi:10.1109/HICSS.2011.88

de Laat, M., Lally, V., Lipponen, L., & Simons, R.-J. (2007). Investigating patterns of interaction in networked learning and computer-supported collaborative learning: A role for Social Network Analysis. *International Journal of Computer-Supported Collaborative Learning*, *2*(1), 87–103. doi:10.1007/s11412-007-9006-4

De Liddo, A., Sándor, Á., & Buckingham Shum, S. (2012). Contested Collective Intelligence: Rationale, Technologies, and a Human-Machine Annotation Study. *Computer Supported Cooperative Work*, *21*(4-5), 417–448. doi:10.1007/s10606-011-9155-x

De Zwart, H. (2014, May 5). During World War II, we did have something to hide. (Translated by Benjamin van Gaalen). Retrieved from https://www.bof.nl/2015/04/30/during-world-war-ii-we-did-have-something-to-hide/

Deakin Crick, R., Broadfoot, P., & Claxton, G. Developing an Effective Lifelong Learning Inventory: The ELLI Project. *Assessment in Education*, 11(3), 248-272.

Deakin Crick, R., & Grushka, K. (2010). Signs, Symbols and Metaphor: Linking self with text in inquiry based learning. *Curriculum Journal*, *21*(1).

Debowski, B., Areibi, S., Grewal, G., & Tempelman, J. (2012). A Dynamic Sampling Framework for Multi-class Imbalanced Data. *Proceedings of the 2012 11th International Conference on Machine Learning and Applications* (pp. 113–118). doi:10.1109/ICMLA.2012.144

Dembo, M. H., Junge, L. G., & Lynch, R. (2006). Becoming a self-regulated learner: implications for web-based education. In H. O' Neil (Ed.), *Web-based learning: theory, research, and practice* (pp. 185–202). Mahwah, NJ: Lawrence Erlbaum Associates.

Deng, L., & Yuen, A. H. K. (2011). Towards a framework for educational affordances of blogs. *Computers & Education*, *56*(2), 441–451. doi:10.1016/j.compedu.2010.09.005

Denil, M., & Trappenberg, T. (2010). Overlap versus imbalance. *Advances in Artificial Intelligence*.

Derry, S. J., Pea, R. D., Barron, B., Engle, R. A., Erickson, F., Goldman, R., & Sherin, B. L. et al. (2010). Conducting Video Research in the Learning Sciences: Guidance on Selection, Analysis, Technology and Ethics. *Journal of the Learning Sciences*, *19*(1), 3–53. doi:10.1080/10508400903452884

Dessus, P. (2009). An Overview of LSA-Based Systems for Supporting Learning and Teaching. In *Artificial Intelligence in Education* (pp. 157–164). doi:10.3233/978-1-60750-028-5-157

Dewey, J. (1933). *How We Think: A Restatement of the Relation of Reflective Thinking to the Educative Process*. Boston: Heath and Co.

Diakopoulos, N. (2014a). Algorithmic Accountability Reporting: On the Investigation of Black Boxes. Tow Center. Retrieved from http://www.nickdiakopoulos.com/wp-content/uploads/2011/07/Algorithmic-Accountability-Reporting_final.pdf

Diakopoulos, N. (2014b). Algorithmic Accountability: Journalistic investigation of computational power structures. *Digital Journalism*.

Diaz, V., & Brown, M. (2012). Learning analytics. A report on the ELI focus session. Retrieved from http://net.educause.edu/ir/library/PDF/ELI3027.pdf

Diaz, V., & Brown, M. (2012). Learning analytics: A report on the ELI focus session. EDUCAUSE Learning Initiative. Retrieved from https://net.educause.edu/ir/library/PDF/ELI3027.pdf

Diaz, V., & Fowler, S. (2012). *Leadership and learning analytics*. Retrieved from https://net.educause.edu/ir/library/pdf/ELIB1205.pdf

Dimitrova, V. (2003). STyLE-OLM: Interactive Open Learner Modelling. *International Journal of Artificial Intelligence in Education*, *13*(1), 35–78.

D'Mello, S. K., Picard, R. W., & Graesser, A. (2007). Towards an affect-sensitive AutoTutor. *IEEE Intelligent Systems, 22*(4), 53–61. doi: 10.1109/MIS.2007.79

Dobrovolny, J. (2006). How adults learn from self-paced, technology-based corporate training: New focus for learners, new focus for designers. *Distance Education*, *27*(2), 155–170. doi:10.1080/01587910600789506

Domingos, P. (1999). Metacost: A general method for making classifiers cost-sensitive.*Proceedings of the Fifth ACM SIGKDD International Conference on Knowledge Discovery and Data Mining*. doi:10.1145/312129.312220

Donker, A. S., De Boer, H., Kostons, D., Dignath van Ewijk, C. C., & van der Werf, M. P. C. (2014). Effectiveness of learning strategy instruction on academic performance: A meta-analysis. *Educational Research Review*, *11*, 1–26. doi:10.1016/j.edurev.2013.11.002

Doran, P. R., Doran, C., & Mazur, A. (2011). Social network analysis as a method for analyzing interaction in collaborative online learning environments. *Journal of Systemics. Cybernetics and Informatics*, *9*(7), 10–16.

Dourish, P., & Bly, S. (1992). Portholes: supporting awareness in a distributed work group *Paper presented at theSIGCHI Conference on Human Factors in Computing SystemsCHI '92* (pp. 541–547). doi:10.1145/142750.142982

Drachsler, H., & Greller, W. (2012, April). The pulse of learning analytics understandings and expectations from the stakeholders.*Proceedings of the 2nd International Conference on Learning Analytics and Knowledge* (pp. 120-129). ACM. doi:10.1145/2330601.2330634

Driscoll, A., & Wood, S. (2007). *Developing outcomes-based assessment for learner-centered education: A faculty introduction*. Sterling, VA: Stylus Publishing, LLC.

Ducate, L. C., & Lomicka, L. L. (2005). Exploring the blogosphere: Use of web logs in the foreign language classroom. *Foreign Language Annals*, *38*(3), 410–421. doi:10.1111/j.1944-9720.2005.tb02227.x

Duffy, T. M., & Cunningham, D. J. (2001). Constructivism: Implications for the design and delivery of instruction. In D. H. Jonassen (Ed.), *Handbook of Research for Educational Communications and Technology*. New York, NY: Simon and Schuster.

DuFon, M. A. (2002). Video recording in Ethnographic SLA Research: Some issues of validity in data collection. *Language Learning & Technology*, *6*(1), 40–59.

Du, H. S., & Wagner, C. (2006). Weblog success: Exploring the role of technology. *International Journal of Human-Computer Studies*, *64*(9), 789–798. doi:10.1016/j.ijhcs.2006.04.002

Duncan, S., & Berland, M. (2012). *Triangulating learning in board games: Computational thinking at multiple scales of analysis.*Paper presented at the Games + Learning + Society (GLS) Conference 8.0, Madison, WI.

Duncan, T., & McKeachie, W. J. (2005). The making of the motivated strategies for learning questionnaire. *Educational Psychologist*, *40*(2), 117–128. doi:10.1207/s15326985ep4002_6

Dunn, K. E., Lo, W.-J., Mulvenon, S. W., & Sutcliffe, R. (2012). Revisiting the motivated strategies for learning questionnaire: A theoretical and statistical reevaluation of the metacognitive self-regulation and effort regulation subscales. *Educational and Psychological Measurement*, *72*(2), 312–331. doi:10.1177/0013164411413461

Durall, E., & Gross, B. (2014). Learning analytics as a metacognitive tool. Retrieved from https://files.ifi.uzh.ch/stiller/CLOSER_2014/CSEDU/CSEDU/Information_Technologies_Supporting_Learning/Short Papers/CSEDU_2014_152_CR.pdf

Duval, E. (2011). Attention please!: learning analytics for visualization and recommendation. *Paper presented at the1st International Conference on Learning Analytics and KnowledgeLAK '11* (pp. 9–17). doi:10.1145/2090116.2090118

Duval, E. (2011) Attention please! Learning Analytics for Visualization and Recommendation.*Proceedings of LAK11 1st International Conference on Learning Analytics and Knowledge 2011* (pp. 9-17). New York, ACM

Dyckhoff, A. L. (2014). *Action research and learning analytics in higher education.* Doctor of Philosophy, Universitätsbibliothek. Retrieved from http://darwin.bth.rwth-aachen.de/opus3/volltexte/2014/5208/pdf/5208.pdf

Dyckhoff, A. L., Zielke, D., Chatti, M. A., & Schroeder, U. (2011). eLAT: An Exploratory Learning Analytics Tool for Reflection and Iterative Improvement of Technology Enhanced Learning. *Educational Data Mining* (pp. 355–356).

Dyckhoff, A. L. (2011). Implications for learning analytics tools: A meta-analysis of applied research questions. *International Journal of Computer Information Systems and Industrial Management Applications*, *3*, 594–601.

Dyckhoff, A. L., Zielke, D., Bültmann, M., Chatti, M. A., & Schroeder, U. (2012). Design and implementation of a learning analytics toolkit for teachers. *Journal of Educational Technology & Society*, *15*(3), 58–76.

Dyckhoff, A. L., Zielke, D., Bültmann, M., Chatti, M. A., & Schroeder, U. (2012). Design and Implementation of a Learning Analytics Toolkit for Teachers. *Journal of Educational Technology & Society*, *15*(3), 58–76.

Dyke, G. (2011). *Which aspects of novice programmers' usage of an IDE predict learning outcomes.* Paper presented at the 42nd ACM Technical Symposium on Computer Science Education SIGCSE '11, Dallas, TX.

Earp, J. B., Antón, A. I., Aiman-Smith, L., & Stufflebeam, W. H. (2005). Examining Internet privacy policies within the context of user privacy values. *Engineering Management. IEEE Transactions on*, *52*(2), 227–237.

Ebbinghaus, H. (1913). *Memory: A contribution to experimental psychology.* Teachers College, Columbia University. doi:10.1037/10011-000

Eckerson, W. W. (2006). *Performance dashboards: Measuring, monitoring, and managing your business.* Hoboken, NJ: John Wiley & Sons.

Edelson, D., Gordin, D., & Pea, R. (1999). Addressing the Challenges of Inquiry-Based Learning Through Technology and Curriculum Design. *Journal of the Learning Sciences*, *8*(3), 391–450. doi:10.1207/s15327809jls0803&4_3

Eduventures. (2013). *Predictive Analytics in Higher Education: Data-Driven Decision-Making for the Student Life Cycle* (White Paper). Retrieved from http://www.eduventures.com/wp- content/uploads/2013/02/Eduventures_Predictive_Analytics_White_Paper1.pdf

Edwards, A. D., & Westgate, D. P. G. (1987). *Investigating Classroom Talk.* Lewes: Falmer Press.

Ehrenberg, R. G., Brewer, D. J., Gamoran, A., & Willms, J. D. (2001). Class size and student achievement. *Psychological Science in the Public Interest*, *2*(1), 1–30. doi:10.1111/1529-1006.003 PMID:26151146

Elias, T. (2011). Learning analytics: Definitions, processes and potential. Retrieved 20 February 2015 http://learninganalytics.net/LearningAnalyticsDefinitionsProcessesPotential.pdf

Elias, T. (2011). *Learning analytics: Definitions, processes, and potential.* Retrieved from http://learninganalytics.net/LearningAnalyticsDefinitionsProcessesPotential.pdf

Elias, T. 2011. Learning Analytics: Definitions, Processes and Potential. Retrieved from http://learninganalytics.net/LearningAnalyticsDefinitionsProcessesPotential.pdf

Ellison, N., & Wu, Y. (2008). Blogging in the classroom: A preliminary exploration of student attitudes and impact on comprehension. *Journal of Educational Multimedia and Hypermedia*, *17*(1), 99–122.

Elvers, G. C., Polzella, D. J., & Graetz, K. (2003). Procrastination in online courses: Performance and attitudinal differences. *Teaching of Psychology*, *30*(2), 159–162. doi:10.1207/S15328023TOP3002_13

Enzai, N. I. M., Kar, S. A. C., Husni, H., & Ahmed, N. 2011. Harnessing Creativity in Teaching and Learning Introductory Programming.*Proceedings of 2011 IEEE Student Conference on Research and Development*, Putrajaya, Selangor, Malaysia doi:10.1109/SCOReD.2011.6148778

Erickson, F. (2006). Definition and analysis of data from videotape: Some research procedures and their rationales. In J. L. Green, G. Camili, & P. B. Elmore (Eds.), *Handbook of complementary methods in educational research* (pp. 177–191). Mahwah, NJ: Lawrence Erlbaum Associates.

Essa, A. (2013). Can we improve retention rates by giving students chocolates? [Blog comment]. Retrieved from http://alfredessa.com/2013/10/can-we-improve-retention-rates-by-giving-students-chocolates/

Essa, A., & Ayad, H. (2012, April 29–May 2). Student Success System: Risk Analytics and Data Visualization using Ensembles of Predictive Models. *Paper presented at theLearning Analytics and Knowledge Conference*, Vancouver, British Columbia.

Essa, A., & Ayad, H. (2012). Improving student success using predictive models and data visualisations. *The Journal of the Association for Learning Technology (ALT). Research in Learning Technology*, 2012, 20.

Estabrooks, A., Jo, T., & Japkowicz, N. (2004). A Multiple Resampling Method for Learning from Imbalanced Data Sets. *Computational Intelligence*, *20*(1), 18–36. doi:10.1111/j.0824-7935.2004.t01-1-00228.x

Eubanks, V. (2015, April 30). The policy machine. Slate Magazine. Retrieved from http://www.slate.com/articles/technology/future_tense/2015/04/the_dangers_of_letting_algorithms_enforce_policy.html

Eynon, R. (2013). The rise of Big Data: What does it mean for education, technology, and media research? *Learning, Media and Technology*, *38*(3), 237–240. doi:10.1080/17439884.2013.771783

Falakmasir, M. H., & Habibi, J. (2010). *Using educational data mining to study the impact of virtual classroom in e-learning.* Paper presented at the Third Annual Conference on Educational Data Mining, Pittsburgh, PA.

Fan, Y. (2014). A revisit to the class imbalance learning with linear support vector machine. *Proceedings of the 2014 9th International Conference on Computer Science & Education* (pp. 516–521). doi:10.1109/ICCSE.2014.6926515

Fancsali, S., Ritter, S., Stamper, J. C., & Nixon, T. (2013). Toward "Hyper-Personalized" Cognitive Tutors: Non-Cognitive Personalization in the Generalized Intelligent Framework for Tutoring. *Proceedings of theInternational Conference on Artificial Intelligence in Education* (pp. 71-79).

Feldstein, M. (2013, November 6). Purdue's non-answer on Course Signals [Blog comment]. Retrieved from http://mfeldstein.com/purdues-non-answer-course-signals/

Feng, M., Heffernan, N. T., & Koedinger, K. R. (2009). User Modeling and User-Adapted Interaction: Addressing the Assessment Challenge in an Online System That Tutors as It Assesses. *The Journal of Personalization Research*, *19*(3), 243–266.

Ferdig, R. E., & Trammell, K. D. (2004). Content delivery in the "blogosphere.". *T.H.E. Journal*, *31*(7), 12–20.

Ferguson, R. (2014). *Learning analytics don't just measure students' progress – They can shape it.* Retrieved from http://www.theguardian.com/education/2014/mar/26/learning-analytics-student-progress

Ferguson, R., & Shum, S. B. (2012). *Social learning analytics: Five approaches.* Paper presented at the Second International Conference on Learning Analytics and Knowledge LAK '12, Vancouver, Canada. doi:10.1145/2330601.2330616

Ferguson, R., Clow, D., Macfadyen, L. P., Essa, A., Dawson, S., & Alexander, S. (2014). Setting Learning Analytics in Context: Overcoming the Barriers to Large-Scale Adoption. *Paper presented at the LAK '14*, Indianapolis. doi:10.1145/2567574.2567592

Ferguson, R. (2012). Learning analytics: Drivers, developments and challenges. *International Journal of Technology Enhanced Learning*, *4*(5), 304–317. doi:10.1504/IJTEL.2012.051816

Ferguson, R., & Shum, S. B. (2011). Learning analytics to identify exploratory dialogue within synchronous text chat.*Proceedings of the 1st International Conference on Learning Analytics and Knowledge* (pp. 99–103). doi:10.1145/2090116.2090130

Fernández, A., García, S., & Herrera, F. (2011). Addressing the classification with imbalanced data: open problems and new challenges on class distribution. In *Hybrid Artificial Intelligent Systems* (pp. 1–10).

Fernández-Gallego, B., Lama, M., Vidal, J. C., & Mucientes, M. (2013). Learning analytics framework for educational virtual worlds. *Procedia Computer Science*, *25*, 443–447. doi:10.1016/j.procs.2013.11.056

Few, S. (2009). *Now you see it: Simple visualization techniques for quantitative analysis*. US: Analytics Press.

Fincher, S. (1999). What are we doing when we teach programming? *Proceedings of the 29th ASEE/IEEE Frontiers in Education Conference*.

Fiocco, M. (2006). An evaluation of a pathway program: The students' view. Paper presented at the Australian International Education Conference. Perth, Western Australia: Perth Convention Exhibition Centre. Retrieved from www.idp.com/aiec

Fitzpatrick, J. L., Sanders, J. R., & Worthen, B. R. (2011). *Program evaluation: Alternative approaches and practical guidelines* (4th ed.). Upper Saddle River, NJ: Pearson Education, Inc.

Florian, B., Glahn, C., Drachsler, H., Specht, M., & Fabregat, R. (2011). *Activity-based learner-models for learner monitoring and recommendations in Moodle*. Paper presented at the Sixth European Conference on Technology Enhanced Learning EC–TEL '11, Palermo, Italy. doi:10.1007/978-3-642-23985-4_10

Foucault, M. (1984). Of other spaces. Utopias and heterotopias. In *Architecture/Mouvement/Continuité, Des Espace Autres* (1967, March). (trans. by J. Miskowiec). Retrieved from http://web.mit.edu/allanmc/www/foucault1.pdf

Fournier, H., Kop, R., & Sitlia, H. (2011). The value of learning analytics to networked learning on a personal learning environment.

Fournier, H., Kop, R., & Sitlia, H. (2011). *The value of learning analytics to networked learning on a personal learning environment.*Paper presented at the First International Conference on Learning Analytics and Knowledge LAK '11, Banff, Canada. doi:10.1145/2090116.2090131

Fowler, F. J. Jr. (1995). *Improving survey questions: Design and evaluation*. Thousand Oaks, CA: SAGE Publications.

Friedman, B., & Nissenbaum, H. (1996). Bias in computer systems. *ACM Transactions on Information Systems*, *14*(3), 330–347. doi:10.1145/230538.230561

Friedman, J. H., & Popescu, B. (2008). Predictive Learning via Rule Ensembles. *The Annals of Applied Statistics*, *2*(3), 916–964. doi:10.1214/07-AOAS148

Friendly, M. (2005). *Milestones in the History of Data Visualization: A Case Study in Statistical Historiography*. Retrieved from http://www.datavis.ca/papers/gfkl.pdf

Fritz, J. (2011). Classroom walls that talk: Using online course activity data of successful students to raise self-awareness of underperforming peers. *The Internet and Higher Education*, *14*(2), 89–97. doi:10.1016/j.iheduc.2010.07.007

Fry, B. (2007). *Visualizing Data*. Sebastapol, CA: O'Reilly.

Fujita, N., & Teplovs, C. (2009). Automating the analysis of collaborative discourse: Identifying idea clusters. *Computer-Supported Collaborative Learning*, 2009, 162–164.

Fusion Charts. (n. d.). *Principles of Data Visualization - What We See in a Visual.* Available: http://www.fusioncharts.com/whitepapers/downloads/Principles-of-Data-Visualization.pdf

Gagné, R. M., & Wager, W. W. >, Golas, K. C., & Keller, J. M. (2005). Principles of instructional design (5th ed.). Belmont, CA: Thompson Wadsworth.

García, S., & Herrera, F. (2009). Evolutionary undersampling for classification with imbalanced datasets: Proposals and taxonomy. *Evolutionary Computation*, *17*(3), 275–306. doi:10.1162/evco.2009.17.3.275 PMID:19708770

García-Solórzano, D., Cobo, G., Santamaria, E., Morán, J. A., Monzo, C., & Melenchón, J. (2012). Educational monitoring tool based on faceted browsing and data portraits. *Paper presented at the2nd International Conference on Learning Analytics and KnowledgeLAK '12*, New York: NY. doi:10.1145/2330601.2330645

García, V., Sánchez, J. S., & Mollineda, R. A. (2012). On the effectiveness of preprocessing methods when dealing with different levels of class imbalance. *Knowledge-Based Systems*, *25*(1), 13–21. doi:10.1016/j.knosys.2011.06.013

Gašević, D., Dawson, S., & Siemens, G. (2015). Let's not forget: Learning analytics are about learning. *TechTrends*, *59*(1), 64–71. doi:10.1007/s11528-014-0822-x

Gašević, D., Jovanović, J., & Devedzic, V. (2007). Ontology-based annotation of learning object content. *Interactive Learning Environments*, *15*(1), 1–26. doi:10.1080/10494820600968203

Gavan, C., & Anderson, M. (2012, October 10-14). Engaging Undergraduate Programming Students: Experiences using Lego Mindstorms NXT. *Proceedings of ACM Special Interest Group for Information Technology Education Conference (SIGITE)*, Calgary, Canada.

Geertz, C. (1988). *Works and Lives: The Anthropologist as Author*. Cambridge: Polity Press.

Gerhard, F. (2001). User Modeling in Human-Computer Interaction. *User Modeling and User-Adapted Interaction*, *11*(1/2), 65–86. doi:10.1023/A:1011145532042

Ghazikhani, A. (2012). Class imbalance handling using wrapper-based random oversampling. *Proceedings of the20th Iranian Conference on Electrical Engineering, (ICEE2012)* (pp. 611–616). doi:10.1109/IranianCEE.2012.6292428

Gibson, R. (2010). The 'art' of creative teaching: Implications for higher education. *Teaching in Higher Education*, *15*(5), 607–613. doi:10.1080/13562517.2010.493349

Godwin-Jones, R. (2012). Challenging Hegemonies in Online Learning. *Language Learning & Technology*, *16*(2), 4.

Goldhaber, M. H. (1997, April). The Attention Economy and the Net. *First Monday*, *2*(4). doi:10.5210/fm.v2i4.519

Goldman, R. (2007). Video Representations and the Perspectivity Framework: Epistemology, Ethnography, Evaluation, and Ethics. In R. Goldman, R. Pea, B. Barron, & S. J. Derry (Eds.), *Video Research in the Learning Sciences* (pp. ix–xiii). New York: Lawrence Erlbaum Associates.

Goldstein, P. J. 2005. Academic Analytics: The Use of Management Information and Technology in Higher Education. EDUCAUSE Center for Applied Research. Retrieved from http://net.educause.edu/ir/library/pdf/ECM/ECM0508.pdf

Gonzalez, M. J. F. (2012) Advantages and Limits of Video Recording as a Tool for Students, Teachers and Researchers in Music Conservatoires. *Proceedings of International Conference on The Future of Education*, Florence, Italy.

Goos, M., Manning, M., & Salomons, A. (2009). Job polarization in Europe. *The American Economic Review*, *99*(2), 58–63. doi:10.1257/aer.99.2.58

Govaerts, S., Verbert, K., Duval, E., & Pardo, A. (2012). The student activity meter for awareness and self-reflection. *CHI Extended Abstracts* (pp. 869–884). doi:10.1145/2212776.2212860

Govaerts, S., Verbert, K., Klerkx, J., & Duval, E. (2010). Visualizing Activities for Self-reflection and Awareness. In X. Luo, M. Spaniol, L. Wang, Q. Li, W. Nejdl, & W. Zhang (Eds.), *Advances in Web-Based Learning – The 9th International Conference on Web-based Learning*, Shanghai, China, LCNS (Vol. 6483, pp. 91–100). Berlin, Heidelberg: Springer Berlin Heidelberg. doi:10.1007/978-3-642-17407-0_10

Graf, S., & Kinshuk. (in press). Dynamic Student Modeling of Learning Styles for Advanced Adaptivity in Learning Management Systems. *International Journal of Information Systems and Social Change*.

Grann, J., & Bushway, D. (2014). Competency map: visualizing student learning to promote student success. *Paper presented at theFourth International Conference on Learning Analytics And KnowledgeLAK '14* (pp. 168–172). doi:10.1145/2567574.2567622

Gray, G., McGuiness, C., Owende, P., & Carthy, A. (2014). A Review of Psychometric Data Analysis and Applications. *Journal of Learning Analytics*, *1*(1), 75–106.

Greene, J. A., & Azevedo, R. (2009). A macro-level analysis of SRL processes and their relations to the acquisition of a sophisticated mental model of a complex system. *Contemporary Educational Psychology*, *34*(1), 18–29. doi:10.1016/j.cedpsych.2008.05.006

Greenwood, D., Stopczynski, A., Sweat, B., Hardjono, T., & Pentland, A. (2015). The new deal on data: a framework for institutional controls. In J. Lane, V. Stodden, S. Bender, & H. Nissenbaum (Eds), Privacy, big data, and the public good (pp. 192-210). New York, NY: Cambridge University Press.

Greller, W., & Drachsler, H. (2012). Translating learning into numbers: A generic framework for learning analytics. *Journal of Educational Technology & Society*, *15*(3), 42–57.

Greller, W., & Drachsler, H. (2012). Translating Learning into Numbers: A Generic Framework for Learning Analytics. *Journal of Educational Technology & Society*, *15*(3), 42–57.

Greyling, J. H., Cilliers, C. B., & Calitz, A. P. (2006, July 10-13) B#: The Development and Assessment of an Iconic Programming Tool for Novice Programmers. *Proceedings of the 7th International Conference onInformation Technology Based Higher Education and TrainingITHET '06*, Ultimo, NSW (pp. 367-375).

Gruzd, A., Haythornthwaite, C., Paulin, D., Absar, R., & Huggett, M. (2014). Learning analytics for the social media age. *Presented at theFourth International Conference*, New York: New York (pp. 254–256). doi:10.1145/2567574.2576773

Guillaume, D. W., & Khachikian, C. S. (2011). The effect of time on task on student grades and grade expectations. *Assessment & Evaluation in Higher Education*, *36*(3), 251–261. doi:10.1080/02602930903311708

Gulbahar, Y., & Ilgaz, H. (2014). Premise of learning analytics for educational context: Through concept to practice. *International Journal of Informatics Technologies*, *7*(3), 12–20.

Gunnarsson, B. L., & Alterman, R. (2012). *Predicting failure*. Paper presented at the Second International Conference on Learning Analytics and Knowledge LAK '12, Vancouver, Canada. doi:10.1145/2330601.2330665

Gunnarsson, B. L., & Alterman, R. (2014). Peer promotions as a method to identify quality content. *Journal of Learning Analytics*, *1*(2), 126–150.

Guo, X., Yin, Y., Dong, C., Yang, G., & Zhou, G. (2008). On the Class Imbalance Problem. *Proceedings of the2008 Fourth International Conference on Natural Computation* (pp. 192–201). doi:10.1109/ICNC.2008.871

Guo, H., & Viktor, H. L. (2004). Learning from imbalanced data sets with boosting and data generation: The DataBoost-IM approach. *ACM SIGKDD Explorations Newsletter*, *6*(1), 30–39. doi:10.1145/1007730.1007736

Gurses, S. (2014). Privacy and security. Can you engineer privacy? Viewpoints. *Communications of the ACM*, *57*(8), 20–23. Retrieved from http://dl.acm.org/citation.cfm?id=2632661.2633029 doi:10.1145/2633029

Hagan, D., & Markham, S. (2000). Teaching Java with the BlueJ environment.*Proceedings of Australian Society for Computers in Learning in Tertiary Education Conference ASCILITE 2000.*

Hahn, J. H., Mentz, E., & Meyer, L. (2009). Assessment Strategies for Pair Programming. *Journal of Information Technology Education*, *8*, 273–284.

Hair, J. F., Black, W. C., Babin, B. J., Anderson, R. E., & Tatham, R. (2010). *Multivariate Data Analysis*. Upper Saddle River, New Jersey: Pearson Education.

Hair, J. F. Jr. (2007). Knowledge creation in marketing: The role of predictive analytics. *European Business Review*, *19*(4), 303–315. doi:10.1108/09555340710760134

Halatchliyski, I., Hecking, T., Göhnert, T., & Hoppe, H. U. (2014). Analyzing the main paths of knowledge evolution and contributor roles in an open learning community. *Journal of Learning Analytics*, *1*(2), 72–93. doi: 10.1145/2460296.2460311

Hamalainen, W., Suhonen, J., Sutinen, E., & Toivonen, H. (2004). *Data mining in personalizing distance education courses*. Paper presented at the 21st ICDE World Conference on Open Learning and Distance Education, Hong Kong.

Hamilton, L., Halverson, R., Jackson, S., Mandinach, E., Supovitz, J., & Wayman, J. (2009). *Using Student Achievement Data to Support Instructional Decision Making (NCEE 2009-4067)*. Washington, DC: U.S. Department of Education, Institute of Education Sciences, National Center for Education Evaluation and Regional Assistance.

Han, H., Wang, W., & Mao, B. (2005). Borderline-SMOTE : A New Over-Sampling Method in. *Advances in Intelligent Computing* (pp. 878–887).

Han, J., & Kamber, M. (2006). *Data mining concepts and techniques*. Burlington, MA: Morgan Kaufmann.

Hanneman, R. A., & Riddle, M. (2011). Concepts and measures for basic network analysis. In Handbook of Social Network Analysis. doi:10.4135/9781446294413.n24

Hansen, D. Ben Shneiderman, & Smith, M. A. (2010). Analyzing Social Media Networks with NodeXL: Insights from a Connected World. San Francisco, CA: Morgan Kaufmann Publishers Inc.

Harford, T. (2014). Big data: are we making a big mistake. *Financial Times*, 28, 1-5.

Haro-garcia, A. De, & Garcia-Perajas, N. (2011). A scalable method for instance selection for class-imbalance datasets. *Proceedings of the Intelligent Systems Design and Applications (ISDA)* (pp. 1383–1390).

Hartley, D. (1995). The 'McDonaldization' of higher education: Food for thought? *Oxford Review of Education*, *21*(4), 409–423. doi:10.1080/0305498950210403

Haythornthwaite, C. (2011). Learning networks, crowds and communities. *Paper presented at the1st International Conference on Learning Analytics and KnowledgeLAK '11* (pp. 18–22). doi:10.1145/2090116.2090119

Haythornthwaite, C., & De Laat, M. (2010). Social networks and learning networks: Using social network perspectives to understand social learning. *Proceedings of the7th International Conference on Networked Learning,* Lancaster University, Lancaster, England.

He, H., Bai, Y., Garcia, E. A., & Li, S. (2008). ADASYN: Adaptive synthetic sampling approach for imbalanced learning. *Proceedings of the2008 IEEE International Joint Conference on Neural Networks (IEEE World Congress on Computational Intelligence)* (Vol. 3, pp. 1322–1328). doi:10.1109/IJCNN.2008.4633969

Heath, J. (2014). Contemporary Privacy Theory Contribution to Learning Analytics. *Journal of Learning Analytics*, *1*(1), 140–149.

Heer, J., & Boyd, D. (2005). *Vizster: Visualizing online social networks*. Paper presented at the IEEE Symposium on Information Visualization InfoVis '05, Minneapolis, MN. doi:10.1109/INFOVIS.2005.39

Heer, J., Viégas, F. B., & Wattenberg, M. (2009). Voyagers and voyeurs. *Communications of the ACM*, *52*(1), 87–97. doi:10.1145/1435417.1435439

Henman, P. (2004). Targeted! Population segmentation, electronic surveillance and governing the unemployed in Australia. *International Sociology*, *19*(2), 173–191. doi:10.1177/0268580904042899

Hershkovitz, A., & Nachmias, R. (2008). Developing a Log-based Motivation Measuring Tool. In *Educational Data Mining* (pp. 226–233).

Hibino, S., & Rundensteiner, E. A. (1994) A Graphical Query Language for Identifying Temporal Trends in Video Data (Technical Report). University of Michigan. Retrieved from http://citeseerx.ist.psu.edu/viewdoc/download?doi=10.1.1.50.1145&rep=rep1&type=pdf&ei=VTE7UZGwCuaM7Qag3YGwCg&usg=AFQjCNFf_jWvyoA5h_L9qvoPS-bd06VsiQ&si

Hijon, R., & Carlos, R. (2006). *E-learning platforms analysis and development of students tracking functionality.*Paper presented at the 18th Annual World Conference on Educational Multimedia, Hypermedia, and Telecommunications ED–MEDIA '06, Orlando, FL.

Hillman, N. W., Tandberg, D. A., & Fryar, A. H. (2015). Evaluating the impacts of "new" performance funding in higher education. *Educational Evaluation and Policy Analysis*.

Hilpert, J., Stemien, J., van der Hoeven Kraft, K., & Husman, J. (2013). Evidence for the latent factor structure of the MSLQ: A new conceptualization of an established questionnaire. *SAGE Open*. Retrieve from http://classic.sgo.sagepub.com/content/3/4/2158244013510305.short

Hirschi, C. (2010). Introduction: Applications of Social Network Analysis. *Procedia: Social and Behavioral Sciences*, *4*, 2–3. doi:10.1016/j.sbspro.2010.07.477

Hmelo-Silver, C. E. (2004). Problem-Based Learning: What and How Do Students Learn? *Educational Psychology Review*, *16*(3), 235–266. doi:10.1023/B:EDPR.0000034022.16470.f3

Hong, W. (2008). Exploring educational use of blogs in us education. *US–China Education Review*, *5*(10), 34–38.

Hostmann, B., Rayner, N., & Herschel, G. (2009). *Gartner's business intelligence, analytics and performance management framework*. Stamford, CT: Gartner.

Hotho, A., Nürnberger, A., & Paaß, G. (2005). A Brief Survey of Text Mining. *LDV Forum.*

Huang, H.-Y., Lin, Y.-J., Chen, Y.-S., & Lu, H.-Y. (2012). Imbalanced data classification using random subspace method and SMOTE. *Proceedings of the 6th International Conference on Soft Computing and Intelligent Systems, and The 13th International Symposium on Advanced Intelligence Systems* (pp. 817–820). doi:10.1109/SCIS-ISIS.2012.6505155

Huang, T. C., Cheng, S. C., & Huang, Y. M. (2009). A blog article recommendation generating mechanism using an SBACPSO algorithm. *Expert Systems with Applications*, *36*(7), 10388–10396. doi:10.1016/j.eswa.2009.01.039

Icke, I., & Sklar, E. (2008). Daisy Map: A Visualization Tool For Student Assessments Data. *Proceedings of the IEEE VisWeek From Theory to Practice Design, Vision and Visualization Workshop.*

Igoe, T. (2007). *Making Things Talk: Practical Methods for Connecting Physical Objects*. Make Books.

Improving the degree attainment of Black and minority ethnic students. (2011, March 17). UK Higher Education Academy, http://www.heacademy.ac.uk/news/detail/2011/improving_BME_degree_attainment

Information Literacy Competency Standards for Higher Education. (2000). Association of College & Research Libraries, Chicago.

ISTQB Exam Certification. (n. d.). *What is Waterfall model- advantages, disadvantages and when to use it?* Retrieved from http://istqbexamcertification.com/what-is-waterfall-model-advantages-disadvantages-and-when-to-use-it/

Japkowicz, N. (2000). Learning from imbalanced data sets: a comparison of various strategies. *Proceedings of theAAAI Workshop on Learning from Imbalanced Data Sets.*

Jayaprakash, S. M., Moody, E. W., Lauría, E. J. M., Regan, J. R., & Baron, J. D. (2014). Early alert of academically at-risk students: An open source analytics initiative. *Journal of Learning Analytics*, *1*(1), 6–47.

Jeatrakul, P., Wong, K. W., Fung, C. C., & Takama, Y. (2010). Misclassification analysis for the class imbalance problem. *Proceedings of theWorld Automation Congress (WAC).*

Jeong, H., & Biswas, G. (2008). Mining Student Behavior Models in Learning-by-Teaching Environments.*Proceedings of the 1st International Conference on Educational Data Mining*, (pp. 127–136). Montréal, Québec, Canada.

Johnson, L., Adams Becker, S., Cummins, M., Estrada, V., Freeman, A., & Ludgate, H. (2013). Horizon report (2013 higher education ed.).

Johnson, L., Levine, A., Smith, R., & Stone, S. (2010). The 2010 Horizon Report. Austin, TX: The New Media Consortium. Retrieved from http://wp.nmc.org/horizon2010/

Johnson, L., Smith, R., Willis, H., Levine, A., & Haywood, K. (2011). The 2011 Horizon Report. Austin, TX: The New Media Consortium. Retrieved from http://net.educause.edu/ir/library/pdf/HR2011.pdf

Johnson, B., & Turner, L. A. (2003). Data collection strategies in mixed methods research. In A. Tashakkori & C. Teddlie (Eds.), *Handbook of mixed methods in social & behavioral research* (pp. 297–319). Thousand Oaks, CA: SAGE Publications, Inc.

Johnson, L., Adams Becker, S., Estrada, V., & Freeman, A. (2014). *NMC Horizon Report: 2014 K-12 Edition* (pp. 1–52). Austin, Texas: The New Media Consortium.

Jones, C., Asensio, M., & Goodyear, P. (2000). Networked learning in higher education: Practitioners' perspectives. *HE Association for Learning Technology Journal*, *8*(2), 18–28. doi:10.1080/0968776000080203

Jovanović, J., Gašević, D., Brooks, C. A., Devedžić, V., & Hatala, M. (2007). LOCO-Analyst: A Tool for Raising Teachers' Awareness in Online Learning Environments. In E. Duval, R. Klamma, & M. Wolpers (Eds.), *Proceedings of the Second European conference on Technology Enhanced Learning: creating new learning experiences on a global scale(EC-TEL'07)* (pp. 112-126). Berlin: Springer-Verlag. doi:10.1007/978-3-540-75195-3_9

Jovanović, J., Gašević, D., Brooks, C., Devedžić, V., Hatala, M., Eap, T., & Richards, G. (2008). LOCO-Analyst: Semantic web technologies in learning content usage analysis. *International Journal of Continuing Engineering Education and Lifelong Learning*, *18*(1), 54. doi:10.1504/IJCEELL.2008.016076

Junfei, C., Qingfeng, W., & Huailin, D. (2010). An empirical study on ensemble selection for class-imbalance data sets. *Proceedings of the 2010 5th International Conference on Computer Science & Education* (pp. 477–480). doi:10.1109/ICCSE.2010.5593573

Kalhan, A. (2013). Immigration policing and federalism through the lens of technology, surveillance, and privacy. *Ohio State Law Journal*, *74*, 1105–1165.

Kardan, S., & Conati, C. 2011. A Framework for Capturing Distinguishing User Interaction Behaviours in Novel Interfaces. In M. Pechenizkiy, T. Calders, C. Conati, S. Ventura, C. Romero, & J. Stamper (Ed.), *Proceedings of the 4th International Conference on Educational Data Mining* (pp. 159–168).

Kargar, M. J., & Azimzadeh, F. (2009). A framework for ranking quality of information on a weblog. *World Academy of Science, Engineering and Technology*, *56*, 690–695.

Kasemsap, K. (2014a). The role of social media in the knowledge-based organizations. In I. Lee (Ed.), *Integrating social media into business practice, applications, management, and models* (pp. 254–275). Hershey, PA, USA: IGI Global. doi:10.4018/978-1-4666-6182-0.ch013

Kasemsap, K. (2014b). The role of social networking in global business environments. In P. Smith & T. Cockburn (Eds.), *Impact of emerging digital technologies on leadership in global business* (pp. 183–201). Hershey, PA, USA: IGI Global. doi:10.4018/978-1-4666-6134-9.ch010

Kasemsap, K. (2015a). The role of business analytics in performance management. In M. Tavana & K. Puranam (Eds.), *Handbook of research on organizational transformations through big data analytics* (pp. 126–145). Hershey, PA, USA: IGI Global. doi:10.4018/978-1-4666-7272-7.ch010

Kasemsap, K. (2015b). The role of data mining for business intelligence in knowledge management. In A. Azevedo & M. Santos (Eds.), *Integration of data mining in business intelligence systems* (pp. 12–33). Hershey, PA, USA: IGI Global. doi:10.4018/978-1-4666-6477-7.ch002

Kay, J., & Lum, A. (2005). Exploiting readily available web data for scrutable student models. *Proceedings of the12th International Conference on Artificial Intelligence in Education* (pp. 338–345). Amsterdam: IOS Press.

Kay, J., & Lum, A. (2006). Exploiting Readily Available Web Data for Reflective Student Models. *Artificial Intelligence in Education.*

Kay, J., Maisonneuve, N., Yacef, K., & Reimann, P. (2006). The Big Five and Visualisations of Team Work Activity. *ITS'06 Proceedings of the 8th international conference on Intelligent Tutoring Systems*, 197–206. doi:10.1007/11774303_20

Keim, D. A. (2002). Information Visualisation and Visual Data Mining. *IEEE Transactions on Visualization and Computer Graphics*, *7*(1), 100–107.

Kelleher, C., & Pausch, R. (2005). Lowering the Barriers to Programming: A Taxonomy of Programming Environments and Languages for Novice Programmers. *ACM Computing Surveys*, *37*(2), 83–137. doi:10.1145/1089733.1089734

Kerly, A., & Bull, S. (2008). Children's Interactions with Inspectable and Negotiated Learner Models Paper presented at the ITS '08: *Proceedings of the 9th International Conference on Intelligent Tutoring Systems*, 5091, 132–141. Springer-Verlag, Berlin, Heidelberg. doi:10.1007/978-3-540-69132-7_18

Kerly, A., Ellis, R., & Bull, S. (2008). CALMsystem: A Conversational Agent for Learner Modelling. *Knowledge-Based Systems*, *21*(3), 238–246. doi:10.1016/j.knosys.2007.11.015

Kerr, I., & Barrigar, J. (2012). Privacy, identity and anonymity. In K. Ball, K. D. Haggerty, & D. Lyon (Eds.), *Routledge Handbook of Surveillance Studies* (pp. 386–394). Abingdon, UK: Routledge. doi:10.4324/9780203814949.ch4_1_c

Khurana, U., Nguyen, V.-A., Cheng, H.-C., Ahn, J.-W., Chen, X., & Shneiderman, B. (2011). Visual Analysis of Temporal Trends in Social Networks Using Edge Color Coding and Metric Timelines. Paper presented at the *Privacy, Security, Risk and Trust (PASSAT) and 2011 IEEE Third International Conference on Social Computing (SocialCom)* (pp. 549–554). doi:10.1109/PASSAT/SocialCom.2011.212

Kim, K., & Bonk, C. J. (2006). The future of online teaching and learning in higher education: The survey says. *EDUCAUSE Quarterly*, *29*(4), 22.

Kirkpatrick, D. L., & Kirkpatrick, J. D. (2007). *Implementing the four levels: A practical guide for effective evaluation of training programs.* San Francisco, CA: Berrett-Koehler Publishers, Inc.

Kitchen, R. (2014b). Thinking critically about and research algorithms. The Programmable City Working Paper 5. Retrieved from http://eprints.maynoothuniversity.ie/5715/

Kitchen, R. (2014a). *The data revolution. Big data, open data, data infrastructures and their consequences.* London, UK: SAGE. doi:10.4135/9781473909472

Klein, H. J., Noe, R. A., & Wang, C. (2006). Motivation to learn and course outcomes: The impact of delivery mode, learning goal orientation, and perceived barriers and enablers. *Personnel Psychology*, *59*(3), 665–702. doi:10.1111/j.1744-6570.2006.00050.x

Knight, S., Shum, S. B., & Littleton, K. (2014). Epistemology, assessment, pedagogy: Where learning meets analytics in the middle space. *Journal of Learning Analytics*, *1*(2), 23–47.

Knowles, J. (2014). *Data Visualisation for Education.* Retrieved from jaredknowles.com/s/KnowlesSDPTalk2014.html

Kobsa, A. (1990). User Modeling in Dialog Systems: Potentials and Hazards. *AI & Society*, *4*(3), 214–231. doi:10.1007/BF01889941

Köck, M., & Paramythis, A. (2011). Activity Sequence Modeling and Dynamic Clustering for Personalized E-Learning. *Journal of User Modeling and User-Adapted Interaction*, *21*(1-2), 51–97. doi:10.1007/s11257-010-9087-z

Koedinger, K. R., Baker, R., Cunningham, K., Skogsholm, A., Leber, B., & Stamper, J. (2010). A Data Repository for the EDM Community: The PSLC DataShop. In C. Romero, S. Ventura, M. Pechenizkiy, & R. S. J. d. Baker (Eds.), *Handbook of Educational Data Mining* (pp. 43–55). Boca Raton, FL: CRC Press. doi:10.1201/b10274-6

Koedinger, K., McLaughlin, E., & Heffernan, N. (2010). A Quasi-experimental Evaluation of an On-line Formative Assessment and Tutoring System. *Journal of Educational Computing Research*, *4*(4), 489–510. doi:10.2190/EC.43.4.d

Kolb, D. (1984). *Experiential Learning as the Science of Learning and Development*. Englewood Cliffs, NJ: Prentice Hall.

Kölling, M., Quig, B., Patterson, A. and Rosenberg, J. (2003). The BlueJ System and its pedagogy. *Journal of Computer Science Education, Special Issue on Learning and Teaching Object Technology*, 13(4), Dec 2003.

Kolowich, S. (2014, January 16). Exactly know many students take online courses? *The Chronicle of Higher Education*. Retrieved from http://chronicle.com/blogs/wiredcampus/exactly-how-many-students-take-online-courses/49455

Koplowitz, J., & Brown, T. (1981). On the relation of performance to editing in nearest neighbor rules. *Pattern Recognition, 13*(3), 31–32. doi:10.1016/0031-3203(81)90102-3

Koponen, J. M. (2015, April 18). We need algorithmic angels [Blog comment]. *TechCrunch*. Retrieved from http://techcrunch.com/2015/04/18/we-need-algorithmic-angels/

Kop, R., & Fournier, H. (2010). New dimensions to self-directed learning in an open networked learning environment. *International Journal of Self-Directed Learning*, *7*(2).

Kosba, E., Dimitrova, V., & Boyle, R. (2005). Using student and group models to support teachers in web-based distance education. *Paper presented at the 10th international conference on User Modeling UM'05*. Springer-Verlag. doi:10.1007/11527886_17

Kosba, E., Dimitrova, V., & Boyle, R. (2007). Adaptive feedback generation to support teachers in web-based distance education. *User Modeling and User-Adapted Interaction*, *17*(4), 379–413. doi:10.1007/s11257-007-9031-z

Kotsiantis, S., Kanellopoulos, D., & Pintelas, P. (2006). Handling imbalanced datasets: A review. *GESTS International Transactions on Computer Science and Engineering, 30*(1).

Kounios, J., Frymiare, J. L., Bowden, E. M., Fleck, J. I., Subramaniam, K., Parrish, T. B., & Jung-Beeman, M. (2006). The prepared mind: Neural activity prior to problem presentation predicts subsequent solution by sudden insight. *Psychological Science*, *17*(10), 882–890. doi:10.1111/j.1467-9280.2006.01798.x PMID:17100789

Kovacic, Z. (2010). Early prediction of student success: Mining students' enrolment data. *Paper presented at the Informing Science & IT Education Conference InSITE '10.*

Kovanović, V., Gašević, D., Dawson, S., Joksimović, S., Baker, R. S., & Hatala, M. (2015, March). Penetrating the black box of time-on-task estimation.*Proceedings of the Fifth International Conference on Learning Analytics and Knowledge* (pp. 184-193). ACM. doi:10.1145/2723576.2723623

Krause, K., & Coates, H. (2008). Students' Engagement in First-Year University. *Assessment and Evaluation in Higher Education*, 33(5), 493–505.

Kraut, A. I. (1996). Planning and conducting the survey: Keeping strategic people in mind. In A. I. Kraut (Ed.), *Organizational surveys: Tools for assessment and change* (pp. 149–176). San Francisco, CA: Jossey-Bass Publishers.

Kretzschmar, R., Karayiannis, N. B., & Eggimann, F. (2005). Feedforward neural network models for handling class overlap and class imbalance. *International Journal of Neural Systems*, *15*(5), 323–338. doi:10.1142/S012906570500030X PMID:16278937

Krumm, A. E., Waddington, R. J., Lonn, S., & Teasley, S. D. (2012). Increasing academic success in undergraduate engineering education using learning analytics: A design-based research project. Retrieved from http://deepblue.lib.umich.edu/bitstream/handle/2027.42/106032/aera2012_krumm_learning_analytics.pdf?sequence=1

Kruse, A., & Pongsajapan, R. (2012). Student-centered learning analytics. Retrieved from https://cndls.georgetown.edu/m/documents/thoughtpaper-krusepongsajapan.pdf

Kubat, M., & Matwin, S. (1997). Addressing the curse of imbalanced training sets: one-sided selection. *Proceedings of ICML, 4*.

Kuh, G. D. (2003). What we're learning about student engagement from NSSE. *Change*, *35*(2), 24–31. doi:10.1080/00091380309604090

Kump, B., Seifert, C., Beham, G., Lindstaedt, S. N., & Ley, T. (2012, April). Seeing what the system thinks you know: visualizing evidence in an open learner model.*Proceedings of the 2nd International Conference on Learning Analytics and Knowledge* (pp. 153-157). ACM. doi:10.1145/2330601.2330640

Lajoie, S. P., Naismith, L., Poitras, E., Hong, Y.-J., Cruz-Panesso, I., & Ranellucci, J. (2013). Technology-Rich Tools to Support Self-Regulated Learning and Performance in Medicine. In R. Azevedo & V. Aleven, International Handbook of Metacognition and Learning Technologies, 28, 229–242. New York, NY: Springer New York. doi:10.1007/978-1-4419-5546-3_16

Lakshmanan, B., Priscilla, A. J., Ponni, S., & Sankari, V. (2011). Evaluation of imbalanced datasets using fuzzy support vector machine-class imbalance learning (FSVM-CIL). *Proceedings of the IEEE-International Conference on Recent Trends in Information Technology* (pp. 1131–1136).

Lam, H., Bertini, E., Isenberg, P., Plaisant, C., & Carpendale, S. (2012). Empirical Studies in Information Visualization: Seven Scenarios. *IEEE Transactions on Visualization and Computer Graphics*, *18*(9), 1520–1536. doi:10.1109/TVCG.2011.279 PMID:22144529

Lambropoulos, N., Faulkner, X., & Culwin, F. (2012). Supporting social awareness in collaborative e-learning. *British Journal of Educational Technology*, *43*(2), 295–306. doi:10.1111/j.1467-8535.2011.01184.x

Landauer, T. K., Foltz, P. W., & Laham, D. (1998). An introduction to latent semantic analysis. *Discourse Processes*, *25*(2-3), 259–284. doi:10.1080/01638539809545028

Lane, J., Stodden, V., Bender, S., & Nissenbaum, H. (Eds.). (2014). *Privacy, big data, and the public good*. New York, NY: Cambridge University Press. doi:10.1017/CBO9781107590205

Larose, D. T. (2005). *Discovering knowledge in data: An introduction to data mining*. Hoboken, NJ: John Wiley and Sons, Inc.

Lauría, E. J. M., & Baron, J. (2011). Mining Sakai to Measure Student Performance: Opportunities and Challenges in Academic Analytics. Retrieved from http://ecc.marist.edu/conf2011/materials/LauriaECC2011-%20Mining%20Sakai%20to%20Measure%20Student%20Performance%20-%20final.pdf

LaValle, S., Lesser, E., Shockley, R., Hopkins, M. S., & Kruschwitz, N. (2011). Big data, analytics and the path from insights to value. *MIT Sloan Management Review*, *52*(2), 21–31.

Leony, D., & Pardo, A., la Fuente Valentín, de, L., de Castro, D. S., & Kloos, C. D. (2012). GLASS: a learning analytics visualization tool. Paper presented at the *Second International Conference on Learning Analytics and KnowledgeLAK 2012* (pp. 162–163). doi:10.1145/2330601.2330642

Lesh, R., Lamon, S. J., Gong, B., & Post, T. (1992). Using Learning Progress Maps to Improve Instructional Decision Making. In R. Lesh & S. J. Lamon (Eds.), Assessment of Authentic Performance in School Mathematics (pp. 343–375(. Washington, DC.

Leung, C. K.-S., Carmichael, C. L., & Teh, E. W. (2011). Visual Analytics of Social Networks: Mining and Visualizing Co-authorship Networks. *Human-Computer Interaction*, 2011, 335–345. doi:10.1007/978-3-642-21852-1_40

Li, L. (2011). Propensity Score Analysis with Matching Weights. *arXiv Preprint arXiv:1105.2917*, 1–17.

Li, I., Dey, A. K., & Forlizzi, J. (2011, September). Understanding my data, myself: supporting self-reflection with ubicomp technologies.*Proceedings of the 13th international conference on Ubiquitous computing* (pp. 405-414). ACM. doi:10.1145/2030112.2030166

Lilley, J., & Rollins, B. (1995) Using undergraduates as teaching assistants in introductory programming courses: an update on the Stanford experience.*Proceedings of the twenty-sixth SIGCSE technical symposium on Computer science education SIGCSE '95* (pp. 48-52).

Ling, C. X., & Sheng, V. S. (2008). Cost-Sensitive Learning and the Class Imbalance Problem. In *Encyclopedia of Machine Learning*. Springer.

Little, B., Locke, W., Scesa, A., & Williams, R. (2009). Report on Student Engagement (February 2009). HEFCE by the Centre for Higher Education Research and Information (Open University). Retrieved from http://www.hefce.ac.uk/pubs/rdreports/2009/rd03_09/

Liu, X., & Zhou, Z. (2006). The Influence of Class Imbalance on Cost-Sensitive Learning: An Empirical Study. *Proceedings of theSixth International Conference on Data Mining (ICDM'06)* (pp. 970–974). doi:10.1109/ICDM.2006.158

Liu, X., Wu, J., & Zhou, Z. (2009). Exploratory undersampling for class-imbalance learning. *IEEE Transactions on Systems, Man, and Cybernetics, Part B*, 39(2), 539-550.

Lockyer, L., & Dawson, S. (2011, February). Learning designs and learning analytics.*Proceedings of the 1st international conference on learning analytics and knowledge* (pp. 153-156). ACM. doi:10.1145/2090116.2090140

Lockyer, L., Heathcote, E., & Dawson, S. (2013). Informing pedagogical action: Aligning learning analytics with learning design. *The American Behavioral Scientist*, *57*(10), 1439–1459. doi:10.1177/0002764213479367

Lohr, S. (2015, April). How much should humans intervene with the wisdom of algorithms [Blog comment]. Retrieved from http://www.afr.com/technology/how-much-should-humans-intervene-with-the-wisdom-of-algorithms-20150407-1mfqiw

Long, S. (2014, February 20). 'Re-purposing data' in the digital humanities [Blog comment]. Retrieved from https://technaverbascripta.wordpress.com/2014/02/20/re-purposing-data-in-the-digital-humanities/

Long, P., & Siemens, G. (2011). Penetrating the Fog: Analytics in Learning and Education. *EDUCAUSE Review*, September/October, 31–40.

Lonn, S., Aguilar, S., & Teasley, S. D. (2013). Issues, challenges, and lessons learned when scaling up a learning analytics intervention. *Paper presented at theThird International Conference on Learning Analytics and Knowledge*. doi:10.1145/2460296.2460343

López, V., Fernández, A., García, S., Palade, V., & Herrera, F. (2013). An insight into classification with imbalanced data: Empirical results and current trends on using data intrinsic characteristics. *Information Sciences*, *250*, 113–141. doi:10.1016/j.ins.2013.07.007

Lovett, M., O. Meyer, & C. Thille. (2008). The Open Learning Initiative: Measuring the Effectiveness of the OLI Statistics Course in Accelerating Student Learning. *Journal of Interactive Media in Education* (Special Issue: Researching Open Content in Education).

Lu, J. (2004). *Personalized e-learning material recommender system.* Paper presented at the International Conference on Information Technology for Application ICITA '04, Harbin, China.

Luan, J. (2002). Data Mining and Its Applications in Higher Education. *New Directions for Institutional Research*, *2002*(113), 17–36. doi:10.1002/ir.35

Luehmann, A. L. (2008). Using blogging in support of teacher professional identity development: A case study. *Journal of the Learning Sciences*, *17*(3), 287–337. doi:10.1080/10508400802192706

Lupton, D. (2014a, July 28). Beyond the quantified self: the reflexive monitoring self [Blog comment]. Retrieved from https://simplysociology.wordpress.com/2014/07/28/beyond-the-quantified-self-the-reflexive-monitoring-self/

Lupton, D. (2014b). You are your data: self-tracking practices and concepts of data. Retrieved from http://papers.ssrn.com/sol3/papers.cfm?abstract_id=2534211

Ma, H., Wang, L., & Shen, B. (2011). A new fuzzy support vector machines for class imbalance learning. *Proceedings of the2011 International Conference on Electrical and Control Engineering* (pp. 3781–3784). doi:10.1109/ICECENG.2011.6056838

Mabbott, A., & Bull, S. (2004). Alternative Views on Knowledge: Presentation of Open Learner Models. In J.C. Lester, R.M. Vicari & F. Paraguacu (Eds.), *Proceedings of the7th International Conference onIntelligent Tutoring Systems* (pp. 689-698). Berlin: Springer-Verlag.

Macfadyen, L. P., & Dawson, S. (2012). Numbers Are Not Enough. Why e-Learning Analytics Failed to Inform an Institutional Strategic Plan. *Journal of Educational Technology & Society*, *15*(3), 149–163.

Macfadyen, L. P., & Dawson, S. (2012). Numbers are not enough: Why e–learning analytics failed to inform an institutional strategic plan. *Journal of Educational Technology & Society*, *15*(3), 149–163.

Macfadyen, L. P., Dawson, S., Pardo, A., & Gasevic, D. (2014). Embracing big data in complex educational systems: The learning analytics imperative and the policy challenge. *Research & Practice in Assessment*, *9*(2), 17–28.

Macfadyen, L. P., Dawson, S., Pardo, A., & Gasevic, D. (2014). Embracing Big Data in Complex Educational Systems: The Learning Analytics Imperative and the Policy Challenge. *Research and Practice in Assessment*, *9*, 17–28.

Macfadyen, L., & Dawson, S. (2012). Numbers are not enough: Why e-learning analytics failed to inform an institutional strategic plan. *Journal of Educational Technology & Society*, *15*(3), 149–163.

Macfayden, L. P., & Dawson, S. (2010). Mining LMS Data to Develop an 'Early Warning' System for Educators: A Proof of Concept. *Computers & Education*, *54*(2), 588–599. doi:10.1016/j.compedu.2009.09.008

Mackinlay, J. D. (1986). Automating the Design of Graphical Presentations of Relational Information. *ACM Transactions on Graphics*, *5*(2), 110–141. doi:10.1145/22949.22950

MacLennan, B. (2007). Evolutionary psychology, complex systems, and social theory. *Soundings: An Interdisciplinary Journal*, *90*(3/4), 169–189.

Mager, R. F. (1997). *Preparing instructional objectives: A critical tool in the development of effective instruction* (3rd ed.). Atlanta, GA: CEP Press.

Ma, J., Han, X., Yang, J., & Cheng, J. (2015). Examining the necessary condition for engagement in an online learning environment based on learning analytics approach: The role of the instructor. *The Internet and Higher Education*, *24*, 26–34. doi:10.1016/j.iheduc.2014.09.005

Manouselis, N., Drachsler, H., Vuorikari, R., Hummel, H., & Koper, R. (2011). Recommender systems in technology enhanced learning. In F. Ricci, L. Rokach, B. Shapira, & P. Kantor (Eds.), *Recommender systems handbook: A complete guide for research scientists & practitioners* (pp. 387–415). Berlin, Germany: Springer–Verlag. doi:10.1007/978-0-387-85820-3_12

Manyika, J., Chui, M., Brown, B., Bughin, J., Dobbs, R., Roxburgh, C., & Byers, A. H. (2011). Big Data: The Next Frontier for Innovation, Competition, and Productivity. McKinsey Global Institute. Retrieved from http://www.mckinsey.com/Insights/MGI/Research/Technology_and_Innovation/Big_data_The_next_frontier_for_innovation

Marchese, F. T., & Brajkovska, N. (2004). Dynamically binding image to text for information communication. *Proceedings of theInternational Conference on Computer Visualization and Graphics* (pp. 707–712). doi:10.1109/IV.2004.1320219

Martin, B., Mitrovic, A., Koedinger, K., & Mathan, S. (2011). Evaluating and Improving Adaptive Educational Systems with Learning Curves. *User Modeling and User-Adapted Interaction*, *21*(3), 249–283. doi:10.1007/s11257-010-9084-2

Marx, G. T. (2001). Murky conceptual waters: The public and the private. *Ethics and Information Technology*, *3*(3), 157–169. doi:10.1023/A:1012456832336

Massingham, P., & Herrington, T. (2006). Does attendance matter? An examination of student attitudes, participation, performance and attendance. *Journal of University Teaching & Learning Practice*, *3*(2), 82–103.

Mattingly, K. D., Rice, M. C., & Berge, Z. L. (2012). Learning analytics as a tool for closing the assessment loop in higher education. *Knowledge Management & E-Learning: An International Journal*, *4*(3), 236-247.

Mayer-Schönberger, V., & Cukier, K. (2013). *Big data. A revolution that will transform how we live, work, and think.* New York, N.Y.: Houghton Miffling Harcourt Publishing Company.

Mazza, R., & Dimitrova, V. (2004). Visualising student tracking data to support instructors in web-based distance education. *Paper presented at the13th international World Wide Web conference on Alternate TrackWWW Alt. '04*. ACM. doi:10.1145/1013367.1013393

Mazza, R., & Dimitrova, V. (2004). Visualising Student Tracking Data to Support Instructors in Web-Based Distance Education. *WWW Alt. '04 Proceedings of the 13th International World Wide Web Conference on Alternate Track Papers & Posters* (pp. 154-161).

Mazza, R., & Milani, C. (2005). *Exploring usage analysis in learning systems: Gaining insights from visualisations.* Paper presented at the Workshop on Usage Analysis in Learning Systems at the 12th International Conference on Artificial Intelligence in Education AIED '05, Amsterdam, The Netherlands.

Mazza, R., & Botturi, L. (2007). Monitoring an Online Course with the GISMO Tool: A Case Study. *Journal of Interactive Learning Research*, *18*(2), 251–265.

Mazza, R., & Dimitrova, V. (2007). CourseVis: A graphical student monitoring tool for supporting instructors in web-based distance courses. *International Journal of Human-Computer Studies*, *65*(2), 125–139. doi:10.1016/j.ijhcs.2006.08.008

McCue, C. (2006). Data Mining and Predictive Analysis in Public Safety and Security. IT Professional, 8(4), 12-18.

McDonald, B., Noakes, N., & Stuckey, B. (2005). *Breaking down learner isolation: How social network analysis informs design and facilitation for online learning*. Montreal, Canada: AERA.

McKenzie, K., & Schweitzer, R. (2001). Who succeeds at university? Factors predicting academic performance in first year Australian university students. *Higher Education Research & Development*, *20*(1), 21–33. doi:10.1080/07924360120043621

McKeown, T., & Ayson, S. (2013, December 4-6). *Unleashing the potential of learning analytics: A project outline and a model to put the student first.* Paper presented at the Australian and New Zealand Academy of Management (ANZAM) Conference, Hobart, Australia. Retrieved from http://funrun.gcc.tas.gov.au/anzam/content/pdfs/anzam-2013-398.pdf

Means, B., Chelemer, C., & Knapp, M. S. (Eds.). (1991). *Teaching Advanced Skills to at-Risk Students: Views from Research and Practice*. San Francisco, CA: Jossey-Bass.

Medina, R., & Suthers, D. (2009). Using a contingency graph to discover representational practices in an online collaborative environment. *Research and Practice in Technology Enhanced Learning*, *4*(3), 281–305. doi:10.1142/S1793206809000726

Mehta, P. (2015, March 12). Big Data's radical potential. *Jacobin Magazine*. Retrieved from https://www.jacobinmag.com/2015/03/big-data-drones-privacy-workers/

Mendes-Moreira, J., Soares, C., Jorge, A. M., & Sousa, J. F. D. (2012). Ensemble approaches for regression: A survey. *ACM Computing Surveys*, *45*(1), 1–40. doi:10.1145/2379776.2379786

Mercer, N. (2004). Sociocultural discourse analysis: Analysing classroom talk as a social mode of thinking. *Journal of Applied Linguistics*, *1*(2), 137–168. doi:10.1558/japl.2004.1.2.137

Merceron, A., & Yacef, K. (2004). Mining student data captured from a web-based tutoring tool: Initial exploration and results. *Journal of Interactive Learning Research*, *15*(4), 319–346.

Merceron, A., & Yacef, K. (2005). TADA-Ed for educational data mining. *Interactive Multimedia Electronic Journal of Computer-Enhanced Learning*, *7*(1), 267–287.

Merceron, A., & Yacef, K. (2010). Measuring Correlation of Strong Symmetric Association Rules in Educational Data. In C. Romero, S. Ventura, M. Pechenizkiy, & R. S. J. d. Baker (Eds.), *Handbook of Educational Data Mining* (pp. 245–256). Boca Raton, FL: CRC Press. doi:10.1201/b10274-20

Messick, S. (1990). Validity of test interpretation and use (Report No. ETS-RR-90-11). Princeton, NJ: Educational Testing Service.

Meyer, K. A. (2014). Student engagement in online learning: What works and why. *ASHE Higher Education Report*, *40*(6), 1–114. doi:10.1002/aehe.20018

Michael, K., & Clarke, R. (2013). Location and tracking of mobile devices: Überveillance stalks the streets. *Computer Law & Security Report*, *29*(3), 216–228. doi:10.1016/j.clsr.2013.03.004

Michael, K., & Miller, K. W. (2013). Big Data: New Opportunities and New Challenges(Guest editors' introduction). *Computer*, *46*(6), 22–24. doi:10.1109/MC.2013.196

Miller, K. (2011, May 3). *Gender Matters: Assessing and Addressing the Persistent Gender Gap in Physics Education*. University of Michigan Department of Physics. Retrieved from http://sitemaker.umich.edu/ecoach/press

Millner, N., Small, T., & Deakin Crick, R. (2006). Learning by Accident (Report No. 1). *ViTaL Development and Research Programme*, University of Bristol.

Mirriahi, N., Gašević, D., Long, P., & Dawson, S. (2014). Scientometrics as an important tool for the growth of the field of learning analytics. *Journal of Learning Analytics*, *1*(2), 1–4.

Mirza, B., & Lin, Z. (2013). One-vs-all for class imbalance learning. *Proceedings of the 2013 9th International Conference on Information, Communications & Signal Processing*, 1–5. doi:10.1109/ICICS.2013.6782785

Mitrovic, A., & Martin, B. (2002). Evaluating the Effects of Open Student Models on Learning. In X. Luo, M. Spaniol, L. Wang, Q. Li, W. Nejdl, & W. Zhang (Eds.), Advances in Web-Based Learning ICWL 2010, LNCS (Vol. 2347, pp. 296–305). Berlin: Springer Berlin Heidelberg. doi:10.1007/3-540-47952-X_31

Miyazaki, D., & Ferenandez, A. (2000). Internet privacy and security: An examination of online retailer disclosures. *Journal of Public Policy & Marketing*, *19*(1), 54–61. doi:10.1509/jppm.19.1.54.16942

Moere, A. V., & Purchase, H. (2011). On the role of design in information visualization. *Information Visualization*, *10*(4), 356–371. doi:10.1177/1473871611415996

Monroy, C., Rangel, V. S., & Whitaker, R. (2013). STEMscopes: contextualizing learning analytics in a K-12 science curriculum. *Paper presented at theThird International Conference on Learning Analytics and KnowledgeLAK '13*, New York: NY. doi:10.1145/2460296.2460339

Monroy, C., Rangel, V. S., & Whitaker, R. (2014). A strategy for incorporating learning analytics into the design and evaluation of a K–12 science curriculum. *Journal of Learning Analytics*, *1*(2), 94–125.

Monson, R., Bunney, D., & Lawrence, T. (2013). MOOCs, learning analytics and learning advisors. *eCULTURE, 6*, 1-14.

Moore, R., Jensen, M., Hatch, J., Duranczyk, I., Staats, S., & Koch, L. (2003). Showing up: The importance of class attendance for academic success in introductory science courses. *The American Biology Teacher*, *65*(5), 325–329. doi:10.2307/4451508

Morozov, E. (2013a, October 23). The real privacy problem. *MIT Technology Review*. Retrieved from http://www.technologyreview.com/featuredstory/520426/the-real-privacy-problem/

Morris, L. V., Finnegan, C., & Wu, S. S. (2005). Tracking student behavior, persistence, and achievement in online courses. *The Internet and Higher Education*, *8*(3), 221–231. doi:10.1016/j.iheduc.2005.06.009

Morrison, G. R., Ross, S. M., Kalman, H. K., & Kemp, J. E. (2011). *Designing effective instruction* (6th ed.). Hoboken, NJ: John Wiley & Sons, Inc.

Morton, K., Balazinska, M., Grossman, D., Kosara, R., & Mackinlay, J. (2014). Public Data and Visualizations: How are Many Eyes and Tableau Public Used for Collaborative Analytics? *SIGMOD Record*, *43*(2), 17–22. doi:10.1145/2694413.2694417

Mota, M. I. G. (2007, October 10-13) Work In Progress - Using Lego Mindstorms and Robolab as a mean to lowering dropout and failure rate in programming course. *Proceedings of the 37th ASEE/IEEE Frontiers in Education Conference*, Milwaukee, WI, USA (pp. F4A-1 – F4A-2).

Muijtjens, A. M. M., Schuwirth, L. W. T., Cohen-Schotanus, J., Thoben, A. J. N. M., & van der Vleuten, C. P. M. (2008). Benchmarking by cross-institutional comparison of student achievement in a progress test. *Medical Education*, *42*(1), 82–88. doi:10.1111/j.1365-2923.2007.02896.x PMID:18181848

Mundfrom, D. J., Shaw, D. G., & Ke, T. L. (2005). Minimum sample size recommendations for conducting factor analyses. *International Journal of Testing*, *5*(2), 159–168. doi:10.1207/s15327574ijt0502_4

Murphy, K. (2014, October 4). We want privacy, but can't stop sharing. The New York Times [Blog comment]. Retrieved from http://www.nytimes.com/2014/10/05/sunday-review/we-want-privacy-but-cant-stop-sharing.html

Nachimas, R., & Hershkovitz, A. (2007). A Case Study of Using Visualization for Understanding the Behavior of the Online Learner. *Proceedings of theInternational Workshop on Applying Data Mining in E-Learning* (pp. 43–52).

Nagappan, N., Williams, L., Ferzli, M., Wiebe, E., Yang, K., Miller, C., & Balik, S. (2003). Improving the CS1 Experience with Pair Programming.*Proceedings of the 34th SIGCSE technical symposium on Computer science education SIGCSE '03* (pp. 359-362). doi:10.1145/611892.612006

Napoli, P. (2013). The algorithm as institution: Toward a theoretical framework for automated media production and consumption. *Proceedings of the Media in Transition Conference* (pp. 1–36). Doi:10.2139/ssrn.2260923

Naps, T. L., Robling, G., Almstrum, V., Dann, W., Fleischer, R., Hundhausen, C., & Velazquez-Iturbide, J. A. et al. (2003). Exploring the role of visualization and engagement in computer science education. *ACM SIGCSE Bulletin*, *35*(2), 131–152. doi:10.1145/782941.782998

Nebot, A., Mugica, F., & Castro, F. (2010, July 18-23) Fuzzy Predictive Models to Help Teachers in e-Learning Courses. *Proceedings of the 2010 International Joint Conference on Neural Networks (IJCNN)*, Barcelona, Spain. doi:10.1109/IJCNN.2010.5596582

New Media Consortium. (2015). Horizon report higher education edition. Retrieved from https://net.educause.edu/ir/library/pdf/HR2015.pdf

New Media Consortium. 2012. NMC Horizon Project Higher Ed Short List. Austin, TX: New Media Consortium. Retrieved from http://www.nmc.org/news/download-horizon-project-2012-higher-ed-short-list

Newman, R. (2008). Adaptive and nonadaptive help seeking with peer harassment: An integrative perspective of coping and self-regulation. *Educational Psychologist*, *43*(1), 1–15. doi:10.1080/00461520701756206

Next Generation Learning Challenges: Learner Analytics Premises. (2010). Retrieved from http://www.educause.edu/Resources/NextGenerationLearningChalleng/215028

Ni, X., Xue, G. R., Ling, X., Yu, Y., & Yang, Q. (2007). *Exploring in the weblog space by detecting informative and affective articles.*Paper presented at the 16th International Conference on World Wide Web WWW '07, Banff, Canada. doi:10.1145/1242572.1242611

Nichols, M. (2010). Student perceptions of support services and the influence of targeted interventions on retention in distance education. *Distance Education*, *31*(1), 93–113. doi:10.1080/01587911003725048

Niemczyk, M. C., & Savenye, W. C. (2001). The relationship of student motivation and self-regulated learning strategies to performance in an undergraduate computer literacy course. (ED 470107)

Nissenbaum, H. (2014). Respect for Context as a Benchmark for Privacy Online: What it Is and Isn't. *Cahier de prospective*, 19.

Nissenbaum, H. (2009). *Privacy in context: Technology, policy, and the integrity of social life*. California: Stanford University Press.

Nissenbaum, H. (2010). *Privacy in context. Technology, policy, and the integrity of social life*. Stanford, CA: Stanford Law Books.

Norris, D. M., & Baer, L. L. (2013). *Building organizational capacity for analytics*. Louisville, CO: EDUCAUSE.

Norris, D. M., Baer, L. L., Leonard, J., Pugliese, L., & Lefrere, P. (2008). Action analytics: Measuring and improving performance that matters in higher education. *EDUCAUSE Review*, *43*(1), 42–67.

North, C. (2006). Toward measuring visualization insight. *IEEE Computer Graphics and Applications*, *26*(3), 6–9. doi:10.1109/MCG.2006.70 PMID:16711210

Northway, M. L. (1952). A primer of sociometry. Toronto, ON: University of Toronto Press.

Novak, J. D., & Cañas, A. J. (2004). Building on New Constructivist Ideas and Cmap Tools to Create a New Model for Education. In A. J. Cañas, J. D. Novak, & F. M. González (Eds.), *Concept maps Theory, methodology, technology, proceedings of the 1st international conference on concept mapping,* Pamplona, Spain.

Novak, J. D. (2003). The promise of new ideas and new technology for improving teaching and learning. *Cell Biology Education*, *2*(2), 122–132. doi:10.1187/cbe.02-11-0059 PMID:12888848

Novak, J. D., & Cañas, A. J. (2006). The origins of the concept mapping tool and the continuing evolution of the tool★. *Information Visualization*, *5*(3), 175–184. doi:10.1057/palgrave.ivs.9500126

O'Neil, H. F. (2005). *What Works in Distance Learning: Guidelines*. Greenwich, CT: Information Age Publishing.

O'Sullivan, D., & Igoe, T. (2004). *Physical Computing: Sensing and Controlling the Physical World with Computers*. Course Technology.

Oblinger, D. G. (2011, September 6). Doing Better with Less. *Educause Review Online*. Retrieved from http://www.educause.edu/ero/article/doing-better-less

Oblinger, D. G. (2012). Let's talk analytics. *EDUCAUSEreview*. Retrieved from http://www.educause.edu/ero/article/lets-talk-analytics

Ochoa, X., Suthers, D., Verbert, K., & Duval, E. (2014). Analysis and reflections on the third learning analytics and knowledge conference (LAK 2013). *Journal of Learning Analytics*, *1*(2), 5–22.

Ochoa, X., Suthers, D., Verbert, K., & Duval, E. (2014). Analysis and Reflections on the Third Learning Analytics and Knowledge Conference (LAK 2013). *Journal of Learning Analytics*, *1*(2), 5–22.

Ohm, P. (2010). Broken promises of privacy: Responding to the surprising failure of anonymisation. *UCLA Law Review. University of California, Los Angeles. School of Law*, *57*, 1701–1777. Retrieved from http://heinonline.org/HOL/Page?handle=hein.journals/uclalr57&div=48&g_sent=1&collection=journals

Ohm, P. (2015). Changing the rules: general principles for data use and analysis. In J. Lane, V. Stodden, S. Bender, & H. Nissenbaum (Eds.), *Privacy, big data, and the public good* (pp. 96–111). New York, NY: Cambridge University Press.

Open University. (2014). Policy on ethical use of student data for learning analytics. Retrieved from http://www.open.ac.uk/students/charter/essential-documents/ethical-use-student-data-learning-analytics-policy

O'Rourke, S. T., Calvo, R. A., & McNamara, D. S. (2011). Visualizing Topic Flow in Students' Essays. *Journal of Educational Technology & Society*, *14*(3), 4–15.

Orriols-puig, A., & Bernad, E. (2008). Mining imbalanced data with learning classifier systems. *Learning Classifier Systems in Data Mining*, *125*, 123–145. doi:10.1007/978-3-540-78979-6_6

Osborne, J. W. (2015). What is rotating in exploratory factor analysis? *Practical Assessment, Research & Evaluation*, *20*(2), 1–7. Retrieved from http://pareonline.net/getvn.asp?v=20&n=2

Panadero, C. F., Roman, J. V., & Kloos, C. D. (2010). Impact of learning experiences using LEGO Mindstorms in engineering courses.[IEEE.]. *Proceedings of Education Engineering EDUCON*, *2010*, 503–512.

Papamitsiou, Z., & Economides, A. (2014). Learning analytics and educational data mining in practice: A systematic literature review of empirical evidence. *Journal of Educational Technology & Society*, *17*(4), 49–64.

Pardo, A., & Kloos, C. D. (2011). Stepping out of the box: Towards analytics outside the learning management system. *Proceedings of the 1st International Conference on Learning Analytics and Knowledge* (pp. 163–167). New York, NY: ACM. doi:10.1145/2090116.2090142

Pardo, A., & Siemens, G. (2014). Ethical and privacy principles for learning analytics. *British Journal of Educational Technology*, *45*(3), 438–450. doi:10.1111/bjet.12152

Pariser, E. (2011). *The filter bubble. What the Internet is hiding from you*. London, UK: Viking.

Pascarella, E., & Terenzini, P. (1980). Predicting Freshman Persistence and Voluntary Dropout Decisions from a Theoretical Model. *The Journal of Higher Education*, *51*(1), 60–75. Retrieved from http://www.jstor.org/stable/1981125?seq=13#page_scan_tab_contents doi:10.2307/1981125

Pasquale, F. A. (2011). *Restoring Transparency to Automated Authority*. Seton Hall Research Paper, (2010-28).

Pasquale, F. (2015). *The black box society: the secret algorithms that control money and information*. London, UK: Harvard University Press. doi:10.4159/harvard.9780674736061

Patterson, B., & McFadden, C. (2009). Attrition in online and campus degree programs. *Online Journal of Distance Learning Administration*, *12*(2).

Pavlik, P., Cen, H., & Koedinger, K. (2009). *Learning factors transfer analysis: Using learning curve analysis to automatically generate domain models*. Paper presented at the Second International Conference on Educational Data Mining EDM 09, Cordoba, Spain.

Pegg, A., Waldock, J., Hendy-Isaac, S., & Lawton, R. (2012). *Pedagogy for employability*. HEA.

Pellegrino, J. W., & Hilton, M. L. (Eds.). (2013). *Education for life and work: Developing transferable knowledge and skills in the 21st century*. National Academies Press.

Perkins, D. N. (1992). Technology meets constructivism: Do they make a marriage? In T. M. Duffy & D. H. Jonassen (Eds.), *Constructivism and the technology of instruction: A conversation* (pp. 45–55). Hillsdale, NJ: Lawrence Erlbaum Associates.

Perkins, D., Hancock, C., Hobbs, R., Martin, F., & Simmons, R. (1989). Conditions of learning in novice programming. In *Studying the Novice Programmer* (pp. 261–279). New Jersey: Lawrence Erlbaum Associates.

PewResearchCenter. (2014). Public perceptions of privacy and security in the post-Snowden era. Retrieved from http://www.pewinternet.org/2014/11/12/public-privacyperceptions/

Philip, R., & Nicholls, J. (2009). Group blogs: Documenting collaborative drama processes. *Australasian Journal of Educational Technology*, *25*(5), 683–699.

Phillips, R., Maor, D., Cumming-Potvin, W., Roberts, P., Herrington, J., Preston, G., . . . Perry, L. (2011, December 4–7). Learning analytics and study behaviour: A pilot study. Proceedings of ASCILITE 2011, Wrest Point, Hobart, Tasmania (pp. 997-1007).

Phillips, J. J. (1997). *Handbook of training evaluation and measurement methods* (3rd ed.). Houston, TX: Gulf Publishing Company.

Phillips, J. J., & Stone, R. D. (2002). *How to measure training results: A practical guide to tracking the six key indicators*. New York, NY: McGraw-Hill.

Phillips, R., Maor, D., Preston, G., & Cumming-Potvin, W. (2012). Exploring Learning Analytics as Indicators of Study Behaviour. In: T. Amiel, & B. Wilson (Eds.), *Proceedings of World Conference on Educational Multimedia, Hypermedia and Telecommunications 2012* (pp. 2861-2867).

Picciano, A. G. (2012). The Evolution of Big Data and Learning Analytics in American Higher Education. *Journal of Asynchronous Learning Networks*, *16*(3), 9–20.

Piech, C., Sahami, M., Koller, D., Cooper, S., & Blikstein, P. (2012). *Modeling how students learn to program*. Paper presented at the 43rd ACM Technical Symposium on Computer Science Education (SIGCSE 2012), Raleigh, NC. doi:10.1145/2157136.2157182

Piety, P. J., Hickey, D. T., & Bishop, M. J. (2014, March 24-28). Educational data sciences: Framing emergent practices for analytics of learning, organizations, and systems. *Paper presented at the4th International Conference on Learning Analytics & Knowledge*, Indianapolis, IN. doi:10.1145/2567574.2567582

Pintrich, P. R. (1995). Understanding self-regulated learning. In P. R. Pintrich (Ed.), *Understanding self-regulated learning* (pp. 3–12). San Francisco, CA: Jossey-Bass Publishers.

Pintrich, P. R., & DeGoot, E. V. (1990). Motivational and self-regulated learning components of classroom academic performance. *Journal of Educational Psychology*, *82*(1), 33–40. doi:10.1037/0022-0663.82.1.33

Pintrich, P. R., Smith, D., Garcia, T., & McKeachie, W. J. (1991). *A manual for the use of the motivated strategies for learning questionnaire*. Ann Arbor, MI: University of Michigan.

Pirolli, P., & Card, S. (2005). The Sensemaking Process and Leverage Points for Analyst Technology as Identified Through Cognitive Task Analysis.*Proceedings of International Conference on Intelligence.*

Pistilli, M. D., Arnold, K., & Bethune, M. (2012). *Signals: Using academic analytics to promote student success*. EDUCAUSE Review Online.

Plowman, L. (1999). *Using video for observing interaction in the classroom. SCRE Spotlights 72*. Edinburgh: Scottish Council for Research in Education.

Plutarch. (100 AD) On Listening to Lectures (De auditu), in Moralia (Vol 1, 3), http://penelope.uchicago.edu/Thayer/E/Roman/Texts/Plutarch/Moralia/De_auditu*.html

Podgorelec, V., & Kuhar, S. (2011). Taking Advantage of Education Data: Advanced Data Analysis and Reporting in Virtual Learning Environments. *Electronics and Electrical Engineering*, *114*(8). doi:10.5755/j01.eee.114.8.708

Pohl, A., Bry, F., Schwarz, J., & Gottstein, M. (2012). Sensing the classroom: Improving awareness and self-awareness of students in Backstage. *Paper presented at theIEEE 15th International Conference on Interactive Collaborative Learning (ICL)*. doi:10.1109/ICL.2012.6402110

Pozzi, F., Manca, S., Persico, D., & Sarti, L. (2007). A general framework for tracking and analyzing learning processes in computer-supported collaborative learning environments. *Innovations in Education and Teaching International*, *44*(2), 169–179. doi:10.1080/14703290701240929

Prati, R. C., Batista, G. E., & Monard, M. C. (2004). Class imbalances versus class overlapping: An analysis of a learning system behavior. *MICAI 2004. Advances in Artificial Intelligence*, LNCS (Vol. 2972, pp. 312–321).

Prati, R., Batista, G., & Monard, M. (2004). Learning with class skews and small disjuncts. *Advances in Artificial Intelligence–SBIA*, *LNCS* (Vol. 3171, pp. 296–306).

Prinsloo, P. (2009). Modelling Throughput at Unisa: The key to the successful implementation of ODL. Retrieved from http://uir.unisa.ac.za/handle/10500/6035

Prinsloo, P. (2014). *A brave new world: student surveillance in higher education*. Presentation at the Annual Conference of the Southern African Association for Institutional Research (SAAIR) Conference 16-18 October, Pretoria, South Africa. Retrieved from http://www.slideshare.net/prinsp/a-brave-new-world-student-surveillance-in-higher-education

Prinsloo, P., & Slade, S. (2013). *An evaluation of policy frameworks for addressing ethical considerations in learning analytics*.

Prinsloo, P., & Slade, S. (2015, b). *Student vulnerability, agency and learning analytics: an exploration.* Presented at the EP4LA workshop during the Fifth International Conference on Learning Analytics and Knowledge.

Prinsloo, P., Archer, E., Barnes, G., Chetty, Y., & Van Zyl, D. (2015). Big (ger) data as better data in open distance learning. *The International Review of Research in Open and Distributed Learning*, *16*(1), 284–306.

Prinsloo, P., Archer, E., Barnes, G., Chetty, Y., & Van Zyl, D. (2015). Big(ger) data as better data in open distance learning. *The International Review of Research in Open and Distributed Learning*, *16*(1).

Prinsloo, P., & Slade, S. (2013, April). An evaluation of policy frameworks for addressing ethical considerations in learning analytics.*Proceedings of the Third International Conference on Learning Analytics and Knowledge* (pp. 240-244). ACM. doi:10.1145/2460296.2460344

Prinsloo, P., & Slade, S. (2014). Educational triage in open distance learning: Walking a moral tightrope. *The International Review of Research in Open and Distributed Learning*, *15*(4), 306–331.

Prinsloo, P., & Slade, S. (2015a, March). Student privacy self-management: implications for learning analytics.*Proceedings of the Fifth International Conference on Learning Analytics and Knowledge* (pp. 83-92). ACM. doi:10.1145/2723576.2723585

Purcell, P. (2007, September 3-7). Engineering student attendance at lectures: Effect on examination performance. *Paper presented at theInternational Conference on Engineering Education (ICEE)*, Coimbra, Portugal.

Puzziferro, M. (2008). Online technologies self-efficacy and self-regulated learning as predictors of final grade and satisfaction in college-level online courses. *American Journal of Distance Education*, *22*(2), 72–89. doi:10.1080/08923640802039024

Qian, Y., Liang, Y., Li, M., Feng, G., & Shi, X. (2014). A resampling ensemble algorithm for classification of imbalance problems. *Neurocomputing*, *143*, 57–67. doi:10.1016/j.neucom.2014.06.021

Quinlan, J. R. (1991). Improved estimates for the accuracy of small disjuncts. *Machine Learning*, *6*(1), 93–98. doi:10.1007/BF00153762

Raca, M., & Dillenbourg, P. (2013). System for assessing classroom attention. *Paper presented at the:Proceedings of the Third International Conference on Learning Analytics and KnowledgeLAK '13*, New York, NY. doi:10.1145/2460296.2460351

Rahman, N., & Dron, J. (2012). *Challenges and opportunities for learning analytics when formal teaching meets social spaces.* Paper presented at the Second International Conference on Learning Analytics and Knowledge LAK '12, Vancouver, Canada. doi:10.1145/2330601.2330619

Raimondo, J. (2013). Analytics' Big Test. *Information Week.* Retrieved from http://twimgs.com/infoweek/green/012813ed/InformationWeek_Education_2013_02.pdf

Reese, D. D., Seward, R. J., Tabachnick, B. G., Hitt, B., Harrison, A., & McFarland, L. (in press). Timed Report Measures Learning: Game-Based Embedded Assessment. In D. Ifenthaler, D. Eseryel, & X. Ge (Eds.), *Assessment in Game-Based Learning: Foundations, Innovations, and Perspectives*. New York, NY: Springer. doi:10.1007/978-1-4614-3546-4_9

Reffay, C., & Chanier, T. (2003). *How social network analysis can help to measure cohesion in collaborative distance learning.*Paper presented at the International Conference on Computer–Supported Collaborative Learning CSCL '03, Bergen, Norway. doi:10.1007/978-94-017-0195-2_42

Reffay, C., Teplovs, C., & Blondel, F. M. (2011). *Productive re-use of CSCL data and analytic tools to provide a new perspective on group cohesion.* Paper presented at the International Conference on Computer–Supported Collaborative Learning CSCL '11, Hong Kong.

Rinkevich, J.L. (2011). Creative Teaching: Why it matters and Where to Begin. *The Clearing House: A Journal of Educational Strategies, Issues and Ideas*, *84*(5), 219–223.

Rittel, H. W. J., & Webber, M. M. (1973). Dilemmas in a general theory of planning. *Policy Sciences*, *4*(2), 155–169. doi:10.1007/BF01405730

Ritter, S., Anderson, J., Koedinger, K., & Corbett, A. (2007). Cognitive Tutor: Applied Research in Mathematics Education. *Psychonomic Bulletin & Review*, *14*(2), 249–255. doi:10.3758/BF03194060 PMID:17694909

Rivera, W. A., Goel, A., & Kincaid, J. P. (2014). OUPS : a combined approach using SMOTE and Propensity Score Matching.*Proceedings of the 2014 13th International Conference on Machine Learning and Applications*, *1*(2), 4–7. doi:10.1109/ICMLA.2014.106

Robinson, C. C., & Hullinger, H. (2008). New benchmarks in higher education: Student engagement in online learning. *Journal of Education for Business*, *84*(2), 101–109. doi:10.3200/JOEB.84.2.101-109

Rodgers, J. R. (2001). A panel-data study of the effect of student attendance on university performance. *Australian Journal of Education*, *45*(3), 284–295. doi:10.1177/000494410104500306

Rojas, I. G., García, R. M. C., & Kloos, C. D. (2011). Orchestration and feedback in lab sessions: improvements in quick feedback provision. *Paper presented at the6th European conference on Technology enhanced learning: towards ubiquitous learning EC-TEL'11* (pp. 424–429). Springer-Verlag.

Romero, C., Ventura, S., Espejo, P. G., & Hervs, C. (2008*). Data mining algorithms to classify students.* Paper presented at the First International Conference on Educational Data Mining EDM '08, Montreal, Canada.

Romero, C. R., & Ventura, S. (2010). Educational Data Mining: A Review of the State of the Art. *IEEE Transactions on Systems, Man and Cybernetics. Part C, Applications and Reviews*, *40*(6), 601–618. doi:10.1109/TSMCC.2010.2053532

Romero, C., & Ventura, S. (2007). Educational data mining: A survey from 1995 to 2005. *Expert Systems with Applications*, *33*(1), 135–146. doi:10.1016/j.eswa.2006.04.005

Romero, C., & Ventura, S. (2013). Data mining in education. *Wiley Interdisciplinary Reviews: Data Mining and Knowledge Discovery*, *3*(1), 12–27.

Roschelle, J., Penuel, W. R., Yarnall, L., Shechtman, N., & Tatar, D. (2005). Handheld tools that "informate" assessment of student learning in science: A requirements analysis. *Journal of Computer Assisted Learning*, *21*(3), 190–203. doi:10.1111/j.1365-2729.2005.00127.x

Rosenbaum, P. R., & Rubin, D. B. (1983). The central role of the propensity score in observational studies for causal effects. *Biometrika*, *70*(1083), 41–55. doi:10.1093/biomet/70.1.41

Rosenbaum, P. R., & Rubin, D. B. (1985). Constructing a control group using multivariate matched sampling methods that incorporate the propensity score. *The American Statistician*, *39*(1), 33–38.

Rubin, V. L., & Liddy, E. D. (2006). *Assessing credibility of weblogs*. Paper presented at the AAAI Spring Symposium: Computational Approaches to Analyzing Weblogs AAAI–CAAW '06, Stanford, CA.

Rueda, U., Larrañaga, M., Arruarte, A., & Elorriaga, J. A. (2006). DynMap+: a concept mapping approach to visualize group student models. *Paper presented at theFirst European conference on Technology Enhanced Learning: Innovative Approaches for Learning and Knowledge SharingEC-TEL'06* (pp. 383-397). Springer-Verlag. doi:10.1007/11876663_30

Rymarczuk, R., & Derksen, M. (2014). Different spaces: Exploring Facebook as heterotopia. *First Monday, 19*(6). Retrieved from http://firstmonday.org/ojs/index.php/fm/article/view/5006/4091 doi:10.5210/fm.v19i6.5006

Saha, S., & Ekbal, A. (2013). Combining multiple classifiers using vote based classifier ensemble technique for named entity recognition. *Data & Knowledge Engineering, 85*, 15–39. doi:10.1016/j.datak.2012.06.003

Salas, E., Sims, D. E., & Burke, C. S. (2005). Is there a "Big Five" in Teamwork? *Small Group Research, 36*(5), 555–599. doi:10.1177/1046496405277134

Saltz, J. S., Roxanne, S., & Turoff, M. (2004). Student social graphs: Visualizing a student's online social network. *Paper presented at the2004 ACM Conference on Computer Supported Cooperative Work. Chicago*, IL. doi:10.1145/1031607.1031709

Santos, J. L., Verbert, K., Govaerts, S., & Duval, E. (2011). Visualizing PLE usage. *Proceedings of EFEPLE11 1st Workshop on Exploring the Fitness and Evolvability of Personal Learning Environments* (Vol. 773, pp. 34–38).

Savage, M. & Burrows, R. (2007). The coming crisis of empirical sociology. *The Journal of the British Sociological Association, 41*(5), 885–899. doi:10.1177/0038038507080443

Savin-Baden, M., & Major, C. H. (2013). *Qualitative Research: The essential guide to theory and practice* (pp. 182–192). Oxon: Routledge.

Scanlon, E., Sharples, M., Fenton-O'Greevy, M., Fleck, J., Cooban, C., & Ferguson, R. et al.. (2013). *Beyond prototypes: Enabling innovation in technology-enhanced learning*. Milton Keynes: Open University.

Scardamalia, M., & Bereiter, C. (1994). Computer support for knowledge-building communities. *Journal of the Learning Sciences, 3*(3), 265–283. doi:10.1207/s15327809jls0303_3

Scardamalia, M., & Bereiter, C. (2006). Knowledge building: Theory, pedagogy, and technology. In R. K. Sawyer (Ed.), *The Cambridge handbook of the learning sciences* (pp. 97–115). Cambridge, UK: Cambridge University Press.

Schaffhauser, D. (2013, September 25). The Power of Predictive Analytics. Campus Technology. Retrieved from http://campustechnology.com/Articles/-2013/09/25/The-Power-of-Predictive-Analytics.aspx

Scheffel, M., Drachsler, H., Stoyanov, S., & Specht, M. (2014). Quality indicators for learning analytics. *Journal of Educational Technology & Society*, 2014, 124–140.

Scheuer, O., & Zinn, C. (2007). How did the e-learning session go? The Student Inspector. *Proceedings of theInternational Conference on Artificial Intelligence in Education* (pp. 487–494(.

Schissel, D. P., Burruss, J. R., Finkelstein, A., Flanagan, S. M., Foster, I. T., Fredian, T. W., & Wallace, G. et al. (2004). Building the US National Fusion Grid: Results from the National Fusion Collaboratory Project. *Fusion Engineering and Design, 71*(1), 245–250. doi:10.1016/j.fusengdes.2004.04.041

Schoenfeld, A. H. (1983). *Mathematical problem solving*. Orlando, FL: Academic.

Schreurs, B., Teplovs, C., Ferguson, R., de Laat, M., & Shum, S. B. (2013). Visualizing social learning ties by type and topic: rationale and concept demonstrator. *Paper presented at theThird International Conference on Learning Analytics and KnowledgeLAK '13*, (pp. 33-37). doi:10.1145/2460296.2460305

Sclater, N. (2014). *Learning analytics - The current state of play in UK higher and further education.* Retrieved from http://repository.jisc.ac.uk/5657/1/Learning_analytics_report.pdf

Seaver, N. (2013). Knowing Algorithms. *Media in Transition, 8*, 1–12.

Seiffert, C., Khoshgoftaar, T. M., Van Hulse, J., & Napolitano, A. (2010). RUSBoost: A Hybrid Approach to Alleviating Class Imbalance. *IEEE Transactions on Systems, Man, and Cybernetics. Part A, Systems and Humans*, *40*(1), 185–197. doi:10.1109/TSMCA.2009.2029559

Seiffert, C., Khoshgoftaar, T., Van Hulse, J., & Folleco, A. (2014). An empirical study of the classification performance of learners on imbalanced and noisy software quality data. *Information Sciences*, 2014, 651–658.

Selwyn, N. (2015). Data entry: Towards the critical study of digital data and education. *Learning, Media and Technology*, 40(1).

Selwyn, N., & Facer, K. (Eds.). (2013). *The politics of education and technology*. New York: Palgrave Macmillan. doi:10.1057/9781137031983

Serrano-Laguna, A., Torrente, J., Moreno-Ger, P., & Fernández-Manjóna, B. (2012). Tracing a little for big improvements: Application of learning analytics and videogames for student assessment. *Procedia Computer Science*, *15*, 203–209. doi:10.1016/j.procs.2012.10.072

Sfard, A., & Prusak, A. (2005). Telling identities: In search of an analytic tool for investigating learning as a culturally shaped activity. *Educational Researcher*, *34*(4), 414–422. doi:10.3102/0013189X034004014

Sha, L., Teplovs, C., & van Aalst, J. (2010). A visualization of group cognition: semantic network analysis of a CSCL community. *Proceedings of theInternational Conference of the Learning Sciences* (pp. 929–936).

Sheard, J., & Hagan, D. 1997. Experiences with Teaching Object-oriented Concepts to Introductory Programming Students using C++. *Proceedings of the Technology of Object-Oriented Languages and Systems (TOOLS'97).*

Sherin, B. (2012). *Using computational methods to discover student science conceptions in interview data.*Paper presented at the Second International Conference on Learning Analytics and Knowledge LAK '12, Vancouver, Canada. doi:10.1145/2330601.2330649

Shirky, C. (2014, January 29). The end of higher education's golden age. [Blog comment}. Retrieved from http://www.shirky.com/weblog/2014/01/there-isnt-enough-money-to-keep-educating-adults-the-way-were-doing-it/

Shmueli, G., & Koppius, O. R. (2011). Predictive Analytics in Information Systems Research. *Management Information Systems Quarterly*, *35*, 553–572.

Shum, S. B. (2012). *Learning analytics*. UNESCO Policy Brief. Retrieved from http://iite.unesco.org/pics/publications/en/files/3214711.pdf

Shum, S. B., & Crick, R. D. (2012). Learning dispositions and transferable competencies: pedagogy, modelling and learning analytics. *Paper presented at the2nd International Conference on Learning Analytics and KnowledgeLAK '12*, New York, NY. doi:10.1145/2330601.2330629

Shum, S. B., & Ferguson, R. (2012). Social learning analytics. *Journal of Educational Technology & Society*, *15*(3), 3–26.

Shute, V. J. (2008). Focus on formative feedback. *Review of Educational Research*, *78*(1), 153–189. doi:10.3102/0034654307313795

Siemens, G. (2004, December 12). Connectivism: A learning theory for the digital age. Retrieved from http://www.ingedewaard.net/papers/connectivism/-2005_siemens_ALearningTheoryForTheDigitalAge.pdf

Siemens, G. (2010). *What are learning analytics?* Retrieved from http://www.elearnspace.org/blog/2010/08/25/what-are-learning-analytics/

Siemens, G. (2011). 1st International Conference on Learning Analytics and Knowledge LAK '11. Retrieved from https://tekri.athabascau.ca/analytics/

Siemens, G. (2012). Learning analytics: Envisioning a research discipline and a domain of practice. *Paper presented at theProceedings ofthe 2nd International Conference on Learning Analytics and Knowledge*. doi:10.1145/2330601.2330605

Siemens, G., & Baker, R. S. J. D. (2012). Learning analytics and educational data mining: towards communication and collaboration. *Paper presented at the2nd International Conference on Learning Analytics and KnowledgeLAK '12*, New York, NY. doi:10.1145/2330601.2330661

Siemens, G., Gasevic, D., Haythornthwaite, C., Dawson, S., Shum, S. B., Ferguson, R., ... & Baker, R. S. J. D. (2011). Open Learning Analytics: an integrated & modularized platform. Proposal to design, implement and evaluate an open platform to integrate heterogeneous learning analytics techniques.

Siemens, G. (2011, January). Learning analytics: A foundation for informed change in Higher Education.*Proceedings of EDUCAUSE Conference*.

Siemens, G. (2013). Learning analytics: The emergence of a discipline. *The American Behavioral Scientist*, *57*(10), 1380–1400. doi:10.1177/0002764213498851

Siemens, G., Dawson, S., & Lynch, G. (2013). *Improving the productivity of the higher education sector: Policy and strategy for systems–level deployment of learning analytics*. Sydney, Australia: Society for Learning Analytics Research for the Australian Government Office for Learning and Teaching.

Siemens, G., & Gasevic, D. (2012). Guest Editorial-Learning and Knowledge Analytics. *Journal of Educational Technology & Society*, *15*(3), 1–2.

Siemens, G., & Long, P. (2011). Penetrating the fog: Analytics in learning and education. *EDUCAUSE Review*. Retrieved from http://www.educause.edu/ero/article/penetrating-fog-analytics-learning-and-education

Simons, H. (2004). Utilizing evaluation evident to enhance professional practice. *Evaluation*, *10*(4), 410–429. doi:10.1177/1356389004050284

Sitthiworachart, J., & Joy, M. (2008). Computer support of effective peer assessment in an undergraduate programming class. *Journal of Computer Assisted Learning*, *24*(3), 217–231. doi:10.1111/j.1365-2729.2007.00255.x

Slade, S., & Prinsloo, P. (2013). Learning Analytics: Ethical Issues and Dilemmas. *The American Behavioral Scientist*, *57*(10), 1510–1529. doi:10.1177/0002764213479366

Small, T., & Deakin Crick, R. (2008). Learning and Self-Awareness: An Enquiry into Personal Development in Higher Education. Vital Partnership and Bristol University, Bristol. Retrieved from http://www.northumbria.ac.uk/sd/central/ar/lts/ltselli/

Smith, D. F. (2014, April 7). Signals Is an Analytical Crystal Ball for Students. *EdTech Magazine*. Retrieved from http:/www.edtechmagazine.com/higher/article/-2014/07/signals-analytical-crystal-ball-students

Smith, V. C., Lange, A., & Huston, D. R. (2012). Predictive modeling to forecast student outcomes and drive effective interventions in online community college courses. *Journal of Asynchronous Learning Networks*, *16*(3), 51–61.

Smolin, D., & Butakov, S. (2012). *Applying artificial intelligence to the educational data: An example of syllabus quality analysis.* Paper presented at the Second International Conference on Learning Analytics and Knowledge LAK '12, Vancouver, Canada. doi:10.1145/2330601.2330644

Sobrinho, W. T., & Goncalves, R. S. (2011, October 1-4). Study of Robotics Singularities using LEGO Mindstorms Kit. *Proceedings of 2011 IEEE IX Latin American and IEEE Colombian Conference on Automatic Control and Industry Applications LARC*, Bogota, Columbia. doi:10.1109/LARC.2011.6086792

Solove, D. J. (2013). Introduction: Privacy self-management and the consent dilemma. *Harvard Law Review* 1880 GWU Legal Studies Research Paper No. 2012-141. Retrieved from http://ssrn.com/abstract=2171018

Solove, D. J. (2001). Privacy and power: Computer databases and metaphors for information privacy. *Stanford Law Review*, *53*(6), 1393–1462. doi:10.2307/1229546

Solove, D. J. (2004). *The digital person. Technology and privacy in the information age*. New York, NY: New York University Press.

Song, E., Petrushyna, Z., Cao, Y., & Klamma, R. (2011). Learning Analytics at Large: The Lifelong Learning Network of 160,000 European Teachers. *EC-TEL*, *6964*(31), 398–411. doi:10.1007/978-3-642-23985-4_31

Spector, P. E. (1992). *Summated scale construction: An introduction*. Newbury Park, CA: SAGE Publications, Inc. doi:10.4135/9781412986038

Spence, R. (2007). Information Visualization Design for Interaction (2nd ed., pp. 17–60). Harlow: Pearson Education Limited.

Sperber, D., & Wilson, D. (1986). *Relevance: communication and cognition*. Cambridge, MA: Harvard University Press.

Spiro, R. J., Feltovich, P. J., Jacobson, M. J., & Coulson, R. J. (1991). Cognitive flexibility constructivism and hypertext: Random access instruction for advanced knowledge acquisition in ill-structured domains. *Educational Technology*, *31*(5), 24–33.

Stahl, G. (2003). *Meaning and interpretation in collaboration*. Paper presented at the International Conference on Computer Support for Collaborative Learning CSCL '03. Bergen, Norway.

Stahl, G. (2009). *Studying virtual math teams*. New York, NY: Springer–Verlag. doi:10.1007/978-1-4419-0228-3

Stefanowski, J. (2014). The Impact of Local Data Characteristics on Learning from Imbalanced Data. In *Rough Sets and Intelligent Systems Paradigms*, 1–13.

Stefanowski, J., & Wilk, S. (2008). *Selective pre-processing of imbalanced data for improving classification performance*. Data Warehousing and Knowledge Discovery. doi:10.1007/978-3-540-85836-2_27

Stella, A., & Woodhouse, D. (2007). *Benchmarking in Australian higher education: A thematic analysis of AUQA audit reports*. Citeseer.

Stiles, R. J. (2012). Understanding and managing the risks of analytics in higher education: A guide. *EDUCAUSE.*

Stiles, R. J. (2012). Understanding and managing the risks of analytics in higher education: A guide. *EDUCAUSE.* Retrieved from https://net.educause.edu/ir/library/pdf/EPUB1201.pdf

Stoddart, E. (2012). A surveillance of care. Evaluating surveillance ethically. In K. Ball, K. D. Haggerty, & D. Lyon (Eds.), *Routledge Handbook of Surveillance Studies* (pp. 369–376). Abindgon, UK: Routledge. doi:10.4324/9780203814949.ch4_1_a

Street, H. D. (2010). Factors influencing a learner's decision to drop-out or persist in higher education distance learning. *Online Journal of Distance Learning Administration, 13*(4).

Subotzky, G., & Prinsloo, P. (2011). Turning the tide: A socio-critical model and framework for improving student success in open distance learning at the University of South Africa. *Distance Education, 32*(2), 177–193. doi:10.1080/01587919.2011.584846

Sun, L.-P., Lv, T.-q., & Pan, L.-w. (2011). Reinforcing Practice Teaching of Software Engineering for Fostering the Creative Talent. *Proceedings of the International Conference on Consumer Electronics, Communications and Networks* (pp. 1548-1551).

Sun, J. C. Y., & Rueda, R. (2012). Situational interest, computer self-efficacy and self-regulation: Their impact on student engagement in distance education. *British Journal of Educational Technology, 43*(2), 191–204. doi:10.1111/j.1467-8535.2010.01157.x

Suthers, D., & Verbert, K. (2013). Learning analytics as a "middle space. Paper presented at *the Third International Conference on Learning Analytics and KnowledgeLAK '13* (pp. 1-4). doi:10.1145/2460296.2460298

Suthers, D. D. (2006). Technology affordances for intersubjective meaning making: A research agenda for CSCL. *International Journal of Computer-Supported Collaborative Learning, 1*(3), 315–337. doi:10.1007/s11412-006-9660-y

Suthers, D. D., Ravi, V., Medina, R., Joseph, S., & Dwyer, N. (2008). Beyond threaded discussion: Representational guidance in asynchronous collaborative learning environments. *Computers & Education, 50*(4), 1103–1127. doi:10.1016/j.compedu.2006.10.007

Swan, K. (2001). Virtual interaction: Design factors affecting student satisfaction and perceived learning in asynchronous online courses. *Distance Education, 22*(2), 306–331. doi:10.1080/0158791010220208

Swenson, J. (2014). Establishing an ethical literacy for learning analytics. *Paper presented at theFourth International Conference on Learning Analytics and Knowledge LAK '14* (pp. 1-4). doi:10.1145/2567574.2567613

Taibi, D., & Dietze, S. (2013). Fostering analytics on learning analytics research: the LAK dataset.

Tait, A. (2015). Student success in open, distance and e-learning. ICDE Report Series. Retrieved from http://icde.org/admin/filestore/Resources/Studentsuccess.pdf

Talavera, L., & Gaudioso, E. (2004). *Mining student data to characterize similar behavior groups in unstructured collaboration spaces.* Paper presented at the 16th European Conference on Artificial Intelligence ECAI '04), Valencia, Spain.

Tan, D., & Liew, S. (2012). A feature selection model for binary classification of imbalanced data based on preference for target instances. *Data Mining and Optimization (DMO)*, (September), 2–4.

Tavani, H. T. (2008). Informational privacy: concepts, theories, and controversies. In The handbook of information and computer ethics (pp. 131-164).

Tavani, H. T., & Moor, J. H. (2001). Privacy protection, control of information, and privacy-enhancing technologies. *ACM SIGCAS Computers and Society, 31*(1), 6–11. doi:10.1145/572277.572278

Tempelaar, D. T., Rienties, B., & Giesbers, B. (2014). Computer Assisted, Formative Assessment and Dispositional Learning Analytics in Learning Mathematics and Statistics. In M. Kalz & E. Ras (Eds.), Computer Assisted Assessment. Research into E-Assessment (Vol. 439, pp. 67–78). CHAM: Springer International Publishing. doi:10.1007/978-3-319-08657-6_7

Tempelaar, D. T., Rienties, B., & Giesbers, B. (2014). In search for the most informative data for feedback generation: Learning Analytics in a data-rich context. *Computers in Human Behavior*. Retrieved from http://www.sciencedirect.com/science/article/pii/S0747563214003240

Tene, O., & Polonetsky, J. (2012). Big data for all: Privacy and user control in the age of analytics. *Northwestern Journal of Technology and Intellectual Property, 239*, 1–36. Retrieved from http://papers.ssrn.com/sol3/papers.cfm?abstract_id=2149364

Teplovs, C., & Scardamalia, M. (2007). Visualizations for knowledge building assessment. *Proceedings of the AgileViz Workshop*.

Teplovs, C., Fujita, N., & Vatrapu, R. (2011). Generating predictive models of learner community dynamics. *Paper presented at the1st International Conference on Learning Analytics and KnowledgeLAK '11* (pp. 147-152). New York, NY. doi:10.1145/2090116.2090139

Teplovs, Chris, & Fujita, N. (2013). Socio-Dynamic Latent Semantic Learner Models. In *Productive Multivocality in the Analysis of Group Interactions* (pp. 383–396). Boston, MA: Springer U.S. doi:10.1007/978-1-4614-8960-3_21

Thanathamathee, P., & Lursinsap, C. (2013). Handling imbalanced data sets with synthetic boundary data generation using bootstrap re-sampling and AdaBoost techniques. *Pattern Recognition Letters, 34*(12), 1339–1347. doi:10.1016/j.patrec.2013.04.019

Thatcher, A., Fridjhon, P., & Cockcroft, K. (2007). The relationship between lecture attendance and academic performance in an undergraduate psychology class. *South African Journal of Psychology. Suid-Afrikaanse Tydskrif vir Sielkunde, 37*(3), 656–660. doi:10.1177/008124630703700316

Tian, J., Gu, H., & Liu, W. (2011). Imbalanced classification using support vector machine ensemble. *Neural Computing & Applications, 20*(2), 203–209. doi:10.1007/s00521-010-0349-9

Tinto, V. (1975). Dropout from Higher Education: A Theoretical Synthesis of Recent Research. *Review of Educational Research, 45*(1), 89–125. doi:10.3102/00346543045001089

Torniai, C., Jovanović, J., Bateman, S., Gasevic, D., & Hatala, M. (2008). Leveraging Folksonomies for Ontology Evolution in E-learning Environments.*Proceedings of the IEEE International Conference on Semantic Computing* (pp. 206–213). doi:10.1109/ICSC.2008.15

Tufte, E. R. (1990). *Envisioning information*. Cheshire, CT: Graphics.

U.S. Department of Education. (2010). National Education Technology Plan. Retrieved from http://www.ed.gov/technology/netp-2010

Uprichard, E. (2015, February 12). Philosophy of data science - Most big data is social data – the analytics need serious interrogation. *Impact of Social Sciences*. Retrieved from http://blogs.lse.ac.uk/impactofsocialsciences/2015/02/12/philosophy-of-data-science-emma-uprichard/

van Barneveld, A., Arnold, K. E., & Campbell, J. P. (2012). Analytics in Higher Education: Establishing a Common Language. Educase Learning Initiative, 1, 1-11.

Van Barneveld, A., Arnold, K. E., & Campbell, J. P. (2012). *Analytics in higher education: Establishing a common language*. EDUCAUSE Learning Initiative.

Van Diggelen, W., Janssen, J., Overdijk, M., Asterhan, C. S. C., Hever, R., Schwarz, B. B., ... (2008). Analyzing and presenting interaction data: a teacher, student and researcher perspective. *Proceedings of theInternational Conference of the Learning Sciences* (pp. 375–382).

Van Hulse, J., & Khoshgoftaar, T. M. (2002). Experimental Perspectives on Learning from Imbalanced Data.*Proceedings of the 24th International Conference on Machine Learning* (pp. 935–942).

van Leeuwen, A., Janssen, J., Erkens, G., & Brekelmans, M. (2014). Supporting teachers in guiding collaborating students: Effects of learning analytics in CSCL. *Computers & Education*, *79*, 28–39. doi:10.1016/j.compedu.2014.07.007

Van Rijmenam, M. (2013, April 30). Big data will revolutionise learning [Blog comment]. Retrieved from http://smartdatacollective.com/bigdatastartups/121261/big-data-will-revolutionize-learning

VanLehn, K., Lynch, C., Schulze, K., Shapiro, J. A., Shelby, R. H., Taylor, L., & Wintersgill, M. et al. (2005). The Andes Physics Tutoring System: Lessons Learned. *International Journal of Artificial Intelligence in Education*, *15*(3), 147–204.

VanZile-Tamsen, C., & Livingston, J. A. (1999). The differential impact of motivation on the self-regulated strategy use of high- and low-achieving college students. *Journal of College Student Development*, *40*(1), 54–60.

Vatrapu, R., Teplovs, C., Fujita, N., & Bull, S. (2011). *Towards a visual analytics for teachers' dynamic diagnostic pedagogical decision-making*. Paper presented at the First International Conference on Learning Analytics and Knowledge LAK '11, Banff, Canada. doi:10.1145/2090116.2090129

Vee, M. H. N. C., Meyer, B., & Mannock, K. L. (2006). *Understanding novice errors and error paths in object-oriented programming through log analysis*. Paper presented at the Workshop on Educational Data Mining at the Eighth International Conference on Intelligent Tutoring Systems ITS '06, Jhongli, Taiwan.

Velliaris, D. M., & Breen, P. (2014, December 2-5). Tailoring graduate attributes to meet the needs of international students in a pathway program. *Paper presented at theConference Proceedings of the 25th ISANA International Education Conference*, Adelaide, South Australia.

Velliaris, D. M., & Willis, C. R. (2014). Getting personal: An autoethnographic study of the professional identit(ies) of lecturers in an Australian pathway institution. In P. Breen (Ed.), Cases on teacher identity, diversity, and cognition in higher education (pp. 87–110). Hershey, PA, USA: IGI Global. doi:10.4018/978-1-4666-5990-2.ch004

Velliaris, D. M., Willis, C. R., & Breen, P. (2015). Academic reflections: Disciplinary acculturation and the first year pathway experience. In P. N. Shrestha (Ed.), *Current developments in English for academic and specific purposes: Local innovations and global perspectives* (pp. 217–235). Reading, UK: Garnet Publishing Ltd.

Ventura, P. R. Jr. (2005, September). Identifying predictors of success for an objects-first CS1. *Computer Science Education*, *15*(3), 223–243. doi:10.1080/08993400500224419

Verbert, K., Duval, E., Klerkx, J., Govaerts, S., & Santos, J. L. (2013). Learning analytics dashboard applications. *The American Behavioral Scientist*.

Verbert, K., Govaerts, S., Duval, E., Santos, J. L., Van Assche, F., Parra, G., & Klerkx, J. (2014). Learning dashboards: An overview and future research opportunities. *Personal and Ubiquitous Computing*, *18*(6), 1499–1514. doi:10.1007/s00779-013-0751-2

Verbert, K., Manouselis, N., Drachsler, H., & Duval, E. (2012). Dataset-driven research to support learning and knowledge analytics. *Journal of Educational Technology & Society*, *15*(3), 133–148.

Verpoorten, D., Westera, W., & Specht, M. (2011). Infusing reflective practice in eLearning courses: Can widgets help? *International Journal of Technology Enhanced Learning*, *3*(1), 93–109. doi:10.1504/IJTEL.2011.039066

Viégas, F. B., Wattenberg, M., & Dave, K. (2004). Studying cooperation and conflict between authors with history flow visualizations. *Paper presented atSIGCHI Conference on Human Factors in Computing SystemsCHI '04*, New York, NY (pp. 575–582). doi:10.1145/985692.985765

Viégas, F. B., Wattenberg, M., McKeon, M., Van Ham, F., & Kriss, J. (2008). Harry Potter and the Meat-Filled Freezer: A Case Study of Spontaneous Usage of Visualization Tools.*Proceedings of the 41st Annual Hawaii International Conference on System Sciences* (p. 159). doi:10.1109/HICSS.2008.188

Villalon, J., & Calvo, R. A. (2011). Concept Maps as Cognitive Visualizations of Writing Assignments. *Journal of Educational Technology & Society*, *14*, 16–27.

Wagner, E., & Ice, P. (2012). Data Changes Everything: Delivering on the Promise of Learning Analytics in Higher Education. EDUCASE Review, 47(4), 33–42.

Wagner, E., & Ice, P. (2012, July 18). Data changes everything: delivering on the promise of learning analytics in higher education. *EDUCAUSEreview*. Retrieved from http://www.educause.edu/ero/article/data-changes-everything-delivering-promise-learning-analytics-higher-education

Wagner, E., & Ice, P. (2012). Data Changes Everything: Delivering on the Promise of Learning Analytics in Higher Education. *EDUCAUSE Review*, *47*(4), 32.

Wang, G. G., & Wilcox, D. (2006). Training evaluation: Knowing more than is practiced. *Advances in Developing Human Resources*, *8*(4), 528–539. doi:10.1177/1523422306293007

Wang, K. T., Huang, Y. M., Jeng, Y. L., & Wang, T. I. (2008). A blog-based dynamic learning map. *Computers & Education*, *51*(1), 262–278. doi:10.1016/j.compedu.2007.06.005

Wang, M., Peng, J., Cheng, B., Zhou, H., & Liu, J. (2011). Knowledge Visualization for Self-Regulated Learning. *Journal of Educational Technology & Society*, *14*(3), 28–42.

Wang, S. L., & Lin, S. S. J. (2007). The application of social cognitive theory to web-based learning through NetPorts. *British Journal of Educational Technology*, *38*(4), 600–612. doi:10.1111/j.1467-8535.2006.00645.x

Ware, C. (2004). Information Visualization: Perception for Design (2nd ed., pp. 3–4). San Francisco: Morgan Kaufmann.

Ware, C. (2005). Visual Queries: The Foundation of Visual Thinking. In S.-O. Tergan & T. Keller, Knowledge and Information Visualization (Vol. 3426, pp. 27–35). Springer Berlin Heidelberg. doi:10.1007/11510154_2

Ware, C. (2012). *Information Visualization: Perception for Design* (3rd ed., pp. 1–536). Morgan Kaufmann.

Warschauer, M., & Matuchniak, T. (2010). New technology and digital worlds: Analyzing evidence of the equity in access, use and outcomes. *Review of Research in Education*, *34*(1), 179–225. doi:10.3102/0091732X09349791

Wasikowski, M., & Chen, X. (2010). Combating the small sample class imbalance problem using feature selection. *IEEE Transactions on Knowledge and Data Engineering*, *22*(10), 1388–1400. doi:10.1109/TKDE.2009.187

Watson, J., & Gemin, B. (2008). Using online learning for at-risk students and credit recovery. Washington, DC: International Council for K–12 Online Learning.

Watson, C., Li, F. W. B., & Godwin, J. L. (2013). Predicting Performance in an Introductory Programming Course by Logging and Analyzing Student Programming Behavior.*Proceedings of 2013 IEEE 13th International Conference on Advanced Learning Technologies* (pp. 319-323). doi:10.1109/ICALT.2013.99

Wattenberg, M., & Viégas, F. B. (2008). The Word Tree, an Interactive Visual Concordance. *IEEE Transactions on Visualization and Computer Graphics*, *14*(6), 1221–1228. doi:10.1109/TVCG.2008.172 PMID:18988967

Watters, A. (2013, October 13). Student data is the new oil: MOOCs, metaphor, and money [Blog comment]. Retrieved from http://www.hackeducation.com/2013/10/17/student-data-is-the-new-oil/

Wayman, J. C. (2005). Involving Teachers in Data-Driven Decision Making: Using Computer Data Systems to Support Teacher Inquiry and Reflection. *Journal of Education for Students Placed at Risk*, *10*(3), 295–308. doi:10.1207/s15327671espr1003_5

Weiss, G. M. (2010a). Data Mining and Knowledge Discovery Handbook. *Data Mining and Knowledge Discovery Handbook*, *1*, 747–757. doi:10.1007/978-0-387-09823-4

Weiss, G. M. (2010b). The impact of small disjuncts on classifier learning. In R. Stahlbock, S. F. Crone, & S. Lessmann (Eds.), *Data Mining* (Vol. 8, pp. 193–226). Boston, MA: Springer US; doi:10.1007/978-1-4419-1280-0_9

Whipp, J. L., & Chiarelli, S. (2004). Self-regulation in a web-based course: A case study. *Educational Technology Research and Development*, *52*(4), 4, 5–22. doi:10.1007/BF02504714

Whitelock, D., Twiner, A., Richardson, J. T. E., Field, D., & Pulman, S. (2014). OpenEssayist: real-life testing of an automated feedback system for draft essay writing. *Paper presented at the #designlearning from blended learning to learning analytics in HE*, Milton Keynes, UK. doi:10.1145/2723576.2723599

Willging, P. A., & Johnson, S. D. (2009). Factors that Influence Students' Decision to dropout of online courses. *Journal of Asynchronous Learning Networks*, *13*(3), 115–127.

Winne, P. H., & Hadwin, A. F. (2013). nStudy: Tracing and Supporting Self-Regulated Learning in the Internet. In R. Azevedo & V. Aleven, International Handbook of Metacognition and Learning Technologies (Vol. 28, pp. 293–308). New York, NY: Springer New York. doi:10.1007/978-1-4419-5546-3_20

Winne, P. H., & Hadwin, A. F. (2013). nStudy: Tracing and supporting self-regulated learning in the Internet. In R. Azevedo, & V. Aleven (Eds.), International handbook of metacognition and learning technologies (pp. 293–308). Amsterdam, The Netherlands: Springer–Verlag.

Winne, P. H. (2005). Key Issues in Modeling and Applying Research on Self-Regulated Learning. *Applied Psychology*, *54*(2), 232–238. doi:10.1111/j.1464-0597.2005.00206.x

Winne, P. H., & Jamieson-Noel, D. (2002). Exploring students' calibration of self reports about study tactics and achievement. *Contemporary Educational Psychology*, *27*(4), 551–572. doi:10.1016/S0361-476X(02)00006-1

Wise, A. F. (2014). Designing pedagogical interventions to support student use of learning analytics. *Paper presented at theFourth International Conference on Learning Analytics And KnowledgeLAK '14*, New York, NY, 203–211. doi:10.1145/2567574.2567588

Wise, A. F., Zhao, Y., & Hausknecht, S. N. (2013). *Learning analytics for online discussions: A pedagogical model for intervention with embedded and extracted analytics*. Paper presented at the Third International Conference on Learning Analytics and Knowledge LAK '13, Leuven, Belgium. doi:10.1145/2460296.2460308

Wishon, G. D., & Rome, J. (2012, 13 August). Enabling a data-driven university. *EDUCAUSE review*. Retrieved from http://www.educause.edu/ero/article/enabling-data-driven-university

Wishon, G. D., & Rome, J. (2012, August 13). Enabling the Data-Driven University. *Educause Review Online*. Retrieved from http://www.educause.edu/ero/article/enabling-data-driven-university

Wolters, C. A. (2010). Self-regulated learning and the 21st century competencies. *Artikel Online*. Retrieved from http://www.hewlett.org/uploads/Self_Regulated_Learning__21st_Century_Competencies.pdf

Wolters, C. A., & Pincrich, P. R. (1998). Contextual differences in student motivation and self-regulated learning in mathematics, English, and social studies classrooms. *Instructional Science*, *26*, 27–47.

Wolters, C. A., Pintrich, P. R., & Karabenick, S. A. (2005). Assessing academic self-regulated learning. In K. A. Moore & L. Lippman (Eds.), *What do children need to flourish? Conceptualizing and measuring indicators of positive development* (pp. 251–270). New York: Springer. doi:10.1007/0-387-23823-9_16

Wong, W.-K., Yin, S.-K., Yang, H.-H., & Cheng, Y.-H. (2011). Using Computer-Assisted Multiple Representations in Learning Geometry Proofs. *Journal of Educational Technology & Society*, *14*(3), 43–54.

Worsley, M., & Blikstein, P. (2014). Analyzing engineering design through the lens of computation. *Journal of Learning Analytics*, *1*(2), 151–186.

Wu, G., & Chang, E. Y. (2003). Class-boundary alignment for imbalanced dataset learning. *ICML 2003 Workshop on Learning from Imbalanced Data Sets II*, 49–56.

Wu, G., & Chang, E. Y. (2005). KBA: Kernel boundary alignment considering imbalanced data distribution. *IEEE Transactions on Knowledge and Data Engineering*, *17*(6), 786–795. doi:10.1109/TKDE.2005.95

Xiaohui, G., & Yaguan, Q. (2010, May 7-9). The Exploration of Teaching about Java Programming.*Proceedings of the International Conference on E-Business and E-Government ICEE 2010*, Guangzhou, China. doi:10.1109/ICEE.2010.1397

Xiong, R., & Donath, J. S. (1999). PeopleGarden: Creating Data Portraits for Users. *Proceedings of theACM Symposium on User Interface Software and Technology*, 37–44. doi:10.1145/320719.322581

Yazzie-Mintz, E. (2009). *Charting the Path from Engagement to Achievement: A Report on the 2009 High School Survey of Student Engagement*. Center for Evaluation & Education Policy, Indiana University.

Yi, J. S., Kang, Y.-A., Stasko, J. T., & Jacko, J. A. (2008). Understanding and characterizing insights: how do people gain insights using information visualization? *Paper presented at the2008 Workshop on BEyond time and errors: novel evaLuation methods for Information Visualization BELIV '08*, New York, NY. doi:10.1145/1377966.1377971

Zadrozny, B., & Elkan, C. (2001). Learning and making decisions when costs and probabilities are both unknown.*Proceedings of the Seventh ACM SIGKDD International Conference on Knowledge Discovery and Data Mining - KDD '01* (pp. 204–213). doi:10.1145/502512.502540

Zagal, J. P., & Bruckman, A. (2007). *GameLog: Fostering reflective gameplaying for learning*. Paper presented at the 2007 ACM SIGGRAPH Symposium on Videogames, San Diego, CA. doi:10.1145/1274940.1274950

Zhang, Y.-P., Zhang, L.-N., & Wang, Y.-C. (2010). Cluster-based majority under-sampling approaches for class imbalance learning. *Proceedings of the 2010 2nd IEEE International Conference on Information and Financial Engineering* (pp. 400–404). doi:10.1109/ICIFE.2010.5609385

Zhao, W.-Y., Chellappa, R., Phillips, P. J., & Rosenfeld, A. (2003). Face recognition: A literature survey. *ACM Computing Surveys*, *35*(4), 399–458. doi:10.1145/954339.954342

Zhuhadar, L., & Yang, R. (2012). Cyberlearners and learning resources. *Paper presented at the2nd International Conference on Learning Analytics and KnowledgeLAK '12*, New York, NY. doi:10.1145/2330601.2330621

Zhuhadar, L., Nasraoui, O., & Wyatt, R. Dual representation of the semantic user profile for personalized web search in an evolving domain. *Proceedings of the AAAI2009SpringSymposium on Social Semantic Web* (Vol. 2, pp. 84–89).

Zhuhadar, L., Yang, R., & Nasraoui, O. (2012). Toward the Design of a Recommender System: Visual Clustering and Detecting Community Structure in a Web Usage Network. *Paper presented at the 2012 IEEE/WIC/ACM International Conferences on Web Intelligence and Intelligent Agent Technology (WI-IAT)* (Vol. 1, pp. 354–361). doi:10.1109/WI-IAT.2012.270

Ziemkiewicz, C., & Kosara, R. (2008). The shaping of information by visual metaphors. *IEEE Transactions on Visualization and Computer Graphics*, *14*(6), 1269–1276. doi:10.1109/TVCG.2008.171 PMID:18988973

Zimmerman, B. J. (1989). A Social Cognitive View of Self-Regulated Academic Learning. *Journal of Educational Psychology*, *81*(3), 329–339. doi:10.1037/0022-0663.81.3.329

Zimmerman, B. J. (2001). Theories of self-regulated learning and academic achievement: An overview and analysis. In B. J. Zimmerman & D. H. Schunk (Eds.), *Self-regulated learning and academic achievement: Theoretical perspectives* (2nd ed., pp. 1–37). Hillsdale, NJ: Erlbaum.

Zimmerman, B. J. (2008). Investigating self-regulation and motivation: Historical background, methodological developments, and future prospects. *American Educational Research Journal*, *45*(1), 166–183. doi:10.3102/0002831207312909

Zimmerman, B. J., & Risemberg, R. (1997). Self-regulatory dimensions of academic learning and motivation. In G. D. Phye (Ed.), *Handbook of academic learning: Construction of knowledge* (pp. 105–125). San Diego, CA: Academic Press. doi:10.1016/B978-012554255-5/50005-3

Zinn, C., & Scheuer, O. (2006). *Getting to know your student in distance learning contexts.* Paper presented at the First European Conference on Technology Enhanced Learning EC–TEL ‘06, Crete, Greece. doi:10.1007/11876663_34

About the Contributors

Mark Anderson has been employed as a Professor in Computing and Information Systems, and has led courses at both undergraduate and postgraduate levels in subjects such as Grid Computing, Distributed Systems and Java Programming. He has also introduced new subjects into the Computing curriculum in collaboration with colleagues, such as Physical Computing to engage the students with programming activities. Professor Anderson has also successfully supervised a number of students through the dissertation/project process and is currently the Programme Leader for BSc(Hons) Computing (Application Development) course and Programme Leader for the MSc Advanced Software Application course. He has also worked with a number of external clients to develop novel solutions for interacting with customers. In this capacity, solutions have been developed using Microsoft Kinect cameras, Leap Motion, mobile devices and embedded systems.

Collette Gavan is the Director of Undergraduate Studies for the computing department, Senior Lecturer and Programme Leader for BSc Computing, Computing (Games Programming), and Computing (Systems and Software). She has led courses at both undergraduate and postgraduate levels in subjects such as programming and Project/IT Management. Before becoming a lecturer, Collette worked for a number of large organisations in roles which have enabled her to develop invaluable skills and experiences which are used to provide real world examples to students within her modules. Collette is currently working towards gaining her PhD at the University of Lancaster, with a thesis entitled "Using Robotics to explore computer programming: investigating student experiences and attainment". The work directly feeds into her teaching and draws upon the innovative experiences that she has designed to engage students within the subject. Collette has introduced new concepts into the introductory programming modules, which are designed to engage and enthuse the students with what is often perceived to be a very challenging subject. This innovative approach builds upon the work within her research to use robotic technology as an enabling mechanism for teaching problem-solving to students. These practices also assist the students in developing critical employability skills within their coursework.

***

Halimat I. Alabi has been a higher education educator for the last decade. This work informs her research in the design and application of visual learning analytics for learners. Currently pursuing her Ph.D., her academic path began with a degree in Acoustical Engineering from Purdue University. She then went into television, working in the newsrooms of PBS, FOX, and CBS stations. Later she obtained an M.A. in Television, Film and New Media Production and an M.Ed. in Mathematics, Science, Social Studies & Technology Education. From there, she went on to work in console game development for Sony Computer Entertainment America and THQ. Her previous experience informs her current research, which draws from theories of design, transformative education, human computer interaction, new media and game theory to help people visually extract meaningful patterns from their learning data.

Catherine Chen received her doctorate from the University of Minnesota. She has been teaching microcomputer applications, business information systems, computer networking, and database management courses at both undergraduate and graduate levels. She has published many articles in referred journals and conferences proceedings, as well as conducted research training workshop. Chen received an Outstanding Teaching Applications Award in 1999, a Best Paper Award in 2000, a Most Accessible Teacher Award in 2001, the Delta Pi Epsilon Independent Research Award in 2003, an Outstanding Immersive Learning Project Award in 2012, and an Outstanding Teaching Award in 2013. Currently, her primary research interests are in pedagogical issues of information systems education, e-learning, and business analytics skills and curricula.

Scott Frasard has been an adult educator for two decades. He has worked in government, academic, and corporate organizations, in local, national, and international settings. Presently, Scott is the Global Manager of Training Measurement and Evaluation at eBay Inc. and also provides consulting work to organizations seeking to better their measurement evaluation strategies and processes. Scott holds a Ph.D. in adult education and a master of education with an emphasis in organizational development, both from the University of Georgia. Scott conducts applied research in alternative methods of evaluation training, identifying factors impacting how training participants rate trainers on post-course surveys, and understanding the role culture plays in shaping trainers' teaching philosophy.

Amit Goel has more than two decades of experience in Research and Development. His research interests are parallel and high performance computing, big data, predictive analytics, machine learning, intelligent agents, virtual worlds, and algorithmic game theory. Amit has published internationally in journals, conferences and book chapters. Amit has worked with large, medium and startup scale companies in different countries. He has been responsible for teams of 5-100 people with 1-50 million USD budgets. He has worked across multiple domains such as travel, education, finance, stock exchanges, banking, human resource, entertainment, medical informatics, infrastructure and energy with core focus on providing advanced solution with scientific problem solving methods.

Jack Halliday was born in Ormskirk in 1993. Jack graduated from Edge Hill University with a First Class Bachelors of Science degree in computing in 2015. He has worked as a Junior Web Developer for Edge Hill Graduate Enterprise and is proceeding to study a Master's of Science degree in IT Management and Information Security.

Jennifer Heath is currently the Director Student Support & Education Analytics at the University of Wollongong in the state of New South Wales, Australia. Dr Heath's journey to this role has included many years as a tenured Informatics academic, more than a decade of IT experience across diverse industries and more recently a focus on the planning, delivery and evaluation of student support and the application of analytics in higher education. The focus of Dr Heath's PhD research was the complex domain of privacy surrounding the secondary use of data and this theoretical work has informed the approach taken to ethics and privacy matters surrounding learning analytics at the University of Wollongong.

Kijpokin Kasemsap received his BEng degree in Mechanical Engineering from King Mongkut's University of Technology Thonburi, his MBA degree from Ramkhamhaeng University, and his DBA degree in Human Resource Management from Suan Sunandha Rajabhat University. He is a Special Lecturer at Faculty of Management Sciences, Suan Sunandha Rajabhat University based in Bangkok, Thailand. He is a Member of International Association of Engineers (IAENG), International Association of Engineers and Scientists (IAEST), International Economics Development and Research Center (IEDRC), International Association of Computer Science and Information Technology (IACSIT), International Foundation for Research and Development (IFRD), and International Innovative Scientific and Research Organization (IISRO). He also serves on the International Advisory Committee (IAC) for International Association of Academicians and Researchers (INAAR). He has numerous original research articles in top international journals, conference proceedings, and book chapters on business management, human resource management, and knowledge management published internationally.

J. Peter Kincaid is founding and current director of the Modeling and Simulation Graduate Program at the University of Central Florida and is affiliated with UCF's Institute for Simulation and Training. During his career, he has worked as a scientist for the US Air Force (AF Human Resources Lab), Army (Army Research Institute), and Navy (Training Analysis and Evaluation Group and NAVAIR Training Systems Division) and as an engineer for a large defense contractor (now Lockheed-Martin). He has held academic positions at two universities and is currently a research professor at UCF. He has published widely in a variety of disciplines, including journal articles in simulation, human factors, engineering, instructional technology and medicine. He developed the widely used Flesch-Kincaid Reading Grade Level formula, which is a feature of MS Word's Style and Grammar Check. Dr. Kincaid's PhD is in human factors from the Ohio State University.

Eeva Leinonen Professor Leinonen is the Deputy Vice-Chancellor of Education at the University of Wollongong.

Amir Manzoor holds a bachelor's degree in engineering from NED University, Karachi, an MBA from Lahore University of Management Sciences (LUMS), and an MBA from Bangor University, United Kingdom. He has many years of diverse professional and teaching experience working at many renowned national and internal organizations and higher education institutions. His research interests include electronic commerce and technology applications in business. He is a member of Chartered Banker Institute of UK and Project Management Institute, USA.

Paul Prinsloo is a Research Professor in the Department of Business Management at the University of South Africa (Unisa). His current research interests include learning analytics, student retention and success and graduate supervision.

William Rivera is CEO and principal research scientist for Cognita Solutions LLC. His research interests include predictive modeling, machine learning, software architecture and engineering and data mining with emphasis on implementing artificial intelligence into software applications.

Richard J Self is a Senior Lecturer in Analytics and Governance in the Department of Computing and Maths at the University of Derby in the UK. He was the School Learning and Teaching Advisor between 2012 and 2014. This role involved critically evaluating the impact of different learning, teaching and assessment approaches on student attainment and encouraging the up-take of good and best practice amongst colleagues in the School of Computing and Maths. He is leading the introduction of Analytics and Data Science, using SAS®, into the curricula of one of the UK SAS Student Academy universities, at both undergraduate and postgraduate levels and the development of a range of Analytics based degree programmes. His current pedagogic research focus is into the impact of the use of Learning Analytics as a means of evaluating the impact of pedagogic choices for teaching and learning styles on the achievements of students. He is a programme committee member of the annual Knowledge Management in Organisations conference. He was one of the two co-chairs of the Big Data & Analytics 2014 conference in Las Vegas in Oct 2014. He co-chairs the Big Data and Analytics Educational Conference 2015 in Puerto Rico. He has presented conference papers on aspects of Student Excellence at a range of recent conferences, including giving the Keynote address at the International Journal of Arts and Sciences Conference in Toronto, May 2014 entitled "Inspiring and Delivering Outstanding Student Excellence."

Sharon Slade is a senior lecturer in the faculty of Business and Law at the Open University, UK. She has a PhD in mathematical control theory and a background in mathematical modelling. She has led work within the Open University on the development of new policy and consent options around the ethical use of student data to shape their support and learning and improve retention and progression and is an Academic lead for the university's Analytics Project. Recent research include papers and chapters establishing an ethical framework for the use of learning analytics within Higher Education, examining the concept of educational triage and broader issues around an ethics of care. Her last two conference papers have been awarded the best research paper award.

Donna M. Velliaris is Academic Advisor at the Eynesbury Institute of Business and Technology (EIBT). EIBT is a specialist pre-university institution where international students work towards the goal of Australian tertiary entrance. Donna holds two Graduate Certificates in: (1) Australian Studies; and (2) Religious Education; two Graduate Diplomas in: (1) Secondary Education; and (2) Language and Literacy Education; as well as three Masters degrees in: (1) Educational Sociology; (2) Studies of Asia; and (3) Special Education. In 2010, she graduated with a PhD in Education focused on the social and educational ecological development of school-aged transnational students. Her research interests and expertise include: academic literacies; human ecology; Third Culture Kids (TCKs); and schools as cultural systems. Donna is first-author of more than 10 book chapters to be published in 2015-2016.

Index

L

M

O

P

R

S

T

V

W

www.ingramcontent.com/pod-product-compliance
Ingram Content Group UK Ltd.
Pitfield, Milton Keynes, MK11 3LW, UK
UKHW050952290926
15470UKWH00005B/1770

9 781466 699830